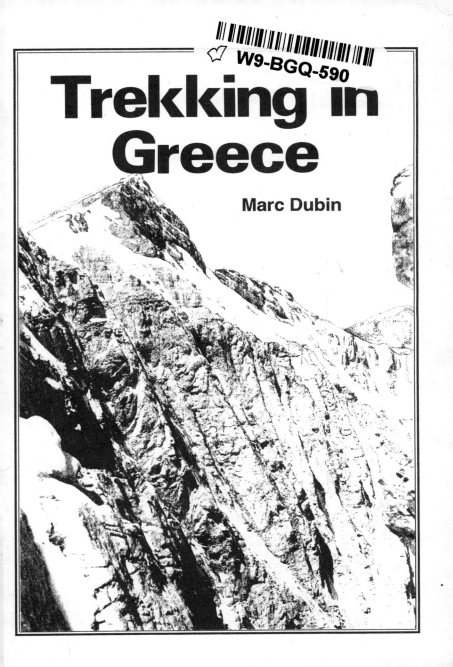

Trekking in Greece

Marc Dubin

Trekking in Greece

1st edition

Published by
    Lonely Planet Publications
    Head Office: PO Box 617, Hawthorn, Vic 3122, Australia
    Branches: PO Box 2001A, Berkeley, CA 94702, USA
                    12 Barley Mow Passage, Chiswick, London W4 4PH, UK

Printed by
    Colorcraft Ltd, Hong Kong

Photographs by
    Marc Dubin (MD)
    Michael Cullen (MC)
    Black and white photographs by Marc Dubin

    Front cover: Below Moní, in from Kalóxilos, Náxos (MD)
    Back cover: Áyios Andhréas church above ancient ruins, Sífnos (MD)
    Title page: Ólimbos: Skolió looms over the Kazánia chasm (from a photograph by Marc Dubin)

Published
    April 1993

Although the authors and publisher have tried to make the information as
accurate as possible, they accept no responsibility for any loss, injury or
inconvenience sustained by any person using this book.

National Library of Australia Cataloguing in Publication Data
    Dubin, Marc S. (Marc Stephen).
    Trekking in Greece.

    1st ed.
    Includes index.
    ISBN 0 86442 159 1.

    1. Hiking – Greece – Guidebooks. 2. Greece – Guidebooks.
    I. Cullen, Michael. II. Title. (Series: Lonely Planet walking guide).

914.950476

Marc S Dubin

Marc was born and educated in California, interrupting university in 1976 to teach English in South America. Though he eventually finished his formal schooling, this maiden voyage sparked a travel habit which has led him to learn (more or less) four foreign languages and visit more than 40 countries on every continent. Travel journalist, author and editor since 1979, Marc has in addition to this title written *Trekking in Spain* and (with Enver Lucas) *Trekking in Turkey* for Lonely Planet, *Greece on Foot* for The Mountaineers (USA), and is co-author of the Greek, Spanish and Turkish volumes of the Rough/Real Guides series, and sole writer of their upcoming Cyprus guide.

He is also an accomplished photographer with numerous publication credits, with a portfolio represented by a London company. Marc has lived in Greece most of each year since 1989, where he still finds time between bouts in the garden and research trips to lead the occasional walking tour.

Michael Cullen

Born in Athens to British parents, Michael was brought up in close contact with both cultures and languages. He claims to have taken his first step in the Greek mountains at the age of three, and has never looked back since. After leading three successful university expeditions to some of the remotest corners of Greece, Michael decided to turn professional; in conjunction with the Athens agency Trekking Hellas, he has been operating walking tours in the Peloponnese and Ágrafo ranges since 1991. Between treks he works as a freelance travel writer; to this book he contributed the sections on the Ágrafa region, Mt Helmós and Mt Zíria, as well as supplementary material for Náxos island.

A graduate in modern languages from Cambridge University, Michael is a fluent speaker of French, German, Greek and English, and thinks of himself as a 'European'. He is also a committed ecologist and a keen photographer.

Dedication

In memory of Kevin Andrews, who loved the Greek backcountry.

From the Author

I would first of all like to express my appreciation to the following readers of my previous Greek hiking guide, whose letters and accounts were invaluable in the preparation of the present version: Maureen Watson of Waymark Holidays (UK), Wolter and Juditha Oosterhuis (Netherlands), Ronald and Justine Ward (Australia), Charles Koutras (USA), Andrew Webb (UK), Carola Scupham (UK), André Le Pennec (UK), Denys Morton (UK), and the late Kevin Andrews (Greece).

On mainland Greece, Toula Chryssanthopoulou of the EOT provided a special introductory letter to Mt Áthos; the Christodhoulos family of Megálo Pápingo, as previously, lent advice and logistical support; Kostas Vassiliou of Robinson Travel provided tips on current conditions in the Píndhos; and Helen Swift (UK) and Marianne Schuppe (Switz) shared the trail with me (and served as models) for two days. In Haniá, Crete, the staff of Aptera Travel and Josef Schwemmberger both provided advice and travel facilities; in the Dodecanese, Marianne and Sotiris Nikolis (Ródhos) and Katerina Tsakiris (Sími) offered gracious hospitality, and Liz Tamalunas (Nísiros) shared what she knew about that isle. Leylâ Akbaba accompanied me on several hikes across Sámos, where I have spent so much time since 1989; also on that island thanks are due to Greg Koutsomitopoulos for help with car rentals, and to my peripatetic neighbour John Peat, also of Hania (Crete) and Toulouse (France), for casting a critical eye on selected chapters. Back in Athens, John Chapple, Julie Hardenberg, Kiveli Petropoulou and the management at Marble House Pension have all helped out in various ways.

Last but not least, I wish to acknowledge my indebtedness to the hundreds of rural Greeks, names never known or unremembered, who over the years have offered company, directions and hospitality with no thought of recompense.

From the Publisher

This first edition of Trekking in Greece was edited by David Meagher and Jeff Williams, and Jeff carried it through production. Proofing was done by Frith Pike and Sally Steward. The maps were prepared by Rachel Black, Vicki Beale and Sandra Smythe. With patience, Rachel made the detailed corrections to the maps and also prepared the cover. Vicki Beale was responsible for the layout and illustrations.

Disclaimer

Although the author and publisher have done their utmost to ensure the accuracy and currency of all information in this guide, they cannot accept responsibility for any loss, injury or inconvenience sustained by any person using this book. In particular, we cannot guarantee that paths described have not been destroyed in the interval between research and publication. All hiking times given exclude rest stops and, unless otherwise stated, assume a trail surface unobstructed by snow. The fact that a trip or area is described in this guide does not mean that it is necessarily a safe one for you or your group. While technical rock-climbing is practised in most of the regions covered, the actual itineraries included have been deliberately selected to avoid the necessity of engaging in these activities. You are finally responsible for judging your own capabilities in the light of the conditions you encounter.

Warning & Request

Things change – prices go up, schedules change, good places go bad and bad places go bankrupt – nothing stays the same. So if you find things better or worse, recently opened or long since closed, please write and tell us and make the next edition better.

Your letters will be used to help update future editions and, where possible, important changes will also be included in a Stop Press section in reprints.

We greatly appreciate all information that is sent to us by travellers. Back at Lonely Planet we employ a hard-working readers' letters team to sort through the many letters that we receive. The best ones will be rewarded with a free copy of the next edition or another Lonely Planet guide that you prefer. We give away lots of books, but, unfortunately, not every letter/postcard receives one.

Contents

MAP LEGEND

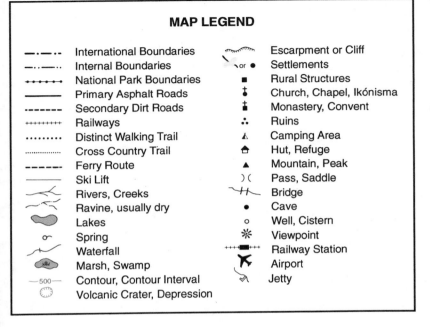

—·—··	International Boundaries		Escarpment or Cliff
—··—··	Internal Boundaries	↘ or ●	Settlements
+·+·+·+	National Park Boundaries	■	Rural Structures
————	Primary Asphalt Roads	⚲	Church, Chapel, Ikónisma
-------	Secondary Dirt Roads	⚱	Monastery, Convent
+++++++	Railways	∴	Ruins
········	Distinct Walking Trail	⚐	Camping Area
···············	Cross Country Trail	⌂	Hut, Refuge
- - - - -	Ferry Route	▲	Mountain, Peak
————	Ski Lift	) (	Pass, Saddle
	Rivers, Creeks	~H~	Bridge
	Ravine, usually dry	●	Cave
	Lakes	○	Well, Cistern
�ോ	Spring	✳	Viewpoint
	Waterfall	+++■+++	Railway Station
	Marsh, Swamp	✈	Airport
—500—	Contour, Contour Interval	⚓	Jetty
☺	Volcanic Crater, Depression		

Introduction

This guide is the result of 10 seasons of hiking in Greece between 1981 and 1992. Since I first visited the country in 1978, enormous changes have taken place – some good, some bad. Sadly, many beautiful trails and trekking routes have been destroyed, and readers of my earlier walking guide (*Greece on Foot*, The Mountaineers, USA, 1986) will not find them in this update. On a happier note, trails are better marked, equipment, information and good maps are far easier to obtain than a decade ago, and foreigners are no longer considered deviants or even potential spies for expressing a desire to explore the Greek wilderness.

Perhaps naively believing that the bulldozers have done their worst, I have made a careful selection of those routes which are likely to still exist five years hence. There is an emphasis on areas very near where people would be going anyway, so most of these walks can be part of a conventional holiday. I have also kept dirt-track walking and tough cross-country scrambles to an absolute minimum, though the treks vary in length from an hour or so to more than a week. All of them are rated as to difficulty and time, and can be accomplished by any reasonably fit person with some outdoor experience.

Most visitors to Greece are devotees of a cult which compels belief that the country is a uniformly flat, hot place, and that all of value can be found at selected archaeological zones or coastal resorts. Until recently few tourists were aware that Greece in fact possesses vast tracts of wilderness unequalled, proportionately, in most other European countries; fully 75% of the land area is classified as montane, nonarable or otherwise uninhabitable.

As information and education has improved, a steady trickle of walkers, some in organised groups but more often as solo travellers, have brushed the beach sand off themselves and ventured inland to often enchanted realms. On returning, they greet with a sceptical smile the tales of woe from those who fell prey to the more exploitative aspects of the mainstream tourist industry. Patrick Leigh Fermor's observation in his book *Roumeli* still rings true three decades later:

Greeks are very conscious of foreign opinion; they tend to shepherd foreigners toward the conventionally acceptable things and away from the backward and the obscure. They need not have these fears. The strangers who form the deepest regard for Greece are not the ones who are bear-led; they are the solitaries whose travels lead them, through chance or poverty or curiosity, along the humble and recondite purlieus of Greek life.

Despite this increase in popularity, the Greek back country still offers something – relative solitude – that has virtually vanished from trails in the rest of Europe, the Americas and the Himalaya. While the mountains here are not imposingly lofty or perennially snow-clad like the Alps, Andes or the Himalayas, they are graced with a severe, craggy, uniquely Balkan beauty and often riotous vegetation at middle altitudes. The more familiar lower elevations of the islands are no less inviting for foot exploration. These landscapes, together with the remaining examples of village, monastic and pastoral culture, guarantee a satisfying and surprisingly varied trekking experience.

Ironically, this surge in interest has developed at a point when most Greeks seem to have permanently turned their backs on their rural patrimony. The bringers of progress, Army Corps of Engineers style, are hard at work. Roads, ostensibly to benefit shepherds or farmers but effectively to service ski lifts, logging operations or military installations, proliferate on most mountainsides and island flanks.

Most of Greece's formerly wild rivers – in particular the Akhelöos, Árakhthos and Agráfiotis in the central mainland – have been extensively dammed, with habitats threatened, villages inundated and rafters or kayakers forced to use a dwindling number of white-water streams. Rarely are the various development projects for the benefit of nearby villages, which continue to wither away; instead they encourage migration to the towns of an increasingly urbanised, centralised and concreted Greece.

As matters stand, little time – less than a generation – remains to enjoy rural Greece as it has been for the past several centuries. Hence this book is as much a memorial document as a guide, for within the next couple of decades will be completed the unravelling of a cultural fabric that began between the world wars, when the drastic depopulation of the Greek hinterlands began to take place.

It is romantic fancy to imagine that the hydroelectric barrages will be completely stopped or that the old villages will ever be revitalised (except as summer resorts), but the use of this book should rescue those old trails that have not succumbed to the road builders or expired quietly under a blanket of scree and foliage.

To those who know and love them, the old pilgrimage cobbles, shepherds' migratory routes and medieval high roads of wild Greece are as valuable a heritage as the Parthenon – and often nearly as old. The Greeks of the 21st century will thank you for preserving the abandoned paths, for a Greece that in all likelihood will be half Athenian will never need them as much as then.

Facts about the Country

GEOGRAPHY & GEOLOGY

Greece, the splintered south-eastern tip of the Balkan peninsula, presents a highly convoluted map outline, with a generally rocky coastline equal in length to that of France, though that nation is four times larger. What we see today is the result of the primordial flooding of the Mediterranean basin which occurred aeons ago, when a debris dam at the Strait of Gibraltar gave way. Inrushing Atlantic waters gradually inundated most of the mountain ranges that segmented the deep, hot depression, a process finished only after the last Ice Age and probably the basis of the Biblical flood account.

Isolated, exposed summits became the Greek islands, with Crete the highest and largest. More continuous massifs on the newly created mainland were still joined to the young Dinaric Alps of future Albania and Yugoslavia, with the important, older spur of Rodhópi shared with Bulgaria.

If the Mediterranean could be drained, the north-western Balkan systems, the Albano-Greek Píndhos, the Peloponnesian ranges, Crete and the Turkish Toros mountains would form one extended, unbroken arc.

No point in Greece is more than 100 or so km from the sea, and the sierras that crisscross the land steepen the grade over which the various rivers must run. Cultivation is confined to narrow zones on either side of the banks, which were seasonally overflowed until the advent of flood-control projects. On the western slope of the Píndhos mountains, which tend from south-east to north-west, rivers flow uniformly and swiftly from north-east to south-west. The main exception is the Aóös which exits north-west to the Adriatic via Albania. On the opposite side of the Píndhos crest, rivers water fertile plains as they drain east or north-east in a more leisurely fashion. The single largest agricultural area here is the breadbasket of Thessalía (Thessaly), once the bed of a prehistoric inland sea. As Greece

curls around the northern Aegean, the courses of rivers with their headwaters in former Yugoslavia or Bulgaria are deflected south as they meander to the sea through gaps in the Rodhópi ranges. On the Pelopónnisos, most rivers are swift, short torrents, except for the Évrotas and Alfíos, which flow in opposite south-easterly and north-westerly directions from sources which almost coincide in the rugged centre of the peninsula.

On close inspection most Greek rock formations turn out to be limestone or schist, with occasional intrusions of gneiss, fleisch or chert, the last in flint-like nodules that look like fossils. Conglomerate and other sedimentary rocks are seen in alluvial areas. The schists are usually folded and tilted into giant, weathered beds, which crack and rain down the terrible scree that constitutes a hiker's nightmare. Limestone is usually karst-type (named after the Carso or Karst region of Italy and Yugoslavia), which is extremely porous and peppered with caves, sinkholes and subterranean rivers. Underground streams often empty some distance out to sea, or conversely channel salt water inland to turn springs brackish. The sieve-like limestone core of most Greek mountains acts as a giant sponge for precipitation, but this means that there are few lakes and that springs above 2000 metres are rare.

Most of the peaks are not much higher (usually 2100 to 2400 metres), and the sheerness and lack of water can limit camping opportunities, but this is partly mitigated by dramatic, sculpted contours verging on the grotesque. Limestone needles and pinnacles, treacherously brittle and razor-sharp, are best admired from a distance. Not all of these evocative contours are the result of ordinary weathering; the appearances of many summits are evidence of glacial action as far south as the Gulf of Kórinthos, a gash-like break in the Píndhos chain which the sea later filled. Large volumes of water are still at

BULGARIA

MACEDONIA

• Falakró

MAKEDHONÍA & THRÁKI

ALBANIA

• Grámmos

Samothráki

• Ólimbos

Áthos Peninsula

Kíssavos •

THESSALÍA, MAGNISÍA & ÉVVIA

• Víkos Gorge Environs & North Píndhos

ÍPIROS

• South Píndhos

Pílion Peninsula

• Akherónda Gorge

SPORÁDHES

Skíathos

• Ágrafa

IONIAN ISLANDS

Íti (Oeta) •

Vardhoúsia • Glóna •

Dhírfis •

• Parnassós

THE STEREÁ

Párnitha (Párnes)

Fónissa Gorge

Erímanthos •

• Helmós

Zíria •

PELOPÓNNISOS

Tínos

• River Gorges of Arkadhía

KIKLÁDHES

Sérifos

Náxos

Párnon •

Sífnos •

• Taïyettos

Folégandhros

CRETE

**Greece
Location of Treks**

South—West Coast

Mt Psilorítis •

Lefká Óri & The Sfakiá Coast

0   50   100 km

work in the mountains, most notably in the Ágrafa region, where only-recently tamed rivers have carved 1700-metre-deep gorges through the rock strata.

Scattered volcanic and geothermal activity is the result of the African tectonic plate burrowing under the European one; a string of extinct or dormant volcanoes, including Méthana, and the islands of Mílos, Thíra and Níssiros, marks the junction. In addition there are numerous hot springs in the northern mainland and the north-eastern Aegean archipelago, where many islands are wholly or partly volcanic in origin.

CLIMATE

Despite its small area, Greece has startling regional variations in climate. Visitors tend to forget that most of the country lies between the latitudes of 35° to 41° north, roughly the same distance from the equator as Japan, California, or New Zealand's north island. Thus it's the overall mildness of the climate that's surprising, not the well-defined areas and periods of harsh weather. Except for the interval from late January to early March, there is always some spot in Greece where conditions are at least tolerable, if not ideal, for a walking visit. More specific pointers are given in the season briefing for most hike write-ups, but the following outline will serve as a useful overview.

In the far north and inland mainland locales away from marine influence, the prevailing climate features hot, muggy summers and bitterly cold, snowy winters that call for a Siberian wardrobe. Luckily, there are buffers of moderate, lingering springs and autumns between the two extreme seasons. The entire western coast, from Methóni on the Messenian cape to the Albanian frontier, experiences gentler but extremely rainy winters that keep the countryside lush all year round, as well as the same hothouse summers.

Weather rhythms of the central and northern Aegean – Magnisía and the Pílion, the Sporádhes, Halkidhikí, Thássos, Samothráki – fall somewhere in between: cold winters with moderate precipitation, and more salubrious in summer. The islands of the eastern Aegean – Sámos, Híos and Lésvos – benefit somewhat from the sheltering effects of the Anatolian landmass just opposite, with much milder winters than their northerly position would lead you to believe.

The southern islands, the lowlands of the Pelopónnisos (Peloponnese) and the Attic peninsula around Athens enjoy a true Mediterranean climate. This is a convenient description for a pattern repeated in several parts of the world lying between 30° and 36° north or south that face a dry, subtropical ocean on the west. Mild and minimally wet winters precede long, hot summers (in Greece, from early June to early October). Vegetation is almost entirely dependent on ground water accumulated during the winter months, when most growth actually occurs; such conditions favour the small-leaved, thorny, evergreen scrub that makes casual visitors from other 'Mediterranean' areas (California, Chile, southern Australia, South Africa...) feel as if they'd never left home.

Attikí (Attica), the coastal Pelopónnisos and most of the islands receive their annual rainfall in sporadic downpours falling at any time between November and March. Only eastern Crete and the southern Dhodhekánisos (Dodecanese) have really brief (February and March) dryish winters, but even this balmy area may be inaccessible owing to storms between it and Athens' seaports and airports. Around most of the islands no particular wind prevails in winter, with warm, rain-bearing southerlies alternating with chilling northerlies. The *alkionídhes* or halcyon days of the ancients, two calm, sunny weeks in mid-January, really do exist and make for fine walking weather. For much of the year, though, the Aegean is buffeted by the infamous *meltémi*, a northerly wind fuelled by high-pressure zones over the mainland, which blows roughly from noon to midnight.

The mountains everywhere – whether Cretan, Peloponnesian or mainland – generate their own microclimates and are pretty much off limits to all but snow campers from November to April. Even as late as June you may have to contend with heavy runoff, huge snow banks or both, depending on the severity of the past winter. Summer alpine thunderstorms, particularly in the northern Píndhos, are inconvenient and common.

This leaves April-June and September-October as the best times for a low-altitude walking visit. Most, though by no means all, of the famous Greek wildflowers bloom in succession from early to late spring while there is still enough shallow ground water. If you come to see them too early, though, March winds will tear you and the pages of your field guide to ribbons. In compensation, the early spring atmosphere attains a lens-like clarity, and photographic opportunities are at their best.

Easter week is a moveable feast in the Greek Orthodox calendar; it can occur anytime from late March to early May, but usually falls in April – and means substantial hassles for the traveller in terms of booked transport and accommodation, especially in the years when Catholic and Orthodox Easters coincide and northern Europeans descend on the country. However, if you reserve in advance, Crete, the southern Pelopónnisos and the Dhodhekánisos offer some of their best walking weather then, in addition to the festivities.

The days lengthen and warm up through May, which marks the unofficial beginning of the swimming season. Sensible trekkers or day hikers will move north with the sun as the land behind them dries to a crisp; heatstroke in the south remains a very real danger until autumn. By June, crampons, gaiters or an ice axe are needed nowhere except on Mount Ólimbos and perhaps two or three other northern peaks.

July and August are the peak months for tourist arrivals; that fact, plus the soaring mercury, frays everyone's nerves. It's a good time to retreat to the alpine hideouts of Ípiros (Epirus) and the Stereá (central mainland), far from the crowds. Nuisance insects, particularly flies and mosquitoes, are tropically profuse, and the humidity can be debilitating, but the long summer days permit extended marches, and wild edible fruits abound in many places.

In addition, numerous city dwellers rebel against hellish metropolitan conditions and retreat to their ancestral villages, where between mid-July and the end of August the wayfarer can partake in an almost nonstop series of religious festivals. Accommodation, expensive now in any event, is to all intents and purposes unavailable, so if at all possible bring a tent with you. (This is sound advice for anywhere in Greece, in midsummer.) There's no lack, however, of liquid refreshment, country-style barbecues, and musical accompaniment more distinguished by decibels than quality.

The worst of the heat relents by mid-September, when the sea is at is warmest for swimming. Autumn in the mountains is spectacular, with turning leaves and piled-up cloud formations; unhappily, the clouds herald erratic weather, and an Aegean storm or two just before the equinox is the rule. In the north virtually uninterrupted wetness begins with almost monsoonal regularity around 1 October, a date often referred to simply as *protovróhia* (first rains). The autumn trekker should return again to the south, keeping in mind that the less expensive types of accommodation officially close on 1 November, and that schedules for all kinds of public transportation are severely cut back.

LAND MANAGEMENT & CONSERVATION

Greece has been inhabited continuously for at least 9000 years, and the results have included intense cultivation of the limited farmland, deforestation by ship builders, goats and arsonists, and ever-increasing population pressure on finite natural resources. The land mass remaining after the primeval flood was heavily forested, but scarcely anything remains of the original growth. Expanding cities and road networks restrict animal ranges so that wild creatures bigger than a fox are rarely encountered. In addition, Greeks are ruthless and thorough hunters and fishers, and autumn – when the

hills resound with gunshots and motorbike handlebars are festooned with dead game – is not for the squeamish. As in most other Mediterranean countries, conservationist notions were completely foreign to Greece until after WW II.

Since then, protection of various plant and animal species has been instituted by the forest service, though it must be said that these rules exist more on paper than in actual fact. Exceptions, where the express prohibitions are occasionally enforced, include the two marine reserves in the Sporádhes islands and off western Sámos, and eight national parks – Samarian Gorge (Crete), Kefallonià (Mt Énos), Mt Párnitha, Mt Íti, Mt Ólimbos, the Víkos Gorge, the Válía Kálda, and the Préspa lakes – though these all conform more to the idea of a North American national forest or a breeding sanctuary than a recreational park. The designation of an area as a reserve has until recently meant relative neglect rather than sensible development for walk-in visitors, and hasn't kept the poachers and bulldozers away. And in any case you should refrain from picking plants everywhere, since many Greek wildflowers are endangered species and you'd need to be a trained botanist to distinguish them from common ones.

On a more grass-roots level, numerous conservation-orientated groups have sprung up in the urban centres, either broadly

Logo of the Greek Protection of Forests society

focused (eg ELPIDA, the Greek Protection of Forests; or a chapter of Mountain Wilderness) or specifically dedicated to saving endangered species such as the brown bear, monk seal or wolf. There are also ecological and mountaineering magazines, the most visible being *Korfes* – the voice of the Greek Mountaineering Federation – which frequently highlights deplorable situations such as strip-mine scarring on Mt Gióna or proposals for megadevelopment in the northern Píndhos, to name prominent, recent examples. In 1988 the 'Attilas', a satirical award modelled on the Nobel Prize, was instituted by Athens ecologists to single out groups or individuals engaging in particularly destructive environmental behaviour; past 'winners' include a minister of agriculture for introducing legislation allowing shepherds to graze in burnt forests, and the director of the public power corporation for his approval of a major dam at the source of the Aóös, in the Vália Kálda national reserve. The conservationist contingent, in rare alliance with the local villagers, has apparently won – for the time being – the battle to preserve the Víkos/lower Aóös area in its natural state, but such victories are rare; the developers are cunning, and have regrouped for an assault on Mount Ólimbos, where some of their proposals for the summit area defy belief.

The greatest obstacle to rescuing the remnants of the Greek natural environment, however, is the gap in outlook between the often hard-pressed rural population and the overwhelmingly urban, upper-class 'birdwatching' contingent. An across-the-board antihunting stance by the city slickers is unlikely to sit well with a shepherd who has just lost a whole flock of goats to hungry wolves. Progress is, and will be, made only when the villagers see that their bread is buttered on the side of wilderness preservation – more likely in mountain tourism areas.

Nowhere are these issues more starkly dramatised than in the recurring tragedy of forest fires, which since 1928 have reduced Greece's forest cover from just under one-third of the land area to just under one-fifth,

with the most rapid loss since 1974. The proposed reasons and agents for the conflagrations which rage through the woods each summer are as numerous as the blazes themselves. Conspiracy theorists, definitely not an endangered species in Greece, have a field day; you may hear variously that the CIA, the KGB, Mossad, the Turks, the PLO, Freemasons, or little green men set off the latest inferno, but the painful, unvarnished truth is that the vast majority of the fires are the result of arson perpetrated by Greeks. Actual motives are simple and sordid: clearing land for grazing or building, speculators forcing intransigent farmers to sell up at depressed prices, dampening tourism on a rival island or at a rival beach, or creating further panic and lack of confidence in the government during the frequent periods of political instability.

Those responsible are often underemployed thugs who hire themselves out to bigwigs needing a 'job' done; that lots of money is frequently behind the arson was demonstrated some years back when time-delay incendiary devices dropped from a private plane were fortunately discovered before detonation in one of the mainland's densest forests. The Orthodox Church and the forest service respectively own and administer vast tracts of land in a quasi-feudal system, pursuing contradictory and erratic taxation, classification, and use policies which only encourage the firebugs – a prime example is the 1988 law permitting grazing in burnt woods whose classification as protected forest had previously been irrevocable. Some sort of administrative reshuffle is imperative to prevent the complete destruction of Greece's dwindling wilderness.

FLORA & FAUNA

Given the uneven (to put it mildly) record of resource management, the abundance of smaller mobile and vegetative wildlife may come as a pleasant surprise. Like so many things Greek, the flora is a mix of the north African, west Asian and south European that meet only here. Some interesting speciations have occurred as a result of the islands' mutual isolation by the Aegean ages ago, and many Greek plants in particular are found nowhere else. There is no point in duplicating the hard work of the excellent field guides listed in the Books section, so the following summary will just touch on what the most untrained visitor can't help but see on a Greek trip. Greek names for the most common trees, often used as landmarks, are given in the Language section.

The prime indicator of Mediterranean and island biomes is the presence of the olive, holm oak, carob, Aleppo pine and cypress, which often share sites on rocky, sunny, limestone hillsides. In the Dhodhekánisos and Crete, juniper will be the largest plant of the *frígana* (low scrub) zone, consisting mostly of spikey, clumpy, low growth; here the kermes oak assumes distorted, almost topiary forms. The larger Valonea oak tolerates volcanic soil, and arbutus – whose fruit used to be made into ouzo – and heath favour acid ground. The two genera of brooms are

not picky, though they prefer to be within sight of the sea. Oleanders line usually dry streambeds but plane trees prefer their water running and usually become huge landmarks at fountains. Naturalised exotic species include palm trees, most famously on Crete; the smelly tree-of-heaven; and the prickly pear cactus, whose (peeled!) September fruit tastes like watermelon.

Closer to the ground, anemones are usually the first spectacular wildflower out in late winter or early spring; irises and several types of lilies follow soon after, as do the poppies which love fallow fields. The spring cyclamen is white and stays in partial shade; rock roses (genus *Cistus*) like dry, sunny slopes. The grotesque dragon arum (*drakóndia*), found near garbage dumps, is characterised by a rotten-meat odour which attracts pollinating flies to a spiky, maroon blossom. Autumn blooms are less numerous but no less colourful; the best are the pink cyclamen; the yellow sternbergia which inhabits rock crevices at ancient ruins; and

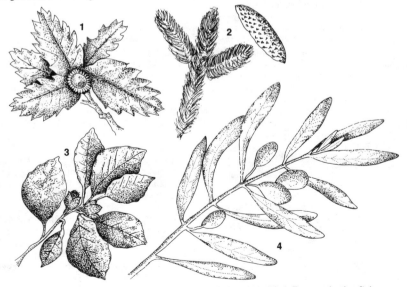

1 *Quercus macrolepis* (oak) **2** *Abies cephalonica* (Cepallonian fir) **3** *Fagus sylvatica* (fig)
4 *Olea europaea* (olive, with fruit)

the sea squill, which sends up metre-high white flower stalks from hidden bulbs. As for the herbs that fill pantries, just follow your nose...

Foothill trees include wild pear, used on Crete to make musical instruments; wild plum *(korómila)*, a riverside delight in Ípiros; and white poplars, a sign of past or present habitation. Not a tree, but ubiquitous, is the twining clematis vine, with its unmistakable fuzzy seed coat. The most majestic alpine conifers are the Cephallonian fir, whose range includes Évvia, the Stereá and the Pelopónnisos as well as its namesake island, and its cousin the silver fir, found only in the north. Mount Pílion in particular is dense with sweet chestnut and beech, the latter also the main deciduous species in Makedhonía and the Píndhos. Among pines, the most common are the black pine, found across most of the mainland as well as Crete, and the Balkan pine, which can grow up to elevations of 2300 metres in northern Greece.

The most conspicuous mid-altitude wildflowers are gladioli, mostly reddish tulips, and violas, all spring bloomers. Of true crocuses there are a dozen examples in Greece, some appearing in spring, some in autumn; the similar colchicum comes out only in autumn, often in the same area, and to confuse identification further many similar

Save our Seals Poster

species can grow at altitudes ranging from 100 to 1500 metres. Small-flowered, reddish lilies enliven the mainland mountains in mid-summer, as do campanulas; contrastingly drab but interesting are carlinas, giant composites growing flush with the ground above the treeline, whose bracts close in moist conditions.

Common island and coastal creatures include dolphins and porpoises, who often follow ferries to the delight of passengers (though a mysterious AIDS-like blight, aggravated by pollution, is killing them off), and pelicans, frequent mascots at fishing harbours. Much wilder and shyer are the endangered monk seal and the sea turtle, the latter nesting only at the island of Zákinthos. You may be surprised to find freshwater crabs, eels and terrapins swimming in streams on islands with a high water table or in mainland estuaries. On the other hand, overfishing and pollution of the Aegean mean that fish stocks are quite depleted, so deceptively clear waters are often quite sterile.

Laurus nobilis (true laurel)

Small mainland mammals are widely distributed: various kinds of rodents get in your pack at night if you're not careful, and hares or rabbits are a favourite hunting target. Hedgehogs seem to have bad luck crossing roads, as the many squashed specimens imply; foxes and badgers are more canny. You're more likely to smell or hear wild boar, weasels or jackals than see them, and the same goes for chamois, which inhabit lofty, inaccessible crags of the Píndhos. Far more often talked about than seen are the Spanish lynx, said to exist only in the western Rodhópi hills and perhaps the Aóös valley, and wolves, which have made a comeback recently and are now blamed for attacking livestock. Locals, pointing to occasional fresh tracks or claw marks on tree trunks, will attempt to scare you with threats of attacks by brown bears; in fact they are timid, with less than 100 left in the Aóös basin of the Píndhos and along the northern frontier. Avoid overnighting in dense forest and you should have no trouble from them.

Monarchs of the air include the golden eagle, the rare lammergeier and two other kinds of vulture, which all gravitate toward cliffs that provide nests and air currents to soar on. The most colourful small birds include finches, bee-eaters and hoopoes; the most luckless are partridges, turtle doves and quail, shot out of the sky in large numbers come September. Partridges tend to cluster near springs, hence the hundreds of *Perdhikóvrisi* (Partridge Spring) place names in the hills; flush a covey accidentally, and the whirring of their wings never fails to startle you. Greece's extensive wetlands support permanent or transient populations of every sort of wading and floating waterbird you can imagine, most notably egrets, herons, ducks and bitterns but also grebes and cormorants. Nocturnal hooters include the tiny Scops owl, the little owl, and the sinister nightjar; ravens and rooks form grim conventions of day-time croakers. More cheerful and domesticated are swallows, which swarm from their mud nests at dusk to catch insects, and the storks which roost on artificial structures throughout the northern mainland – both are tolerated since they're considered to bring good luck.

On the ground you'll see orange-speckled fire salamanders promenading after rains; six species of frogs; lizards ranging from finger to arm size; and the surprisingly noisy Greek land tortoise, which you should not take home as a pet (as some attempt to) since they're protected. In lakes and ponds of the northern mountains, newts suspend themselves comically just below the surface of the water.

POPULATION & PEOPLE

Greece is commonly reckoned to have just under 10 million inhabitants, though the exact number of Greek people is almost impossible to tally due to the overriding phenomenon of the Greek diaspora. Virtually as many Greeks live outside the country as in, principally in the USA, Australia, Canada, Germany and England, but also in most other EC countries, Africa and many of the former Communist states of Eastern Europe. The emigration began during Ottoman times, reached a peak during the first seven decades of this century, and only recently abated with the world economic slowdown. Consequently there are numerous Hellenes abroad who retain Greek citizenship, returning to spend the summer or even to vote, but whose lives are firmly based elsewhere. Their payments to relatives back in the 'old country' support what until recently was largely a remittance economy.

Add to this the semi-established groups of Greek Orthodox refugees from Cyprus, Istanbul, Albania and even Central Asia and you can see the futility of assigning hard and fast numbers. A near-zero population growth rate provokes anxiety in the face of the mushrooming birth rate in neighbouring Turkey, the hereditary enemy, and the labour shortage for menial jobs has attracted many Filipinos and others from South-East Asia looking for work.

Until 1950 Greece was predominantly an agrarian nation, with daily life played out in a village or small-town setting, but the transformation to an urban and overseas remittance culture had actually begun following the disastrous 1919-22 Asia Minor War, after which nearly 1½ million refugees poured into the country, concentrating overwhelmingly in and around Athens and Thessaloníki. From then on there was no turning back, and today the two major cities – plus half a dozen others over 75,000 – constitute nearly two-thirds of the population. The effect on values, whether monetary, ethical, civic or aesthetic, has been cataclysmic, to say the least; the combined factors of war, earthquakes and profiteering have guaranteed that Greek cities are generally among the ugliest in Europe.

Most remote villages are today merely summer holiday centres, with only a skeleton crew during the other eight months or (in extreme cases) complete abandonment in winter. This lifestyle has required only small modifications to existing habits, since there had always been a certain amount of seasonal migration: the cooler, higher pastures and hamlets reserved for the summer months, with residence lower down being the norm when the grazing season was over.

In terms of the people themselves, it should be stressed that a 'pure Hellene' is a romantic fiction last trotted out for use by the colonels' junta, since centuries of invasion, immigration and subsequent assimilation point to cultural durability and Orthodox religious identity rather than racial continuity. The average Greek is such a complex amalgam that they probably couldn't dissect their ancestry into its components even if they tried. There are more minority groups in Greece than is commonly realised, and the backcountry visitor will probably run across at least a few of these subcultures.

Greece was originally populated from the 6th to the 2nd millennium BC by successive waves of settlers from Asia Minor and the Levant. Thereafter, aside from a few citizens of the western Roman Empire, there were not many newcomers until the Slavs from the northern Balkans raided the then declining Byzantine (eastern Roman) Empire in the 7th to 10th centuries AD. The Slavs soon lost their separate ethnic identity, leaving only a handful of place names as far south as the Pelopónnisos to mark their coming.

Shortly after, the less assimilable Vlachs, purportedly nomads from present-day Romania (then known as Walachia, hence Vlach), appeared and dispersed themselves in Ípirios and parts of Thessalía and Makedhonía. (According to a contending theory, they are descended from locals trained as mountain-pass guards by the Romans; after the empire dissolved, their barracks Latin evolved into a dialect mutually intelligible with standard Romanian.)

There used to be two types of Vlachs, or Rumaní as they prefer to be called. (*Vlákhos* in the mouths of many Greeks is an insult, equivalent to yokel or bumpkin.) The so-called Kutso-Vlachs until recently spoke their dialect of Rumaniká as their first language, but today, despite optional education in the tongue for school children, it is dying out and only older adults tend to be proficient in it. These people are concentrated in the central Píndhos, from Métsovo (their 'capital') to the Akhelóös river valley, and in the villages of the Aóös river basin, particularly the east-bank settlements of Vovúsa and Samarína. Natives of villages above the snowline have alternative winter quarters lower down in Thessalía or western Makedhonía. Until recently there existed numbers of less prosperous and less settled Karagunídhes or Arvanito-Vlachs, who spoke Albanian in addition to Rumaniká and Greek, but any distinction is vanishing as this subgroup is steadily absorbed into mainstream Greek culture.

Another conspicuous mainland 'tribe' is the Sarakatsáni, strictly Greek-speaking nomads, possibly of aboriginal or Pelasgian (first-settler) origin, who formerly wandered through most of northern Greece but whose range is now restricted. Until a few years ago they were true nomads, migrating between summer pastures in the Píndhos and winter grazing in the lowlands. The government has of late required them to establish permanent winter dwellings, but they still return each summer to the mountains, where they may rent pastures from the villagers, often the now nearly sedentary Kutso-Vlachs with whom they are not on good terms. They are quite welcoming to outsiders, though, and it is probable that summer trekkers in the Píndhos will happen upon their temporary colonies or meet them on the trail.

Albanian Christians arrived in Greece around 1300, repopulating the islands of Spétses and Ídhra, the Peloponnesian mainland opposite, and portions of Ádhros, Évvia and Attikí. Albanian and medieval Greek cultures were so alike that assimilation was rapid, although spoken Albanian only disappeared from Attikí after 1950. Recently the clock has been turned back, so to speak, as tens of thousands of Orthodox refugees, mostly young and male, poured across the frontier into Greece during 1990 and 1991 in response to chronic persecution and new political turmoil in Albania. Once again Albanian is heard frequently on Greek streets, and will be for some time yet since the newcomers' Greek is often rudimentary, the consequence of decades of suppression of Hellenic culture by the Hoxha regime. For the moment they are hired as day-labourers at disgracefully low wages by Greek farmers and builders, and all manner of vice and bad habits are ascribed to them – unhappily not without basis. When Prime Minister Mitsotakis declared Greece a refuge for the Albanian Orthodox in 1990, the Albanian authorities took the opportunity to unload some of their more hardened criminals on the Greeks, just as Cuba's Castro did whenever American presidents did their give-us-your-huddled-masses-yearning-to-be-free number. Mass arrests and deportations have been the result as the Greek police attempt to separate the genuine, legal refugees from the others.

As most visitors will soon be told in an aggrieved tone, the Ottomans conquered most of the provinces of what is now modern Greece by 1425 and stayed as occupiers for almost four centuries. During that period intermarriage, voluntary or otherwise, was not unheard of, and the influence of things Turkish on cuisine, language and music (though not Orthodox Christianity or folklore) was enormous. All of the ills of modern Greek society are laid at the imperial rulers' door, and to some extent this is true, but stable, indirect rule permitted the semi-autonomous wealthier communities of the Dhodhekánisos, Ípiros, Thessalía/Magnisía and the eastern Aegean to thrive in a way not seen before or since. The long interaction between the two cultures is too complex to summarise or dismiss in a paragraph, but suffice it to say that both parties also benefited from mutual contact.

With each northward extension of the frontiers of the modern Greek state, Greek Muslims (a more accurate term than Turk) were either killed or fled over the border to Ottoman territory. By the harsh terms of the 1923 Greco-Turkish Treaty of Lausanne, all remaining Greek Muslims – some half a million – were forcibly exchanged for nearly three times as many Anatolian Orthodox, many of these Greek in religion only as their way of life and language were completely Turkish. The only exceptions were the Tsamídhes (an Ipirote Muslim group expelled in 1944 for collaboration with the Axis), the bilingual Muslims of Ródhos and Kos (many of them expelled from Crete between 1913 and 1923, and 'inherited' by the Greeks when they regained the Dhodhekánisos in 1948), and – most importantly – the ethnic Turks of western Thráki (Thrace), who today number about 100,000.

For many years their neighbours and the central government treated them relatively well – by comparison with Bulgarian policy towards their Turkish minority, or Republican Turkish handling of Kurds and Christians – but recently old Ottoman rivalries, resentments and hatreds have resurfaced. There were bloody communal riots in early 1990 and a political trial of two community leaders at the same time in which a former MP (one Thracian seat is always considered 'Turkish') was convicted of sedition. Developments in neighbouring Bulgaria, where a specifically ethnic Turkish party is now a partner in the new coalition government (in direct contrast to the former regime's persecution and expulsion of Turks), has the Greeks quaking in their boots, fearful of a pan-Thracian Muslim movement on both sides of the hard-won border. (After WW I there had been a peace treaty and a partial exchange of Greek and Slavic populations between Greece and Bulgaria.) To complicate the picture, there also exists along the same frontier a group known as the Pomaks, some 30,000 Muslims speaking a bizarre hybrid of Bulgarian, Turkish and Greek. Because of alleged collaboration with the Bulgarian occupiers during the last world war, the Greek government quite literally trusts them only as far as they can see them, and they require special permits to leave their home area.

Another recurring Greek nightmare involves the Orthodox Macedonian-speakers, who live along the current Greco-Yugoslav border. Just where and what Macedonia is and whether its people are Hellenic or Slavic is the focus of an ongoing, three-way propaganda war between Bulgaria, Greece and (insofar as it continues to exist) Yugoslavia.

Archaeology plays a big role in the argument; finds at northern Greek digs are political dynamite, pressed into service at the Thessaloníki museum in an well-executed 'educational' exercise demonstrating that ancient Macedonia – including that portion well inside modern Yugoslavia – was incontrovertibly Hellenistic. Most impartial scholarship backs the Greek position, but the outcome, in view of the current Yugoslav turmoil, is by no means certain.

The concept of an independent Macedonian state was endorsed by the leftist rebels during the 1945-49 Greek Civil War, and (allegedly) by a certain proportion of Macedonian-speaking Greeks. Thereafter, the rump state of Yugoslavian Macedonia (the Greeks still disparagingly call it the Republic of Skopje, after its capital), had to suffice, and the 1950s Greek regime, assuming all of them guilty of treason, made life miserable for its Macedonian minority until the bulk of them emigrated to Canada and

Australia. Only since 1975 have the Macedonian-speakers begun to trickle back to their old villages, and to use their dialect in public without fear of harassment. As 'Yugoslav' Macedonia proceeds to act in practical terms on its Unilateral Declaration of Independence of September 1990, there's no telling what the outcome will be. It seems as if Greece and her neighbours are doomed to yet resolve, one way or another, messes left over since the disintegration of the Ottoman Empire.

Other Greek minorities, fortunately, are more scattered and advance no territorial claims. Gypsies can be found almost everywhere in Greece (particularly on ferries), although they concentrate in Thessalía, Makedhonía and Thráki, where they are usually Muslim rather than Orthodox Christian. They have long since traded in their horse carts for trucks in which they rove the countryside, peddling watermelons, cheap bedding or linen and plastic garden furniture.

Other Greeks view them ambivalently, appreciating their musicianship – most of the great mainland instrumentalists are of gypsy origin – but as a rule looking down on them as beggars and swindlers. As a result it is a problematic community, undereducated and underemployed due to a vicious circle of discrimination and their own low self-esteem.

Catholics are a legacy of the Venetian penetration of the Aegean following the piratical Fourth Crusade of 1204. Today they live principally on the islands of Tínos, Syros, Thíra and Náxos, or in Athens. Often Italianate last names distinguish them from their Orthodox neighbours, though little else; on Tínos and Syros especially, the adherents of the two churches get along peacefully.

The Jewish communities of Ioánnina, Halkídha and Ródhos are some of the oldest in Europe, dating back to the Roman era. The Sephardic Jews of Thessaloníki, Vólos, Lárissa, and Thráki were invited there by the Ottoman sultan Beyazit II in 1492 following their expulsion from Spain and Portugal.

The Jewish enclave in Athens is a more

recent phenomenon, being mostly German Jews who accompanied King Otto of Bavaria to Greece in the 1830s. There were many other Jewish centres in Greece prior to WW II, but the Nazis massacred 80% of them in 1944-45, so that today only about 5000 Jews remain.

Taken together, these various interesting minorities total less than 5% of the entire Greek population. Nonetheless they are conspicuous and important out of proportion to their numbers, and any visitor to Greece will derive satisfaction from an informed glimpse of those who would otherwise just be mysterious oddities. It is also sobering to contemplate that, at any given moment, Greece is host to anywhere from a few thousand to almost a million foreigners, mostly concentrated in Athens and the southern islands. While individually transient, travellers and foreign residents must be considered an important demographic component of the country into the foreseeable future.

LANGUAGE

Modern Greek is not one of the easier languages to learn, falling somewhere between German and the Slavic tongues in difficulty, according to informed assessment. However, travelling in the style advocated by this guide assumes a willingness to acquire at least the rudiments, since it can be potentially dangerous to stroll off into the Greek yonder without being able to understand at least the gist of the usually detailed directions offered by villagers. In addition, many readers may not be able to obtain the instructional materials cited in this section, let alone attend formal courses, so the following glossaries are quite thorough.

If you can't make the time to learn Greek systematically or to commit the phrases below to memory, I strongly urge you to at least master the script transliteration table, since the majority of rural, business and bus signs, not to mention phone books, are not in Roman script.

Greek Alphabet

Greek uses a special alphabet of 24 letters,

the basis of both the later Cyrillic and Roman scripts. Some of the characters are the same as in our alphabet, but many of their phonetic values are different and there are a couple of deceptive look-alikes. A monotonic accent system replaced the classical threesome back in the 1980s, and the dominant stress is now indicated by a simple acute accent over the appropriate syllable. Proper accentuation is critical in Greek, often being counter-intuitive and frequently the only distinction between otherwise identical words: *mílo* (apple) versus *miló* (I speak) is just one of numerous examples.

You'll notice that there are diphthongs made of certain Greek vowels; an umlaut breaks these into the component parts, eg the river Aóös is pronounced 'Ah-ohs', rather than 'Ah-ooos'; similarly *tsaï* (tea) is pronounced 'ts-eye' rather than 'tseh', which is how such a vowel group would ordinarily come out. Sometimes the umlaut is the primary stress, sometimes not, in which case another accent is shown.

Pronunciation

A α	'ah' as in tall
B β	'v'
Γ γ	approximately 'g' (a unique soft palatal), but 'y' before certain vowels
Δ δ	'th' as in 'these'; rendered as 'dh' in this book
E ε	'e' as in 'bed', rendered 'eh' if final to emphasise that it's never silent!
Z ζ	'z'
H η	'i', but as the vowels in 'tree'
Θ θ	'th' as in 'throw'
I ι	'i' as above
K κ	'k'
Λ λ	'l'
M μ	'm'
N ν	'n'
Ξ ξ	'ks' when initial, 'x' as in 'box' when medial or final
O o	'o'
Π π	'p'
P ρ	'r'
Σ σ ς	's', sometimes 'z' before certain consonants
T τ	't'

Υ υ	'i' as above; varies (see next section)
Φ φ	'f'
Χ χ	hard 'h' when initial, 'kh' when medial
Ψ ψ	'ps'
Ω ω	'o'

Double letters, whether diphthongs or consonant clusters, often have entirely different values.

αι	'ey' in the vowels of 'train'
ει	'i' as described above
οι	'i' again as above
ου	'u' as in rule, often rendered on signs as '8'
αυ	'av' but often 'af' before certain consonants
ευ	'ev' but often 'ef' in same conditions as above
ηυ	'iv' or 'if' as above
γγ	'ng' (always medial)
γκ	'ng' when medial, hard 'g' otherwise
μπ	'mb' when medial, 'b' if initial
ντ	'nd' when medial, 'd' if initial
τζ	'dz' or 'j'

The presence of any of the last three clusters usually indicates a word's Turkish, Italian, Slavic or other foreign origin.

Learning Materials

The following reasonably priced paperback books are generally available in university bookstores in North America and the UK, and most probably in Australia, New Zealand and South Africa.

The best compact dictionary for travellers is the palm-sized *Collins Gem Greek-English English-Greek*, inexpensive and usually available on both sides of the Atlantic. Their coat-pocket-sized model *Collins Contemporary Greek-English English-Greek* is identical in coverage so don't load yourself down with it. The bulkier and more expensive *Oxford Dictionary of Modern Greek* is an acceptable second choice. Don't get seduced by the smallness of the *Divry's Handy Greek-English English-Greek*

Lexicon, whose usage and outlook is stuck somewhere back in the 1950s.

For a crash self-instructional course, *A Manual of Modern Greek* by Ann Farmakides (Yale University Press) is the best available in North America; there's an intermediate sequel and a reading primer for those who master the basics. The entire three-volume set costs close to $100 but is well worth it. *Demotic Greek* by John Rassias and Peter & Chrysanthi Bien (University Press of New England) is a distinct second choice. You may have to settle for *Colloquial Greek* (Routledge) or *Modern Greek* by S A Sofroniou, part of David MacKay's ageing Teach Yourself series, the latter really most useful as a quick brush-up for those who have studied Greek formally. In the UK you should try either for the Farmakides set or find *Breakthrough Greece*, a book and two cassettes issued by Pan, the best self-teaching course available.

Greek being what it is, even decent phrasebooks are of limited usefulness (and virtually nonexistent in North America). The best choices in the UK are either *Greek Travelmate* (Drew) or *Greek at Your Fingertips* (Routledge), the latter with more grammatical orientation. Going out of print, but worth looking for in Athens, is Tom Stone's *Greek Handbook*, an excellent emergency manual that's a combination cultural guide, phrasebook and dictionary. It's light years ahead of any Berlitz or Hamlyn product, and the author intends to reissue it soon.

Transliteration & Grammar

Since many Greek letters have no exact Latin equivalents, the art of transliteration will always be controversial. Some favour an orthographic approach, which dutifully traces the evolution of each letter through the ages and uses its Roman descendant, despite the fact that the value of the letter has changed completely. Then there is the quasi-phonetic school, which vainly substitutes the nearest 'international' (usually Germanic) equivalent, such as 'ch' for 'hi', the hard-aytch sound. I have even seen ridiculously pedantic systems littering pages with double or even triple vowels, with or without y's, in frantic attempts to duplicate the Greek sound. The spellings used in this book assume some familiarity with the ah-eh-ee-oh-oo for a-e-i-o-u vowel schema of most Romance languages, and if you've ever suffered through high-school Spanish, Italian or French, you'll utter comprehensible noises with the transliterations below – do not be flustered if you see other systems. Mine are phonetic and do not always correlate, letter for letter, with the word spelling in the Greek alphabet. The transliteration of place names has followed, with some small departures, the conventions of *The Times Concise Atlas of the World*.

Personal names are handled a bit differently, since the Greeks adhere to their own system in business cards or foreign-language tourist literature. The principal variation here is my substitution of 'u' for their 'ou', 'h' or 'kh' for 'ch' and 'dh' for 'd'.

Greek, like Latin and German, has three genders and swarms of different declensions for the singular, plural, accusative and genitive forms. Adjectives must agree in number and gender with nouns; except for numerals and nationalities, they are cited in the neuter singular below to simplify matters, while nouns are given in the nominative singular case. An exception has been made in the case of active staffed monasteries or convents, which are listed in the genitive, because their formal titles are 'The Holy Monastery of Such-and-Such', the last four words commonly used in speech. Rural churches or tiny one-cell monasteries active only on their feast days are referred to in the nominative. Like many other languages, Greek has both familiar and formal second person forms of address, which are here indicated by the abbreviation sg/pl (for singular/plural, which these forms also are).

Greetings & Civilities

Good morning/day.
kalí méra
Good evening.
kalí spéra

Good night.
kalí níkhta
Health to you. (standard greeting, parting, toast)
ya su/sas (sg/pl)
Rejoice. (the greeting of the early Christian fathers, still common in rural areas)
hériteh
Welcome! (literally, 'It is well that you have come.')
kalós ílthes/ílthateh! (sg/pl)
To which the response is literally, 'We have found you well.'
kalós sas vríkameh
Goodbye. (a Venetian loan-word similar to Spanish *adiós*)
adío
Health and joy. (a very casual parting equivalent to 'bye')
ya hará
See you soon. (as the French *au revoir*)
kalí andámosi
Bon voyage.
kaló taxídhi
May you go towards the good. (formal farewell uttered by the stationary party)
na pas sto kaló
The good hour to you.
kalí óra su/sas (sg/pl)
Good strength. (said to someone seen undertaking a difficult task)
kalí dhinamí
Have a good rest. (what people are likely to say to you when they find out where you've been trekking!)
kalí ksekúrasi

Small Talk

How are you?
pos íseh/ísteh? (sg/pl)
How are you? (more informal)
ti kánis/kániteh? (sg/pl)
What's up? (rather casual)
ti yíneteh?
Fine, and you?
kalá, keh esí/esís? (sg/pl)
Please.
parakaló
Thank you (very much).
efkharistó (polí)

You're welcome. (literally, 'I also (thank you).')
keh egó

(It was) nothing. (same idea as above)
típota

Pardon (me).
signómi

OK. (used exactly as in English)
en dáxi

Certainly
málista

Yes.
neh

Standard phone greeting
bros!

No.
óhi

Greeks' Questions

Where are you (sg/pl) from?
apó pu ísey/ísteh?

Are you (m/f) married?
pandhremén(os)/(i) ísey/ísteh?

Where are you (sg/pl) going?
ya pu pas/páteh?

Can we treat you (sg/pl) to something?
na su/sas kerásumeh káti?

Nationalities

The first parenthetical ending is masculine, the second is feminine. In all cases you can make a complete sentence with the verb *ímey* (I am).

American	*ámerikan(ós)/(ídha)*
Canadian	*kanadh(ós)/(éza)*
English	*ángl(os)/ídha)*
Australian	*austral(ós)/(ídha)*
New Zealander	*néa Zilandh(ós)/(í)*
Dutch	*olandhéz(os)/(a)*
German	*yerman(ós)/(ídha)*
Austrian	*avstriak(ós)/(í)*
Swiss	*elvet(ós)/(ídha)*
French	*gáll(os)/(ídha)*
Irish	*irlandh(ós)/(í)*
Swedish	*souidh(ós)/(éza)*
Danish	*dhan(ós)/(éza)*
Finnish	*finlandh(ós)/(éza)*
Norwegian	*norvig(ós)/(í)*

Israeli	*israïlin(ós)/(í)*
South African	*nótia Afrikan(ós)/(ídha)*

Requests

Can I leave this here for a while?
boró na afíso túto edhó ya lígo?

Can I camp around here?
boró na kataskinóso edhó péra?

How far is it to...?
póso makriá íneh ya...?

I'm looking for the path to...
yirévo to monopáti ya...

Where is the toilet?
pu íney i tualéta?

Is there... (a bus, beach, trail)?
ékhi...?

Are there... (tickets, apples, etc)?
ékhun...?

There is/are.
ékhi/ékhun

There isn't/aren't any.
dhen ékhi/ékhun

The verb *ipárkhi/ipárkhun*, which has a similar meaning to *ékhi/ékhun*, is also common.

Accommodation

I'm staying...days.
méno...méres

single, double, triple (room)
monóklino,dhíklino, tríklino

double bed
dhipló kreváti

room with a window/shower
dhomátio meh paráthiro/dus

(hot) water
(zestó) neró

Can I wash clothes?
boró na plíno rúha?

sheets, blankets, pillow
sedónia, kuvértes, maxilári

key
klidhí

light bulb, lantern, candle
lámba, fanári, kerí

Numbers

Counting in Greek is made somewhat challenging by the fact that some, but not all, numbers are declined according to the three genders.

1	énas, mía, éna – also the indefinite article
2	dhío (invariable)
3	tris, tría – m/f, and neuter
4	tésseres, téssera – again m/f, and neuter
5	pénde
6	éxi
7	eftá
8	októ
9	ennéa or ennyá
10	dhéka
11	éndheka
12	dhódheka
13	dhéka tris/tría
14	dhéka tésseres
20	íkosi
24	íkosi tésseres/téssera
30	triánda
40	saránda
50	penínda
60	exínda
70	evdomínda
80	ogdhónda
90	enenínda
100	ekató(n)
118	ekató(n) dhéka-októ

When necessary, Greek uses masculine and feminine endings for the multiples of hundred, and for one thousand, since the numerals are grammatically adjectives defining the item counted. First the neuter forms, then some more complex examples:

200	dhiakósia
300	trakósia
400	tetrakósia
500	pendakósia
600	exakósia
700	eftakósia
800	oktakósia
900	enniakósia
1000	hílii, hílies, hília

Multiples of a thousand take a special, invariable form:

| 2000 | dhío hiliádhes |

| 4403 dhrakhmés | tésseres hiliádhes tetrakósies tris |

(since the unit of money is grammatically feminine)

| 8614 'masculine items' | októ hiliádhes eksakósii dhéka-tésseres |

Time

What time is it?	ti óra íney?
It's...o'clock.	íney...i óra.
At what time...?	se ti óra...?
At...o'clock.	stis...óres
one hour	mía óra
half-hour	misí óra
three hours	tris óres
a quarter (of an hour)	éna tétarto
one minute – elastic unit of time in Greece	éna leptó
20 minutes	íkosi leptá
When?	póteh?
Never.	potéh (note accent difference)
now	tóra
later	argótera
always, continually	pánda, sinéhia
today	símera
yesterday	kthes
day before yesterday	prókthes
tomorrow	ávrio
day after tomorrow	metávrio
dawn	hárama, ksimerómata, avyí
sunset	iliovasílema
dusk, twilight	súrupo
morning	proï
afternoon	mesiméri
evening	vrádhi

Weather

good/bad weather	kalós/kakós kerós
It's sunny.	ékhi ílio
clouds, it's cloudy	sínefa, sinefiázi
rain, it rains	vrokhí, vrékhi
major storm	fortúna, kateyídha
downpour, squall	bóra
calm at sea	bonátsa

lightning	*astrapí*
thunder	*vrondí*
snow, it snows	*hióni, hionízi*
mist, fog	*omíkhli*

Hiking Equipment

altimeter	*ipsómetro*
backpack	*sakídhio*
backpacking store	*kataskínosis/ kámping/katástima*
boots	*arvíles*
compact stove	*gaziéra, kaminéto*
compass	*pixídha*
crampons	*krampón* (also plural)
flashlight, torch	*fakós*
foam pad	*stromáki*
gaiters	*gaïtes*
gas cartridges	*gazákia, boutilákia*
ice axe	*pioléh*
matches, lighter	*spírta, anaptírio*
parka	*bufán*
pocketknife	*souyás*
rain poncho	*kagúla*
sleeping bag	*ipnósakkos*
down	*pupulénio*
fibre-fill	*poliéster, sinthetikó*
tent	*skiní*
walking stick	*bastúni, mangúra*
water canteen	*pagúri*
windbreaker	*andianemikó*

Directions

a bit more, further	*lígo pió, lígo akóma*
above/below	*(e)páno apó/káto apó*
across from, opposite	*apénandi*
adjacent	*dhípla*
before/after	*prin/metá*
between, among	*metaxí, anámesa*
beyond	*péra*
big/small	*megálo/mikró*
flat/sheer	*lío/apótomo*
from...until, up to	*apó...méhri, os*
here/there	*edhó/ekí*
level/uneven (land)	*omaló/anómalo*
near/far	*kondá/makriá*
nice, pretty	*oréo*
unpleasant/ugly	*áskimo*
right/left	*dhexiá/aristerá*
straight ahead	*katefthía, ísia*
towards	*pros*

uphill/downhill	*aníforo/katíforo*
upper/lower	*áno/káto*
wide/narrow	*fardhí/stenó*

Rights of Way

road, way	
(vague general term)	*dhrómos*
goat trace	*katsikódhromos*
proper trail	*monopáti*
mule track	*muláriko*
cobbled path	*kalderími*
forest logging road	*dhasikí odhós*
rock stairway, ladder	*skála*
government-maintained road other than a dhasikí between villages (literally 'public')	*dhimósio*
dirt/asphalt	*homaténio/ásfalto*

Trail Science

altitude, trig point	*ipsómetro*
contour lines	*ipsometrikés kambíles*
crossroads, fork	*stavrodhrómi, dhiastávrosi, dhiakládhosi*
map	*hártis*
marker cairn	*kutrúmbulo*
metres, km	*métra, hiliómetra*
Saint...(m/f, plural)	*áyios/ayía, áyii...*
scale	*klímaka*
shortcut	*koftó*
sign, placard	*pinakídha, tabéla*
switchbacks, zig-zags	*kangelákia*
waymark(s), blaze(s)	*simádhi(a)*

Landmarks & Features

agricultural plain	*kámbos*
alpine refuge	*kataffyio*
antiquities, ruins	*arkheótites, arkhéa*
aqueduct, canal	*idhragoyío*
boulder	*kotróni, lithári*
bridge	*yéfira, yefíri*
can-on-a-string	*sikláki*
castle, fortified elevation	*kástro, frúrio*
cave	*spiliá, spíleo*
cemetery	*nekrotafío*
chasm, sinkhole	*hásma*
church	*eklisía*

cirque, often pond	*lútsa*
cliff	*gremmós*
clump of trees	*sistádha*
couloir	*lúki*
crag	*vrákhos*
crest, watershed	*korifógrammi*
cultivated field	*horáfi*
dry gully	*ksiropótamos*
dry-stone walls	*ksirolithiés*
burnt area, clearing	*kséfoto*
forest	*dhássos*
gorge	*farángi*
gravel	*halíki*
gulch, cavity, clearing	*lákka*
high plateau	*oropédhio*
hill, knoll	*lófos, ípsoma*
house	*spíti*
hut, cottage	*kalívi*
fountain, tap	*vrísi*
isolated rural chapel	*ksoklísi*
lake	*límni*
marine cape	*akrotíri*
marsh, swamp	*báltos*
meadow	*livádhi*
monastery or convent	*monastíri, moní*
mountain(s)	*vun(ó)/(á)*
narrows	*sténoma*
open pool or tank (East Aegean idiom)	*havúza*
pass, saddle	*pérazma, dhiásello, avkhínas*
peak (in Rumaniká dialect)	*tsúka*
phone or power poles	*kolónes*
quarry	*latomío*
rain cistern	*stérna*
ravine, canyon, defile	*langádhi, langádha, harádhra*
ridge	*rákhi*
river	*potámi*
riverbank	*ókhthi*
rock (the substance, sg)	*pétra*
sandy beach	*ammudhiá, paralía*
scree (pile)	*sára*
sea	*thálassa*
seashore	*yialós*
sheep pen, corral	*mándhra, strúnga*
shepherds' colony	*stáni*

side, other side	*meriá, álli meriá*
slope, hillside	*playá*
smaller stream	*révma, riáki*
soccer field	*yípedho*
spring of water	*piyí*
summit, peak	*korfí*
threshing circle	*alóni*
tower	*pírgos*
tree	*dhéndhro*
concrete, capped reservoir	*dhexamení*
valley	*kiládha*
vineyard	*ambéli*
waterfall	*kataráktis*
wayside shrine	*ikónisma, i konostási*
well	*pigádhi*

Civic Units & Places

all-in-one store, grill and phone booth of a mountain village	*magazí*
café, coffeehouse	*kafenío*
city, large town	*póli*
community records office	*kinotikó grafío*
county	*eparkhía*
district of larger entity, habitation	*sinikía, sinikismós*
hamlet	*horiudháki*
main town of an island, usually called by the same name as the island	*hóra*
mountain-village inn	*ksenón(as)*
plaza, village square	*platía*
province	*nomós*
roadhouse, isolated eatery	*exohikó kéndro*
town hall	*dhimarkhío*
village	*horió*

People

abbess	*iguménissa*
abbot	*igúmenos*
bag & zipper mender	*tsandadzís*
café proprietor	*kafedzís, magazís*
cobbler	*tsangáris*
foreigner, also guest	*ksén(os)/(i)*

guard, warden	*fílakas*
field warden	*agrofílakas*
forest ranger	*dhassofílakas*
hunter	*kinigós*
monastery	
guestmaster	*arhondáris*
monk	*kalóyeros, monahós*
nun	*kalógria, monahí*
police officer	*astinómos*
shepherd	*tsombánis, voskós, ktinotrófos*
village headman	*próedhros*

Trees

pine	*pévko*
Balkan pine	*róbolo*
fir	*élato*
beech	*oxiá*
poplar	*lévka*
linden	*flamúri*
chestnut	*kastaniá*
wild walnut	*karidhiá*
wild plum	*koromiliá*
Valonea oak	*valanidhiá*
kermes oak	*purnári*
juniper, cedar	*kédhros*
cypress	*kiparíssi*
carob tree	*harupiá*
olive tree	*eliá*
plane tree	*plátanos*
oleander	*pikrodháfni*
palm tree	*fínikas*

Beasts, Birds, Bugs

badger	*asvós*
bear	*arkúdha*
bee	*mélissa*
butterfly	*petalúdha*
chamois	*agriéga*
deer	*eláfi*
donkey	*gaïdhúri, gaïdharos*
eagle	*aetós*

field mouse	*pondíki*
flea	*psílos*
fly	*míga*
fox	*alepú*
frog	*vátrahos*
gnat	*skgrípa*
goat	*katsíki, gídha*
hare	*lágos*
hawk	*yeráki*
hedgehog	*skanzókhiros*
horned owl	*búfos*
horse	*álogo*
jellyfish	*tsúktra, médhusa*
little owl	*kukuváyia*
lizard	*sávra*
long-eared owl	*mikróbufos*
louse	*psíra*
lynx	*língas*
mosquito	*kunúpi*
mule	*mulári*
newt	*trítona*
partridge	*pérdhika*
pigeon	*peristéri*
rabbit	*kunélli*
rat	*aruréos*
salamander	*salamándhra*
scorpion	*skorpiós*
sea urchin	*akhinós*
sheep	*próvato*
sheep guard-dog	*mandróskilo*
snake	*fídhi*
spider	*arákhni*
stork	*pelargós, leléki*
tick	*tsimbúri*
tortoise	*helóna*
turtle dove	*trigóni*
viper, adder	*okhiá*
vulture	*órnio*
wasp, hornet	*sfíka, sfigóna*
weasel	*nifítsa*
wolf	*líkos*

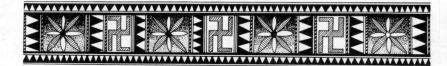

Facts for the Trekker

VISAS & IMMIGRATION

Holders of any European Community (EC) passport will experience no special formalities upon entering Greece; US citizens, Canadians, Australians, New Zealanders and virtually all western European nationals receive a passport stamp valid for a stay of 90 days, while those from South Africa get 60 days.

Non-EC nationals who wish to stay longer than the allotted automatic tourist visa allows can do one of two things. Not strictly legal, but most commonly practised, is to leave the country for one of its neighbours (usually Turkey, Yugoslavia or Bulgaria) for a few days and then reenter for a new stamp. The more legitimate option, obtaining an *ádhia paramonís* (residence permit), involves visiting the nearest police station with six passport photos and personalised pink bank-exchange receipts proving that you can support yourself without working in Greece. In the largest cities you go not to an ordinary police station, but to the Ipiresía Allodhapón (Aliens' Bureau), open from 8 am to 1 pm Monday to Friday. In Athens it's at Halkokondhíli 9, near Platía Káningos; in Thessaloníki the address is Politekhníou 41.

If you overstay your initial period but then leave on your own (ie are not deported), you will be fined a certain amount – $6 or so per month of total stay – upon exit, which in effect retroactively extends your tourist stamp.

MONEY

In such a tourist-friendly country as Greece, exchanging foreign currency is usually a fairly painless and rapid exercise, with a variety of options and strategies available. Things get a bit creaky only if you are well off the beaten track, where banks are less apt to have the routines down pat. All banks are open from 8 am to 2 pm Monday to Thursday, with a 1.30 pm closure on Friday – provided, of course, that they're not on strike, a not uncommon condition. Certain banks in big cities or in frontier towns keep short evening or weekend morning hours; these include Athens, Dhelfí, Iráklion, Thessaloníki, Pátra, Corfu, Ródhos, Kos, Skiáthos, Alexandhroúpoli, and any international airport. Note that the land-crossing frontier posts at Kípi (Turkey), Promahónas (Bulgaria), Evzóni and Níki (ex-Yugoslavia) and Igoumenítsa (ferries from Italy/Croatia) seem to keep no extraordinary banking hours, so buy some Greek money in advance if you'll be arriving at these places at odd times. Post offices also change money; see the Post entry in this chapter for opening hours.

Most brands of travellers' cheques are easily exchanged, though commissions – which depend on the amount being transacted, and to a certain extent on the particular bank – can vary considerably, from $2 to $5, so ask first. Converting cash incurs much lower charges, but then the rate given tends also to be less favourable.

If you have a European bank account, Eurocheques are often the most convenient and economical way to go: the commission works out slightly more than for travellers' cheques, but then you don't pay a charge upon purchase and you get the most advantageous inter-bank rate when the cheque is presented for payment. They're also honoured at post offices when the banks are on strike and no-one can work out the rate for the various currencies. In a similar vein, you can use post offices to draw money out on a northern European Girobank account.

Plastic is widely honoured for large purchases, vehicle hire, and plane or ferry tickets, usually without fuss or extra charges. The cash-dispensing machines of a few banks can accept foreign credit cards, provided you know your PIN number. The widest network is that of Trápeza Písteos (Credit Bank), which takes Visa Cards, as well as British Barclay Cards; much more restricted are those of the Emborikí Trápeza (Commercial Bank – Visa) and the Ethnikí Trápeza (National Bank – MasterCard). Using such machines for an emergency infusion of cash is far easier, cheaper and quicker than having money wired from overseas.

Try not to get stuck with large amounts of extra Greek money on departure – nonresidents are only allowed to reexchange the equivalent of $100 back into foreign currency without formality. If you need to reconvert more, you'll have to have saved pink, personalised exchange receipts to more than cover the amount you wish to repurchase. These are not given out routinely, so if you think you'll be wanting them ask for one each time you exchange money. Even if you present the necessary receipts, massive red tape and off-putting commissions (as much as $10) are further disincentives. If you must, the best place to do it is an airport arrivals exchange booth – they'll have a wide range of foreign money on hand.

Currency

The Greek currency is the *dhrakhmí* (plural dhrakhmés; abbreviated to dr), which comes in denominations of one, two, five, 10, 20, 50 and 100 (coins), and 50, 100, 500, 1000 and 5000 (notes). Nobody much bothers about the 1dr and 2dr coins any longer, the 50dr note may soon be discontinued, and a 10,000dr note is being contemplated. Beware of the limited number of pre-1975 (junta era) notes floating about; these are no longer legal tender.

Dhrakhmés are often referred to in slang as *fránga* ('francs'). Each denomination has a special descriptive name which you should recognise:

5dr coin	*táliro*
10dr coin	*dhekáriko*
20dr coin	*ikosáriko*
50dr coin/note	*penindáriko*
100dr note	*katosáriko*
1000dr note	*hiliáriko*

Exchange Rates

A$1	=	148dr
C$1	=	170dr
DM1	=	133dr
FFr1	=	39dr
NZ$1	=	111dr
SwFr1	=	146dr
Turk (lira)100	=	2.6dr
UK£1	=	331dr
US$1	=	215dr

Costs

Even for outsiders (let alone residents) Greece is no longer a particularly inexpensive country in which to travel or live, though it compares with Portugal as one of the cheapest EC nations. Domestic inflation hovers around 20% annually, with frequent, unannounced hikes in the prices of everything from meat to ferry tickets, as the current government tries to amortise the extravagance of the 1981-89 regime. The dhrakhmí devalues against most foreign currencies at just under the inflation rate; thus prices in this book are cited in US$, values likely to remain approximately correct for some time to come.

Decent accommodation will usually set you back $10 to $16 a single or $17 a double. Count on $2 for a continental breakfast, and $6 to $10 per person for main meals. Drink is cheap – $1 for a beer, less than $4 for a decent bottle of wine – as are city buses, which work out at $0.30 to $0.70. Trains are also inexpensive – perhaps $6 for a 200-km trip – but long-distance coaches cost more than double that. Domestic ferry boats are fairly reasonable, particularly the B-class cabins, and you'd be hard pressed to spend more than $40 for one on the longest trips (19 hours). Inland plane flights are affordable, once in a while, at $35 to $70 per trip.

In summary, if you hide out in the hills trekking all the time, cooking store-bought food on your campstove, staying in your tent, and hitching around, it's possible – though by no means easy – to survive on $14 a day. A more realistic figure, however, allowing for occasional indulgences in comfortable hotels, meals out and fast transport, entails a minimum budget of $900 per month. You can reduce these figures somewhat if travelling with another person.

An international student or youth card often nets you discounts on museum and site admissions and certain types of air and rail transport; ask.

POST & TELECOMMUNICATIONS
Post

Post offices *(takhidhromía)* are usually near the middle of town and open Monday to Friday from 7.30 am to 2 pm. In the largest cities and tourist centres, hours are often extended into the evening and weekend mornings.

Post boxes are bright yellow with black lettering, the same as the postal service logo. Outgoing mail is quite reliable, with items taking from three to six days to reach other EC countries, from five to nine days for North America, and slightly longer for Oceania. Registered, express and small-package services are reasonable; fax is not, at about $15 per page.

You can have your inbound mail sent to the poste restante division of any Greek post office. Unclaimed letters (you'll need some

ID to pick them up) are returned to the sender after 30 days. Incoming mail service can be terrible, especially on islands without airports – allow 12 to 16 days for airmail delivery from Australia and New Zealand, and 15 to 25 days from the UK or North America.

Telephones

Greek telephones are abysmally bad, on a par with eastern European or Israeli services, and for similar reasons. You generally have to try four or five times to get a line out of a particular area code, with echoes, cut-offs and one inaudible party being the norm. To add insult to injury, rates are among the most expensive in the EC though reductions took effect in 1992. The telecommunications entity, OTE, claims it will be installing a couple of million digital exchanges in the 1990s, but so far only the posher suburbs of Athens have benefited and, as ever, relief will come last to the more remote provinces. This program was set even further back during the mid-1980s, when funds earmarked for infrastructure improvement were embezzled by a former OTE director. Greece lost a quick chance for state-of-the-art exchanges when Greek Euro-deputies recently 'persuaded' their colleagues in Brussels to award the modernisation contract to a small, unproven home company rather than a northern European one, thus guaranteeing a new cycle of delays and cost overruns.

Phone booths per se are being phased out, though still common are fat red counter-top phones which take a 10-dr coin for local calls. You generally make long-distance calls from a street-corner kiosk or *períptero*, or (much quieter) the confines of an OTE station booth. The latter have variable hours depending on location: from 7 am to almost midnight in the biggest cities, down to 7.30 am to 3 pm in the tinier towns. It's preferable to use them, since periptera, while open long hours, often levy a 15% surcharge on the already outrageous basic rates. Don't ever call out of a hotel, where the supplement is usually a whopping 50%. Local calls made from a períptero cost 10dr, just like on the red phones.

Careful dialling makes all the difference to whether you get through or not. Hit a single zero to get onto the country-wide net, and a second one to reach the perennially overloaded international circuits. Medium fast blips at this point mean you failed, try again; if you get a 'sorry, all lines busy' recording, wait a longer while. A uniform, seashell-to-ear type hiss means success. Next dial the Greek area code, or the foreign country code (1 for the USA/Canada, 44 for the UK, 61 for Australia, 64 for New Zealand, 27 for South Africa), then wait for a distinctive series of six clicks. If you don't hear them you haven't got through, and if you continue dialling without waiting for them you won't get through. Finally, dial either the Greek subscriber number, or the area code and subscriber number in the overseas place without interruption.

Rates within Greece are 9dr per unit, with 15 to 18 units elapsing per minute; a cheap rate applies from 3 to 5 pm and 10 pm to 8 am, plus Saturday afternoon to Monday morning. As a rough estimate, one minute costs $2 to Australia or North America, $1 to all of north-western Europe, and $0.65 to the Balkans and Turkey. There is no off-peak period for international calls.

Greek phone numbers cited in this book have been given with the initial zero included in the area code. If you are attempting to reach any of these numbers from overseas, omit it.

TIME

Greece is two hours ahead of GMT, seven hours ahead of US Eastern Standard Time and eight hours behind Australian Eastern Standard Time. Daylight saving is observed from 4 am on the last Sunday in March until 4 am on the last Sunday in September; the change is not well publicised, and every year people miss ferry boats or planes – beware! Be also alert, especially when phoning home, to the fact that in early April, and for most of October, Greek daylight saving does not coincide with North America's (and in autumn, England's); at these times the difference is one hour from England, six or eight hours from New York.

BANK HOLIDAYS

Watch out for the following public holidays, when in fact nothing is likely to be open:

1 January
Ayíos Vasílios
6 January
Epifánia (Epiphany)
Katharí Dhevtéra
(first Monday of Lent – varies from mid-February to late March)
25 March
a combination of Evangelismós (Annunciation of the Virgin) and National Day
Easter (Páskha) weekend
the Friday through the Monday, variable in spring
Whit Monday (Pentecost)
seven weeks plus one day after Easter
1 May
Protomayiá
15 August
Apokímisis tis Panayías, Assumption of the Virgin
28 October
Óhi Day, marking Greece's entry into WWII
25-26 December
Hristúyenna (Christmas) and Sínaxis tis Panayías (Meeting with the Virgin); if Christmas and New Year's Day fall on weekends, many working days on the previous and following weeks are also holidays.

BUSINESS HOURS

Business hours are likely to cause grief to the uninitiated foreigner. It is difficult to be very specific about Greek opening hours, except to say that they change constantly with the seasonal and political climate, and to not count on getting anything done except between the hours of 10 am and 1 pm, Monday to Friday.

In theory shops are open during the warmer months on Monday, Wednesday and Saturday from approximately 8.30 am until 2 or 2.30 pm, and on Tuesday, Thursday and Saturday from 8.30 am to 1 pm and again from 5 or 5.30 to 8.30 or 9 pm. But exceptions, owing to personal or professional idiosyncrasies, are the rule – proprietors tend to shut early at noon; bakeries and pharmacies are never open in the evening, nor do the latter operate on Saturday morning (though a list is posted showing the nearest night-duty one).

Butchers are not supposed to sell meat, only cheese and deli items, on summer evenings (though many do, on the sly); conversely, any small shop selling milk can stay open as long as it likes.

In recent years the government, against fierce resistance from retailers, imposed (on Athens and Thessaloníki at least) a unitary schedule during the colder months of the year – approximately 9 am to 7 pm daily, with closure on certain days at 6 pm. This was done to reduce the pollution resulting from four, rather than two, daily commutes, but adjustment problems still persist.

It is rumoured that, in accordance with EC directives for uniform post-1992 commercial practices, afternoon rests everywhere in the country will soon go by the board. This would be a shame, since the siesta is one of the Mediterranean's great contributions to civilisation, and the summer climate (as you'll see for yourself once there) virtually demands one.

By contrast, white-collar offices work 9 am to 6 pm schedules across the calendar, and all government ministries keep year-round 8 am to 2 pm hours. Museums and archaeological sites have completely unpredictable hours, depending on their popularity, staff funding and the whim of the keeper; count on 10 am to 1 pm as a minimum, with Monday the most frequent day of closure. Monasteries close for an afternoon siesta whose length varies with the season, and will likely be exempt from any mandates from Brussels.

In terms of timekeeping, intercity buses and planes are usually very prompt – don't dawdle. Trains and ferries start out with good intentions, but are typically half an hour behind by the end of their run. Punctuality in personal or business appointments depends a great deal on where you are and on how business-suit professional your contact is.

Socially, Greeks are largely nocturnal (thus the afternoon naps) and often need to be coaxed out of bed in the morning. Patience is a virtue to cultivate, and – cynical as it may sound – have alternative plans ready if your party doesn't show up within a reasonable time of your agreed meeting. Late July until early September is a bad time to see anyone or get anything done in the larger cities, which are half empty then – this is Greece's official vacation period (see Religious Festivals) and everybody who can manage it is out in the mountains or on the islands.

WEIGHTS & MEASURES

Greece uses the metric system, except for two particularities: interisland distances and speeds are given in nautical miles (*mília* or *kómvi*), and plots of land are sold – and, more tragically, forest fire damage is estimated – in *strémmata*, equal to 1000 sq metres or about one-fourth of an acre.

ELECTRICITY

Electric current in Greece conforms to continental European standard, ie 220-240V AC out of a double (unearthed) or triple (earthed) round-pin socket. Travellers from Britain, Oceania or North America will require the appropriate plug adapter and, in the latter case, a voltage regulator.

RELIGIOUS FESTIVALS

The major festivals of the Greek Orthodox church come in clusters, with the principal concentrations in late winter, spring and midsummer. This doesn't mean that the calendar is inactive otherwise; every locale has its patron saint, whose day is the occasion for observances of some sort. The *paneyíria* (festivals) listed here are either important nationwide spectacles or fervently celebrated events in rural spots where trekkers are most likely to be. An important concept to understand is the *paramoní* or evening before the festival date; most of the drinking and dancing takes place then, so if you show up on the actual calendar day you'll usually have missed the party.

Áyios Vasílios (St Basil), 1 January – Mostly an indoor, family holiday; adults play cards for money, and bake a cake, called the *vasilópitta*, with a coin in it; finding it in your portion brings luck. Parades on the seafaring islands of Híos and Ándhros. The typical New Year greeting is '*Kalí hroniá*'.

Epifánia (Blessing of the Waters), 6 January – Reconsecration of the water in church baptismal founts and at seaside or lakeshore locations. A priest or bishop used to hurl a crucifix over the water, and the young men swam for the honour of recovering it, but unseemly tactics among the contestants is causing the custom to die out.

Apókries or Karnaváli (Carnival), late January to early March – Especially on the seventh weekend before Easter, many mainland towns – particularly Pátra and Náussa – celebrate Carnival with parades, masking and mischief. Premier Aegean observance is on Skíros, where the Goat Dance is enacted by young men festooned with heavy bells and swathed in hairy pelts and goatskins.

Katharí Dheftéra (Clean Monday) – The seventh Monday before Easter is the first day of Lent, marked by a mass exodus to the country for picnics and kite flying. Last binges of music and meat eating before Lenten austerities.

Megáli Sarakostí (Lent), the seven weeks before Easter – Not observed rigorously in urban areas, but even there seafood and greens dominate menus. Observance in rural areas can be strict and it may be difficult to find animal protein in the more remote tavernas (octopus, squid and sea urchin are substituted). Weddings are not conducted and music is not played in the villages.

National Day, 25 March – A mixed secular/religious festival commemorating both the beginning of the Greek independence uprising and the Annunciation of the Virgin Mary. In sizeable provincial towns there will be parades and evening folk dancing. Services are held at any church named Evangelizmós or Evangelístria (Annunciation),

the most famous being on Tínos island, where a wonder-working icon of the Panayía (Virgin) is carried in procession over the sick, who kneel before it.

Páskha (Easter), variable, usually April – This is the grandest holiday in Greece, though observance varies from place to place. Throughout Megáli Evdhomádha (Holy Week) you should wish friends '*Kaló Páskha*' (Happy Easter); the entire week is a build-up to the Sunday event, with rites and customs specific to each day. Most obvious to outsiders are the Maundy Thursday practice of dyeing eggs red, and placing them in *tsourékia* (baked spicy bread twists), and the Friday preparation of the Epitáfios (Christ's funeral bier) by the women of a parish, who completely adorn a wooden catafalque with woven flower sprays. This is carried in solemn candlelight procession on Friday evening, following the poignant service of the Descent from the Cross. In many parts of Greece effigies of Judas Iscariot are burnt at a stake during this period. The candlelit Anástasi (Resurrection) ceremony at midnight on Saturday is among the most beautiful ceremonies in Christianity; the standard greeting after the event, if you can hear anything above the din of firecrackers, is '*Hristós anésti*' ('Christ is risen'). In the small hours of Easter Sunday, after the midnight service, the Lenten fast is broken with a meal of *mayerítsa* (lamb tripe, rice and dill soup). Lambs slaughtered the day before are put to the spit on Sunday afternoon, and the party usually lasts well into Monday.

Áyios Yióryios (St George), 23 April, or the Monday after Easter if that falls later – The dragon-slaying saint is the patron of the Greek army and of shepherds. Barbecues, dancing and games are held at Aráhova at the base of Mt Párnassos. Shepherds sacrifice a prize animal to the church at this, the start of the pastoral year; grazing leases are agreed on and flocks head up the mountains.

Protomayiá (May Day) – In Greece this is still a holiday with pagan/magical rather than Marxist associations. There are excursions to the country to weave wreaths, which are hung on front doors and cars. The garlands are credited with various magical properties and are saved until...

Áyios Ioánnis Pródhromos (St John the Baptist), 24 June – A thinly disguised summer solstice festival: bonfires are lit the evening before, the May wreaths are tossed in, and children take turns leaping over the flames.

The close spacing of the following festivals between late July and early September brings Greece effectively to a standstill – the

'Artistic' site admission ticket

best strategy is to join in the fun and not have any plans to get things done.

Ayía Marína (St Marina), 17 July – A very important rural saint; today essentially marks the harvest of the first fruits.

Profítis Ilías (Profit Elijah), 20 July – Processions on the evening of the 19th to any of the numerous hilltop chapels dedicated to this patron of the weather. Frequently an all-night vigil, with music and feasting.

Ayía Paraskeví (Holy Preparation), 26 July – An important bacchanal in rural areas, particularly Ípiros, where the saint's chapels are everywhere. Áyios Pandelímon, 27 July, and Metamórfosi tu Sótiros (Transfiguration of the Saviour), 6 August, are nearly as popular.

Apokímisis tis Panayías (Assumption of the Virgin), 15 August – Probably the most important and widely celebrated feast after Easter. Particularly fervent observances at Ayiássos on Lésvos, Páros, Tínos, and most mountain villages which are bound to have a church dedicated to the Assumption nearby. It is highly inadvisable to try travelling by any conveyance for several days before or after the 15th without having made reservations well in advance.

Yénnisis tis Panayías (Birth of the Virgin), 8 September – Any Marian monastery not dedicated to the Assumption will be dedicated to the Birth of the Virgin, with correspondingly lively festivities today.

Ípsosi tu Timíu Stavrú (Elevation of the Holy Cross), 14 September – The last big summer festival commemorates the Byzantine empress Helena's finding of the True Cross in Jerusalem.

Áyios Dhimítrios (St Demetrius), 26 October – The pastoral year traditionally ends on this day (though the mountains tend to empty a week or two before), and the first wine is tapped. Dhimítrios is the patron of Thessaloníki, where a major cultural festival precedes the day.

Óhi (No!) Day, 28 October – Civil holiday commemorating the dictator Metaxas' apocryphal one-word answer to Mussolini's ultimatum in 1940. Parades, folk dancing, etc.

Hristúyenna (Christmas), 25-26 December – Like New Year's, this is a private, indoor festival, with pork the traditional evening meal rather than turkey. However the day is becoming increasingly commercialised in west European style with every passing year, though in some areas you may still see children going from house to house singing *kálanda* or carols.

Name Days

In addition to the saints listed previously, there must be a good 100 others whose feasts are observed by the church. This concerns you insomuch as Greeks prefer to celebrate their *yiortí* or saint's name day rather than their birthday, and the traditional congratulation, if you learn it's an acquaintance's day, is '*Hrónia pollá!*' (Many happy returns!).

Other Events

You may be invited to a wedding or baptism, which are similar enough to non-Orthodox rites, but some Greek funerary customs may take getting used to. Do not be alarmed if you see people tucking bones into metal ossuaries in country churchyards – it is customary to unearth the dead after three years and make room for the newly deceased. Similarly, you may be approached by the bereaved and offered *kóliva*, a mixture of sugar, cinnamon, wheat, barley, rice, pomegranate seeds and other ingredients. This special food, symbolic of the resurrection, is offered to everyone met on various anniversaries of the death date, and you should politely accept your handful.

ACCOMMODATION

There's an abundance of lodging for most tastes and wallets in Greece. All of it is rigorously controlled and rated by the local authorities, so standards are generally fairly high – it's rare to find any roach traps or scabies-laced sheets.

Rented Rooms & Pensions

Readers will probably be most interested in *enikiazómena dhomátia* (rented rooms), of which *pansions* seem a recent subset. On the islands and mainland coasts, they're often clearly marked in three or four languages. Average prices are about $14 a single, and a little more for a double – bona fide singles are in fact rare and solo occupancy tends to carry a heavy penalty. Maximum permissible prices must be posted on a placard, either in the room or the entrance lobby. Extra amenities such as en suite bathrooms, kitchens, gardens, balconies, laundry areas and complete furnishings other than the bed are generally present, reflecting the increasing competitiveness of Greek tourism. Hot water comes either from a solar roof heater (ie there won't be any between 10 pm and 9 am) or a *thermosífono* (electric boiler) which you'll have to work yourself. All this wonderfulness must be paid for, however, and you may occasionally find that rented rooms are as expensive, or more so, as those in a hotel of a comparable category.

The managing family may or may not live in the same building, but you will very likely have met them, crooning that particularly Greek mantra 'Room?! Room?!' when the boat or bus pulls in. Sadly, as tourism in Greece becomes more of an industry, the former routinely personable relationships between host and guest have become something of a rarity. However, you will at least once on your journey run across an old-fashioned proprietor, curious, friendly, helpful and – accustomed to a hardier and less ostentatious clientele – not in awe of their guests. A good landlord or landlady can make all the difference with respect to how much you get out of your stay somewhere: regional pride is highly developed in Greece, and a gregarious, sympathetic host is a veritable storehouse of information on local history, beauty spots, culinary and garden specialties and, yes, walking trails.

Hotels

Wherever and whenever there are no dhomátia, as on the mainland or between 1 November and 1 April, you must rely on hotels of roughly the same price range. These are more impersonal, but single rooms are slightly more common. In the D and E-class establishments, shared bathrooms off the hall are the rule; a C-class hotel by definition must have en suite facilities and a small breakfast/drinks bar. For those travelling as a pair, these can often be very good value – sometimes as little as $17 for two, since price depends as much on location as on amenities.

Inns

An inn or *ksenón(as)* is a vague designation covering both the highest and lowest end of the market. When the national tourist organisation renovates traditional dwellings

and rents them out for near-Hyatt rates, it designates these establishments as ksenónes. Occasionally rural municipalities build a modern ksenón from scratch to house summer holiday-makers who don't have a local ancestral home of their own, and again these are not usually particularly cheap. In some mountain villages, though, they can be both very basic and inexpensive. A *ksenón neótitos* is a youth hostel, of which there are 20 official (and as many more unofficial) scattered throughout Greece. None, except one noted in the text, are near any hiking areas, and at about $5 per person they are not really worth considering if two of you can fill a hotel or dhomátia double room for only slightly more.

Alpine Shelters

The Greek mountains are dotted with over 40 *katafýia* (refuges). Unfortunately, very few are continuously staffed (those that are staffed are discussed in the specific chapters) and you must contact the responsible branch of the pertinent alpine club to rent keys for a shelter. This is generally an expensive undertaking – up to $40 a night – and not really worthwhile unless you have a large group.

Some of the mountain huts are wonderful base camps, equipped with stoves, blanketed bunks, meeting-and-eating areas and fully appointed kitchens; others are mean little hovels or glorified saloons for the drive-in trade. In addition, most were built at a time when approaches to the mountains were quite different, and today many find themselves well off preferred hiking routes. Accordingly they will be discussed in detail only when really useful.

Traditional Hospitality: Monasteries & Village Settings

Greek monasteries and convents have a long-standing tradition of hosting single visitors of the appropriate sex – married (let alone unmarried ones) couples are very seldom accommodated. Especially on the islands, however, this custom is on the wane, since there and on the mainland monastic hospitality has been abused by both Greeks and foreigners vandalising unoccupied but unlocked cloisters. Leaving aside the obvious exception of Mt Áthos, where there are well-defined procedures for obtaining permission, your chances of obtaining shelter are better if the place is truly remote and you are either Orthodox or a Greek-speaker sincerely interested in the way of life. Dress modestly, show up well before dusk, and ask permission from the abbot, abbess or the guest-master. You'll be expected to share quarters with other religious pilgrims, possibly invited to church services, and fed the same, often barely edible fare as everyone else.

In extremely isolated areas where there is no lodging whatsoever, it still occasionally happens that you are put up for the night by village families. Alternatively, you can ask permission to sleep in the school (especially during summer recess) or an unused room of the *kinótiko grafío* (community records office) and it will usually be granted. Barring that, you will be shown a place to sack out – on a *kafenío* terrace or in someone's garage – unmolested.

Camping

Partly because of sanitation problems and fire hazards, partly to harrass gypsies, and partly to ensure trade for hotels and legitimate campsites, 'freelance' camping is actually illegal in Greece. However, this law is rarely enforced as long as you are discreet and exercise a modicum of respect for the local environment and inhabitants. Patronage of local grocery shops and restaurants generally renders you immune from official harassment, and the tavernas may offer you the use of toilets or even showers into the bargain. Where there are no mountain huts or indoor accommodation available (the last a distinct possibility in midsummer), you'll be obliged to camp. Most rural people are fairly tolerant of tent colonies, even going so far as to show you the best place to pitch on the edge of their village. After all, the mountain-dwelling guerrillas of the independence war are enshrined in the pantheon of national heroes, and the summer colonies of rustically

sheltered shepherds are their direct descendants.

Organised campsites, of which there are hundreds, vary considerably in appearance, facilities and price. The impromptu ones set up by individuals or a village are significantly cheaper than the rather plastic-fantastic regimented places managed by the national tourist authority. Somewhere in between fall the perfectly acceptable B and C-class sites that have some sort of official sanction. Charges for a tent and two people, though, can sometimes nearly approach the price of an inexpensive double room, so camping between treks is not always the best-value option.

FOOD
Local Cuisine

Careful choice when eating out is rewarded in Greece, where restaurant quality and prices run the gamut from exorbitant oily slop to unique delicacies served for little more than it would cost to make them yourself. Obviously you're more likely to encounter clip joints and cut corners in a resort setting; often the little holes-in-the-wall with a simple grill and rickety tables under a reed awning are the best. Certainly study the menu first (if there is one) to see if the establishment is within the bounds of reason, but common sense and your nose are equally useful. Prices in fact do not vary that much; a local clientele, fresh-looking food and decent portion size are more critical. It is common practice, especially among foreigners, to head for the kitchen where you point to what you want: end of language-barrier problems. Establishments without written menus can be an opportunity for misunderstandings or attempted fleecings; it's best to settle the price for the most expensive items (main courses, wine) and hope for the best with side dishes.

Eateries tend to come in several different varieties:

estiatória ('restaurants'), mostly urban lunchtime places that specialise in the more complex oven-casserole dishes

kafenía, which serve only coffee, tea, ouzo and beer

ouzerí or *ouzádhika*, which concentrate on a range of *mezédhes* (fancy dips, hors d'oeuvres and seafood bits) to complement alcohol

psistariés (grills), which confine themselves to meat items and a limited number of salads or side dishes

tavérnes, combinations of the two, and most common in resorts

zakharoplastía or patisseries, which emphasise sticky cakes and occasionally offer continental breakfast; a *galaktozakharoplastío* will sell milk-based desserts and yogurt as well.

The fare itself tends to be hearty rather than elegant, a reflection of the peasant culture from which it has grown. Recipes rely heavily on olive oil, pasta, vegetables and dairy products; vegetarians should do OK, since animal fat is not used in cooking. The seafood can also be very good, though alas – except for the sorts listed below – it is no longer remotely cheap. The following 'menu master' has no pretentions to exhaustiveness, but is drawn up with an eye (and a tongue) for what is most nourishing for trekkers on or between treks, most appetising, most commonly found, of best value, and most in agreement with my own prejudices. You may discover other favourites – bon appétit!

Village Breakfasts

trakhasnávhes – sweet- or sour-dough dumplings in hot milk

yiaúrti – yoghurt, preferably *próvio* or sheep-milk based

Street Snacks

kalambóki – roast corn on the cob, mainland staple from July to September

kástana – chestnuts, sold roasted at corner stalls from October to midwinter

suvláki – chunks of pork or lamb, best served in *píta* bread with garnish

spanakópita – spinach filling in a filo crust

tirópita – savoury cheese turnover, in crust as above

Vegetables & Vegetable Dishes

angináres – artichokes (March-April)

arakádhes, bizélia – peas (usually canned)

bámies – okra (expensive)

briám – ratatouille, heavy on the *patátes* (potatoes)

dolmádhes – stuffed grape or cabbage leaves; the former are vegetarian, the latter usually not

fasoládha – bean soup

fasolákia – fresh runner (snap or string) beans

florínes – marinated red Macedonian peppers

horiátiki – so-called Greek salad of tomato, pepper, cucumber, onion, cheese, and olives

hórta, vlíta – steamed wild greens served in lemon and oil

kolokíthia – zucchini, steamed or deep fried

kukiá – horse (broad) beans (April)

lákhano – cabbage (November-February)

melidzánes imám – eggplant slices smothered in rich sauce

marúli – lettuce (November-April)

pandzária – beets (October-April)

róka – rocket greens (raw salad)

yemistá – stuffed tomatoes or peppers (vegetarian)

yígantes – large haricot beans

Dips

dzadzíki – yogurt/cucumber mash, heavily garlicked and herbed

melidzánosalata – mild eggplant purée

taramá – fish roe pâté, popular during Lent

Meat – Grilled, Fried, Baked, Boiled

biftéki – hamburger patty, best grilled

brizóla – pork or veal chop, best grilled

gídha vrastí – goat pot-au-feu – a rural dish

keftédhes – meatballs, with mint, egg and breadcrumbs, fried

kokorétsi – spit-roasted innards and offal

kondosúvli – spit-roasted lamb served in big bony chunks

kotópulo – chicken, grilled or baked

lukániko – country sausage, excellent, grilled or fried

païdhákia – lamb or goat chops, grilled

salingária – snails, fried whole in oil and herbs

sikóti – liver, usually fried; prefer beef to pork

Specialities Containing Meat

dzudzukákia – mincemeat torpedoes baked in sauce

musakás – eggplant, potato and ground lamb casserole under béchamel sauce

paputsáki – a cheese-topped variation of mussakás suitable for vegetarians

pastítsio – baked macaroni and mincemeat pie

patsás – tripe/trotter soup; better than it sounds, very restorative after an all-night ferryboat trip

yuvarlákia – meat and rice balls in *avgolémono* (egg-lemon sauce)

yuvétsi – generic term for any baked-clay casserole containing *kritharáki* (a pasta like Italian *orzo*) and meat chunks

Seafood

galéos – dogfish steak, similar to shark, often frozen

garídhes – shrimp, usually fried or steamed

gávros – anchovy-like sardine
gópes – bogue, a small but meaty, cheap fish
kalamária – squid, fried or stuffed
ksifías – swordfish, beware of *galéos* masquerading as this
ktapódhi – octopus, grilled, stewed or marinated
marídhes – whitebait, tiny, cheap fish eaten head and all
péstrofa – trout, farm-raised in Ipiros

Preparation Terms
tis óras – grilled, cooked to order
kokinistó, stifádho – stewed
vrastó – boiled, steamed
sto fúrno – baked
tiganitó – fried
ksidháto – marinated
psitó – roasted

Dessert & Fruit
The only remotely decadent element of Greek cuisine is the sweets. Many Levantine introductions are tasteless concoctions of sugar and flour, but several desserts are outstanding.

bakalavá – honey and nuts between filo sheets
buǵátsa – sweet cheese pie
ergolávo – almond macaroons
galaktobúriko – custard pie, with little crust
karpúzi – watermelon; summer taverna finale
kidhóni sto fúrno – baked quince; autumn taverna dessert
kurabiédhes – sugared almond cookies
kréma – plain pudding
lukúmi – Turkish delight, standard welcome titbit at monasteries
mustalevriá – grape-must pudding, autumn vineyard speciality
pagotó – ice cream, usually Italian-style; Turkish *kaïmáki* style is better if you can find it
rizógalo – rice pudding - usually excellent

Drinks
kafés illinikós – 'Greek' coffee, served with the fine, boiled grounds at the bottom of the cup
tsaï vunú – 'mountain' tea, brewed from a type of sage
bíra – beer, usually in 33 or 50 cl bottles, rarely draught
krasí – wine; comes as
    levkó, áspro – white
    kókino – red
    kokinélli – rosé
    retsína – flavoured with pine resin
    híma, varelísio – bulk local wine, often very good
neró – water

oúzo – anise-flavoured liqueur
rakí – firewater made from grape stems and crushings
tsikudhiá – Cretan distilled spirits laced with terebinth
tsípuro – mainland variation, standard greeter at monasteries

Food for the Trail
You needn't necessarily weigh down your luggage with packets of expensive, freeze-dried backpacker's food from home, since Greek grocery stores stock a variety of adaptable and (usually) appetising basic materials. With a little imagination much is possible: for example, a small can of shellfish and some instant mashed potato as thickener/extender added to a pot of cream of mushroom packet-soup approximates chowder; a sausage cut into rice, lentils, and red pepper powder will put you right in New Orleans.

Food shopping hours are roughly the same as for other establishments, with Monday, Wednesday and Saturday evening closure the rule, except in small villages where shops keep late afternoon hours daily. It's almost impossible to buy groceries on Sunday except in major tourist centres or in very small villages where the *magazí* doubles as the *kafenío* and is thus open at least in the evening. You may find village stores shut on workday mornings because the proprietors are out in their fields or orchards, running the shop only as a sideline. So if at all possible always do your rural restocking the night before.

The former system of specialisation, whereby different foodstuffs were sold in various types of shops, is fast losing ground to French/American style 'soupermarkets', and in many places it's easiest to resign yourself to filling a list from such establishments. In the larger towns, good stalls of the traditional sort are found in the central bazaar. In Athens this is centred around Evripídhu and Athinás streets; a good outlet for dehydrated and canned items is at Evripídhu 34. If you hate the thought of cans, head a block over to Aralus at Sofokléus 17, a rare Greek health-food store which carries an array of muesli, oat flakes, dark bread, noodles and grains, plus dry fruits and nuts, in bulk or lightly wrapped. Other such shops are the Kendro Fizikis Zois keh Iyias, nearby on Panepistimíu 57, with a good snackbar as well, and To Stakhi, Mikrás Asías 61-63, Ayíu Thomá, Ambelókipi, near the US and Australian embassies; take a No 3 or 13 yellow trolley to get there. (Most conventional supermarkets have a small diet section featuring products by Fytro, a company specialising in health/vegetarian items.) Thessaloníki's old market is a warren of alleys bounded by Egnatías, Dhragúmi, Aristotélus and Tsimiskí.

You should stock up on comparatively esoteric items like oatmeal, powdered milk, or whole-grain bread in the larger towns, or wherever you see them, carrying them about cheerfully until needed. In the villages the range of foodstuffs can be very limited. Incidentally, *bakáliko* is the spoken word for grocery store, but the sign out front will read *pandopolíon* in the formal katharévousa.

In the following lists, a brand may be given if the product is unique in some respect or if it will help the shopkeeper identify it; this does not necessarily imply an endorsement.

Dehydrated & Powdered Items

gala skóni – powdered milk; almost always French Regilait brand in a box

kakáo skóni – cocoa powder; Van Houten is the best imported make, Pavlidhes is an acceptable local variety

kafés stigméos – instant coffee, which tends to be Nescafé, in small cans or individual-serving packets

músa, pudínga – instant mousses or puddings that must be beaten for double the stated instruction time; make with cold spring water and let stand 20 minutes for best results

patátes puréh – instant mashed potatoes

súpa – envelope soup, mostly Knorr, sometimes Maggi brand; flavours include *karóta* (carrot), *manitára* (mushroom), *aspárago* (asparagus)

tsaï se sakulákia – English or Ceylon tea in sachets; bulk tea is rare

votanikó tsaï – herbal tea; *hamomíli* (chamomile), *faskómilo* (sage), and *tsaï vunú* ('mountain tea') are commonest kinds

zákhari – sugar, usually sold in bulk

Staples

elyés – olives; Kalamata variety best

fakés – lentils; quick-cooking protein

hilopítes, kritharáki – square egg noodles and *orzo*-type pasta, both crumble-proof

ksirá fasoliá – dried beans, less practical for small stoves

méli – honey; sold in different sizes, including spill-proof breakfast packets

músli – German, Swiss and British brands are expensive but fairly widely available

rízi – rice, sold prepackaged and in bulk, mostly quick-cooking

plighúri – bulgur wheat, usually expensive Fytro brand or rarely more reasonable Serafeim (Kórinthos) or in bulk; very rapid cooking

vrómi 'Koaker' – Quaker oats to you, always tinned; 'Texas Oats', in a plastic bag, is much cheaper and commonly available in summer.

Bread

Psomí (bread) subdivides into *mávro* ('dark'), *starénio* ('wheat'), and *horiátiko* ('village'). The first two types, at least, are neither particularly dark or wheat-y but virtually indistinguishable from the sawdust-loaves so prevalent in Greece. In many towns, at least one bakery prepares *sikálino* (rye bread) for the benefit of diabetics, and this is usually very good. In Athens, the bakeries at Veïku 45 and 75, a km south of the Acropolis, have excellent genuine whole-grain loafs worth going out of your way for. A *karvéli* is a round loaf, a *frandzóla* is a long loaf. Also sold by weight in bakeries are *kulúria*, hard or soft, sweet or salty, sesame-sprinkled rolls, doughnuts and pretzels, as well as *butímata*, a catch-all term for rich but not too sweet biscuits heavy on the butter, cinnamon and molasses. Both tend to crumble on the trail, however.

Semi-Perishable Items

allandiká – generic term for any cured sausage

avgá – eggs, sometimes sold preboiled

lukániko – country sausage, must be quite dense to keep well

tirí – cheese, of which the most trail-practical is the hard *graviéra*. *Kefalograviéra* is an extra-hard variety intended for grating over pasta. *Kapnistó* is smoked gouda or edam and keeps well.

tsalámi – salami; the dry *típos Levkádhos*, similar to Italian-style, keeps best

Tinned Goods

hirinó kréas – imported Polish, Danish or Yugoslav pork meat; cook it

sardhélles – sardines; not all brands sold with a key

skumbrí – mackerel, usually in tomato sauce

tónos – tuna; Rio Mare brand seems best

You can also find squid and octopus, stuffed grape leaves, beef-and-peas, and other 'ready meals' in tins, but the cumulative weight is prohibitive and any tinned good is best considered a flavouring accent.

Fresh Produce
The only things likely to leave your pack more or less unsquashed are:

akhládhia – pears (little green ones)
kerásia – cherries
kremídhia – onions
mandarínia – tangerines
míla – apples

Liquids
himós – juice, now sold almost exclusively in one-litre or 200 ml cartons; main brands, in roughly descending order of preference, are Balis (with such exotic strains as kiwifruit, carrot, grapefruit and pineapple), Ivi, Amita, and Florina
krasí – wine: if you can fill a small container from a store supplying wine *híma* (in bulk), it's well worth it

Snacks
Ksirí kárpi is the generic term for nuts and dried fruit. In any sizeable town there will be at least one stall that sells nothing but, as well as street pushcarts (less economical packaging). Nuts in particular are known as *tragana* (crunchies).

amígdhala – almonds
ananás – pineapple slices
banána – banana chips
beríkoka – apricots
biskótes – cookies; the biscuit industry has diversified in recent years, so you can now get 'organic' style as an alternative to the all-chemical, filled-sandwich types. Allatini is a typical American-style label.
dhamáskina – prunes; pipless is *horís kukútsi*
fistíkia – peanuts or pistachios: ambiguous, most people qualify peanuts as *araviká fistíkia*
fundúkia – hazelnuts
mandoláto – egg/nut nougat
pastélli – sesame/honey and peanut/honey bars
síka – figs
stragália – dried chickpeas (garbanzos)
stafídhes – seedy black raisins
sultaníncs – pale seedless sultanas

HEALTH
Insurance
Emergency-room care at *yeniká nosokomía* (public general hospitals) in Greece is usually free for most foreign nationals, but the care is not always the greatest, and private clinics are as costly as anywhere else in the world. So a travel insurance policy that covers medical prbolems as well as theft and loss, is a wise idea. The international travel policies handled by STA or other student travel organisations are usually good value. Some policies offer lower and higher medical expenses options, but the higher one is chiefly for countries like the USA which have extremely high medical costs. Check the small print:

1 Some policies specifically exclude 'dangerous' activities, which can include scuba diving, motorcycling, even trekking. If you're planning to use this book in the field then you don't want that sort of policy.
2 You may prefer a policy which pays doctors or hospitals directly rather than you having to pay at the time and claim later. If you have to claim later, make sure you keep all documentation. Some policies ask you to call (reverse charges) a centre in your home country, where an immediate assessment of your problem is made.
3 Check if the policy covers ambulances or an emergency flight home. If you have to stretch out you will require two seats, and somebody has to pay for the extra one!

Sunburn
At high altitudes, or on the Aegean, you can get sunburnt surprisingly quickly even through cloud cover. A hat provides needed protection, and zinc oxide or some other barrier cream protects your nose, lips and earlobes, plus the back of your hands and neck. Calamine lotion is good for mild sunburn.

Prickly Heat
Prickly heat is an itchy rash caused by excessive perspiration trapped under the skin. It usually strikes new arrivals whose pores have not yet opened sufficiently to cope with greater sweating. Keeping cool but bathing often, using a mild talcum powder or even

resorting to air-conditioning may help until you acclimatise.

Heat Exhaustion

Dehydration or salt deficiency can cause heat exhaustion or heat cramps. Take time to acclimatise to the high temperatures and low humidity of the Greek summer, make sure you get sufficient liquids, and heed the seasonal recommendations for each hike! Salt deficiency is characterised by thirst, fatigue, lethargy, headaches, giddiness and muscle cramps; in this case plenty of water with glucose or sugar added may help. Vomiting or diarrhoea can deplete your liquid and salt reserves.

Anhidrotic heat exhaustion, caused by an inability to sweat, is quite rare, and unlike other forms of heat exhaustion is more likely to strike people who have been in a hot climate for some time.

Heat Stroke

This serious, sometimes fatal condition occurs when the body's heat-regulating mechanism breaks down completely and the body temperature rises to dangerous levels. Long, continuous periods of exposure to high temperatures can leave you vulnerable to heat stroke, and you should avoid excessive alcohol intake or strenuous trekking when you first arrive in Greece.

The symptoms are feeling unwell, not sweating very much or not at all, and a high body temperature (39 to 41°C). If sweating has ceased, the skin becomes flushed and dry. Severe, throbbing headaches and lack of coordination will also occur, and the sufferer may be disoriented or aggressive. Eventually the victim will become delirious or convulse. Hospitalisation is essential, but meanwhile get the victim out of the sun, remove their clothing and cover them with a damp sheet or towel, and then fan them continually until their skin is cold to the touch. If they are conscious, give water to which glucose has been added.

Cold

Too much cold is just as dangerous as too much heat, particularly if it leads to hypothermia. When trekking in Greece be prepared for cold, wet or windy conditions at any time of the year; never venture into the hills unprepared, even for a short stroll, since thunderheads can billow out of a clear sky on an hour's notice.

Hypothermia occurs when the body loses heat faster than it can produce it and the core temperature of the body falls to a dangerous level. It is surprisingly easy to progress from very cold to dangerously cold due to a combination of wind, wet clothing, fatigue and hunger, even if the air temperature is above freezing. It is best to dress in layers; silk, wool and some of the new artificial fibres are all good insulating materials. Less obvious is to always feel comfortable as you walk along; if you're too warm you'll sweat into your superfluous clothes, which will just make matters worse if the temperature plunges later. A hat is important, as a lot of heat is lost through the head. A strong, waterproof outer layer is essential, since keeping dry is vital. Daypacks should also be stocked with basic supplies, including food containing simple sugars to generate heat quickly, and lots of fluid to drink.

Symptoms of hypothermia are exhaustion, numb skin (particularly on feet and fingers), uncontrollable shivering, slurred speech, irrational or violent behaviour, lethargy, apathy, stumbling, dizzy spells, muscle cramps and erratic bursts of energy. Irrationality may take the form of sufferers claiming they are warm and trying to take off their clothes.

To treat hypothermia, first get out of the wind or rain, and replace wet clothing with dry, warm clothing. Drink hot liquids – not alcohol – and eat some easily digestible high-calorie food. This should be enough during the early stages of hypothermia, but if it has gone further it may be necessary to place the victim in a warm sleeping bag and get in with them. Do not rub the patient, place them near a fire, or remove wet garments in the wind. As soon as possible, put the victim in a warm (not very hot) bath.

Intestinal Troubles

Most people seem to get stomach troubles at least once during a short visit to Greece; this is probably due to unfamiliar or slightly-past-its-prime food rather than to the water, which is world-famous for its purity and good taste. The only places to avoid collecting water while on trek are just below villages (the piles of garbage will generally put you off anyway) or downstream from a an alpine shepherds' colony, since grazing animals can harbour giardia. This intestinal parasite causes stomach cramps, nausea, bloated stomach, watery, foul-smelling diarrhoea and frequent gas. The symptoms can appear several weeks after you have been exposed to the parasite, and often disappear for a few days before returning; this can go on for several weeks more. Metronidazole, marketed commercially as Flagyl, is the drug of choice, but should only be taken under medical supervision. Ordinary antibiotics are useless.

Cuts, Bites & Stings

Cuts & Abrasions The main sources of these in Greece are bramble thickets and sharp rocks, the latter both on mountainsides and under water. Even shallow scratches should be cleaned thoroughly, since in the warm Greek summer they may become septic and take a long time to heal. If possible avoid bandages or Band-Aids, which may keep a wound wet. Deeper injuries must be disinfected with an appropriate solution such as mercurochrome, or an antiseptic gel.

Dog Bites Dog bites should be treated as soon as possible, especially if your tetanus shots are not up to date. Rabies has not been eradicated from Greece. See Dogs later in this chapter.

Snake Bites Greeks have an overdeveloped, mostly superstitious fear of snakes (*fídhia*) and tend to kill any on sight. In fact the only poisonous species is the *okhiá* (adder), *Vipera berus*, which has mottled dorsal marking in grey, brown or red. The young hatch in the spring, and both they and the adults tend to sunbathe on or near pathside stone walls, To minimise your chances of being bitten, always wear boots, socks and long trousers when passing such structures or through undergrowth. Don't put your hands into holes and crevices that you can't see into, and be cautious when collecting firewood.

Adder bites will not cause instantaneous death, and antivenin should be available from the nearest *agrotikó yatrío*, the state-run rural outpatient clinic. Keep the victim calm and still, wrap the bitten limb tightly, as you would for a sprained ankle, and then attach a splint to immobilise it, before seeking medical attention.

Tourniquets and sucking out the poison are now comprehensively discredited.

Insect & Spider Bites or Stings Unless you're allergic to them, bee and wasp stings are painful rather than dangerous. Greek hornets seem to be able to sting you repeatedly (bad news) but at least don't leave stings in (the good news). Calamine lotion will give relief, and ice packs can reduce the pain and swelling. There are poisonous spiders in Greece, but antivenins should be available.

Scorpions have notoriously painful stings. They are quite common in the drier parts of Greece, often sheltering in shoes and clothing or under ledges.

In indoor accommodation, mosquitoes, gnats, midges and other winged pests will torment you all night unless you've lit *fidhákia* or *spíres* (pyrethrin incense coils). These work well but make the room reek; you may prefer a topical repellant, which is your only option when trekking or camping. In some places, electric devices (Spira-Mats) which vaporise an odourless insecticide pad are available and work very well.

Ticks

Greece has lots of ticks, with the main season between April and June. You should always check yourself, especially socks and trouser cuffs, if you have been walking through a tick-infested area. Be particularly wary of boulders and logs you may sit upon.

Vaseline, alcohol, oil or a heated wire-tip will persuade a tick to let go; don't just yank them off, since a head left stuck in the skin will become septic. Ticks spread a number of bacterial and viral diseases, including typhus, so you should clean them off as soon as possible.

Scabies & Lice

At the lower end of the scale, some hotels will cut corners in the matter of laundering bedding, in which case you run the risk of picking up scabies. This is an extremely contagious parasitic infestation caused by a microscopic mite; the initial symptoms, appearing three to seven days after exposure, are small raised bumps behind the ankles and on the back of the hand. Very quickly the colonies spread to the forearms, between the thighs and around the waist in particular, announcing themselves with redness and intense, fiery itching which worsens after dark, often preventing sleep. The bigger 'bites' scab over, bleeding profusely if scraped off.

In Greece, the inexpensive but unfortunately not very effective over-the-counter remedy is Benzogal lotion, with benzoyl benzoate the active ingredient; it is also highly irritating to the skin, causing rashes and welts difficult to distinguish from the actual condition. Much better if you can get them (in the UK) Derbac or Derbac-M lotion, laced respectively with the pesticides carbaryl or malathion, or (in North America) Kwell, which contains the powerful pesticide lindane. This last product is the best but has been banned in much of the world.

Treatment with any of these lotions consists of a full-body application, which is left on in a thin film for 24 hours before bathing. A second application is suggested a few days later. The mites and their eggs should in theory be killed by then, but the itching will not go away completely for about 10 days – and often many mites survive. They have lately become resistant to most available lotion formulas, so that stubborn cases (meaning almost all infestations) eventually require intensive treatment, specifically a week of daily lotion applications. Formulas may have to be blended to get rid of all resistant individuals; sunlight is helpful too, though ultraviolet radiation by itself will only slow the spread of the condition, not stop it entirely. Scabies has reached epidemic proportions in much of northern Europe, causing major headaches for health officials, and tourism has spread it quickly to the Mediterranean.

Equally important is the handling of all clothing and bedding worn or slept on during the infestation. These must be washed in hot water, with hands retreated immediately afterward; items that can't be laundered, like coats and mattresses, must be dry-cleaned and ironed with a hot iron (though you'll surely have long since left the guilty hotel).

The same products listed are also used to treat body, head or pubic lice, which you are much less likely to pick up. After application of the lotion to the afflicted area you may want to comb the nits (empty louse-egg shells) out of the hairs in question.

Marine Hazards

Armadas of jellyfish periodically besiege the Greek coasts, particularly in autumn, making swimming then a nerve-wracking activity. A variety of pain-relieving over-the-counter formulas are sold in Greek pharmacies, but failing that, home remedies include vinegar, baking-soda poultices and (it is claimed) urine.

If you graze against one of the many sea urchins that perch on Greek shore rocks, or worse step on one, the spines will lodge porcupine-style in your anatomy. If not removed, especially from feet, all but the tiniest fragments will fester or at least make subsequent hiking painful. Set to work with a sewing needle, the finest blade of your pocket knife (both sterilised) and olive oil introduced dropwise into the punctures. The oil floats the hollow, barbed spines, which can otherwise introduce bacteria deep into the flesh. Olive oil is also perfect for removing tar from your feet, quite a lot of which washes up on Greek beaches from time to time.

WOMEN TRAVELLERS

Women travelling alone in rural Greece are usually treated with respect. Hassles do occur but they tend to be a nuisance rather than threatening.

Greeks rarely travel alone and so have difficulty understanding why anyone would want to do this, but they have been sufficiently exposed to foreigners to accept such 'strange' ways. This applies also to women travelling with a male partner to whom they are not married. In rural areas it is a good idea to dress conservatively, although it is perfectly OK for women to wear shorts, short skirts etc in tourist areas. If you are pestered, ignore the guy, and you'll find that the hint is usually taken.

The status of women in Greece has been improved by several reforms introduced by PASOK, including civil marriage, divorce by consent, legal abortion and the abolition of the dowry system. But remember that changes in attitude are slow in rural areas.

DANGERS & ANNOYANCES
Safety

Greece is one of the safer places in which to travel, with crimes against persons (especially foreigners) exceedingly rare; when it does happen the perpetrators are often other foreigners. The Greeks' reputation for honesty certainly contributes to the country's popularity among tourists. In the larger towns there are burglary rings, but this will probably not concern you – even car break-ins are not the norm.

In the hills and remote islands, problems are virtually unheard of, though some of the northerners will attempt to scare you with one-third-true stories of hungry Albanian refugees brandishing sharpened spoons, lying in ambush in the forest. The main culprits here are four-footed, not two-footed, food thieves, field mice especially. Always secure your belongings in a beast-proof fashion before turning in for the night.

Alpine Common Sense & Assistance

As yet there is no formal mountain rescue service in Greece, and each year unprepared or imprudent hikers suffer the fatal consequences in every season. When necessary, army helicopters are summoned to conduct searches, but they take a long time to arrive and this is likely only near the bare handful of staffed refuges with two-way radios. Be conservative with route decisions, heeding this book's warnings, and always trek within the limits of daylight and your capabilities. If you're kitted out with the items in the Equipment List entry, you should never find Greek conditions dangerous, though they may certainly be less than ideal for enjoying the hike.

Lightning

Greek topography is ideal for redistributing air masses so as to threaten hikers, and there have been a number of recent fatalities from summit and meadow strikes. Seek shelter, if possible, in low-lying wooded areas or *deep* horizontal caves.

Dogs

Sooner or later, hikers in Greece will have to contend with the ferocious *mandróskila* (sheepfold watchdogs). They've been bred to intimidate bears, wolves and livestock rustlers, so they're unlikely to be impressed by you. In addition, they're often underfed and badly treated by their masters and so have become that much meaner. While scarcely any are actually rabid, it is worth going to some length to avoid being bitten by them.

Avoid turning your back on dogs, if there aren't enough of them to completely surround you. Facing your assailants, back away slowly but steadily until enough distance has opened up between you and them to resume normal walking. Dogs seem to like nothing better than to sink teeth into fleeing ankles, calves or buttocks.

Light artillery can be useful. Try shying plum-size rocks toward, but not *at*, the beasts. The best throws are those that bounce once just in front of their snouts; this keeps them distracted and eyes-down, during which time you can sneak a bit further away.

A stout walking stick can double as a club

in an emergency – even the most resolutely charging dog will be given pause by a sound whack across the snout. Shepherds aren't too thrilled if you abuse their pets – they like to reserve that right for themselves – so use violence only as a last resort.

Finally, avoid travelling in the mountains after dark – canine viciousness increases as the sun goes down. Also, never parade through flocks of sheep at any hour of the day: give them a wide berth. If you don't, you may be bitten without so much as a preliminary bark. An Englishman was badly mauled above Tsepélovo (Ípiros) in 1982 because he insisted on photographing a flock close up. If worst comes to worst and you are bitten, you can derive some small consolation from the fact that the animal is not stray and can be tested for rabies if need be.

BOOKS
'OP' means out of print – consult a major library or second-hand bookstore.

General & Regional Guidebooks
For an extensive coverage of the region and approaches from northern Europe, see Lonely Planet's *Mediterranean Europe on a Shoestring*, *Western Europe on a Shoestring* and *Scandinavian and Baltic Europe*. For more specific reading on Greece itself, try the following books.

The Rough/Real Guide to Greece Mark Ellingham et al. (Penguin, London and Prentice Hall, New York, 1992). Despite the British title, a sophisticated guide for travellers of all but luxury budget levels, now in its fifth, definitive edition.

The Rough Guide to Crete John Fisher (Penguin, London, 1991). Specific coverage of the 'Big Island'.

Greece (Hachette World Guides, Paris, last edition 1964.) It is worth scouring used book stores for this fossil since it has excellent listings of Byzantine and medieval castles and churches often lost in the shuffle to older antiquities, and points you to a surprising number of trails (some paved over since then).

Delphi and the Sacred Way by Neville Lewis (Michael Haag, London/Hippocrene, New York, 1987). An excellent companion for the Parnassós area, part history, part personal anecdotes and site visits, and lots of short walk directions.

Deep into Mani by Greenhalgh, Peter & Eliopoulos, Edward (Faber & Faber, London, 1985). Two more wartime resistance members return to the Mani 25 years after Leigh-Fermor's visit (see later) and find village life, as well as many monuments, disintegrating.

Aegina, Paros, Naxos, Patmos by various authors (Lycabettus Press Publications, Athens). Not the complete backlist but merely those titles of most interest to walkers; all have simple maps and walking-excursion descriptions.

Ethnology, Sociology & Anthropology
The Cyclades, or Life Among the Insular Greeks by James T. Bent (Argonaut Press, Chicago, 1965; OP). Bent and his wife spent a year in this archipelago back when it took a year to visit them all. Still *the* English-language monograph for anyone interested in Cycladic folklore or archaeology.

Honour, Family, Patronage: A Study of a Greek Mountain Community by John Campbell (Oxford University Press, 1964; OP). More precisely, a study of Sarakatsan transhumants in western Zagória during the late 1950s. Not entirely outdated.

Portrait of a Greek Mountain Village by Juliet DuBoulay (Oxford University Press, 1974; OP). One of Campbell's students lived in the remote Evvian hamlet of Ambéli. Indispensable for understanding the interior landscape and daily life of rural Greeks.

The Metamorphosis of Greece since World War II by William McNeil (University of Chicago Press, 1976/Basil Blackwell, Oxford, 1982; OP). Exactly as the title implies; specifically, analysis of demographic trends and case studies of change in six villages.

Modern Greek Folklore and Ancient Greek Religion: A Study in Survivals by John Cuthbert Lawson (University Books, New York, 1964; OP). This is to Greece what *The*

Golden Bough is to the world – and Lawson's conclusions have stood the test of later scholarship better than Frazer's.

Rainbow in the Rock: The People of Rural Greece by Irwin T Sanders (Harvard Unversity Press, 1962; OP). Outstanding, moderately analytic introduction to Greek geography, demography, sociology and folklore that confirms surface impressions of life in the hills.

The Nomads of the Balkans by A Wace and M Thompson (Methuen, London, 1914; OP). The classic study on the Vlachs.

General History & Political Science

A Short History of Modern Greece by Richard Clogg (Cambridge University Press, 1979). A 200-page distillation of salient events since 1454.

The Unification of Greece, 1770-1923 by Douglas Dakin (Ernest Benn, London, no date; OP). One of the better one-volume accounts of the foundation of the modern Greek state and its expansion.

Greece in the 1940s: A Nation in Crisis edited by John O Iatrides (University Press of New England, 1988). Collection of forty important essays from different perspectives on various topics.

Tangled Webs: The US in Greece 1947-1967 by Yiannis Roubatis (Pella Publishers, New York, 1987). Chronicles the growing post-war American involvement, and the US's role in the establishment of the military para-state which dominated Greek civilian politics during this period and long after.

The Rise and Fall of the Greek Colonels by C M Woodhouse (London, Granada, 1988; OP). Perhaps the best account of the period, benefitting from long hindsight.

Memoirs, Travelogues & Expeditions

The Flight of Ikaros by Kevin Andrews (Penguin, New York/London, 1984). Conceivably the best book written about Greece in English. Whether breaking bread with a Royalist death-squad member, officiating as a godfather, or laid up in a sanitarium, Andrews as 'Ikaros' is shattering, unsentimental and unforgettable. Generous hiking

accounts, including a harrowing ascent of Mt Ólimbos.

Journey to a Greek Island by Elias Kulukundis, (Cassell, London, 1968; OP). And a journey back through time and genealogy by a diaspora Greek two generations removed from Kássos, poorest of the Dhodhekánisos. A delightful exploration that reads like nonfiction García Márquez.

Bus Stop Symi by William Travis (Rapp & Whiting, London, 1970; OP). Chronicle of three years' residence on the isle during the mid-1960s by an English couple. Travis got to know the local scene well, but erroneously prophesied that the place would never become touristified.

The Stronghold by Xan Fielding (Secker & Warburg, London, 1953; OP.) British ex-commando revisits WW II haunts in Sfakiá Crete; jolly reunions and some hikes retraced in the western Crete section of this book.

Epirus by Nicholas Hammond (Oxford University Press, 1967; OP). The best study of this area by yet another parachuted-in wartime guerrilla and scholar, if you can afford the price rare copies fetch.

Journals of a Landscape Painter in Greece and Albania by Edward Lear (Century, London, 1988). Vivid accounts of 1848-1849 journeys through Ottoman Macedonia, Epirus and Albania by the gifted writer and water-colourist. Lear trekked and lodged routinely in conditions rather more demanding than you'll find in the humblest Greek mountain hamlet today.

The Station by Robert Byron (Century Books, London, 1984). The author of the classic *Road to Oxiana* actually made his debut, at the age of 24, with this light-hearted account of a season on Áthos in the company of the equally young David Talbot-Rice, who went on to become a premier Byzantine scholar.

Áthos: The Holy Mountain by Sidney Loch (Molho Bookstore, Thessaloniki, 1971). The male half of a missionary couple who dwelt in Ouranopoli's Phosphori tower from 1928 onwards recounts his hikes on the mountain. Despite original posthumous publication in 1957, it's still a good source for recent Athonite history and the legends surrounding various ikons and monasteries.

Mani and *Roumeli* by Patrick Leigh-Fermor (Penguin, New York/London, 1984) This comrade-in-arms of Fielding's is an aficionado of the vanishing minorities, relict communities and disappearing customs and beliefs of rural Greece. Tantalising scholarship interspersed with strange tales.

Natural History Field Guides

Flowers of Greece and the Aegean by Anthony Huxley and William Taylor (The Hogarth Press, London, 1989). The leading English-language field guide.

Flowers of Greece and the Balkans by Oleg Polunin (Oxford University Press, 1987). Stronger on the alpine flora, and recently out in a paperback printing.

Let's Look at Northern Greece by Michael Shepherd (Ornitholidays, Bognor Regis, UK). A useful booklet put out by a UK bird-watching holiday group.

Wildflowers of Greece, Trees and Shrubs of Greece, Medicinal Plants of Greece, Birds of Prey of Greece by George Sfikas (Efstathiadhis, Athens, 1976-present). These are generally more useful than their appearance in tourist shops would suggest; available overseas in the UK only.

Bookshops

Except for those few titles published in Greece, do your book shopping before arrival – foreign publications are prohibitively expensive once there. It is worth noting that US editions of copublished works are invariably cheaper whether new or second-hand, in the latter case because there's little demand for them in North America. Not so in Britain, where recently lapsed – let alone antiquarian – titles are hot items and thus expensive.

In the London area, two bookstores with a specifically Greek focus are: the Hellenic Book Service (☎ (071) 267 9499), 91 Fortess Road, London NW5 1AG, and Zeno's Greek Bookshop (☎ (071) 836 2522), 6 Denmark Street, London W1.

You should be able to find just about everything in this bibliography at one or the other store – though at a price in the case of second-hand volumes. In the USA, it's best to raid used book outlets in university-orientated towns. Quality bookshops in Greece are listed later in the Map Retailers entry.

MAPS

For many years obtaining maps for walking in Greece was a paranoid, dismal subject. Because of ongoing security considerations, maps of a scale better than 1:200,000 were virtually unobtainable without resorting to stealth. Recently the situation has improved enormously, so that for the most popular walking areas you can get at least one, and sometimes two, Greek-published maps – either one produced by *Korfes* or one issued by the military mapping service. (Mt Áthos is a special case, with the best cartography done by individuals in Vienna and Thessaloníki. Crete is also an exception, with the best available products published in Germany.) For other regions where *Korfes* has not published a map or the military forbids the sale of its sheets, you'll have to resort to British or Italian military quads produced before or during WW II. However, with persistence and resourcefulness you can indeed assemble a collection of detailed maps for every square metre of Greek territory should you so desire.

The Korfes Maps

Strictly speaking, there is only one gazetting source in Greece: the *Korfes* maps are based entirely on the army set described later. The magazine pays a yearly fee to the military for the right to duplicate the cartographic information, and until recently did little or nothing to update or correct it, merely adopting wholesale the original base map's numerous errors. Only since 1988 has there been any effort to ink in new roads, alpine shelters, dams, etc and to highlight paths. Furthermore, the hierarchy of trail tracings is totally unreliable – the squiggly solid or dashed black lines in use generally bear no relation to the actual width and surface of the right of way. Worse, paths are shown where there are none, or vice versa; refuge staff and others involved in helping trekkers assert that many people have been led badly astray or even seriously injured by taking these maps at face value. Springs and wells shown may have long since dried up or been abandoned. The maps in this book are more reliable than the corresponding *Korfes* sheet, since they have been tested and corrected in the field.

Still, the *Korfes* maps are far better than nothing, and they cover virtually all of the alpine areas of mainland Greece. At the start of each regional write-up, the appropriate *Korfes* map is cited by the issue number it appeared in. The maps themselves are almost all at a scale of 1:50,000 and have been included as a stapled-in centrefold in each issue of *Korfes* since 1981, with various cosmetic improvements as budgetary considerations allowed: colour maps since 1982, and both Latin and Greek script for most place names since 1989. The sheets, sized according to the mountain range and with a 20-metre contour interval, are considerably more convenient and portable than the army products.

The *Korfes* office sells them separately from the magazine (though they cost the same as the entire magazine, $2.50); all maps from issue No 45 onwards are still in print, though if you are in Athens you might phone the magazine (☎ (01) 24 69 777) for up-to-date information. Mail-order business is conducted with foreign customers; enclose a bit more than $2.50 per map to cover postage and handling. Annual subscription rates are $25 for overseas and $16 within Greece. It may be easier to track down old map sets through one of two foreign outlets: Stanford's (☎ (071) 836-1321), 12-14 Long Acre, London WC2E 9LP, or Map Link (☎ (805) 965-4402), 25 East Mason Street, Santa Barbara, CA 93101, USA. Stanford's is a more likely source since Map Link suspended their *Korfes* purchase program in 1988.

YIS Maps

Your alternative are the products of the Yeografikí Ipiresía Stratú (YIS), the army mapping service. They produce an array of series covering all of Greece, though the most popular is the set of 387 sheets at 1:50,000 (the 1291 quads at 1:25,000 are unhappily not available to the public). YIS maps are the standard ordnance survey size and thus somewhat unwieldy on the trail; furthermore, none of them have been updated or reverified since the early 1970s, and with their rather dense four-colour layout they're somewhat harder to read than the earlier *Korfes* printings. Exact coverage is 15 x 15 minutes, with contour interval of 20 metres.

YIS sells its maps from a special ground-floor sales office on its premises at Evelpídhon 4, 113 62 Athens, just north of the Pédhion Áreos. To get there take any yellow trolley bus (except for Nos 1 or 6) from downtown Athens, and get off at the stop called 'OTE' on Leofóros Patissíon; the No 15 actually goes right by YIS. Public hours are Monday, Wednesday and Friday from 8 am to 12.30 pm; sign in with the gate sentry and leave some ID with him. A pocket-size foldout index is available on request, and you indicate your preference by quad title (the numbering systems are in the throes of change and not reliable). The maps cost 800dr (about $4.50) each, and service, once purchase is sanctioned, is computerised and rapid.

Formalities involve filling out a one-page form stating why you need the maps, with a signed promise not to copy or resell them; if you don't speak or write Greek you can enlist the help of staff. EC passport holders should encounter no obstacles to purchase, except that as of this writing nearly half the country – Crete, the Dhodhekánisos, north-eastern Aegean, Skíros, the Ionian islands and anything near the northern frontier – still falls within a forbidden zone. Staff have indicated that after 1992, and theoretically uniform rights within the EC, even this limitation will be dropped. When listed in the hike write-ups, all YIS map titles that for the moment still have restricted distribution are indicated with an asterisk.

Non-EC nationals may have to go upstairs for an interview with an officer in charge, who may attempt to discourage them from buying the quantity or scale of maps requested. Having been through this a couple of times, I can only suggest that you stay as cool and polite as possible. Once back downstairs you are treated no differently than any other customer.

Crete Maps

Harms, a German cartographic publisher, is preparing a series of five maps, covering Crete at a scale of 1:80,000. So far, however, only two of the sheets are available – one of them, No 3, gazetting the popular Mt Psilorítis area.

Early Italian & British Maps

For regions where *Korfes* and *Harms* maps are not published or YIS sheets are out of bounds, you'll want to lay hands on Italian or British military maps drawn up during the first half of this century.

For the Dhodhekánisos, under Italian occupation from 1913 to 1943, the Italian-prepared set, published by the Instituto Geografico Militare in Firenze from 1927 onwards, is your best choice. Sheets for each island of the archipelago are at a scale of 1:25,000, with a 10-metre contour interval.

Because of that, and the calligraphic labelling style, they have a busy, antiquarian appearance, but don't let that put you off – they are perfectly reliable for natural features and villages, and a surprising number of the trails traced still exist.

The main problem using them is the fact that all the place names have been Italianised – eg Terrarossa for Kokinokhóma, San Demetrio for Áyios Dhimítrios – so you'll spend some time decoding between two possibly unfamiliar languages.

You can find sets of these quads in the map collections of major university libraries; I got mine from the University of California at Santa Barbara, though strangely the larger campus at Berkeley does not seem to have them in its holdings. Staff will photocopy the sheets you need for a nominal charge at most.

In the UK you can find them in the map room of the Royal Geographical Society in London, but read on for a discussion on how that institution works.

For Crete, the Ionian islands and the eastern and northern Aegean islands, you want maps prepared by the British War Office in 1943-44 just before, and after, the departure of the Axis forces. These have a 1:50,000 scale, with the contour interval varying from 20 to 40 metres. They're well-produced and easy to read (more so the wide-interval sheets), with a logical transliteration system and useful glossaries, but generally do not show trails, only roads. Still, considering their age, they are reasonably accurate, often more so than the newer YIS quads.

The main obstacle to their usefulness, however, and that of the Italian sets which are often stocked with them, is their limited accessibility and high cost. In the UK they are only available to the public through the map curator of The Royal Geographical Society (☎ (071) 589 5466), Kensington Gore, London SW7 2AR. The present curator, Mr Francis Herbert, or his staff will photocopy necessary maps for you, but this is a comparatively expensive undertaking at £2 to £4 per sheet! Also, in 1991 and 1992 there were rumours that because of funding constraints access to the Society's map division would be further restricted in some way, either on a fee-per-enquiry basis or closure to non-Society members altogether. You should phone ahead to find out about the current policy and opening hours.

Even assuming that the Society is still inclined to provide service, you must obtain permission to copy their set from the British military authorities, under the terms of an agreement with Greece. Compile a list of the maps you want, citing by number and sheet title, and send it with a covering letter to the Military Survey; Acquisition & Library Group; Block A, Government Buildings, Hook Rise South, Tolworth; Surbiton, Surrey, KT6 7NB. The people in charge of such permissions Barry Thomas and P Ayers (☎ (081) 330 7959, ext 5336; fax 337 3533).

A license to make up to five sheets is usually given. Within a few days you should receive a form letter by return mail approving your request. This is apparently not automatic; it is wisest to present yourself as a researcher, scholar or leader of an expedition – which could, of course, mean just you and a few friends on trek.

Incidentally, the British wartime sheets are the only detailed maps of Greece to show magnetic declination from true north; throughout the country it is 3° or less, so in this guide magnetic north has been treated as true north.

Small-Scale Overview Maps

For a general, journey-planning map of Greece, the best is that produced by Freytag & Berndt at a scale of 1:650,000. Michelin No. 980, at 1:700,000, is a distinct second choice because of its numerous errors.

For specific regions, Freytag & Berndt is again generally the best, with titles for the Pelopónnisos (1:300,000), Pílion (1:100,000) and the Cyclades (1:150,000) being of particular interest. Also worth considering is the Reise und Verkehrsverlag (RV) 1:300,000 effort for the mainland and select islands, much better than their 1:800,000 country-wide map; it is distributed in the UK by Bartholomew. Until *Harms* completes its series, the most useful overview of Crete is provided by Nelles at a scale of 1:200,000 – it has contour lines and occasionally correct path tracings.

Map Retailers

Sources for specialist hiking maps have been introduced above; of these, Map Link and Stanford's will also carry the small-scale maps mentioned. There are no map or travel bookstores per se in Greece; maps are sold either at general book retailers or through tourist shops at a considerable mark-up from their overseas price. Two good possibilities for touring maps are: Eleftheroudhakis (☎ (01) 32 29 388), Níkis 4, 105 63 Athens, near the downtown Platía Síndagma (you can also buy most Lonely Planet titles there); and Molho, Tsimíski 10, Thessaloníki. It

also helps to know that Efstathiadis has the distribution rights for Freytag & Berndt within Greece and that, repackaged with a local cover, these maps are more or less reasonably priced.

A Note on Nomenclature

A potential source of confusion when interpreting maps is the existence of one or more alternate names for many places. Names given on maps are sometimes in *katharévousa* (formal, legal/ecclesiastical language) spelling, with word endings different from those in the *dhimotikí* (literary and spoken Greek), eg Karyaí rather than Kariés. Many locales have an alias of Italian, Turkish, Vlach or Slavic origin. The policy in this book is to cite first the name best understood in the area and to list important alternatives immediately following in parentheses. In recent decades Greek governments vigorously pursued a Hellenisation campaign, promoting classical place names over medieval ones. During the 1930s especially, the Metaxas dictatorship attempted, with mixed results, to suppress the majority of foreign place names on the mainland.

Thus, after having spent some time in Greece, you'll begin to recognise a list, so to speak, of bureaucratically 'approved' place names, which is not terribly long. When villages aren't named for the patron saint of their main church they're apt to be called by certain common geographical or botanical features. Livádhi (meadow), Dháfni (laurel), Kriovrísi (cold spring) and Áyios Ioánnis (St John), of which there must collectively be a thousand in Greece, are the worst offenders. You may have to qualify the name of the village you're looking for with a province name if there seems to be any confusion.

GREEK MOUNTAINEERING ORGANISATIONS

Mountaineering and hiking in Greece, like almost everything else, is factional, the result being a number of alpine and walking clubs. The Ellinikós Orivatikós Síndhesmos (EOS, the Greek Alpine Club, ☎ (01) 24 61 528), Kentrikí Platía 16, 136 71 Akharnés (not in

Athens, but in a suburb to the north, in the same offices as *Korfes* magazine) is the largest and most widespread organisation, but there are also the Síllogos ton Ellinikón Oriváton (SEO, Association of Greek Climbers) (☎ (031)224 710), Platía Aristotélous 5, Thessaloníki; the Ellinikí Omosphondhía Hionodhromías keh Orivasías (EOHO, the Greek Mountaineering and Skiing Federation) (☎ (01) 32 34 555), Milióni 5, Kolonáki, 105 63 Athens; and other smaller groups. These abbreviations will be used throughout the book. Other branches of these organisations are cited in the specific hike accounts when necessary.

Provincial alpine club offices tend on the whole to be receptive to foreign hikers, though their main reasons for existence are to organise excursions for Greeks, mark and maintain nearby trails, and rent out the keys for any unstaffed huts under their control. Since most staff are volunteers and otherwise employed, EOS branches in particular tend to open only on weekday evenings (8 to 11 pm is a common schedule) and Saturday mornings.

Enthusiasm must in many cases stand in for lack of funding and political clout, and (as far as you're concerned) a language barrier. Only very recently have clubs been able to halt any inappropriate types of high-altitude development, and larger battles still loom. Don't expect branch personnel to be well informed on any mountains except those in the immediate area, though often you will be pleasantly surprised by Greeks who have trekked in many regions of the country and whose knowledge is not limited.

TREKKING INFORMATION

The most popular trekking and climbing periodical in Greece is *Korfes*, issued every other month, and available from many street-corner períptera for about $2. In Athens back issues are sold at the I Folia tu Vivliu bookstore, in the arcade at Panepistimíu 25-29, and at the Alpamayo alpine shop nearby at Panepistimíu 44. You should try these outlets before traipsing out to Akharnés to riffle through the publication office's backstock.

Korfes has grown from humble beginnings in 1976 to a four-colour, relatively slick, large-format magazine. Critics charge, with some justification, that in trying to be all things to all readers it has lost focus: too many features on straight tourism and other activities unrelated to alpinism, girlie-model ads for questionable products, etc. On the other hand *Korfes* has always made itself heard, on the conservationist side, in the growing number of alpine development controversies in Greece. Another obvious limit to usefulness is the fact that it's in Greek; foreigners are principally interested in snagging copies for the detailed alpine maps which each issue contains (see the Maps entry following). Since early 1989, a short description in English and German has appeared on the reverse of each map, detailing points of interest and possible walks in the area shown.

In general there's no point bothering the various local offices of the National Tourist Organisation (Ellinikós Organismós Turismú or EOT) for trekking information, since they simply don't have it. The only exception is the Ioánnina branch, which may have some photocopied *Korfes* maps for the northern Píndhos. The EOT has, however, published one pamphlet entitled *The European Rambler Trails – the E4 in Greece*, but even in this case the text has been written by EOHO personnel. The information as such is reliable but the E4's routing is not always the most imaginative.

LONG-DISTANCE TRAILS

There are in fact four long-distance trails in Greece: the E4, which winds from Flórina in Makedhonía to Yíthio in the southern Pelopónnisos, and which may soon be extended the length of Crete; the E6, essentially a short spur between Igoumenítsa and Flórina, taking in Métsovo, the Vália Kálda and part of the Aóös valley on the way; the O3, in the northern Píndhos between Zagória and Mt Smólikas; and the Pausanias Trail, a four-day randonée route between Pátra and ancient Olympia. The two E trails, known as *Evropaïká monopátia* (European paths), or *monopátia megalón dhiadhromón* (long-distance paths) are indicated by yellow tree diamonds with black borders and lettering, or by yellow stripes on rocks.

Signposting on the E4 was begun in 1987 and completed in 1990, but already weather and malicious hunters or vandals have taken their toll on the waymarks. It has to also be said that much of the E4 is just plain drudgery, relying overly on forest roads at the expense of proper trails nearby which wither from lack of use. Accordingly, only those really useful scenic sections are incorporated and discussed in the trek write-ups following. The O3, marked either with black-on-yellow diamonds or red-and-white chevrons on boulders, is by contrast an often challenging sequence of paths and cross-country sectors. It is discussed in detail in the northern Píndhos chapter.

You can get further information on each section of these long-distance paths from the alpine club responsible for their upkeep.

TRAIL SCIENCE
Getting lost is an integral part of the Greek backcountry experience, since paths, while usually marked in some fashion, are often not done so well enough. No matter how good a trail sense you possess, it will happen to you eventually – Greeks, unless they inhabit the mountain or island in question, are certainly not exempt either. Of necessity you'll become a competent tracker of the correct route after a period in the Greek woods, but until then (and forever after), mental toughness, judgement and a sense of humour will serve you in as good a stead as boots and pack. A light attitude definitely helps when you're trudging through a drizzle, uncertain whether still on the trail or on a natural rock ledge, with darkness and hostile dogs approaching. At such moments rescuers in the guise of hairy-cloaked shepherds with portable radios and coffee in thermoses tend to materialise out of the mist, but it's not good to tempt fate. The following pointers will help you stay on course.

Bona fide trails were originally built to serve points of economic or religious importance, and primarily continue to do so (the more recent construction of mountain huts has kept other paths alive). Thus, alpine paths tend to halt at the highest summer pasture, with cross-country scrambling from there on; if a mountain has a summit path, it's probably because of a shrine on top. In the case of two villages on opposite sides of a mountain, a point-to-point foot route generally survives, but it's often badly deteriorated if cars can easily skirt the range. Worse, the old paths were often so well routed and designed that they provided the right-of-way for modern roads and now lie bulldozed under tonnes of rubble. In luckier instances the old trail may persist, paralleling the new road or cutting across its switchbacks. Even where there are no roads, many old paths were dynamited and blocked by the central government during the 1946-49 civil war to hamper the movements of the insurgents.

Since Greece's accession to the EC, and the increase in grant money lying about, the country has been gripped by a positive mania for road building, often where it's least needed; the main highways deteriorate while dirt tracks strangle every mountainside.

Everyone in the Greek ecological and trekking community has their theories about who's responsible – the military, preparing for another Balkan or civil war; the former PASOK government, dispensing road grants in an effort to buy votes; municipality big shots, raiding community coffers to open a track to their own summer villas or sheep pen. Some combination of these three is close to the truth, and there's general agreement on at least one point: more roads are not essential, since virtually every village in Greece that's still inhabited has at least one road connection. Their continued proliferation, wandering aimlessly through the landscape and often left unfinished, seems symptomatic of the country's general directional crisis; the mentality seems to be that, if everyone has their own road, like a TV or a new car, then all will be well.

Trails still regularly used by festival pilgrims or other hikers are frequently marked with red – more rarely blue or yellow – paint splodges. Occasionally, painted metal discs or squares are used, and piling rocks to make a cairn *(kutrúmbulo)* is also practised. Cryptic initials with arrows, or summits shown schematically as triangles, can be critically important: eg MΠ and HΠ can translate as Monastíri Prodhrómou and Profítis Ilías. Similarly, hieroglyphics can be dangerously meaningless, as is the common K plus a number, a surveyors' mark signifying *Ktíma* (plot) such-and-such. Power or phone lines often serve also as waymarks, since rural electrification and telecommunications projects long pre-date the current craze for roads – and the linesmen got into the bush using the nearby trail, of course.

Old cobbled trails *(kalderímia)* usually lead somewhere, though sometimes no further than the nearest hilltop shrine. If you need to know the dedication of a particular rural church *(ksoklísi)*, as when matching it to a name on a map, the patron's ikon is usually on a raised dais to one side of the *témblon* or altar screen. Well-used trails descending from grazing areas become heavily oxbowed over the years, just like old rivers, with multiple, potentially confusing interconnections and shortcuts. Just follow the general bearing of the path.

The unsignposted fork is the hiker's perennial nightmare; you may have to choose among three or even four turnings. Goat or sheep traces, speckled with their droppings and often criss-crossing a hillside in a fish-net pattern, are usually bad news – there's no guarantee that humans have ever been that way. Manure from pack animals is a good sign – they rarely march anywhere unaccompanied by humans. A path with weedy or overgrown sections has not necessarily been abandoned. Conversely, beware of the trail that looks too good to be true: it may merely lead to a chapel, spring or private dwelling and stop there. The correct path is often the one that's visible from afar but seems to vanish under close inspection; that has recent, but not too fresh, lolly and cigarette wrappers ground into its surface (you may, for the first time ever, be relieved to see rubbish in the wilderness); and that trundles on meadow after meadow, always skirting extinction in a network of aimless livestock traces or abandoned terraces, but somehow continuing miraculously in the right direction.

On the islands, many trails lie between double dry-stone walls or (less likely) alongside a single boundary wall. Many isles, especially in the Kikládhes, have old loop paths located roughly halfway between the shoreline and the island's summit. Convoluted or long islands, logically enough, often have old foot routes paralleling the long axis, slightly off centre. If you have gone astray on an island, don't try the old trick of following watercourses downhill; you'll likely as not end up in a blind cove, with the prospect of a climb back out.

Don't plan a cross-country traverse through apparently trackless regions without a good map and compass, plus preferably Greek language skills and enough prior experience in such terrain so that nothing takes you completely by surprise. Impassable, yawning chasms and sheer cliffs are common Greek topographical features, and the presence of either will obviously add hours to what would seem from a road map to be a relatively straightforward point-to-point trek. Such obstacles are especially common in the southern Píndhos, the Ágrafa, western Taïyettos and Crete's Lefká Óri, where completing itineraries may involve vertiginous ridge walks.

Many locals will express surprise at finding you hiking by yourself, if that is your preference. Greeks are notoriously gregarious and to them there is something suspect about people who prefer their own company, but their distress is partly motivated by concern for your safety.

It bears repeating again and again that the Greek mountains can be lethal – every year a handful of both Greek and foreign climbers die, the latter lulled by the apparent mildness of the climate into taking chances with the unforgiving terrain. Don't – and if you choose to go solo, tell someone where you're headed. The disadvantages of going alone are evident, but if you want a greater chance of glimpsing wildlife, and more extended interaction with those you meet along the way, there's no better strategy.

OVERSEAS & GREEK TREK OUTFITTERS

This guide contains all the information you need to hike on your own with confidence and full enjoyment of your surroundings. However some readers may prefer not to hike alone, in which case the companies listed here can provide you with companions on one of their scheduled departures, or a custom-tailored itinerary.

UK Outfitters

Exodus Expeditions, 9 Weir Road, London SW12 0LT (☎ (081) 675 5550). Main emphasis on eight-to-12 day loops in the northern Píndhos.

Explore Worldwide, 1 Frederick Street, Aldershot, Hants GU11 1LQ, (☎ (0252) 344 161). Píndhos trips as in the preceding listing, plus expeditions in western Crete.

Ramblers Holidays, PO Box 43, Welwyn Garden City, Herts AL8 6PQ, (☎ (0773) 31133). Although the clientele can be on the older side, some unusual and more imaginative-than-the-norm destinations are offered – among them Kefallonía and Itháki.

Sherpa Expeditions, 131a Heston Road, Hounslow TW3 0RD (☎ (081) 577 2717). Broadly similar Píndhos routes to that of their main rival Exodus, plus (according to demand) itineraries on Crete.

Waymark Holidays, 44 Windsor Road, Slough SL1 2EJ (☎ (0753) 516 477). As with Ramblers, a somewhat geriatric pitch, but again the company's offerings tend to change over the years, sampling a good selection of the islands (Híos, Mílos, for example) and patches of the mainland.

US Outfitters

Avenir Aventures, PO Box 2730, Park City, Utah, UT 84060 (☎ (801) 649-2495, 1-800/367-3230). Spring and autumn walking tours on Sámos and Sími, in smallish groups.

Greek Outfitters

Martha Tours, Panayiótu 14, 156 69 Athens, (☎ (01) 65 33 597). At the moment this operator seems to be dormant, but in the past they organised tours to 'name' destinations such as Crete's Lefká Óri and Mt Ólimbos.

Robinson Travel, Ogdhöis Merarkhías 10, 454 45 Ioánnina (☎ (0651) 29 402 or 74 989). Currently the local subcontractor for Sherpa, but owner-manager Kostas Vassiliu also assembles trips for walk-in trade and knows the north Píndhos well.

Trekking Hellas, Filellínon 7, 105 57 Athens (☎ (01) 32 34 548). Variable length walking tours of Helmós, Zíria and Taïyettos on the Pelopónnisos, and in the Ágrafa range of the Stereá, designed and led by Michael Cullen, the main contributor to this guide.

ATTITUDES TOWARDS TREKKERS

The dominant demographic trend in Greece this century has been massive rural depopulation, so as a backcountry tramper you are both going back in time and bucking the tide. An Athens cobbler once introduced me to acquaintances as 'the man who's always going up into the mountains we've tried so hard to leave'.

As you step off the bus at the end of the line, the hum of *platía* (plaza) discussions and *távli* (backgammon) games may subside as all eyes rivet on you and your luggage. To those assembled you are a distinct oddity, but established convention may inhibit them from addressing you. (In Greece the approaching party always greets the stationary group; this custom still applies strictly in the wilds but is beginning to break down in villages.) Once the ice is broken, questions – fuelled by roughly equal proportions of good heartedness, boredom, curiosity, and wariness – come back-to-back: 'Where are you from?' and 'Where are you headed?' are the standard openers, with 'Why are you alone?' (if that's the case) as a sequel. A benevolent examination of your equipment may follow – walking sticks are always conversation pieces, as are high-tech packs and sturdy boots – but such scrutiny rarely becomes annoying. Rural Greeks are not covetous, and this absence of menace contributes to the enjoyment of hiking in Greece.

At this point, someone who's visited your home town as a sailor or who has a close relative there may turn up, lending with their reminiscences a veneer of sophistication to what may be a rustic scene indeed; somebody at the next table may have only a hazy idea of global geography ('New Zealand? Is that near South Africa?'). Some returned expatriates and pensioners can have overly fond memories of the lands where they made their nest eggs and acquired the rudiments of what they consider culture, and may wish to bend your ear about how provincial Greece is or their neighbours are; they should be gently but firmly put off. An unconventional answer to the routine question 'Well, is it better here or in your country?' can induce blessed silence. They, or someone of like sentiments, may pop another and more insidious question: 'Why are you going on foot when they just built a new road to your destination?'

The query underlines a logic prevalent throughout the developing world – namely, that nobody could possibly trek for pleasure. Walking is associated with backwardness and toil, with the hand implements and 12-hour days that were the rule before progress conferred its mixed blessings on rural Greece. Additionally, the old byways seem to bear connotations of outright shame, as leftovers from the bad old days when the Turks ruled (never mind that some of the finest architectural and engineering feats of medieval Greece – delicate bridges, finely paved kalderímia, and handsome mansions – were completed during the supposedly sepulchral *Turkokratía*).

Country Greeks, like many peoples eking out a subsistence living, regard their surroundings as a work place and a resource, a treasury of water, pasture, timber, game, honey and herbs, and usually not something to be enjoyed for its own sake.

These subtle but nonetheless real attitudes may account for any resistance met when asking villagers for directions. On rare occasions you may be initially told that no path exists, and to use the road. Sometimes this is true; in other cases the locals may have sized you up and decided that the terrain ahead is beyond your capabilities. At such times you may have to deliver an oral resumé of your hiking experience, perhaps noting successful passage of an arduous or faint section of trail

the day before that your audience is likely to be familiar with. Or give as 'references' acquaintances who have done successfully what you wish to do now – they may be remembered. This may elicit complete instructions for continuing on your way, delivered, however, with an air of 'Since you insist...'.

Part of this hesitancy can be attributed to a Greek host's natural instinct to spare a visitor the unpleasantness of getting lost, but you can't discount the element of embarrassment over the past. The permanent committee of kafenío busybodies, like the chorus in ancient Greek drama, will always be ready to offer negative advice or express doubt as to your eventual success, which doesn't help your state of mind as you plunge onward into the little known. If you find yourself in such a situation, persist until you find a sympathetic villager (or six or seven pessimistic opinions in a row) – there is almost always a way.

Fortunately such hesitation in giving instructions is rare. A request for assistance, even if delivered in halting Greek, generally yields an elaborate, unequivocal response, assisted by the full repertoire of Greek hand gestures to ensure comprehension. To banish any ambiguity you may be escorted to the edge of the village and have assorted landmarks along the distant path pointed out to you.

Directions may be given in tandem with hospitality *(filoxenía)*; much has been said and written about this legendary Greek trait, and it generally applies doubly in rural areas. Fruits of the season are routinely offered to wayfarers passing villagers' front doors; more involved invitations may result in all-day or all-night drinking, eating or even staying sessions. It's polite to always accept a coffee or stronger drink; more elaborate offers may require some discretion or diplomacy. (You should not attempt to reciprocate on the spot, but a postcard from your home town upon return will be hugely appreciated, and pinned on the wall for posterity.)

Extraordinary generosity is deeply rooted in the Greek pysche and goes back thousands of years. In the more distant past a stranger represented an unknown, possible hostile power and the bestowal of food and shelter was a method of placation; who could tell if the visitor might not be a god in disguise, come to check on mortals' behaviour? Certainly a residue of these sentiments persists, but today the open-handedness is largely an expression of faith and pride. A shepherd might offer you the last bowl of milk, confident that tomorrow will surely bring another. In their capacity to set a table for you or order you a drink, any Greek is your peer, be you a mule driver or a visiting dignitary.

Filoxenía, and that fraction of the pessimists' mutterings that has a solid basis, will be jointly responsible for the 25% extra you should routinely add to any estimate of time given to reach your destination. Mountain Greeks, up to amazingly advanced ages, cover ground with yard-long strides that will leave you (especially if pack-laden) breathless. Even assuming you can match their pace, you will always be delayed by weather, wildflowers, dogs, or other chance encounters.

You are enjoined by courtesy to at least exchange a few words with any person you meet on the trail, and it's the least you can do by way of thanks for someone who gives you supplementary directions or shows you that hidden spring when you're dying of thirst. If they sense they have an interested audience, those left behind in the mad rush to Athens can tell awfully good tales – anything from a personal history of the last war to the current activities of the EC in the neighbourhood, by way of a local bestiary and catalogue of legends. You will have learned far more than from any tourist office or library book and relieved the monotony of the days that press down on isolated monks, barley threshers or high meadow dwellers who ordinarily have only transistor radios for company (though Walkmans are making their appearance in some of the wealthier stánes).

Urban Greeks may already be one or two generations removed from their rural ancestry, and the separation may be sufficient to lend a nostalgia for the country that is usually absent in the villagers themselves. You may find carloads of townees or walking parties stopping you, the apparently well-equipped foreigner, to ask for directions. Intentions are commendable ('We've never been up here and decided to have a look.') but the shepherd's savvy and the inclination to meet the mountains on their own terms may be lacking. Once in a while you come across an individual, perhaps a village innkeeper or an alpine club branch official, in whom the desire and the know-how are happily wedded. Such acquaintances, and the resulting added appreciation of the landscape, are to be cherished.

Although hospitality may initially overshadow all other considerations, and differences between you and your hosts are not dwelt upon, extended discussions may bring assorted resentments and irritants of Greek pride to the surface. There are small bones, never far out of reach, to pick with citizens of several nations. Americans may be taken to task for their government's support of the 1967-74 junta, and for their continued perceived interference in local affairs; the behaviour of German and Italian occupying forces in WW II has not, and will not, be forgotten; and Anglo-Greek relations have been badly strained by events in Cyprus and within the Greek resistance between 1942 and 1947. (On the other hand, Canadians, Australians and New Zealanders may find themselves feted almost everywhere they go, especially in Crete.)

The traits of the marketplace may lead some merchants to squeeze extra dhrakhmés out of visitors considered easy marks. You are at some disadvantage in countering this, since as a foreigner your earning power is double or triple that of a Greek; a visit to a grocery store, a clothes shop and electrical appliance outlet respectively will provide you with a current scale of values and clue you in as to what people are up against economically of late.

Food and transportation prices are to a large extent government-set and nationally standardised. Just about anything else, from souvenirs to boot repairs, is negotiable within small limits – gauging those parameters is part of learning the ropes.

EQUIPMENT LIST

If you were to do every trek in this guide, you would find it advisable to carry all of the following items. Most of them will come in handy even for short island hikes. If you need to acquire or replace certain articles while in Greece, you'll find a discussion of Greek alternatives in the Local Hiking Equipment entry, and a glossary of their names in the Language entry.

Clothing

2 pairs lightweight, loose cotton trousers
1 pair heavier-duty pants for high-altitude use (corduroy, wool, part synthetic, etc.)
1 pair shorts or cut-offs
1 warm-weather hat or cap, brimmed all around, reflective colour
1 long-sleeved cotton turtleneck top, sweatshirt, or similar
1 shell windbreaker, warm-up jacket, wool-lined water-resistant coat, or GoreTex product

The last two items, used in layers as you choose, should protect you in most conditions encountered from early June to late September below 2200 metres. However, outside these months at higher elevations in northern Greece, add the following:

1 down or fibre-fill parka
1 pair gloves, lined and waterproof
1 hat/cap, wool or similar, to extend down over ears

Footwear

socks – assortment of cotton/synthetic (85%/15%), polypropylene/natural fibre (various formulas), and wool (90 to 100%) pairs to handle all conditions.
hiking boots – one pair medium-duty or stronger, leather upper, over-the-ankle, Vibram or equivalent sole. Do not be seduced into buying 'state-of-the-art' synthetic-upper boots – they provide poor ankle support in the Greek scree piles, are steamy in the warm Greek climate, and let in water like a sieve. If you are North American and don't already own boots, buy a pair in Britain or Greece, where choices and prices of quality leather boots are far better.
kick-around shoes, sneakers or lightweight walking shoes – for evenings at camp and strolling through town

leather conditioner – natural oil-based or wax-based types are preferable to silicone formulas

Camping Gear

Backpack Your backpack should have a minimum capacity of 60 litres (3660 cubic inches), and should be designed to effectively carry up to 18 kg on long treks.

I exchanged my external frame pack in favour of internal frame models some years ago. While my new choice has numerous advantages (easier loading on buses, convertibility to 'suitcase' guise, lack of metal parts to break/bend), I could carry heavy loads more efficiently with an old-fashioned design. Slit-sockets are handy for suspending your foam pad, tent poles, sleeping bag, etc. Really soft (ski-touring) packs are not the best for milder Greek conditions, as your back will be quickly sweat-drenched.

Tent You can get away without a tent in western Crete and the southern Pelopónissos, but elsewhere, particularly rainy Ípiros, it is a wise if not mandatory accessory. This is one item not to scrimp on; as a minimum bring a free-standing dome tent of ripstop nylon with a securely mounting fly. Cheapo models from military surplus or similar outlets which must be tied to trees (usually absent at preferred sites) are not going to cut it. Remember that capacity is usually overrated: a 'two-person' tent usually holds one person and gear comfortably, a 'three-person' houses two people plus some baggage.

Other recommended gear includes:

daypack – suffecient to carry snacks, map, extra clothes, water container, toilet paper, sunglasses, etc; get one with well-padded straps and back so that contents don't dig into yours
camera belt pack – various companies make serviceable carriers for up to two bodies and most lenses; this is the most efficient way to carry opticals while on trek, and it will pay for itself within a month in terms of falls cushioned and repairs thus avoided

walking stick – A stout walking stick is quite versatile, preventing many a fall on slick scree slopes, protecting knees on downhills, and doubling as an ice axe for spring snowbanks. Some people use ski poles, others high-tech tipped items from outdoor stores, but you can improvise in the Píndhos, where below the treeline there is usually suitable beech deadfall or discarded branches near logging sites. Beech cracks as it dries out but remains phenomenally strong, as does poplar wood. In western Crete sticks are made from *abelítsia*, a dwarf elm-like tree, *Zelkova cretica*.

ground pad – medium-density; blue foam, Carimat or Therm-a-Rest type

sleeping bag – three-season, down or fibre-fill according to personal preference

poncho/cagoule – large enough (eg 250 cm x 150 cm) to fit over you and your pack, and perhaps double as a groundsheet

camp stove – a butane-burning one; see discussion in next section

cooking utensils – steel sets are quite safe, as opposed to aluminium ones which could be toxic, but food, especially eggs, sticks badly; in either case carry cooking oil with you in a small (50 mL) plastic bottle

cutlery – in addition to the obvious, wide wooden tongue depressors make excellent impromptu spatulas

egg case – for six eggs

water container – solid or soft models; see discussion in Local Hiking Equipment for more details

Odds & Ends

nylon stuffsacks – a few of assorted sizes, with drawstrings

plastic bags – especially flat, sturdy ones large enough to protect maps

sunglasses

swimming goggles

compass and metric altimeter – essential for orientation

compact flashlight – AA batteries are common, bulbs less so; spares for North American makes like Tekna or Maglite will be tough to find, there's easier maintenance for Eveready Durabeam or Philips items

candle lantern – great morale booster after dark, saves flashlight batteries. Avoid models that take weird-shaped candles; you won't find replacements in Greece.

camp mirror – for looking like the folks in the outdoor catalogues, and possibly emergency signalling

parachute cord, three to four metres – for use as a clothesline, and for swinging mess-pots down into wells to collect water

Nalgene or polyurethane bottles – a pair or more: large for storing laundry powder, medium for mixing up dry milk or holding leftovers

tape – strong, lightweight, fibre-based product such as 3M Micropore; not terrific for surgical use but unsurpassed for mending maps and book bindings since it's archival and won't crinkle, turn colour or fall off like cellotape

first-aid kit – at a minimum, should contain an elasticised bandage to wrap sprains; sterile dressings; bandages and gauze for minor abrasions; medical adhesive tape; topical antibiotic/antiseptic; itch-suppressant ointment to keep you from scratching bug bites; insect repellent, a preventative for the last-noted problem; lip balm; sunblock, an absolute necessity, factor 15 at a minimum; moleskin (old boots, not to mention new ones, will find fresh spots to abrade at unpredictable moments); cuticle scissors, used with the blunt end of a thick sewing needle, deal effectively with ingrown big toenails; dental floss; adhesive strips; painkillers (aspirin or paracetamol); tweezers

sewing kit – assorted needle sizes and thread gauges, for emergency repairs to pack or clothing

Swiss Army or similar pocketknife

timepiece with loud alarm – if not a wrist watch, then a little quartz clock running on an AA battery

pocket or wallet calendar – very easy to lose track of days in the hills (unless that's intended...)

money belt – in Greece, more for convenience than for safety; keep it in your pack unless you're overnighting in a refuge

photo film – E-6 type is easily available in Athens or Thessaloníki, but it's slightly expensive. Processing, however, is good and reasonably priced in Athens (very costly and dodgy quality elsewhere)

waterproof felt-tip marker – for labelling rolls of film and addressing large envelopes, also useful for emergency messages

Last, but not least, bring spares and replacements for everything that could conceivably be impossible or tedious to find overseas and doesn't weigh much or take up room. Examples include eyeglasses (or prescription at least), contact lenses, bootlaces, widgets for backpack, photocopy of front passport page, special medications or cosmetics, odd-sized flashlight bulbs.

LOCAL HIKING EQUIPMENT

Were you to decide in the middle of a conventional vacation in Greece that you wanted to go trekking, or should you lose all of your hiking gear, you could be in far worse countries from the point of view of outfitting yourself. The Greek mountaineering equipment industry is in its infancy and quality is not consistent, but various importers ensure that you can get all sorts of Italian, Austrian, French, Dutch and German items – a far cry from the situation a decade ago, when you couldn't even replace a lost pocketknife.

Backpacks
You would be at some disadvantage only concerning backpacks; the Greek brands Polo and Crest (about $150 for a large model) are not exactly state-of-the-art, and your other choices tend to be either the Spanish Serval, Irish Lowe or Swedish Fjäll Räven makes.

Sleeping Bags
You can find German down Asta bags for about $135, as well as other Dutch or French models like Selva for slightly more. Phenix L.S.D. is the main Greek manufacturer. Decent foam pads 180 cm in length are easy to find, costing about $12.

Boots
The range of footwear is excellent: Austrian Dachtstein, Italian Asolo and Duilo, or various Greek lightweight boots are all widely available. Prices are quite competitive, certainly compared to North America; you might get Italian boots for under $120, and they will be still in very good condition two years later. Biwell, the Austrian boot conditioner, is usually in stock.

Fluid Containers
There's less choice with water and beverage containers. The best solution is the porcelain-lined aluminium bottle with a spring-loaded, leak-proof cap made by Laken (France); they're expensive in Greece, upwards of $10 for a one-litre model. Alternatives include even more expensive bottles by Salewa, or Spanish wine *botas* and German water 'camels' imported by Crest, which have good insulating properties but of course can't be filled by immersion. Avoid the shabby green military surplus bottles sold in hunting stores and flea markets; they leak unbearably.

Stove
Only one brand of stove makes sense, and that's the French-manufactured Camping Gaz Bleuet 206. It is widely sold for about $15, not only in better backpacking stores but also through the Petrogaz chain of home stove and appliance retailers. The same outlets provide service and spare parts; don't waste your time looking elsewhere for a windshield, for example. In Athens, Petrogaz is at Leofóros Singrú 174, on the No 10 trolley line; in Ioánnina, there's a Petrogaz franchise on Odhós Karamanlí just west of the castle gate – nearly every sizeable town has one. The 190 mL cartridges which fit this stove are found everywhere, even in the most remote mountain villages, for the lowest price in Europe (about $0.60 apiece). Two things to watch out for, however: don't buy the very cheapest of the half a dozen brands, since they tend to burn inefficiently or worse pop their safety seals for no good reason. Make sure that cartridges purchased have special grooves or a tapered top; other shapes are intended for blowtorches or the disappearing Koffee-Gaz line of tabletop stoves, and will not fit the Bleuet 206.

Other Equipment
Polo brand tents are okay but not cheap (well over $200 for a decent dome model); South-East Asian imports tend to be of poor to fair quality, so it's best to come equipped. You can find a good selection of imported windbreakers, anoraks and parkas, as well as wool hiking socks. Altimeters and compasses are expensive and should if possible be purchased before arrival. Swiss Army knives, the German J A Haenckls line, and various lesser brands are widely sold in hunting and novelty shops as well as outdoor stores at typical European prices.

BACKPACKING STORES
In an emergency you can try replacing gear at a *katástima athlitikó* (sporting goods

store) or a *katástima kinigís* (hunting store), or head for the ski and sports floor of the Klaoudatos department store, which has branches in Athens, Thessaloníki, Vólos and Pátra.

If you have a choice in the matter, though, head for a proper backpacking and camping store. Athens monopolises the directory below, as it does most other aspects of Greek life.

All listings are meant to be suggestions only and are not necessarily exhaustive, nor do they constitute an endorsement. I would appreciate hearing of any new finds especially out in the provinces.

Athens

Pindos, Leofóros Patissíon 52, within sight of the Mavromatéon bus terminal and very near the YIS map division. State-of-the-art, if a bit expensive, equipment; also pack repairs. The oldest mountaineering shop in Athens.

Army & Navy, Kinéttu 4, 105 55 Monastiráki (☎ (01) 32 50 875). Not really, as the name implies, army surplus, but a general outdoors shop in the heart of the flea market, good for mess kits, stoves, boots, and gadgets.

Alpamayo, Panepistimíu 44, 106 79 Athens (☎ (01) 36 27 032). A good, new, small store with well-balanced offerings and back issues of *Korfes* as well.

Adventure, Voukurestíu 11. High-tech mountain gear.

Kazos, in the arcade between Stadhíu 3 and Koraï 4. A bit expensive because of the location but a good range of socks, bottles, knives, etc.

Marabou, Sólonos 74 (☎ (01) 36 15 438). Software (tents, sleeping bags and parkas) only.

Crest, Dhistómu 23, 104 44 Kolonós (☎ (01) 51 47 690). An importer specialising in software and raingear, plus their own packs; Kolonós is a district behind the railway stations.

Kataskinotis, Ayías Triádhos 8, 143 41 Néa Filadhélfia (☎ (01) 25 11 925). A long-established store with a big stock whose main disadvantage is its distance from downtown; take a No 6 yellow trolley there.

Kinitro, Sofoklí Venizélu 70A, 152 32 Halándhri (☎ (01) 68 44 076). Well out of the centre and listed mostly for completeness.

Selena, Anastasíu Vrettú 4, 136 71 Akharnes (☎ (01) 24 43 793). A small, new import co-op on the lines of REI in the USA; a select list of discounted items every month, sold by mail order, with a catalogue page printed in each *Korfes*. You're encouraged to join for about $100 – worth thinking about if you'll be living in Greece for a while.

Voronof, Menándhru 28, Platía Omonías. Not a camping store at all but virtually the only boot repair shop in Greece with machinery capable of penetrating soles and uppers simultaneously for welt stitches.

Elsewhere

Petridhis, Vassilíu Iraklíu 43, Thessaloníki. As much a travel gadget and luggage store as a camping outlet.

Egastirio Belezakis, basement of Venizélu 23, Thessaloníki. Again not a backpacking store, but a good workshop for having packs, specifically burst zippers, mended.

Christos Karistianis, Skalídhi 9, Haniá, Crete (☎ (0821) 26 869). Specialty boots and boot repairs.

Getting There & Away

Besides flying to Greece, you can reach the country overland by train, bus or car from northern Europe, or (less gruelling) a combination of one of those three methods and a ferry hop over from Italy. There are also handy, if overpriced, ferry links from Turkey to certain Greek islands.

AIR

Athens has the busiest airport, with the largest number of scheduled and charter flight arrivals. Thessaloníki, Corfu and Rhodes are the only other destinations for scheduled flights, and fares to there are distinctly more expensive. Other airports well served by charters and near areas of particular hiking interest include Haniá (Crete), Rhodes, Sámos, Skiáthos and Corfu.

An international air departure tax has been instituted as from November 1992. It is a whopping 5000 dr, or $25 at current rates, and only transit passengers and children under 12 are exempted. If you buy a ticket in Greece, the sum is automatically added to the ticket price; for others, the fee will be collected at the airport. The monies are supposed to go to the construction of a new airport at Spata, though court challenges from tour operators and other EC countries can be expected.

Similarly, a 10,000 dr departure tax for travel to any non-EC country is still mooted for 1 January 1993, though this too is being contested by travel agents who stand to lose a lucrative business in day trips to Turkey – obviously the main target of the measure. If it sticks, people flying home to Australia or the USA, or popping over to Egypt or Israel, could find themselves looking at coughing up 15,000 dr ($75). Vociferous complaining to tourist authorities may be a suggested counterattack.

To/From the UK & Northern Europe

The package holiday, pioneered in the post-war decades when European currency export restrictions spawned a host of (mostly British) dodges for getting around the law, still dominates much of Greece; if you shop around carefully you can benefit handsomely from the industry without necessarily being tied down by it.

There are, however, a couple of catches that need paying attention to. Greek aviation law stipulates that a return charter ticket must be for a minimum of three days and a maximum of four weeks, and that it be accompanied by an accommodation voucher for at least the first few days of your stay. In practice the voucher is a dummy one and you wouldn't be able to use it if you tried. Upon arrival it is usually a fairly simple matter to extend your stay for up to six weeks, providing space is available on the return flight. However the authorities periodically crack down, and in any case the charter industry's days are numbered. With the impending deregulation of European fare prices it will probably disappear by 1997, driven out of business by suddenly cheaper scheduled flights.

In the meantime, you can find charter seats from the UK at off-peak periods for UK£120-150 return, rising to well over UK£200 in high summer. Prices from the Netherlands and Scandinavia are slightly more, and from Germany somewhat less.

Your alternative is to take a scheduled flight, which has numerous advantages: better departure times and in-flight service, and longer validity (up to a year for a round-trip ticket if you're willing to pay for it).

Since Athens is a major international air hub, just about every airline passes through at some point, but some have a particular reputation for bargains on the London-Athens route.

Two of the best are KLM, with a daily connecting service via Amsterdam, and Kenya Airways, whose once-weekly flight can be had in off season for as little as UK£160 return. Among east European air-

Top: North Píndhos: Dhrakólimni with peak and col of Astráka in rear (MD)
Bottom: Zíria: Lake Stimfalía as seen from Mikrí Zíria (MC)

A	E	H
B	F	I
C	F	J
D	G	K

A: *Lilium heldreichii* (MD)
B: *Crocus cancellatus* (MD)
C: *Sterbergea lutea* (MD)
D: *Crocus sieberi* (MD)
E: *Urginea maritima* (MD)
F: Stork (Makedhonía) (MC)

G: *Aubrietia detoidea* (MD)
H: *Anemone coronaria* (MC)
I: *Cistus parviflorus* (MD)
J: *Dracunculus vulgaris* (MD)
K: *Cyclamen graecum* (MD)

lines, MALEV, LOT, CSA and Balkan Bulgarian have historically undercut others, but reaching Athens with them involves layovers of three to seven hours in Budapest, Warsaw, Prague and Sofia respectively, and since the demise of Marxist command economies in the east it's not clear what will happen to their fare structures – currently about UK£220 open return outside of high season. It's always worth contacting British Airways and Olympic Airways, which between them share the direct London-Athens route; especially outside of summer they often have very competitive deals on return flights – say, UK£250 for an eight-week APEX ticket in April-May, well worth the extra 33% over the price of a charter ticket for its relative flexibility.

For up-to-the-minute prices and agents in Britain, consult the classified pages of such magazines as *Time Out* or *LAW*, or the travel sections of *The Observer*, the *Sunday Times* or the *Evening Standard*. Some agencies worth trying in London include Alecos Tours (☎ (071) 267 2092), 3a Camden Rd, London NW1; Goldair (☎ (071) 287 1003), 321-322 Linen Hall, 162-168 Regent St, London W1R 5TB, or Springways Travel (☎ (071) 976 5833), 15 Gillingham St, London SW1V 1HN. All of these are reliable enough bucket shops and consolidators – outfits which buy up and resell seats which the airlines reckon they can't unload for full price.

If you're a student or under 26, you might contact specialist youth/university agencies who will often be able to knock another 10 or 15% off the sample fares quoted; even if you don't meet their age/status criteria, such outlets can still be a very good source of deals. Moreover, student/youth flights are exempt from the accommodation voucher requirement and can be sold legally as one-ways: combining two of these, each costed according to the period in which it falls, results in long-term, reasonably priced tickets. Two established agencies in London are STA (☎ (071) 937 9921), whose head office is at 86 Old Brompton Rd, London SW7 3LQ, and USIT/Campus Travel (☎ (071) 730 3402), 52 Grosvenor Gardens, London SW1 0AG. Both have numerous other locations throughout the UK as well as Eire; in Dublin try also Joe Walsh Tours (☎ (01) 78 9555), 8-11 Lower Baggot St.

To/From the USA

Fares to Athens from the USA are just competitive enough to make it worth your while to fly directly, though one-ways and cheap long-term tickets are rare indeed. Scheduled flights, whether through the airlines themselves or a consolidator, far outnumber the limited number of charter services.

When you are hunting for a ticket, scan the Sunday travel supplements of major newspapers to get an idea of the price range. The best ones are those in the *Los Angeles Times*, *San Francisco Chronicle*, *Miami Herald*, *Chicago Tribune*, *Washington Post*, *Boston Globe* and *New York Times*.

Only four airlines offer services from the USA to Greece: the national flag carrier Olympic Airways, direct from New York-JFK and Boston only (connecting service to Chicago); TWA, from a number of cities via Paris to Athens or direct from JFK; United Airlines has a direct twice weekly service to San Francisco from Athens; and Delta, again from a number of points via Frankfurt, though their mooted direct Newark-Athens service has not yet materialised. One advantage of flying Olympic is that you'll land at the western terminal used by Olympic's domestic flights to the islands and mainland towns, thus eliminating the necessity of shuffling five km around the runway by bus or taxi between Olympic's hall and the eastern terminal reserved for all other air companies.

You'll probably find that minimum APEX fares from east-coast cities weigh in at about US$750; add another $100 or so if you start from Dallas or Chicago. Charters out of California are more common, and good value at $700 to $900 for a round trip; an APEX ticket on a scheduled flight will run well over $1000, though at slack periods you can find $US700 deals.

Reliable and consistent consolidator agents include:

Access International, 101 West 31st St, Suite 104, NY 10001 (☎ (1-800) 825 3633) or 55 E Washington St, Suite 220, Chicago, IL 60602 (☎ (312) 977 4800);

TFI, 34 west 32nd St, New York, NY (☎ (1-800) 825 3834);

Airkit, 16 California St, San Francisco, CA 94111 (☎ (415) 362 1106) or 1125 W 6th St, Los Angeles, CA 90017 (☎ (213) 957 9304).

Student and youth fares are handled through three reputable agencies – Nouvelles Frontières, STA and Council Travel – and usually amount to the same as those advertised through the consolidators' newspaper adverts. There are certain differences in style and emphasis between the three outfits. Nouvelles Frontières is the most flexible if not always the cheapest, welcoming non-student/non-youth clients; STA isn't obsessed with your student status but is more wary about booking over-32s; Council Travel offices often refuse point-blank to deal with older, non-student customers.

Nouvelles Frontières' head office is at 12 East 33rd St, New York, NY 10016 (☎ (212) 779 0600), with two other branches in Los Angeles and San Francisco; STA has six outlets nationwide, half of them in California (eg 920 Westwood Blvd, Los Angeles, CA 90024 (☎ (213) 824 1574); and Council Travel's headquarters are at 205 E 42nd St, New York, NY 10017 (☎ (212) 661 1450 or (1-800) 223 7401), with 27 branches around the country, primarily in California, Massachussetts and New York.

To/From Canada

Because of the large Greek community in Canada, more-or-less reasonably priced flights are available on Olympic from Toronto and Montreal to Athens via New York twice weekly from each starting point. APEX tickets will set you back about C$1100 to C$1500 depending on the time of year. A number of other carriers provide stopping service via various European cities.

The student/youth outlet Travel CUTS (Voyages CUTS in Québec) may be worth a call – head office: 187 College St, Toronto Ontario M5T 1P7; (☎ (416) 979-2406), with

20 other branches across Canada. Their fares out of Vancouver, Montreal or Toronto should be a good 33% cheaper than full-price tickets, and one-ways may be available.

To/From Australia & New Zealand

Again, because of the huge numbers of Greeks in Australia there's no shortage of scheduled services to Greece. There are no direct flights, however; everybody makes a stop in Rome, Singapore or Bangkok on the way, though you usually won't have to change planes. The main carriers serving this route are Olympic, Alitalia, Qantas, Singapore and Thai International; typical year-round frequencies for each company are twice weekly, but each airline tends to fly on slightly different days, so coverage across the week is pretty good. Count on A$1500 return as a minimum.

If, and only if, you're short on money or plan to visit some Asian countries in between, it may be worth having a more complicated ticket written out with somewhat dodgier companies like Bangladesh Biman, EgyptAir or Air India. Their flights, though, tend to become multistop marathons, annoying unless you intend to take advantage of stopover privileges.

Students and under 30s would do well to contact branches of STA across Australia – head office: 1a Lee St, Sydney 2000, (☎ (02) 212-1255), or its affiliate STS in New Zealand – headquarters at 10 O'Connell St, Auckland, (☎ (09) 39-9191).

TRAIN

There are no less than five rail entry points to Greece at the northern and eastern borders, but only two are of major importance. The Idhoméni/Gevgelija crossing on the old Yugoslav frontier north of Thessaloníki funnels most of the major expresses coming from Munich, Budapest and Belgrade, the only European cities with direct connections to Greece. The Píthio/Uzunköprü crossing on the Turkish border sees just one slow, if popular, train from Istanbul. In theory there is a through service from Bucharest and Sofia, but there will be a change of lines and trains just beyond Greece's Promakhónas frontier post. All services pass through once daily.

From Britain, there are in theory two basic routes: one via Belgium to Munich, the other through Paris and Venice to Belgrade. Each crossing takes about 3½ days with minimal stops and changes, and service standards decline rapidly upon entering Slovenia, Croatia and Serbia – the recent civil war not having improved matters any. At the time of writing all through services are being routed on a day-to-day basis, via a long detour through Hungary to reach Belgrade. If war or sanctions have ruled out Belgrade as a stop, then you will have to buy a ticket through Bucharest and Sofia as well, en route to Thessaloníki. Even at the best of times, it's really only worth the trip if you plan to take in other countries along the way on the same ticket, or if you're under 26.

The least expensive return fare from the UK is an Interail pass, good for a month's free travel on all European railways (50% discount in the country of purchase, and reductions on certain ferries). Prices are currently UK£180 for under 26s and UK£260 for the recently introduced seniors version; there are also two-week passes that are not such good value at UK£180. If you plan to stay more than a month in Greece, not touring extensively the rest of Europe, you might consider a simple Eurotrain ticket, valid for two months with stopover privileges en route. These fares, available in Britain through USIT/Campus Travel, are slightly cheaper than Interail but not available to over 26s. North Americans will find that a Eurail pass is simply not worth the money for a single journey to and from Greece.

If you insist on the train, there are a couple of things you can do to make life more pleasant en route. Take a shower during the two-hour layover in Venice; get a couchette between Belgrade and Athens; and have the bulk of your luggage checked through to Athens, saving you the trouble of hauling it around at every change of wagons. Or – most sensibly – take a train to Italy instead and complete the trip by ferry (see Italy-Greece Ferries below).

BUS

If for some reason you can't get a reasonable flight or train ticket, an absolutely last resort will be a long-distance coach. It's worth avoiding the rock-bottom agencies, drive-by-night outfits in all senses of the words; a reliable, licensed service such as Eurolines will set you back about UK£100 one-way or UK£180 return from the UK, less any youth reductions. Departures tend to be two or three times weekly, the trip taking four days in all, with rest stops theoretically every five or six hours. Frankly the coaches fall into the never-to-be-forgotten, never-to-be-repeated category of experience, and the cost of meals and incidentals on the road will wipe out any savings over a cheap charter – not to mention a day or two wasted on arrival recovering from the ordeal.

CAR

For trekkers in particular who generally construct point-to-point itineraries, coming by car is not always worthwhile except in the North Píndhos or Mt Ólimbos where loop hikes are quite feasible. In some places, like the Pelopónnisos or Crete, a car parked back at your often-remote starting point becomes an outright inconvenience (though rural break-ins are not the norm).

If you value your sanity and the car's health, take the quickest route across the continent from Britain to Italy and a ferry from there on. Yugoslavia, even before its troubles, had a nasty reputation for poor road safety. Check with your insurer and the RAC or AA for current requirements and conditions en route, allow two or three driving days to one of the Italian ferry ports, and fill your car with petrol in France to avoid the exorbitant Italian fuel prices.

ITALY-GREECE FERRIES

There are regular ferries from Venice, Ancona, Bari, Brindisi and Otranto to Igumenítsa in Ípiros and Pátra at the northwest corner of the Pelopónnisos; most services allow a stopover on Corfu, and some midsummer boats will let you halt on Kefaloniá and Paxí instead. There is also a very useful once or twice-weekly Minoan Lines boat from Ancona to Kefaloniá, Pireás, Páros and Sámos, and a direct Bari-Iráklio (Crete) link at least every 10 days year-round.

The northerly Italian embarkation points are mostly worth knowing about if the Italian train system is on strike (most common south of Ancona); the ferry companies are well aware of the high price of Italian petrol, and what you save on fuel you will more than spend on ferrying a car the extra distance. Also, boat frequency tends to improve as you move further south, from twice-weekly at Venice or thrice-weekly at Ancona to nearly daily at Bari or daily (except January to March) at Brindisi.

Accordingly Brindisi is the most used crossing point, with the greatest selection of companies and fares and the longest operating season. Shop carefully – there are often significant price differences and conditions for drivers, rail-pass holders, students, youths, etc. From Brindisi to Igumenítsa (an 11-hour trip), count on low season fares of UK£25 per passenger without discounts and UK£40 for a car; taxes are extra. Advance reservations for cars are essential in midsummer, and now advisable year-round given the extra pressure on the boat services caused by the Yugoslav turmoil. Any competent UK travel agent will point you to the representative of the ferry company in Britain. Historically the cheapest hop over is from Otranto, but this operates only from May to October and you may find the extra rail distance there will wipe out any savings.

Boats tend to leave between 9 and 11 pm in the evening, and Italian trains seem perversely talented at leaving you in the ferry ports early in the morning; the most pleasant, interesting town in which to be stuck for the day is Bari, with Brindisi a distinct second.

TURKEY-GREECE FERRIES

There are five short-haul ferry crossings from Turkey to Greece: Ayvalık-Lésvos, Çesme-Híos, Kuşadası-Sámos, Bodrum-Kos, and Marmaris-Rhodes. They are all fairly similarly priced at $20 to $25 single, $30 to $35 open return per foot passenger, $50 to $75 each way per car. An additional tax of about $5 is levied both leaving and entering the Turkish side if the port is controlled by the Turkish maritime company; currently Ayvalık and Çesme are exempt from this. Of these services, only Marmaris-Rhodes and Çesme-Híos operate in winter (twice weekly); the Lésvos crossing ceases between September and May, and the Kos and Sámos services function unpredictably according to demand (about once a week) between early November and mid-April.

A word of warning: if you have entered Greece on a charter flight, you will invalidate the return half of your ticket by spending even one night outside the country – that means Turkey. The Greek government, having subsidised cheap landing fees for charter lines, is loathe for you to spend your money elsewhere. Day trips are OK, though, and the package industry in the frontier islands takes due advantage of this. Passport checks for foreign stamps on exit from Greece are not always thorough, but you could be unlucky, and it would be embarrassing, to say the least, to be denied boarding.

Greek Exit Taxes

Upon leaving Greece on the island-Anatolia ferries listed above, or on any of the boats to Italy, you will pay an exit tax, currently 1500dr; foreign currency is generally not accepted, so don't spend your last dhrakhmí. Often, though, the amount is collected when you buy your ticket, and you should be issued a small chit to keep as a receipt.

Two new taxes are slated to be introduced in 1993: a $15 airport tax, supposedly to help fund construction of a new airport at Spáta near Athens, and a whopping 10,000dr levy, replacing the 1500-dr port tax on the Aegean-Turkey services. Travel agents are fighting the latter, so far without success.

Getting Around

Public transportation of all kinds is still a fixture of life in Greece, and while no longer especially cheap it's considerably less costly than renting a vehicle or bringing your own. Promptness, vintage of the conveyance, and condition of the roads, rails or seas are unpredictable; in general, the further off the beaten track you venture, the less standardised things get.

If you're going to be spending a lot of time in Greece, it might be worth begging a slightly old copy of the travel-trade publication *Greek Travel Pages* (GTP), a fat paperback revised monthly. These invaluable compilations of trivia usually can be found in the lobbies of better hotels and travel agencies. They contain schedules and fares for virtually every ferry, train, bus and plane moving into, out of and around Greece.

AIR

If you're in a hurry, you can fly to most corners of Greece with Olympic Airways' domestic services. Flights cost roughly three to four times the basic deck-class ferry passage to an island, and up to five times the basic train fare to a mainland destination. That said, the longer hops (eg Athens-Sámos, Athens-Haniá) can be good value, and it's difficult to spend more than $90 on an internal flight – $60 is a more typical fare. If your time is limited you'd do well to consider flying at least in one direction.

In a drive to make Olympic a profit-making entity, turbo-prop ATR 42s and 70s, Dornier 228s and Short 330s have replaced jets on most internal routes which were hived off to the subsidiary Olympic Aviation. Their relatively small capacity means that seats are at a premium in season – book with foresight. (The big Boeings and Airbuses are reserved for high-volume or more remote airports such as Crete, the Dhodhekánisos and northern Greece.) Many peripheral routes between islands have been axed in the campaign against red ink, replaced by sea-level hydrofoil services, but the network as a whole still expands and contracts to some extent with the seasons – frequencies can be five times greater in summer on the same route.

Domestic baggage weight allowance is only 15 kg – a potential problem if you're off for a trek – but if you're arriving on an international flight which connects more or less directly with your onward internal flight, you are entitled to 20 kg. In practice the levying of excess baggage charges is pretty rare – the Greek public, with its twined bundles, hatboxes and lumpy duffles gets away with murder – but if you are nabbed the fees are pretty lenient at about $2 per excess kg. Weight and carry-on piece limits are more strictly enforced on the new generation of small planes.

Check in at least 45 minutes ahead of flight time at the Athens Olympic (western) terminal, especially in summer, when things get chaotic. If you have to pay excess baggage, this will delay you another 10 minutes while you hunt out various counters for payment and documentation.

As part of the general cost-cutting measures in hard times, your destination airport may no longer have any sort of bus service into town – Athens, Haniá, Kos and Thessaloníki are the only exceptions now. All the other Olympic-run shuttle services were eliminated recently, much to the delight of the taxi drivers who stand to gain; check if there are any public bus links before submitting to their tender mercies.

BOAT

Boats *(karávia, vapória* or just plain *féribot)* lend a distinctive romance to travel in Greece; no other country has such an extensive ferry network because no other nation, except Indonesia and the Philippines, has so much territory in insular form. Inter-island steamers are notorious for their erratic time-keeping, sensitivity to weather and general fickleness, so extended ferry travel is not for those on a tight schedule. If you are planning an 'If-this-is-Tuesday-this-must-be-Míkonos' island-hopping itinerary, you are going to come to grief. Flexibility, a sense of humour and a large backlog of reading or letter-writing should be standard equipment, along with a current copy of *The Thomas Cook Guide to Greek Island Hopping*, which while not flawless is invaluable. Much the same can be said for the mimeographed weekly schedules handed out by the central Athens tourist office, covering departures from Pireás, Lávrio and Rafína, or the Vólos and Thessaloníki offices' printouts. It's amazing how many novice travellers appear in a mainland or island port expecting a connection that may never have existed, or conversely unaware of one that does.

Harbour quays are generally lined with competing agencies, each flogging a particular shipping line or lines; the only impartial source of information is the *limenarkhío* (port authority). Their offices, usually within sight of the water, maintain complete, up-to-the-hour, posted schedules of all craft docking and sailing within their jurisdiction. They also are the first to monitor the weather report, since departures of even the largest boats tend to be cancelled if winds get above Force 7 or 8 on the Beaufort scale. They also have phone numbers of every other port authority in Greece; if you're drawing a blank on information about service from the next island – common, since local agents can't or won't tell you – phone ahead to make sure you won't be stranded. Most port policemen don't speak much English, but occasionally you can convince them to make such a call for you.

It's unwise to buy a ticket until the vessel you intend to board is confirmed to be on its way. If you want a cabin berth or room for a car, though, you should enquire as to whether space is selling out (not unheard of in summer). Fares once purchased are not refundable or transferable except to another boat run by the same company. Deck class – also known as tríti (3rd) – is adequate for daytime crossings; if the weather turns bad,

you're always welcome in the 'low-class' bar or lounge.

Summer nights see numerous backpackers sacked out on deck, but new boats acquired lately seem expressly designed, with their glaring lights and extruded-plastic benches, to frustrate such enterprise; on these boats you'd do well to consider a bunk in a B-class cabin. They're not outrageously expensive (eg $35 for the 13-hour crossing from Athens to Sámos including the basic fare of $18) when you consider that you'd pay at least $9 for your share of the cheapest hotel double.

Meals on board have improved greatly in recent years; the food on the overnight boats to Crete, the eastern Aegean islands and the Dhodhekánisos is usually moderately priced and often decent, and the only time you might want to brown-bag it is on the short hops to the inner Kikládhes or Argo-Saronics where the galley can't be bothered dishing appetising lunches.

In addition to the big liners, there are swarms of smaller excursion boats and *kaíkia* with licences to move perpendicular to the main shipping lines or supplement them in the high season – such services are very sensitive to demand, and you won't find them running in winter. The Ministry of Transport sets prices each year for all trajectories and routes, for all bona fide ferries; despite what an agent may say there will be little or no difference between his prices and anyone else's, and you can almost always buy a ticket on board without penalty (again despite dire warnings to the contrary). Where things get blurred is in the matter of excursion boats, which are essentially chartered and exempt from ministry guidelines; thus they can charge what they like. Similarly expensive, but more on the order of a scheduled service, are the hydrofoils which link Rafína or Flísvos marina at Pireás with the Kikládhes, Pireás with the Argo-Saronic and the lower Pelopónnisos, and Ródhos/Kos with the other Dhodhekánisos, Sámos, Híos and Lésvos. They are twice as fast and more than double the price of conventional steamers, but provide a rough ride in heavy seas and are not for the seasick-prone. Accordingly they also don't run in winter.

On the opposite end of the scale, an important term to remember is *ágoni grammí* (unprofitable line). These are routes or ships which the government subsidises to run to sparsely populated places, and which may either have no agency at all or agencies that are very reluctant to publicise them. Unfortunately from the traveller's point of view, these lines are often among the most useful and interesting in the Aegean. The limenarkhío will tell you where to find such boats and their agents, if any.

TRAIN

Trains *(tréna)* are administered by the Organismós Sidherodhrómon Elládhos (OSE or *oséh*), the state railway organisation. The rail system had fallen on hard times in recent years, with Peloponnesian service in particular retarded owing to century-old ties and rails, but there are signs of hope as management has lately implemented various reforms to attract customers and bring OSE into the black: true intercity expresses *(amaxostihiés piótitos)* on the Athens-Volos, Athens-Thessaloníki and Thessaloníki-Alexandhrúpolis lines, sleeper-only

Greece, Ferry & Railway Routes

(tréno-ksenodhohío) overnight services between Athens and Thessaloníki, and a new generation of rolling stock all around.

Second-class fares on ordinary (non-express) trains, which are of most interest to hikers, are less than half those on buses, with an even greater discount for round-trip tickets. First class is recommended for long journeys when 2nd-class gets packed out; it's still about 50% cheaper than a coach. Always buy train tickets in advance *and* request a seat reservation, regardless of the length of the trip. Reservations are free of charge; the wagon and seat numbers are on the back of your brown ticket. You will often pay a supplement for express services, your receipt being an extra grey stub. Even so, the basic 2nd-class fare for a trip Athens-Pátra won't exceed $6 ($9.50 for the round trip). Rail-pass holders must secure reservations like everyone else and may be required to pay supplements.

You'll find that, while day trains invariably leave promptly from the *initial* station of a run, they can be half an hour late or more by the end of the line. Food service is scarce and costly and cars can be badly heated in winter on the short-hop departures; if you have a choice go for the new top expresses.

Despite the fact that Greece's rail network – originally built partly by the Ottomans, partly by the Italians and partly by the Germans – is relatively skeletal, quite a number of jump-off points for hikers are well served by train. Services, if applicable, are indicated in the Access section of each hike write-up. Free wallet-size, comprehensive but Greek-only schedules are issued every May but they're quickly exhausted, so I have tried to be fairly explicit about current timings.

BUS

Avocado-green buses *(leoforía)* serve almost every town and rural village, though in some cases there may be a gap of days between departures. In towns, buy your ticket in advance at the station; on rural lines and small islands, ticket-sellers come around once you're under way. Prices usually work out at about $0.09 cents/km, though there are local variations – on Crete it's closer to 12 cents. Buses run on time, so be there when they tell you to be.

The single, nationwide bus company is universally referred to by its acronym KTEL, so if you can't find the station, ask where the *ktel* is. It is organised by province (KTEL Lakonías for the area around Spárti), with the main station or stations in the provincial capital and substations in the capitals of *eparkhíes* (counties) if a concentration of villages warrants it. This can lead to some confusion as to where exactly your bus departs from. For example, Iráklio on Crete has three stations: for coast-road services, villages in the south-east of the province, and villages in the south-west. KTEL Ioánnina has two stations in the capital, one for Athens and the south-east villages, the other for lines toward Makedhonía and the northern villages, plus a substation in Kónitsa.

All villages are served by the KTEL of the province in which they happen to be; if a village you're trying to reach lies in the neighbouring province, you'll generally have to use that province's KTEL, even though the place may be just over the border and easier to reach from your side! Thus there are often 10 km to 30 km gaps between services in the vicinity of provincial frontiers, which you have to bridge by walking, taxiing or hitching.

As a general rule, buses from provincial or county capitals tend to follow the school and market day: from the village to the regional centre early in the morning, and back to the hamlet after school and morning shopping, finishing about 1.30 or 2 pm. There are, however, numerous exceptions to this: the bus may reverse the pattern, heading to the village at dawn, or only make several trips weekly, at odd hours. A typical Sunday pattern is from the capital to the village for the benefit of townspeople going to visit relatives or attend to smallholdings. In the more remote rural areas, Sunday or holiday bus services are severely limited or non-existent, and some extremely depopulated or isolated villages have no service whatsoever.

TAXIS

Where there is no public transit you'll be looking for someone with whom to share a taxi, which may be too expensive otherwise. Taxis on an island should be metered or have standard set fares, but between towns on the mainland or Crete bargaining is the rule. If the driver is returning home empty from a drop-off, he may offer you a ride for the equivalent of the bus fare or a bit more, just to pay for the petrol; count your blessings. A metered or standardised stretch will cost you about $7 to $10 per 10 km – up to ten times what the bus would cost. The flag falls at 200dr, and double tariff applies once outside city limits or after midnight. Luggage attracts a small extra charge, as does entering an airport or a seaport.

Within city limits, meters must always be used – it is illegal to quote a flat (inflated) rate, a ploy commonly tried on foreigners outside airport arrival terminals. You should, however, be familiar with the Athens institution of the group taxi. Flag a half-full car by shouting your destination at the driver; if it suits him, he stops for you. Memorise the meter reading when you get in, then pay the difference plus the minimum when disembarking – each passenger pays as if they were riding alone.

HITCHING

Hitching *(otostop)* is usually quite easy if you're toting only a daypack, but I've several times waited a couple of hours for 70-km rides with a full pack. Rides are, as ever, easiest to come by in remote regions where traffic is primarily pick-up trucks and vans, and where everyone knows that the bus may not be a feasible alternative. Hitching on commercial vehicles is technically illegal, so you may find that, if offered a ride in a large van, particularly in the payload area, you'll be left on the outskirts of the upcoming town so as not to be seen at police checkpoints. In really rural areas it's common for extra passengers to ride in the back of pick-ups, and nobody gives a damn.

The Pelopónnisos misses being an island by only six km, the width of the isthmus of Kórinthos connecting it to the rest of mainland Greece. Today considered isolated and away from the centre (politically as well as geographically), it is in many ways the heart of Greece.

Ancient ruins and medieval monuments are thicker on the ground here than anywhere else in the country. It was on the Pelopónnisos that the standard of revolution was first raised in 1821, and most of the decisive battles of the war of independence were fought on the peninsula or just offshore. Until the acquisition of Thessalía in 1881, the Pelopónnisos formed the most important chunk of Greece's non-island territory.

The scenery itself, whether the Maniot near-desert, the orchards and river valleys of Arkadhía or the sandy Messenian capes, is unsubtle and dramatic, painted in bold swatches always weighted by the mountains that invest the outline of the Moreás (the medieval name, still used) like the bones of a hand. A great wall of consecutive peaks – Zíria, Helmós, Panahaïkós, Erímanthos – cuts off the middle from the Kórinthos gulf, with the two great 'fingers' of Taïyettos and Párnon flanked by the lesser hills of Messenía and the Argolid 'thumb'.

The northern and western shores of the Pelopónnisos absorb the brunt of winter precipitation; in summer a heaviness and languor in the air suggest correctly that the Adriatic and the softer contours of Italy are not far away. Water becomes more of a preoccupation as one journeys south and east; its extreme lack culminates in the study of austerity provided by south-western Taïyettos and its extension, the Máni.

The Peloponnesian people, benefiting from the relative natural wealth of their home, are strongly attached to their villages and lands, which are in general not languishing as on many of the islands or in Ípiros. Although they have a poor reputation with other Greeks – a common reproach is *ólo embório*–'all business (and no other values)' – at least some of this can be ascribed to jealousy of the disproportionate role that locals have played in national affairs recently. Outsiders will find them to be almost unfailingly hospitable and helpful, particularly (as always) in the remoter settlements.

Zíria (Killíni)

The second-highest mountain range of the Pelopónnisos is arranged in a 'U' around the Flamburítsa valley, with a distinctive plateau just north of the highest peak. Zíria is bounded on the west by the Ólvios River, to the south by the basin of Stimfalía, and on the north and east by more densely inhabited valleys whose streams drain to the gulf.

The two names of the range stem from a Slavic word for acorn in the case of Zíria, and the ancient Greek term for cavity and sinkhole, *kyllos*, which became Killíni in the modern language. In the pre-Christian era the mountain was sacred to the god Hermes who, legend has it, was born in a cave on the heights; Pausanias found traces of his cult, a favourite of travellers, persisting when he passed by in the 2nd century AD. Accordingly Zíria has always been viewed with a more trusting eye than precipitous Helmós to the west, or Taïyettos to the south; the slopes here are mostly gentle and smooth, devoid of the fatal associations with the kingdom of the dead on Helmós or the fickle nereids at Taïyettos.

The main summit, then, is a barren and rather uninteresting dome of rock, perhaps the acorn of the Slavic imagination. In winter, however, its open slopes and the 1600-metre-high plateau of Ksirolívadho below are transformed into the best cross-country ski routes in southern Greece. After snowmelt the plain is dotted with a pair of temporary lakes, one of them suitable for a cold, late-spring dip.

KSIROLÍVADHO & AROUND

As for trekking, the best opportunities are offered by the Mikrí Zíria ridge (the eastern flank of the 'U'), which allows dramatic vistas over the isthmus and gulf of Kórinthos, and the forested Flamburítsa valley, thus far untouched by roads.

Itineraries up top are easily combined with a trip to the Fónissa Gorge (see Other Excursions later in this chapter) on the coast below; here a 300-metre-deep chasm eventually narrows to form a giant cavern.

Rating & Duration

All traverses fall into the easy-to-moderate category, owing to the fairly gradual elevation changes. Allow two to three days on and around the mountain.

Season

The Zíria uplands are most interesting in late spring or early summer, when the lakes have water and snow still drapes the mountainsides.

Supplies

These are best obtained in Athens, though you can snare minor items in Tríkala.

Maps

Korfes 82, *Zíria*, or YIS 1:50,000 *Kandhíla*, *Dhervénion* (the very southern edge) and *Neméa* (its western edge).

Access

Tríkala, the main village on the northern side of Zíria, has a twice-daily bus service from Ksilókastro at 5.15 am and 2 pm, returning immediately after the 38-km journey. Ksilókastro straddles the main Athens-Pátra bus and train routes.

Tríkala actually consists of three *sinikíes* (settlements): Káto, Méso and Áno Tríkala. The upper neighbourhood, a popular summer resort but relatively empty in winter due to its 1100-metre altitude, supports the

Hotel Asteria (☎ (0745) 91 207) and Kostas Korkaris's rented rooms (☎ (0743) 91 396), both open most of the year.

Stage 1: Tríkala to Ksirolívadho Refuges via Kleftáki Peak

(3 hours)

A 10-km dirt road built in 1986 leaves Áno Tríkala at its southern end, passing the monastery of Ayíu Vlasíu and leading all the way to the rocky Ksirolívadho plateau and a pair of mountain refuges. It's far more interesting, though, to head up west through dense pine forests and then curl around south to reach this plateau by the seasonal lake called Límni Dhasíu.

Leave the village on the path leading west from the Hotel Asteria, keeping left, to meet a dirt track after 10 minutes. At the first hairpin right, keep going north-west for five minutes on a small track to a gully; here a small trail climbs up the left (south) bank for five more minutes, crosses an aqueduct and reaches an uneven track of grey earth just below a left bend. It continues opposite, climbing up through pines and taking the right of a fork until, 25 minutes along, it joins a large dirt track at a hairpin bend. Follow the road up to the left and, after 100 metres, you should see various paths appearing between the pine trees on your left. To diminish an irritating road walk, strike west up the leftmost of these trails, though some 40 minutes from Tríkala you rejoin the road at another hairpin curve above a field and a concrete trough. Across the road, the path slips down and left before resuming a steady west-north-west climb; 20 minutes later you hit the road again.

A left fork here leads directly, within four km, to the lake. However, it's better to follow the road system first right and then left as far as a right bend on a forested north-south ridge at 1400 metres. You'll have a fine perspective south-west down the Ólvios river valley, with Mt Helmós beyond. This river, curiously enough, flows away from the coast toward the plain of Feneós, where it promptly disappears. The path for the Ksirolívadho begins from this viewpoint.

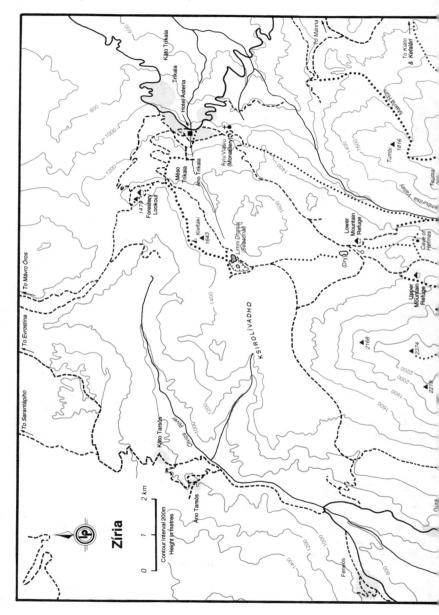

Káto Trikala
Trikala
Hotel Asteria
Áyiu Vlasiu (Monastery)
Méso Trikala
Áno Trikala
To Mavro Óros
To Kiáto & Kefalári
To Mavra Óros
1479
Forestry Lookout
Kiefráki
Kiefráki 1643
Limni Dhasíu (Sébachia)
Tumbi 1816
Manna Valley
To Mavra
Lower Mountain Refuge
Tsuma
Lambúnga Valley
Cave of Hermes
(Dry)
Upper Mountain Refuge
KSIROLÍVADHO
2168
2374
2218
1400
To Evrostína
To Sarantápiho
Káto Tarsós
Ólvios River
Áno Tarsós
Gúra
Fengós
Zíria

2 km

Contour interval 200m
Height in metres

0   1   2 km

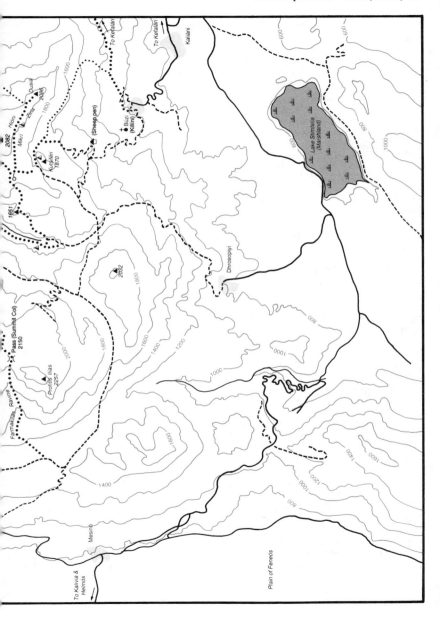

Ten minutes away to your right stands a fire-spotting tower and a path to the 1479-metre trig point.

Head south through the pine trees on the ridge for a few minutes until the view on your right reappears by some piles of sand. Bear right onto a generally flat and pleasant path with an overall west-south-west direction, ignoring the small right-hand options at the outset (the second one passes a seasonal spring if you're desperate). Keep climbing gently between (and sometimes over) the pine trees; after 40 minutes, keep low through a thickly wooded patch, and five minutes later a grassy balcony overlooks the Ólvios and surrounding forests. Another 10-minute climb brings you to another panoramic rocky rim; here the path curves left (south-west) slightly and hugs a band of composite rock for five minutes before veering right to meet the 1600-metre lip west of Kleftáki (1643 metres), some two hours out of Tríkala.

The secondary peak (about 1630 metres) is a worthwhile 15-minute hop up to the north-east; the panorama includes (clockwise from south-west to east) the whole Helmós range from outrider Mt Durduvána to the main ridge, nearby Mt Marmáti, Mt Vardhúsia beyond the gulf, the tabletop summit of Mávro Óros, Mt Parnassós and Mt Elikón across the sea, the peninsula of Perakhóra, Mt Yeránia above the isthmus of Kórinthos, and the mountains of Attikí behind. At your feet, in the opposite direction, lies Límni Dhasíu, your next destination, with Ksirolívadho sprawling south of it.

To get to the refuges, leave the lake at its southern end, following the road south for one km, and when the road bends right simply continue south for two km over the gentle hummocks and boulders until you reach a thistly field and a stony road. The upper shelter, which sleeps 16, is just discernible two km ahead, at 1700 metres; the lower and larger (30-person) refuge hides five minutes down a track to the left (east), behind a bluff, at 1550 metres, next to a spring. More accurate description is impossi-

ble since the terrain is so monotonous; a compass, a watch and a bit of mental arithmetic are the best locators. Total walking time out of Áno Tríkala shouldn't exceed three hours. If you need the keys for either of the mountain huts, contact the EOS branch in Éyio (☎ (0691) 25 285) for the lower hut, and in Kórinthos (☎ (0741) 29 970) for the upper one.

If you want to visit the mythical birth-cave of Hermes, continue south along the rim above the Flamburítsa valley for half an hour; you should intersect a small track, from whose left-hand terminus the cave lies about 10 minutes east along a narrow path.

Stage 2A: Ksirolívadho to Gúra via the Summit Col

(4½ hours)

A walk of about half an hour separates the lower from the upper mountain huts; from the high hut a path winds south, then west, within an hour to the saddle between Profítis Ilías (2257 metres) and the anonymous summit 2374. A detour to the top will consume another 90 minutes each way; the last water is just before the col, off to the south. From the pass at 2150 metres, a trail (and later a track) continues west down the Farmakílas ravine to the village of Gúra, a 2½ or three-hour descent.

From Gúra, you can link up with the Helmós routes by either taking the daily bus at about 2.15 pm to Feneós village and walking either to Ayíu Yioryíu monastery or straight up to Dhiásello (see Helmós, Southern & Western Approaches, Stage 1A). Alternatively, you can return to Kiáto on the coast via the 2.45 pm bus, which connects with the 5.30 pm Athens-bound service.

Stage 2B: Ksirolívadho to Kefalári or Búzi via Flamburítsa

(6½ hours for full stage)

Follow the track to the rim of the plateau, 10 minutes south-east of the lower refuge, and then down towards the Flamburítsa Valley until it fizzles out after another 10 minutes. From here drop 30 metres down a stony gully onto a slender trail which wends its way approximately south-south-east among young pines. At times it's invisible, but as long as you keep descending gently in the same direction you'll reach a stream at about 1250 metres within an hour of quitting the refuge.

It is possible to return to Tríkala from here by following an old woodcutters' path downstream. This keeps to the true left bank for about half an hour, until a stone cairn, where the stream drops sharply into a narrow gorge and the path starts a gentle ascent. Apart from the numerous fallen trees blocking the way, and occasional washouts, this trail is a very pleasant stroll through the woods, with fine views across to the forested slopes below Túmbi. Keep above the green meadows on your right, which hide nearly a dozen species of orchids in May, and you'll reach the main Tríkala-Ksirolívadho road, six km above the village, in just over an hour from the streambed.

For those interested in walking straight from Tríkala to the Flamburítsa valley, you can follow the above path in reverse, locating it through a breach in the left earth bank above the road, just after a right hairpin curve. Allow 1½ hours for the initial six km of dull road-tramping, passing Ayíu Vlasíu monastery en route, and a similar amount of time for the path section as described previously.

To go upstream from the point where the trail drops down to Ksirolívadho, use a small path switching from bank to bank, carpeted with bright yellow daisies in late spring and beautifully shady in summer. After a second hour's stroll the valley opens out, the stream splits into a web of trickles, and lush grass dotted with flocks and huts replaces the black pines. Skirt the left edge of the basin for about 500 metres, then bear due east just before a large gully and descending track. Follow the stream for a few minutes before veering left (north-north- east) again and then climb steeply through fir trees on a network of goat trails.

At about 1650 metres, at the last ridge before the spur leading up to Tsúma Peak (2021 metres), turn right (east) and follow the path past the treeline (about 1700 metres elevation) on the southern slope of a steep valley. The trail then curls left (north) among heather and thistle, crossing seasonal seeps, and next climbs east up a gully to a reliable improved spring at about 1850 metres. The spring, with its final stunted tree, looks across at the bare limestone slopes of Tsúma. It makes a good resting spot after the hour's climb from the head of the valley floor, some three hours from the Ksirolívadho refuges.

Descents to Búzi & Mánna Another path leading north from the moss-flecked boulder (mentioned previously) bisects the Mikrí Zíria massif at about 1950 metres, drops slightly to the Túmbi spur and then descends north-east to the flatlands along the Makriá Húni streambed. However, leaving the Mikrí Zíria in this direction will entail quite a long hike to the closest village, Mánna.

Fifteen minutes beyond the spring you come to a large boulder flecked with fluorescent green moss. From here starts the descent to the village of Búzi (Killíni). Descend south-west to the saddle below a gentle 1930-metre knoll, and then south to the valley and lone plum tree in front of Kutsiféri peak (1870 metres). From there a jeep track heads south-west down to a dirt road linking Búzi and Gúra.

Descent to Kefalári To reach Mikrí Zíria's highest point, Dusiá (2086 metres) from the spring, continue east from the boulder on the faint trail. Enjoy the sight of Lake Stimfalía which nestles below you to the right, and the jagged array of peaks stretching south towards Argos. Narrow-leafed shrubs gradually yield to grassy patches or late snow (the ridge on your left is indeed called Hióni, or 'snow'). Half an hour along, a left turn brings you to the main crest where there's a splendid view to the north. Dusiá is an easy 10 minutes of rockhopping east-south-east, with more wide-angle views over its plunging slopes.

The final descent to Kefalári village starts from the saddle between Hióni (2082 metres) and Dusiá. It lurches down through a knee-jarring boulder field in a north-easterly direction. Until you make the treeline, don't waste time looking for an easier way (the old path has long since vanished), but try to keep on the first or second bluff to the right of the central gully. You should find a variety of trails taking you north-east through the dense pine forest to the edge of level ground. If you haven't reached this cultivated plateau within two hours of leaving the saddle, you probably drifted too far right (south-east).

Assuming you do reach it, turn right at the edge of the plain – you may pass a well – until coming to a track among the fields; adopt this and after 30 minutes you hit the Tríkala-Kefalári dirt road, with an arc of cliffs to your right and Kefalári below you. To avoid the large switchback, leave the road about 500 metres further down and head straight for the northern extremity of the village, where you'll arrive some 6½ hours out of Ksirolívadho.

In Kefalári there's an inn run by a Mr Liga (☎ (01) 36 07 093 for information). Other accommodation is down on the main asphalt road to Kiáto, one km east of the village (☎ (0747) 22 280). A bus passes along this main road at around 4.30 pm daily and terminates in Kiáto in time for you to catch the 5.30 pm Athens-bound bus from there. Alternatively, you can head west by train or bus to the mouth of the Fónissa Gorge.

OTHER SUGGESTED EXCURSIONS NEAR ZÍRIA
Day Hike in the Fónissa Gorge
Driving along the expressway between Kiáto and Dhervéni, you can't help but notice a series of low jutting cliffs, unusually textured so as to seem a painted backdrop for a Western. This is a geologically young area, formed less than a million years ago when the narrow coastal strip was still submerged; as it was thrust upwards, water from the rising mountains to the south cut through the still-soft marl and clay to form intricate ravines and abrupt edges. By far the most impressive of these is the Fónissa ('Murderess') Gorge.

Access Either take one of the four daily buses from Athens to Dhervéni (the 10.30 am is convenient), alighting 1½ hours later in Káto Lutró (8 km past Ksilókastro), or use a local bus or train from Kiáto (six trains daily between 9.20 am and 8.30 pm).

Route Directions As you leave the Káto Lutró village 'centre', just before the primary school, a signposted asphalt road turns inland (left) towards Vrisúles. Follow this under the highway and immediately turn sharp left onto a dirt track, which runs east alongside the highway. Veer right at the first fork and then follow the main track through citrus groves, about 100 metres west of the river bed. Just where the track makes a right turn and becomes impassable for ordinary cars (about three km from the coast), you must strike left five minutes through reed plantations to an aqueduct.

The best method of proceeding from here is to walk up inside the conduit, holding onto the sides if necessary; you're going to get wet feet later on in any case, so bring a spare pair of quick-draining shoes. After an elevated section you land on top of a concrete dam. From here on you simply walk up the river until it is impossible to continue any further. In summer or autumn this would be about one hour, after which a three-metre waterfall bars your way; otherwise deep pools and minor cascades may make you decide to turn back earlier.

At various stages the sides of the chasm close in so much that it becomes dark (bring a flashlight); shafts of light pierce the gloom, illuminating boulders trapped between the walls as they fell. There is little danger of them falling further, though there is a slight chance of smaller stones being dislodged by earthquakes or even goats. The alarmingly slimy creatures which may brush your ankles are harmless water snakes (if that's any consolation!).

If you're up to some technical climbing, there's a full account of a complete south-to-north traverse of the gorge, a two-day affair involving slippery rappels, in *Korfes* 88 (March/April 1991).

Helmós (Aroánia)

The linchpin of the northern Peloponnesian barrier mountains is a complex mini-sierra in its own right, situated exactly halfway across the peninsula. The eastern summits (Neraïdhálono, Aëtorákhi, Psilí and Korfí) and the western ridge (the longer but lower Neraïdhórakhi) are connected by an intermediate zone called Apáno Lithária. This great horseshoe encloses a deep, north-flowing canyon, supposed in ancient times to contain the source of the mythical river Styx (Stigós). It is this defile, plus the wild forests on the north flanks of the Stygian canyon, that distinguishes Helmós from adjacent mountains. Besides trees – junipers, pines, firs and deciduous species are all jumbled together – Helmós hosts seasonal explosions of flowers and rare endangered butterflies.

All of the northern Peloponnesian ranges trap moist air from the nearby Kórinthos gulf; thus Helmós is apt to be misty and damp even in summer, though wind sighing in trees and crags creates the illusion of running water when there is none. Most available water is in fact at the bottom of the legendary valley, eventually attaining enough volume as the infant Kráthis River to sustain a handful of villages at the lower margins of the great forests. The relative isolation of these settlements, plunged in a wilderness even more complete in some ways than the mountain, is emphasised by the frequent lack of customary name signs at the outskirts of each community. The northern Helmós villages are as high as those on Zíria (about 1100 metres), and the metre of winter snow drives the inhabitants down to balmier quarters at Akráta on the coast.

For such a remote area, Helmós has been the target of more than its share of development activities. A ski resort has been established on a high plateau north-east of Nerädhórakhi, and a dirt road – one of the highest in Greece – opened from the lifts, past the tiny alpine refuge, to the very summit itself! A waterworks utility track has pressed far into the Styx valley, with only the sheerness of the head of the canyon saving it from a similar fate. With a bit of discrimination, and using less obvious trailheads, however, it is possible to construct satisfying trekking traverses perpendicular to the growing network of roads.

Rating & Duration

Whether trekking at high or low altitudes, the routes are all moderately strenuous, particularly the passage of the Styx canyon in either direction or ridge-walking above the Dhiásello of Zarúkhla.

With four days at your disposal you can see most of the mountain by following the route from Zakhlorú to Tsivlós, Peristéra, Apáno Lithária, Planitéro and Spíleo Límnon. On a long weekend you could easily trek from Káto Lusí to Apáno Lithária, Gaïdhurórakhi and Dhiásello.

Season

These treks are best attempted in summer.

Supplies

Get these in Kalávrita, Dhiakoptó or Akráta; the high Helmós villages have little in the way of groceries.

Maps

Korfes 80-81, *Psilí Korfí* and *Avgó*, or YIS 1:50,000 *Aíyion, Kandhíla* and *Dháfni*.

NORTHERN APPROACHES

Tackling Helmós from the north gives you the chance to savour the middle elevations of some underrated foothills. Within a short distance of one another you have a celebrated monastery, one of the Pelopónnisos's few natural lakes, and a daunting gorge. And you can also climb to the waterfalls of the Styx valley from this direction, without having to cross over Helmós's summit ridge.

Access

Zakhlorú Reaching the base of Helmós is certainly half the fun. You can take any KTEL bus plying between Athens and Pátra to the town of Dhiakoptó, asking the driver

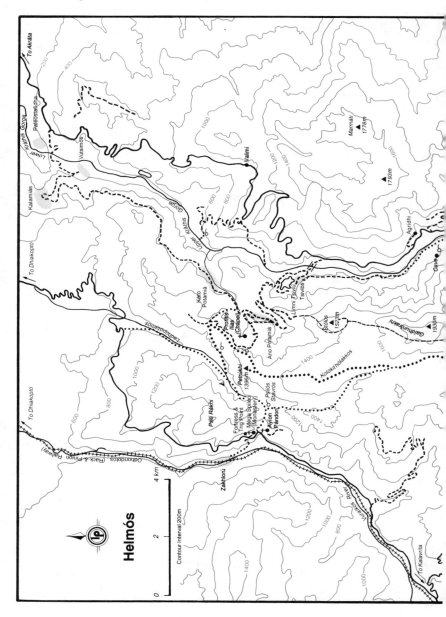

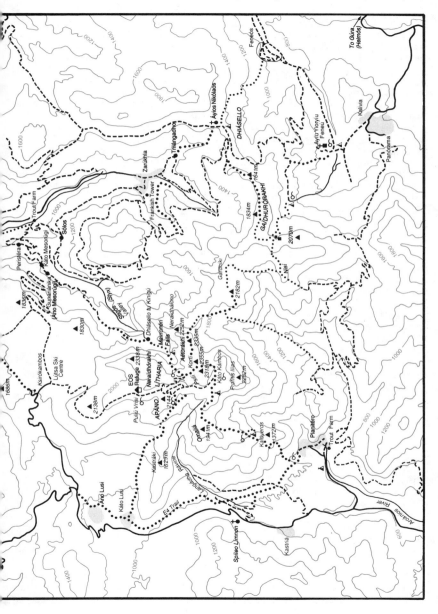

to drop you on the bridge over the rack-and-pinion railway (*ston odhondotó*), where steep stairs in the embankment lead off the highway to the tracks and the village centre. Alternatively, you can catch one of the seven daily trains serving the same route, though these take nearly twice as long.

At Dhiakoptó you'll board one of the four daily departures (currently 7.45 and 10.42 am, 12.15 and 15.08 pm) of the famous rack-and-pinion railway which snakes up the Vuraïkos River gorge towards Kalávrita. This amazing feat of engineering, which climbs over 700 metres in 22 km, was designed by an Italian firm in the 1890s. Although the original steam locomotives and wooden cars are long gone, the ride – with its tunnels, rickety trestles, roaring cataracts, and narrow ledges – is not to be missed. The third rail is noisily engaged at the start of each particularly tough grade; passengers bounce from one side of the carriage to another for the views, and risk decapitation by sticking their heads out the smudgy windows.

However, some people do miss the ride, preferring instead to walk the first 13 km up to Zakhlorú, where the route described in this section begins. Hiking along the right-of-way is a popular outing, leaving one at leisure to study the twisted rock formations and shepherds' caves overhead, but make sure you leave just after a train does, since there are several tight spots along the tracks where there wouldn't be room for both a string of walkers and a carriage! The hike up from Dhiakoptó to the tiny hamlet of Zakhlorú takes 3¾ hours.

At Zakhlorú you can stay and eat either at the Romantzo Hotel (☎ (0692) 22 758), an inn run by cousins next door (☎ (0692) 22 789), or at the Messinia, 100 metres beyond.

Zakhlorú to Límni Tsivlú via Méga Spíleo Monastery & Mt Petrúkhi
(6 hours)
From the terrace next to the Messinia inn, follow a steep but well-defined path towards the monastery of Méga Spíleo. After half an hour's climbing you collide with the hairpin bend of a dirt track and, continuing upwards on this, next hit the asphalt road between Kalávrita and the coast. Bearing left (north) onto this, you reach the paved driveway for the monastery within 10 minutes, and the building itself five minutes later, a total of 45 minutes out of Zakhlorú.

Nestling under a cliff, the monastery is perched in front of the large cave which has given the cloister its name. A miraculous ikon of the Virgin, apprehended in a vision by the hermits Simeon and Theodhoros and the shepherdess Evfrosini, prompted its foundation in the 4th century, though the place has been burnt down and rebuilt so many times you'd hardly know it. Méga Spíleo was once an immensely wealthy monastery, which accounts for its rich treasury containing gold-filigree crosses and relics of various saints; the ikon, said to be painted by either Luke the Evangelist or Luke the Beatified (a difference of nearly a millennium!), has lately been returned to a small chapel. Currently there are just five resident monks, who run a guest quarters for men only (☎ (0692) 22 401).

From the large bell near the main building, a path leads up past the guest wing and the chapel of Ayíon Pándon, towards a monument to local civilians executed by the Nazis during WWII (1943 saw similar massacres at nearby Rogí and Kavlávrita). Turn instead left off the main path onto a steeply pitched trail, just after the chapel and a battered sign. This trail climbs abruptly over some old stone steps to a ridge, and then curls north around a narrow ledge to a fork, where potable water gushes out of a pipe into a barrel.

Here a left-hand trail brings you next to a fortress, and beyond that to a dramatically situated cross and a trig point; in summer you can watch red kites and kestrels, with their characteristically U-shaped wings, hovering in front of the cliffs.

The right-hand fork follows the pipe to the Psilós Stavrós saddle at 1150 metres. This path is generally quite level and passable, but does have two narrow, steep sections for which a reasonable sense of balance is required. You should allow one hour from the monastery to the saddle, where more spring water flows through a system of troughs.

From this saddle the adventurous can follow the ridge north to a landmark rock pierced by a large hole (Psilí Rákhi), or south towards the main Helmós massif. The way towards Petrúkhi, a rocky, fortified-looking peak seen to the north-east, starts down the other side of the saddle on a steep incline covered with slick stones. Ignore the boastful display of goats perched precariously among the looming rocks above, and take the slope slowly and carefully.

Some 30 minutes beyond the ridge, the path flattens out among some fields on the left (west) bank of the Ladhopótamos stream, down to a trickle by September. To avoid getting tangled in brambles, it is best to follow the stony riverbed north until reaching a green, thistly patch, where the bed narrows and water reemerges from it after a short stretch underground (in summer). Here a small, shaded path leaves the valley on the right (east) bank and heads north-east, alternately through fir trees and open bracken slopes, reaching a spring with troughs in about half an hour, or two hours from Méga Spíleo.

As the trail climbs, the river drops rapidly below, giving you a sense of accomplishment tempered by the sight of Petrúkhi's vertical walls above you to the south. From the fountain keep right when in doubt (the steeper alternative, usually) and you should reach a second ridge at about 1100 metres and a north-south dirt track in about 20 minutes. From here you may glimpse the rugged massif of Marmáti to the south-east, last habitat of the Peloponnesian wolf, and to the north the Kórinthos gulf and sometimes the mountains on its far side. Áno Potamiá village lies hidden below you to the right (south), with the lake of Tsivlú lurking behind a lip beyond.

Follow the main track (or preferably the path on the ridge running parallel to it) southwest for about two km (30 minutes), until shortly before the cliffs begin, some three

hours from the monastery. Here the 45-minute, nontechnical ascent of the peak sets off from the ridge; scramble up from the road if necessary. The well-trodden path climbs south through fir trees to a ledge next to a distinctive outcrop. Here you may need to remove (and replace) some branch fencing in order to proceed, veering right (south-west) past an ivy-covered cave-sheepfold and right (west) again past steep, thistly slopes to a north-south crest at about 1350 metres.

From here the Ladhopótamos valley and the Psilí Rákhi palisade above Méga Spíleo are clearly visible to the west; on a clear day you can also see Mt Erímanthos to the south-west and Mt Panahaïkos to the north-west. The 1396-metre trig point of Petrúkhi is reached by following a smaller, overgrown path north for five minutes, climbing up the ledge to your left where it is lowest and continuing west for a couple of minutes. The easterly summit, though marginally higher, is only for climbers who enjoy crumbly rock.

Descent is by the same route, returning you to the track just over four hours from Méga Spíleo. Well-equipped trekkers who aren't interested in the lake can follow the main path south along the ridge to reach the Kolokithólakkos plateau (1500 metres) in one hour or the Ksirókambos plateau (1660 metres) in about four hours.

After rejoining the dirt road, follow it south to the well-frescoed chapel of Profítis Ilías, built into the rock face and garnished with a spring and plane tree. Then the road winds down about four km, making a total of five walking hours from Méga Spíleo, to the summer village of Áno Potamiá at about 900 metres, where the *agrofílakas* (guard), Panayiotis Seflas (☎ (0696) 61 379), may be able to find you a bed – but don't expect cooked meals.

To get to Límni Tsivlú, cross the river and head north-east up the road towards the lip, where the track branches right to the southern portion of Áno Potamiá and Stólos peak, and left to the lake, which at 720 metres will mark the sixth hour of walking on the day.

As you approach the lake on the dirt track,

cutting two switchbacks if desired, the first right turn takes you around the shoreline counter-clockwise to Tsivlós village, while the second leads to various points, some suitable for camping, on the water's edge; the summer temperature is usually just right for a refreshing swim.

The main trail continues by a seasonal café overlooking the lake (owned by Lambis Sakelaropoulos (☎ (0696) 51 237, food on request), past another right fork for the village, over the Kráthis River and onto the asphalted road linking the coast with Zarúkhla, at the head of the Kráthis valley. At the junction you can try hitching, summon a taxi (☎ (0696) 22 959, 31 892 or 31 052) from Akráta, or coincide with the bus which passes by only on Tuesday, Thursday and Saturday mornings.

Onwards to the Stigós (Styx) Valley If you intend to proceed up the Stigós (Styx) valley (reversing the itinerary set forth in Stage 2A of the Southern & Western Approaches section), and transportation up-valley is not forthcoming, it's possible to walk to Peristéra from Tsivlós in about three hours. Take a bad dirt road south out of Tsivlós village for five km until it stops near a cave and a spring on the west bank of the Kráthis River. Beyond this point, despite appearances to the contrary on the *Korfes* and YIS maps, you are best advised to follow the river closely upstream as far as the trout farm and sideroad bridge off the asphalt. There are inns or tavernas (or both) in most of the villages clustered up on the west bank; for details see the Southern & Western Approaches section.

Day Hike in the Kráthis Gorge

If you want a different sort of adventure than that provided by the mountain itself, the most inaccessible and untrammelled gorge of the Pelopónnisos is not far from Tsivlós. It's not certain whether anyone has even attempted a complete traverse of this 13-km gash in the limestone strata. When you mention the place, locals tend either to give you blank looks or tell you to take the road. Nonethe-

less it is possible to walk the upper section of the gorge, but only in late summer and with a light load. Even then, be prepared for a good four hours of boulder-hopping with wet trousers and scratched legs. That said, the sight of the precipices overhead amply compensates for the difficulty.

Map YIS 1:50,000 *Dhervénion* – though it won't be much help on a rock-by-rock, minute-to-minute basis!

Route Directions To begin, follow the river downstream from the bridge of the side road from Tsivlós. After the first right-hand bend, some 1½ km or an hour along, you reach a concrete weir where a bulldozer track descends from the asphalt road to your right (east). Soon afterwards the fun begins, as the first *sténoma* (narrowing) forces you into waist-deep water and onto narrow ledges. Another 500 metres of relatively easy walking brings you to the second and main sténoma. The trickiest obstacle here is a pair of metre-high cascades separated by a large boulder. Climb around to the right of the boulder and down into the pool, then duck left under an arch formed by two larger rocks. If all goes well you should reach the next open section, where a smaller creek tumbles down from Káto Potamiá village to the west, within 2½ hours of the weir.

About a km further down, a larger waterfall near the remains of a bridge makes further progress difficult. The best 'out' is 500 metres before this, where the western bank is at its lowest and an incline of scree is seen on the eastern bank. Scramble up the latter and, near the top, turn left onto a slim trail for two minutes. Next bear right (east), climbing through dense scrub, to the first of three consecutive fields. Just above these you'll meet a disused track, by a metal-trough spring hidden among the oaks. Follow it left (downhill) for 10 minutes, after which you intersect a larger track at a sharp bend next to a concrete-trough spring. If you can arrange it locally, have a car and dry clothes waiting for you here (and at least tell someone beforehand that you're attempting the gorge); otherwise you face a two-km uphill tramp to a point on the asphalt road three km west of Valimí village.

If you wish to investigate the lower half of the gorge, be warned that this is even more drastic than the upper part. It's best tackled as an out-and-back hike from Paleostafídha (near Akráta) or, if the first sténoma beneath the Vútsimos bridge is impassable, from the village of Vútsimos.

SOUTHERN & WESTERN APPROACHES

Helmós is a classic instance of a Greek mountain whose most time-honoured approach has lost caste in the face of road-building, high-elevation development, and a new generation's interest in low-altitude rambling as opposed to peak-bagging. Accordingly, nobody walks the three hours up from Kalávrita to Ksirókambos on the now almost-vanished trail, cut to ribbons by the paved road to the ski resort at Lútsa. And the tiny refuge an hour above at Puliú Vrísi, despite (or perhaps because of) a dirt-track continuation of that road, sees little use. Currently the most satisfying and direct routes to and from the high ridge of Apáno Lithária are those of Gaïdhurórakhi, Káto Lusí and Planitéro.

Access

Gaïdhurórakhi For Gaïdhurórakhi ridge, take the Tuesday, Thursday or Saturday morning bus from Akráta to the end of the line at Zarúkhla, proceeding on foot to the saddle as discussed in the account. In Zarúkhla you can overnight in a refurbished Frankish *pírgos* (☎ (0606) 51 252), or more cheaply in a simple village house (☎ (0696) 22 731).

If you're coming off Zíria via Gúra, a good spot to break the journey before tackling Gaïdhurórakhi is the monastery of Ayíu Yioryíu Feneú, a couple of dirt-track km above Kalívia village, at the edge of the Feneós plain. Built around 1600 by monks from Ioánnina, it would not seem out of place – except for the frescoed chapel – plonked on the lawn of an Oxbridge college. With

advance notice in Greek, the two remaining monks can host you in spartan but character-filled old rooms (☎ (0747) 41 226).

Other Villages The villages of Káto Lusí, Kastriá and Planitéro are served by a 1 pm, Monday-to-Friday bus from Kalávrita. The two villages are also linked by a section of the E4 trail, and near Kastriá you can visit the newly opened Spíleo Límnon ('Cave of the Lakes'): the waters of its underground river are so saturated with calcium that the mineral has formed dams enclosing a series of mini-lakes.

Stage 1A: Dhiásello to Apáno Lithária via Gaïdhurórakhi
(10 hours)

Not to be confused with the namesake ridge north of Ksirókambos and the ski lifts, this is probably the most spectacular and strenuous approach to the Helmós high peaks. It sets off from the saddle (imaginatively named Dhiásello, or 'Saddle') roughly halfway along the dirt road between Zarúkhla and the plain of Feneós.

The best way to get there from Zarúkhla is to follow the dirt road south-east past the hamlet of Trilángadho. After two km, or 100 metres before the road leaves the valley at a right hairpin bend, you'll see a stream coming in on your left. The path to Dhiásello climbs the angle between this and the main stream, at first very steeply, later flattening out between tall pines. Nearly two hours out of Zarúkhla, you'll come out on the saddle at Áyios Nikólaos chapel; head west for 15 minutes until meeting a triple fork in the dirt-track system, and take the centre option.

Follow this bulldozer track further west for 15 minutes, until it veers right and you adopt a path branching left (south-west) and worming up the forested ridge. This brings you, just under an hour after quitting the main road, to the foot of the 1641-metre cone – worth the hop up for views over the Feneós plain. After another 10 minutes along or just north of the ridge, dip to a north-south col ribboned by another path. Before you looms a steep, stony hill, best attacked from the right (north-east). Leaving the last trees, follow the now-sharp hogback west to the 1834-metre feature, 90 minutes along. Beyond this the ridge becomes more sheer and the surface treacherous; the next 20 minutes, left of the secondary peak to a 1770-metre saddle, must be taken carefully. With sheer drops to either side, this is not a hike to attempt in windy conditions.

Beyond this saddle, the abrupt cliffs of the lower Gardhíki peak (about 2130 metres) bar further progress west along the watershed. Instead, drop down to the left (south) towards a plateau at about 1600 metres with some pastoral buildings. From there it's possible to attain the 1840-metre col between Nisí and Gardhíki by zig-zagging up the rocky slopes to the west of a gully.

If you're coming from the monastery of Ayí Yioryíu Feneú, follow the road down to just before the junction and spring, then turn right onto an abandoned track heavily camouflaged by broom. After climbing for about an hour, you emerge onto a large track; turn left and proceed for about two km to road's end at a spring among firs. Visible paths then lead to the plateau described above, some three hours out of the monastery.

However you arrive at the 1840-metre col, you'll take the only path west, along the base of the cliffs north of 2070-metre Nisí, and above some large fingers of scree. After half an hour and a short uphill section, drop five minutes through shrubbery to a large path visible above a sheer drop. From here you can look west to the 100-metre cliff below the terraces of Mayéru, whence 80 Austrian and Polish soldiers were thrown to their death by Greek resistance fighters in the Yermanogrémi slaughter of December 1943, thus (say some) provoking the more notorious Kalávrita massacre in retaliation.

The path you are on leads left within another half hour to two shepherds' huts, also called Nisí, and the end of a side road branching off the main Planitéro-Kalívia link. If you have a full day ahead of you and can handle some steep scrambling among Helmós' most forbidding and untrodden peaks, you can bear right instead to reach

Apáno Lithária near Point 2252 of Neraïdhálono in six to seven hours, passing the Gardhíki peak system en route.

Follow the well-defined path east-north-east, below the fingers of scree, to the Hondrólakka gully beneath the col mentioned above. From here on the trail must be characterised as intermittent. After crossing the gully, it heads north, just below the bulky cliffs of Gardhíki's southernmost peak (often called Vrákhos) and above a messy scree slope. Opposite you at about 1900 metres is a small cave behind three fir trees, where one of the three Austrian soldiers who escaped the Yermanogrémi incident sheltered before being located and shot. In front of you are the rocky needles of Orniópirgos ('Vulture Tower'), where vultures were reportedly seen until the 1980s. Hugging the cliffs, the path veers right (north-east) and deposits you, after a steep and slippery climb, on the 2000-metre col between Orniópirgos and Vrákhos.

Head north up the ridge to a triple-needled rock; clamber down the other side, over an apparently man-made step of rocks, and skirt Orniópirgos along its north-eastern base. Soon you reach the gentle spine leading up to Gardhíki's main 2182-metre peak. This last half hour is a beautifully airy ridgewalk and a pleasant end to the gruelling three-hour climb from Nisí col or pastoral hamlet.

From the trig point, head south-west down a gentle ridge until you intercept a path after half an hour. Here, at 2000 metres, you will find a roofless pen and, two minutes to the north, a spring with a wooden trough. Here, unfortunately, the path towards the main peaks of Helmós drops nearly 400 metres in elevation before climbing back steeply to the ridge east of Aetórakhi, in order to avoid the plummeting overhangs north-west of Point 2182.

From the spring, descend the slope for five minutes before picking up a well-defined path heading down and right (north). You may even spot some faint red arrows pointing back the way you came, until you cross a gully at about 1600 metres. Here the main trail loses more altitude and bends back west to reach the terraces known as Mayéru in about two hours. Maintaining your altitude from thereon, head north-west to the the highest firs, and then climb north-east to a 1950-metre col.

Turning right (south-east), you can climb the rocky pyramid of Kutulópirgos ('Head-Banging Tower'), which is the prominent summit visible from the Kráthis river valley near Peristéra.

Turning left, you begin the technically difficult scramble to Neraïdhálono, at first skirting the peaks to the south-west and then to the north-east. This section is not to be underestimated: full packs are a bad idea, a pitch of rope a good one (if only for security).

Two to three hours from the spring and pen you reach a gap; the main summit-line between Neraïdhálono and Aetórakhi is half an hour's climb north-west up the now-stony ridge.

Stage 1B: Káto Lusí to Apáno Lithária
(4 hours)
A number of goat trails lead east from the village, crossing some deceptively deep gullies. The most direct route climbs up the first valley to the south of the main square and follows its south bank for 30 minutes to a concrete-roofed cistern. From there, the main path continues almost due east through fields, then fungus-plagued forest. There is no waymarking; simply follow the most-trodden trail of loose stones, adopting a safe middle option when things get bewilderingly divergent.

Gradually the path becomes steeper and curves right (south-east); you may notice two inconspicuous red well covers. At about 1600 metres the dry gullies have become deeper, particularly the one on your right separating you from Kastráki spur. As the trees thin out you should see a bare col in front of you at 1670 metres; aim east-south-east over this to hook onto the spur at about 1700 metres. Here, two hours out of Káto Lusí, you have a fine view south across the Langádha ravine to the Omaliá massif (1941 metres).

Keep scrambling east up the spur; the old

zig-zagging path is still visible in places. After 30 minutes the trail has appeared again, bends right (south-east) again and traces a well-defined course between steep slopes on the left and vertiginous outcrops to the right.

The third hour out of Káto Lusí should see you just beneath a tiny spring and wood trough, which may both dry up by September.

Five minutes later you draw abreast of a strategic spur often well defended by goats; do not follow the lower path on the right, but climb left (north-east) for a few minutes up the spine before resuming eastward progress. This higher trail crosses two muddy seasonal rivulets, after which you must veer left (north) up the stony, thistly slope to a 2050-metre plateau just south of Point 2144. Here, an hour from the spring and four from the village, you'll be greeted by barking sheepdogs and maybe a shepherdess.

To reach the EOS Refuge from here, take the track to the main dirt road, which you then follow north-north-west for two km. The hut is tiny (12 bunks) and fairly primitive; for keys and information, visit or phone the Kalávrita EOS Branch (☎ (0692) 22 611).

Stage 2A: Apáno Lithária to Peristéra via the Stigós (Styx) Valley
(4½ hours)
If, instead, you fork right 10 minutes above the stáni, the track system winds east then south over the end of Neraïdhórakhi to a unique cluster of giant outcroppings, the namesake boulders of Apáno Lithária. (If you're following the track rather than going cross-country or attempting to find the old path, make sure to bear left twice.) In their lee is an older rock corral and a recently built sheep-pen.

To find the trail down into the Styx valley, put your back to the boulders and point slightly left of dead ahead. You should pass, within 150 metres, a reliable pool spring in a patch of green turf; just below this gushes a fountain with a properly fitted spout.

Cross to the right (east) bank of the drainage which can truly be said to be the very head of the canyon. The faint trail plunges down a rock spine, swerves right past a dripping rockface and crosses a mud bed, all that's left when a seasonal pond evaporates. Some people coming up in the opposite direction (from Peristéra) choose to camp on its grassy margin. The descending route then slips over the saddle beyond the pond and continues down the ravine for only a few more moments before crossing to the left side of the watercourse just over 30 minutes from the stáni.

Further progress along the eastern (right) bank is hindered by a nasty drop just beyond a small stone pen; the only possible access to points downstream proceeds faintly on the western flank of the ravine, now several hundred metres wide. Turning a corner, the path brings you face-to-face with the 200-metre, orange-stained, plant-flecked cliffs of the Mavronéri Falls. The still-faint trail now zig-zags down the slope south-east of the cascades, reaching their base one hour out of Apáno Lithária.

The Mavronéri Falls (as the waters of the Styx are known locally) dwindle to a shower in late summer but still administer a mandatory, immortality-conferring (says the myth) ablution to those entering the small cave at the base of the cliff. Inside, there is year-round water (which you must lap from the rock) and an astonishing quantity of greenery and flowers. Don't be so distracted, though, by the other-worldy grandeur into forgetting that Mavronéri is quite far up the side of Neraïdhórakhi – just under 2000 metres up, to be exact – with the bulk of the trek down still before you.

To either side of the cave the path vanishes under messes of scree. You slither and slide down this for about 25 minutes to the canyon bottom. Here the old trail has been eroded out of existence, and you are forced to cross the stream and climb the opposite bank. Follow the top of the bank left (north), passing stunted trees, and drop to the stream just beyond a large sloping slab of rock. To your right are two more waterfalls; opposite you may see cairns marking the foot of the 15-minute scramble up to the resumption of

the old path. Climb this section one at a time and with care, as the loose stones are easily dislodged.

Turning right just below an overhang will bring you out at a ledge, with a painted arrow on the first stump at treeline; there's another soon after, and the trail rapidly clears up. Within a few moments more you reach the Dhiásello tu Kinigú ('Hunter's Pass', not to be confused with the Dhiásello above Zarúkhla). Here you can gaze north towards the villages and back at the Stygian cliffs, which from this angle appear stained quite black as well as orange, and also at the involved banding of the cliffs on the eastern side of the much-widened and deepened valley.

From here on, yellow-and-black markers (courtesy of EOS) are common. In the 50 minutes below the Dhiásello tu Kinigú there are no complications except several washouts of the path. Then there's a meadow on a knoll; 15 minutes beyond, you cross a dry gully and, shortly after, the first permanent stream since the Mavronéri.

Just past this, some two hours below the falls, oaks begin and the path disappears under an unsightly modern bulldozer track constructed supposedly to service an aqueduct which has been brought down from somewhere below Mavronéri. The path reappears briefly later on by a goat pen, then succumbs for good. Near the highest house of Gunariánika (Áno Mesorúgi), an EOS tree-marker pointing against you reads 'Pros Ídhata Stigó' (To the Styx Waters). Finally, 3¼ hours below them, you come to the platía of Peristéra, having passed another 'Ídhata Stigós' marker. The total descent from Apáno Lithária is thus something over four hours.

Peristéra is a friendly village with one taverna and a comfortable inn (☎ (0696) 22 827). Beds are at a premium in summer, however; if you have no luck here you'll have to walk 20 minutes down the road to Káto Mesorúgi, where there's another inn (☎ (0696) 51 219) upstairs from a taverna. If this is full you have one last chance in Sólos, 20 minutes by path across the young Kráthis stream – walk a few paces along the road out of Mesorúgi, then bear down towards the river just past the town-limit sign.

Sólos is graced by two lodgings, eateries, and the unusual church of Áyios Yióryios, which bears an inscribed '1806' over the door. Such Latin-influenced, rectangular churches are peculiar to certain remote districts of the Pelopónnisos, and are virtually the only tangible heritage of the Frankish occupation of the Moreás during the 13th century. They generally feature a square belfry, single-gabled roof, and a side door rather than the customary Greek front entrance, with only a slightly protruding apse as a nod to the Orthodox creed.

These villages only have bus services three days a week. Having done the traverse in the direction indicated, most trekkers will find it no inconvenience to spend an extra day recuperating at an inn or perhaps taking strolls to the two hamlets not stayed in. The countryside is idyllic, and according to the season you may be plied with apples, walnuts, ouzo or titbits from the grill.

If you choose to reverse the above itinerary – and this seems a popular strategy, since that way you handle the slippery bits to either side of the falls going uphill – it will take you 5½ hours to reach just Mavronéri, with another 90 minutes of tough ascent beyond that to the first feasible campsite. Plan your day with time to spare.

Stage 2B: Apáno Lithária to Planitéro
(3½ hours)

You'd be most interested in this sector as a way off the mountain if you'd hiked up the Styx valley, or possibly to complete a loop back to Káto Lusí with the E4; scenically it can't compare with the hikes starting or ending at Dhiásello or Káto Lusí.

From the saddle south of the big boulders, where the north-easterly fork of the dirt track currently ends, aim south-south-east on a path skirting the 2318-metre peak to its north-east. After 20 minutes, you reach the col between this and the highest point of Helmós, 2355-metre Psilí Korfí, barely worth a half-hour detour. Instead, follow the

clear path heading south across loose pebbles for half an hour more to the Káto Kámbos, where shepherds make and store cheese in summer. Follow the extreme southerly end of the high-altitude track network for five minutes or so before dropping left to a large walled spring, an hour from the first col.

Beginning here, a soggy path runs west along a creek for 500 metres before sliding up and left to cross a nameless spur pointing north-west. Follow this, either on the ridge or just to the left, until you come out on the saddle before the 1941-metre peak of Omaliá, 45 minutes from Káto Kámbos. Next drop 100 metres south down the steep, earthy slope to link up with a trail leading south-south-west over muddy seeps. Keeping to the left of the Omaliá massif, the path, still revetted in places, allows a good look at the sheer flank of Profítis Ilías (2282 metres) to the east. About an hour from the saddle, or nearly two from Káto Kámbos, you veer right to traverse the blunt nose of Omaliá on messy rocks, and end up just below a spring at 1600 metres.

Once to this point it's best to dispense with the path as it meanders off to the west, and instead head cross-country directly south down the Kalóyeros spur, passing some meadows and ruined houses. Within 30 minutes of the spring you will have passed the 1372-metre point and begun the final, steep, 400-metre descent south-west towards Planitéro. The ground levels out at about 900-metres, where fields replace forest; at about the 850-metre level you intersect the E4, which you adopt going south-east past a spring to the northern end of the village.

Planitéro has a limited number of rooms (☎ (0692) 31 696) and two tavernas, by the clinic and the church. Alternatively, you can follow the concrete road south down to the sources of the Aroánios River, where there's a trout farm.

Onwards to Káto Lusí

Hiking north-west towards Káto Lusí requires three hours. The Spíleo Límnon is about two hours along; just after you cross the mouth of the Langádha ravine, and a dirt track, turn up left onto the paved road, and left again when you hit the asphalt. The sidetrack to the grotto is indicated at a bend.

Erímanthos (Olonós)

The westernmost of the Peloponnesian mountains is essentially a long, rugged sierra, tending from south-west to north-east.

Geologically Erímanthos is more closely related to the Píndhos and other north mainland ranges than its neighbours, something borne out as well in the matter of small wildlife, both fossilised and still living. Another un-Peloponnesian characteristic is the presence of many springs at 1600 to 1700 metres elevation – though not, of course, up on the high ridges.

Manifold nomenclature is, as ever, a potential source of confusion. Some Greeks call the entire massif Olonós (or sometimes Olenós) after its highest peak, and reserve the label Erímanthos for just the south-western end of the peak-line, around 2124-metre Profítis Ilías. Furthermore, the main summit is variously cited as 2224, 2222 or 2221 metres in altitude, and on many maps has the alias Granítis. To make life easier, Olonós refers here only to the main peak.

Although plenty of rivers drain off the range, and the Vuraïkós River clearly separates it from Helmós, Erímanthos seems best defined by the ring of roads around it, linking Pátra with Kalávrita, and Trípoli with both.

Mythology is relatively silent on the subject of Erímanthos, except that the capture of the Erimanthean boar was the fourth labour of Hercules; he supposedly ran it to ground in one of the mountain's many ravines and took it back to King Eurystheus in a net. It seems the big pig was a pet and protégé of Artemis, who also favoured the mountain for hunting.

RIDGE WALK & OLONÓS SUMMIT

The principal attraction for the trekker is the chance for a lengthwise traverse involving plenty of ridge walking, though a more conventional summit climb from a high plateau is also on offer.

Rating & Duration

All outings qualify for a moderate rating, owing mostly to the long walking days and the need for good orientation skills. It is possible – just – to trek the length of the watershed between two trailhead villages in one very long summer day, but it's more sensible to break a traverse in two with a bivouac somewhere in the vicinity of the highest peak.

Season

This trek is best done in the long days of summer, for maximum daylight.

Supplies

Get these in Pátra or Athens; the foothill villages have a very limited selection of goods.

Maps

Korfes 79, *Erímanthos/Olonós*, or YIS 1:50,000 *Trópaia* and *Kértezi*.

Access

There are daily buses from Pátra to Erimánthia at 5 am, noon and 4 pm; once weekly, on Saturday, it may continue the final seven km to the actual south-western jumping-off village of Kaléndzi.

Four buses a day ply the route Pátra-Kalávrita, passing through or very near the trailhead settlements of Míkhas, Áno Vlasía and Káto Vlasía on the way.

Stage 1: Kaléndzi to Psilí Túrla
(6 hours)

Kaléndzi, 900 metres up on the west flank of Erímanthos at the margin of the fir forest, enjoys a fine setting with views across the coastal plain to the gulf of Pátra. It's the birthplace of George Papandreou, intermittent prime minister of Greece in the post-war years; the upper of the two café-grills, identified by a plaque, was the house where he grew up. (The villagers are considerably

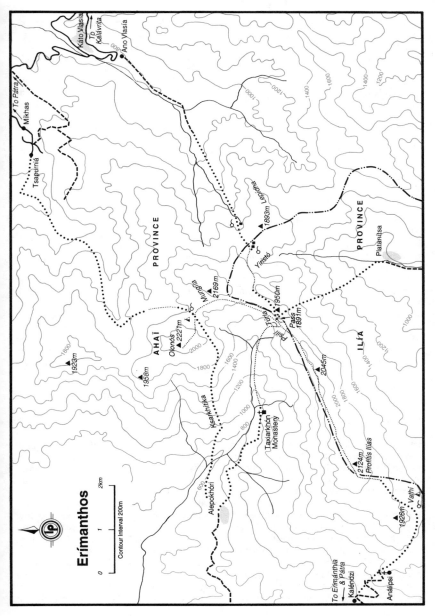

Erímanthos

Contour Interval 200m

0   1   2km

To Káto Vlasiá
To Kalávrita
Áno Vlasía
To Pátra
Miknas
Tsapurniá

PROVINCE

Lepídha
1893m
Yirísto

Mungila
2169m

AHAÏ
2221m
Olonós

1958m
1923m

Ksafkhítika

Alepokhóri

Taxiárkhon Monastery

PROVINCE

Platanítsa

Pass
1891m
1950m

2045m

ILÍA

2124m
Profítis Ilías

1926m

Vathí

Kaléndzi

To Erimanthía
& Pátra

Análipsi

more reticent about the doings of his son
Andreas, also prime minister from 1981 to
1989.) Despite the light winter snowfall, the
winter population is skeletal, with most of
the villagers tending fields in Erimánthia or
gone to the bigger cities.

There's a relatively expensive inn, with
doubles only for about $20, in the upper
left-hand portion of Kaléndzi; otherwise
you're dependent on rural hospitality, which
may take the form of a bedroll on the terrace
of the taverna where you ate.

Just shy of the big hotel there's a park with
a statue of the elder Papandreou and a
popular museum; here mountaineers have
marked the beginning of the path up the
mountain with a somewhat vague sign
('Erimanthos 7 hr') in Greek and English.
They mean Olonós peak, for which seven
hours is not a bad working estimate. From
the central fountain, bear left up a narrow
lane to another sign pointing to Erímanthos.

Head up the indicated trail, helped by
occasional red arrows, to a large antenna.
Here the recently bulldozed road and a building site muddle the route, so it's best to turn
left onto the road, following it until just past
a concreted spring where it hairpins right and
the trail reemerges on the left. Avoid ascending into the gully on your left (north); climb
towards the right, passing some goat pens on
a slope, after which the trail and red arrows
reassert themselves.

Now you have pleasant progress through
the forest; the trail crosses the road neatly
when necessary, heading for a saddle to the
left of a fir-tufted knoll. There's a spring at
about 1350 metres, and the trail and road
merge just after; the latter ended 80 minutes
along at about 1450 metres when I passed
through, but by now it may have been
extended all the way up to the Vathí valley.

Continue east-north-east on the now well-
engineered path which allows good views
over the coastal plain to the west. Just over
two hours above Kaléndzi you should reach
the stáni and spring at Vathí at about 1560
metres. Fill your bottles, as there's no more
water along the route until the vicinity of
Olonós peak. Trails of a sort exit the valley

via the saddle at the far (north-eastern) end,
but once there you'll have to bear left cross-
country up a spur to the main watershed,
attaining the trig point of Profítis Ilías (2124
metres) some two hours after leaving Vathí
spring. Here you'll get your first look at the
distinctive sugarloaf of Olonós summit to the
north-north-east.

From Profítis Ilías, simply stroll about two
more hours along the ridge proper, with a
world of toy-like villages revealed to either
side. At the end of this period, when the
hogback becomes impassable, you are
forced down to the left, towards grassy
natural ramps, and then right to round the
base of the sheer end of the ridge. Faint
livestock traces enable you to accomplish the
whole descent.

Having arrived at a distinct pass in the
2000-metre-plus watershed, you'll need to
make a choice. Shepherds' trails lead south-
east toward the valley of Platanítsa, and less
distinctly west towards the ravine draining
first to the monastery of Taxiárkhon and then
to Alepokhóri village. If for any reason you
need to cut short your walk, Alepokhóri is a
better destination, both for transport connections out and the village's preserved
vernacular houses. However, most trekkers
will want to continue with one of the two
final sectors described as follows.

Stage 2A: Psilí Túrla to Áno Vlasía via Yiristó

(4½ hours)

Pick your way around alternating dark and
red rocks to the base of Psilí Túrla (about
1900 metres); negotiate this around its left
(west) side, towards Olonós. A faint path
emerges, rounding the peak via a small pass
in the vicinity of a lone tree. Once on the far
side, you've an easy cross-country traverse
across a waterless valley to the next low
ridge, three hours from Profítis Ilías, from
where you've a clear view of the two huts
comprising the stáni of Yiristó.

More faint trails take you round the head
of the next ravine, converging on the spring
just below the cottages some eight hours
from Kaléndzi. The shepherds here can point

you on the onward course, but if they're not around simply go past the huts and descend the ravine draining north-east off the far side of aptly named Lepídha ('The Blade'). Do not approach the first sparse trees on the other side, but bear slightly west down to another pastoral hut and spring some 30 minutes beyond Yiristó.

Here a decent path resumes, taking you for 80 minutes through fine forest until it meets a bulldozer track. Another 45 minutes or so on this brings you to Áno Vlasía, for a total walking time on the day of 10½ hours – closer to 12 when you figure in lunch and other stops. It's really something to do in one go only in the longer days of summer.

Áno Vlasía is identical to Kaléndzi in its elevation and the number of tavernas, but there is no accommodation of any category – you'll have to camp or rely on village hospitality.

Stage 2B: Psilí Túrla/Yiristó to Míkhas via Olonós

(4¼ hours)

Peak 2221 is in fact difficult to reach from the vicinity of Psilí Túrla, especially with a heavy pack, owing to steep slopes in between. You might want to consider either camping at Yiristó and backtracking slightly to climb the peak as a day hike, or reversing the following itinerary, approaching on a day hike from Míkhas.

Still, for purists, here it is: to avoid the yawning canyon between Psilí Túrla and Olonós; proceed as for Stage 2A to just past the lone tree, then carefully traverse north-north-east around the gentler Mungíla ridge beyond for 90 minutes until reaching a sizeable grazing plateau, with springs and huts, at 1820 metres. You should camp here and climb the peak, a 2½-hour job, the next morning.

From this high plain, descend over a scree slope at first and then more gradually north past more pastoral colonies, and then curve westward to enter the head of the canyon leading down to Míkhas. Here you'll see fragments of an abandoned aqueduct which once supplied that village. It's then simply a

matter of heading north-east until reaching Tsapurniá, the hamlet next to Míkhas, some 2¾ hours after leaving the plateau at the base of the peak. Míkhas is a popular summer retreat, with tavernas and at least one inn.

If you reverse Stage 2B, you'll need almost four hours to get to the highest stáni from Míkhas. Finally, it's useful to know that there exist fairly well-trodden paths from the foot of Olonós down to Alepokhóri via the spur of Ksarkhítika; count on five hours to get there.

River Gorges of Arkadhía

Arkadhía (Arcadia) still exists, both as an administrative division of modern Greece and as a concept. The ancient population occupied a corner of the Greek popular imagination similar to that of the Druids or the hoarier Celts in north-western Europe. Contemporaries considered them with a mixture of scorn for their alleged primitiveness and fearful respect for their religious capacity. Not the Olympian pantheon per se but earlier, earth-deities held sway here, mostly in animal form with a veneer of Hellenic culture applied. Pan presided above all in unadulterated guise, while wolves – or perhaps werewolves – were venerated on Mt Líkeon, poised between the two hikes described here. Stranger than the gods were their rites, which in the case of the wolf cult included human sacrifice.

The countryside does such a reputation justice, being far more majestic than the trite phrase 'Arcadian idylls' can possibly conjure; certainly the ancients were discussing it as much as they were the rustic inhabitants. 'Idyllic' doesn't apply to the climate, however, which is relatively harsh and damp, more central European in feel. Forests, orchards and villages teeter over river valleys that are deeper, moodier and shaggier than their lowland counterparts; two of the best can only be visited on foot.

LÚSIOS RIVER VALLEY

As Greek canyons go the Lúsios is not long – barely five km in the really sheer parts – but it is rich in historical, religious and artistic associations, not to mention intrinsic natural beauty. Several monasteries cling to the sides, and two towns that were hotbeds of revolutionary activity in the 1820s overlook either end of the narrows. Just below these lies the site of ancient Gortys, one of the more underrated antiquities in Greece.

Recommended day hikes begin in the town of Stemnítsa (Ipsúnda), which makes an excellent base for exploring the area whatever your level of activity. In addition to its appealing domestic architecture and a handful of medieval churches, Stemnítsa long had a role as one of the leading metalworking centres in the Balkans. Today, a single workshop and training academy attempt to carry on the tradition.

Map

YIS 1:50,000 *Dhimitsána.*

Access

Stemnítsa has fairly poor public transport links, with just one daily bus connection in each direction with Trípoli, the provincial capital. Dhimitsána is only slightly better served, with two buses in each direction. There is no link over the nine km of road between the two towns, except in the early morning when the Trípoli-bound bus sets off from Dhimitsána and passes through Stemnítsa. If you plan to traverse the entire length of the gorge, you'll have to arrange for a taxi to pick you up at the far end and shuttle you back to base.

Stage 1: Stemnítsa to Monastery of Ayíu Ioánni Prodhrómu

From Stemnítsa's central square (elevation about 1100 metres), walk about 15 minutes out along the asphalted road to Dhimitsána. Near the customary town-limits sign you should see four park benches by the side of the road; the trail down into the Lúsios Gorge starts just before the fourth one. Soon after the descent begins, the surface becomes that

of a kalderími; 20 to 25 minutes along you pass a fountain. You're treated to fine views west and south over not only the Lúsios but also the Alfíos river valley in the middle distance, as your route gradually curves west, and then north.

Some 40 minutes below Stémnitsa you will debouche onto the main dirt road to the monastery; turn left, trot about 200 metres, and then bear right at a junction. After five minutes down this turning, the road ends by a rather stark modern chapel, two fountains and the monastery garage; the final, well-trodden access path to the monastery drops for 15 minutes from behind these structures. Total elapsed time from Stemnítsa won't exceed one hour 15 minutes; if you need to reverse these directions, count on 90 minutes going uphill.

Founded in the 11th century, Prodhrómu (as it's generally abbreviated) is one of those swallow's-nest monasteries with which the Orthodox church loves to adorn wild, cliffside settings such as this. Despite the large surface area of the cantilevered exterior, once inside the place is surprisingly small: the diminutive, frescoed katholikón (main church) never held more than the dozen monks currently in residence, mostly from Arkadhía. Four of them are young and committed; Nikiforos and Galaktis, if they're still there, tend to see to foreign visitors. If you want to stay the night, let them know in good time, as the guest quarters are small and often swamped by carloads of pilgrims.

Stage 2: Monastery of Ayíu Ioánni Prodhrómu to Ancient Gortys

From the monastery's lower gate at about 500 metres elevation, take the path heading down into the river canyon, and almost immediately make a left (southward) turn, shunning for now the option upstream. It's 20 minutes down well-graded switchbacks to the bridge over the Lúsios River, formerly known as the Gortynios after the nearby ancient city. Once on the west bank, you've 20 minutes more of up-and-down hiking to the 11th-century chapel of Áyios Andhréas (350 metres). The fields and woods here are

Top: Lúsios Gorge: The Asklipion of ancient Gortys, seen from the south (MD)
Left: Hélmos: Northerly Gaïdhurórakhi seen from typical local church, Kráthis valley (MC)
Right: Lúsios Gorge: The 17th-century monastery of Néa Filosófu (MD)

Top: Ágrafa: Western ridge as seen from Kukurúdzos (MC)
Bottom: Ágrafa: a house of Trídhendhro village, with the crags of Katarakhiás behind (MC)

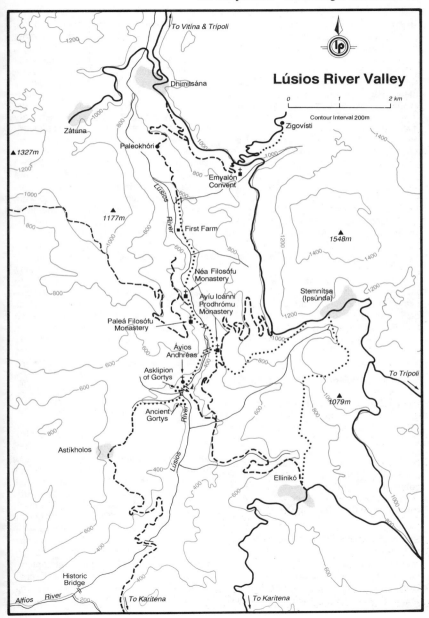

all monastery property, which accounts for the unusually high quality of the path up to now; there's no other way of getting to these holdings directly from Prodhrómu.

The Asklipion (or therapeutic centre) of ancient Gortys lies just in front of the lone, tile-roofed farmhouse visible west of the chapel. A vast sunken excavation contains the foundations of a temple, plus the 'clinic' itself, its cobbled floors and a peculiar round bathhouse with wall niches still well preserved; both apparently date from the 4th century BC.

The ancient town proper, with only sparse foundations remaining, lies still further south on the same bank of the rushing Lúsios, but separated from the Asklipion by a small stream ravine. Your trail continues there and eventually to the village of Atsíkholos, though 20 minutes beyond the ruins it becomes a rather boring jeep track.

On the way in you can't have helped but notice an old bridge over the river in the vicinty of Áyios Andhréas. There is good camping on the turf of the left (opposite) bank, though you'll want a tent as the nights are cold and damp all year round.

From Gortys you can take a return loop to Stemnítsa or hike to Dhimitsána.

Stage 3A: Ancient Gortys to Stemnítsa
(3½ hours)
A track from the far end of the bridge twists up for about seven km to the village of Ellinikó. From there a proper trail leads north for two more hours back to Stemnítsa, making a loop walk possible, but the prospect is made less than attractive by the dreariness of the track walk and the almost complete lack of trail short cuts of the switchbacks. Most trekkers will prefer to carry on with the following alternative.

Stage 3B: Ancient Gortys/Prodhrómu to Dhimitsána
(3¼ hours)
Retracing your steps upstream from Ancient Gortys to the split in the path just belowAyíu Ioánni Prodhrómu monastery requires half

an hour. Having adopted the right-hand fork not taken previously, 30 minutes more should see you over a higher river bridge, then up a narrow but clear path to just under the derelict monastery of Paleá Filosófu, established in 960! A few moments of scrambling up the cliff gets you to this well-camouflaged eyrie, ruined except for the church, home to frescoes no longer, only bats. The exterior, with ornamental tilework and fresco patches, is more interesting.

Back on the main trail, it's 10 minutes further to the grounds of Néa (New) Filosófu, dating from the 17th century and modern only in relation to its neighbour. This revels in a commanding setting overlooking the river gorge, but today the church is locked and disused; there are, however, excellent frescoes inside, and if you won't be content with a peek through the window grille, ask for a set of keys at Prodhrómu.

Don't be fooled by the jeep track passing near Néa Filosófu – the onward trail to Dhimitsána drops inconspicuously, and precipitously, from just behind the apse of the church. The first 20 minutes down to the river are frankly terrible, making it unlikely you'd want to drag a full pack through here. Ford the Lúsios at the point where scraps of cloth may be draped over two trees on the opposite bank; whether these are deliberate waymarks or flood flotsam is hard to say. There are nice swimming holes near the ford, though in spring you may have no choice but to swim across anyway.

The path improves on the far side, but it's always somewhat bush-clogged. After another half an hour, through the terraces below an abandoned cliff-base lean-to and past a potable brook, you'll reach your first tended farm, after which the path gradually improves to motor-trike width and standard.

From here you face just over an hour's walk to Dhimitsána, making for a total of 2¾ hours from Prodhrómu. Keep to the same (east) bank upon passing a bridge; thereafter you start to climb again appreciably, from about 600 metres near the river to about 800 metres at Paleokhóri, the first hamlet you'll reach. This is about a km shy of Dhimitsána; from here on it's plain sailing to Stemnítsa via Emyalón convent.

NÉDHA RIVER GORGE

Greece is full of rivers that disappear underground, and gorges of every size and description, but nowhere else in the country is there such a satisfactory combination as in this remote corner of the peninsula.

The Nédha River, barely 30 km in length from the point where it springs from the sides of Mt Líkeon, is hardly a major flow, but size is not everything, as the following demonstrates.

Map

YIS 1:50,000 *Néa Figália*, but very optional – follow the route directions and you can't go wrong.

Access

Take one of the two daily buses from Pírgos, or Megalópoli (the latter at noon and 7 pm), to Andhrítsena, and from there arrange with a taxi driver for a transfer to the hamlet of Figália. Make sure he understands that you don't want the village of Néa Figália, but the place south of the Apollo Temple at Vassae, to where drivers are well used to shuttling customers.

The final turn-off is at the equally small hamlet of Perivólia, two km before Figália. The track narrows progressively until a point, just before the hamlet, where there are some park benches, an ikónisma (shrine) and a sign ('Perivólia 2') pointing back the way you've arrived.

Figália to the Gorge, return

Bid farewell to your taxi and bear right (west) past the benches rather than entering Figália (500 metres altitude), which has limited facilities. After 200 metres turn right onto a path whose beginning is charmingly strewn with marble artefacts of ancient Figália.

Shrubbery to one side may obscure an incongruous Greek highway department sign reading 'Platánia, 5 (km)'; anything less like a modern road would be hard to imagine.

Take the first two possible right forks among the scrub oak. Between this pair of choices the boundary walls of ancient Figália almost block the trail, and the proper bearing stays quite close to and just under them.

Figália was a minor trading post on the way to nearby seaports, but wealthy enough to construct the temple up the hill as a token of gratitude for deliverance from a plague. Here though, aside from the boundary walls termed Cyclopean after the only beings who presumably could have manoeuvred the giant stones into place, little remains other than various marble fragments and statuary unearthed over the years.

About 25 minutes beyond the 'Platánia, 5' sign, the trail comes to a stone ikónisma on a knoll. Step behind it and bear left down a slope and across a dry stream bed; once on the other side the path, partly cobbled and well shaded now, begins plunging steeply into the Nédha Gorge, and the river gradually becomes audible. Twenty minutes below the wayside shrine you arrive at a corral just above the river.

The main path continues down to a bridge (about 200 metres elevation) and then up the far bank within an hour to Platánia village (550 metres), with rudimentary amenities and the possibility of transport south into Messinía Province. For the moment find an inconspicuous trail veering back right (west) at a sharp angle.

This little side-turning is badly overgrown but well grooved into a rock ledge overlooking the swirling waters of the Nédha. Just under an hour below Figália you arrive at impressive waterfalls and pools at the confluence of the Nédha and a tributary coming in from the north. A few tiny, damp chapels cling to the cliffs beyond the main swimming hole, but they're hardly worth the climb. You can inch out along the outflow of the side stream and peer around a rocky corner at the famous *stómio* (aperture) of the Nédha, where thousands of litres of water disappear hourly into a distinctly vaginal tunnel, not to reappear above ground for 10 km.

The site has been holy since before recorded history; it was variously regarded as an entrance to Hades, an oracle of the dead and an appropriate spot for worshipping various goddesses. That the ancient Arcadians had some fairly unusual rites and deities has already been noted, but the Figálians excelled in this respect; Pausanias and others reported local worship of Eurynome, an avatar of Artemis in the form of a mermaid, and of Black Demeter, a version of the goddess with a horse's head in token of her rape by Poseidon Hippios. Gazing around you, and at the anatomically suggestive topography, anything seems possible. Today the stómio is considered consecrated to the Virgin, and on 15 August modern villagers cast stones into the abyss in lieu of the former vegetable and animal offerings, but this must be considered an Orthodox dilution of long-standing worship; no other setting in Greece is as primordially pagan.

A final note on more practical matters: currently the vicinity of the swimming hole is still in a pristine state, and locals are happy to show visitors the way down if necessary. Crowds of trippers strewing garbage or behaving in a manner inimical to rural values would change attitudes. You can't camp at the junction of the rivers anyway – if you need or want to, there is some space near the bridge.

Taïyettos

Taïyettos occupies most of the south-central finger of the Pelopónnisos, its crest dividing the provinces of Messinía and Lakonía. It's a vast chunk of reef limestone, with a scattering of less permeable strata which force springs to the surface. Lakonía comes out much better in the water bargain, with the lion's share of permanent springs and some dense stands of fir and black pine. The Messinían slopes are unrelentingly arid even after a wet winter, and to accomplish any of the long-distance traverses described you'll want a fluid-carrying capacity of at least three litres per person, kept full at every opportunity.

Despite the problematic water supply and occasional wearying nature of the terrain, the rewards are great: in few other places in Greece do you get such a true sense of wilderness. Botanically the range is interesting, with a wide spectrum of habitats from east to west as well as up and down; if you're a herbal connoisseur, you'll be interested in buying or gathering the local *tsaï vunú* (mountain tea), the best in the country.

Taïyettos has always figured prominently in Greek religion and folklore. Its original name was Taleton, a Doric word whose meaning has long since been lost. The current nomenclature stems from one Taygete, depending on sources either a daughter of the Titan Atlas or a member of Artemis' retinue. The mountain was in fact sacred to the Olympian twins Artemis and Apollo. In more recent times the party of Artemis has been disguised as the *neraïdhes* (forest nymphs), those terrors of lone shepherds, who danced on the heights by moonlight and hurled to his death any male mortal unlucky enough to witness their revels. The summit shrine of Apollo was rededicated to his descendant Profítis Ilías (the Prophet Elijah) with the onset of Christianity, and although observance has sadly declined in recent years, the best such festivities in Greece are still held up top each 18-20 July.

AROUND TAÏYETTOS

Despite its savage appearance, particularly from the east, the enormous Taïyettos Range is arguably the most popular hiking area in Greece after the Píndhos, western Crete and Mt Ólimbos. Looking up from the town of Spárti or Byzantine Mistrás, it's hard to resist the urge to explore the crags and ravines overhead. Indeed gorge-walking is an integral part of getting across the mountain; there are two principal gorges west of the watershed, Ríndomo and Víros, plus a host of smaller tributaries. Although these canyons make various loop itineraries possible, it must be said that a little of them goes a long way, and you'll perhaps wish them all an hour or two shorter than they are.

Rating & Duration

Any crossing of the Taïyettos watershed is a strenuous exercise, owing to long walking days and sharp altitude changes, so you should be reasonably fit and have experience with high mountain conditions. Because of the position of the various trailheads, and the way the gorges and ridges are arranged, you'll want at least four and probably five days to tour the mountain. You can organise the stages in a number of ways, for example Anavrití to Profítis Ilías/Ayía Varvára, Ayios Dhimítrios, Víros and Kardhamíli; or Kardhamíli to Víros, Ayios Dhimítrios, Ayía Varvára, Anavrití, Ríndomo and Pigádhia/Vório.

Season

The area is best hiked either in spring (but not so early that run-off is a problem in the gorge systems) or autumn, when heat is not a factor. Because of the scarcity of water west of the crest, midsummer treks are inadvisable.

Supplies

These are best obtained in Spárti or Kardhamíli, though Anavrití has certain staples such as lentils, sausage, cheese and wine.

Maps

Korfes 85-86, *Taïyettos – Profítis Ilía (2407 m)* and *Taïyettos 2031 m*, or YIS 1:50,000 *Spárti, Kalamáta, Kardhamíli,* and *Xirokámbion* – quite an expensive, bulky armful, which should predispose you to the *Korfes* products.

Access

Depending on the season, six to 10 daily buses depart from the take-off point marked 'Mistrá' three blocks south-west of Spárti's central platía. Don't get off in Mistrás unless you wish to see the exquisite Byzantine ruins there; stay on the vehicle as it bears south-east, tracing the foot of the mountain for four

km more to the large village of Áyios Ioánnis. A portion of the marked E4 trail climbs from Mistrás up to Anavrití, the main eastern Taïyettos trailhead, but it's mostly dull jeep track underfoot and you're well advised not to miss the spectacular preliminary trail out of Áyios Ioánnis.

Kardhamíli, an important resort on the Messinían gulf and the preferred trailhead south-west of Taïyettos, is served by four well-spaced daily buses plying the stretch between Kalamáta and the provincial border at Ítilo; for some reason there are five going back in the opposite direction, Kardhamíli being roughly halfway in between.

Stage 1: Áyios Ioánnis to Imerotópi/Boliána via Anavrití

Trekking begins not in the platía of Áyios Ioánnis, but two km above – you'll probably want to take a taxi the final distance. Instruct the driver to drop you at the *trívio* (rock-crushing mill) whose tailings are plainly visible as a huge scar on the hill west of the village, at 400 metres elevation.

You'll pass the church of Áyios Yióryios, flanked by cypresses, on the second bend above the mill. Watch carefully for traces of path cutting up to the straight part of the third curve, and then continuing to join up with the first clear section of the old wide, revetted kalderími directly over the mill. The true base of the path has been obliterated by the asphalt road, but by heading uphill away from the small ravine carrying power pylons up to Anavrití, you're guaranteed to intersect it.

Once established, this venerable trail curls into the chasm just north, then bears west as a spectacular corniche route. Climb steadily, veering progressively more to the south until, about 40 minutes above the rock mill, Anavrití appears. Fifteen minutes later, the path, having lost its cobbles some while ago, ends at a bend in a narrow dirt lane. One hour along you'll draw even with the first house in the village, and shortly afterwards a sign saying 'Kalós Ílthate' welcomes you to the village as you collide with the paved road in.

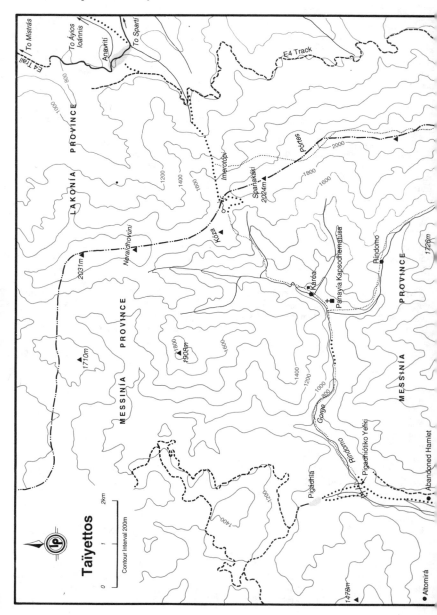

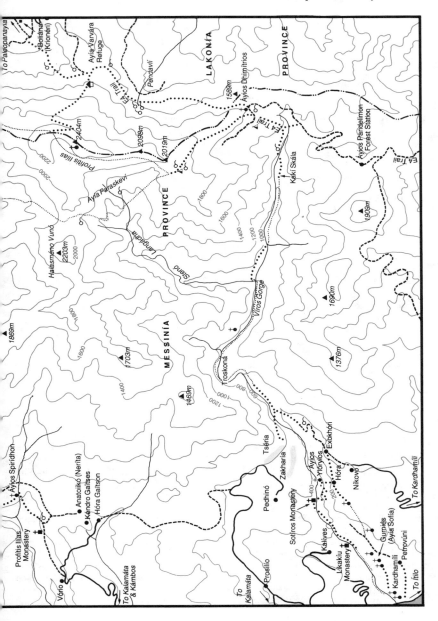

Allow one hour 10 minutes to the platía at just over 800 metres.

Anavrití is an attractive, friendly village that has come down considerably in the world. During the first half of the 20th century it was a major centre for rope manufacture, leatherworking and shoemaking, supplying most of the Pelopónnisos with these products; post-war events put a stop to that, and now the permanent population is less than 10% of the former 3000.

Just east of the square is a good-value hotel/restaurant run by the Kostianis family (☎ (0731) 21788); out of peak season you can bargain for a single/double with bath for $8/13. There are also two magaziá, where you can buy a limited range of basics for the trail and also get a rough-and-ready meal.

From the delicious fountain on the platía (where you should fill water bottles), head up past the two-belfried church of Áyios Nikólaos, winding under imposing houses without falling off to the left or right. After 15 minutes you'll reach the *dhasikó* (forest) road, next to the Forest Service picnic grounds of Aï-Lías (850 metres). Turn left (south); you may see occasional E4 markers.

You'll reach a sharp kink in the road 45 minutes out from Anavrití; bear up, just past the bend, through a bulldozed landslide zone to find an inconspicuous trail, on a natural ledge at the base of the rock wall behind. Turn right (west), and you'll soon see a variety of fluorescent tree stickers and orange paint splodges on rocks, installed by EOS Spárti.

Over the 45-minute climb up from the road the path improves fitfully and fir trees provide much-needed shade, until reaching a distinct thinning of the forest among terraces at 1250 metres; the flank of Spanakáki peak looms ahead. Just over an hour above the forest track you'll notice a large orange EOS placard on the hillside, proclaiming the following more-or-less correct route times: Spanakáki, 2024 (metres), 2 hours; Profítis Ilías (along the ridge), 7 hours 30 minutes; Neraïdhovúni, 2031 (metres), 4 hours 30 minutes.

You have arrived at Imerotópi and must make a choice. You can trek south, following the promptings of the EOS sign, to the summit of Taïyettos, but you'll need to carry a few litres of water and to get a very early start to make it to the peak (not to mention the alpine hut at its base). Furthermore, this is very advanced ridge-walking, with some nastily exposed sections which would be no-go in wet or windy conditions. If you're compelled to turn back, you'll have to follow the E4 to the refuge – a not terribly inspiring seven-hour walk, mostly on the forest road from the point where you left it to clamber up to Imerotópi.

The alternative to these routes is to slip over the low, relatively easy pass to the west and pursue the stage described following. Patrick Leigh Fermor, in Chapters 1 and 2 of *Mani* (see Books), has interesting things to say about Anavrití, the pass in question, and what lies beyond it.

Stage 2A: Imerotópi to Pigádhia & Vório

To reach the pass just north of Spanakáki Peak, bear right away from the EOS placard at Imerotópi, up the south (true right) flank of a shallow vale. The trail is now very intermittent at best. Upon reaching a grassy hollow with a ruined stone bivvy, go slightly left to reach the correct saddle at 1750 metres, 3¼ hours out of Anavrití. (Don't go right or straight ahead from the stone hut – this leads to a false pass.)

From the proper gap you'll see Kóza summit and beyond Neraïdhovúni to the north; before you lies a forbidding jumble of gorges, spurs and knife-edged ridges, eloquently described in *Mani* and four decades later still showing little trace of human presence other than a dirt road or two on the horizon.

Down to the left (south) you should glimpse patches of descending path, with a spattering of mule or donkey droppings – proof that large animals get through here, and that this is the correct way. Drop down about half an hour to a patch of bracken, then make a hairpin north to merge with a wider, more gradually descending path to a vital spring at 1650 metres, one hour below the saddle. You must find it, since there may be no other dependable water until the end of this stage; look for trees and unusually green grass next to an extensive trough system in a rock hollow. It's a wonderful lunch stop, but would be a difficult campsite.

Just the other side of the spring, painted red arrows and dots reappear, guiding you rather perversely, it seems, across a spur to the west and then down a scree-littered gully to the bed of the main gully at 1250 metres. It's a fairly awful stretch, but the main gorge appears to be impassable above the point where you finally return to it, and there are a few crumbled sections of medieval trail near the bottom.

Descending occasionally sharply along the drainage bed, you've 50 minutes more to the junction, at about 1000 metres, with another more gently pitched ravine draining directly off Neraïdhovúni. Come down at an abandoned grove of dead walnut trees above some terracing and some ranks of suggestive plane trees, but alas there's no open water here. Turn sharp left or south, initially through some small, turfy pasture and later along the bed of the gully itself. Bits of trail leading off up the banks are only apt to get you into trouble, and there is no potable spring (despite notations on maps) at the abandoned huts of Karéa.

It's 45 minutes to the ksoklísi of Panayía Kapsodhematúsa, perched on a triangle of high ground at 980 metres altitude exactly where the Ríndomo ravine enters from the south-east. Here there's a cistern with a bucket, an outbuilding that's unlocked, and a porch for shelter – all in all a good place to spend the night. Total elapsed walking time from Anavrití will be 6¾ hours.

The church takes its unusual name from a legend pertaining to the time when the tiny settlements passed on the way in were not so abandoned. The inhabitants were threshing wheat gathered from the high terraces at an *alóni* (threshing cirque) by the church, and neglected to observe the 15 August festival in the Virgin's honour. She decided, it seems, to teach them a lesson: sparks rained

from the horseshoes of the draft animals treading the grain, which caught fire and was destroyed. Hence the name Kapsodhematúsa ('Our Lady Who Burns the Bales').

Sidetrip: Ríndomo Hamlet If you stay at Kapsodhematúsa, an interesting day hike can be made the next morning, before continuing with the main itinerary, to the tiny hamlet of Ríndomo, 30 to 40 minutes up the gorge of that name. Half a dozen houses and a church face each other on each bank of the ravine, amid terraces and walnut orchards. You could camp here, but don't depend on there being running water – a spring in the gulch above the church on the southern (true left) bank is unreliable, and often there's only stagnant water in a garden tank below the chapel or filled jerry cans near some of the dwellings. Ríndomo has long been notable as the last surviving local summer colony without road access, though it seems a road is being blasted in to disturb the place's tranquility. Judging from the ripe cheeses stored in some basements, people linger here until the first winter storms.

Continuing along the main route, 10 minutes below Kapsodhematúsa, the bed of the Ríndomo ravine plunges impassably, forcing you up onto a stretch of kalderími on the south bank. After 20 minutes bear right and down at a fork, following a waymark; you're now poised at a tremendous lookout over the canyon, its sides most heavily vegetated at this point.

Stop to drink it in, since the hour after you hit bottom again is fairly boring. Sections of faint path to either side spare you treading on the knobbly pebbles for moments at a time. Altitude is lost very slowly; the walls of the gorge narrow dramatically with increasing frequency, so that the bed of the watercourse is sunless even at midday during much of the year.

Some two hours below Kapsodhematúsa, the renowned Pigadhiótiko Yefíri (Pigadhian Bridge), a miniature flying buttress, spans a particularly narrow gap and blends into the surrounding rock. This is a critical junction, though your choice may be made for you by the following considerations.

You can continue straight under the bridge, as Leigh Fermor reports having done, though he's vague about exactly how he got out of the gorge to end up in Kámbos on the coast. It's better to adopt the ramp-like path on the left which quickly becomes a kalderími and takes you up to the little span at 650 metres. Turning right onto it and heading up the side canyon here brings you within an hour to the all-but-empty village of Pigádhia, from where you'd also have quite a time getting any transport out, eventually ending up in or near Kalamáta some 23 km distant. It's probably wisest to continue straight on the path, though this too has its own set of complications.

Just beyond the older bridge is a modern bridge, giving more access to a trickle of water which may be coming down from Pigádhia. Your route now curls south as the gorge bed drops steadily and scenically away from you to the west; all would be well from here on if some idiots hadn't decided to blast a road to Ríndomo through here in 1991, above the trail, blocking it with tonnes of rubble just moments before I passed through. (For more on how and why such roads get built, who benefits and who pays, see the discussion in Facts for the Trekker.)

Locals claim that, since the dynamite wielders have also obstructed the power corporation's right-of-way, they'll be compelled to clean up after themselves. Seeing is believing, as that would be a first in Greece; more likely the rock slides across the trail will stabilise after winter rains, permitting safer passage.

Assuming you can fight your way through the mess as I did, you'll thread through a romantically set, abandoned canyon-side hamlet and then drop gently on the progressively more overgrown path to a shady gulch and the dilapidated chapel of Áyios Spirídhon, 45 minutes beyond the bridges. From here you've 15 minutes more up a cobbled surface, partly overlaid with concrete, to the monastery of Profítis Ilías atop its 688-metre hill, which you've been able to

see for some time now. At the top of the grade gushes a welcome spring, whose run-off you'll have also noticed much of the way up from Áyios Spirídhon. You can try to visit the monastery, which has worthy frescoes inside, but like most such treasures in Greece it's usually locked.

For all intents and purposes quality hiking ends here, three-plus hours below Kapsodhematúsa, as a web of more or less drivable dirt and concrete tracks radiates away from the spring. Your main decision now will be how to get down to the coast and its bus lines. You can bear right (west) at the fountain onto a narrow dirt lane which leads within 20 minutes to the village of Vório, from where a paved road – and possibly taxis

Taïyettos: Áyios Spíridhon, 18th-century church in medieval acropolis of Kardhamíli

– descend eight km to Kámbos, a major stop on the bus route.

Going left instead takes you, after a like period of time, to the triple village of Gaïtses, shown on most maps as Kéndro; Kéndro is actually the name of the westernmost sinikía, but you'll have arrived in Anatolikó (Neríta), with Hóra just beyond. While they make a pretty sight splashed against the hillsides, they can't (except for their tall belfries) compare architecturally with the settlements around Kardhamíli. Indeed, there's little point in visiting them unless you're trying to get back to Kardhamíli on foot – they're further up the mountain than Vório.

A dirt road leads south from Hóra Gaïtson to both Prosílio on the coast route and to Tséria on the Víros Gorge, a rather boring two-hour walk in either case if you're compelled to do it – arrange a ride if possible, and don't expect any buses.

Stage 2B: Imerotópi/Boliána to Ayía Varvára Refuge & Profítis Ilías

The following description assumes that you've elected to ridge-walk from Imerotópi to the main summit of Taïyettos, or to take the forest road glorified as the E4 (from beyond Anvrití) to Boliána, the formerly favoured approach to the alpine shelter at Ayía Varvára.

Fewer and fewer climbers hike up the dreary, dusty 10-km dirt road from Paleopanayía in the Évrotas valley to Boliána (Krionéri on some maps) and the now-ravaged trailhead there. In spite of the protests by EOS Spárti club members, the forest road system was extended some years ago virtually to the door of the Ayía Varvára refuge, and while much of the former trail is still intact, partially incorporated into the E4 routing, inevitably it has suffered both aesthetically and maintenance-wise. The elderly Nikos Dusmanis, who used to run a rustic summer coffeehouse at Boliána (a place name, not a village) for mountaineers, is no longer the fixture he was for decades. Still, if you have wheeled transport to this point, it's worth knowing about what remains of the path up.

Some 20 minutes beyond Nikos' inn, the dirt track forks; bear left with the signposting towards the refuge, and the E4 forest road to Anavrití will be straight ahead. Nearby there's a picnic grounds and a reliable water source, the last on this leg of the trip. You'll have to walk uphill on this turning for about 25 minutes until seeing a sign saying 'EOS Spárti, Katafíyio' pointing to the new trailhead. Soon E4 markers appear, and at just under 1400 metres altitude is the sporadic spring of Trípolos; another half an hour further on you'll find the weak (often dry) fountain of Ayía Varvára at 1550 metres. Some two hours above the main Anavrití-Boliána track, the trail and jeep road meet 50 metres before the EOS refuge at 1600 metres, admirably sited on a meadow facing the rising sun.

The hut is often in use on weekends and holidays from May to October; obtain keys and reservation information from EOS Spárti on Akropóleos 3 (☎ (0731) 22 574). The weather is usually mild enough, however, to make camping on the grass out front an attractive prospect; lots of people do during the July festival when the shelter's capacity of 28 is exceeded. Water can be more of a problem: if both the Ayía Varvára spring and the refuge cistern have run dry (not uncommon by September), there's another, more reliable spring 15 minutes downhill (south) along the onward E4 (not back towards Boliána). This waters an attractive hollow, with plane trees, a stone-lined irrigation pond and a walnut grove below, but it's too damp and steep to camp next to.

Sidetrip: Climb of Profítis Ilías from Ayiá Varvára

Climbing from the shelter to Profítis Ilías peak takes 2½ hours on a variably marked path. Despite EOS maintenance, many of the metal arrows along the way tend to be faded or twisted 90° to 180° off kilter by wind or snowpack, so it's not as straightforward a walk as it might be. The surface is decent, but there is no water beyond the hut.

The path begins from the hut's left rear corner as you face it; after 15 minutes you reach the treeline at 1800 metres and bear right (north) across a rocky hillside. Within another 25 minutes you'll cut through a large sloping meadow and then abruptly across a tiny gully. A few moments above the gully, skirt a small bog ringed by bracken; a few straggly pines grow 200 metres to your right. For the next half hour the path picks its way along a hogback heading north-west towards a distinct secondary peak just in front of you. It then worms up a slight crevice before turning abruptly left (south) onto a natural rock ledge on the eastern face of the ridge leading up to Profítis Ilías.

The next 40-minute stretch involves an easy ascent along this shelf, with the summit cone in plain sight before you. During the last few moments of this section the path switches back towards the north-west, aiming for a distinct pass at the low point of the saddle between Profítis Ilías and the secondary peak. Just beyond this notch lies a meadow which could serve as a campsite for those coming south along the watershed from Imerotópi. The final push to the 2404-metre trig point, along the north-western slope of the mountain, takes about 25 minutes.

On the summit are some relatively sturdy rock shelters mostly bereft of their former corrugated-iron roofs, and the chapel of Profítis Ilías, conceivably built from the same stones that once constituted the pagan shrine. Along with the entire crest, the peak forms part of the border between Lakonía and Messinía provinces. Spárti, the Párnon Range and the Évrotas flood plain lie below and to the east; on the west yawns the maze of canyons in the Messinían foothills, punctuated by 2179-metre Halasméno Vunó ('Wrecked Mountain'), joined to your vantage by a rocky spur. The only view comparable to it in desert-like grandeur is that from the top of Egypt's Mt Sinai, but here you have the added bonus of the sea in the form of the gulfs of Messinía and Lakonía, extending in bright ribbons to either side all the way south to the tip of the Taïyettos peninsula at Cape Ténaro. This unusual setting can produce striking optical phenomena at sunset and sunrise, a good argument for ridge-walking down from Imerotópi and spending a summer night here. The shadow of the pyramidal peak (as well as yours) projects far to the west at sunrise, and multicoloured bands appear on the surface of the ocean towards sunset.

Returning to the alpine shelter takes about two hours; if you're covering this route downhill for the first time with a full pack, allow plenty of daylight, since the path can be somewhat tricky to find if you haven't been over it before. It's unwise to contemplate entering the gorge system to either side of Halasméno Vunó from here with a full pack; follow the instructions in the description of the next stage for the safest way across the crest hereabouts. If you doubt this, you might scramble a few moments south along the ridge to a sheer spot and a cross marking where a 38-year-old shepherd fell to his death, and was buried, in 1982.

Stage 3: Ayía Varvára Refuge to Áyios Dhimítrios

(2 hours)

From the refuge the E4 heads east, then south for 15 minutes to the spring noted earlier; there it bears south-west for a similar period of time to the cluster of springs at Pendavlí (1300 metres). This spot, one of the wettest on Taïyettos, takes its name ('Five Canals') not just from the multiple runnels here, but from the tradition asserting that when Christ was fleeing his pursuers in Gethsemane, he leaped the intervening ocean to this place at one bound. To break his fall he stretched out a hand, and from the holes punched by his fingers and thumb, abundant water has flowed ever since.

From the walnut orchards and ruined cottage foundations at Pendávli, the E4 – which is not any of the several new bulldozer tracks going east downhill – continues south for one hour 20 minutes to Áyios Dhimítrios. After an initial gentle grade, climb sharply to a ridge at 1550 metres. Beyond, on the Messinían side, the trail nearly disappears, but you're within sight of the easternmost cottages of Áyios Dhimítrios, 15 minutes below.

It's difficult to get badly lost crossing the watershed in either direction; just aim for that ridge crowned by a giant slag pile painted with E4 markers. Waymarking throughout this stretch is adequate, employing green or red paint dots and cairns as well as the standard black-on-yellow diamonds, but the trail surface needs a thorough tidying up. Nonetheless this is a very useful and safe link between Ayía Varvára refuge and Áyios Dhimítrios, poised in a forested bowl at the head of the Víros Gorge.

You should emerge from the trees near the namesake chapel and dribbly spring of Áyios Dhimítrios (1500 metres), served by forest road from the Messinían shore. This summer/weekend 'resort' for the villagers of Kardhamíli and Exokhóri consists of about a dozen plaster, metal-roofed cottages scattered in the trees; it's a beautiful spot to camp, but if you're tentless a vacant front porch can offer some protection. There's usually at least one family about from April until the first snowfall in November. Sadly, the inhabitants themselves report that one of their number is a bit of a thieving magpie, a rarity in Greece, so keep your gear secure.

Sidetrip: Another Approach to Profítis Ilías

Áyios Dhimítrios serves as a jumping-off point for climbing Profítis Ilías for those who've come up the Víros Gorge from Kardhamíli. This is a rather more difficult summit route than the ascent from Ayía Varvára refuge, and should only be attempted in settled weather. However, to my mind it is also more attractive, and if you have some time to spare at the end of a walking day it's well worth strolling up at least as far as the first saddle to the north.

To begin, find a log cabin (the only one at Áyios Dhimítrios) in the western group of huts, on the forest road. Head north-east uphill to find some boulders splashed with green paint, then bear north-west to pick up a faint path. Once past the highest hut in the colony, belonging to a certain Pavlos, cairns

appear. Don't lose altitude to your left; over the first 45 minutes the correct path curls around the head of gulch to the treeline, where some seeps in the turf off to the left at about 1750 metres accumulate in a drinkable pool or two.

You've 20 minutes more, or just over an hour total, to the saddle at 1950 metres, with fine perspectives on Profítis Ilías to the right, and Halasméno Vunó across the basin of Ayía Paraskeví. Between the turf springs and the ridge you'll pass a plug of rock which, seen from above, looks remarkably like a sphinx wearing a French beret – a good landmark for the descent.

To continue to Point 2404, veer right on the saddle towards some slab-like pinnacles, where a faint trail resumes. Following this under the 2019-metre point and then along the watershed itself, it's two more hours to the top. Good scrambling skills and a head for heights are required at certain points, as there are some partially exposed sections that are unsafe in wet or windy weather; even on a fair day you may find it necessary to drop a bit to the left (west) during the second hour of ascent.

Don't take a full pack up here; the only trekking route feasible from the first saddle is down into Ayía Paraskeví, then up the shoulder to the east of Halasméno Vunó, where a weak spring dampens the hillside. Count on an hour to this point, and another two beyond to Ríndomo hamlet; the main reason for doing this traverse would be if you wanted to link up the heads of both the Taïyettos gorges.

Stage 4: Áyios Dhimítrios to Kardhamíli via Víros Gorge

(7 hours)

From the lowest house of Áyios Dhimítrios, almost due south of the log cabin mentioned previously, adopt a neglected forest track and follow occasional E4 markers. After 10 minutes follow the markers as they dip left to stay with a trail zig-zagging down the slope. About half an hour along you reach the floor of what appears to be a small gully but which is actually the head of Víros. The

E4 markers bear off slightly to the left, across the gulch; you should go right or west onto what quickly becomes a delightful woodland path through black pines. About 40 minutes along you'll pass a spring in a hollow just off the trail at about 1220 metres; this is the only reliable, easy-to-get-at water until you're nearly finished with this stage!

Cairns continue to guide you down the north (true right) flank of the upper Víros gorge, until just under an hour out you cross to the southern bank.

Over the next 20 minutes or so the trail slips through boulders in the shade of tall firs, until the first hints of cobbles show themselves; this is the top of the Kakí Skála, a marvellous feat of engineering left over from ancient times when this path was one of the principal connections between Sparta and Messene. Suddenly you emerge at the top of a sharp drop, the kalderími flanked by boulders on the canyon side, some 70 minutes out of Áyios Dhimítrios; this is also the best photo opportunity of the valley spreading before you.

The term Kakí Skála, or 'Evil Stairway', of which there are many in Greece, refers here as always to the grade to be surmounted, not the quality of the path underfoot, which is (as here) usually excellent. The revetted section is actually quite brief; after skirting an abandoned section of the skála (don't get stuck on this if you're ascending) you'll find yourself down on the canyon floor again at about 1000 metres, next to a final cairn.

Soon, nearly one hour 20 minutes along, there's a corral on the left bank, where cows might be grazing at the mouth of a small gully. The people at Áyios Dhimítrios will tell you that there is good water up the gully, but it's neither visible nor audible from the main watercourse and it's only something to look for if you're desperate.

The worst drop is over, and at about 900 metres elevation you negotiate a narrow, dank rock gallery with seeps on the walls, uncollectable except by the swarming gnats. Another side gully enters, again on the south bank, just over 2¼ hours along; you'll see pipes which run down from an unfortunately dry spring somewhere above. The fir trees thin out as you leave the gorge floor for a 20-minute section of welcome trail up on the north (right) bank.

After about 2¾ hours a major tributary canyon, the so-called Stenó Langádha starting up at Ayía Paraskeví, joins the Víros Gorge from the north; Halasméno Vunó will be in plain sight. There's a well on the south bank, but no bucket or rope is provided. Abandoned terraces soon appear, as well as a chapel up on the north bank, correctly shown on available maps, about 40 minutes below the union of the two gorges.

Progress now is tedious rather than difficult; you can take advantage of brief bursts of trail, mostly on the south bank, to spare yourself walking on the volleyball-sized riverbed stones. You can also speculate on what fear or poverty drove people to scratch out a living in such a desolate place, even granting that there was more water about back then. Particularly eerie is Troskoná, a cluster of ruined houses at about 700 metres, some four hours along the route.

Once past the derelict hamlet, the Víros nearly doubles back on itself in a brief, north-west to south-east reach. After twisting around to its original bearing, leave the watercourse finally a bit less than five hours along in favour of a sandy path on the southeast bank. Just as a kalderími snaking up to Tséria village on the right bank pops into view, a faded arrow on a boulder points you up and left towards Exokhóri.

The 45-minute way up to Tséria (not including the 10-minute drop down from the arrow to the gorge floor at 450 metres) is very enjoyable, but best reserved for part of a day-hike out of Kardhamíli; Tséria itself, while equally attractive, has only a taverna and a few magaziá, no place to stay, and a four-km gap between it and the main road at Prosílio. You could, with some initial clambering, attempt to follow the Víros gorge its entire distance to the sea at Kardhamíli, but it's a while before it flattens out, and by now you will have in all likelihood had enough gorge for the time being.

So it's best to head up the left-hand path,

passing a much-appreciated spring, until merging with a new track after 20 minutes. Take this the remaining 20 minutes of the 5½-hour traverse to Exokhóri (500 metres), which has little more than Tséria in the way of facilities (including an afternoon bus that doesn't run every day). It is, however, the start of a very pleasant final walk into Kardhamíli. Like Kéndro Gaïtses across the Víros, Exokhóri is a triple village: Exokhóri proper, Níkovo on the south-west, and Hóra to the west, all swathed in olive groves.

Beginning in Hóra district, head downhill on the central cobbled lane; after three minutes bear right at a fork, and then five minutes later make another right in the direction of a hilltop chapel. Even if your stamina is flagging after six-plus hours on the road, it's well worth making the five-minute detour to this dilapidated shrine of Áyios Yióryios for the look it allows straight up the way you've come and down into Víros. (You'd also have missed this panorama if you'd stayed on the gorge floor.)

Return to the main kalderími, which snakes down to the monastery of Sotíros in the canyon after 20 more minutes. Having skirted the worst of the terrain between here and the junction below Tséria, you have a relatively simple route through another set of narrows below Sotíros, past another monastery (Likakíu), until emerging at the north end of Kardhamíli, nearly seven hours after leaving Áyios Dhimítrios.

If you bear left at the first fork below Hóra you'll also get to Kardhamíli safely in about the same elapsed time, though you don't have the spectacular canyon views and you will find the middle of the trail has been fairly well chewed up by bulldozers. The left-hand path ambles along the edge of a high (about 400 metres) agricultural plateau just below Hóra, before ending after some 20 minutes at a ksoklísi. Between here and another tiny chapel visible below you'll have a similar period of lousy cross-country hopping through olive terraces – not a cheerful prospect if darkness is approaching. Briefly adopt a tractor track leading down from the second chapel, then bear right onto what's left of the trail, which is soon cut to ribbons by a new dirt road. After scrambling down to this, take either the left or right fork to Petrovúni with its fortified tower- houses, or to Gurniés (Ayía Sofía). The latter, whose alias stems from its magnificent 17th-century church, is reached nearly 45 minutes below Hóra.

From just in front of that small church, a fine kalderími leaps the final 40 minutes (and 300 metres) downhill to the main highway Kardhamíli. Ten minutes before the bottom you'll pass a double, rock-cut Mycenean tomb, in legend that of Castor and Pollux; just beyond stand the monuments of Kardhamíli's medieval acropolis. The foremost of these is the graceful 18th-century church of Áyios Spirídhon, constructed partly from the stones of the ancient town and adorned with a typically exquisite Maniote belfry. You have definitely arrived in the Éxo (Outer) Máni, one of the most fascinating parts of Greece, and a subject fit for – and amply covered in – other volumes (see Books in Facts for the Trekker, especially Greenhalgh's *Deep into Mani*).

By this point, though, sightseeing will probably be the last thing on your mind, and all of these wonders – as well as the kalderími between Petrovúni and Kardhamíli – are best reserved for more casual walks on another day, along with any portions of the described route that you missed on the way down. Kardhamíli generally has enough beds to go around (except in August), an excellent pebble beach, and three or four tavernas. Purists bemoan its comparative development since the 1970s, but as these things go in Greece it's a mild case, and there is still no five-star hotel or a bank – just a post office.

For those wishing to reverse this stage, it's eight trekking hours from Kardhamíli up to Áyios Dhimítrios – barely an hour longer than the downhill course, since the gorge bed can't be rushed in either direction, and with sharp altitude changes confined to the upper Víros, around the Kakí Skála.

Párnon

Dominating the south-eastern Pelopónnisos, the Párnon massif (Párnonas) is a long but low range extending nearly 40 km from the convent of Malevís to a pass near the village of Kosmás, beyond which the mountain gives one last gasp before expiring in the sea of olives on the Évrotas river basin. It has a more montane feeling than its modest elevation implies, forming a formidable enough barrier between the highlands around Spárti and Trípoli and the eastern coast of Arkadhía. Broad as well as long, much of Párnon is surprisingly remote; early in the year Taïyettos, hovering like a snowy morning ghost to the west, may be your principal landmark.

Closeness to the Argolid gulf means drifting nocturnal mists, and damp rather than dry day-time heat. The humidity promotes thick forests (duly exploited) up to the 1700-metre treeline, and riotous spring wildflowers.

TRAVERSE VIA KRÓNIO

The north end of the summit ridge, around 1934-metre Krónio (Megáli Túrla), is the most interesting, providing the focus for a challenging two-day hike from Vamvakú village to the Malevís convent. South of the highest peak, however, the terrain is too sliced up by forest roads to be of much interest as a high-quality trek.

Rating & Duration
This trek is moderately strenuous, requiring some scrambling at points.

Season
The best time is late spring or early summer, as you'll need long days to complete the first stage out of Vamvakú by sunset, assuming you arrive by bus.

Supplies
Get them in Spárti; Vamvakú has little to offer.

Maps
Korfes 84, *Párnonas – Megáli Túrla*, or YIS 1:50,000 *Ástros*.

Access
There's just one daily bus from Spárti to Vamvakú, Monday to Saturday, departing at about 2 pm from the terminal at Ayissiláu 47,

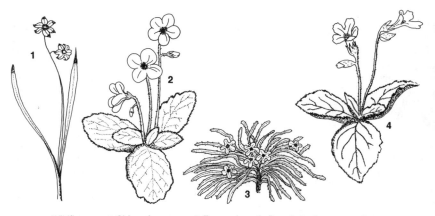

Wildflowers: **1** *Chionodoxa nana* **2** *Ramonda nathaliae* **3** *Anchusa caespitosa* **4** *Haberlea rhodopensis*

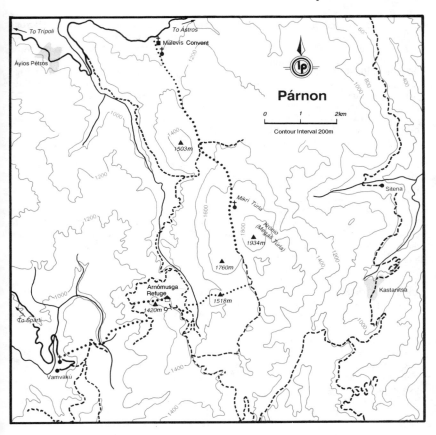

across from the produce market and near the Hotel Sparti; the ride takes two hours.

Stage 1: Vamvakú to Arnómusga Refuge

(2½ hours)

Once in Vamvakú (900 metres), start from the church on the central platía and find a prominent concrete staircase heading up and north-east. Soon the steps become a wide mule path that almost immediately crosses a dirt road and then plunges up a slope covered with chestnut trees. Keep a yawning gulch to your left and aim for the ridge above you.

This you reach after a half-hour climb, to be rewarded by a view over a long, fertile valley of potato fields nestled between the north-south lengthwise ridges of Párnon.

Your trail drops down, crosses another road, and almost instantly intersects it again. Amble right about 50 metres and again dip down the resumed trail in the direction of an audible river at about 1050 metres. Just over an hour out of Vamvakú, ford this stream (there's no bridge) and head up a dry gulch on the opposite bank. About 100 metres up this gulch you should see a rusty, jerry-rigged aqueduct just overhead; do not go under it, but take a prominent left some 30 metres before it.

Now there's a one-hour climb, initially through thick stands of broom but later through orchards and past a spring. As the path levels out it becomes extremely faint, but even if you lose it you should meet a dirt dhimósio (inter-village track) within the hour specified. Turn left onto this and proceed for 10 to 15 minutes until you reach the high point of the track, on a pine-clad ridge.

Make a reckoning of the ridge line (the track crosses it perpendicularly) and plunge right (east); after a moment you'll see red metal arrows that have been nailed to trees by EOS Spárti. There's no distinct trail; just keep exactly to the ridge line without meandering right or left. Some 200 metres beyond the last red blaze and a concrete benchmark, and half an hour after leaving the dhimósio you should reach the imposing Arnómusga refuge. Total walking time from Vamvakú will be 2½ hours.

The refuge is superbly sited at 1450 metres in a thinning fir and pine forest, with views of the sunset and the main crest of Párnon. There's enough flat ground for camping, and water is fetched from a spring five minutes downhill and south (follow a sign saying 'Piyí, EOS Spárti' nailed to a tree). The front terrace of the hut offers some wind shelter, though if you want the keys you'll have to contact EOS in Spárti (☎ (0731) 22 574 or 24 135).

Stage 2: Arnómusga Refuge to Krónio Summit

(3½ hours)

Hike down the shelter's driveway past a soccer field (!) until you find another tree-marker saying 'Krónion 3½ ora'. Head down the path indicated, meeting another road within 100 metres. The trail resumes slightly to the right; 15 minutes from the refuge there's a spring at the edge of an orchard, alongside the forest road to Áyios Pétros village.

Another red tree-marker prompts a left turn onto the road; after a few more moments

you'll see an ambiguously orientated sign on the left: 'Krónion 3 ora'. This is the cue to head to the right down a ridge covered with Scotch pine; there is no clear trail any longer. Twenty minutes past the orchard spring you'll ford a creek at about 1250 metres; this is the last dependable water until Malevís convent!

Turn right (south) up an overgrown drover's track on the opposite bank, keeping a sharp eye out for one last EOS Spárti sign on a tree at the base of a mostly denuded, 1500-metre bluff to your left. Just claw your way up the slope; it's a fairly brutal cross-country exercise, whether you head straight on or angle around. Moving most directly, it will take you about 45 minutes to meet the last stretch of forest road on the western side of the watershed – and have done with the only unpleasant portion of the trek.

Turn left (north) onto this track and follow it for 35 minutes until it ends at the base of Krónio (Megáli Túrla) and the head of a valley rising up to the 1700-metre *oropédhio* (alpine basin or flats) at the base of the peak. It's a pleasant 25-minute crossing on sheep traces to a small chapel at the far end of the high meadow. There is no spring up here, only a metal-lidded well between Krónio and the little ksoklísi, some 300 metres from the latter. However, its water is foul and larvae-infested even in spring, and can only be used, if boiled, in emergencies. In spring you may still find patches of snow suitable for melting on the mountain's flanks.

Seen from the coast to the east, Párnon's summit has a symmetrical triple profile, and up close it's obvious why. Beyond the dubious well a low saddle separates the northerly peak of Mikrí Túrla from Krónio and Rússa Pétra to the south; the true summit is the middle knob.

Sidetrip: Krónio Summit

To climb Krónio, take off your pack and leave it among the saddle's boulders. Inch up the grade to the trig point; this will require an extra hour for a round trip. Weather permitting, you'll be treated to panoramas of the Argolid and its gulf to the east, Taïyettos and

Lakonía Province to the west, and a large depression to the north beyond Malevís.

Stage 3: Krónio Summit to Malevís Convent

(2½ hours)

Locate the terminus of a proper path immediately behind and below the little chapel, approximately in the middle of a livestock-frayed trail network. All this soon resolves into one obvious right-of-way – it's sporadically red-blazed, but the waymarks are orientated towards uphill hikers. An hour's uneventful descent through a delightful mixed forest is interrupted by a logging road.

Go straight across it, continuing along a juniper-tufted ridge before dipping down into a quilt of potato fields at about 1350 metres. Keep most of these to your left and make for the top of a canyon in the landscape ahead. There's really only one notch where you can easily leave this plateau; it's flanked by boulders and dashed with red paint, and a trail of sorts picks up half-heartedly.

Initially descend gradually north, with a terraced slope on the left; soon you must avoid bearing right and uphill in favour of dropping in the opposite direction across a pasture, changing to the other side of the gully. Presently you'll see a couple of reassuring tree-arrows; begin following the actual bed of the drainage before changing sides again. About 45 minutes below the logging road, at just under 1200 metres elevation, any trace of trail vanishes, as do waymarks.

Keeping clear of dense stands of trees above and below, choose a median cross-country course through a vast series of steep terraces belonging to Malevís. The dome of an outlying chapel of the convent tantalises and guides you. Finally, 2½ hours after leaving the high plateau, you'll arrive on the grounds of Malevís, a much-rebuilt, white-elephantine structure. Weekend visits are inadvisable, since religious retreats often fill most available beds. At other times you can request a bunk or two from the abbess. No food is available, however.

Leaving Párnon

Daylight and stamina permitting, you may prefer to hitch or walk eight km west to Áyios Pétros, which has a normal hotel, tavernas, and a view back at the recently climbed mountain. Alternatively, you can hitch or take a bus east towards Ástros and its beach annex Paralía Ástrous, 33 km away. However, there is no Sunday bus service in any direction, and hitchable traffic is patchy on the road east of Malevís. Since the Párnon watershed is also the provincial boundary between Lakonía and Arkadhía, westbound buses eventually end up in Trípoli, which can be a problem if you want to return to Spárti.

One possible solution is to descend to Ástros and there catch one of several daily buses coming from Árgos, going all the way down the coast to Leonídhi. From Leonídhi a single daily bus (about 1 pm) continues up a dizzying road as far as Kosmás (1200 metres), the southernmost of the Párnon villages. It's a peaceful place on an exposed pass, with tufts of firs and extensive cherry and chestnut orchards; there are two tavernas and an inn as well. Recrossing the provincial border, you've 16 bus-less km down to Yeráki, the first town in Lakonía with public transport back to Spárti. Twice weekly, on Tuesday at noon and Saturday at dawn, the Kosmás bus goes all the way to Spartí. You can hitch, take a taxi or walk the recently improved road – stretches of old path still run parallel to it.

This may sound like an awful lot of trouble, but it's a beautiful circuit that can be accomplished in rather less time than it took to hike Párnon. Chances are you'll want to break the journey anyway between Ástros and Kosmás, at any of several beach resorts.

The Stereá

Stereá Elládhos (literally, 'mainland of Greece') is in some ways an obsolete label, more appropriate back when most of Greece was islands or the Pelopónnisos, and the territory from Athens to the Turkish-held Balkans was the full extent of her Continental holdings. In his companion volume to *Mani*, Patrick Leigh Fermor proposes Roumeli as a substitute name, but this Ottoman term, meaning 'the land of the Rum' (Greek Orthodox Christians), is even less specific, so Stereá will probably retain its place of honour among such venerable geographic catch-alls as Appalachia and the Midlands.

Whether rockily denuded or heavily forested, most of the terrain is dramatic and thinly populated. As you proceed west from the Attic Peninsula towards the island of Lefkádha and the Amvrákikos Gulf, communications and settlements grow progressively more sparse, so that by the time the Ágrafa region is reached, many of the villages seem truly forsaken by both God and humans. The inhabitants of the Kravára, an isolated region west of Vardhúsia and south of Ágrafa, long had a reputation as itinerant beggars and snake-oil peddlers, so poor was their land.

Today most Stereáns earn a much better living, whether from olives, bauxite, sheep, tobacco, grain or timber, and (except around ancient Delphi) tourism has made little impact on one of the least visited parts of Greece. Accordingly the people may seem a bit reserved or even indifferent towards outsiders, especially compared to the ebullient or even obsequious islanders, but in general they are no less friendly once you get to know them. But do keep in mind that the civil war and natural disasters have been particularly harsh on the area, that development came late by Greek standards, and that until recently there wasn't a lot of anything to spare in many villages. So don't be surprised to find conventional accommodation and restaurants almost nonexistent or geared towards native emigrés up for a summer visit.

Párnitha (Párnes)

Párnitha, a low but heavily wooded range just north of Athens was a hunting forest, military training ground and protective barrier for the ancient city. Today, with the modern metropolis of nearly four million beginning to scale its foothills, this range has become the 'lung' of Athens and the closest escape from urban life. Even before the era of the notorious *néfos* (the chronic Athenian smog pall) there was a tuberculosis sanatorium on Mt Párnitha, and recently most of the summit area was declared a national park. Every year a marathon is run around the mountain, and weekend rock climbers swarm over the sheer cliffs at Varimbópi and Arma. But casual walkers will be happy to learn that Párnitha is endowed with a network of relatively well-maintained and marked trails giving access to an area far wilder and greener than its slight distance from the capital would suggest.

Rating & Duration
All of the easy outings described are designed to be completed in one day or less; staying at the Báfi hostel will greatly extend your range. You might try some as training walks before heading out into higher, more trackless territory.

Season
You can tour Párnitha most of the year, weather permitting – spring with the local wildflowers is best, while in high summer it's crowded and hot. It can be delightful even on a sunny winter day, crunching about in the snow between storms.

Map

Korfes 54, or YIS 1:50,000 *Kifisiá.*

Access

Bus No 726 departs frequently from the corner of Sturnára and Akharnón streets in central Athens, bound for the outlying suburb of Akharnés, a 45-minute trip. Here you change to a less regular No 724 bus (same ticket) to the remoter district of Thrakomakedhónes. Line 714 departs from the same city terminal for the chapel and spring at Ayía Triádha, passing through Metókhi.

To approach Mt Párnitha from the north, take any of the 15 daily local trains towards Halkídha, alighting at Sfendháli (Malakássa) railway station, four stops out of Athens.

Trek 1: Thrakomakedhónes-Ayía Triádha Loop via Báfi

(5 hours)

From the last, highest stop of bus No 724, walk uphill about 10 minutes to a stone wall guarding a hairpin turn to the east. Using a gap at the lower end of the wall, plunge down briefly to the bottom of the Húni ravine (550 metres), which exits Párnitha here. The path

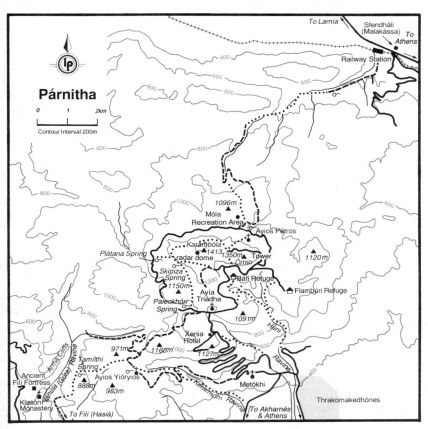

is clearly visible on the far bank of the gully and is waymarked by an assortment of red or white blazes, or even paint-tin lids.

Some 50 minutes along, after trading Mediterranean scrub for the famous fir forest, you'll reach a junction at about 800 metres altitude: right leads to the springs at Kirá and Katára, and to the refuge at Flambúri; straight ahead goes to Báfi. Keep straight, shunning left and right options 1¾ hours along in favour of the middle path; the Báfi hostel (1160 metres) should now be visible.

You'll arrive there two hours out of Thrakomakedhónes, having in the last moments curled around the head of a stream gully. The hostel (☎ (01) 24 69 050 or 24 61 528) is open most days in summer, on Friday evening and weekends in winter, and at other times by arrangement. When the refuge is shut you can get water from a tap around the back (except in winter when it freezes up). It's always wise to phone ahead if you want to stay, as reservations are often necessary and alpine club members (Greek or foreign) may be given preference. If it's full you may be referred to the less convenient Flambúri shelter (☎ (01) 24 64 666).

To continue the route, head north-west across the Báfi shelter's car park to join the paved Párnitha ring road, and turn right. After 300 metres along this, turn left onto the trail marked 'Móla'. This worms up to the saddle between 1350-metre Órnio, crowned by a monstrous tower, and Karambóla, Párnitha's 1413-metre summit, with an air force installation on top. Change sides of the mountain at a chapel, crossing the ridgetop dirt road to follow the path downhill through the densest forest yet. Snow lies late and thick on Párnitha's north slope, and you'll want gaiters and a walking stick in March, but in compensation, wonderful crocuses and other species emerge as the drifts melt.

At another signed junction 45 minutes past Báfi, bear left (right goes within 20 minutes to Móla) to continue towards Skípiza spring. The next hour is spent beautifully skimming first the north, then the north-west, flanks of the mountain, with

views as far as Párnassos on a clear day. After an initial level section, climb left over the tip of the summit ridge, just below an artlessly camouflaged radar dome, and drop steeply down to Skípiza, 'the place of the eagles' in Albanian. Ignore the blue-marked path veering down to the right – stick to the trail marked with elderly red or rusty discs.

This fountain, in the heart of the mountain at 1200 metres, also marks a four-way trail junction; stand with your back to the spout to orientate yourself. Straight west goes within 20 minutes to the Platána spring on the main circle road; back up behind you goes back east to Báfi; while the south-easterly path, marked with white then red waymarks, heads for Ayía Triádha. Take this south-easterly path, and roller-coaster through a series of ravines before descending steadily southwards along a creek bed to emerge on the paved ring road after an hour at the Paleokhóri spring (1000 metres).

At Paleokhóri, distinguished by some funny ventilator pipes sticking out of the ground, turn left (east) and walk along the asphalt for 15 minutes to Ayía Triádha (1000 metres), where the highway up from Akharnés meets the ring road. There's a chalet-restaurant here where you could treat yourself to a post-hike meal, assuming an early start – the No 714 bus down to town leaves from the stop next to the chapel and spring at 4 pm sharp.

If you miss it you can try hitching down, or there is a path from near the Xenia Hotel (one km south) down the Ayía Triádha ravine, which avoids five km of switchbacks on the highway.

Once at the bottom, either continue on foot to the strip of hotels and tavernas in Áno Akharnés served by the No 729 bus, or walk east to lower Thrakomakedhónes for the No 724 back to central Akharnés.

Trek 2: Sfendháli (Malakássa) to Móla (4 hours)

The long (four-hour) but more gradual ascent of Párnitha from the railway line transects the entire rich plant community of the mountain, from the low-altitude arbutus and

Aleppo pines to the majestic Cephallonian firs of the higher slopes. However, a warning – this area was devastated by fire in September 1992, so you can expect at least some of the terrain described following to be affected.

Coming out of the railway station (about 300 metres), head up a track well away from the east (right) bank of a ravine; at a junction after 15 minutes turn right, to stay with the general bearing of the valley. A bit over half an hour along is a spring – the last reliable water for a while. Powerlines appear overhead, and the track dwindles to a path as it drops much closer to the ravine bed.

Just over an hour out, cross a side gully coming in from the south, and a few minutes later briefly change to the other side of the main drainage. Eighty minutes along, the powerlines march up a second tributary running south from the flanks of Párnitha; stay with your stream. Over the next 15 minutes the route negotiates a set of narrows, with the path following the bed of the gorge briefly before clambering up on the north-western bank.

Some 2¼ hours along, you and the somewhat overgrown trail emerge from the gallery to meet a dirt road which has come down along the left bank of the gully; make a left onto this. You'll have to follow it for the best part of an hour, though the mix of high and low-altitude vegetation – you're at 700 or 800 metres here – is some consolation.

Near the head of the ravine, where the track bends around north, a faint trail picks up, heading off to the south-east; if you can't find it, just follow the streambed. The path improves going uphill, until just shy of four hours along it leaves you by some power poles at the edge of the large meadow which forms the heart of the Móla picnic and recreation area (1050 metres).

Up on the main circuit road you'll find the chapel of Áyios Pétros, and a spring opposite. The well-marked trail to Skípiza or Báfi begins just to the west, behind a clump of poplars. Within 20 minutes you should be up at the trail forking below Órnio described above.

A reversed itinerary (Móla to Sfendháli) takes three hours 20 minutes.

Trek 3: Metókhi to the Yanúla (Gúra) Ravine via Áyios Yióryios
(4¼ hours)

This route combines alpine hiking with the chance to visit various monuments in the Yanúla ravine, which furrows Párnitha on the south-west.

The walk actually starts a bit below the chapel at Metókhi, in the vast picnic grounds at about 500 metres; the trail is blazed in green. It's just under two hours, following the Keramídhi ravine, up to the spring and ksoklísi of Áyios Yióryios. From Áyios Yióryios, head north-west along the forest road for about 15 minutes towards Point 971, obvious as a rocky knoll. Leave the track before this, turning west onto a path with sporadic cairns and blazes.

Over the next 15 minutes the path begins to curl down and south; don't bear too far left, but aim for the conical hill of Point 888. The path, now emblazoned with red discs, is easier to find once you're well under way, and skirts this hill on its north side. Take a left as you emerge into the Yanúla ravine, and within 40 minutes of leaving Áyios Yióryios you should be having a drink at the cliff-base Tamílthi spring (800 metres).

South from the spring the path is well-trodden and blazed, though as the gorge widens out it becomes a wider lane about half an hour past the spring. The much-rebuilt but originally 14th-century monastery of Klistón ('Of the Closed-in Places') monastery should be visible on the far bank of Yanúla, tucked under the Árma cliffs. To visit it you'll have to finish your descent to the paved road; turn right and proceed for 25 minutes to Klistón. Above it, accessible by scrambling, is the 4th-century BC fortress of Filí, built to defend a pass in the ancient route between Athens and Thebes.

When you've finished sightseeing, the nearest facilities – and buses back to the Akharnón/Sturnára terminal in Athens – are in Filí village, three km south of the side road to Klistón. Most locals, and the bus signs themselves, know Filí by its Albanian name Hasiá. From the Tamílthi spring directly to Hasiá, allow 1½ hours.

Parnassós

With any number of Parnassós or Montparnasse streets, districts, bars and parks as namesakes throughout the world, Parnassós is perhaps the most famous peak in Greece after Mt Ólimbos. Since earliest history the entire mountain was sacred to the god Dionysus, as well as Pan; later the range, and the Delphic oracle at its base, also became associated with Apollo and the Muses. Not surprisingly, the environs of the mountain were heavily populated in classical times; a half-dozen or so modern villages are the direct descendants of ancient towns.

Geologically, Parnassós (Parnassus) is a jagged chunk of karstic limestone, with the very limited number of high-altitude springs and the swiss-cheese pattern of *dolines* (sinkholes) that is typical of such material. The south abutment drops sharply into the olive-swathed valley of Plístos; about three-quarters of the way down, the Delphi archaeological zone is tucked into a nook at the base of cliffs. The northern flank, indented by the Velítsa canyon, descends more gradually toward the Kifissós and Sperkhiós river valleys. Bands of fir trees drape the mountain at their preferred altitude of 800 to 1300 metres.

The 2457-metre peak itself, though not the highest in the Stereá (Gióna and Vardhúsia nearby are both loftier), is uniquely situated to provide a giant-relief-map perspective of Greece. However, this 360° panorama is likely only in summer, and often not even then. Weather near the summit is consistently wet or blustery from the end of September to the start of June.

A CLASSICAL GREEK WALK

Unfortunately, the actual appeal of Parnassós for trekkers no longer matches its hoary reputation. The traditional ascent of the mountain, related in slightly fictionalised form in John Fowles's *The Magus*, used to be from the villages of either Dhelfí or Arákhova, but you'll get little joy out of this approach today in the wake of an excessive campaign of road-building in the south-western corners of Parnassós, and the expansion of the ski resort in the north-west quadrant. There is arguably nothing more dismal than a ski lift in summer, and you're advised to spare yourself the sight of it twice by including the length of the Velítsa ravine as at least one leg of your trek – if not both. In any case the mountain shows what is left of its majestic character only in the north-east, as seen from the flanks of the canyon.

Rating & Duration

A two-day traverse of the mountain as suggested, from north-east to south-west, falls in the moderate category, mostly because of the long second day. Similarly, a long single-day hike out of Tithoréa gets a moderate grading.

I've detailed a north-east to south-west traverse, rather than the other way around, because the way down is slightly easier to find going in that direction – and what better post-climb reward than a pilgrimage to ancient Delphi (and a chance to brag about where you've been)?

Supplies

Because of the number of tourists about, you can get a wide range of these in modern Dhelfí; Tithoréa is a bit more basic.

Maps

Korfes 75-76, or YIS 1:50,000 *Amfíklia & Arákhova*.

Access

For the north side of the mountain, several stopping trains daily serve Káto Tithoréa from Athens or Thessaloníki, with the final four km up the hill to Áno Tithoréa best covered in a taxi (about $4 more).

From Athens, the best-timed trains leave

at 10 am and 1.15, 2.40 and 5.10 pm; from Thessaloníki, at 6.58 and 10.50 am.

Modern Dhelfí, south-west of Parnassós, is easily reached by bus from Athens (four or six daily), less so from Pátra or Thessaloníki (maximum of three daily, with a change at Itéa or Ámfissa respectively).

Dhávlia, the eastern trailhead, has its own railway station beyond the Tithoréa one, but it's eight km below the village, making the taxi shuttle up a rather expensive one; an alternative is to take one of the early-morning trains from Athens to Livádhia, the provincial capital, and then do the final distance on the afternoon bus. This is a popular strategy for those who've been unable to secure seats on an Athens-Dhelfí coach (a common problem in summer); it's far preferable to stand in a bus aisle for the 44 km from Livádhia to Dhelfí than the whole way from the capital.

Stage 1: Áno Tithoréa to Liákura Summit

(5¾ hours)

Áno Tithoréa is a pleasant hill settlement often referred to by its medieval name of Velítsa, still the term of choice for the giant ravine nearby. Ancient Tithoréa was an important city, mentioned by Pausanias, and you can still see extensive stretches of vine-cloaked, 4th-century BC wall below the platía. During the modern Greek war of independence, a cave high up on the true left bank of the Velítsa ravine was the lair of that guerrilla captain of ambiguous loyalty, Odysseus Androutsos, and his sidekick, the English adventurer Edward Trelawny. (For a complete account of their rather lurid doings, consult *Delphi and the Sacred Way* by Neville Lewis.)

On a practical level, Áno Tithoréa is not entirely ideal as a hiking base; while a handful of stores and tavernas provide for you, there is at present only one lodging, in the ground-floor apartment of Ioannis Mintzas, 300 metres west of the platía. The capacity is six persons, best booked for two days at about US$6 per person; it's generally not available during the school year, when

the teacher rents the entire flat. It is best, in fact, to plan on camping out somewhere near town.

Leave town from the platía (420 metres), heading south-west on various narrow driveways. The foot trail proper begins by the waterfall (really a leak in an aqueduct) and some park benches overlooking the Velítsa ravine that limits Tithoréa to the south-east. Another partly covered concrete aqueduct crosses the path a few minutes past the waterfall, and 100 metres beyond the water channel you bear left into the canyon, following some orange dots on path-side rocks. Do not proceed further up the wider, apparently main path – this dead-ends at the lair of Androutsos and Trelawny, and despite anything else you may hear, the following route is the *only* way up to Liákura.

Here, in its lower reaches, the Velítsa ravine, listed on some maps as the Kakórema or Ksirórema, is interesting but not breathtaking. After a 10 to 15-minute descent to its usually dry bed, change sides where the aqueduct (also usually dry) spans it. Natural rock steps worm up the opposite bank, roughly following the course of the aqueduct, and finish their climb right next to the channel at the edge of a large plateau.

Follow the waterworks for 20 minutes more to the unsightly concrete ksoklísi of Áyios Ioánnis at 700 metres. (Below this chapel the aqueduct divides, water being diverted on a day-by-day basis to either of the two branches. If you're descending from the summit area, be sure to follow the left fork to reach Tithoréa.) About 300 metres above Áyios Ioánnis the foot trail resumes among some firs just uphill from a bulldozer-scraped area and the aqueduct, which is the last dependable water supply for some time. Count on a one-hour walk from the village to the start of the alpine trail (though the track may well have been extended recently some distance higher), and don't be too dismayed by the initial condition of the route; matters improve dramatically above Áyios Ioánnis.

After a stiff half-hour climb through thick forest, the grade lessens and the trees thin out to permit views of one Parnassan crag after

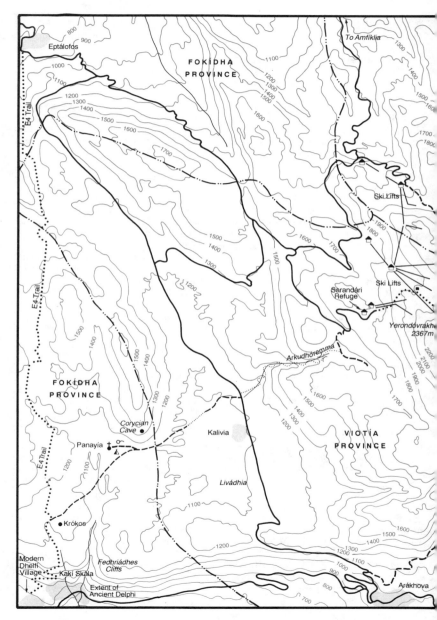

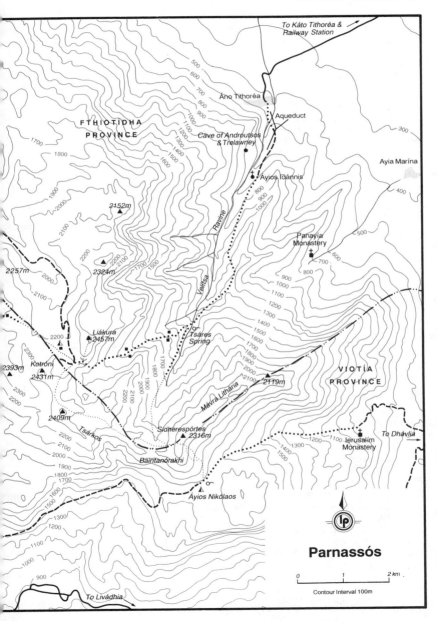

Parnassós

0   1   2 km

Contour Interval 100m

another filing in a stately procession to the top on the opposite side of the now-impressive chasm. Some two hours above Tithoréa, a high waterfall at the base of those crags contributes to the perennial sound of rushing water in the canyon bottom. Twenty minutes further, the path scales a sparsely treed 1200-metre ridge and briefly runs along the crest; you have perspectives north-east over the valley containing Ayía Marína village and the isolated monastery of the Panayía, while straight ahead looms the eastern spur of Parnassós.

Soon the dry ridge widens into a high, stony pasture; when trees reappear, some 2¾ hours out, the trail veers inconspicuously to the right – do *not* go steeply up left or straight from the pasture. After forsaking the pasture, the correct route runs levelly for a period along the gorge and then gradually dips further into Velítsa. The canyon has narrowed considerably and rises to meet the trail just below treeline at 1400 metres, approximately 3½ hours along. Cross the ravine where the permanent Tsáres spring flows – this is the last reliable water until you're on the far slope of Parnassós.

Go straight or slightly right (south-west) on the opposite bank and climb 30 minutes more up scree-laden switchbacks to a small stáni of two huts and some corrals just at treeline. You must bear right here, going straight up the hill across from the second corral, to begin a cruel half-hour climb up to another stáni perched at 1850 metres on the south-east slope of the main defile leading down from the Liákura saddle. The grandeur of the escarpments that enclose you on all sides compensates somewhat for the slow, painful progress on this leg of the walk; so also do occasional orange waymarks, but these are orientated primarily for those descending.

After the last stáni, the valley on your right (north), a tributary of the Velítsa ravine, closes; the grade becomes gentler; and the path crosses to the right (north-west) flank of what is now merely a gently inclined couloir, where it stays for the final hour up to the saddle at 2240 metres. At the very end

you've a brief scramble up a boulder slide to a notch in the ridge. Your total elapsed hiking time from Tithoréa to this point should be 5½ hours.

For the summit, turn right (north); red paint splodges guide you up for the 20-minute scramble to the top at 2457 metres. A compass enables you to identify features of the living map that surrounds you upon arrival at the trig point. All of the following landmarks will, of course, be visible only in optimum conditions.

NW to NE – Timfristós peak is a bald, almost cylindrical knob; Ólimbos, Kíssavos and Pílion merge to the north-east.

NE to SE – The Pagasitikós gulf shines in front of Mt Pílion; the Maliakós and Évvian gulfs merge and are the closest bodies of water; beyond long, skinny Évvia floats in the Sporádhes archipelago; Párnitha hides Athens to the south-east.

SE to SW – The Kórinthos gulf basks in the foreground of the northern Peloponnesian ranges of (east to west) Zíria, Helmós and Panaïhakó.

SW to NW – Returning to the mainland, the prospect west is interrupted by the neighbouring peaks of Vardhúsia and Gióna, both higher than Liákura.

If the afternoon weather is poor, you can give yourself another chance of seeing the view by camping in the plateau south-west of the peak, described in the next stage, and repeating the summit climb at dawn.

Stage 2: Liákura Summit to Dhelfí via Kalívia

(8½ hours)

Just beyond the saddle at the base of Liákura, a jeep road twists along the base of the crest; cross it, aiming for a shepherd's cottage with a mortared roof which, if unoccupied, makes an acceptable overnight shelter. Exit the stáni going north-west, attaining a slight saddle with a small meadow just beyond. On the other side of this, curve slightly west with little altitude change to run parallel to the ridge of Yerondóvrakhos (2367 metres) which has appeared on your left. You'll soon pass an enormous vertical pinnacle supporting a cluster of crude shelters; cut straight through the patch of turf beyond, but skirt another one encountered just afterwards.

Emerging at the top of a low, rocky spur, the route heads downhill on fairly well defined rock steps splattered with red arrows pointing against you. At the base of this stairway sits another stone hut (2200 metres) which can sleep three on a raised platform. Normally its loose-beam-and-sheet-metal roof is stacked to one side; be sure to dismantle it again after use so that the weight of winter snow doesn't damage it.

Once past this hut, occasional red dots mark a proper path with a neat stone edging, though this becomes badly muddled just after reaching the last pylon of one of the ski lifts. Upon meeting the top of a bulldozer track, bear south-west and skirt the top of the graded run to find the stone huts and a corral of a final stáni.

Keeping the ski runs well below you to the right, continue through a gully between two slight rises; a cairn and a red dot orientated away from you mark the entrance of this trough. At its exit you should see a large cairn liberally splashed with red paint; here the path plunges sharply down to a stunted tree, where you bear left (south-east) towards a second small tree about 400 metres distant.

The three-building ski complex of the Athens Ski Club at Sarandári should now be in plain sight, and your path ends just above it at about 1840 metres, between the fourth and fifth pylons of the ski lift. (For the benefit of those ascending, a schematic peak and an arrow are painted on a rock here.) Total walking time from the notch at the foot of Liákura shouldn't exceed four hours; count on an extra half hour if you reverse this itinerary.

Once on the asphalt driveway here, walk a few moments down to true treeline and the rather forlorn and little-used EOS shelter at Sarandári (1800 metres). Proceed down the asphalt 20 minutes more, around a single hairpin, until seeing a rough dirt road taking off south (left) at about 1700 metres. Turn onto this and follow it about 15 minutes down a shallow ravine flanked by forest to a meadow. Veer right (west) until reaching a saddle to your right (west), perhaps noting a

rusty marker pointing back up to the Sarandári refuge.

From the head of the incipient ravine (marked as Arkudhóremma on some maps) carry on west, then south-west, on a faint and sporadic path, until you come out on the paved Arákhova-Eptálofos road at a bridge (1100 metres), some 90 minutes after leaving Sarandári. There is a taverna nearby, virtually the only amenity here; Kalívia itself, 10 minutes down the road, is a strictly pastoral community.

To continue, simply move west-south-west across the vast plateau before you, the livádhia of Arákhova, devoted to grain-growing or grazing according to season; at the rear of this high plain is a prominent ridge. As you proceed toward a break in the trees ahead, meeting a dirt track in so doing, you'll be able to spot the famous Corycian Cave, long sacred to Pan and the nymphs, above you to the right, at the tip of the ridge. A half-hour scramble off your basic route brings you to a large cavern – Neville Lewis estimates the first chamber to be 60 metres long by 12 metres high – and it may possibly have figured in the local ancient rites of Dionysus, celebrated by women in November when Apollo was absent from the lower sanctuary. After exploring the area, return to the dirt track and continue west.

About an hour after leaving the asphalt you'll find a seasonal pond, a spring and a chapel of the Panayía near a flat grassy spot that could make an emergency camp. An agricultural track continues south-west into the firs to a group of stock-watering troughs and pastoral shelters in an area known as Krókos (1150 metres) – another possible campsite if darkness is falling. Join up here with the E4 long-distance trail coming south from Eptálofos; simply turn left onto the marked path, and start to lose elevation in earnest.

About one hour from Panayía the route edges the top (1000 metres) of the Fedhriádhes cliffs which plummet abruptly to the sanctuary of Delphi; angle right with the waymarks to the top of the famous Kakí Skála, another of those magnificently wrought ancient stairways, built in this case to allow Pan's devotees access to his cave. Most of it is kalderími surface, but some sections are carved from the living rock.

Some 2¾ hours from the road, or nearly 8½ hours of walking from Liákura saddle, you'll end up at the upper left-hand corner of the Delphi archaeological site and its perimeter fence, very near the Philomelos fortifications. You have arrived at Delphi in a manner that few of the whisked-in coachloads of tourist could possibly imagine. Just below you, at the edge of modern Dhelfí is a house (600 metres) once occupied by the poet Angelos Sikelianos, with his bust out the front – a useful landmark if you wish to reverse the itinerary.

Alternative Approach from Dhávlia
Parnassós is occasionally climbed from Dhávlia, or more precisely from the convent of Ierusalím (850 metres), seven road km above the village. From there a trail leads without ambiguity or complications west then west-south-west for three hours up to high pastures at Áyios Nikólaos (1800 metres), a good campsite where there are a couple of springs, shepherds and the end of a jeep track up from Arákhova.

To the north tower the rotten ridges of Baïtanórakhi and Mávra Lithária, with an inconspicuous pass (Sidherespórtes) separating them at about 2200 metres. There's no trail up from Áyios Nikólaos; the grade is sharp, the surface dubious, and really it's only for lightly laden purists. On the other side is the top of the valley not followed from Tsáres spring when coming up from Tithoréa, but don't bother dropping into it – just ridge-walk north-east, avoiding sinkholes, to the base of Liákura. Allow 2½ hours from Áyios Nikólaos to the base of the summit.

Íti (Oeta)

This underrated mountain is blessed with far more meadowlands, forests and water than

the harsh norm for central Greece, and actually displays many characteristics of ranges in Makedhonía. In fact, Íti marks the end of a high-precipitation belt extending south from the Albanian frontier through the Píndhos and Ágrafa. The northern part of Íti has been set aside as a national park, and the best hiking is also up the abrupt escarpment on the northern slope of the mountain into this lush territory.

Most of the summit area consists of rolling meadows, and the highest peak of Pírgos is not striking; however, a secondary summit was in mythology the site of Hercules' self-immolation and accordingly has been dubbed Pirá (Pyre). From the heights you continue south over a variety of surfaces towards a handful of villages between Íti and Gióna, the nearest other Sterean massif.

Rating & Duration/Season
Allow at least 1½ days to cross the range from north to south, as described below. Íti's springs run even in mid-summer, which features balmy nights and only some day-time discomfort on the initial ascent.

Orientation skills necessary for the territory south of Pírgos push this trek into the moderate category.

Supplies
Get these in Lamía or Ipáti.

Maps
Korfes 67, or YIS 1:50,000 *Lamía* and possibly *Sperkhiás*.

Access
The best path begins in the village of Ipáti, reached almost hourly by buses from Lamía. However, it's not necessary to catch the bus in town; hikers coming from the direction of Athens or northern Greece should take a train to Lianokládhi, the station halfway between Lamía and Ipáti. The most convenient trains leave Athens at 7.20, 10 am, 1 and 2.40 pm; from Thessaloníki, try for the 7 am, 11.30 am or 1 pm departures. Walk east from the terminal (take a right out the station door) to the crossing guard's booth

by the tracks – this is an official stop for Ipáti-bound coaches.

In Lamía itself there are three separate bus terminals: one for long-distance coaches of the Athens-Thessaloníki line, one for service west to Karpeníssi and south to Amfissa, and one for service to local villages, Ipáti being one of these. By the time you locate the appropriate terminal you'll probably agree it's a bit easier to use the train.

Once on the bus make sure that you're set down at the end of the line, the pleasant hill town of Ipáti, and not at the sulphurous spa below. Upper Ipáti was once sufficiently important to prompt construction of a small medieval castle, when it was called Pátrai; today it attracts enough Greek vacationers to support two hotels and an array of tavernas.

Stage 1: Ipáti to the Trápeza Refuge
(4 hours)

From the spring on the central platía (400 metres), start up the steep, paved street heading south. This snakes through the highest houses of Ipáti; always stick to the principal, concreted right of way. A few metres past the highest point in this road, turn left onto a prominent mule track; after another 200 metres, turn right opposite a final, rustic house with a water tap into its front corral. Initially the climb is severe, but an aqueduct running alongside the path provides coolant for baked heads.

Soon the aqueduct meanders off to the left, and shortly after you must take a narrower fork to the right. Confidence is restored by the sighting of a few red dots as the trail plunges onwards, deeply grooved into the terrain by generations of livestock. Owing to their hooves, the path is usually double or triple – just maintain a middle course.

The first fringes of Íti's fir groves offer valuable shade about an hour above Ipáti, and some 15 minutes beyond the beginning of the trees you'll reach a meadow with a vigorous stream and the ruins of an old mill (about 850 metres). Bear off here across a denuded hillside towards the resumption of the trail among some trees; don't dip into the stream valley to the south. After another

1½ hours of steady climbing through monumental firs, a marshy spot announces the Amalióvrisi spring (about 1300 metres) near the top of the initial rampart separating you from the Sperkhiós river valley. A rusty blue sign to one side points along the path continuing to Trápeza.

Immediately above Amalióvrisi you could camp quite nicely in the large meadow of Amaliólakka; the trail itself skirts the south edge of the turf and veers off across the top of a gully to begin a stiff, half-hour climb up to Perdhikóvrisi spring. The way is often obscured by the wildflowers that grow in profusion, even in midsummer, at the base of firs draped with moss. Perdhikóvrisi (unmarked) is a muddy, stomped-about place with none of the masonry or charm of its lower neighbour; it lies just below a forest road which you cross at about 1600 metres, guided by red paint dots.

The path resumes feebly on the far side, recrossing the road again almost instantly and twisting steadily up through more firs on a carpet of mid-altitude turf and blossoms. About 30 minutes after first tangling with the road the path is often imaginary, so look out for the red blazes. The road does its best to submerge the trail with multiple switchbacks, and after a few minutes the red blazes – and probably your patience – give out.

Resign yourself to following the road a final 10 minutes to the 300-metre-long driveway leading to the alpine hut, strikingly situated on a small canyon-bound plateau (hence the name Trápeza, which means 'bank' or 'table'; 1800 metres) with views of the setting and rising sun. The total hiking time from Ipáti is four hours, but you should allow more leeway than usual since the steep grade prompts longer rests.

The keys for the 24-person refuge can be obtained from EOS Lamías, Ipsilándu 20 (☎ (0231) 26 786), though camping under the trees nearby is idyllic. There is a rather weak spring about 300 metres west of the shelter; a tree-sign pointing to it is nearly wrecked, but a well-worn trail betrays the location of the fountain.

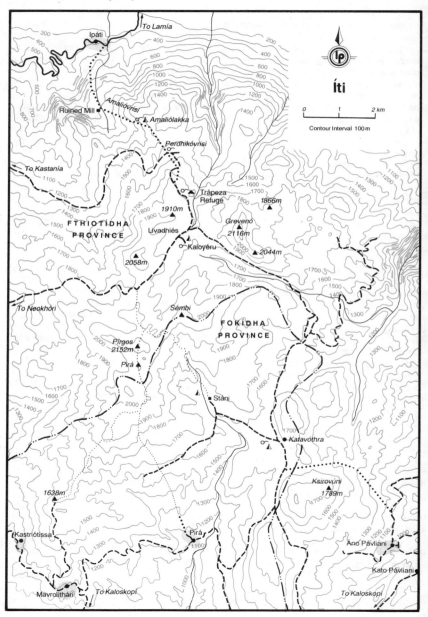

Top: Ágrafa: Crossing the Kustésas stream, between Vrangianá and Trováto (MC)
Left: Ágrafa: Curious sheep, Latómika ravine, below Valári village (MC)
Right: Ágrafa: Wobbly plank bridge below Trídhendhro village (MC)

Top: North Píndhos: The Pírgi (towers) of Astráka, above Mikró Pápingo (MD)
Bottom: North Píndhos: Morning view of Gamíla as seen from Smólikas (MD)

Stage 2: Trápeza Refuge to Anó Pávliani via Pírgos Peak

(6¼ hours)

From Trápeza, walk 25 minutes up the road to the grassy Livadhíes highland that surrounds most of Iti's major peaks, keeping a stream to your left, and then bear right at a fork in the vicinity of two weedy ponds. Pírgos, the official 2152-metre summit of the range, is sandwiched by two lesser heights, and while directly in front of you is still some km distant.

Some 20 minutes past the little ponds, a sign marks a side route going left to the Kaloyéru spring and picnic area (camping feasible); after perhaps pausing for water, continue along the main track in the signposted direction of Neokhóri village. Half an hour beyond Kaloyéru the road broaches a high saddle (1950 metres), from which a small stáni is visible below and to the left; Pírgos and its satellites hover just to the south.

Leave the road here for an easy 45-minute cross-country lope, occasionally on shepherds' traces, to the base of the peak; there's a final puddle-spring about 15 minutes past the saddle. A quarter of an hour's scrambling covers the distance from the foot of the summit to the trig point, which you should reach no more than 2½ hours after leaving the Trápeza refuge. In clear weather you can glimpse many of the important peaks of the Stereá deployed from south-east to south-west, but under most circumstances the distinctive cone of Gióna and the jagged crenellations of Vardhúsia further west are the most prominent.

Pirá, Hercules' reputed final resting place, is the next peak south of Pírgos; from there it's a three-hour walk to the villages of Pirá or Mavrolithári at the southern edge of the range. For Mavrolithári, keep to the faint paths just below the ridge line and resist the temptation to lose altitude into the tempting valleys east of the summit zone; for Pirá you will have to pick your way down, mostly cross-country, over partly forested slopes, avoiding a drop to the left. The principal problem with descending to either of these places are the marginal facilities and poor bus services out.

Most trekkers will prefer to drop down into the territory east of Pírgos, initially using the saddle between it and neighbouring Sémbi (2086 metres). Then a steep, virtually trail-less descent leads to a meadow with some tracks, plainly visible from above. One hour below Pírgos, you should pass a stáni tenanted by some shepherds from Mavrolithári; you will probably make their acquaintance, since their dogs are not easily deterred.

Just below the sheepfold a large road and a watercourse intersect your track; turn left. Tramping 45 minutes further brings you to a vast, flat expanse distinguished only by a trough-spring on the right. An incline on the left slopes down to Katavóthra ('the Swallow-Hole'), a deep natural drain at the base of a prominent cliff ahead and the exit point for all water on this plain. Some locals refer to the entire plateau here as Katavóthra; the hole itself (1540 metres) lies just the other side of an important forest road which runs north to the left fork you passed just south of Trápeza.

Turn right (south) onto the forest road and proceed about 10 minutes to a conspicuous rise. On your left (east) you'll see the faint beginnings of a trail which threads its way between the hill above Katavóthera and 1789-metre Ksirovúni. After a 90-minute descent along this trail, mostly through forest that's an antidote to the duller parts of the day's walk, you'll arrive in Áno Pávliani (1050 metres), an attractive village set among firs and apple orchards. Totting up the elapsed walking time from Trápeza to here gives a total of just over six hours.

When I was last there, the villagers seemed rather indifferent to outsiders, and it took some time to flush out lodgings above the Grill Morgonis in Káto Pávliani, one km below. Things may have improved with the opening of a mountaineers' lodge by Fivos, an excursion club in Athens (☎ (01) 32 34 461 for reservation information).

Gióna

The striking topography and landscapes of Gióna ('John's Peak', in Albanian) live up to its statistical promise as the highest peak (2510 metres) of the Stereá. It is an extensive range as well as a high one, reaching south almost to Ámfissa and the Kórinthos gulf, and north nearly to Íti. A low pass separates it from Parnassós on the east, but to the west Gióna drops precipitously in a series of huge cliffs to the Mórnos river valley, on the other side of which sprouts the Vardhúsia massif.

Until recent years the mountain's wildness matched its size and ruggedness, but lately the bauxite mining cartel hereabouts has expanded its operations from the northeastern quadrant of the mountain to disfigure most of Gióna with roads and tailings. Environmentalists and mountaineers have protested vigorously, proposing a national park to protect the remaining unspoiled areas, but so far to no avail; the mining interests (partly French-owned, it seems) are too powerful, and however many (or few) jobs they create are badly needed in the depressed local economy.

Thus far, however, these activities are not obvious along most of the recommended traverse, though this could change rapidly, as there seems no limit (other than a fall in the global price of bauxite) to the aluminium company's appetite.

TRAVERSE VIA VATHÍA LÁKKA

The highlights of Gióna remain the Lazórema canyon and the Pláka cliffs above Sikiá; the view west from the summit ridge atop those same palisades over the Mórnos valley; and a passage through the Rekká ravine, a 10-km gravel-floored chute between beetling cliffs.

There are said to be wild goats on the crest, if the miners' heavy machinery hasn't scared them away by now. The vegetation and landforms at the top of Lazórema ravine hold their own with the best in Greece, and despite Gióna's limestone strata, spring water is more plentiful in the alpine zones than lower down. The air is dry, however, and you'll probably use up half a stick of lip balm.

Rating & Duration

The recommended traverse in either direction takes two days; I'd suggest doing it as described, since the Rekká ravine would be extremely tiresome to ascend. Because of the sharp altitude changes and the often rough walking surfaces, the trek carries a strenuous rating.

Season

Midsummer is clear but quite hot.

Supplies

Get these, in order of preference, in Ámfissa, Lidhoríki, Sikiá or Kaloskopí.

Maps

Korfes 63-64, or YIS 1:50,000 *Lidhoríkion* and *Ámfissa*.

Access

Kaloskopí Trekkers continuing from Íti must somehow cover the 10 road km between Pávliani and the village of Kaloskopí (Kukuvítsa), and if possible a bit beyond. There is no bus service between the two communities, but three mornings a week (Monday, Thursday and Saturday at last look) the bus connecting Pávliani, Pirá and Mavrolithári can take you halfway, to the turn-off south for Kaloskopí. In the early morning you can often get a lift from the bauxite ore trucks that rumble up the northern flank of Gióna to within a reasonable distance of the actual trailhead above Kaloskopí. In any case try to avoid the hot, dusty and flyblown two-hour-plus walk – money for a taxi is well spent.

Kaloskopí is not much to write home about, though recently an inn (☎ (0265) 91 518) and a taverna have opened to supplement the pair of small magaziá which always existed.

Víniani Víniani (Káto Prosílio) is the closest habitation to the mouth of the Rekká ravine, but from the trekker's point of view is not terribly well appointed: no formal restaurant or lodging, a limited range of tinned goods in the magazí, and mediocre bus connections (7 am to Ámfissa, 1.15 pm return). Those interested in hiking up (rather than down) Rekká should hire a taxi in Ámfissa for the 17-km trip, since arriving with the afternoon bus will not allow you enough time to reach the alpine zone and the best campsites before dark. Alternatively, you can spend the night at more attractive but less convenient Prosílio (Sigdhítsa), 1½ km south-west,

where there are rooms in a private house and a summer taverna.

Sikiá Seventeen km up the Mórnos valley from Lidhoríki, Sikiá (Sikéa) is perhaps the most popular jumping-off point for expeditions up the mountain, but it too leaves a bit to be desired from the practical standpoint: while there are two tavernas and a small magazí, there is no longer an inn, and you're reduced to begging permission to sack out in the school (☎ (0266) 22 009 for the community office). You can camp a short distance

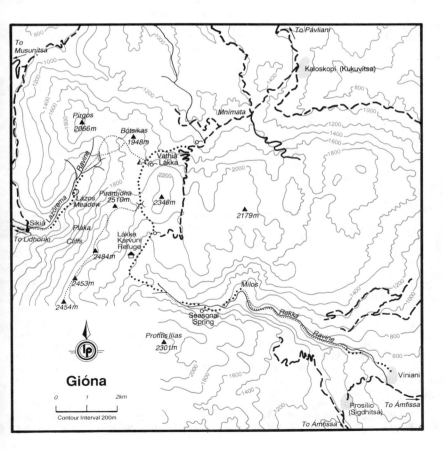

Gióna

0   1   2km

Contour Interval 200m

up the Lazórema, on a terrace near the aqueduct. Furthermore, there is a bus service to/from Lidhoríki only two or three times weekly, depending on the whim of the KTEL.

Stage 1A: Kaloskopí to Vathiá Lákka
(4 hours)

The following will really be of interest only to those who are coming directly off Íti. The route as described still existed at last check a few years ago, but it is quite likely that you'll soon find bulldozer tracks pushed all the way up to Vathiá Lákka.

By foot or (better) taxi, take the uppermost of two dirt roads leading south-south-west out of Kaloskopí (1100 metres); after about 30 minutes or two km you'll reach a triple junction at 1300 metres. Ignore the options bearing hard left or doubling back to the right; on a placard erected by the bauxite company, a rusty, barely discernable arrow accompanied by the legend 'Giónas' points toward the correct turning at about 'two o'clock'. If you manage to hitch with an ore truck you'll probably be set down here, as most turn left.

About 1¼ hours past this sign, or just under two hours on foot out of Kaloskopí, the forest road becomes impassable to vehicles in the vicinity of an unreliable concrete-trough spring. A taxi would leave you at a turnaround just before the dry spring (there may be some beehives here); the entire area between the first junction and here is known as Mnímata. Five minutes beyond, a healthy spring burbles out onto the track, which dwindles hereafter to a chaos of boulders, branches, animal tracks and manure until, 2½ hours above Kaloskopí, you come upon a giant pit in which snow persists until late summer.

A few minutes above the snow hole, do not follow a switchback left or east, but bear right onto an apparent dead end. Almost immediately, red dashes in the trees above you to the left mark the start of the foot track (1400 metres). The worst climbing is over after 30 minutes along the trail, and the aptly-named Piramídha summit of Gióna pops into

sight. Next tackle an inclined pasture crisscrossed by rivulets, and a bit less than four hours from Kaloskopí you'll pass the last spring on this approach, at just under 1900 metres.

Within another 15 minutes you'll arrive at Vathiá Lákka, a 1950-metre-high level pasture at the base of Piramídha, eminently suitable for camping as long as you avoid the thousands of sheep turds. A low hogback on the west divides the plateau from the top of Lazórema (see next section); from here you can watch moody sunsets and sunrises on the jagged contours of Vardhúsia across the Mórnos valley.

Stage 1B: Sikiá to Vathiá Lákka via Lazórema
(4 hours)

The way from Sikiá begins from the car park at the north end of the village (750 metres); simply turn up into the ravine coming in from the north-east. Soon you should be up on the south-eastern (true left) bank, walking parallel to an aqueduct. You might want to retrieve some water from it.

About half an hour along you face the first hard grade of scree; once atop this the trail continues on the same bank of the gully, emerging in the wonderful Lázos meadow at about 1100 metres. The palisades of Gióna tower more than 1000 metres above you to the right, while lower down firs are dotted about like live Christmas trees. It is a wonderful spot to linger in.

Near the top of the meadow, some 90 minutes out of Sikiá, another stream comes in from the north-west at about 1200 metres; this is the last reliable water until you reach Vathiá Lákka. This is also the last you'll see of a decent path. From here on it's simply a matter of creeping up the main drainage, first north and later north-east, to the saddle above you which runs from 2066-metre Pírgos through 1948-metre Bótsikas and merges with the low ridge at the western edge of Vathiá Lákka.

This is a two-hour-plus process, much of it on loose scree that slows you down considerably; the confining valley, however, makes it difficult to go badly astray – just stick to the watercourse if in doubt. Finally, you'll reach a small corral; up and over the lip just beyond lies Vathiá Lákka, four hiking hours above Sikiá.

Stage 2: Vathiá Lákka to Víniani via Piramídha & Rekká

(6¼ hours)

Facing Piramídha from Vathiá Lákka, you'll notice a saddle to the left (south-east); it takes about 45 minutes, assisted by waymarks on a faint trail, to cover the distance to this pass (2200 metres). From it you can spy the head of the Rekká ravine and the Gióna alpine hut at Lákka Karvúni hundreds of metres below; beyond them, the partly forested outline of 2301-metre Profítis Ilías closes the southern horizon. To the right, the main crest of Gióna, half a dozen summits in all, culminates in Piramídha, the northernmost and closest to your vantage point.

Another 45-minute trail-less scramble brings you to the graffiti-embellished trig point. Beyond the peak, the western face of Gióna forms sheer walls that plunge dizzyingly into the canyon carved by the Mórnos (which, dammed further down, supplies Athens with most of its water). Vardhúsia, on the far side, rises far more gradually. Sikiá is tucked out of sight unless you move slightly south along the summit ridge.

From the eastern end of the saddle at the foot of Piramídha, a faint but occasionally marked trail curls down to the level of the mountain refuge at Lákka Karvúni. Twenty minutes down, scree and steepness lessen as the route curves onto the edge of a high meadow above the valley draining off Piramídha. A red-painted 'Katafíyio' on a rock outcrop followed by red dots indicates the location of a powerful spring that surges out of a long steel pipe 10 minutes below, the last easily accessible water until Víniani.

The shelter stands some 45 minutes below the watershed at 1800 metres, but its sponsor, the Pezoporikós Ómilos Athinón (Athens Hiking Club) (☎ (01) 36 34 549), Hariláou Trikúpi 51has let it slip into disrepair; for emergencies a side stable is

permanently open. There is supposedly a spring five minutes north of the refuge, but I have never found it. Ascending from the hut to the saddle, count on a 75-minute climb; it's best to curl right, then left, in the reverse of the directions for the descent, rather than charging up the steep incline directly below the saddle.

With your back to the front door of the refuge, head for the last handful of firs at the treeline on the slopes to the right; the path to Víniani carries on there. You've a one-hour descent to the floor of Rekká: the first 20 minutes across the split upper reach of the canyon uses an adequate trail, but the balance of the hour is spent wrestling with faint double and triple parallel animal traces laden with scree. Just as you emerge onto the Rekká ravine at the point where it divides (1450 metres) you'll notice a couple of cairns, a critical landmark for those perverse enough to hike up the gorge.

After about a 15-minute march down the bone-dry gravel bed of the watercourse, a genuine trail cuts in on the left (north) bank at the point where the drainage gets jumbly and impassable. Soon it's apparent that the path was once an excellent kalderími, now much deteriorated by slides and tree falls but still generous by Greek alpine standards.

Just over 1½ hours after leaving the shelter, cross to the right (south) bank of Rekká – only stumps of a bridge remain but the drop to the ravine floor is slight. High above you, slightly further along, a spring flows at the top of a scree pile and the base of a reddish cliff, but it may stop in late summer. The two-hour mark in the descent finds you recrossing to the northern side, and within another half an hour the built-up kalderími ends just before thick water pipe sallies into the Rekká from a side canyon at 1100 metres.

The confluence of the two gorges, known as Mílos, was the site of a bloody ambush by ELAS (Greek Popular Liberation Army) guerrillas in 1942 or 1943. A company of 33 Italian soldiers had been ordered to march from the east to the west side of Gióna; a shepherd, seeing the party moving up the Rekká ravine, sped up the mountain to tip off the *andártes* (rebels), who fell on the Italians at dawn while they were still asleep.

In reprisal the Italian command ordered the burning of Prosílio, at the mouth of the gorge, thus according it the dubious distinction of being the first of several hundred Greek mountain villages to be vengefully destroyed by occupying troops during WW II. Rather than rebuild in Prosílio – which remains half inhabited today – most of the population relocated downhill to Víniani, which had been insignificant until then.

Follow the water main down Rekká away from this haunted spot; 20 to 25 minutes along the gravel bank or three hours below the refuge, oak and other scrubby trees replace fir as the primary species. Thirty minutes further on, a sharp drop in the ravine bed is marked by a rusty 'danger' sign above a bauxite tailings dump, and the preferred trail bears slightly uphill and right, following the water pipe.

After skirting the tailings, descend again to the watercourse; the walls of Rekká diminish steadily to either side, and ore cablecars swing overhead in the distance. Four-plus hours below Lákka Karvúni, the ravine ends (or begins) near a stock trough and a path on the left (north) bank, 15 minutes before Víniani.

Remember that there is no available water on the gorge floor itself; the source of the sealed aqueduct at Mílos is virtually inaccessible. Hiking up Rekká from Víniani is certainly not out of the question – this was the preferred approach to Gióna back when the mountain hut was built in 1959 – but the canyon seems to extend forever even in its best moments, and the monotony of the lower reaches, plus the sharp grade and loose surface under foot, would be pretty demoralising going uphill. At least 5½ walking hours in daylight should be allowed for safely reaching Lákka Karvúni from Víniani.

Vardhúsia

The remotest of the central Greek ranges, Vardhúsia has also the most rugged outline, something that makes it a favourite of both winter alpinists and technical climbers. Coming into Greece from northern Europe on a jet, you can often make out Vardhúsia's distinct profile poking out of the clouds. The summits are arranged in a few groups scattered around an extensive high pasture, with the foothills extending well north towards the Sperkhiós valley and south to the giant dam on the Mórnos.

Nonetheless, there is an enjoyable traverse route or two, the favourite being from east to west (or vice versa) between the villages of Artotína and Athanásios Dhiakós. The E4 long-distance trail crosses the mountain in a relatively sensible course, and you'll log some of it when piecing together itineraries, particularly the recommended day hike out of Artotína.

Rating & Duration
The preferred day hike is easy except for one steep descent from a pass, and possible cross-country work thereafter. The one-day traverse of the range between Athanásios Dhiákos and Artotína with a full pack gets a moderate grading.

Season
Vardhúsia is a slightly wetter mountain than Gióna or Párnassos – July, August and early September are good walking months, when the weather is driest.

Supplies
Get supplies in Náfpaktos, Ámfissa or Lidhoríki if possible; Artotína and Athanásios Dhiákos have a much more limited stock.

Maps
Korfes 65 or YIS 1:50,000 *Lidhoríkion*.

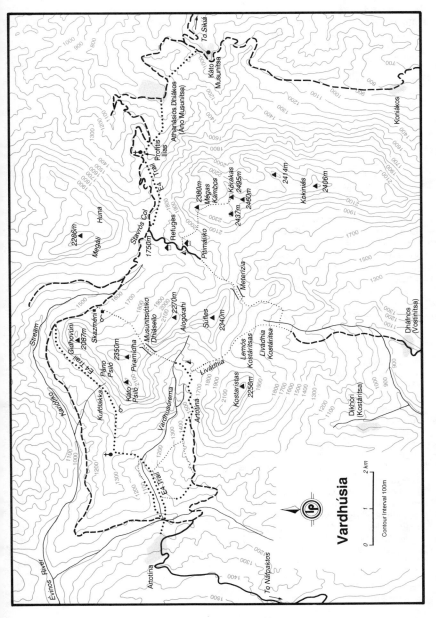

Vardhúsia

0   1   2 km

Contour Interval 100m

Access

The bus service to Athanásios Dhiákos (Áno Musunítsa) from Ámfissa/Lidhoríki is as spotty as that up to Sikiá; if you're coming down off Gióna and wish to append Vardhúsia onto your route, you may find yourself getting a taxi or walking from Sikiá. The latter is a 4½-hour business, involving a crossing of the Mórnos river and bushwhacking up the other side to Káto Musunítsa, with a proper trail only in the last 45 minutes to Áno Musunítsa.

Artotína is served by a daily (except Sunday) bus from Náfpaktos, coming up at around noon and returning the next morning – a beautiful but arduous two-hour journey.

Trek 1: Athanásios Dhiákos to Skazméni and Kórakas via Stavrós Col

Athanásios Dhiákos, so named for a revolutionary war hero supposedly born here, is known equally often by its old name of Áno Musunítsa. The village, at 1000 metres, is rather undistinguished in architecture but beautifully set in mixed forest. There's a taverna plus two inns (☎ (0265) 63 214, Ioannis Ravanis; 63 201, Kostas Mastolos), and since the place is now a popular summer resort on the E4 trail, it might be wise to phone ahead.

The E4 trail leaves Athanásios Dhiákos (Áno Musunítsa) at its south-western corner, heading west up a ravine past a water-pumping station. The path collides with the road up to the high Vardhúsian meadows about 45 minutes along, but quickly resumes from a sharp bend. After one hour 15 minutes you'll come to a clearing at just over 1400 metres, with an ikónisma dedicated to Profítis Ilías.

There follows another very brief section of dirt road, and then the trail continues off another bend right, keeping left of the twisty road for the remainder of the 2½-hour course up to Stavrós col at 1750 metres. This is an appropriate spot to orientate yourself using a map.

Two alpine refuges lie 25 and 45 minutes respectively south of the saddle (Stavros col), at Pitimáliko; the lower, smaller one is

controlled by the Athens Hiking Club (☎ (01) 36 34 549), the upper one by EOS Ámtissa (☎ (0265) 28 577). However, the refuges are badly placed for trekkers and are mostly of interest to those wanting a base for ascents of the highest peaks, which rear up evocatively to the south-west, the highest being 2495-metre Kórakas.

If you're willing to camp somewhere in the meadows to the west of the summits, you can make the three-hour return trip up to the summit of Kórakas. The classic route leads east of the higher hut at 1850 metres, up a scree pile, to the gap descriptively called Pórtes ('Doors'). Beyond is the plateau of Mégas Kámbos (2300 metres), where you'll bear left for the final push to the top.

North of Stavrós col squats the bulk of Megáli Húni (2286 metres), forming one flank of the Kariótiko ravine which exits the alpine zone to the north-west. The other bank consists of the Gidhovúni (2087 metres) and Piramídha (2350 metres), joined by a false pass. The real pass, the Musunitsiótiko Dhiásello, is further south, between them and Alogórahi (2270 metres).

At the base of all this are the scattered concrete huts of the stáni called Skazméni. The entire landscape between your vantage and Skazméni consists of grassy hummocks oozing a dozen or so springs; according to the shepherds, more than 6000 sheep are grazed here in summer by the community of Musunítsa, making it one of Greece's largest surviving pastoral areas.

Although water is plentiful, level space for camping up in these pastures is at a premium. The alternative is to plan a village- to-village traverse, or to content yourself with the day hike outlined below.

Trek 2: Day Circuit from Artotína
(8 hours)

Artotína is an attractive, surprisingly large village, whose variously styled houses are draped in tiers on an east-facing hillside at 1150 metres. The view towards the mountain is impressive, whether by moonlight (if you're lucky) or in the fading afternoon light. There are two rather basic grocery shops, two very carnivorous tavernas, and persistent rumours of an inn run by a Mr Vassilis Kotronis (though I was unable to find it, and the locals encouraged me to camp nearby).

From behind the church on the platía, drop down onto a concrete drive, making a hairpin turn right just past the public toilets. Carry on downhill for a few minutes, passing a sunken fountain on the right, then bear left 50 metres beyond. The drive quickly becomes a path with the characteristic black-on-yellow E4 waymarks.

It's 25 minutes from the church to the river below the village, at about 1000 metres. Cross on two crude plank-and-mud bridges, with the Vardhusórema coming down directly in front of you from the peaks ahead to meet your stream. The E4 trail continues behind what appears to be a dilapidated mill and some nut trees on the south bank of the Vardhusórema, not along the tempting-looking path staked out by a blue ikónisma on the north bank – if you take that one, you soon end up walking in an aqueduct.

The proper trail crosses to the north side

of the valley about 45 minutes along, climbing north-east to meet that aqueduct at about 1150 metres, one hour 15 minutes from Artotína. Once past the channel you curl north; use the E4 waymarks, since the trail is in a bad condition here. You'll emerge on a broad saddle at about 1325 metres, where there's an ikónisma dedicated to saints Konstantinos and Eleni; bear east or right. The peaks of Gidhovúni and Káto/Páno Psiló rear up in the direction of travel.

There's a weak spring just under 2½ hours out from Artotína by the narrow path, with little elevation change since the saddle. After a quarter of an hour more, leave the trees for now and cross a permanent stream at Kufólakka (1500 metres); the bare cliffs of Páno Psiló are at their closest to the route here. Another rivulet laps across the trail at about the three-hour mark, just before the north point of Gidhovúni.

Finally, three hours 20 minutes along, one of the most unspoiled portions of the mountain ends abruptly as you hit the road coming up from the Kariótiko valley. You're obliged

Vardhúsia: Súfles peaks, above Artotiná Livádhia

to follow it for about half an hour to the edge of the Skazméni uplands, where a concrete shepherd's cottage sits by a stream at 1625 metres, an E4 diamond sits on a pole, and a rock-painting proclaims 'Water/Piyí 2 minutes'. It's a good spot for lunch.

To circle back to Artotína, head up to the plainly visible Musunitsiótiko Dhiásello at 2000 metres; it's 45 minutes, mostly trailless but easy. There are views across to Kórakas, the two shelters, Stavrós col, assorted pastoral buildings, and many ugly new tracks on the far side of the highlands. You can also see your eventual destination, Artotína, plainly to the west.

That was the easy part; the descent from the pass is fairly uncomfortable, with steep scree slopes that would be worse than a nuisance with a heavy pack. It's 45 minutes again down to the 1700-metre crossing of the ravine draining off toothy, photogenic Súfles (about 2300 metres). The stáni at the Artotiná Livádhia appears a few minutes ahead, some 5½ hours out of Artotína itself.

Here a decent path resumes, exiting past a hut and a corral, dropping into another ravine whose far side is peppered with caves. Climb out of this, only to dip into yet another, beyond which a plunging rock spur of Kostáritsa peak must be circumvented; the path does this with a quick zig-zag. Rounding a bend, you'll see the end of the new road just ahead. From here, there are two choices to return to Artotína.

Take a fork right and down, cued by a cairn, some 35 minutes out of the stáni. From about 1500 metres the path gradually loses altitude, then dwindles to nothing. It's easy and humiliating to get lost here, as I did, ridiculously close to Artotína. To avoid doing the same, angle down steeply right when the trail seems to disappear, and head through the boulders and the sparse trees to link up with the E4 running along the Vardhusórema.

Staying up high results in being forced up onto the road by the terrain, which soon features a sheer bluff plunging to the desired stream. When the road bends left and south, you must go down straight into the trees at this curve, using hunters' trails to reach the Vardhusórema some 7¼ hours out. You'll be back at the mill and nut trees a half-hour later, and back in the village eight walking hours after starting off.

If you only have a day at your disposal, this is a wonderful introduction to the mountain, passing through some of its more scenic, isolated corners.

The Ágrafa

One of the remotest corners of Greece, the Ágrafa ('Unwritten Places') supposedly earned its name by successfully excluding imperial tax collectors and census takers throughout the Ottoman occupation, thus remaining a cipher on the Sultan's records.

Locals are always keen to tell visitors about feats of daring and skill during this period: Greek mountain rebels defeating legions of Turks single-handedly, or outrunning them on vertiginous paths. Although the blurring effect of intervening centuries and the noted Greek tendency to hyperbole have clearly embellished the facts – for starters, it seems that general civil disobedience and the condition of being 'unwritten' dates back to Byzantine times – the kernel of truth to these tales has maintained the locals' sense of independence, regional patriotism, and continuity in ethnic make-up.

Their prickly spirit is mentioned in Homer's Iliad, where the 'Dolopes' took an active part in the Trojan campaign; later they were invaluable in repelling the numerous invasions of the Gauls.

During WW II, these mountains of Evritanía Province were, along with those of Ípiros, the main centre of resistance to the Axis occupation and, a few years later, a stronghold of the leftist rebels. Perhaps the most gruesome reminder of these times is the plaque beneath the summit of Pláka peak which commemorates a winter night in 1947, when dozens of soldiers from both sides in the civil war froze to death; some bodies were reputedly found in a final embrace for warmth with a foe.

As in the case of the Maniots around Taïyettos, this martial valour is matched and abetted by a harsh, forbidding landscape. A montane wall nearly 2000 metres high surrounds the central Agrafiótis valley on all sides except the south, where the namesake river flows into the reservoir of Kremastón. To either side the Akhelóös and Tavropós (Mégdhovas) rivers have carved almost equally deep gorges into the mountains, making access even more difficult.

Not surprisingly, the area is still conspicuously blank on present-day road maps. Until 1971 the central Ágrafa was still inaccessible to vehicles; a fair-weather-only track led as far as Márathos village in the south, but no further. Towards the end of the junta years, roads and electricity reached the larger settlements to the north, while in the early 1980s PASOK-channelled EC funds paid for bulldozer tracks to the remotest shepherds' colonies.

Consequently, contemporary trekkers have at their disposal an extensive and intricate system of paths and kalderímia, which are only now beginning to decay. Many have been cut by roads or bulldozed out of existence, others have been destroyed by washouts and landslides and never repaired, and doubtless a few have simply been forgotten. But there remain a substantial number which are a pleasure just to tread on. Typically these worm between sheer rockfaces and roiling torrents, with a mix of lime and mud as a binding agent. Equally impressive engineering spectacles are the old arched bridges (where they have not been replaced by ferroconcrete spans); the carefully masoned and fitted stones redirect gravitational force toward the termini, keystone-fashion, to allow a strong, freestanding structure.

Recent history and culture has not been so glorious for the Agrafiots. In 1966 a severe earthquake destroyed many of the old stone houses, and in a few cases (eg Monastiráki) left entire villages uninhabitable. In response, the Greek government offered interest-free loans for the inhabitants to establish new homes in and around Alíartos, on the plain of faraway Viotía Province, where a new irrigation system had been constructed. This, in combination with the general post-war drift to the cities, led to wholesale depopulation of the area.

Nowadays, the carefully built-up infrastructure of centuries is dying a slow death. In a region known for its secret academies during the Turkish era, primary schools run out of children and close down or, as in the case of Trídhendhro, continue with three pupils. Old paths and bridges are neglected by the proud owners of 4WD vans.

Ironically, roads are still being opened to connect hamlets like Lípa, whose population will soon dwindle from single figures to nothing. Indeed the inertia of bureaucracy and grantship seem infinite; the government has recently revived plans to divert much of the flow of the upper Akhelóös river to Thessalía, inundating most of the upper Akhelóös valley with yet another redundant dam and starving its delta, though opposition from EC environmentalists and from downstream farmers/fishers who stand to lose their silt promises to be strong.

Arguably the only positive, or at least relatively harmless, contribution is from urban emigrants returning with enough money (and local pride) to build new houses, but these generally bad-taste seasonal chalets merely accentuate the sadness of the abandoned traditional dwellings.

Rating & Duration

Although the Ágrafa has been split into three traverses of roughly three days each, with five to eight hours of walking on the daily stages, none of it is very easy and some is downright strenuous or requires a good head for heights. Experienced hill and ridge walkers will be delighted.

Season

The Ágrafa is not only one of the wetter regions of Greece, but winters tend to hang on longer here than in most other places. Snow arrives in early November and stays until the end of March, though flurries until May are not unusual, and one older resident of Vrangianá remembers a snowstorm on 28 June 1928. Winter weather tends to come from the south-east, meaning that the eastern watershed is often snow-covered when the western crest is lightly dusted.

The numerous rivers are running at full spate in April, during thaw; they're kept to respectable levels by midsummer thundershowers – finding drinking water is never a problem. Accordingly your best chances of clear dry weather are, as in much of Greece, in May/June and September/October.

Supplies

Get supplies in the closest provincial capitals (Karpenísi or Kardhítsa) before setting out. Once in the Ágrafa, you cannot expect to top up with anything other than the instant coffee, two-year-old tinned meat and the occasional egg which are the standbys of the magaziá in the poorer villages.

Maps

Korfes 89, 92, 93, 95 and 96, or YIS 1:50,000 *Ágrafa. Korfes* Nos 90, 91 and 94 are *very* optional.

EASTERN RIDGE: MAVROMÁTA TO VRANGIANÁ & TAVROPÓS RESERVOIR

This spectacular and airy traverse route can be done either as a strenuous two-day hike, camping at Kamária, or as a more leisurely three-day walk, sleeping in the villages of Ágrafa and Vrangianá.

Access

Dháfni A bus leaves Karpenísi daily at 1 pm and takes you as far as Dháfni village, except on Friday when it braves the final 12 km to Mavromáta. Otherwise you can hitch or take a bus to Néa Víniani, just off the main Karpenísi-Agrínio road, and walk some or all of the way on from there, as follows.

As you leave the new settlement of Víniani on the Kerasokhóri-bound road, turn right onto a dirt track (opposite the driveway into the centre). This track, once the only link with the old village and now barely passable

on muleback, takes you directly to the tumbledown old hamlet within half an hour. After the 1966 quake, all the inhabitants moved nearer to the main road to establish the new village on flatter ground; recently a few locals have begun refurbishing their former homes, whose 30 cm-thick stone walls still stand intact. The locked but dramatically situated church is accessible on a path which curves up from the right (south).

If you follow the same track out of Paleá Víniani, a left turn takes you up to the new road in five minutes. Committed walkers keep low and right onto another abandoned and rock-strewn track, past a spring, to what you might call an X-junction. Turning sharp right brings you down to the Tavropós river, just upstream from a small gorge and an old bridge.

For Dháfni, go straight ahead down a proper dirt road for 25 minutes as far as the bed of the Gavrenítis tributary, near a sunken double-arched bridge. As you cross, look up to spot some power lines spanning the canyon here, the pride of the local power corporation engineers. The road, once again impassable for vehicles, climbs on the far bank for 45 minutes to deposit you on the new road, just before the Dháfni town limits sign. You've another 10 minutes of walking to the main square and magazí, where there's food and the possibility of a bed (☎ (0237) 31 246).

This sounds like, and is, a fairly boring bit of road-tramping, but the shortcut described saves you twice as much meandering via the new way. If there's time to spare in Dháfni you can follow the bulldozer track from just north of the village past Sotíros monastery and down to the Tavropós – about two km. Just downstream is a *karélli* or *peratária*, a fine example of the alternative Agrafiote way to cross a river. You stand or sit in a box suspended from a wire, and propel yourself from one bank to another by turning a wheel – or by paying the keeper to do so.

Stage 1: Mavromáta to Morforákhi

(5½-7 hours without sidetrips)
Leave the village (860 metres) by the church,

and follow the path uphill (west), bearing left, to a track within five minutes. Round a right-hand bend to a larger track, cross this and go straight up the bluff in front of you. A few minutes later cross the track again, and some 30 minutes out of town meet the pathfinder's nightmare: terraced fields.

Veer almost 90 degrees right, up the spine towards Kópsi peak, and enter the firs. The path and spur curve back left and take you to more terraces about an hour along – keep left (south-west) here. The path describes a large, clockwise arc with an old threshing cirque at its centre, and ends up entering the forest again just before the first stream. Half an hour's pleasant walk (nearly two hours out of Mavromáta) through firs brings you to the road again, 100 metres before the paired turn-offs to Áyios Dhimítrios and a stáni on the Yerúkos col (1570 metres).

Now that you have cleared the treeline, several short cuts (the original path) are visible between the bends. One starts just after you reach the road, crosses the gully on the right, passes a spring and rejoins the road at the col itself. It continues north straight up the slope, crossing the road once, to approach a hut and circular fence. From here, follow the road to the next saddle, from where you can survey the western watershed of the Ágrafa, and then to a third, higher saddle (1600 metres), some 2½ hours into the hike.

Sidetrip: Kópsi Peak This peak is just east, is less than an hour away. To reach it, head round the western flank of the first hump to a saddle; ignore the level path on the left and ascend the spine for a few metres before skirting the flank on a higher path. Passing a cirque, you reach the spur north of the summit in half an hour. Bear hard right and traverse to the spur west of the peak in another 10 minutes; the 1941-metre trig point stands a similar walking time to the east up a spur.

When you return to the road you'll see trails leading steeply up to and along Kafkiá ridge towards Prosiliakó (1864 metres). If you don't have a good head for heights, you'll want the easy, boring option of sticking to the road north-east of the crest here, bearing right at a fork, to the small leaky hut just before Fidhóskala.

If you prefer watersheds, be warned that the edge gets particularly sharp around the second peak (1705 metres); after you have passed it to your left, you have to take some long steps onto small, loose rubble. If you lose your nerve, there are bail-out trails to the road between each of the peaks; if you disdain them, you eventually come out safely at the 1670-metre col east of Prosiliakó.

Sidetrip: Prosiliakó Peak The summit, which dominates the village of Márathos to the west, can be reached in half an hour on a path curling around the mountain on the north side. Another, formerly important path leads south from the saddle, at first along and then to the right of a large spur, to the nearly deserted hamlet of Gávrina in about two hours.

Follow this same path (from Prosiliakó saddle) 15 minutes in the other direction down to a track above a spring; head right to a bend within 10 minutes, from where the brick-like stones of the Fidhóskala are clearly visible to the north, and veer left cross-country along the ridge until reaching the leaky hut mentioned above – about 90 minutes in all from the col below Kópsi.

However you get there, this hut (1600 metres) is always open and, despite a leaky roof, could be used as an emergency shelter. Hop left onto the crest and follow the path which twists its way upwards (Fidhóskala means 'Snake Stairs'). After climbing within half an hour to the 1700-metre contour, it levels out in a depression, with higher points – including a cairn and a 1740-metre peak – to your right. The further you proceed, the flatter the terrain and the more expansive the panorama. The most impressive skyline is to the west, where (left to right) the peaks of Liákura, Ftéri, Korúna, Pláka, Sínoro, Korífi and Delidhími form a serrated silhouette.

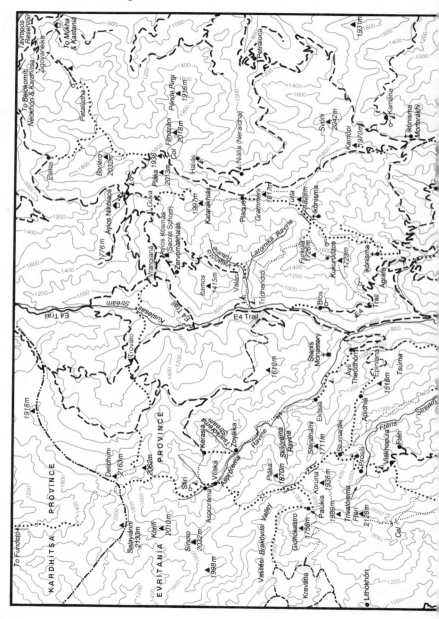

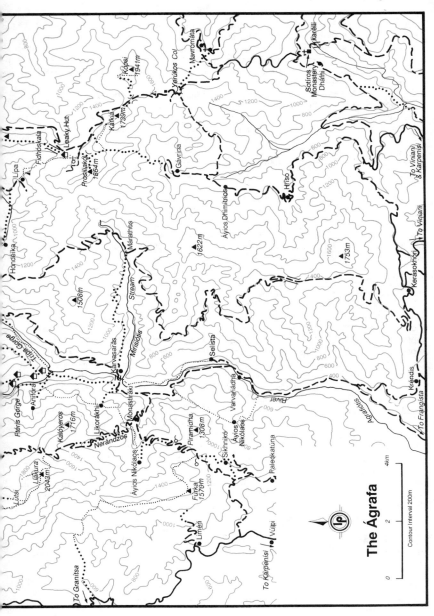

The Ágrafa

Contour Interval 200m

0   2   4km

About one hour beyond the hut, descend to meet the road again by Morforákhi, at about 1680 metres; 500 metres in front of you is a triple junction, near an ikónisma also called Morforákhi. Those without full gear should turn left to Ágrafa village (10 km of road-walking, 2½ hours), though you could also have arrived there by trail from the hut south of Fidhóskala – see the Fidhóskala to Ágrafa-via-Lípa route decribed later in this section.

Campers should bear right towards Kamária hamlet (two km, 30 minutes); this is half a dozen or so shacks at about 1500 metres, seasonally inhabited by shepherds, around a single tree in an otherwise bare landscape. There is a spring, but little else for the traveller. You should budget a total of 5½ hours or 6¾ hours walking time from Mavromáta, depending on whether or not you ridge-walk at Kafkiá and Prosiliakó.

Sidetrip: Svóni Peak The pointed peak to the north, Svóni (also called Maráthia, 2042 metres) can be climbed fairly easily from the south-east, starting at the saddle on the Kamária to Kardhítsa track, about 1500 metres from Kamária. It's an hour of careful work along, or just right of the ridge up to the 2042-metre summit, highest point on the eastern ridge. If visiblity is poor, beware of the sharp drop beyond the trig point – there's nothing but 1000 metres of air between you and a river valley to the north-west!

Stage 2A: Morforákhi to Vrangianá
(5¼ hours without sidetrips)

To reach Vrangianá, continue initially straight along the ridge from Morforákhi ikónisma, cutting the switchbacks of the dirt road as it ascends the slopes of Karnópi. On the way you'll pass the remains of a fort built during the civil war by the royalist government to oppose guerrilla movement hereabouts. An hour along, at about 1900 metres up, the road switches to the western flanks of the mountain, and it's worth the extra effort involved in forsaking it for the 1970-metre peak and the chance to follow the ridge. Cross the road again after half an

hour more and stay on the ridge. Dodge the relatively minor knobs of Túrla and Gramméni on their right, then skim the road again 2¼ hours along. A trail from Ágrafa village comes in behind you to the left here.

Sidetrip: Sarakatsan Stánes At this point, in good weather and with an early start, you may want to detour east a bit to visit the Sarakatsan stánes of Niálla (Neraïdha) and Haliás, east of the road, though this will involve a considerable altitude loss since both are at about 1500 metres. Whether this is worth it to you depends on the appeal of vernacular stone architecture; the eight sturdy houses and church of Niálla are certainly more impressive than anything at Kamária. Haliás is much the same, and either one makes a wonderful campsite, though too far from Mavromáta to be reached in any but the longest summer days.

The next summit is the more formidable Katarakhiás (1997 metres), with stomach-twinging drops to the west. From the road, zig-zag up the spine on goat traces to the trig point (another hour); the north-western peak group is separated from you by an unbridgeable bite out of the crest. The descent is best made by following a spur initially east, and then north-east, as far as the first col (1850 metres, 25 minutes from the top). This point is also accessible via a grid of goat trails skirting the eastern slopes and passing some soggy spots in the turf, courtesy of trickles.

Now you can descend, more or less directly, to Vrangianá. A path picks its way north-east, down a boulder field towards a hump within a quarter of an hour. A more prominent path descends left to a small plateau, though the right-hand option around the hump (which becomes progressively pointier as you pass it) is faster. The two trails link up, and the joint path heads due north, dropping rapidly to a dirt track at about 1500 metres just over an hour from Katarakhiás summit.

Turn left on the track, taking it to the end at Gúva, where there's a tidy white hut. Here a path drops 200 metres in altitude, along the north-eastern bank of the gully, before intersecting the upper Valári-Vrangianá road. A side turning from this, continuing down the ravine, brings you to the bottom end of Vrangianá some 90 minutes below Gúva, and 5¼ hours from Morforákhi/Kamária.

Though virtually deserted now, Vrangianá (1000 metres) was a thriving metropolis with 3000 residents three centuries ago, with a secret school for imparting Greek language and culture; a clutch of churches date from the same period. There are a couple of magaziá – at the one run by Mr Alexakis (☎ (0441) 93 380) you can eat and make arrangements to sleep in the spartan school rooms; at the other (☎ (0441) 93 391), 500 metres up the road, Takis Christou has unusually detailed and accurate information on local paths and tracks.

There is, however, no bus service; the closest link (to Kardhítsa) is from the village of Neokhóri, a good 20 km away.

Stage 2B: Morforákhi to the Tavropós Reservoir

(6½-7 hours)
Instead of heading to Vrangianá, you can follow the eastern Ágrafa crest beyond Katarakhiás as far as the reservoir on the Tavropós river. Follow the initial Stage 2A directions but, instead of ascending Katarakhiás, keep on the road when you skirt it past Gramméni for about three km, curving over a col around Point 1938 of Pláka. Where the road begins wiggling north-east towards Áyios Nikólaos saddle, above Vrangianá, adopt a path heading north off the bend, just left of the ridge leading up to Borléro peak (2032 metres).

After 25 minutes, change to the other side of the ridge (this is the best jumping-off point for a peak-bagging trip to the summit, allow 90 minutes) and skirt the top of a beech forest on the eastern flank. Another 15 minutes takes you to the beginning of a large scree patch that's much easier to traverse than it first appears. Within 75 minutes of leaving the road you'll intersect the eastern spur of the distinctive Borléro pyramid and follow it for 10 minutes more down to its lowest point.

Here another path to the left leads along the 1600-metre contour to the saddle north of the summit, and then steeply (but clearly) down to the summer hamlet of Élatos on the Vrangianá to Belokomíti road.

To reach the Tavropós reservoir, ignore the path to Élatos and follow the ridge east through thick stands of beech, past a natural boulder archway and onto a grassy corridor between rock walls. In summer this habitat is buzzing with small animal life and brimming with wild herbs, and there are excellent views of Flindzáni (Kalívia, 2018 metres) and Pénde Pírgi to the south. Half an hour from the trail division you'll drop to the col just south of Petalúdha knoll at about 1750 metres. Turn right (east) and keep to the northern bank of the gully; the tracery of paths sliding down right leads to some possible springs and a grazing patch for cows.

Within another 25 minutes the trail bears sharp left at the first stunted trees, and then comes to a fork. Right (and down) takes you through thick bracken to the beginning of a track in 15 minutes; left (and slightly up) leads through thick grass to a reliable spring in 10 minutes, and then east for the same amount of time to the same track. This is impassable for ordinary vehicles, but makes a relatively pleasant hour's walk past Zigoyanéika hamlet to the main road around the reservoir. Allow an elapsed hiking time from the vicinity of Morforákhi of 9¼ hours – something to attempt in one go only in the weeks either side of the summer solstice.

Neokhóri, with its bus connections, is about five km to your left. The dam (800 metres) is three km in the opposite direction (right or south-east), with as much distance again to Múkha village, where there is a magazí and rather expensive accommodation (☎ (0441 (94 074). Kastaniá village, with more buses (and asphalt) back to Kardhítsa, lies five km east of Múkha.

If the idea of a swim at this stage appeals, follow the track leading north from the edge of the village (by the school gate). Pass a small branch left, and take the second, larger one, which brings you to the reservoir shore in 20 minutes.

The leg between the reservoir and the eastern crest of Ágrafa is most worth considering in reverse (ie uphill), as a way of getting quickly to grips with the centre of the region without the long slog up from Karpenísi. Coming from the dam, the stánes of Haliás or Niálla described as sidetrips from Stage 2A are perfectly placed for your first night's camp.

AGRAFIÓTIS VALLEY: MONASTIRÁKI TO TROVÁTO

If you're torn between doing the eastern ridge route to Vrangianá described previously and the Agrafiótis river route described here, you might consider reversing the following directions to do both. (A link route between Fidhóskala and Ágrafa is described later, immediately after Stage 1.) Certainly you'll gain a more complete picture of the region, and have the possible advantage of being able to store extra gear in Karpenísi.

Access

Monastiráki If you don't have a car, the only reliable way to reach Monastiráki is on foot. There are two approach tracks: one from Kréndis village (daily bus from Karpenísi at 1 pm) and one from the Karpenísi to Granítsa road near Vúlpi (daily buses along it at 5 am and 1 pm).

The first is longer (about 20 km) but offers a greater chance of a lift, at least as far as Varvariádha. Once there, you can walk the final distance to Monastiráki in one of two relatively pleasant fashions. Beyond Selísta, the hamlet one km beyond Varvariádha on the east bank of the Agrafiótis river, a narrow trail leads 2½ km upriver to a point opposite a ravine carrying the road up to Monastiráki; cross the Agrafiótis and make your way uphill using the short cuts mentioned in the description of Stage 1.

Alternatively, a path about 750 metres before Varvariádha leads west from the road and up a ravine to the hamlet of Áyios Nikólaos, and then down to the river road south of the side ravine to Monastiráki – rather roundabout, but if your ride sets you

down before Varvariádha, actually not much longer than tramping the road from there.

The second side road starts from between Vúlpi and Liméri, passes above Sikhnikó (Kefalóvrisi) hamlet, crosses the 1150-metre pass between Fúrka and Piramídha peaks, and then descends (an old path provides short cuts) to Monastiráki village after 10 km.

Monastiráki Village

Monastiráki (750 metres) was once a thriving community of 500 people, but of all the Ágrafa villages suffered the most from the 1966 quake. Many houses lost their wood-and-tile roofs, replaced by ugly corrugated iron sheets. Now the village has shrunk to a dozen permanent families; the rest have moved to either Aliártos or the USA. In mid-August the streets resound to the twang of Americanised voices belonging to relatives who have returned for the summer and whose children, born abroad, can only speak pidgin Greek with their grandparents.

One of the hold-outs, 82-year-old Maria Bakoyianni, rebuilt her house single-handedly and claims to have carried the entire structure in pieces on her back from the end of the road to its site on the hill near the new church. Faced with such hardships, it is little wonder that 90% of the population opted for emigration.

Luckily the remaining 10% are hospitable and enterprising enough to keep the village functioning and accommodate passing guests. To be sure, ring Maria or her husband Hristos (the mayor) on the communal phone (☎ (0237) 98 263), especially if your are planning to stay long or come in droves. As ever in the Ágrafa, bring any special foods with you – there's only the most basic stuff here.

Sidetrips: Around Monastiráki

Near Monastiráki is a group of year-round waterfalls, whose distant roar accompanies your every step in the village. Even in August their waters, spewing straight out of the rocks, are too icy to suggest a dip; in winter, strangely enough, their temperature rises enough to make bathing a remote possibility. To reach them, either follow the bulldozer track west out of the village and walk upstream from the ford, or take the kalderími up from the magazí and branch left onto an aqueduct after a couple of minutes.

The kalderími, incidently, ends up on the dirt road to Ftéri village, joining it at the large bell of the unlocked but windowless church of the Panayía. You can follow the road north-north-west, cutting across the switchbacks on the old path through dense oak woods, to broach the shoulder of the Nerándzos spur after 90 minutes and the 1600-metre col west of Liákura an hour later. For more instructions on the western crest of Ágrafa see the Western Ridge: Trováto or Epinianá to Monastiráki later in this chapter.

If Monastiráki is too big and busy for your tastes, you can visit the even more ghostly hamlet of Áyios Nikólaos to the west: only one house out of 30 or so is still inhabited (or indeed habitable). For an hour-long roundtrip, follow the old aqueduct (conspicuous on the rockface opposite Monastiráki) and return by the path. The aqueduct, now abandoned, was once a focus of communal life; every spring, after snowmelt, everyone from the youngest child to the oldest granny would take take a few days off work or school to help repair the channel, forming human chains over a km long back to the village centre.

To intersect it, turn left off the cobbled path to the Ftéri road, some five minutes above the magazí. After crossing the stream above the waterfalls, the channel maintains a level southward course across the steep slope above the village before rounding the corner. At times you have to walk inside the aqueduct, stooping slightly to avoid banging your head on the overhanging cliff. The best-preserved houses are above the end of the conduit.

The return path starts from the lowest house on the southern slopes of the valley containing Áyios Nikólaos, and takes you to the road bridge over the stream; taking right forks would take you up to the old Monastiráki-Sikhnikó path, which you may have become acquainted with as a means of arrival in Monastiráki.

A final possible day excursion involves taking the old trail north-east out of Monastiráki via Likorákhi on a winding course down to the Agrafiótis river at the bridge of Karvasarás (apparently a corruption of caravanserai). This trail is probably too dilapidated to drag a full pack over, but it's OK in at least one direction to this point. Once across the streambed and beyond Karvasarás (all of a dozen cottages at just under 500 metres), a path leads up the Mirisiótis stream to Márathos village (800 metres) within two hours. Return to Monastiráki via the same route.

Stage 1: Monastiráki to Ágrafa via the Trípa Gorge

To reach the Agrafiótis valley from Monástiráki with a full pack, you can eliminate the uppermost switchbacks on the road down to Varvariádha by taking the old path. From the magazí, follow the road about 10 metres south and turn left onto the cobbled path by a water tap. As you clear the edge of the village, keep left past some terraces. After 15 minutes another left fork gets you to the second hairpin; the right fork crosses more terraces and half-collapsed houses to the bottom curve in 10 more minutes. The road is the only choice for the last 800 metres through the narrow cleft to the riverside road (480 metres) from Varvariádha to the upstream villages.

Turn left onto this, passing a waterfall tucked away in an enclosure to your left, to where a steep valley comes in on the left at a right-hand bend of the Agrafiótis (about one km along the valley road and 800 metres before the Karvasarás bridge). Walk north-west up the little tributary past a well-camouflaged sheepfold, keeping to the north-eastern bank. After a few moments a path materialises, twisting its way steeply up through oaks, to curl back east to an outcrop 100 metres above the river within 15 minutes.

Beyond this point the path passes alternately through oak forest and open scree, keeping 100 to 150 metres above the west bank of the Agrafiótis. Occasionally the old masonry is visible, but in other areas (particularly at large scree slopes) it has slid out of existence, and demands careful footwork. Being still the sole link between Anifóra hamlet and the vehicle road, it should always be passable, but in summer, when a bulldozer track runs alongside the Agrafiótis, the upper path may become obstructed – check locally before setting out.

About one hour after leaving the road you'll start the descent towards the river again from a shrine on a grassy bluff. Fifteen minutes later you reach some ruined houses and the old bridge crossing the Ftéris stream at about 500 metres. This bridge was an important junction in former times.

A very enticing but badly crumbled path leads up alongside the Ftéris stream, passing some spectacular waterfalls on the left, to the mouth of an extremely narrow gorge in half an hour. This cleft, while not as 'subterranean' as the Fónissa gorge on Mt Zíria (see the Pelopónnisos), is no less dramatic and inaccessible. From July to October you can wade, swim and scramble your way through the chilly water to where the canyon broadens out about 200 metres upstream; those who cannot bear retracing their steps should continue another two km until the concrete bridge mentioned later in this stage, to make a four-hour loop via Anifóra village.

A second, higher path winds prominently up the salient to the highest houses of Anifóra (Tsilísta) within an hour; turning left five minutes above the last house, you can continue past the saddle to another fork, 80 minutes above the old bridge. The right-hand option passes a threshing cirque, winds up a terraced gully and reaches Stúrnaraki hamlet (see Western Ridge) in another three hours.

The left-hand path drops to cross the same gully 50 metres lower down, curls around a rocky spine adorned with a shrine, and jolts down a boulder field to a concrete bridge over the Ftéris stream, one hour out of Anifóra. Originally this was a well-trodden route connecting Anifóra with Ftéri village, but the remaining section up the latter is now

badly overgrown with the bracken (ftéri) which gives the place its name.

Yet a third trail branches right off the Anifóra path to take you to a worrying 200-metre-high wall of rock to Epinianá village. This serves as a good bail-out if the main Tripa Gorge is impassable because of high water. The route starts about 200 metres after the first inhabited house of Anifóra, next to two ruined huts. Turning right, you climb steeply through stands of oak for half an hour, before reaching some more dilapidated houses and terraces. Looking up to the north-east you get your first glimpse of a hut on the skyline, nearly 300 metres above you, where the path finally levels out. Fix this hut in your sights and attack the rocky spine slightly left of dead ahead on a zig-zagging kalderími; the views back from the top merit the hour's stiff climb. Now the path maintains its 1000-metre altitude through forests and fields, passing a walled spring after an hour, to the end of a dirt road one km south of Epinianá. From the old bridge below Anifóra to Epinianá itself, allow a good four hours.

To reach the Trípa ('Gap') Gorge of the Agrafiótis, follow the river upstream past tempting pools and boulders tumbled down from the road, which follows the eastern bank north of Karvarsarás. Even in summer, when the rough jeep track is opened next to the river, the going is slow and you should allow a good hour for the two-km stretch to the Trípa. Suddenly the canyon narrows to a few metres wide, and you are forced to walk in the river, avoiding the main current, for about 200 metres. The water levels is likely to be chest high in April, waist high in June, and knee high by September. Budget 15 minutes for this short passage, not least for the time taken to marvel at the beauty and luxuriant greenery. Waterfalls pour through flower-flecked moss, while frogs and fish dart out of your way. Halfway along you'll see tunnels bored in the walls overhead; these were part of a hydroelectric installation which thankfully (and typically) was never finished.

Once clear of the Trípa, continue upstream for 500 metres, keeping on the eastern bank.

At a group of poplars before a right curve, a path leads steeply up and right before running parallel to the river 50 metres above it. Half an hour from the Trípa you'll pass a steeply descending creek, where the path deteriorates. At a larger stream five minutes beyond, you are best off scrambling 10 minutes up the gully to the Trídhendhro-Ágrafa-Varvariádha road junction. Ágrafa village lies three km along the uppermost road (Epinianá is a bit further on the lower road).

Ágrafa sits on a small plateau at about 850 metres, bathed in the sound of rushing water and surrounded by the peaks of the eastern ridge and its outriders Kukurúdzos and Prosiliakó. Thanks to its strategic position and such rare facilities as a post office, reliable telephone and officially rented rooms (☎ (0237) 61 009), but no hot water, it makes a good base for exploring the surrounding wilderness.

In addition to the nearby gorges of the Agrafiótis, Ftéris and Asprórema streams, there are two paths to the eastern summits. The stages of ridge-walking thus covered can be done either as individual day trips using different ascent and descent routes, or strung together in a two-day hike involving an overnight stay at Kamária or Niálla.

Sidetrip: From Ágrafa to Eastern Ridge via Kukurúdzos

(4 hours)

This is the easiest of the spectacular approaches to the eastern ridge, and arguably the most beautiful stretch of path in the entire Ágrafa. At the post office, continue east on a trail parallel to the road's direction until rejoining the latter. Follow that to 100 metres beyond a bright white shrine, turn left onto a rubble-strewn track, and follow this until it fizzles out next to a conduit. This point is also reachable by following the path which skirts the upper margins of the village from above the platía; either way it takes 10 minutes.

From here the trail zig-zags up the hogback, repeatedly crossing the aqueduct, to a church on a grassy clearing overlooking Ágrafa. Another five minutes alongside the aqueduct brings you to an ikónisma built atop the torrent; a path on the left takes you back to the western extremity of the village. Follow the water uphill for another 15 minutes to a fork in front of a wire fence; bear left here. The right-hand option follows the aqueduct for another 45 minutes or so before ending near some cottages.

The trail climbs gently up the eastern flank of Kukurúdzos ('Corn Cob' in Turkish and certain Slavic dialects) to a spring at about 1300 metres, some 90 minutes along. You are now actually in the lee of Furkúla peak, and the path veers north-east to skirt a 1530-metre spur and come out, just under two hours into the day, on a saddle between it and Túrla summit, where there is an ikónisma.

Here you've a choice of onward routes. Making a hairpin left onto a westerly path takes you alongside the spur leading to Furkúla as far as an earthy saddle, with three sides of a low rectangular shelter remaining. Follow the now-narrow path along the south-east flanks of Furkúla, and up to the lowest point on the ridge between that peak and Kukurúdzos, just below a stone hut. Here, 45 minutes from the ikónisma mentioned above, you can pursue a cross-country course to Kukurúdzos, eventually dropping south-west to a road at a point about 1500 metres north-east of Ágrafa. Because of the surface underfoot and the extra distance, you'll need more than four hours to complete this loop.

For longer circuits, proceed on the main path east-north-east from the ikónisma, just left of the saddle; after five minutes you cross onto the southern side and then curl back north to a spring with some wooden troughs, within as much time again. Just above the spring there's another junction: keeping left (north), a clear path traverses the ridge of Gramméni to intersect the watershed and its road in 1¼ hour, or nearly four hours out of Ágrafa.

Turning right (east-south-east), another trail skirts the southern base of Túrla and ends up just east of this summit within an hour, on the crest route discussed earlier in the Morforákhi to Vrangianá route description. This path is fine as far as the foot of some rocky outcrops roughly halfway along, after which it narrows and clings to ledges before meeting a small bluff pointing south-west within 15 minutes.

It zig-zags messily up this spur for five minutes, then skates north-north-east to a col east of Túrla, another landmark on the eastern ridge traverse.

Link Trail: Fidhóskala to Ágrafa via Lípa

(4½ hours downhill)

This route links the eastern ridge with the Agrafiótis valley, but it could also form part of a day hike up from Ágrafa village.

From the leaky hut at 1600 metres just south of Fidhóskala (see the Mavromáta to Morforákhi route description), head south for five minutes along the ridge to a dirt track, which you follow right for 10 minutes to just above a concrete spring. Drop down to this and descend on the ridge to the right (east) of the left-most stream visible, then cross the watercourse and adopt the left bank until broaching the forest just over half an hour below the spring.

Within another quarter of an hour cross a clearing and wind down to the stony bed of the stream. After another few minutes through plane trees and more forest you'll reach a gate and the edge of Lípa hamlet (1100 metres), an hour below the ridge spring.

Only one windowless but sturdy house remains, on a high terrace to your left. Follow the right-hand edge of the terraces for five minutes, cross an aqueduct and again zig-zag down to the stream bed. A few metres beyond this is crossed by the dirt road to Gavrolisiádha (one km) and Ágrafa (seven km).

Turn right onto this, a far as the first spur (15 minutes); when the road curves north-north-east, go west straight along the spur, past some ruined houses. This route later narrows so much that locals call it the *sírma* (wire). After five minutes the ridge comes to an abrupt edge; leave it on your left to follow the steep path down west-south-west. Within

15 minutes more you'll come to another ruin, just before the confluence of your stream and one coming down from Gavrolisiádha. The path bears right above some terraces and brings you down to the tributary at 900 metres in five minutes, or just under two hours below the eastern ridge.

From here you are well-placed to explore the gorge below – it is apparently possible to reach a lonely house on its terraces a km away, if not Hondéïka itself (as much distance again) via the gorge. This route, however, has not been verified, so don't slide down any waterfall you couldn't climb up again if necessary!

It's safer to cross the stream coming down from Gavrolisiádha and start the climb up the boulder field opposite. The trail resumes on your right, tracks left after five minutes above a solitary plane tree, and then hugs the rocks to the left for similar distance. Next a sharp turn left (south) brings you to a spur in five minutes. Henceforth the path clings to the mountainside between 100 and 200 metres above the main stream, threading alternately through oak forest and open rock.

After half an hour some downhill steps bring you to the trickiest section: a steep and crumbly slope of scree and earth, which doesn't seem to have a path or ledge. A trail does in fact exist, but you can see why it is compared to a wire – in places it is no more than 20 cm wide. Naturally great care must be taken, though as long as both Gavrolisiádha and Hondéïka remain inhabited this slope should be passable.

Five grunting minutes later you'll find yourself once more on a broad path, albeit a steeply climbing one. Keep high at the next hut, and the beautifully constructed kalderími switchbacks towards the stream staircase-fashion. Half an hour beyond you reach the first ruined houses of Hondéïka (also called Miálo, 800 metres), with a dry-stone ikónisma on an outcrop. From here small paths lead down to the stream within five minutes. Take the right-hand one, cross two wooden bridges, and a few moments later – 3¾ hours of hiking below the eastern crest – you are in the hamlet.

The five remaining families have maintained their property superbly; there are flowerpots on balconies, and the aqueducts and gutters are in good repair. Unfortunately the uninhabited dwellings have been allowed to collapse, and will soon be completely reclaimed by nature.

To continue to Ágrafa village, follow the vehicle track to the creek ford. Beginning here, a cleverly built path leads down the rock face on the western bank of the watercourse, though after just 10 minutes you hit another track which winds among plane trees for five minutes until linking up with the Ágrafa-Márathos road 50 metres south-east of a concrete bridge. Proceed 50 metres on the other side of the brige, and turn right onto another steeply-climbing trail. At the first house, 15 minutes along, a side trail branches right – ignore it, keeping left alongside a fence.

Soon you reach yet another track; bear right to stay with the path, keeping the fence on your left, as far as the village, which remains hidden until the last moment of the 4½ hour course down the mountain. You emerge diagonally opposite the post office. If you are reversing this itinerary for some reason, the road describes three sides of a rough square starting from the post office; the path takes off from the second left bend.

Stage 2: Ágrafa to Trováto via Valári & Vrangianá

(7½ hours)

Initially you have a choice of routes north. Purists could follow the directions already given to the saddle east of Furkúla, and then to the stáni north of the spur. From there a cross-country route leads down to Valári village in two hours.

Easier, but duller and not much quicker, is to follow the portion of the E4 long-distance route out of Ágrafa. Ten km of dirt road ends in Blos (Papapostóli) hamlet (900 metres); there, at the first house near a cistern, keep left on a well-marked but steep 40-minute path down to the Agrafiótis. One km upstream, ford with the characteristic E4 diamonds where the river is shallowest and pick

up a dirt track leading to the main riverside road below Trídhendhro. If you'd rather keep your feet dry, cross on a wobbly wooden bridge 500 metres further upstream and cut through the plane trees to the village.

Just to your right are the lowest houses of Trídhendhro (750 metres), including a magazí with a few beds (☎ (0237) 61 002, Mr Papadhopulos). The main group of houses lies, more or less unaffected by recent development, about 15 minutes up the hill.

Unhappily for trekkers, the direct road between Vrangianá and Trídhendhro will have been completed by 1993, so the best onward option is to follow the Latómika ravine to Valári village and take the track from there. One km north of the Trídhendhro magazí, lurch down a plane-clogged gully to the river, remembering that leaves often cover empty spaces. Cross the concrete slab bridge and walk 200 metres right along the grassy bank, with its fine camping, to the mouth of the Latómika. It's a beautiful but slow 1½ km upstream along the mule path to the union of the two rivulets 75 minutes out of Trídhendhro; the northerly one, the Valariótis, is worth a pause to explore some enclosed sculpted pools.

The path to Valári, another local engineering marvel, winds up the salient between the two streams, starting from your right and then changing to overlook the Valariótis. Half an hour from the junction you ford that stream, walk a minute upstream and follow the nettly path (usually more of a running ditch) into the village (950 metres). Foreigners are rare beasts, so you may be invited in for a glass of *kraniá* (Cornelian cherry) or *karídhi* (walnut) liqueur – favourites of the priest, whose recipe consists of half a bottle of fruit, half a bottle of sugar turned regularly, and given three months of sunshine. Failing that, the lowest house also doubles as a magazí.

The unavoidable road leaves the top of the village to cross the ridge below Ítamos hill and draws even with the first houses of Vrangianá, the district called Zervomakhalás, after six km. Moving from here to the central part of the village on the northern side of the valley, you pass the clandestine school of Áyios Kosmás. In Ottoman times, this (along with another in Fúrna village, across the Tavropós) was one of the most important of such institutions, with such luminaries as Yannulis (1596-1682) and Anastasios Gordhis (1654-1729), though their teachings were probably as much military as cultural or religious.

Once over the stream, head for the abandoned school and church; just above these are the two magazí described in Stage 2A of Eastern Ridge: Mavromáta to Vrangianá.

From the saddle above and north-east of the main cluster of houses, a path descends steeply through firs, crossing a small creek twice, to reach the Kustésas stream (really the upper reaches of the Agrafiótis) near some terraces in 40 minutes. It then plunges down the steep sandy bank to the log bridge (no handrail) and curves left (south-west). Finally the trail clears up, climbs and bends right (west) to the side-stream below Trováto, 85 minutes out of Vrangianá. Trováto is 15 minutes up a wet path to the west, or over 5½ hiking hours from Blos. Trováto is well placed as a base for the western ridge routes following, but there do not seem to be any formal overnight facilities, though there is a magazí.

WESTERN RIDGE: TROVÁTO OR EPINIANÁ TO MONASTIRÁKI

For more casual walkers, the western summits are best viewed from a distance; trekking on them is a delicate, steep business requiring full equipment. The only possible shelter is in the small and dwindling hamlets of Asprórema and Vlakhopúla. Those who take this as a challenge can use the hamlets as bases for exploration, along with the few reliable paths connecting them.

Stage 1A: Trováto to Asprórema via Delidhími Peak

Take the path climbing west through patchy trees, past the highest cluster of huts, and within 90 minutes reach a road at about 1400 metres; go right along the road for about 500 metres to a boulder-studded field on your left. Cross this and take the visible path leading up and west. An hour from the road you'll curl slightly left to reach a gully; keep on the southern bank until about 1800 metres elevation, then veer north to a grassy saddle. Next you've a stiff half-hour climb west-south-west up the main crest. From there the 2163-metre summit of Delidhími (Avgó), highest peak in the Ágrafa, is half an hour north, or 4½ hours from Trováto.

From the north-west flank of Delidhími a recognised route leads west and north within four hours to the village of Fundotó, and access to the mountains of the Akhelöös watershed. To get to Asprórema, take the goat trail traversing the west flank of Delidhími at the 1900-metre level, starting from the saddle west of the peak. This heads down along and just west of a spur to reach the upper huts of Asprórema, also known as Sfirí at about 1200 metres; there is water and the possibility of camping here.

Stage 1B: Epinianá to Asprórema
(4¼ hours)

Epinianá (Piyianá) is connected to the outside world by road, and boasts the area's only official accommodation, newly opened in late 1992; for details call the village *próedhros* or head of village, Theodhoros Avrambos, on (0237) 61 212. Epinianá also marks the start of the easiest and most spectacular route into the heart of the western mountains, following a stone path perched dramatically on the south bank of the Asprórema ravine.

Begin from the first hairpin bend on the Epinianá-Ágrafa dirt road, about 500 metres below the village square. Ignoring left and right forks, you will pass a small shrine after about 20 minutes, with a view across the valley to Stánis monastery. Locals proudly tell of its magical ikon, originally from Stános village near Amfilokhía, which escaped the clutches of thieves and returned of its own accord to the monastery.

Bearing left (west), the path continues past a small stream to a conspicuous saddle below Eklisiá hamlet, an hour- plus out of Epinianá. The hamlet has a total population of one old lady (summer months only), but the saddle makes a good campsite, with water from a second rivulet crossing the path a couple of minutes further on.

The trail, now heading north-north-west, maintains its 800-metre contour into the narrowest section of the gorge. This is where the present headman of Epinianá remembers hanging in a harness from a tree, chipping away at the rockface to fill in the damaged sections of the path. Thankfully his work has lasted well and you can enjoy an obstacle-free hour's walk, dropping gently to meet the river next to a side gully called Skilórema. At this point the Asprórema stream is spanned by a plank-bridge.

Upstream from the plank, the agile can follow the riverbed as far as Asprórema. The first km or so takes you through a narrow S-bend which is impassable in spring; thereafter it is, at worst, slightly overgrown with oleanders. Most people, however, will follow the proper path on the north bank, initially zig-zagging up a steep boulder field, then dropping behind a saddle to river level. You'll repeat the process twice on a smaller scale, the third climb bringing you to the first ruined walls (and soon after, the one permanently inhabited house) of Zoyéika. From here a well-trodden path heads briefly north to the hamlet of Kerasiá, with road connection to Trováto.

Whether reached by the streambed or the north-bank path, Zoyéika is just over an hour from the plank-bridge, or a good three hours' march from Epinianá. Five minutes further north-west you cross the permanent trickle of the Tsarkórema and drop to the stony main riverbed again half an hour from the lone house. There is no formal path here, but within half an hour you should reach the junction of two streams. A path on the far bank of the left-hand one climbs in 40 minutes to Vriská, the largest of the settlements that constitute Asprórema village. (If you keep right instead, you pass another tributary, with excellent pools for a dip; an old path winds up the angle of the stream junction to some ruined houses and a watermill.) The uppermost houses of Asprórema, called Sfirí district, lie a further 20 minutes up the main rivered. Campsites abound along this stretch.

Sidetrip: Sfirí of Asprórema to Delidhími Peak

From the huts known as Sfirí, a path winds up the left flank of the blunt spur to the north. After an hour, it crosses the now-sharp spine at 1500 metres and forks. Keep left, recross the hogback and traverse the stony slopes to your north, while climbing steadily. Although the going is at best uneven, the trail is clear all the way to the col between the 2163-metre summit and Salayiánni, its slightly lower neighbour to the west. From this pass Point 2163 of Delidhími is a stiff 40-minute climb east, or 3¼ hours from Sfirí, but the panorama of bleak and jagged mountains from the top is ample reward.

Descent to Trováto These directions essentially reverse the ascent of Stage 1A. Descend south for 20 minutes, cross-country, along Delidhími ridge until shortly before the 2062-metre hump. Now drop steeply east-north-east towards the middle of three spurs, until picking up a faint trail which drops into the gully on your right. Cross this, and the path clears up to lead you east over boulder-strewn fields to a north-west-to-south-east-tending dirt road within an hour, or two hours from the peak. Walk 100 metres right along this road to pick up more trails on the far side, which continue east to Trováto within 90 more minutes.

Stage 2: Vriská of Asprórema to Sturnaráki

(4 hours)

From the highest of the rather makeshift huts of Vriská 'neighbourhood', a path climbs steeply south-south-west, initially through firs, then up a slippery hogback. Half an hour uphill it slips left into a sheep pen, then resumes course to reach a gently sloping meadow called Pína ('Hunger') in another half-hour. Cross this heading west and pick your way over some boulders to the foot of a steep ridge; on your left you should spot a crude gate of branches and thistles, designed to keep the horses which graze locally from straying up any of the forbidding peaks around. Climb over this barrier and follow the path south to where it intersects with the sharp ridge between Pláka and Sínoro peaks at about 1700 metres elevation, within 10 minutes or 1¼ hours from Vriská, respectively.

From this point it is possible to detour one hour south-east along the watershed to Pláka summit (1870 metres) or, with climbing gear, two hours north-west to Sínoro summit (2032 metres).

The onward path to Sturnaráki bisects a grassy meadow before slipping off the west side of the ridge and contouring south-east on a steep stony slope. Although the terrain is uneven and demands concentration, the route is clearly visible under normal conditions. An hour from the meadow you reach a col with views east over the Skilórema valley. The path turns two small summits on their west side, then splits into two parallel options which rejoin at a third col, 75 minutes from the meadow. To the south are the imposing bulwarks of Korúna peak (1938 metres), which is only climbable from the south-west.

At this col another path leads south-west in 40 minutes to the hamlet of Palúkia, with a single resident family in summer. From there you can head back to civilisation, either west-north-west along the Brakóvrisi valley to Vasilési village, or over the pass between Gidhókastro and Ftéri peaks to Krevátia hamlet. Both settlements are a short hitchhike away from Lithokhóri village, with its daily 6.30 am bus connection to Karpenísi.

To finish the basic stage at Sturnaráki, follow the path south-east from the col, dropping slightly through occasional clusters of nettles (*tsuknídha* in Greek, if someone's warning you...). Passing above the summer dwelling of a shepherd and two noisy dogs, you reach the pass between Korúna and needle-shaped Sfendhámi (1711 metres) within half an hour. Next the path winds down to a small spring (usually dry after August) in 15 minutes, then straightens up

and bears south-east to derelict Sturnaráki in another 40 minutes, or four hours from Vriská. All that remains of the dozen houses is one hut, several walls and an alóni (threshing cirque).

Loop to Epinianá It is possible to avoid Stage 3 by adopting a well-defined path continuing east-south-east. After 25 minutes, fork left and climb to the hamlet of Apidhiá, on the crest of Tsúma spur, reached an hour along. A newly built road takes you back down to Epinianá in another hour, allowing the construction of a loop itinerary.

Stage 3: Sturnaráki to Monastiráki
(7½ hours)

To continue with the main traverse, adopt the lower path at Sturnaráki bearing west-north-wests towards the gully, and slog down this for about 20 minutes. At about 1200 metres altitude, an almost imperceptible trail appears to your right and climbs gently south up the overgrown slope. Within half an hour you round a sharp corner at a shrine. Hereafter the route clears up, and drops down a gritty slope past the ruined houses of Prosíli to the Trivalórema valley in half an hour. At the first tributary five minutes downstream, a continuing path climbs through fern-covered terraces opposite to a dirt road leading on to the few occupied houses of Vlakhopúla, reached just over two hours from Sturnaráki.

These shacks are the only remaining habitations of what used to be a large village; some stone walls and churches are still visible further downhill. Small groups can expect water and shelter in the summer months, and happily exchange novelty foodstuffs for cheese and milk.

The path south to Liákura and beyond sets off from the highest shack at the end of the bulldozer track in from Monastiráki. Seen from below, it traces a distinct line in the scree as far as the meadows below Lútsi ridge.

From this point, you bear north along the watershed for Ftéri peak (2128 metres), but this a four-hour trip, involving some Grade

2 climbing and probably the use of rope, so it's really only something to be attempted in good weather as a day trip out of Vlakhopúla campsite. Most trekkers will prefer the stiff scramble one hour south-east to Liákura (2043 metres), followed by another rather dull hour descending east over trail-less slopes to the saddle on the Vlakhopúla-Monastiráki dirt road. Monastiráki itself lies two more hours below, for a fairly arduous 7½-hour trekking day. If you're lucky you may glimpse one of the numerous golden eagles that soar above the pinnacles of Kalóyeros, east of the road.

Completion of Traverse: Ftéri to Monastiráki

To complete a full western traverse, branch right at the ridge above Ftéri and follow it west towards the peak of the same name. A broad zigzag south and then north-west brings you out after nearly three hours at the first main col south of the 2128-metre trig point, but it's still an hour's scramble past two smaller peaks to the top.

Alternatively or additionally, you can continue south from the col on the easterly flank of the Lútsi ridge, and cut up to the last saddle before Liákura peak at 1900 metres.

From here Liákura's 2043-metre summit is a steady half-hour climb to the south-east, and the pass on the Ftéri-Monastiráki road a rather boring hour-long descent east over trail-less stone and scrub. Monastiráki village lies two more hours below, for a fairly arduous 7½-hour trekking day.

Ípiros

The character of Ípiros (Epirus) is determined by the rugged, thinly populated Píndhos (Pindus) range which, together with its extension (the Ágrafa) makes up nearly a quarter of the northern Greek mainland. In antiquity, mountainous Ípiros was considered the limit of the civilised world; few traces of ancient culture have been unearthed aside from the shadowy oracles at Dhodhóni (Dodona) and Akherónda (Ephyra).

The Romans and their heirs the Byzantines had little use for the rugged province lying to one side of the Via Egnatía which linked the eastern and western empires, though the area enjoyed a brief period of importance during the 13th and 14th centuries when the Despotate of Epirus was a leading contender in the struggle to resume the leadership of the Byzantine Empire following the expulsion of the Latins from Constantinople.

During late Ottoman times Ípiros was the lair of the colourful but ruthless Ali Pasha, who governed a virtually independent domain centred on Ioánnina, which since the Byzantine collapse had become a refuge and showcase of medieval Greek culture. Union with modern Greece came late (1913) and shortly after was put to the test by the Italian invasion from Albania on 28 October 1940. The Greeks astounded the Allies and Axis powers alike by soundly thrashing Mussolini's legions, and only irresolution, a Píndhos winter and Hitler's subsequent blitzkrieg from Yugoslavia prevented Greece from annexing the long-coveted ethnic Greek area of Vória Ípiros (Northern Epirus), which despite a continuing, low-key propaganda war between Greece and Albania seems destined to remain part of the latter.

Another, and more lastingly destructive, set of circumstances prevented Greek irredentist aims from being realised with respect to Vória Ípiros. The WW II experience in Greek Ípiros was among the most bitter in Greece, which is saying a lot when you consider that nearly 10% of the population country-wide either starved to death or were killed outright by occupying troops or their fellow Greeks. In Ípiros, 1942-44 resistance activities, retaliatory destruction of villages and the subsequent mayhem of the 1946-49 civil war not only convinced outside powers that Greece was unfit to govern northern Ípiros, but consigned Greek Ípiros to subsequent decades of misery and under-development until the late 1970s.

This is all the sadder because it was not always so. From the 15th to the 19th centuries the isolating Píndhos fostered the growth of a fabulously wealthy and cultured society of semi-autonomous villages in and around the district of Zagória, whose traders, weavers, woodworkers, jewellers and masons were famous beyond the borders of the Ottoman Empire. The inaccessibility of the heights simultaneously discouraged depredations by the Turks, who preferred to leave the prickly mountaineers alone in exchange for nominal tribute. In recent years the montane barrier (Zagória is a Slavic word meaning 'behind the mountains') has worked against the vigour of the rural Ípirote communities, and indeed all Greek alpine villages; the wartime destruction, poor communications, lack of livelihood and seemingly punitive government neglect have rendered many moribund.

Attempts to reverse this decline have focused on touristic development of the 46 traditional Zagórian villages and certain others in the southern Píndhos, still architecturally intriguing though otherwise left desolate by the lapse of Ottoman privileges. An abundance of local limestone, schist and wood has been transformed into Hansel-and-Gretel housing that is all of a piece; street paving, walls and roofs blend together in a uniform grey which, rather than being depressing, is an example of perfect adaptation to environment.

Natural Ípiros is no less impressive. Wild rivers such as the Aóös, the Thíamis, the Akherónda and the Árahkthos furrow the terrain, often separating densely forested peaks towering hundreds of metres above the water. The Víkos Gorge, an 11-km cleft in the flank of Mt Astráka that compares favourably with the more publicised canyon of Samariá in Crete, slices through the heart of Zagória. Where there are no forests – a common condition on the west-facing slopes – the limestone skeleton of the mountains protrudes in various uncompromising forms.

The people, as ever, reflect the landscape: *Ipirotikó kefáli* ('Ipirote head') has long been a byword for stubbornness and resolute resistance to outsiders bent on harm. But Ípirots honour the peaceable stranger to sometimes inconvenient degrees – indigestion and hangovers are frequent consequences of accepting invitations to village bacchanalia. In moderate quantities, local dairy and meat products are among the best in Greece, produced by the Vlach and Sarakatsan shepherds who tenant the high meadows in summer.

South Píndhos

Looking east from Ioánnina at dusk, an imposing alpine wall glows in the setting sun on clearer days. This is the south Píndhos, which extends in an unbroken series for nearly 30 km south from the Katára pass which separates them from the eastern and north Píndhos. The three main peaks of this massif, Peristéri, Kakardhítsa and Dzumérka, are on average nearly as high as their counterparts near Albania, and rather more forbidding. Slopes facing the Árakhthos valley lie in a bit of a rainshadow and tend to be barren, while the Ahelóös watershed by contrast is heavily forested.

FROM THE ÁRAKHTHOS TO THE AKHELÓÖS WATERSHEDS

Not surprisingly, the harsh territory south of Katára is less visited than the more popular mountains to the north-west, but if you pick your routes carefully the rewards can be great. Regrettably I have jettisoned a description of a stage across Peristéri from Anthokhóri to Siráko, since the landscape there has been recently bulldozed beyond recognition, but the wildness and steepness of Dzumérka and Kakardhítsa, as drastic as anything in southern Europe, seems so far to have protected it from the road crews. Four to seven-hour stretches without encountering another human can be expected, and even then the shepherds or rural labourers will be dwarfed by the desolate surrounding grandeur.

Villages on the selected route are a bit larger and more prosperous than those of the western Stereá and Ágrafa, but scarcely better equipped to accommodate outsiders; foreign tourists are a rarity. The first trek covers the distance between Siráko and Prámanda, since Siráko and its neighbour Kallarítes should not be missed, but if you have the choice and the pertinent maps it's probably better to begin in Prámanda, trek around or over Kakardhítsa to Gardhíki or Dziúrdzia, and loop back to Matsúki and Kallarítes as a final leg.

Rating & Duration

The initial trek between Kallarítes and Prámanda is easy, but anything beyond – up and over Dzumérka or Kakardhítsa – falls squarely into the difficult category, owing to the faint paths, sharp grades and long traverses. You should have the listed YIS maps, and preferably experience with this sort of terrain – a crossing of Gamíla (see the Northern Píndhos section) is good preparation.

Season

Because of the high-altitude passes and long trekking days, this itinerary is best done after the summer solstice, up to late August. The passes on and between Dzumérka and Kakardhítsa are prone, even in midsummer, to chilling high winds which the locals claim have blown over laden mules in the past – be prepared.

Supplies

Get supplies preferably in Ioánnina; Prámanda has a large shop, but if – as is likely – you pass through at afternoon nap time, its usefulness will be largely theoretical.

Maps

Korfes 40-41 is unfortunately out of print. Use YIS 1:50,000 *Ágnanda* and *Prámanda*, for the route detailed, plus *Kastanéa* for the eastern slope of Kakardhítsa.

Access

Siráko has rather strange bus services from the Bizaníu station in Ioánnina: Tuesday at 5.45 am and 1.30 pm, returning at 8 am and 3.45 pm, and Friday at 4 pm, returning at 6.15 pm.

Prámanda is served daily from Monday to Friday in a more normal fashion, at 5 am and 3.30 pm, with immediate turnaround at the village. Two days a week, usually Tuesday and Friday, the Prámanda bus may continue to Kipínas hamlet, just below Kallarítes, or to Matsúki, south-east of Kallarítes, from where it is possible to walk across a river gorge in about two hours to Kallarítes.

Trek 1: Siráko/Kallarítes to Prámanda
(4¼ hours)

It's well worth coinciding with the sporadic bus service to Siráko (1050 metres), since it and its neighbour Kallarítes are much the most attractive settlements of the south Píndhos. The well-preserved mansions, archways and churches bear a strong resemblance to those of Zagória, but the barren, cliffside, almost fortress-like setting of Siráko is quite a contrast to the gentler slopes and greenery west of the Aöós. The village is also the birthplace of a few national political figures and poets, and has several statues of those who made good.

In terms of practicalities, English-speaking Vassilis Vaïtsis (☎ (0651) 53 290) owns the Siráko grill and rents out five beds between May and October. If the inn is full you can usually get permission to sleep in the school during summer.

To begin, follow the single street-lit walkway east out of town. Just past the next-to-last inhabited house on the cliff-face overlooking the Hrússias stream, and just before a clump of three or four walnut trees, bear right onto a path passing just under the last small occupied house of Siráko. A 20-minute descent along a progressively clearer step-trail brings you level with the river (about 900 metres), right by an abandoned mill and a modern metal bridge. The scenery is riveting and the cool depths of the gorge are a balm on a hot day.

As you begin your climb up the opposite cliff face you'll catch sight of another, much larger empty mill a few hundred metres upstream. Part of the 50-minute ascent to Kallarítes from the river is via a ladder inside a tunnel hewn into the rock, a bit of engineering the villagers are justly proud of. Once through this stone gallery you'll have a comprehensive view back over Siráko.

Kallarítes (1050 metres) is less enclosed and greener than Siráko, facing south over the gorge of the river which from here on is known, logically enough, as the Kallarítikos. Like Siráko it is a Kutsovlach village and, not to be outdone by its neighbour, it has long been renowned as a cradle for goldsmiths and silversmiths, specifically most of the ones still operating in Ioánnina. Also in Kallarítes, there are two good psistariás on the generously laid-out cobbled platía, and one rather basic ksenónas (inn) (☎ (0659) 61 251) with half a dozen beds.

To move on towards Prámanda, descend south-east from the square via the lane leading away from the Melissa grocery store. The cobbled way zig-zags down for half an hour to a spring, and 20 minutes further to a fine old bridge over the river at just under 800 metres. Sadly, just the other side of the bridge, you'll stumble upon the leading edge of the ugly new road, which by the time you read this will have found its way – hopefully not on top of the kalderími – into Kallarítes.

Turn left through the mess of junctions here, following the river as much as possible, and within 25 minutes you'll pass under the uninhabited monastery of Kipínas. This is

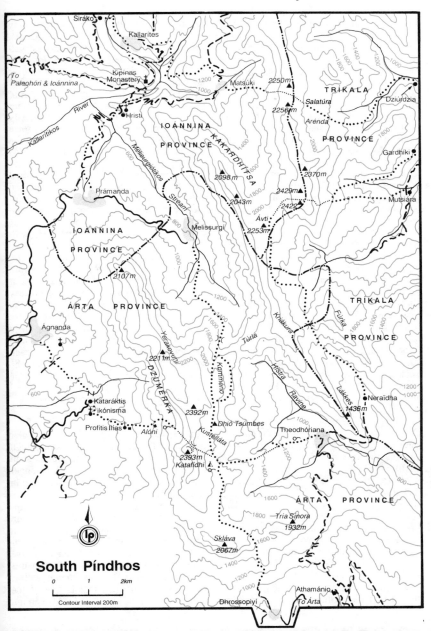

South Píndhos

0   1   2km

Contour Interval 200m

one of the swallow's-nest type of monastery, peeking as it does from a perch some metres up a cliff face; parts of the structure date from 1381. Just below it, by the side of the road, lies a peculiar cave concealing an icy river running through down to unplumbed depths. Mt Kakardhítsa looms above the dense forests on the far side of the Kallarítikos.

Beyond Kipínas the landscape opens out and becomes less dramatic; bracken, oak and plane comprise the main vegetation of the river's flood plain. Beyond, a prominent spur of Kakardhítsa dominates Hristí village, huddled down by a tributary of the Kallarítikos. About 15 minutes past the cave, and a full 1½ hours out of Kallarítes, you should leave the road just short of a combination shed-haystack-terrace garden in favour of a path switchbacking down a scree slope to a grove of plane trees. A full 15 minutes below the road you'll cross an appealing stone bridge (550 metres) which no bulldozer will ever molest.

Once on the opposite bank, climb for half an hour up an old cart track to a modern chapel on a knoll overlooking Hristí; just before reaching this ksoklísi you'll notice the Hristí-Matsúki road above and to the left. From here, a 15-minute downhill scramble along the degenerated trail lands you on a rockslide spilling onto a road junction just above the church and platía of Hristí, a dull modern village with a single magazí, at 650 metres.

Since the extension of the road beyond Prámanda to Hristí and Matsúki, the onward path has fallen into disrepair, but it's still possible to follow much of it, saving considerable time. Cross the bridge over the Melisurgiótikos stream; the path begins with a sharp left uphill, just above the irrigation ditch and a bit to the left of the power poles. It's 20 minutes of hot work, snaking up through semicultivated terraces and fern brakes, until you intersect the road again. Follow this uphill for another 20 minutes until reaching an ikónisma and a concrete shelter on the right.

The trail reappears some 15 metres behind these landmarks, climbing up the ridge with the aid of intermittent cobbling. It quickly mounts above the road to about 700 metres, permitting a good look at the north-west wall of Dzumérka towering above Prámanda, some of which is already visible. After another 20 minutes the old trail is swallowed by the road again just about two km short of the village; however, 10 minutes farther along, the path resumes to the left. A mostly dirt surface leads within 30 minutes, for a total of just over four walking hours on the day, through a mix of open scrub and fir. At the outskirts of the village there's a drop to a streambed and a bridge, then a gradual uphill past kitchen gardens and chicken coops until your path merges with the concrete lane (Ikopróti Fevruaríu) leading up to the platía at about 800 metres.

A simple inn (☎ (0659) 61 393) with about 15 beds is on your right just before two barber shops north of and below the square. The proprietor is Christos Papatheodhorou. You can eat fairly well, if carnivorously, at a handful of psistariés, and a good grocery and a milk bar are south of the platía, past the bus stop. Prámanda is the main market centre for the Kallarítikos valley and is large enough to warrant such detailed directions – the town is spread over several ridges, each with its own view of the others and the canyons below.

Trek 2: Melissurgí to Theodhóriana via Dzumérka

(8½ hours)

This has recently become the most popular traverse of Dzumérka (Tzoumérka), though there are several other trekking options, such as the approach of Trek 3 or a slightly longer trek parallel to the watershed and ending in Dhrossopiyí.

Continuing from Prámanda (see description of Trek 1), your day will end or begin with the Árta provincial KTEL's afternoon or morning bus to Melissurgí, six km southeast along the road. This is an attractive village of old stone houses at 850 metres altitude in the head of its stream valley, graced with a basilica that is one of the biggest in the Píndhos. There is also an inn

Top: Áthos: Courtyard of Meyístis Lávras, morning (MD)
Bottom: Áthos: View over Ayíu Paṅdelímonos monastery interior (MD)

Top: Áthos: Ayíu Pávlu seen from its bay, with Áthos peak behind (MD)
Left: Ólimbos: Waterfall just above Priónia, along the E4 from Litókhoro (MD)
Right: Ólimbos: Trekkers en route to the base of Stefáni peak (MD)

and a taverna on the main square, run by Christos Pappas, plus a smaller hostel – both are likely to be filled by visiting relatives in summer.

The start of the path up the mountain is well-marked with red blazes, with the initial cluster of plane trees by the wooden bridges over the river yielding to pines further up. But within an hour the trees thin out, and you've nearly three hours of climbing to a pass at 1750 metres, known simply as the saddle of Melissurgí.

(If you intend to climb Dzumérka's summit, aim for a westerly gap immediately north of the bluff called Komméno, and not the one which overlooks a sharp drop into the sources of the Hístra ravine.)

Next you round Komméno on its eastern flank without gaining much altitude, but then you need to climb substantially, to 2100 metres or so, to pass Dhió Tsúmbes to its west, some six hours along. Despite waymarking the path is generally not clear, being used until recently only by shepherds and guerrillas. Within another half an hour you will be near the stánes of Kustelláta plateau (described in detail in Trek 3); make camp here for the night, since you won't have time to ascend Dzumérka and also get down safely to a village.

On the most popular route east from the stánes and trough-spring to Theodhóriana, the path widens a bit before starting to switchback down towards the bed of the ravine. It doesn't quite make it, instead levelling and straightening out as it passes yet another shepherds' colony 300 metres to the left in the canyon floor itself. Theodhóriana has plunged out of sight; all that's visible to indicate settlement are a ksoklísi or two in some fir trees ahead.

One hour or so below the trough spring, the ridge whose crest you've been following since skimming the canyon floor ends abruptly. About 300 metres beyond the last traces that could definitely be ascribed to humans rather than animals, watch for a rock at about 1400 metres with a red 'K40' painted on it. This marks the spot where the trail from the canyon-bed stánio comes up to

round the 'snout' at the edge of the ridge – thorny groundcover blocks further forward progress, so the new path is hard to miss.

Turn right onto it; as it wiggles down through abandoned terracing, Theodhóriana pops into view once again. A copse of willows shades a good spring and a hairpin left turn 45 minutes below the meeting with the new path; just after, the trail crosses the runoff from the fountain to stay on the same bank as the village.

Theodhóriana (950 metres) is a friendly community, one of the southernmost Kutsovlach villages in the Píndhos. There are a couple of stores and an abundance of grills, including one specialising in roast chicken. Christos Papadzikos (☎ (0689) 73 402) runs the central kafenío and lets eight beds upstairs; conditions are spartan but at least the quilts are warm. There is a bus to Árta at 6.15 am, returning in the afternoon.

Trek 3: Ágnanda to Theodhóriana via Kataráktis and Dzumérka
(9 hours)
This option has the advantage of being the one traverse of Dzumérka peak which can be safely completed in a single long day, thus relieving you of the necessity of hauling a lot of gear, but there is a fairly nasty climb above Kataráktis up to the summit crest.

A direct three-hour path from Prámanda to Ágnanda reportedly still exists, but I didn't bother with it; most hikers will need a vehicle start to complete the walk in one day. Prámanda-Ágnanda bus connections are good owing to the fact that Melissurgí is in Árta province, while Prámanda lies squarely within the *nomós* (prefecture) of Ioánnina: thus you have double coverage, the Árta KTEL running past Ágnanda in the early morning and afternoon, and the Ioánnina KTEL offering service at dawn and in the evening.

If you need or want to stay in Ágnanda, Theofanes Kapelis (☎ (0659) 31 476) has rooms, but only in midsummer – the rest of the year he may be absent. So it's best to plan on an immediate departure for Kataráktis.

Ágnanda (700 metres), nearly as large as

Prámanda, is divided into a lower town (in whose platía the bus halts) and an upper district, where a square abuts the kinotikó grafío and the primary school. Leave this platía via the street named after Napoleon Zervas in the direction of the large church visible to the south. Rather than pass this church, bear left and slip behind a single, modern, yellow-tan house. Just above this building, turn right onto an ample trail which snakes up the scrubby slope between fenced corrals and past a ruined house.

About half an hour along, your path is subsumed into an even wider donkey trail coming up on the right. Within 10 minutes you'll top the ridge you've been climbing and come out onto a wide jeep track – the junction's marked by a white ikónisma at just under 900 metres.

Turn left, and this track ends almost immediately; however, the footpath jumps down to the right and presses steadily on. Cross the first streambed encountered, heading straight across rather than veering left. In contrast to some of the hot, exposed terrain around Hristí, this is superb walking country alive with oak, juniper and fir. The apparently sheer walls of Dzumérka, framed by 2211-metre Yerakovúni on the left and the main Katafídhi summit (2393 metres) on the distant right, impressively dominate the scenery.

As you complete an hour's walk out of Ágnanda, the landscape flattens and the forest opens onto an expanse of sandy meadows and flat rocks where the trail becomes tentative. Suddenly the houses of Kataráktis come into sight, banishing any doubts about orientation as the route begins to lose altitude. Soon you're across a creek bed and should pass another ikónisma 15 minutes downhill from the meadows. The alpine vegetation ends abruptly and you begin traversing badly eroded hillsides, passing many small dams which under the circumstances must be reckoned as too little, too late.

You'll cross a running stream on the rim of one flood-control device, just upstream from the ruined supports of a bridge long since swept away. After skittering a few

moments over a final scree slope, dip down to a concrete bridge (740 metres) over the principal watercourse hereabouts. Beyond this point it's obvious how Kataráktis ('Waterfalls') got its name – running sluices and gushing springs are heard, if not seen, on all sides, and if you carefully scan the cliff walls above you can count several cascading torrents.

Finally, two hours after leaving Ágnanda, you should arrive in the grassy, informal platía of Kataráktis (820 metres). It is a village blessed with good orchard land and an open, plateau-top setting in addition to its hydraulics.

Dhimitrios Panutsis runs a small inn a block west of the platía, though it is often full with visiting village relations taking summer holidays here. There is also a daily bus connection with Árta – good to know about if you wish to begin crossing Dzumérka from here or are coming down from the mountain.

Leave the Kataráktis platía from its southeastern corner and head south through a maze of lanes until you reach the edge of the inhabited plateau and are able to overlook a sizeable stream canyon. With the water on your right, descend to the bridge at the bottom, first noting a lone house on the wooded ridge above the far bank. A few moments above the bridge, an ikónisma marks a fork – make a hard left turn onto a narrow path which passes just a few metres to the left of the solitary dwelling as it climbs the ridge.

Within 45 minutes of crossing the river, low scrubby bushes give way to terraced pasture. The trail is faint and hard to trace; as a rule do not wander off right, but keep to the line of this ridge forming the south wall of the canyon on your left. There are occasional red paint splodges, but these are less helpful than a small church of Profítis Ilías and an outbuilding atop a small 1100-metre knoll at the end of some bulldozed curves. The ksoklísi marks the end of the first hour of hiking.

Line up the chapel and the outbuilding for the next leg of the journey; your preliminary goal is the gap in the peak line ahead, the stream's point of exit into the gorge and also where the 'proper' trail begins its way up to Katafídhi summit. The next half an hour involves a tough climb up the ridge line, whose pitch has greatly steepened. During the following 30 minutes up to the two-hour mark out of Kataráktis, the grade lessens and you get an assist from an old disused aqueduct, which directs you up through turfy pastureland to the stáni named Alóni (1400 metres) consisting of two huts – one sturdy, the other crude.

North of these you should see the waterfall at the head of the gully; more importantly, you must also find the initially faint trail starting just above the aqueduct as it loops off towards the falls. During its first 30 minutes, this path is clearly waymarked in red as it zig-zags up the right side of the ravine, but as the route levels out into a boggy meadow at 1750 metres, the path disappears and blazes become rare. Halfway up the grassy slope to the south of the meadow, a pile of boulders marks the entrance to a grotto spring. This is the only dependable water on the way (the waterfall is too difficult to get at), so you should carry adequate water for the three hours that it takes to arrive here from Kataráktis.

From here on it's line-of-sight to the saddle just north of Katafídhi peak, which is finally visible again. The next 90 minutes is spent in a gruelling climb up the only partly grassy spur pointing to the base of the peak. Keep a large stáni well to your right; there is no easier way up from its stone pens. The last 20 minutes of the scramble are not for those with a fear of heights, as you toil on all fours up miserable scree piles which end only up on a tiny ridge joining the two points of the peak. The western (right-hand) knob is a bit lower than the true 2393-metre summit, which offers some comfort in the form of alpine grass with good footing. The turfy spot is your springboard for the final few moments' push up to the top, but if you wish merely to continue on the route, veer away from a small natural arch and round the north side of the summit, using little goat walkways in the grass.

A generous four hours after leaving Kataráktis, you'll emerge on the main north-south crest of Dzumérka to catch tremendous views over the Ágrafa to the south and east, Kakardhítsa to the north, and much of Ioánnina province to the west. The red roofs of Theodhóriana peek reassuringly from out of the grey rock fields some km down the mountain. Immediately below you stretches the Kustelláta plateau, which has two stánes separated by a nasty-looking gully.

Clamber down the rockslides on the east flank of Katafídhi as best you can and direct your steps towards the southerly (right-hand) stáni. Faint trails furrow the turf of Kustelláta, starting especially from the vicinity of the left-hand sheepfold, but you should link up, no more than an hour down the mountain, with a clear trail coming south from Melissurgí as outlined in Trek 2, crossing the head of the gully at about 1850 metres. This is the only safe way to get to the southerly stáni; further up Katafídhi the slopes are too steep, and below the trail crossing the gully quickly becomes impassable.

Less than 30 minutes from the top of the ravine you'll reach the potable trough spring of the sheepfold (1900 metres), the first water since the cave spring. From here on follow the directions at the conclusion of Trek 2.

When you reach Theodhóriana, you'll finish just over three hours below Katafídhi, and seven-plus hours from Kataráktis, a little below the platía.

Alternative Descent to Dhrossopiyí It is possible to bear 90° south from Kustelláta to adopt a trail heading down to Dhrossopiyí (Vulgarélli), but this is an appreciably longer (over four hours) descent than that to Theodhóriana and should only be attempted with an early start out of Kataráktis or Melissurgí.

This alternative route heads more or less due south to the base of 2067-metre Skláva, then wiggles south-east to drop off Skláva's shoulder, between it and Tría Sínora (1932 metres) before finally following a stream canyon down to Dhrossopiyí. There are several hotels in this village, which has the same bus service as Theodhóriana.

Trek 4: Theodhóriana to Gardhíki via Kakardhítsa

(9½ hours)

If you wish to ascend Kakardhítsa while in the area, you'll need to shift to the hamlet of Neraïdha (1000 metres), an hour or so's walk around the Lákkes ridge from Theodhóriana. From Neraïdha, a path leads up within two hours to a 1750-metre saddle north-north-east of the village, between the hills of Kriákura and Fúrka, beyond which you will continue in the same direction, without losing unnecessary altitude into the river canyon beyond, to the pass known as Ávti at 2050 metres, some five hours out of Neraïdha.

From Ávti the best route heads north-east towards the small gap between Point 2422 and the highest summit of 2429. East of here, very faint paths drop down along either bank of the ravine draining off the summit area, either to Mutsiára (Athamaní) at its mouth, or Gardhíki, well north of the ravine. Large Gardhíki (1000 metres), with its several stores and bus service to Tríkala, is the more popular target, a full 3½ hours below the summit.

This is a moderately difficult traverse, lengthier than the Kataráktis-Theodhóriana route, though there are more trees once you're on the Akhelóös side of the mountain, a relief after the barren expanses of Dzumérka.

Dziúrdzia to Matsúki While the Gardhíki route is the quickest way on and off the summit itself, the forbidding Kakardhítsa crest is more gradually approached from Dziúrdzia (Ayía Paraskeví), the next village north of Gardhíki. A traverse over to Matsúki, near Kallarítes, requires at least six trekking hours, slipping over a saddle just north of Point 2256, above the pastures of Salatúra and Arénda.

North Píndhos

This rugged territory, containing two of Greece's most impressive mountains, extends north-west from Ioánnina and Métsovo to the Sarandáporos river valley at the base of Mt Grámmos, enclosing an area of more than 1000 sq km. No discussion of trekking in Greece would be complete without the inclusion of the northern Píndhos, which (except for western Crete) is virtually the only large region of the country where foreigners come specifically to hike. Accordingly the area, especially the Zagorokhória (Zagórian villages) is not exactly unknown, being featured in the catalogues of perhaps a dozen European trekking-expedition outfitters, and some of the locals are beginning to get a bit blasé – and greedy – in the face of a steady traffic of foreign (and Greek) walkers. The plus side of this is that facilities such as trails, village inns and maps are of a higher standard than almost anywhere else in alpine Greece, and despite the increase in popularity, the area is still blissfully uncrowded compared to the Alps or the Pyrenees.

Strictly speaking, the term Zagória usually applies only to the area west and south of the Aóös river, the main reference point for this itinerary. One can stretch the definition a bit, as patriotic villagers do, to include a few settlements on the east bank of the Aóös, but since they were all burnt down by the Germans in 1943-44, they can't compete with their western cousins in architectural interest, and their appeal lies mostly in their status as home to Kutsovlachs. The foothill villages, Zagórian or not, are conveniently spaced so that, with proper planning and a willingness to pay sometimes inflated prices, you can sleep in a bed most nights and avoid the necessity of lugging many days' worth of food with you. A tent is still a must – see the Season information.

Besides Sámos, the north Píndhos is the corner of Greece which I know best, and the following basic route, based on several seasons of experience, has been designed to touch all the highlights on strictly a path or cross-country surface. So the itinerary charts a somewhat convoluted course around and over Mts Gamíla and Smólikas, the defining massifs of the north Píndhos and two of the highest in all Greece. I have also followed the lead of foreign and local trekking companies, who have recently abandoned previously used track-walking sections in the east Píndhos now that better alternatives (specifically the E6 overland trail) have become available.

The long, serrated crest of Gamíla (Tímfi) forms a barrier between the two main plant communities of the north Píndhos, partly because it catches more than a fair share of the wet weather which here tends to come from the north-east. A usually dense mix of black and Balkan pine, with some hardwoods and Macedonian fir, thrives on the serpentine and fleisch strata north and east of the palisades, and on Smólikas. But to the south and west, in central Zagória, mostly beech, scrubby oaks and low shrubs like juniper take root – evidence of more porous limestone-based soil. At lower elevations near the Aóös, hornbeam, maple, linden, chestnut, alder, wild plum and arbutus run riot, forming dense thickets. Closer to the ground small edible fruits, especially wild strawberries and raspberries, complement the usual array of wildflowers and are a selling point for midsummer treks.

You cannot rely on seeing much of the shy local fauna but they are there: the obvious newts of the alpine lakes, birds of prey in the gorge cliffs, elusive chamois of the summits, protected but illegally hunted bears in the woods, and even the occasional wolf pack – which ate 120 goats above Pápingo one recent, snowy Christmas.

It's almost inevitable, though, that a touristic prize as rich as the north Píndhos would become the focus of ongoing battles between conservationists and developers. The progressive depopulation of the villages, which began after the end of Turkish rule in 1913, has been slowed or halted by the establishment of a local timber industry, and provincial/municipal or EC subsidies to shepherds as well as by the growth of tourism. Logging and grazing generally mean roads, incompatible with trekkers' interests, and make a mockery of the precepts of the two national parks in the area: one centred on the Víkos gorge, the other at the sources of the Aóös. Of the two, grazing is far less destructive, and recently the herders were in rare alliance with the big-city mountaineers, local tourism personnel and ecologists in the successful effort to halt the destruction of Gamíla.

Specifically, rather outrageous proposals to build a ski lift on Astráka col, open a road from Pápingo to Tsepélovo, erect a dam on the Aóös near Stomíu monastery, and string a téléférique up the mountain above Stomíu,

Σώστε την ελληνική ΑΡΚΟΥΔΑ....

οι φίλοι της ελληνικής ΑΡΚΟΥΔΑΣ

Friends of the Greek Bears logo

were defeated by the unlikely coalition, with input as well from overseas groups such as the European Kayaking Federation. Considerable bitterness was generated locally, with the Ioánnina-based would-be ski moguls fulminating in print against Athenian bunny-lovers and the treacherous ministries of tourism and agriculture, which withdrew their support from the scheme. The issue seems dormant for now, but could be revived given the recent change in government.

So far local development on the ground has taken the sensible form of trail blazing and refuge staffing and construction, and will hopefully remain at that level.

As they are, the north Píndhos compare well to any other wilderness in Continental Europe, and deserve a visit whatever your level of trekking commitment.

Rating & Duration

However you piece together the suggested stages of the two main walks, this is a strenuous expedition if done in full, taking a minimum of eight days to complete. Sample itineraries include a challenging route encompassing Monodhéndhri, Víkos, Pápingo, Astráka, Karterós, Vrisokhóri, Paliosélli, Smólikas, Samarína, Dhístrato and Vovúsa, which is basically from eight to nine days plus extra time for day hikes out of a base, and the possibility of extension to Métsovo on the E6 trail; the easy start, used by some tour companies, of Elafótopos to Vitsikó, Pápingo, Astráka, Tsepélovo, Gúra and Vrisokhóri; and the alternate Aöös crossing via Lákka Tsumáni, Stomíu, Kónitsa, and a bus to Paliosélli, in either direction. In short, the possibilities are pretty endless and you can mix and match to suit your abilities and schedule.

Season

Snow is a factor to contend with on the peaks until the end of May or (in a wet year) early June. Midsummer fruits partly compensate for muggy Julys and Augusts, when tourists also fill the limited amount of village and refuge accommodation (one reason to take a tent – the other being frequent thundershow-

ers). They are outnumbered only by the biting flies and mosquitoes, which have multiplied in recent years owing to some subtle ecological or climatic change. You'll especially want insect repellent and/or an itching salve in the north Píndhos.

Potable water, at least, is never a problem; the protovrókhia (first rains) arrive with clockwork regularity in the last week of September, so don't plan a trek after the equinox. On balance, mid-June and early September are the best times in a normal year.

Supplies

Two to three days worth of meals should be purchased at the outset in Ioánnina. However well equipped for tourists the Zagorian villages appear to be, they're still villages, with a limited range of groceries. Of the communities en route, Monodhéndhri, Pápingo, Kerásovo and Paliosélli have middling stores, Samarína and Tsepélovo are quite good, but the cupboard is absolutely bare in Vrisokhóri and Vovúsa.

Maps

Korfes 55 (Víkos and western Gamíla), 56 (Gúra and Vrisokhóri area), 57 (Smólikas), 58 (for the E6 route Samarína-Dhístrato), 59 (E6 on to Vovúsa and Vália Kálda) and optionally 60 (E6 from Vália Kálda to Métsovo). These were compiled from the YIS 1:50,000 sheets *Tsepélovon**, *Métsovon**, *Kónitsa** and *Pendálofos**.

Photocopies of Nos 55 and 56 are generally available from the tourist office in Ioánnina (across from the post office) or from the EOS chapter (near the OTE office at Molaïmidhou 6, open in the evening).

However, a strong warning needs to be sounded: they are old (1984-85) and as usual unedited, with numerous potentially dangerous errors. Schematic sketch maps from various sources, collected by the EOS office in Megálo Pápingo and a particular inn in Mikró Pápingo, are more authoritative and should at least be glanced at.

Access

Two daily Monday-to-Friday buses, at

6.30 am and 4 pm, link Ioánnina with Monodhéndhri, the best place to start a north Píndhos traverse. The bus takes more than an hour to cover the 37 direct km from Ioánnina, since it usually detours to the villages of Asprángeli, Káto and Áno Pedhiná and Elafótopos, giving you a like-it-or-not tour of western Zagória. Both morning and afternoon departures are popular, often selling out, so get tickets in advance – the day before should be enough leeway.

The Zozimádhu 4 terminal in Ioánnina, from where the Zagória services leave, has become more chaotic, not less, since the increase in tourist (and Albanian refugee) traffic, with schedules posted in Greek only and ticket-window staff not conspicuously helpful. If you're intimidated by the prospect, visit the more sympathetic tourist information booth downtown, which hands out Roman-alphabet schedule sheets.

THROUGH VÍKOS GORGE & AROUND MT GAMÍLA

For a combination of showcase villages and alpine scenery, this area is unbeatable in Greece. Despite an increase in trekker traffic and a minimally improved trail, the famous gorge is still wild enough to get lost in. Gamíla itself, with the longest crestline in the country except for Taïyettos and Ágrafa, has a variety of approach routes, and except for some bleak grazing land (outside national park boundaries), is often compared to the Italian Dolomites.

Monodhéndhri & Environs

Monodhéndhri is one of the more attractive and strikingly situated Zagorokhória, perched as it is on the brink of the Víkos gorge. Yet somehow it seems shabbier and more ruinous than the two Pápingos, and for obscure reasons more popular with foreigners than trendy Greeks. In terms of accommodation there is one luxury ksenónas (☎ (0653) 61 232 or (01) 68 16 417) as well as four more modest ones, though there are only two places to eat: one is a grill by the upper platía that doubles as the bus stop, and

the other a more traditional place on the lower main plaza.

If Monodhéndhri is full up and you've come on the afternoon bus, you have two options: descend 15 minutes on a short-cut path to the adjacent village of Vítsa, where there are two more inns, one run by Ioánnis Papakhristos, or camp in the Víkos gorge – of questionable legality and not really possible until you're at the springs of the Voïdhomátis.

In any case it would be a shame to rush along the gorge in the twilight, since Monodhéndhri is worth an hour's look around before starting off. The single most outstanding attraction is the recently restored cliff-top monastery of Ayías Paraskevís, not actually in the village but signposted 700 metres beyond it, poised above the 350-metre drop into Víkos. For the dedicated, a trail creeps 400 metres further, along a hair-raisingly sheer plummet, to caves used in centuries past by hermits and persecuted Christians.

Many people are a bit disappointed by the perspective on the Víkos gorge available from inside as you traverse it, and indifferent photographs are the rule. The really good lookouts are above: one at the Oxiá site, near Monodhéndhri and served by a road, the other more or less opposite at Belóï (see Sidetrip: Around Tsepélovo).

Stage 1: To the Pápingo Villages via the Víkos Gorge

(13½ km; 6½ hours)
The route through the gorge is fairly well marked with O3 diamonds, though sometimes not well enough, and still qualifies as a challenging adventure. The start of the path is marked on Monodhéndhri's lower platía (1070 metres) with a sign reading 'Víkos Arísti Pápingo 10 km' and a schematic pedestrian hieroglyph; the figure of 10 km is misleading, since that is only the distance to the end of the gorge narrows, and you've at least another 2½ km to walk up to the Pápingo villages.

Starting off, a recently strewn kalderími takes off from the rear left of the handsome

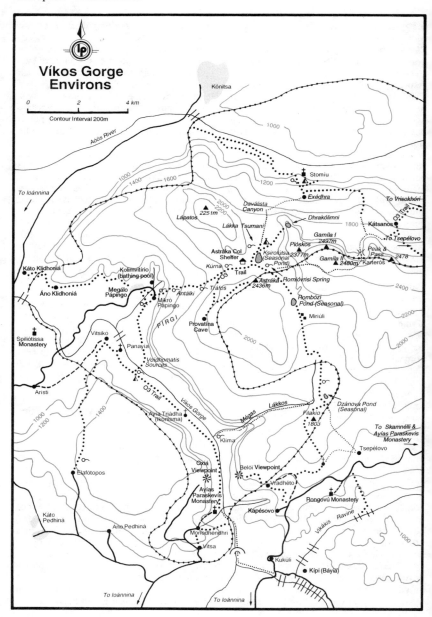

Víkos Gorge Environs

0   2   4 km
Contour Interval 200m

Kónitsa
Aóös River
To Ioánnina
Stomiu
Exédhra
To Vrisokhóri
O3 Trail
Daválista Canyon
Lápatos 2251m
Lákka Tsumáni
Dhrakólimni
Kátsanos
Astráka Col Shelter
Ksirolútsa (Seasonal Pond) 2377m
Plóskos
Gamíla I 2497m
Gamíla II 2480m
Peak & Pass
Karterós
2478
To Tsepélovo
Káto Klidhoniá
Kolímvitírio (bathing pool)
Kúrna Trail
Astráka 2436m
Romióvrisi Spring
Áno Klidhoniá
Megálo Pápingo
Antálki
Trápos
Rombózi Pond (Seasonal)
Mikró Pápingo
PIRGI
Provatina Cave
Miriúli
Spiliótissa Monastery
Vitsikó
Panayía
Voïdhomátis Sources
Aristi
O3 Trail
Víkos Gorge
Mégas
Lákkos
Filakió 1803
Dzánova Pond (Seasonal)
Ayía Triádha (Ikonísma)
Klíma
To Skamnélli & Ayías Paraskevís Monastery
Tsepélovo
Elafótopos
Oxiá Viewpoint
Béloï Viewpoint
Vradhéto
Ayías Paraskevís Monastery
Kápesovo
Rongóvú Monastery
Káto Pedhiná
Áno Pedhiná
Monodhéndhri
Vítsa
Víkakis Ravine
Kukúli
Kípi (Báyia)
To Ioánnina
To Ioánnina

church of Áyios Athanásios on a due east bearing. The grade is slight at first, but then steepens markedly as the cobbled surface vanishes; be careful here early in the day, when the sun has not yet had a chance to burn off the slippery damp underfoot.

It's just under an hour down to the bed of Víkos (about 680 metres). A number of O3 trail diamonds take you briefly across to the far (east) bank, then back onto the west (true left) side of the gorge. Now you skim along north a few tens of metres above the floor of the ravine, with the trail very hesitant at this point; soon, however, it firms up, crosses a rockslide, and dips to the watercourse again one hour 20 minutes out of Monodhéndhri. Cairns rather than O3 waymarks guide you through the pumpkin and automobile-size boulders on the gorge floor, with a return to the west bank, and a proper path, 90 minutes along. Now there's a 25-minute climb up to a grassy saddle at about 675 metres, guarded by a small rock pinnacle to the east, with the best views en route up and down the gorge – also a good place for a long rest or snack.

As it descends from this point the path is slippery and in poor condition, and at one point seems to disappear altogether, but resist the temptation to drop to the streambed again – cairns pointing you that way are criminally deceptive and will only land you in plenty of trouble. When it reasserts itself, the trail takes you through a dense growth of maple, beech and chestnut, about 20 metres above the level of the gorge, without veering significantly uphill.

After nearly 2½ hours you'll draw even with the Víkos gorge's major tributary, the Mégas Lákkos; you know you're close when moss festoons branches, ferns carpet the sunless ground and frogs hop across damp rocks. The frogs depend, as you do, on the Klíma spring (580 metres), from which water gushes out in quantity at the junction of the two canyons. This is the only reliable water en route, so top up. You can't camp here – too much stony, uneven ground – but you won't find a better place for a lunch stop in the gorge.

Past Klíma the path stays closely parallel

North Píndhos: Church of Áyios Athanásios, Monodhéndhri (at head of trail into Víkos Gorge)

to the river bed, trundling through banks of shrubbery and tiny clearings. You'll pass the ikónisma of Ayía Triádha on the right, opposite a small and unreliable well, at just over three hours. Beyond this point the gorge gradually opens out, the landscape becomes more arid, and pastures appear more regularly.

Just over four hours along, there's a critical junction; what seems to be the main trail begins heading up and left, acquiring a cobbled surface, on its 45-minute way to Vítsiko hamlet (see Elafótopos to Vitsikó option) – if you look carefully you can even see a street-light pylon on the rim overhead. You should instead bear right onto a large paddock, worming past a corral thrown together with bits of stick and cyclone fencing. Your ears will help with orientation as well, since the springs of the Voïdhomátis ('Ox-Eye') river make an audible racket just beyond the pasture.

The O3 route crosses the gorge at the source of the river, but before moving on, a description of the area is in order. The springs (about 450 metres) feed the river draining the north end of the gorge, a favourite venue for beginners' rafting and kayaking classes. The water boiling out from the base of the 1700-metre-altitude cliffs north-east of the canyon are among the coldest in Greece, and reputedly good for the digestion, but you'd really have to be an otter or a polar bear to actually enjoy a dip.

Curiously the source of the river is mobile; as the summer wears on the springs surge out progressively further downstream, presumably as the water table lowers. Tracer-dye experiments have shown that the water percolates nearly 1300 metres down from the tops of the cliffs above in about a week. Early in spring the water level can be so high that you'll have to detour considerably upstream to reach the continuation of the O3 path on the eastern bank.

Unfortunately, the environs of the springs are not as pristine as they once were, thanks to the droppings of sheep grazed by an Albanian refugee shepherd. It is said that he'll be moved on by 1993, but in the meantime the turds – thousands of them – make the water suspect for drinking unpurified, and camping on the adjacent turf less appealing. It's not clear whether pitching a tent here is legal (you're within the boundaries of the Víkos National Park), so it's best to do so only in emergencies. A somewhat more savoury location is the green in front of the ksoklísi of Panayía – to get there, walk three minutes up the kalderími towards Vitsikó, and then seven more minutes along a narrow side trail.

You can't, incidentally, get to the chapel easily by following the river, and it's impossible to follow the Voïdhomátis much further downstream owing to a sheer-walled gallery between here and the Arísti-Pápingo river bridge. Here's an instance where the rubber-raft contingent has it over you; I have heard that you would float under a fine old stone bridge which once carried a long-abandoned trail between Vitsikó and Megálo Pápingo.

To continue to the Pápingo villages, cross the Víkos bed at or near the Voïdhomátis source, cued by the timely O3 diamond on the slope opposite. The trail here has been tidied up in recent years, and zig-zags obviously up for some 40 minutes to a saddle at about 675 metres, staked out by a rock 'mitten' or 'castle' (depending on your imagination) and an undeniable stone 'index finger' for the clean of mind. The view down into the Voïdhomátis river from here is exceptional, convincing you that the narrows really are impassable to hikers, among other things.

Beyond the viewpoint, the trail traverses an enormous rockslide to an obvious notch to the left of a promontory ahead, then curls left and down towards another tributary canyon of Víkos. Some 80 minutes beyond the Voïdhomátis springs, there's an important division. Right, following the O3 waymarks, leads to the two masoned springs at the edge of Mikró Pápingo within half an hour. Going left, descending as per the schematic-water-tap sign to a small basin-spring just before the sculpted rock bed of the stream, and then climbing up the other side, brings you to Megálo Pápingo in 25 minutes.

The *Korfes* and YIS depiction of trails in the area, incidentally, is particularly inaccurate and cannot be trusted. Before the local paths were improved between 1985 and 1988, the Megálo/Mikró split used to be back near the 'mitten', but the upper trail has been abandoned and allowed to be covered by landslides – this is the one shown, after a fashion, on maps.

In any event you should allow for 6½ hours of walking from Monodhéndhri to either of the Pápingos, a reduction of an hour or more from the days when the route was barely marked and the trail immediately above Voïdhomátis and below Monodhéndhri was almost non-existent.

Elafótopos to Vitsikó (Bypass of Víkos Gorge)

Some English tour companies favoured this route back in the days when they reckoned the southern portion of the gorge too daunting for their clients. Now that the canyon route has been cleaned up considerably, the only reason to use this option is for an early spring traverse, when the Monodhéndhri end of Víkos may be submerged under dangerous quantities of snowmelt. While not in the same league scenically as the canyon, the bypass trail surface is excellent and there is the advantage of fine views into the chasm from Vítsiko. Sadly, there are rumours afoot that this path will soon be bulldozed into a road.

Elafótopos (about 1100 metres), an underrated and well-preserved Zagorian village, has two kafenía which can provide very simple meals (ie breakfast) on short notice, and one functions as a grill on summer evenings, but overnight lodging may be impromptu at best.

Before getting under way, first find a peculiar church north-east of Elafótopos, set apart from the village at the base of a hillock covered with roofless walls and small, low stone huts. The church gate, inscribed 'Pazedhros' (presumably the family that donated it), opens onto a courtyard with a curious fountain; a hole in the wall weeps continuously, and beside it is a plunger-spigot that you work to fill canteens for the 2½-hour walk to the next water.

The trail begins just to the left of the chapel, and passes – within a 10-minute initial climb – a shaded wall fountain, a covered reservoir and a masonry-lined livestock wallow. This route is heavily used by herders and at the outset consists of many parallel traces, but after a good 30 minutes the way becomes much more discreet, giving weedy hollows below and to the left a wide berth. There's a crest of sorts about 45 minutes above Elafótopos, and after a final backward glance at the village rooftops, you proceed more or less levelly across consecutive, 1300-metre-high, flyblown meadows.

Descending from these pastures, the path is a bit ambiguous; a little over an hour along, you must make two consecutive left forks in the once again well-grooved right of way. Soon you negotiate a brief series of switchbacks dipping down into a clump of oaks. By 2¼ hours, the path has settled into a consistent north-north-east bearing through stunted oaks and large boulders, towards Vitsikó (not yet visible). The route continues to drop gradually through another meadow, meeting a lone tree and an ikónisma on the 950-metre ridge directly above Vitsikó, 2¾ hours out of Elafótopos.

From this vantage the two Pápingo villages and the hoodoo Pírgi ('Tower') rock spires above them are plainly visible, as of course is the hamlet at your feet. It's another 20-minute downhill scramble to the niche fountain at the outskirts of Vitsikó (900 metres); this spring also marks the top of the kalderími heading down within half an hour to the landmark corral near the Voïdhomátis springs. There is a moderately priced 20-bed inn (☎ (0653) 41 176) here run by Kostas Karpouzis.

Most maps show the hamlet as Víkos – I am not being perverse, but am using the old local name to avoid any confusion with the canyon. Incidentally, when the government officially renamed the place, presumably in its Hellenisation drive, they outsmarted themselves – merely replacing one Slavic toponym with another, since Víkos is derived from the medieval Slavonic *vik*, 'shout' or 'cry'.

Pápingo Villages & Environs

The two Pápingos, Mikró and Megálo, both at about 950 metres, are if anything more impressively situated than Monodhéndhri or Vitsikó, and their superlative beauty has earned them, like most of the Zagórian villages, the status of protected traditional communities. This means that architectural homogeneity is supposed to be maintained, with repairs and renovations carried out in the original materials. Nonetheless, a monstrous concrete hotel creeps closer to actionable completion in Megálo Pápingo.

Their settings, at least, opposite (Megálo) and under (Mikró) the massive limestone bulwarks known as the Pírgi are faultless, and the villages are hardly undiscovered. Mikró, comprising some 30 houses, is the calmer place, except perhaps at the 8 September festival, with an incipient English expat colony who have bought ruins to restore for jaw-dropping prices. Megálo, roughly twice as large, tends to get too busy with Greek city-dwellers and trek groups in August, a good time to avoid it; the local festival, also a crowded time, is from 18 to 20 July.

The EOS reps in Megálo Pápingo are Koulis Christodhoulos and his English-speaking son Níkos; they are quite knowledgeable about trails in the area and have a collection of sketch maps worth perusing. In addition they are in CB contact with the alpine refuge up on Astráka (see Stage 2 later) – if you wish to reserve a bunk up there, the procedure is to phone them, and they'll radio up the mountain and have the space confirmed or denied.

The family also runs the magazí and a charming, idiosyncratic lodge with 17 beds (☎ (0653) 41 138 or 41 115). If it is full, common in the high season, Kalliopi Ranga, on the opposite side of the village, on the street leading south from the church and bus stop, has a small modest pension (☎ (0653) 41 081) and offers meals. These are probably the two least expensive establishments, at about US$21 to US$32 per double; half a

dozen other outfits, providing over 100 beds, pick up from there, and you can spend US$60 a night at some of the sumptuously restored 'traditional ksenónes', once part of an EOT scheme which has since been privatised.

There are just a handful of inns in Mikró Pápingo, including the least expensive Agnandi (☎ (0653) 41 123) at about US$20 a double, and the 50% more costly Dhias (☎ (0653) 41 257), run by Kostas Tsoumanis who is also the EOS rep for the village; he too is in CB contact with the mountain hut. Don't be tempted to camp on the lawn of the village church; so many people were doing this that there is now a sign up forbidding it. If you need to pitch a tent, there is an excellent place a short distance up the trail (see the description which follows for Stage 2).

A rather tedious, three-km asphalt road links the two villages, taking 45 minutes to walk, but the time-saving path via the old (1854) Lákka bridge in the canyon separating them has recently been cleared and signposted. Another valuable short cut begins in Megálo Pápingo, just behind the uppermost cluster of high-class ksenónes. The best reason to venture up the road at all is the *kolimvitírio* (natural swimming hole), roughly halfway along. The sign indicating it was removed at my last visit, but you can't miss the spot – there is usually a knot of parked cars at the appropriate bend in the road. A two-minute walk gets you to a deep, though not overly wide, pool whose natural level has been augmented by a skilfully constructed rock dam. The usually brisk water is best savoured at midday.

If you're finishing your trek in Pápingo, bus services in and out tend to be erratic. Currently they leave Ioánnina on Monday, Thursday and Friday at 5 am and 3 pm, with a turnaround at Megálo Pápingo one hour 45 minutes later; on Sunday there is a single outbound service at 9.30 am, returning from the village in the late afternoon. On its way in or out the same bus passes through the village of Arísti, six km below Pápingo across the Voïdhomátis, and three dirt-track km below Vitsikó.

Though not nearly so well preserved as the two Pápingos, Arísti is a pleasant village with accommodation; there's a cultural festival during the latter half of August, culminating in a religious feast on the 29th.

Sidetrip: Walk to Klidhoniá If you are marooned in Pápingo by uncooperative bus schedules, a reasonable trail leads west and down to the main Ioánnina-Kónitsa highway in considerably less time than it would take to trudge along the 19-km side road through Arísti. The route passes through the almost completely desolate village of Áno Klidhoniá, until recently, one of the few remaining in Zagória without road access. This path is used by several tour companies faced with the public transport problem, and has recently acquired some minimal red waymarking.

Leave Megálo Pápingo by the street running west below the Christodhoulos café terrace. After passing a small ksoklísi, you dip into two successive streambeds; avoid little goat paths to the left when climbing out of the second creek gully. Thirty minutes beyond Megálo Pápingo you'll come to an ikónisma of Áyios Trífonos on a ridge.

Here bear right and uphill; the trail becomes untidy, then levels out and neatens, finally tilting downhill past a lone, five-metre-high plane tree which stands out among the scrubby vegetation. An hour's walking should suffice to complete the descent into, and quick crossing of, the largest (and last) ravine encountered en route.

The path again deteriorates as it climbs out of this gully, on its way to an as yet invisible pass. Beyond this next saddle, attained 90 minutes out of Megálo Pápingo, the trail surface again improves and Áno Klidhoniá comes into view. You can choose either the right or left of an impending fork. The left-hand alternative passes a substantial chapel shaded by some tall oaks, but shortly after the trail fizzles completely and you have to cover the last 20 minutes cross-country to the village.

Áno Klidhoniá is not a terribly uplifting sight, a virtual ghost town of some 25 crumbling houses whose roofs are mostly collapsed. The fountains are dry or capped except for the inevitable plane-shaded one in the central platía. The site is fully exposed to the elements, with a climate congenial only for the vineyards still tended; perhaps three families remain here. Recently a road was bulldozed in which fortunately did not affect the trail; it will more likely spark a wave of restoration of derelict houses by outsiders than any renaissance of village life.

From the platía, continue west, hiking parallel to the phone lines of the lone subscriber, towards a little chapel on the edge of the plateau ahead. Pass under this ksoklísi as you stumble upon a grand view over the flood plain of the Voïdhomátis and Aóös rivers, which mingle some km west of the Ioánnina-Kónitsa road, also laid at your feet. Mt Nemertska in Albania towers beyond the plain west of the road.

Beginning at the chapel you've an hour-plus descent, for a total of three out of Megálo Pápingo, on a well-defined but often steep and uneven kalderími, to the thriving community of Káto Klidhoniá. Ioánnina lies 52 km to the south, Kónitsa 11 km to the north; the bus stops for both directions are within sight of the Mamadhakis petrol station.

Stage 2: Papíngo Villages to Astráka Col

Make your way to Mikró Pápingo, if you're not already there, and find a large blue placard at a three-way junction in its limited network of cobbled streets. The sign, with an arrow pointing up and left (north-east), gives these fairly accurate estimates to some popular destinations:

Refuge	3 hr
Provatína Cave	3½ hr
Dhrakólimni	4 hr
Gamíla Peak	5½ hr

Ten minutes out of town, the shrine of Áyios Pandelímon surmounts an alcove where the delicious Avragónios spring erupts in twin jets; the usual plane tree shades a flat, grassy terrace which would be a good contingency campsite. Just past Áyios Pandelímon, a sign ('Katafíyio') points to the right of a fork. After a 40-minute hike through a mixed forest of oak and two kinds of juniper, you arrive at Antálki spring.

Some goat-eroded switchbacks above the fountain are perhaps the hardest portion of the demanding climb to Astráka col. Beyond Antálki the forest thins out gradually to the treeline at about 1700 metres; keep your eyes peeled for chunks of jet scattered on the path.

The weak Tráfos spring lies at about 1550 metres, one hour above Antálki; the featureless ridge of Lápatos (2251 metres) extends to the north, while the infinitely more compelling Pírgi looms in the opposite direction. Tucked between one of the closer 'Towers' summits is the mouth of the Provatína cave, 405 metres deep and the second-longest straight-drop sinkhole in the world; currently only a *cenote* in Yucatán beats it. The nearby Épus cave is over 447 metres deep, but its drop occurs in several stages.

Some 20 minutes above Tráfos (two hours beyond Mikró Pápingo), ignore for now the red arrows pointing right towards the Astráka peak trail, and instead proceed straight towards the col and refuge. The strong spring of Kúrna (1800 metres) burbles 20 minutes beyond the junction, and 20 minutes further, a total of 2¾ hours above Mikró Pápingo, you'll reach the EOS shelter, perched strategically on the saddle joining Lápatos and Astráka.

Megálo Pápingo has finally reappeared to the west, but Astráka to the south, Gamíla to the east and the Lákka Tsumáni valley with the seasonal pond of Ksirolútsa at the base of the two peaks are much more immediate. A small conical rise on a green ridge beyond the Tsumáni stáni marks the direction of Dhrakólimni, the famous, luminous lake of the Gamíla range.

The EOS refuge is permanently staffed from mid-May to mid-October, and the 25 bunks are frequently full of overseas trek groups or Greek rockclimbers. If there's a vacant space, fees for nonmembers of the alpine club are a bit on the expensive side – over US$7 – and so are meals, with additional charges (in theory) for everything from camping within sight of the place to using their water (pumped up at some expense from Lákka Tsumáni). If you have your heart set on staying, contact the EOS reps in Megálo/Mikró Pápingo well in advance. If you're carrying your own tent, there are much better campsites down at the southern end of Ksirolútsa, within a short distance of the Romióvrisi spring.

Sidetrips: Around Astráka Col
Most people take a day to explore the environs of the refuge; it's time well spent, and a relief from the previous two stages. The most obvious and popular excursions are to Dhrakólimni and the peaks of Astráka and Gamíla.

Dhrakólimni The trail up the distant slope to Dhrakólimni is clearly discernible from the col, owing to steadily increasing use, and is now haphazardly waymarked. To start over there, proceed downhill (north-west) from the refuge towards Ksirolútsa; about 10 minutes along, at a fork in the trail, a guy-wired sign gives four destinations (Vrisokhóri, Gamíla, Stomíu, Dhrakólimni), four conventions of waymarking, and as many route-time estimates. Most of the latter are sound (except for Stomíu's), but alas the waymarking as shown barely exists except for the O3 to Vrisokhóri, and the sign-key must have been included against some hopeful future.

It takes 15 minutes to reach the northern end of Ksirolútsa, where the trail fades out within sight of the huts and corrals of the stáni. A giant bog below and north of the shepherds' colony literally crawls with hundreds of amphibians and insects; several springs feed this marsh. The easternmost one, at the foot of the grassy ridge leading up to Dhrakólimni, more or less marks the beginning of the 40-minute path.

As the sign indicates, it's a full hour's walk to the lake, more of a weedy tarn, at 2050 metres. 'Weedy tarn' doesn't quite do it justice – it's actually very appealing, is quite deep in the centre, and admirably reflects two peaks arranged like saw-teeth to the south-east: Plóskós (2377 metres), and Gamíla (2497 metres). Beyond scattered, barrel-like cairns which surround the lake, there's a sheer 350-metre drop into the Aóös basin, where a carpet of forest extends to the base of Smólikas, 10 km away. There are no level campsites on the tilted shore and you really oughtn't camp there anyway, since the fragile environment couldn't support such pressure. No-one will mind, though, if you brave the chill, clear water for a swim with orange-bellied, lacy-gilled newts.

Astráka Peak To reach Astráka, backtrack from Dhrakólimni towards Pápingo approximately 20 minutes to the fork below Kúrna spring. Turn left and follow the marked side trail for about 45 minutes, then leave it where red arrows deviate across a rocky area (the main branch probably continues to Provatína). From a small green hollow just beyond the rocks, follow a hogback east-north-east another 30 minutes up to the main crest, marked by a row of barrel cairns similar to those at Dhrakólimni. The apparent ridge turns out to be the edge of a vast, hummocky upland which culminates, some distance to the left, in Astráka peak.

Bear left and follow more scattered red arrows towards the highest visible cairn, which is still a bit below the summit. The final 45-minute climb is rather uneventful until you approach another, previously unseen line of cairns perched on the brink, where you can contemplate the sheer wall, beloved of technical climbers, dropping to Lákka Tsumáni. From the 2436-metre trig point, Dhrakólimni is just visible; in clear weather the Albanian Píndhos and Smólika close off the horizon north-west and north-east respectively, while Gamíla hunches just across the way.

The total time necessary for the climb from the Kúrna junction is two hours, with the return taking half an hour less. Ordinarily it should be straightforward except after a rain, when the hectares of reef-limestone beds will be slick and treacherous.

Gamíla Peak The approach to Gamíla is from the O3 trail to Vrisokhóri, with the exact turn-off point discussed in Stage 3. Because it is a five-hour-plus round-trip from Astráka col (three hours up, two down), it's difficult to do this and any other sidetrip in the same day, let alone reach Vrisokhóri afterwards. You could just conceivably fit it in as a detour from Stage 3B, Astráka Col to Tsepélovo, assuming a very early start. The climb up is rather dull compared to that for Astráka peak – the perspectives from the top over the Aóös valley are the thing.

Stage 3A: Astráka Col to Vrisokhóri via Karterós Pass
(8¾ hours)
Red dots and O3 diamonds mark much of this traverse, but they scarcely make it much easier – this is a long, challenging day. Incidentally, the waymarks are strongly biased in the direction the description is written – it would be difficult to reverse the itinerary for that reason, as well as the killing altitude change coming up from Vrisokhóri.

At the signposted junction below Astráka col, bear right down to the southern end of Ksirolútsa (about 1800 metres), past the obvious campsites. Begin climbing the lowest point in the rock-studded slope ahead; about 50 metres beyond the edge of the level turf, a somewhat moveable spring, Romióvrisi, gurgles in a shallow ravine. Fill up, as this is the last reliable water for almost seven hours.

Just under half an hour along you'll level out in grassy pasture at about 1925 metres. Follow the O3 markers which take you a bit left of what seems to be the more obvious trail (which is the route to Tsepélovo); veer east towards the two summits of Gamíla. After a gradual climb to a point one hour out at about 2000 metres, from where the Rombózi pond is visible to the south-west, you bear sharply north-east. A series of cairns marches up a ridge to Gamíla I (2497 metres) and the false pass next to it; you

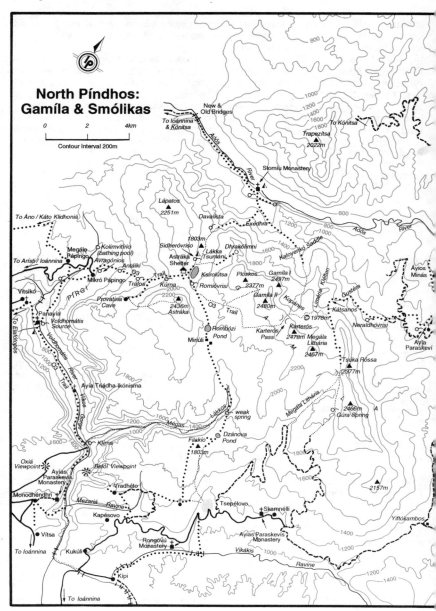

North Píndhos: Gamíla & Smólikas

0   2   4km

Contour Interval 200m

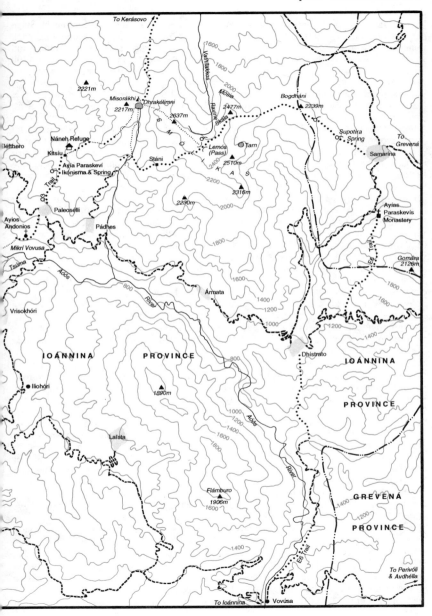

should fall off to the right (east-south-east), towards Gamíla II (2480 metres) and still-unseen Karterós peak.

Painted waymarks have temporarily disappeared; the trick is to curl around the southern 'nose' of Gamíla II, helped by a single, pointy cairn, to begin skirting a line of low, east-to-west cliffs on your left. O3 blazes reappear in strength one hour and 45 minutes along at about 2125 metres; just over two hours out, you've a slight elevation loss into a small, grassy vale.

Coming up on the 2½-hour mark, try not to lose or gain further altitude as you roller-coaster across the heads of various ravines. Some apparently perverse waymarking is justified as you turn sharply north into a defile, sheer-walled on the side you've come from except at the point of entry. Red dots multiply, and just under three hours into the day you attain the Karterós pass, between Karterós peak and Gamíla II, at about 2350 metres.

Rest and enjoy the view across the Aóös basin, because you'll need all your wits about you for the nasty, scree-laden half-hour drop into the cirque of Kopánes. At the bottom of the couloir, bear right across a permanent snowbank, to traverse an equally arduous (and nearly as hazardous) boulder slide; it's fully 3¾ hours to the first place you'd think to sit down, at about 2100 metres. At the four-hour mark you'll finally exchange the last rocks for the grassy neck of Liméria Kléfton ridge; the whole morning's exercise is rewarded by the dramatic line-up of sheer alpine walls around you, ending with Gamíla I to the north-west.

Circle around along the grassy slope, without losing altitude into the gulch to the east (shown as the hole '1978' on the *Korfes* map). Once past this you begin to descend fairly sharply, on traces of a path past the first trees, into the high valley shown on maps as 'Lútsa' but more properly known as Kátsanos, after the family who grazes animals here. Local topography forces the route the longest way around, almost to within sight of the Tsúka Róssa pass (this is

discussed as an alternative route in Stage 3C), after which there's a doubling back down a drainage to a seasonal pond and crude shepherds' shelter at just under 1700 metres, well over five hours into the day.

Now you're confronted by another ledge or lip at the edge of the Kátsanos pasture. Bear left to find the zigzags down and off it; 5¾ hours along, cross the unfortunately dry canyon of Gustéra at about 1500 metres, and continue through newly regenerated mixed forest. The path, clear since the dry streambed, twists along enjoyably, allowing glimpses through thin spots in the trees across to Smólikas and the villages at its base. A little beyond a lightly burnt patch of woods is Neraïdhóvrisi (about 1275 metres), 6½ hours out – a delightful spot where the water spills from a mossy rock face, nourishing damp-loving flora on all sides.

Beyond this much-needed water, the path goes up and down rather tiringly before smashing into an ugly new logging road seven hours on; walk along it about 100 metres, then cut down and left onto the resumption of the trail. Within another half an hour you hit the road again, and must trudge along it for 15 minutes before the next resumption of the path. You should hunt for the remaining O3 placards, which were apparently installed shortly before the road was bulldozed, rather than testing every likely-looking path debouchement at the road's edge.

Next you'll cross a much older road, and Vrisokhóri pops into view. Slippery, extensive schist-mica badlands, where it's easy to get briefly lost, take until over the eight-hour mark to cross. You leave these behind at a bridge over a stream at about 1025 metres, then soon cross another bridge, from where there are good views of Tsúka Róssa above and to the south-west.

At 8½ hours the ksoklísi of Ayía Paraskeví beckons; there's room for two tents in the yard, and a spring adjacent, but the mosquitoes are ferocious. A three-spouted fountain and a flat space under an adjacent mulberry tree at the edge of the village 10 minutes beyond is your only other option, since the centre of Vriskohóri (8¾ hours, 1000 metres) has little to offer.

There's no inn or taverna, only a rather meagre magazí where you can get cold beer and tinned goods. Here you can understand what western Zagória was like 20 years ago; the locals' steadfast indifference to tourism is admirable in certain ways, but at the end of a gruelling day it is most likely to be exasperating. Perhaps in the near future some enterprising local will establish lodging or a taverna to cater for the stream of trekkers coming off Gamíla.

Stage 3B: Astráka Col to Tsepélovo
(5 hours)
Some readers may be intimidated by the prospect of the problematic Karterós Pass; many trekking tour companies are, and route their customers through an easier pass to the east, with two days' hiking sandwiching an overnight or two in the attractive village of Tsepélovo. I say 'two' because it's worth spending an extra day hunting out the exquisite 18th and 19th-century bridges in the valleys downstream from the village.

This stage is identical to Stage 3A until the point, about half an hour along from the Astráka shelter, where the O3 wanders off to the east. Watch for traces on the slope to the right, on the same side as Astrákas mountain, which seem to merge into a natural path – natural in the sense that the flat, seemingly artificial surface seems chiselled out of the limestone strata.

One hour along, after traversing the multi-branched upper reach of a gully, you reach the large Rombózi pond (about 1925 metres), buttressed by a stone dam and set squarely in the middle of the high plateau linking Astráka and Gamíla; ahead and behind are broad vistas of the territory covered and yet to come. At the southern end of the pond is a little gap – slip through this to descend a natural staircase down to the stáni of Miriúli (about 1900 metres). The canine welcoming committee is particularly hysterical here, so steer clear of the buildings until the last possible moment, when you'll have to pass within a few metres of them.

Here is another notch in the landscape and a second, even more distinct natural stairway which drops over limestone badlands. After a few hops and jumps between sheer gullies on either side, the countryside flattens out a bit and the trail continues just under the shadow of a low limestone bluff to the right. The descending gully on your left begins to drop off more and more sharply, and about an hour past the saddle pond your path plunges left. Within 15 minutes it has switchbacked down to the bottom of a dry wash at about 1650 metres, the lowest elevation on this stage until the very end.

From the ravine bed, climb about 20 minutes until finding, on the left, a very weak spring (1700 metres) oozing out from a tiny crevice, garnished with maidenhair ferns and protected by an overhanging rock. This spot, shaded until past midday by high cliffs to the east, is an excellent lunch stop and the place to survey the beginnings of the Mégas Lákkos gorge in front of you. The traverse of Mégas Lákkos is reportedly a three-hour cross-country exercise, ending by the Klíma springs at its mouth.

From the maidenhair spring the path begins climbing in earnest, rounding a corner with the best views of Mégas Lákkos and then zig-zagging up the mountainside before you to a small, 1750-metre pass half an hour above the spring. Mégas Lákkos recedes from view, and after a few moments clambering up and down through a patch of dirt you meet another pond, that of Dzánova.

Skirt it and proceed until, about 45 minutes past the spring, you emerge on a 1700-metre lip overlooking the ravine leading down to Tsepélovo. An obvious trail bears right past 1803-metre Filakío (Kazárma); this leads to a point between Vradhéto and Tsepélovo described in the following section Sidetrip: Around Tsepélovo, and is used by some excursion groups as an alternative way to the village. However, the most direct route involves plunging doggedly straight downhill; it's a fairly nasty one hour 15 minutes down scree slopes to Tsepélovo.

Sometimes there's a clear right of way,

sometimes not; initially you can use any of several parallel traces on a grassy hillside, but eventually you'll find yourself at the top of a juniper-studded outcrop flanked by two shallow gullies. Begin zig-zagging carefully down the nose of this to the main canyon's bed, where a proper jeep track picks up on the Tsepélovo side. At the top of this final grade, a lone fir tree stands guard over a ksoklísi – just before, turn right onto the cobbled way that skirts the edge of the ravine as it heads downhill into town. You should arrive about five hours after leaving Astráka col.

Tsepélovo (1100 metres) compares well with Monodhéndhri, Elafótopos or the Pápingos as an architectural showcase, and additionally is something of a regional centre, supporting a secondary school and a stable population of about 600. But most of the time the village, whose name means 'Place of the Hammer' in old Slavic, is a sleepy community whose quiet is disturbed only by the mutterings of summer thunder and the tolling of the hours from the church clocktower.

In Tsepélovo, Alekos Gouris (☎ (0653) 81 214) has an inn and a store, and prepares simple suppers. He speaks English and is the resident expert on the nearby mountains. When trek groups fill his lodge you can stay at the Ksenonas Alexandhros, run by his relative Fani Tsiavalia. There are two daily (Monday to Friday) buses to Ioánnina, early in the morning and at 3.15 pm; they return from Ioánnina at 8.30 am and 2 pm, passing through 80 minutes later.

Sidetrip: Around Tsepélovo

It's highly worthwhile interrupting a traverse to visit the famous monasteries and bridges below Tsepélovo. While there are historic bridges throughout Greece, Zagória, with more than 60 of them, has by far the best concentration. You can return via the tiny hamlet of Vradhéto, which until quite recently was accessible only via an ingenious kalderími of successive hairpin turns hacked out of a steep cliff.

The monasteries of Rongovú and Ayías Paraskevís are 30 minutes respectively south

and east of Tsepélovo, the former below, the latter above the paved road, which is the easiest way of getting to them. Ayías Paraskevís is the older by half a century (1697), and contains fine frescoes; Rongovú has perhaps the finer setting, overlooking the Vikákis ravine, where the following day hike passes through.

To begin, head out of Tsepélovo on the asphalt towards Ioánnina, and leave this before the first sharp curve about 10 minutes along, in favour of a path heading down the left bank of the same ravine you'd crossed to enter the village in Stage 3B. It's 20-plus minutes down to the stream, following the remnants of the old kalderími to Kípi village.

At the bottom you'll find two bridges, the so-called Palioyéfiro downstream, and the Hatsíou span upstream. The Palioyéfiro or 'Old Bridge' is a perilous, vegetation-flecked contraption so named because nobody is certain when it was built, though it long precedes the Hatsíou span (1804) which was erected to replace it. Evidently some *arkádhes* or bannister-rocks on the newer one, a few of which survive, made all the difference for the nervous!

Once on the far bank, follow the watercourse downhill for about an hour until reaching the next bridge, that of Kondodhímou (the original builder) or Lazarídhi (a miller who had his mill nearby). This structure, dating from 1753, funnelled traffic from a now almost-forgotten trail descending from Kapésovo.

Kípi (Báyia) village itself, the low elevation for the day at about 750 metres, is just a km or so beyond the Kondodhímou bridge, and is has enough interest and amenities to merit a lunch stop. The magazí as always is on the square. Very close, over a tributary ravine known as Kusiárya, is a small, 1764-vintage bridge carrying a now badly overgrown trail up to Kukúli. Don't bother with this path, at least for the moment, but instead carry on downstream until you happen upon one of the most famous bridges in Ípiros, the three-arched Kaloyerikó or Plakídhas bridge.

This fairy-tale structure owes its dual

nomenclature to several phases of construction and repairs. Expenses for the original 1814 stone bridge were defrayed by a monk (*kalóyeros*) at a monastery in Vítsa, but it was repaired in 1866 – as a plaque on the side explicitly states – by brothers Alexandhros and Andhreas Plakidhas of Kukúli, and again in 1912 by the latter's son Evyenios in memory of his father. Therefore, this was possibly the last great Zagórian civic works project before the end of the Turkish era.

The last major bridge on the day's walk is 20 minutes below the Kaloyerikó, at the point where the sideroad for Kípi joins the Ioánnina-Tsepélovo asphalt. This is a particularly quirky span, built between rocky narrows at what in effect is the head of the Víkos gorge; one approach ramp had to be bent 90° to the main axis. It was originally erected in 1750 by one Noutsos, a Greek deputy of Ali Pasha, with money extorted from his coreligionists, and repaired by his son; later the bridge came to be known after the miller Grigoris Kokkoros, who took advantage of the snowmelt torrents in the narrows here and maintained the bridge until 1910.

Incidentally, it's perfectly possible to enter the Víkos gorge from here if there is little or no water, passing under yet another bridge, the double-arched Misíou (1748), which serves an old trail between Vítsa and Kukúli.

Some hiking parties prefer to enter Víkos this way, though this will add a good four km and two hours to a lengthwise traverse.

From the Kókkoros bridge most walkers submit to 4½ km of road-walking up towards Kapésovo (Kepésovo), or hope to coincide with the afternoon bus going uphill. A bit past Kapésovo there's a sideroad marked 'Vradhéto 6 km'; bear left onto an obvious path about 30 metres down this. The next 15 minutes involves a descent to the bottom of the Mezariá ravine, where you cross a tiny, anonymous bridge. Now there's a 45-minute climb to Vradhéto, the first half hour of this on an incredibly tightly coiled, revetted stair path which skilfully conquers a palisade – definitely a premier Zagórian

North Píndhos: Cliff-scaling *kalderími* to Vradhéto

engineering feat on a par with any bridge. In the last 15 minutes the grade slackens and the path dims.

Vradhéto is small and high (over 1200 metres) – one sleepy magazí, seven winter inhabitants – and distinguished mainly by its unusual church; the belfry is short and rectangular, contrary to the slender, tall hexagons favoured elsewhere in Zagória.

A 40-minute walk beyond Vradhéto will take you to the place called Belóï, a lookout over the southern part of the Víkos gorge. A livestock track heading first west and then north out of the hamlet ends within 15 minutes, after which you should bear left (west) across pastureland, being careful not to lose unnecessary altitude in numerous small gullies.

To return to Tsepélovo from Vradhéto, walk east about one km on the road and, at the point where the road bears straight down and right (south), turn left onto a trail heading east. After about 30 minutes you'll see a rocky crag ahead, topped by a cross and an isolated belfry belonging to a tin-roofed ksoklísi at the base of the outcrop. The tour groups' long way around into Tsepélovo from the north apparently links up with your itinerary here.

By the chapel, the trail veers left briefly,

Zagórian Bridges

The stone-built bridges of Zagória usually rank as the biggest surprise for visitors to the region, who often mistakenly attribute them to the Turks and wonder why such intricate structures, colossally expensive in their time, came to be in a province so depopulated and economically depressed this century. Some might wonder why they are there at all, spanning boulder-strewn canyons that are bone-dry an hour after a summer thunderstorm, owing to the porous limestone strata.

With a few exceptions, the Zagórian bridges were not Turkish-sponsored, but an aspect of the brief Greek Orthodox cultural flowering which occurred here during the three centuries prior to the incorporation of Ípiros into modern Greece in 1913. Members of leading families could travel outside the Ottoman Empire without interference and amass large fortunes, which went not only towards construction of the handsome Zagórian mansions but also to various community service projects, principally the bridges.

These date primarily from the 18th and 19th century, and in pre-automobile days the spans were the sole and essential links between the various villages as well as between the Zagórokhoria in general and the outside world. What may seem to the summer tourist a canyon little wetter than a Saharan wadi, is from December to April frequently a raging torrent; often water mills for grinding grain were built into the foundations of the larger bridges. Where money allowed and stream flow warranted it, double or even triple arches were provided.

It's not always obvious from their position which village sponsored each bridge; for example, the triple-arched Plakídha span was funded and maintained by worthies in Kukúli, an hour's walk north, and not by those in Kípi around the bend, who saw to the Kondodhímou bridge upstream, among others. Similarly, the Kókkoros single-arch structure by the modern road was the responsibility of Kapésovo and Vradhéto. To give an idea of the scale of investment relative to the local economy, the Plakídha bridge supposedly cost 20,000 **grosia** (an Ottoman coin) to build; back then a sheep, worth about $200 today, was valued at 8 grosia, and a typical day-labourer's wage was one grosi. Adjusting for inflation and the change in values over two centuries, the Plakídha bridge is a half-million-dollar project!

Though the funding for the bridges may have been local, the knowledge of the craft was not – the master masons hailed mostly from poor and remote communities elsewhere in Ípiros, such as Pirsóyanni and Vúrbiani on Mt Grámmos, and Áganada, Prámanda and Huliarádhes on or near Mt Dzúmerka. These men travelled all summer throughout Greece in work parties known as **bulúkia**, mending previous masterpieces as well as erecting new ones, but their wanderings were halted by the new Balkan frontiers and virulent ideologies of this century. Trade secrets were passed from father to son in a special argot, so the knowledge died out with the last of the artisans; now when a historically listed bridge needs repair (not often, since they were cleverly designed to be self-supporting without mortar), it's a job for specialists of the national archaeological service. ■

then plunges right, along the opposite side of a gully; in this vicinity it was once a well-maintained kalderími but is now mostly crumbled. Tsepélovo (a difficult village to photograph except from this vantage) appears, and the path, deteriorating by the minute, begins manoeuvering down the slope towards a walnut grove near the floor of the same ravine crossed at the end of Stage 3B, except about 200 metres downstream.

You'll enter the village just over two hours after leaving Vradhéto, in the vicinity of house No 86.

Stage 3C: Tsepélovo to Vrisokhóri via Tsúka Róssa Pass
(9 hours)

A dirt-road system has been built in the last decade above both Tsepélovo and Skamnélli to serve the stánes of the Gúra valley, so the first half of the distance to the pass can be covered in a vehicle. Alekos Gouris may be willing to provide this service to trek groups; otherwise it's nearly two hours, up the main gully heading north-north-east from Tsepélovo, to the potholed badlands known as Megála Lithária (not to be confused with

the 2467-metre peak of that name between Karterós and Tsúka Róssa).

Continue up through this a few minutes and you'll meet another dirt track coming up from Skamnélli village, along the eastern side of a slight ridge separating the two ascent routes. The nose of the hogback overlooks a large cirquė extending between 2000 and 2150 metres, with the apparent weak spot in the alpine wall ahead, just left (west) of Tsúka Róssa summit, your way out. First, however, locate the plentiful Gúra spring which erupts at the base of its namesake peak, watering a pasture that is home to some of the best wildflower displays on Gamíla. Gúra ('Spring of Water', in Albanian) is a fairly common place-name in Greece's northern mainland.

If you've walked the whole way from Tsepélovo, you'll need 3½ hours to reach the Tsúka Róssa pass (2340 metres); Tsúka Róssa means 'Red Peak' in Rumaniká idiom. Off to the right is a false pass which gives on to nothing but a stupendous drop into the valley enclosed by Tsúka Róssa and Gúra – if you're for some reason reversing this stage, don't be fooled by it! The stáni of

North Píndhos: Parade of goats on the Plakídhas bridge near Kípi

Kátsanos lies 90 minutes below the pass, and from there on the route is identical with that of Stage 3A. Easier though it may be, it still requires the same amount of elapsed walking time – nearly nine hours – and a consequently early start from Tsepélovo.

Stage 4: Vrisokhóri to Paleosélli
(3 hours)

The O3 as currently marked from Vrisokhóri across the Aóös river was recently (and senselessly) bulldozed, so the long-distance committee is planning to reroute the trail further west. Most likely it will follow the existing path described.

Just before Vrisokhóri's main church and plane tree, a cobbled street takes off down and to the left; within a few moments this becomes a wide mule track, then a decayed kalderími. About 25 minutes out of town, cross an old bridge over a running stream at about 800 metres, and shortly after another, smaller one. During the next 10 minutes you thread through a schist gully to the shack-like ksoklísi of Áyios Minás, astride a pass.

I was told to shun the paths going off to the left, and did, but in retrospect they would probably have worked as well as the route actually followed, ending up at the mouth of the same tributary ravine to the Aóös. The sure (but roundabout) way involves bearing right onto a fainter ridge trail. Eroded and slick, this falls off slightly to the left before reaching a saddle at the base of the conical Tsúma hill, some 50 minutes along. Here continue slightly to the left (west) to find a path through scrub and forest; don't lose or gain altitude initially, until you come out at the tip of a partly forested, eroded spur plunging to the river. At this point the path is faint to nonexistent, but gets you to the bed of the Aóös (600 metres) one hour 15 minutes along.

The best place to ford the river is downstream next to some copses of low trees on the south (true left) bank and the probably debouchement of the alternative path down from Áyios Minás; even in August the water is knee high and the current swift, so check in Vrisokhóri about levels before setting out.

Once on the far bank you'll see an abandoned orchard with an equally derelict aqueduct at its rear – the place is called Mikrí Vovúsa. A potable stream trickles under the aqueduct; the trick is to go either well left or just right of the creek ravine, up steep spurs, to intersect what appears to be an important trail some 50 minutes above the river at 900 metres. This seems to be coming up from a point on the ridge enclosing Mikrí Vovúsa on the west, but the locals will probably assure you after the fact that the steep, tortuous, just-barely-a-trail up the eastern spur is the most direct ascent.

Pass a weak spring in a grassy hollow some 25 minutes later, and then almost immediately the rural chapel of Áyios Andónios. Within another like period of time, you draw even with the lowest fields of Paleosélli, parallelling the bank of a permanent stream, to reach the western edge of the village, three walking hours out of Vrisokhóri.

Paleosélli

Paleosélli has a couple of simple stores and cafés, but these observe a strict siesta between 1.30 to 6.30 pm – no exceptions, and hardly consoling as you plod along sweaty and hungry. Things are a bit better after dark, when a small (two-room) but comfortable ksenónas operates above the combination post office/OTE. This is managed by the Politistikós Síllogos (Cultural Club) of Paleosélli (☎ (0655) 71 216). One of its members, Sotiris Rouvalis, is in residence most of the summer and is eager to provide assistance to trekkers. The club also controls the use of the wooden refuge at Náneh.

The locals claim that before WW II all of the Kutsovlach villages of the Aóös valley, from Eléfthero to Vovúsa, equalled or exceeded those of central-western Zagória in grandeur; with an abundance of local timber for long spans and carved interiors, the mansions here were huge and sumptuous. They were all burnt by the Germans in a one-week period in the winter of 1943-44, and the civil war completed the humbling of the district.

When reconstruction finally occurred, it was in the jerrybuilt tin-roofed style of the depressed 1950s.

Paleosélli was additionally famous for its vineyards, which flourished on sunny, south-facing slopes down by the Aóös, but with the population gone the forest has closed in on the old terraces (as you discovered coming up from the river). The climate has become cooler and damper, and the local grapes now ripen with difficulty.

Another peculiarity of the Rumaniká-speaking communities of the Aóös basin is the prolongation of the nationwide 15 August festival until 19 August – the so-called *Vlakhopanayía* celebration. Don't expect a free bed anywhere in the area until after the 21st, and don't except to stay sober (the villagers coax a very lethal red wine out of the remaining vines).

Paleosélli is served by a daily bus from Kónitsa at 2 pm, which returns from the end of the line at Dhístrato around 6.30 am the next day. Three mornings a week (the exact day tends to change each year) there is an additional outbound morning departure from Kónitsa. Indeed, if you're pressed for time and don't like the sound of the crest routes over Gamíla or the river crossing between Vrisokhóri and Paleosélli, you could do worse than get one of those buses to the foot of Smólikas.

OVER MT SMÓLIKAS

Mt Smólikas (2637 metres), Greece's second-highest point, is also one of its most imposing mountains, and has lately become relatively popular with Greeks and foreigners alike. Tucked in the heart of its lunar limestone-and-serpentine grandeur are two lakes: one easily accessible and favoured by campers, the other isolated and frequented only by shepherds watering their flocks. The range is quite extensive – a good 400 sq km of territory above 1700 metres – and is home to small wildlife: field mice, hares, chamois, birds of prey, plus the occasional larger mammal. The two-day trek across is one of the more demanding portions of a northern Píndhos loop, but is also among the most

rewarding in terms of scenery, campsites and chances for sidetrips.

Stage 1: Paleosélli to Dhrakólimni of Smólikas
(4 hours)

It used to be that Pádhes village, three km east of Paleosélli, was the favourite ascent base for Smólikas from the Aóös valley, but recently a road was bulldozed from Pádhes to approximately the 1600-metre contour. The trail up from the village still exists, but cut to ribbons as it is by the new track, you'd get little joy in hiking the first three hours. Now that the O3 is marked from Paleosélli instead, and a fine new refuge has been built above that village, the route described is far more appealing.

The well-trodden path starts along the stream splitting Paleosélli, at 1150 metres. Go up the true left (east) bank, then pass a red-roofed hut (perhaps a water mill) with a funny orange pipe leading into it. Cross the creek on an upper bridge, then curl up to a spring and ikónisma just 10 minutes above the village.

Half an hour along you'll reach a meadow at 1300 metres after taking the right-hand fork at a large water main; sporadic, well-worn O3 diamonds offer some assistance. One hour out, the ikónisma of Ayía Paraskeví stands next to an emergency shelter (one side's open to the view) and the Túrku spring at 1400 metres. The availability of water has not been a problem up to now, and with the now-exposed aqueduct nearby, you could camp almost anywhere in the idyllic pastureland.

Beyond Ayía Paraskeví the trail climbs more sharply through the woods; as you arrive at another meadow with some corrals and huts – the stáni of Kitsíu – O3 and other waymarks forsake what seems to be the main trail and circle cross-country above the structures. Certain signs give decreasing distances to the mountaineers' hut at Náneh (1650 metres), finally reached one hour 45 minutes along.

The recently built wooden refuge has 12 bunks but can hold twice as many people if need be; there's a heating stove inside and a reliable water tap and privy outside. It's an excellent campsite if you can't be bothered with the key or the shelter is full.

The actual spring of Náneh, which supplies the refuge faucet, spills out at 1750 metres, following a pretty climb through Balkan pine forest with plenty of mushrooms on the ground. O3 diamonds take you east-north-east towards the hint of a ridge, but first you get to a sloping pasture where the trail disappears. You should see a gap in the trees and a notch in the ridge above you; aim for the gap (1900 metres), turning left as you attain it 2¾ hours out of Paleosélli.

Just under three hours out you arrive at another saddle a bit to the north; from here the somewhat cleaned-up path takes off to the right (east of the ridgeline), allowing a glimpse of the valley leading down to Pádhes. As you start the fourth hour of walking, the distinctive summit cone of Smólikas pops into sight, which is just as well since the last O3 marker leaves you stranded without a clue.

Head up to the ridge, which will be on your left, as the trees thin out; you must climb to about 2100 metres, then drop slightly to yet another saddle (at about 3½ hours out), where an old path from Pádhes comes up from the east to intersect your route.

Now there's another obligatory climb up to about 2150 metres; near the highest, last clump of trees, some cairns are reassuring.

Your course, on a northerly bearing for some time now, curls north-east as a clear path threads through an erosion zone, around Point 2217 of Misorákhi. Rather abruptly you almost step right into Dhrakólimni at 2150 metres, nestled in a natural bowl four walking hours out of Paleosélli.

Dhrakólimni This heart-shaped lake at the foot of Smólikas summit has the same name as the tarn on Gamíla, because popular legend asserts the guardian spirits of both dwell at the bottom in the form of a dragon (*dhrákos*). Deep as they both are, the lakes aren't quite big enough to hide a Nessie, unless you allow for

a mutant among the hundreds of newts rippling the surface of the water.

There are just four or five level, dryish campsites on the turfy shore, so get there early in summer, as it's a relatively popular spot. From the top of the slopes enclosing the lake you can watch vivid sunsets over Greek and Albanian ridges and canyons; at dusk the steady breeze dies (fortunately, since this is one of the coldest camps in Greece) and the only sound after dark, until late in summer, is that of snowmelt cascading from the base of the peak to the north-east. In the morning it's well worth climbing the knoll to the east to glimpse the wall of Gamíla glowing in the sunrise.

By noon a hasty swim can be contemplated, but you may have sheepdogs and sheep from a nearby stáni for company. I've never been sick from drinking the water, but the squeamish might boil/purify it, or drink from a small pothole spring near the lake's edge, at one of the lobes of the 'heart'.

Sidetrip: Smólikas Peak

The classic and most direct route to the 2637-metre summit begins from the viewpoint knoll east of the lake, above the base of the 'heart'. It's a tough climb, over a crumbly surface on a grade of nearly 100%, requiring one hour 15 minutes. A slightly more moderately pitched ascent can be accomplished from the stáni north of and below the lake by following another ridge, running parallel to the headwaters of the drainage in the stáni, up to the trig point. The views are as you'd expect, and one afternoon many years ago I glimpsed a chamois very near the top.

Stage 2A: Dhrakólimni to Kerásovo (& Vice Versa)

(2½-3hours)

This section is one of the easiest and most enjoyable routes on the mountain, and constitutes a quick way off it or an alternative to Paleosélli as an approach.

The path begins, predictably enough, at the stáni below and north of Dhrakólimni, at about 2000 metres – it's fairly obvious in the first trees beyond the rivulet-laced pastureland. The description of the downhill course will not be meticulous since it's almost impossible to get lost in this direction. The only distinctive landmark is a healthy spring about one hour 20 minutes down the mountain. Two and a half hours along, your path ends at the eastern edge of Kerásovo, quite near the church of Ayía Paraskeví, also the official name of the village.

Kerásovo village itself is a fairly interesting community, set on a ledge at 950 metres overlooking the Vurkopótamos (Kerasovítikos) stream. Its houses seem to have escaped destruction during the 1940s, but nevertheless life fled from the place after the civil war and it's as seasonally inhabited as any other highish mountain village.

There is just one inn (☎ (0655) 41 215) with some of the most expensive beds in Ípiros and a managerial attitude problem to match; it would only be worth the price asked if you could pack three people in a triple.

Sympathetic villagers will point you to acceptable campsites north-east of town – there's a good terrace near a spring along the old trail to Fúrka. Eating out you have more choice – either the inn's restaurant or the immensely popular bar-pizzeria, with open-air dining. There's a weekday afternoon bus from Kónitsa which returns the next morning at either 7 or 8 am, according to the driver's whim.

Reverse Itinerary If you are starting an ascent from Kerásovo, bear right onto the start of the path just past the chapel and a seasonal bar-pizzeria, and then right again at an immediate fork to be confirmed with red dots. After crossing the last fields of Kerásovo and a damp meadow, the trail broaches a pine forest about 45 minutes along. Another half an hour gets you to a stream crossing the trail, and within 15 minutes more you'll reach the spring mentioned in the downhill summary, which feeds the stream.

Just under two hours out of the village the path veers abruptly right across a grassy slope, forsaking what appears to be the main path in favour of a narrower one. Within 20 minutes of this turning, a mixed forest of beech, fir and pine begins; the trail shifts gradually right to follow the east (true right) bank of a watered canyon upstream, towards the bare ridge above.

You reach the treeline after just under a three-hour climb; just beyond, a potable stream laps the base of the pastureland below the lake, tucked out of sight among the bare spurs overhead. The stáni itself huddles by a final spring almost exactly three hours above Kerásovo. The inhabitants are friendly and will doubtless point you along the final stretch unbidden. From their pens you've a 20-minute trail-less clamber up to Dhrakólimni, the way now marked with cairns and a few red dots.

Stage 2B: Dhrakólimni to Samarína
(5½-6½ hours)

You have two choices regarding onward progress from the lake to Samarína. If you can endure the process of dragging a full backpack up to the summit, you will save considerable time if not effort – though the subsequent ridge-walk is also only comfortable with a relatively light load. The alternative is to descend the ravine draining south-east off the viewpoint knoll east of Dhrakólimni, to the point where the old trail up from Pádhes cuts in – a more conservative process, but one involving a sharp loss and recovery of altitude. From the low ridges south-south-east of the lake, below the viewpoint, you'll find the easiest way into the stream canyon draining off of them. It's an hour-plus descent, with no trail, along the bed of the main watercourse to about the 1800-metre contour, where the old principal path up from Pádhes crosses the stream. If the river does a quick S-bend and plummets suddenly, you've passed it – retrace your steps for about 400 metres.

Turn east uphill onto the path; about five minutes above the stream a smaller brook pours across the trail. You emerge from the forest, with a hard left turn, to describe a gentle arc along the top of a lush meadow before curling back right to a stáni 45 minutes above the river at nearly 2000 metres, on the western bank of a major creek draining directly off Point 2637, prominent to the north. The place is inhabited from May to October by some shepherds from Samarína, and it's a good idea to stop and check your bearings with them, though if you look carefully in the few trees further east you'll see strategic yellow blazes on select trunks.

Once under way again, it's just over an hour to the high pass of Lemós (about 2400 metres) which carries most foot traffic across the watershed. Just on the other side is an initially intimidating prospect over the harsh Vathílakkos ravine and a moonscape sloping down to it, not to mention the continuation of the summit ridge which curls around to enclose you on the right (east). A few moments below, in the centre of this bleak zone, a tiny spring – welled in by rocks and about half a metre across – is worth knowing about, but the site's too exposed for camping.

In the next 45 minutes you descend, then climb a natural rock stairway (the Skála) dangerously littered with scree. Point 2477 of Mósia hill hovers above a tiny spring seeping from the rocks – barely enough for people, but sufficient for wild animals whom you may see sipping if you approach quietly. As you round the corner onto a plateau-like ridge sloping down to the north-east, red blazes supersede the yellow convention, supplemented by a line of cairns which some kindly hands have dribbled through an otherwise nondescript boneyard of football-sized rocks.

Abruptly there's a steep portion of path worming down through a notch in the terrain before escaping out onto a bare hogback. On your left yawns a steep drop into a dry gully – it's easy to stray off course if visibility is poor. As the trail zigzags laboriously down this saddle towards an exposed pasture at about 2200 metres, look right (south) out over an equally avoidable drop-off to see the second, nameless tarn of Smólikas, about the same size as Dhrakólimni, nestled at the base of Point 2510. There's no side trail to it, however, and it would be a difficult though by no means impossible scramble to it.

The treeline is reached at about 2100 metres, some two hours below Lemós (five hours total thus far), and with it some protection from the winds which may have been buffeting you since the pass. Next, there's a fairly level 20-minute portion along a windy meadow south of 2239-metre Bogdháni (Vúzi), where some hardy, gnarled pines grow in whatever shelter they can find below the altimeter. Once over a subtle col, dip five minutes to a small rivulet (the Bogdháni spring) among the serpentine-and-schist beds, which makes a good rest stop. After another 25 minutes you'll have dropped through an increasingly forested landscape to a beautiful alpine clearing at about 1900 metres, where the strong Supotíra spring spills picturesquely into a log trough next to the path.

In its final 45 minutes the path plunges through thick stands of black pines until suddenly you emerge on a bare slope leading down to now-visible Samarína. Pass a flat-roofed water-pumping station, a soccer field, and a solid stone building that's the municipal ksenónas, and you're at the edge of the village some 6½ hours from Dhrakólimni.

If you choose to approach the critical Lemós saddle along the summit ridge, you'll need at least 90 minutes up towards Point 2637 with a full pack, then another 40 minutes along the watershed, avoiding all obstacles by following faint traces just south of and below the crest. From Lemós onwards the route is the same but the cumulative walking time will be nearly an hour shorter. It's not as intimidating as it sounds – organised trek groups do this ridge-walk on a regular basis, sparing themselves possible ugliness and confusion resulting from the recent roadworks near the river.

Samarína At 1475 metres, Samarína can safely lay claim to being the highest village in Greece, but local pride stuffs the ballot box, so to speak, by asserting an altitude of 1650 metres (nonsense, as any good map will show). Excluding Métsovo it is also the largest (if seasonal) community of Rumaní in the country. Like most such villages above

1000 metres in the northern Píndhos, it's occupied only from mid-May to mid-October, with all residents except a snowbound guard retreating to winter quarters near Árgos Orestiádha and on the Thessalian plain.

The village was in bad odour with just about everyone during the 1940s, and suffered accordingly. First the central government accused the locals (mostly wrongly) of collaboration with the Italian invaders, on the basis of linguistic affinity and a few cases where Rumanika-speakers willingly acted as guides and interpreters. Then the place suffered the same incendiary reprisal at the hands of the Nazis as its neighbours over in the Aóös valley. Anything left standing was done for during the civil war, so there remains little of interest to see aside from the late 18th-century church (always spared) at the base of the village. Inside, an intricately carved témblon and lurid frescoes of the Apocalypse (a favourite didactic subject) compete for your attention. Outside, a husky black pine has planted itself, and flourishes, in the roof of the apse!

Samarína is principally a social phenomenon; on any given summer night up to 4000 people stroll and frolic in the central platía and the half-dozen tavernas giving onto it. Perhaps as many sheep mill around the surrounding hills, formerly driven up from Thessalía on the hoof during the spring but now transferred more prosaically by pick-up truck. They are the source of the excellent local cheese and meat (though oddly, not yoghurt).

Besides multiple restaurants, Samarína can offer the aforementioned ksenónas above the village (usually booked solid until mid-September, when it shuts); some simple rooms above the taverna on the eastern side of the square, and the Hotel Kiparíssi, way down the hill near the old church. There's also an OTE post should you have the urge to phone home. Bus service is nonexistent, and even if there were any it would be to Grevená, capital of the province in which Samarína falls – no help if you have to return to Ioánnina. By far the best way in and out is on foot, as in Stage 3.

Reverse Itinerary If for any reason you need to reverse the crossing of Smólikas, landmarks and times are as follows. From the ksenónas, keep left of the bunker-like pumping station and, just below the edge of the forest, link up with a prominent livestock trace looping around and up into the outermost trees, one of which sports a red metal arrow. Once safely under way, the Supotíra spring is an hour along; Bogdháni rivulet and peak are 90 minutes and two hours out respectively; and the tilted tableland with cairns, beyond the lake-cirque on the left and gully to the right, is three hours beyond Samarína. The 'Skála' done in this direction is particularly treacherous; the Lemós pass is broached just over four hours into the day.

Dropping to the Samarinot stáni and the river, keep right of a ravine which opens up in the high turf beyond – the overly inviting, cairned trail down its left bank leads to Ármata. From the pass it's just under an hour to the *mándhra* (synonymous with stáni), on the far bank of the stream pouring off the main peak, and another half an hour to the river. Turn right here and follow the drainage up for just over an hour until forced up by the increasingly narrowed canyon onto a steep, grass-slick hillside to the left. Dhrakólimni is just 10 minutes further north, or nearly 7½ hours out of Samarína.

You'd save more than an hour by bearing west from Lemós pass and following the watershed to the summit and the final descent to the lake.

Stage 3: Samarína to Vovúsa via Dhístrato

(9 hours)

This stage has replaced an old shuffle over Mt Vassilítsa to the village of Avdhélla, with a boring road-tramp from there to Perivóli and Vovúsa. Proliferating roads, hotels and ski lifts have negated whatever interest the section over the mountain once had; all credit is due the local overland trail committees for blazing the alternative, which as the E6 heads almost due south along the Aóös valley to Vovúsa and beyond.

Initially, you must follow the main dirt

dhimósio south-south-east out of Samarína as far as the monastery of Ayías Paraskevís (1200 metres), 40 minutes along. The frescoes here are the equal of the ones in the pine-tufted church in town. Carrying on, the E6 crosses the tributary to the Aöös and climbs slightly up the shoulder of 2126-metre Gomára, an outrider of Vassilítsa, then drops down to a long-established forest road on its south flank, within sight of Dhístrato (1000 metres). The whole exercise won't take over four hours.

There is food and accommodation in Dhístrato, which is also the terminus of the bus route to and from Kónitsa, but with an early enough start out of Samarína you might consider continuing to Vovúsa the same day, within five more hours. The E6 traces a course above the eastern (true right) bank of the river on a mixture of trail and forest-track surface, according to groups who have done it (I have not). There's little altitude change involved, and the way is marked, but you should still probably have a tent (and the appropriate *Korfes* maps) on hand, since there's nothing between the two villages except dense forest.

Vovúsa Vovúsa is the only Píndhos village built directly on the Aöös, and is low enough at 1000 metres not to be snowed in completely during winter. That fact, and the sawmill a short distance upstream, ensures that the place is inhabited all year round. The village is most famous for its graceful bridge dating from 1748, which links its two neighbourhoods. Unhappily that's about the size of Vovúsa's architectural attractions, since it (like most of its neighbours) was burnt down in 1944. Only one house escaped unscathed, and it's now maintained, with interior trappings, as an informal museum. Here more than in most of the Rumaní villages you'll sense the effects of commercial, cultural and sentimental ties with Romania, including (former) partial funding of standard Romanian language classes for the young. At the same time there's a big US connection – summertime sees large numbers of Georgians and Texans on temporary visits to their ancestral haunts.

There are several simple tavernas but really only one place to stay: Oreo Perivoli, a giant, rambling hotel overhanging the river. The bus service out, if you're ending your trek, is decent – on Tuesday, Wednesday, Friday and Saturday to Ioánnina at 6 am, with a 2 pm departure on Sunday. (Except for Sunday, when the bus leaves Ioánnina at 8.15 am, the inbound service from Ioánnina is at 2 pm the day before the 6 am return trip).

Despite its murky greenness, the river here is pleasantly warm for swimming, and there are suitable pools upstream.

OTHER TREKS IN THE NORTH PÍNDHOS
Vovúsa to Métsovo via the Válla Kálda
(14 hours – 2 days)

It is more than possible, however, to continue a trek for two more days to Métsovo via Mts Avgó and Flénga, and the wild Válla Kálda which separates them. I have not been beyond Mt Avgó, but with the recent opening of the E6 and the availability of better maps, this itinerary is less mysterious than it once was.

The first step is to climb 2177-metre Avgó, which towers about Vovúsa; this is a four-hour undertaking along faint trails east of the village which have recently been reclaimed from the bush. Mr Chronis Dhrougias in Vovúsa can provide a guide service if necessary.

The route climbs initially up half-forested spurs of the mountain in just over three hours to a flat, round meadow at about 1800 metres, where the tiny Tóska spring bubbles up in a sandy pothole sheltered by boulders. In the old days it's claimed that young men and women of Vovúsa and the nearby village of Perivóli used to meet secretly here on warm summer evenings, away from the disapproving gaze of their elders – so the place is still known as Koritsolívadho, the 'Maiden's Meadow'.

Once past this romantic spot, the best approach to the peak itself heads up through gnarled trees on the left, nearly atop the hogback that drops steeply off to the north. Half an hour beyond, you cross a trough-like pasture leading like a bowling alley up to the base of Avgó proper, which from this angle resembles more the tip of a US football than an egg (*avgó*). An obvious trail tackles the final stretch to the 2177-metre trig point, which seems higher than it really is in its dramatic isolation. Up the top there's a fire-watching tower, either never finished or utterly vandalised; in any case the spot's an ideal target for lightning strikes, and two youths were killed there in a storm in 1982.

To continue into the Vália Kálda ('Warm Valley' in the Vlach language), leave the peak heading south-east towards a broad saddle at about 2000 metres; from there you drop as best you can on a southerly bearing into the Arkudhórema (about 1350-1400 metres) which drains the Vália Kálda. Make a camp for the night near the confluence of this stream and the Zestó Potamáki, since you will have been hiking for nearly seven hours.

The following day you'll continue south-south-west up to 2159-metre Flénga, where two small ponds hide on the north slope. A lightly cairned path reportedly draws you up a long spur beginning above the river junction. Count on spending four morning hours to enjoy the mountain and its lakes.

The usual finish to a trek is an east-south-easterly route along Flénga's extension, the so-called Mavrovúni, but this is among the most lightning-blasted terrain in Greece and can only be recommended in settled weather. If conditions are unstable you'll have to dip down into the headwaters of the Aóös, skirting the hydroelectric project here, and climb up the southern bank to meet the Greveníti-Métsovo forest road.

Assuming you get through safely – this is easy, enjoyable, broad-ridge walking at the treeline – the Mavrovúni ridge dips within three hours to a saddle over which passes the dirt dhimósio between Miliá and Métsovo. Miliá is the closer and has an inn, but if you can possibly manage to flag a passing vehicle to Métsovo, do so – you'll have a far greater choice of creature comforts there, as well as regular buses to Ioánnina or Tríkala.

I am not sure which option the E6 now takes, but trek groups are beginning to pass through here regularly in summer, and you won't be badly lost or endangered as long as you have the appropriate maps, imperfect as they are.

Kónitsa to Lákka Tsumáni via Stomíu Monastery
(4¾ hours)
This is an extremely useful link trail which can be done dovetailed with a bus ride from Dhístrato or Kerásovo to Kónitsa; or just for its own sake; or in reverse as a very economical way to connect Gamíla with Smólikas without having to conquer the crest itself. The path, which previously had a very bad reputation, has recently been minimally waymarked and is now within the capabilities of most hikers.

A short distance downstream from the river fording between Vrискhóri and Paleosélli, the Aóös river squeezes between the precipitous bases of Gamíla to the south and Trapezítsa to the north in a tight gorge about six km long. The upstream half is virtually inaccessible except to river rafters, but the lower portion is threaded by a good path leading from Kónitsa up to the cliff-top monastery of Stomíu, which overlooks the narrowest point of the canyon.

The Aóös canyon falls squarely within the Víkos National Park, and the dense forests clinging to the sheer palisades above the river reportedly offer safety to various endangered species such as lynx, bear, roe deer and birds of prey. Unfortunately, illegal hunting continues unabated, and reporting the often brazen offenders to the authorities will probably have little effect.

From the Kónitsa bus stand, walk south and downhill on the main road through town, passing the new town hall on your left. The vast flood plain of the Aóös will sprawl to your right.

Leave the main highway at the point where it curves around the Dhendhro taverna in favour of a narrow driveway heading south through a thinly built-up residential district.

At the bottom of the slope here, near the river, stand a ruined mosque and dervish tomb plus several other constructions from the Ottoman era. The most famous of these is the huge stone bridge, the largest such in Greece, spanning the Aóös where it exits the confines of the gorge. It was built relatively recently (1871) by two craftsmen from Pirsóyanni, and the enormous cost (the contemporary equivalent of \$3 million) was funded, unusually, by the donations of both local Muslims and Orthodox Christians. One of the master masons, Zioga Frondzo, was apparently a bit of a wag; asked by a German engineer which polytechnic he'd attended, he supposedly replied, 'The Kráppa Poly' (Kráppa being a pastureland in Pirsóyanni). The retreating Ottoman army intended to destroy the bridge in 1913 but fortunately was unable to do so.

Before you cross the 20-metre-high, 40-metre-long arc (elevation 480 metres), mind the bell hung from the middle – it was installed this century as a warning device after several travellers were blown off the top to their deaths by high winds. If it's clanging, use the ugly wood-and-iron cart bridge alongside.

Once on the southern bank take the bumpy dirt-and-cobble track running upstream parallel to the river, which is quite popular with Greek weekenders out fishing or innertubing. Fifteen to 20 minutes later, watch closely to the right of the track for the start of the old roller-coaster kalderími up to the monastery. It's 90 minutes on a varied surface to Stomíu, with one small but vigorous cascade about 20 minutes below it for filling water containers. The trail, despite not begin terribly efficient about getting there, allows fine views of the palisades of Mt Trapezítsa opposite, and deserves a try in at least one direction if you're walking the river canyon only as a day trip.

The alternative is to stay with what in fact is the local waterworks track, which is soon disrupted by concrete retaining walls, weirs, and mains supplying Kónitsa, as opposed to the nice old stairways and fieldstones of the

upper route. This is 10 to 20 minutes quicker, however, and considerably easier with a full pack. There is a point about 45 minutes along where the two alternatives come within five metres of each other – lots of red dots and arrows flash back and forth – so you can also change over if you regret your initial choice. Just before the waterfall the trail joins the wider track for the final stiff climb; if you descend to the bottom of the grade here, you'll find some of the more secluded swimming spots on the river. In July and August you'll be showered with wild arbutus, cherries and hazelnuts as well.

Stomíu monastery (650 metres) is visible almost from the moment you adopt the high trail at its outset, and on arrival proves to be improbably perched on a high but cultivatable bluff surrounded on three sides by air and the river. The place dates from 1774, but recently it was rather tastelessly restored, with a tin roof and gaudy paint job replacing the previous stone tiles and muted colours. The katholikón or main chapel is of minimal interest. Although two young Albanian caretakers and a single part-time monk absolutely rattle around the place, you can't count on it being open, or on monastic hospitality. The setting is really the thing: most visitors camp in the surroundings, with two springs to choose from.

The onward path up to Lákka Tsumáni begins just behind the modern fountain outside the monastery gate – it is not the wide, obvious lane heading left and slightly down to the second spring, where it ends. Once under way you climb within 15 minutes to an excellent viewpoint of the monastery and the gorge; five minutes later you bear right onto an apparently minor path, following a red arrow. Yet another five minutes further, at about 850 metres elevation, repeat the manoeuvre onto an even narrower trail, prompted by a tree with a red blaze. (The 'main' paths lead south-east, vaguely parallel with the Aóös, to the Kaloyerikó saddle, where there's another trail division: down goes to the abandoned monastery of Ayía Triádha, up goes to Kopánes and Liméria Kléfton ridge.)

The end of the first hour should see you atop a spur where the trees thin out, a welcome red blaze reassures you from a rock, and the tip of a rocky spur overlooks the canyon. Climb more gently than previously along the spur, heading south; 90 minutes out of Stomíu you arrive at an abandoned stáni and stone pen in a clearing at about 1250 metres. Here the trail fizzles; to carry on, bear right and head up the punishingly steep incline into the trees, keeping an eye out for paint splodges. You're heading west now, as the grade mercifully slackens, and 2¼ hours along you'll reach a rock pile marking a small pass at the head of a grassy slope. This is Exédhra outcrop, an ideal rest stop to take in the very satisfactory landscape overhead. The dense, mixed forest of lower down, with its hazelnuts, has been replaced by scattered pines clinging to the Gamíla crags.

The path descends slightly, heading south-west now, for the level crossing of the frayed upper reaches of an unfortunately dry ravine system. Within 25 minutes you'll be up on Davalísta ridge with its ruined stone pastoral hut; from there you've a good look at Lápatos and the valley up which you'll be going to reach the Lákka Tsumáni. The *Korfes*/YIS map tracing of the paths, not great during the first hour above the monastery, is by now completely out to lunch – disregard it.

What's actually involved is a traverse, with little net altitude change but considerable up-and-down, at the base of the formidable cliff face on your left. It's not so claustrophobic, since you can see across the plain of Kónitsa to Mt Grámmos to the northwest. You arrive at the mouth of the Lákkos Davalístas canyon leading up to your destination, 3¼ hours past Stomíu. There's year-round water here, but wait until it's more accessible further up – don't try to fetch it on first hearing.

A brief flurry of red dots on rock walls, then cairns, point you south up the canyon, which is actually a triple one; as you near the top, you want to be on the spur separating the eastern-most watercourse from the central

one. Some energetic mountaineers have even hacked steps out of the dirt over the worst bits. Once you've squeezed past some boulders to emerge on thistly turf, a trail of sorts resumes to the edge of the Lákka Tsumáni uplands at about 1725 metres, four hours along.

Another half an hour of walking brings you to the Sidheróvriso spring, beyond Point 1803, from where the Astráka col refuge pumps its water. Signs warn you off camping in the immediate vicinity of the fenced precinct, but there's excellent turf about 100 metres east and downstream.

Since the uphill elapsed time from Stomíu will be under five hours, the estimate of six hours down given on the guy-wired sign below Astráka refuge is completely unreliable. I met a party of three at Stomíu who claimed to have descended in three hours, but that is pretty manic – 3½ to four hours is a more sensible pace. In any event this is a beautiful forest walk, far shorter than any other approach to or exit from Gamíla.

Grámmos

The melancholy of this high, bare range at the extreme norh end of Ípiros is magnified by its historical and geographical associations. It was the last stronghold of the leftist rebels from 1947 to 1949, and also marks the frontier with troubled Albania. Appropriately for a border mountain, Grámmos as seen from the south (the usual first view) forms a sheer, even-topped wall separating Ípiros from Makedhonía as well as Albania.

Towards the end of the civil war, massive aerial bombardment was undertaken by the royalists to dislodge the communists, simultaneously with the first use of US-supplied napalm (helpfully dropped from US-piloted planes and used in several other valleys nearby). The turf on the highest ridges seems only partly regenerated from this thorough ploughing-up, and every climber will stumble upon spent cartridges, machine-gun bases and other rusty paraphernalia among the rebel bunkers near the summit. Although trench warfare of this sort is now obsolete, it is still a grim and current warning to those further up the peninsula who would plunge the Balkans in blood once again. The three mementos I pocketed appear to be British-made, lest UK readers be inclined to feel superior over those nasty US warmongers.

The Greeks still heartily resent the British and US interference (and arguably instigation) in their civil war, and Grámmos still attracts large numbers of people who are making a political statement or pilgrimage as much as a mountaineering expedition. For the Greek (and European) left, the battles were a heroic last stand in the face of imperialism; for the right it was a final victory over satanic evil on a par with Saint George's skewering of the dragon. Only in the last decade has the emotional charge of the issue lessened, as the nationwide celebrations on the anniversary of the final royalist victory were cancelled, and some sort of reconciliatory/rehabilitative steps were taken by the former socialist government.

ALONG THE FRONTIER

The Albanian-border factor is still very much alive, however, and must be heeded. For years it was technically illegal to hike on the mountain, though dozens of people did so if they were discreet enough to avoid the military patrols. Since 1984 no formal barriers have existed, but security is again an issue since the tidal wave of Albanian refugees in 1990. The traffic in misery has once again subsided to the previous level of a few a week, but the small conscript garrison stationed in Plikáti (the trailhead village) must now be in a continual state of alert. As opposed to the former cat-and-mouse game with the authorities, *do* let on that you intend to climb Grámmos – some of the Albanians managing to slip over the frontier now are famine-hungry, dirt-poor, and could be tempted to do some fairly desperate things. Although a Greco-Albanian border war is probably not on the cards, a conflict with the former Yugoslav Macedonian republic

could cause some local spill-over effect in the form of the area's being sealed off.

Despite this depressing past and uncertain future, Grámmos makes a rewarding outing, either as a day hike or a traverse. It is, after all, the fourth-highest peak in the land after Ólimbos, Smólikas, and Kaïmaktsalan on the former Yugoslav border; the wildflowers are superb; and the eastern part of the range is spangled with a number of small lakes. There's also a fair-sized tarn north of the peak, lying partly in Albania. Until recently the glimpse of that realm from the top was as much as most people ever saw of it, and an added attraction to the hike.

Safety Warning

Stick to the routes described, and don't go to places where there is no visible ground disturbance – there are reportedly still unexploded mines on Grámmos.

Rating & Duration

A day hike out and back from Plikáti is easy; point-to-point treks over to Grámmos village or the hamlets around the Aréna group need an extra full day and qualify for a moderate grading.

Season

The area is best in early summer, when snow streaks add some spice to the otherwise bare upper ridges, and when wildflowers outnumber flies instead of vice versa later on.

Supplies

Plikáti's larder is pretty basic; if you want specialty stuff to cook, get it in Kónitsa or Ioánnina.

Maps

Because of security considerations, maps are not what they should be. The one in *Korfes* 62 was reduced to a scale of smaller than 1:150,000, owing to pressure from the military; the YIS 1:50,000 sheet *Grámos** will probably stay restricted until doomsday.

Access

A bus runs from Kónitsa to Plikáti, the

highest village in the Gorgopótamos river valley, daily except Sunday at 2 pm. If you descend from Smólikas via Kerásovo and intend to hike on Grámmos next, bear this in mind so that you get down the 10 km of side road in time to flag down the passing afternoon bus.

All things considered, it's less risky to get to Kónitsa from whatever direction by 2 pm; from Ioánnina there are at least seven coaches daily, but only three or four arrive in time. If you miss the specific departure for the villages of Pirsóyanni, Vúrbiani, Gorgopótamos and Plikáti, it's a simple matter to get a Kastoriá-bound bus or a lift to the turn-off below Pirsóyanni, but you'll stand a good chance of walking most of the 20 km from the main-road junction to Plikáti.

Plikáti itself is a friendly village of mostly old stone houses, where the women are traditionally attired. This is the last village on the Greek side of the Mávri Pétra ridge leading up to Grámmos proper, and a remote, end-of-the-world feeling is accentuated by broad panoramas over the Gorgopótamos valley, closed off at its head by the bald barrier of the watershed glowing orange in the twilight.

There are two inexpensive – and spartan – inns on the main platía, and more comfortable rooms at the Pandopolio Agapi. This store also fixes simple meals on short notice; more substantial fare, such as a post-hike chicken dinner, can be ordered in advance.

Stage 1: Plikáti to Grámmos Summit Ridge
(3 hours one way)
Proceed north out of Plikáti (1240 metres) on the principal jeep track; 10 to 15 minutes out of the village, just after crossing a small brook, bear left onto a narrower path. After five minutes walk, take a second left onto a kalderími that threads through well-irrigated

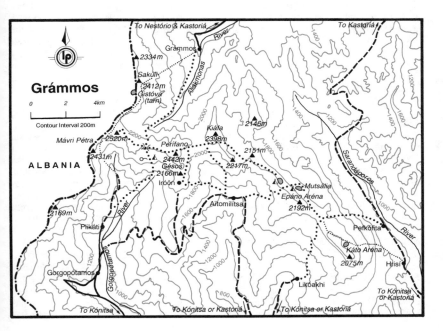

fields and orchards; the cobbles may in fact be ankle-deep in water. Mávri Pétra ridge, extending from Point 2169 to Point 2431, roughly parallels the way on your left.

Half an hour along, cross from the western (true right) bank of the stream to the eastern side and begin climbing steadily north-east through lightly wooded meadows. The asymmetrical summit of Grámmos – formerly known by the Rumaniká name Tsúka Pétsik, but now merely Point 2520 – looms before you. About one hour 15 minutes beyond the river crossing, the trail steepens noticeably, begins switchbacking up a grassy hillside devoid of trees, and reaches a beech grove watered by a powerful spring at its high end. A little over two hours above Plikáti you'll reach a stáni, after which the trail deteriorates markedly.

Angle up the ridge behind the shepherds' colony, passing a cairn a bit above and to the right, and then bear left (north) towards the primary Grámmos watershed. The secondary peak of Perífano (2442 metres) and the Iróön (a large white memorial to the royalist troops who fell in battle here) are clearly visible to the right. Twenty minutes above the stáni a spring feeds a sizeable pond, and 15 minutes higher the last water on the Ipirot side of the watershed surfaces as a trickle in a sheltered patch of turf that makes a good lunch halt.

A bit further, roughly three hours from Plikáti, is the saddle in the crest connecting Point 2520 and Perífano. To the south you can distinugish the peaks of Smólikas and Gamíla, and of course Plikáti village; on the northern side of the ridge, a vast canyon opens out. This is the infant Aliákmonas, one of Greece's major rivers, which is born virtually at the foot of Point 2520. You can also clearly see the village of Grámmos, the goal of the next stage. Stash full packs, if any, somewhere below the crest if you're not trekking to the north beyond the summit.

Sidetrip: Summits (1 hour) A good, plain trail runs much of the way along the crest, connecting various points of interest. Perífano summit is reached by a 30-minute

detour east of the pass, half of this on the path and the rest a cross-country scramble over packed scree and turf. The secondary peak, scarred by a handful of caved-in bunkers, gives you a new perspective on Point 2520 off to the west, and your first good look at the eastern portion of the range.

From the saddle it's 45 minutes on a westerly bearing to the base of Point 2520. The ridgetop trail adheres closely to the crest except for a stretch, 15 to 25 minutes along, where it swings south, and then north again above a catastrophic landslide area. Twenty minutes more of walking just north of the watershed brings you to the summit marker, etched with the polyglot initials of hundreds of climbers and surrounded by stove-in bunkers, dozens of ammunition boxes, and machine-gun mounts, which litter the entire mountain but nowhere so profusely as here. One of the collapsed structures, facing Plikáti, is said to be the remains of a ksoklísi honouring the Virgin.

The ridge running more or less perpendicular to the one you've just walked up is in effect the Greek-Albanian frontier, and the dirt road visible just to the west lies well within Albania. This road was originally opened by the Italians to facilitate their bungled 1940 invasion of Ípiros, and was later used by the Albanians to supply the rebels during 1948-49. The fertile, intensely cultivated valley to the west, with its rivers, ponds and giant utilitarian buildings, provides a striking contrast to the wilderness on the Greek side. The border zone may appear deserted, but don't let that fool you into attempting extended forays into Albania. Armed guards may still lurk in foxholes nearby, and their reaction under current conditions is unpredictable – anything from demanding that you help them escape, to shooting at you just for the fun of it.

Downhill Route To return to Plikáti, completing this stage as a day hike only, descend south-south-west along the frontier ridge through the wildflower-studded (with mostly violas and gentians) turf that has overgrown the numerous gun emplacements and dugouts. To your left the south flank of Point 2520 drops off sheerly – the heavy erosion is possibly the result of the wartime bombardment – and the steepness compels you to remain on the watershed for some 20 minutes until reaching a saddle, where the grade allows you to veer further east into Greek territory.

Even then it's close to two hours down miserably loose slopes, with no sign of a trail, along the western bank of the Gorgopótamos headwaters, before a stáni and the first beeches show themselves. After another 40 minutes of hiking, essentially in the riverbed, change sides where a jeep track appears on the opposite bank. Follow this east for 20 minutes more until you meet the trail used in the ascent. Descent from the peak to Plikáti by this route takes 3½ hours; the ascent, especially with a full pack, is not recommended.

Stage 2A: Grámmos Summit Ridge to Grámmos Village

(4 - 4½ hours)

The continuation to Grámmos (Grámosta) village is pretty straightforward – from the saddle between Point 2520 and Perífano, a fairly distinct trail drops down into the head of the Aliákmonas valley, following the western (true left) bank of the canyon for nearly four hours before arriving in Grámmos (1380 metres). This, like most of the communities on the Makedhonía side of the mountain, was abandoned after the civil war.

Today there is only a semblance of life in summer, when a few people come up to graze thousands of sheep in the huge valley here, even more remote and Asiatic-seeming than the one around Plikáti. There is a magázi, and something – if only the porch of the new church – can be arranged for a night's sleep, but there's no bus out. The closest service from Kastoriá stops at Nestório, nearly 40 km away. The magazí has a phone with which you can summon a tough taxi if a ride in a shepherd's truck is not forthcoming.

It's arguably only worth getting stuck here

if you take a longer route down, via the border ridge north of Point 2520 to Gistóva, the most hidden lake of Grámmos. Closely following the frontier (on the Greek side), you'll arrive after just under two hours at the lake at about 2200 metres altitude, secreted just south of 2412-metre Sakúli. It can't be seen from any of the main peaks, so you'll just have to stumble on this small tarn, about half the size of Dhrakólimni of Smólikas.

From the little lake you continue northeast toward Grámmos village, arriving there after 2½ more hours.

Stage 2B: Grámmos Summit Ridge to Aréna Peaks & Beyond

(7½ hours)

A more complete tour of the massif can be had by going east from Perífano, leaving Grámmos at one of three hamlets with better connections to the outside world. The miniature lakes and forests of the Aréna group are some of the most beautiful spots on the mountain.

From the eastern flank of Perífano you can see the pastoral hamlet of Aïtomilítsa, down in a valley to the south-east. You have a choice of descent routes: south to the civil war memorial on Gésos ridge (2166 metres) and then winding down east to Aïtomilitsa (Déndsko, 1430 metres), or heading east to the southern base of Kiáfa peak (2398 metres), where you veer south to the hamlet. The first route has somewhat better trails owing to people visiting the monument, below which also passes a forest track linking Gorgopótamos and Aïtomilítsa. Either way you'll need 2½ hours, starting from Perífano.

Aïtomilítsa is quite rustic, with no bus service along the 17-km track to the main road, and no formal lodging; the single kafenío is the only amenity. If you're properly equipped, it's probably better to continue along the crest to the Aréna peaks rather than unnecessarily losing altitude to the hamlet. From Perífano it's nearly three hours, via Kiáfa and Points 2217 and 2151, to the gentler north-eastern slope of Epáno Aréna. From the saddle between Perífano and Kiáfa ('Pass', in Albanian), threaded with a trail up from Aïtomilítsa, you turn Kiáfa peak on its southern flank and Point 2217 on its north-east. About halfway along, between Points 2217 and 2151 – sometimes called Kiátra Láïsa and Kanelopúlu respectively – there's a stáni and a spring.

Beginning from Aïtomilítsa, you've a two-hour climb up to the same point, via the stáni of Kazáni, at just under 2000 metres. Epáno Aréna itself (2192 metres), garnished with more crumbling machine-gun emplacements, is another half an hour overhead to the south. On the relatively flat ground north of the mountain you'll find first the odd-tasting Trakosára spring, a litre of which is supposed to weigh considerably less than a kilogram. Very close by is the lake of Mutsália at about 1800 metres, an ideal campsite surrounded by beech forest.

The massif of Aréna ('Sand' or 'Dirt' in Rumaniká) extends further south-east, away from the main Grámmos crest; the name's something of a misnomer, for while the middle elevations are friable enough, the summits poke out bonily from the surrounding forest. The south-western face of Epáno Aréna in particular is sheer rock, and you must continue looping around clockwise from the lakes for 90 minutes to emerge on the large saddle between the two Aréna peaks. Here paths from two villages – Likórakhi to the south-west, Pefkófita on the east – meet your route. You can descend to either in about 2½ hours.

Stamina and daylight allowing, you could also continue along the ridge for an hour to the north-eastern slope of Káto Aréna, where there's yet another small tarn, but the 2½-hour descent from there to the nearest village of Hrisí is complicated by thick vegetation and a loose surface underfoot – it's best to use the more obvious paths from the saddle for your final descent. All of the settlements around Káto Aréna are fairly primitive, but at least you're only a few km away from the Kónitsa-Kastoriá highway and main-line buses.

Another Suggested Trek in Ípiros

AKHERÓNDA RIVER GORGE

Just a few km inland from the oracle of Ephyra at the placid mouth of the bird-lively delta of the Akherónda river, the same stream displays quite a different character. Behind the flood plain of Fanári, the Akherónda has hacked a course through the mountains of Súli, swirling in unnavigable eddies at the base of deep cuts in the rock strata. Here you can understand why the ancients considered that the river sprang from the depths of Hades and thus had their oracle of the dead a little way downstream.

The path up the gorge is still well maintained and marked – it even has a name, the Skála Dzavélenas. In the days before roads it was the principal thoroughfare into the heart of Súli, a region famed for its 18th and 19th-century defiance of Ali Pasha. While perhaps not in quite the same league as the Víkos or Samarian canyons, the Akherónda gorge is certainly a respectable wilderness, so if you're being bored at a coastal resort near Párga and looking for an easy day's adventure inland, you won't find better.

Rating & Duration

The basic route of this one-day hike is easy; trail-less expeditions up the main course of the Akherónda will be moderate.

Supplies

Get picnic staples in Párga or Préveza – Glíki is not up to much, store-wise.

Map

No map is provided in this guide; use YIS 1:50,000 *Paramithía*.

Access

The hike starts from near Glíki, on the inland side-road between Préveza and Paramithía; there's just one daily bus to Préveza at 1 pm. If you're coming from the Párga area, you might take the one daily morning bus to

Paramithía and then a taxi the final 20 km, but you'd have quite a time getting back. The gorge is occasionally offered as an excursion by tour companies out of Párga, and that might very well be your best bet for return transport.

Route Directions

The river bridge, a few hundred metres south of Glikí village itself, is flanked on one side by a reasonable café-grill suitable for a lunch before or after the trek, and on the other by a sign, 'Skála Dzavélenas', pointing up a dirt road. After just under a km along this road, bear left at a hairpin right for 200 metres towards the chapel of Áyii Theódhori (elevation 60 metres), and within 10 minutes – about half an hour from Glikí – you'll reach a laboriously wrought tunnel, where the wider track ends and the *skála* or engineered path begins. Below you the canyon walls have abruptly squeezed together, and upstream a carpet of forest covers an undisturbed wilderness, surging up to the plainly visible castle of Kiáfa.

Over the next half an hour you'll climb slightly to a saddle at just under 200 metres, then descend north-east to a stone-and-concrete bridge over the Akherónda (80 metres), cross a much older span over the Tsangariótikos stream (known locally as the Piyés Sulíu or 'Suliot Springs'), and pass a ruined house or mill.

Next you make a hairpin left, following red paint splodges (courtesy of the Swiss tour company ESCO Reisen, as one graffito proclaims) to begin a hot climb through oak trees. Now on a northerly bearing, you eventually level out at around 300 metres about one hour 15 minutes along, hiking parallel to the course of the Tsangariótikos far below you. Take a right fork away from some shepherds' huts on the hillside below, following the red blazes, and 90 minutes out of Glikí you bear hard right (east) up yet another ravine, towards the hamlet of Samoníva (Samonídha). Within 20 minutes more you'll arrive in the tiny, poor hamlet (420 metres), the path having yielded to a dirt track just below by the cemetery.

There's a well behind the community records office (kinotikó grafío), but usually not a bucket; for a proper kafenío you'll have to road-walk three km north to the half-abandoned village of Súli. In the opposite direction, this dirt road leads after half an hour up to the castle of Kiáfa, one of a handful erected by the Suliots during their protracted wars with Ali Pasha and his allies.

The downhill return to Glikí takes a bit less time, about 1½ hours. You could conceivably extend the outing by following the Akheróndas upstream from the vicinity of the river junction, old bridge and ruined house, and faint paths do take off along the north-eastern bank below the waymarked left curve uphill. But you'd be strictly on your own, in all senses, until drawing even with the village of Tríkastro, high up on the south-west some 2½ hours upstream – assuming, of course, that you can get through. Something for committed explorers only.

Makedhonía & Thráki

Makedhonía (Macedonia) and Thráki (Thrace) are the borderlands of Greece, until recently a moot buffer zone; only between 1913 and 1922 were the two regions annexed and confirmed as Greek territory. They have served as a corridor for every group bent on Balkan settlement or conquest, from the Dorians, Persians and ancient Macedonians themselves up to the Germans and Bulgarians in this century. The receding tides of empire have left a patchwork of religious, ethnic and linguistic minorities that have long since vanished from southern Greece. It's still useful to regard the north of Greece as Byzantine or Ottoman as much as Hellenic, with all the attendant connotations of nationalist intrigue and retrograde behaviour on the part of both the authorities and the allegedly oppressed groups.

The most current wrinkle is Greece's vociferous objection to the Skopje-based ex-Yugoslav republic styling itself as Macedonia, a geographical title to which the Greeks claim sole proprietorial rights. The issue is not as absurd as it might seem to outsiders, since between the 1870s and the 1910s Greece was involved in a sometimes three-way struggle (the *Makedhonomákhes*) involving Hellenic, Slavic and Muslim armed bands battling for control of the area. During their occupation of long-coveted Thráki during WW II, the Bulgarians made a point of defacing ancient Greek ruins – critical evidence of a millennial Greek culture here. Although Greco-Bulgarian relations have since then been good, all the players are still in place, so to speak, with great potential for future instability.

In the lowlands the usual Greek rocks defer to hummocky hills and straight, tree-lined roads. It is by and large productive real estate, which partly explains why it has been fought over so often. As a rule there is more than enough water, often too much; lakes, rivers, swamps and estuaries speckle the landscape. Corn, rice, tobacco and fruit trees rule, encouraged by muggy summers of almost narcotic intensity. Mountains are sometimes densely forested and always carpeted with a thick turf, thanks to heavy winter snowfalls. Here it hits home, in many ways, that Greece is indeed a Balkan nation.

Falakró

This massif in eastern Makedhonía forms the heart of the province of Dhráma and is also the most northerly of the major Greek mountains. Falakró ('Bald') is something of a misnomer, since where the slopes are not forested they are carpeted with luxuriant grass, flowers and herbs all the way up to the 2232-metre summit – despite the fact that springs are rare in this limestone hulk. The upper pastures are even lush enough to support that Greek highland rarity, cattle. The principal summits form an impressive horseshoe shape around a deep ravine, with plenty of scope for gentle ridge-walking and interesting traverses.

Many of the place names in the range are Turkish or Bulgarian, a reminder that this area was securely wedded to Greece only after WW I. That fact, the proximity to Bulgaria, and the haze that frequently obscures the river valleys below, combine to leave an impression of Falakró as an eerily beautiful if somewhat moody mountain at the threshold of eastern Europe.

Rating & Duration
A point-to-point outing from Vólakas to Dhendhrákia or Ksiropótamos via Áyio Pnévma and Point 2232, or to Pírgi via Kartál Bunár, is a moderate two-day undertaking, implying an early start out of Vólakas.

More strenuous excursions from Pírgi towards the high peaks assume your willingness to camp in the summit area, and mean a long second day back down to Pírgi.

Season

Snowpack will linger late in spring – that's why there's a small ski resort here. Wild strawberries await the summer hiker in the meadows near Bámbitsa, and beeches are ablaze with autumn foliage colour.

Supplies

Get your supplies in Dhráma.

Maps

Korfes 52 or YIS 1:50,000 *Potamoí** and *Dhráma**.

Access

From Dhráma there are two daily weekday buses (early morning and afternoon) to Vólakas, a village on the north-west flank of Falakró. Otherwise you can take an *agoréo* (collective taxi), of which there are two; these charge rather less than the cost of chartering a whole car by yourself, and leave in the morning and at noon except on Sunday. The agoréa are usually parked in Dhráma's bazaar, in front of Proïno Patsas restaurant, 300 metres north of the Néa Zoí Hotel.

Failing either of the above, you should take any bus toward Nevrokópi and descend at the crossroads just past the Km 27 marker. From this junction it's a six-km hitchhike to Vólakas (slightly less walking since you can short-cut several road bends).

There are also two daily departures, but not on weekends, from Dhráma to the village of Pírgi on the south-west flank of Falakró.

SUMMIT TRAVERSE

Stage 1: Vólakas to Point 2232 via Áyio Pnévma

(5¼ hours)

Vólakas (830 metres), surrounded by a quiltwork of fallow and exploited fields, is a large community of decidedly un-Greek appearance. This is hardly surprising, since the inhabitants, many tow-haired and freckled, are descended from Greek-speakers who came here from Bulgaria in the 1920s as part of the population exchanges. There is no hotel as such in the village, but if benighted

you can ask at one of the two kafenía about renting a bed.

Almost any trail heading south-east (but not due south) out of the village will do, but try to start on the prominent one beginning between the grammar school and the *yimnásio* (secondary school), both just off the main square. After an hour of gradual climbing through fields, pine patches and then thick beech, it joins what appears to be a more important trail coming up from the north. The beeches disperse a bit and soon give way to more numerous, loftier black pines, and after another half an hour these thin out as you arrive on the bare Kurí ridge (1400 metres). A road winds its way past the tiny locked shelter here, on its way up to the Falakró ski centre.

The path now switchbacks up the slope just above the road cut, doubling back on itself as it adopts a north-east bearing. This delightful route, through stands of pine alternating with slopey meadows, is marked with occasional blue dashes on tree trunks and rocks; the grade is gentler than it was below Kurí. The area is known as Bámbitsa ('Little Granny', in Bulgarian). Once you've cleared the treeline at about 1700 metres you can enjoy views west over the way you've come; to your right (east) the road makes a prominent hairpin turn south-east. A large hotel is slated to be built here, though financing has not yet been confirmed; still, hikers should not be surprised in the future to find the path disrupted or destroyed locally.

Soon the small orange Horós refuge (also locked) appears at 1700 metres; you should pass it about one hour after leaving Kurí. From Horós the trail, faint in places, turns sharply above and behind the hut to continue roughly east. Pylons of the ski lift should now be visible, and they make good orientation points – keep them slightly to your right. The path attains its highest elevation (about 1825 metres) in a flat, spongy pasture and then begins the descent into the Áyio Pnévma plateau, now at your feet.

The first prominent landmark is the chapel of Áyio Pnévma, a bit below and to the left of your course; a spring, the only one on the

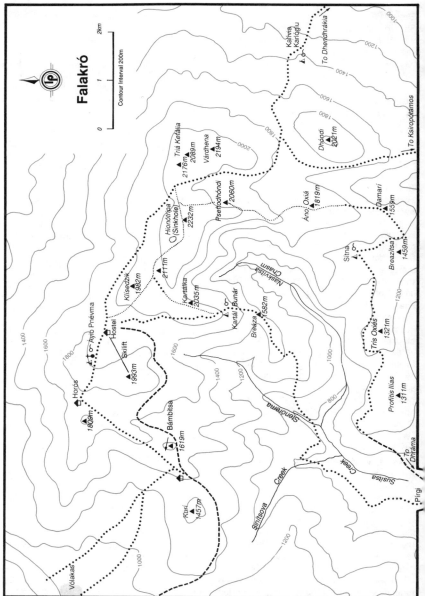

Falakró

Contour Interval 200m

0   1   2km

Kalívra
Karióglu
To Dhendhrákia

To Ksirópotamos

Dhrópti
2021m

Triá Kefália
2176m
2089m
Várdhena
2194m

Hionótripa
(Sinkhole)

Psefdodhóndi
2060m

Ánó Oxiá
1819m

Damari
1559m

2232m

2111m

Breazítsa
1459m

Kilisedzík
1982m

Sitná

Kartálka
2035m

Neskvítsa
Chasm

Kartál Bunár
1582m

Áyio Pnévma

Hostel

Skilift

1993m

Breáza

Slanóráma

Tris Oxiés
1321m

Horás
1809m

Profítis Ilías
1311m

Bámbitsa
1619m

To
Dhíama

Sinítsova
Creek

Susítsa
Creek

Kbrí
1457m

Pirgí

Volakás

route, issues from beneath its foundations. Next you pass cattle sheds, stock troughs and finally, 45 minutes above Horós, the giant hostel at the base of the ski run (1760 metres). Total elapsed trekking time from Vólakas won't exceed 3½ hours.

This huge (70-bed) refuge is open every winter weekend and holiday for the ski trade, but only on request in summer. For information ring EOS Dhráma (☎ (0521) 33 054); otherwise you must plan on tenting down somewhere in the meadows here.

It's 1¾ hours cross-country to the highest peak, ignoring for now the trail described below and in the next stage, and relying instead on a more southerly route closely hugging the main crest. After scaling Klísedzik ('Little Church', in Turkish) slightly south of its peak, follow the ridge line fairly closely, pausing to admire the precipitous drops into the Naskvítsa chasm to the south, and also the odd Hionótripa, a double-barrelled sinkhole full of ice and snow. This is found between the peak of that name and Point 2232. In pre-electricity days Hionótripa ('Snow Hole') was a perennial source of refrigeration for hospitals and banquets; the ice gatherers were lowered the necessary 30 metres on ropes.

Your hiking surface here is both enchanting and tiring, consisting as it does of a dense turf in which you sink up to your shins. At the right times of year, the grass is speckled with a rainbow of wildflowers. From the top of Point 2232 there are commanding views south over Naskvítsa (Bulgarian for 'Washtub'), north (weather permitting) over the Néstos River valley into Bulgaria, and west over Makedhonía. To the east your panorama is cut short by the secondary peaks Tría Kefália and Várdhena.

To vary a return to Áyio Pnévma, scamper down the grassy slope north-east of the peak to the trail visible below, between Point 2232 and Tría Kefália. As you turn left onto this path it's initially very faint and clogged with vegetation, but after dropping down through a gully it becomes more noticeably grooved into the turf, and there are even occasional orange waymarks. Extensive beech forests,

and purported bear country, lie 100 metres below on your right. Once over a spur of Klísedzik the ski lodge appears, and the orange blazes soon disappear, their task accomplished.

Stage 2: Point 2232 to Ksiropótamos or Dhendhrákia
(4-5 hours)

If you instead turn right on this last-mentioned trail below Triá Kefália, you would within an hour reach the saddle between Várdhena and Dhóndi, the next peak south. From there you can continue south along the west flank of Dhóndi, avoiding excessive altitude loss into the Damarí Ravine, to arrive after five more walking hours in the village of Ksiropótamos, nine km from Dhráma.

Alternatively you can slip east through the Várdhena-Dhóndi saddle and descend toward the pastures at Kalívia Karlóglu, and continue from there to the village of Dhendhrákia, some 20 km from Dhráma and four hours from the saddle.

LOOP HIKE FROM PÍRGI

Trails beginning and ending in Pírgi are more challenging, but also more scenic than those linking Vólakas to the peak area – it's worth doing at least part of this circuit, going up or coming down. Since there's 12 hours of hiking involved for the full circle, it's too much to do as a day trip.

Leave Pírgi (640 metres) by the forest road heading north-east toward the Sítna meadows; soon this becomes a path, skirting on their north the low peaks Profítis Ilías and Trís Oxiés to arrive at the Sítna spring (1280 metres), some 2½ hours out of Pírgi. Another 40 minutes suffices to take you from the meadowlands up to the 1450-metre ridge just west of Breazítsa Peak.

Next bear sharply north toward 1819-metre Áno Oxiá summit, then negotiate the watershed up to Point 2232 via Pseftodhóndi (2060 metres), shunning drop-offs left and right into Naskvítsa and Damarí respectively. From Point 2232, reached some six hours after leaving Pírgi, wade cross-country through the turf to Hionótripa peak, then follow the edge of Naskvítsa south past Kartálka Peak, and finally plunge sharply down to the Kartál Bunár (Turkish for 'Eagle Spring') at about 1700 metres.

Here you meet a very faint trail from the north linking the spring with Áyio Pnévma – a two-hour trip in either direction and a useful link for combining Vólakas ascents with the following.

The onward southern path threads across the thin neck of land joining Kartálka with 1582-metre Breáza; this ridge is one of the finest spots on Falakró, perfectly positioned for perspectives of Point 2232 and the Naskvítsa ravine. Just below Breáza there's a *dhexamení* (capped water tank) at around 1500 metres; the trail now switches to the southern slope of Breáza and begins to curl west down towards the Stenórema gully draining off from the north. Follow this ravine briefly, bear right (west) before its union with the Susítsa and Sinítsova streams, and finish out on the western bank of the joint streams as they pass Pírgi. You'll arrive here four hours below Kartál Bunár.

Áthos Peninsula – Monasteries of the Áyion Óros

On the easternmost of the three peninsulas of Halkidhikí, which dangle south from the main area of eastern Makedhonía, a fragment of Byzantium and the Middle Ages persists. The roughly rectangular, 400-sq-km territory of Áthos is a theocratic, semi-autonomous republic devoted to the glorification of God and the maintenance and dissemination of Orthodox doctrine.

Early History
The verified Christian history of Áthos extends back to the 8th century AD, when the first hermits settled at present-day Karúlia and other spots on the peninsula. In 963, Saint Athanasios founded the first com-munal-living arrangement, the monastery of Meyístis Lávras, and the number of monasteries multiplied to nearly 40 within a short period. Soon the Áyion Óros became a powerful religious and political entity which most Byzantine (and later Slavic) rulers patronised, courted and in some cases retired to upon abdication or deposition.

At the height of its power in the 15th and 16th centuries, after the demise of the Byzantine Empire, Áthos supported a population of 20,000 monks. The number of fully fledged monasteries was fixed irrevocably at 20, though no limits were set on smaller dependencies.

All this happened despite considerable turmoil from the 11th to the 14th centuries. The most distinctive feature of the Holy Mountain, the *ávaton* doctrine which forbids access to all female mammals, was codified as an imperial edict in 1060 after a time of famine, when nomadic shepherds were found camped in the fields of the relatively wealthy monasteries and renting their wives and daughters to needy monks. Raids and sackings by pirates and Latin adventurers occurred repeatedly during the 13th and 14th centuries, and considerable, often violent Catholic pressure was brought to bear upon Áthos during the time of the proposed union of the eastern and western churches.

With the fall of Constantinople, Áthos assumed heightened importance as a reliquary of Byzantine culture, and by adroit diplomacy managed to preserve its special status during the centuries when the rest of the Balkans were under stricter Ottoman rule. Turkish Istanbul was as assiduous in paying respects to the Mountain – thus hoping to defuse a potential hotbed of Greek nationalist sentiment – as the Orthodox emperors had been. In the end, however, this did not render the place immune from the promptings of modern nationalism, and Áthos revolted, or tried to revolt, with the rest of Makedhonía in 1822, and thus lost most of the privileges carefully cultivated in the preceding years.

By the end of the century internal conflicts between Slavic and Greek monks reached a new pitch, as imperial Russia attempted to exert greater influence here – and this has revived as an issue with the demise of communism.

In 1926, Áthos assumed its present status as a state-within-the-Greek-state. The 20 'ruling' monasteries, ranked with few changes since the 14th century in a strict hierarchy, were still as in times past to send a representative each year to a central supervisory council, the *Ierá Epistasía*, where policy matters were deliberated. But all foreign monks were required henceforth to take Greek citizenship, a civil governor was appointed from Athens, and a small police force deployed to keep order among religious pilgrims and the large number of lay workers – as well as among the occasionally fractious monks.

Nearly all of the villages at the still-secular foot of the Áthos Peninsula – Ierissós, Néa Ródha, Uranópoli, and the island hamlet of Amolianí, off Tripití jetty – were resettled, as was much of the Halkidhikí Peninsula, with refugees from around the Sea of Marmara in 1923. To do this, quite a bit of land belonging to the Athonite monasteries was expropriated by the Greek government at the time.

Until emigration to northern Europe began in the 1950s, and the revival of monasticism commenced some two decades later, there was often considerable tension between the villagers and Áthos, with the threat, implicit or otherwise, of further takeovers on the peninsula itself in the air. This has evaporated as the refugees' descendants find themselves at the hub of a tourism boom, and no longer have as much need to farm or fish as before.

The villages themselves tend to be ugly and functional, a legacy of a catastrophic earthquake in 1932 as much as the pressures of tourism.

Modern Áthos

In the early 1960s the Holy Mountain was at its lowest ebb ever, a quaint anachronism with barely a thousand elderly, poorly educated monks; since then there has been a modest revival, with numbers rising to about 1700 younger, more committed brothers. This is attributable in part to the increasing appeal of the contemplative life in a blatantly materialistic age, but principally to a wave of sectarian fervour which has swept both Áthos and world Orthodoxy in general. Active recruitment and evangelising has resulted in a crop of novices from every continent, a trend particularly noticeable at such monasteries as Simópetra, Filothéu and Vatopedhíu.

Less admirable, in the eyes of certain observers, were the actual details of the zealots' often tactless transformation of Áthos. Supposedly lax idiorrhythmatic houses (described in the Glossary later in this section) were compelled, allegedly sometimes by force, to become cenobitic as the price of their revitalisation. There has undeniably been a massive campaign of logging, road building, and construction of modern premises, the sale of the timber helping to fund 'improvements'.

Even more disturbing were charges set forth by an English monk, Maximos, who lived at Meyístis Lávras for two years and then left to write a book documenting them (*Human Rights on Mt Áthos: an Appeal to the Civilised World*, published by Stylite Publishing, Hopkins Passage, Welshpool, Powys SY21 7SE, UK). This pamphlet and its appendices seem to demonstrate, in addition to the coercive nature of the wave of transitions to cenobitic status, various unpleasant trends.

The Greek civil authorities, on and off the Mountain, appear to impair the efforts of non-Greek monasteries and dependencies to recruit novices and receive novices from their home country, in violation of the rights of minorities guaranteed under the 1923 Treaty of Lausanne and in a confusion of the aims of Hellenism and Orthodoxy. The purported tyranny of abbots over their monks, in the form of a lack of confidentiality of correspondence and phone calls, and restricted access to publications from outside and to travel documents, is also decried, as well as inadequate civil policing which has supposedly led to a number of 'disappearances' and the looting of treasures from dying monks' cells and hermitages.

Other monks, most of whom wish to remain anonymous, concede that Maximos is essentially correct but exaggerates by a factor of two. In the Greeks' defence it might be said that the Slavic monasteries can be just as beastly to foreigners; for example, four non-Slavic novices recently left the monastery of Hilandaríu, one after another, in the face of Serbian chauvinism. The Greek-Slav conflict is merely a mirroring of the general turmoil in the southern Balkans, and can be seen as a continuance of something which Slavic communism merely threw in the deep-freeze for 40 years – though you'd hope the Greek government to be more pleased at the foreseeable boost to Orthodoxy than annoyed at the minimal threat to the Hellenic character of the Mountain.

As for superiors' interference in the day-to-day lives of the monks, it has been noted acidly by a friend of mine that one joins a monastery to learn obedience and humility (towards the abbot, among others) and not to exercise one's rights.

If all this politicking strikes you as incongruous in a commonwealth supposedly devoted to serenity and spiritual perfection, it's worth recalling that doctrinal strife has always been part of Athonite history – and the history of any religion. In a perverse sense, the ongoing (or in some cases renewed) controversies are a sign of health, insomuch as Áthos, and who controls it, are once again considered to have universal importance.

A PILGRIMAGE AROUND ÁTHOS

As for the monastic buildings, art and landscape themselves, they are simply magnificent. Nearly all of the monasteries are outstanding examples of an architectural and aesthetic genius that will not be seen again. In Greece you come to expect monasteries in stark, forbidding settings relieved only by the spring that keeps the community alive. While several of the Athonite monasteries are stereotypical rock-bound citadels,

fortified against the attentions of pirates, many – especially those built inland – are almost obscured by lush greenery. So it's something of a novelty to trek through the copses and thickets, often verging on jungle, that festoon much of the peninsula. The streams and vegetation that run riot here seem to mock the austerity of the monastic life and reintroduce some of the feminine principle cast out by the ávaton.

The monks are not insensible to this beauty, and refer to the Áthos as the Garden of the Virgin, thus doctrinally justifying the ávaton without reference to early scandals. Indeed, the place had been consecrated to the Panayía after an apocryphal visit in which she cast out the pagan goddesses and claimed the Mountain as her own.

The grey, bony peak of Áthos (2030 metres) towers above the dense growth at the southern tip of the peninsula like a monk aloof from the world – it's an eminently worthwhile climb to the summit. The northeastern shore and summit ridge catches the brunt of wet weather and is accordingly thickly vegetated by a carpet of deciduous trees, ivy, brambles and other creepers; butterflies, as well as less pleasant biting flies, abound. Crossing the peninsula, this becomes fir, oak and chestnut forest at middle elevations, with much of the southwest-facing shore cloaked in Mediterranean scrub.

In midsummer, lugging a heavy pack the considerable distances between each monastery must be reckoned a contemporary form of religious penance, but in any season the stunning scenery, still undisturbed in the remoter corners of the peninsula, provides ample distraction. Often you hike just above some of the last unspoiled coastline of the Aegean, with only a distant power pylon to hint of the 20th century.

The best walking tends to be around the southern tip of the peninsula, where no roads go or are ever likely to, and between the northerly monasteries, where extensive sections of medieval trail also survive, cutting perpendicular to any tracks. Closer to the administrative capital Kariés, the countryside has been thoroughly messed up by roads that make for deadly boring walking and which have spelled doom to the trails even when those have not been bulldozed; in the jungly climate, paths close up in two or three years unless used constantly. Even equipped with the better maps listed below, you should always confirm trail condition and walking times with the monks before setting out. More sadly, fire damage and garbage piles have become a factor – routes have been selected to direct you away from the former, but there's no controlling those responsible for the latter (mostly Greek pilgrims, it seems).

Securing a Permit to Visit Áthos

Since the early 1970s a permit system for entry to the Holy Mountain has been in effect, instituted as much to screen out 'undesirables' as to regulate the traffic of visitors, which had exceeded the monasteries' capacity to offer hospitality. Only Greek nationals and, to a certain extent, foreign Orthodox pilgrims are exempt from this requirement. It is most important to note that *only males over the age of 18 are allowed to apply*, though minors may visit accompanied by an adult. The former ban against the 'beardless', presumably a check against women sneaking into Áthos in disguise, has been dropped, but very long hair is still met with disfavour. If you are a clergyman of any recognised heterodox denomination, your application must first be vetted by the Ecumenical Patriarch in Istanbul, and will probably be regarded with extreme suspicion.

The initial step in acquiring a permit to visit and stay on Áthos is to obtain a letter or recommendation from your embassy or consulate in Athens or Thessaloníki. Pertinent embassies and high commissions in Athens are:

Australia
    Sútsu 37, 115 21 Athens
Canada
    Yennadhíu 4, 115 21 Athens
Denmark
    Vasilísis Sofías 11, 106 71 Athens

Netherlands
    Vasiléos Konstantínu 5/7, 106 74 Athens
South Africa
    Kifissías 124, corner Iatrídhu, 115 10 Athens
UK
    Plutárhu 1, 106 75 Athens; also represents New Zealand
USA
    Vasslísis Sofías 91, 115 21 Athens

Consulates in Thessaloníki are:

Netherlands
    Komnínon 26
UK & all Commonwealth nations
    Venizélu 8
USA
    Níkis 59

This letter should be purely a formality, though the UK consulates levy a UK£15 charge (the US embassy letter is gratis). Try to have yourself described in the studiously courteous form-text as a university-level scholar in art, music, religion or architecture. At a pinch 'man of letters' will do, as it covers just about any male graduate.

Take this letter to either the Ministry of Foreign Affairs in Athens (Zalakósta 2; Monday, Wednesday or Friday from 11 am to 2 pm; Room 73, 3rd Floor) or to the Ministry of Makedhonía and Thráki in Thessaloníki (Platía Dhikitiríu; Monday to Friday from 11 am to 2 pm; Room 218). In exchange for the letter you will be issued a provisional permit valid for four days on Áthos, which must be used 'within a reasonable amount of time' and which will have a date stipulated for the start of your visit.

This may not be the day of your choice in high summer, when it's all but mandatory to apply at least six weeks in advance. Each of the ministries described above is allotted ten slots for foreigners of all nationalities on each day of the year, for a total of 20 new arrivals on Áthos per day. If your day – or week – of choice is full up in one city, there is a slight chance that there may be space in the other, though this can't be counted on.

Access
Once in Thessaloníki, you'll need to take a

Halkidhikí KTEL bus to either Ierissós, Néa Ródha or Uranópoli, the villages nearest the border between secular Greece and the Holy Mountain. For many years this service departed from a terminal at Karakási 68, reached by a No 10 bus from the city centre, but recently the provincial KTELs have been gathered, one by one, into a giant new joint station out at the end of Ikosiogdhóïs Oktovríu, in the south-western Sfayiá district, reached by bus No 31. Contact the tourist office (☎ (031) 513 374) to see what is the current status of the Halkidhikí KTEL.

There are seven daily departures between Thessaloníki and these three settlements, but if you're setting out on the day your permit commences, only the earliest (6 am) service connects with the 9.45 am ferry out of Uranópoli, on the south-western coast, to Áthos. In midsummer, the boat schedule may change to two departures at 7.45 am and noon, but this cannot be relied on – it's best to call the port authority (☎ (0377) 71 248).

The single daily boats out of Ierissós and Néa Ródha on the north-eastern shore (three weekly in winter) leave at 8.30 am (Ierissós) and 8.45 am (Néa Ródha). This is earlier than the first bus through, so you'll have an overnight there and the opportunity to see if the weather, prone to be stormy on this coast, forces a cancellation. If this happens you'll be able to shift to Uranópoli, 17 km south, by taxi or with the first daily bus, in time to catch the other ferry.

From Uranópoli, one of three ferries – the *Ayios Nikolaos*, *Poseidon* or *Axion Esti* (the last a car ferry carrying monastic service vehicles) will take you first to the following ports of call: the *arsanás* (fortified coastal annexe) of Zográfu, the arsanás of Kastamonítu, Dhokhiaríu monastery, Ksenofóndos monastery, Ayíu Pandelímonos monastery, and Dháfni, the harbour hamlet on the south-west-facing coast of Áthos. The *Axion Esti* generally heads back the way it came almost immediately, at around noon.

There is a quick onward connection with a smaller boat which continues down the same coast, stopping at Símonos Pétras monastery,

Osíu Grigoríu monastery, Dhionisíu monastery, the arsanás of Ayíu Pávlu monastery, and the arsanás of Ayías Ánnas. On alternate days this same caïque continues from Ayías Ánnas to Meyístis Lávras monastery, stopping at the *skíti* (smaller dependency) of Kavsokalívia, and returning the same day to 'sleep' at Ayías Ánnas before making its 8 am run towards Dháfni the next day. Uranópoli to Dháfni takes about 90 minutes, and the extra distance to Ayías Ánnas another hour.

The single boat from Ierissós and Néa Ródha always calls at the arsanás (see the Glossary in this section) of Hilandharíu and the monasteries of Esfigménu, Vatopedhíu, Pandokrátoros, Stavronikíta and Ivíron; most days it carries on to the arsanádhes of Filothéu and Karakálu monasteries, and Meyístis Lávras Monastery. From Ierissós to Ivíron the journey takes nearly 2½ hours, and to Meyístis Lávras another hour. The return trip usually leaves Meyístis Lávras between 2 and 3 pm, from Ivíron rather earlier.

A single derelict bus runs between both Ivíron and Dháfni to the capital at Kariés, located more or less in the geographical centre of the peninsula. This was of critical importance in the days when you had to obtain your permit here, but now that this has been changed it's mostly used by residents of the Mountain on business.

Although walking is an essential part of the Athonite experience, it's well worth knowing about the various boat shuttles: they are inexpensive, atmospheric, and (since many visitors are unused to trekking) a great boost for the footsore. If you do not manage to complete the full trekking loop as suggested, try to use each of the ferry lines once – the feel of the boat clientele and the appearance of the Mountain are strikingly different on the two sides.

Entry & the Dhiamonitírion

Your actual disembarkation on Áthos and the final permit formalities will be as described here, regardless of what you might read elsewhere – the protocol was changed suddenly in 1991.

At your very first port of call – the arsanás of Zográfu on the south-western coast or the arsanás of Hiladharíu on the north-eastern shore – all passengers will be ushered off the boat to the police post, where your ministry permit and a fee (currently 2000dr, 30% less for students) will be exchanged for a rather impressive-looking document called the *dhiamonitiríon* ('permit of sojourn'). This entitles you to stay at any of the main monasteries and skítes free of further charge. You are now at liberty to leave the boat, or stay with it to any destination further down the same coast. It is no longer necessary to go up to Kariés unless you specifically wish to, and this new streamlined procedure has essentially granted visitors an extra half-day which was formerly spent getting necessary paperwork attended to in the capital before setting out to any monastery.

Many visitors wish to arrange for an extension of the basic four-day period. There is little point in asking for one, either upon arrival in Áthos or later on in Kariés, since such a request will be routinely denied. In practice, however, nobody is terribly concerned if you stay five days or even a week,

except perhaps in midsummer when monastic accommodation can get quite crowded. It is rare that monastery personnel ask to see your dhiamonitiríon, let alone scrutinise it carefully. Conversations with several monks – in the course of requests to have them sponsor my application for an extension – elicited the plain truth that the four-day term was originally imposed to discourage gawkers and others with frivolous motives. If you are regarded as a sincere pilgrim – and most foreign-born Orthodox are – and move on to a different monastery each day as the regulations require you to, there are no untoward consequences of a do-it-yourself 'extension'. On the other hand, if the monks think you are presumptuous or you behave inappropriately in any way, no amount of time remaining on your permit will persuade them to grant you shelter – as signs here and there repeatedly remind you 'hospitality is not obligatory'.

Monastic Life & Your Adaptation to It

If you study your dhiamonitiríon carefully you'll notice one of Áthos's more subtle peculiarities – the date will be 13 days 'behind', since the Holy Mountain observes the Julian calendar. The time of day is in even more of a muddle: on the north-eastern shore of the peninsula, 12 o'clock is set as the hour of sunrise – which of course changes seasonally – while on the south-western side clocktowers may show both hands up at sunset. Note, however, that Vatopedhíu keeps 'worldy' time, as do most monks' wristwatches.

Although all 20 monasteries now have telephones and road connections with Kariés (and often their arsanádhes) and many have electricity, these innovations have made little difference in the highly ordered daily schedule of a cenobitic institution. This is probably the most disorienting aspect of Athonite life for newcomers, and (as already noted) the sun and stars are better guides to surrounding activity than a clock.

Both you and the monks are expected to go to bed early, within an hour or so after sunset whatever the season – if there is a

Dhiamonitírion ('Permit of Sojourn' for Áthos)

Glossary of Athonite Terms

Arkhondáris Guestmaster of a monastery or skíti, who attends to all visitors; similarly, **arkhondaríki**, the guest quarters themselves.

Arsanás, plural **arsanádhes** Harbour annexe of each monastery or skíti, guarded by a fortified tower, where boats anchor; they can be a considerable distance from the institution in question. Even most coastal monasteries have one, since they too were usually built a bit out of reach of medieval pirates.

Askitírio A hermit's retreat, often just a cave.

Cenobitic The type of monastery where monks worship and eat all meals together, hold all property in common and have rigidly scheduled days. These communities best exemplify the Orthodox monastic ideal as formulated by Saint Basil.

Dhíkeos Literally, the 'righteous one' – nominal head of an idiorrhythmatic foundation.

Dhókimos A novice monk.

Evloyíteh 'Your blessing', the proper Orthodox greeting to monks met on the trail, to which the reply is '**O Kírios**' ('The Lord (blesses you))'. If you say '**evloyíteh**' it will be asssumed that you're Orthodox, so it's a bit pretentious if you're not – use '**hériteh**' instead.

Fiáli The covered fount for holy water in the courtyards of most monasteries; many are very ornate.

Idiorrhythmatic These foundations are more individualistic: the monks prepare their own meals, study or worship when and as they wish, and are allowed to offer small crafted articles in exchange for 'donations'.

The idiorrhythmatic rule arose during the Ottoman era as a protective response to confiscatory taxation and other economic pressures, but the new generation of monks has proclaimed this adaptation obsolete, and over the past decade most of the remaining idiorrhythmatic monasteries have reverted to cenobitic status. Pandokrátoros is the last bastion of the old order, and unlikely to continue as such after the current elderly tenants pass away.

Igúmenos Abbot, the head of a cenobitic monastery.

Kalíva Cottage – the smallest unit of a skíti or a kélli, usually home to between two and six monks, with their own chapel nearby. These individuals, while often quite welcoming to passers-by, are under no obligation to be so – they have chosen to live in such units as a retreat.

Katholikón Main church of a monastery.

Kellí Agricultural colony of a monastery or a skíti, usually inhabited by just a few farmer-monks.

Kiriakón Central chapel of a skíti, where the residents worship together on Sundays.

Narthex (Greek **nárthikas)** Vestibule or porch of a church; sometimes there are two, in which case you have the **esonárthikas** (inner narthex) and an **exonárthikas** (outer one).

Skíti Smaller dependency of a monastery, either a compact cloister or a collection of scattered cottages.

Trapezaría Refectory or dining room, often painted with lurid frescoes of the Last Judgment to keep monks from paying too much attention to their food. You may be invited simply to **trápeza** (set table).

generator it will be shut down to get the point across. Sometime between 2 and 3 am the brothers awake for solitary study and meditation, followed by *órthros* or matins, the first religious service of the day, about an hour or two before dawn. You'll know it's that time from the (un)godly racket of bells and *símandra* (wooden or iron gongs struck with a mallet). The noise seems calculated to wake the dead, and metaphorically that's what it's doing. In Orthodox cosmology the monastery is a Noah's Ark of salvation from the flood of Sin, and the mallet and plank of the símandro are the tools of Noah the carpenter calling all creatures to come and seek eternal safety.

To either side of sunrise there is another quiet period, followed by the *akoluthía* or main liturgy. The morning meal is served at some point between 9.30 and 11 am, again depending on the season. Afterwards the community exits to the fields, sawmills and workshops for manual labour until the late afternoon, with a brief pause at midday. *Esperinós* or vespers is celebrated more than two hours before sunset in summer, much less in winter; the evening meal falls between this and the short *apódhipno* or complines service. All monastery gates are locked at dark, which means that you *must* reach your destination by sunset or risk a night out with the wild boars (and, it is said, a few jackals and wolves).

Monks eat in silence except for the voice

of one of them reading a chapter from the Gospel. If you've been invited to share a table, eat as quickly as you politely can, because on cue everyone rises in unison, there's a closing grace, and the group files out, leaving any uneaten food. Sometimes monasteries make exceptions for late arrivals and allow them to finish undisturbed, or will serve them leftovers; others solve the potential problem by furnishing meals separately to the non-Orthodox. A few houses, realising that guests with a long walking day ahead of them cannot wait until 9.30 am or later for sustenance, considerately provide a 'self-service' table of bread rusks, cheese and coffee from sunrise onwards.

The Holy Mountain grows much of its own food, and the meat-free monastic diet is based on vegetables, cheese, coarse bread and pasta, with occasional treats like hélva (semolina or sesame sweetmeat) or fruit thrown in. The Sunday morning meal is traditionally the heartiest of the week, with wine accompanying fish. No animal products or oil are allowed on Wednesday or Friday, or during the numerous fasts punctuating the year, particularly Lent; despite the best of intentions these lean periods can't help but affect the fare offered to pilgrims.

Food adequate to sustain your level of physical activity, and where you can get it, may become a conversational preoccupation among heathen visitors to Áthos. As a general but not infallible rule you'll do better at the inland monasteries away from the tourist boat routes, and worst at the idiorrhythmatic skítes where cooking for large groups is not a highly developed skill. You should be at least partly self-sufficient in food, especially dried fruits, nuts, sweets and hard-boiled eggs, both for the times when you miss a set meal and for the long walks between institutions. There are a few basic shops in Kariés for buying such snacks, but to save valuable time stock up in advance elsewhere.

Upon arrival at a monastery or large skíti you'll ask for, or be met by, the arkhondáris, who will provide the traditional welcome of a *tsípuro* (distilled spirits) and a *lukúmi* (Turkish delight) or two.

Lately, guestmasters tend to speak at least one foreign language, especially English, a reflection of the increasing numbers of educated novices and those from Australia or Cyprus. If you wish to stay the night let him know immediately, since guest wings can fill early in the day in summer; if there's no room, you may have to hoof it to the next monastery before dark. The accommodation itself varies from rather spruce doubles or quads to barn-like dormitories; bathrooms are always down the hall, and showers are so rare as to be remarkable. You'll be given sheets and enough blankets for the season, so spare the weight of a sleeping bag from your pack unless you intend to camp out on Áthos peak.

Incidentally, idiorrhythmatic skítes and kelliá are only loosely bound by the dictum of monastic hospitality, if at all, and you really need to know one of the inhabitants personally to be asked to stay the night. Moreover, the farm cottages constitute the last refuge of those monks wishing to follow a more independent path and avoid the orphanage-like regulations of a large institution, including the obligation to interact with outsiders; respect their privacy unless invited in.

Many visitors come away from Áthos with their feathers slightly ruffled, annoyed by what they consider as monkish curtness or bigotry; for their part many monks reckon that the heterodox are still just as barbarian as they were in the days when the Fourth Crusaders sacked Constantinople. To minimise the occasions for mutual perceptions of disrespect, observe the following guidelines, and try to comprehend at least the bare outlines of your hosts' admittedly all-pervading world view.

You should be fully clothed at all times, even when going from sleeping quarters to bathroom; other dress-code items include no hats inside monasteries, no shorts ever, and sleeves that come down to mid-bicep. (The police in Dháfnes and Kariés may even dun you if a T-shirt sleeve hikes up under a backpack strap.) If you swim (in bathers, of course), do so where nobody can see you.

Smoking at most foundations is forbidden, though a few allow you to light up out on the balconies; it would be reckless to do so on the trail, given the chronic fire hazard, and you might just want to swear off tobacco as a spiritual exercise for the length of your stay. Singing secular melodies, whistling, and raised voices are taboo; so is standing with your hands behind your back or crossing your legs when seated, both considered arrogant stances. If you want to photograph monks you should always ask permission, though so many people haven't done so in the past that photography is forbidden altogether in several places. It's wise not to go poking your nose into corners of the monasteries where you haven't been specifically escorted, even if they seem open to the public, since the monks get rather upset if they find you there.

Quite a lot of smutty tittering and speculation occurs in outside circles about the extent of homosexual behaviour on Áthos. The truth is that there are certainly no fewer monks of gay inclination than you'd expect in a population of 1700, and probably more. Though theory is not necessarily practice, Áthos has long been a stop of sorts on the European gay travel circuit, and while certainly no Míkonos, the undercurrents are there for those with the antennae to pick up on them. It used to be very trendy for members of the Greek gay community at large to have a boyfriend on the Mountain, and a certain amount of special leave for 'study in the world' was wangled by young monks with possible ulterior motives. However, all this has presumably been one of the targets of the reformers' wrath, and you should consider very carefully before responding to invitations for indulgence. If you're caught, probably the worst you can expect is to be frogmarched to the first boat out and banned permanently from re-entry; the monk will face expulsion from what for years may have been his only home.

Monasteries and their inhabitants vary a good deal in their handling of visitors, and their reputations, deserved or otherwise, precede them as a typical subject of trail gossip among pilgrims. There have recently been many drastic population transfers – the inmates of Stavronikíta moved en masse to Ivíron, for example – so if you are on a repeat visit to Áthos, nothing will be as you remembered. As a heterodox you may be politely, or less than politely, ignored, with signs at many institutions specifically forbidding you from attending the holy liturgy or sharing meals with the monks.

Other monasteries are by contrast very extroverted, putting themselves at the disposal of guests of whatever creed. If this seems the case, do respond to it, as this will often be the only way to get a view of treasures and shrines kept under lock and key. There is often a very soft-sell evangelical effort in the form of a reading library of pamphlets and books on Orthodoxy in foreign languages, usually worth perusing.

As for human interactions, it's not unheard of to be subjected to extreme chauvinism and disarming gentility at the same place within the span of 10 minutes, keeping your head spinning and making it very difficult to draw conclusions about Áthos in general and monasteries in particular. If you have the cheek to be non-Christian as well as non-Orthodox, and seem to understand enough Greek to get the message, you'll probably be told bluntly at some stage that you'll burn in hell unless you convert to the True Faith forthwith; Jews are viewed with particular ire. (The Greek pilgrims, incidentally, not having had training in getting a handle on their passions, can be worse than the monks in this respect.)

Offensive as this is, considering your possibly voyeuristic motivations for being on Áthos it's helpful to remember that the monks are expecting religious pilgrims, not tourists, and that their stance is that of a true believer, however genial, with little room for tolerance. If you're not an Orthodox pilgrim, about the most politely you can expect to have yourself described by a monk is *se anazítisi* (in quest of a spiritual path).

Even among themselves the monks discuss the miracles and life history of some saint depicted on a refrectory fresco with the keenness of football fans reeling off the career stats of the home side's star striker. For them it's a given that the holy ikons protect and punish, fly through the air, cross the sea or root to the spot to make their wishes known. To many monks these events are of unquestioned reality, and you are the disturbing hallucination. The entire world is a manifestation of their faith, in a manner that lay headshrinkers would dismiss as paranoid delusions but for the monks merely proves the validity of the Gospels.

Two examples are worth quoting. Sydney Loch in his wonderful book *Athos: the Holy Mountain* (Molho Bookstore, Thessaloníki, 1971) relates the anecdote of the abbot of Dhokhiaríu who, having observed 30 years of utter calm on the sea at Good Friday, concluded that it was in mourning for the dead Christ. More recently there was an uproar involving a proposal to introduce high-tech identity cards for the monks, incorporating bar codes. Someone had read that in certain countries the initial access field had the numerical value of 666, or the Mark of the Beast of the Apocalypse, and this news caused a sensation among many, who either refused outright to consent to carrying the Mark, or who concluded that the Last Days were imminent. (No wonder some abbots feel impelled to restrict reading material.)

Many things will probably never change on Áthos: the raving fanatics juxtaposed with the serene, gentle monks who seem to be living a foot off the floor, the bell concerts as the sun melts into the gulf, the swishing of monks' cassocks in the dark as they file to church, the strangeness of the lack of women and children. You may not want to return, but because of heightened awareness from the mortification diets, the bizarre timekeeping, and the natural beauty, you will never forget your time here.

Rating & Duration

Conditions on Áthos make essentially easy or moderate hiking days seem difficult. Your morale and attitude will be improved if you bring along snacks to supplement the monastic diet, and scale down over-ambitious plans. Much of your day will be taken up moving from one community to the next, and even so you would need several visits to Áthos to walk all of the remaining paths.

Because of the number of possible entry and exit points, walking permutations are pretty varied. The dirt road which links the port of Dháfni and the monastery of Ivíron via Kariés not only cuts the peninsula roughly in half, but also divides the monasteries into two equal groups – not so arbitrary as it seems, since the two halves feel very different, and the remaining path system seems to reflect the split.

Possible recommendable itineraries include, going clockwise: Day 1, Boat from Uranópoli to Arsanás Zográfu, then hike to Zográfu or Hilandharíu; Day 2, to Vatopedhíu, overnight Pandokrátoros; Day 3, walk via Stavronikíta to Ivíron, boat to Meyístis Lávras; Day 4, walk to Panayía chapel and overnight, or to Ayía Ánnas via Katunákia, or to Ayíu Pávlu; Day 5, climb summit of Áthos, then north to Dhionisíu, or Ayíu Pávlu to Osíu Grigoríu or Símonos Pétras; Day 6, depart on morning boat.

Or, more ambitiously clockwise: Day 1, Boat from Ierissós to Esfigménu, walk to Vatopédhiu, overnight there or at Pandokrátoros; Day 2, walk to Ivíron via Stavronikíta, boat to Meyístis Lávras; Day 3, walk to Ayía Annas via Katunákia; Day 4, dawn ascent of peak, descend to Dhionisíu/Osíu Grigoríu; Day 5, boats as far as Ksenofóndos, then on foot to Dhokhiaríu and Zográfu; Day 6, depart from Arsanás Zográfu or – more energetically – Arsanás Hilandharíu.

Going anticlockwise: Day 1, Boat from Ierissós to Arsanás Hilandharíu, hike to Zográfu by evening; Day 2, walk via Kastamonítu and Dhokhiaríu to Ksenofóndos, pick up midday boat to Símonos Pétras or Osíu Grigoríu; Day 3, coastal hike to Ayíu Pávlu or Ayía Anna; Day 4, dawn ascent of Áthos Peak, continue to Kavsokalívia or Meyístis Lávras; Day 5, afternoon boat from Meyístis Lávras to Ivíron, possible walk to Pandokratóros; Day 6, walk to Vatopedhíu, afternoon boat out.

Season

Midsummer on Áthos is worth avoiding if you have the choice, as are weekends – at both times Greek pilgrims arrive in biblical hordes, and you'll face intense competition from other foreigners for the allotted permits. May or June are excellent times: Áthos summit sports a few attractive snow patches still, the heat at sea level is tropical only at midday, and long days permit the completion of ambitious itineraries. The peak, incidentally, can only be safely climbed between May and September. Early autumn is also a pleasant time to visit.

Supplies

Get these in Thessaloníki or Uranópoli beforehand.

Maps

The single best map of Áthos is unquestionably the two-sided, topographic product entitled *Áthos (Agion Oros)*, compiled by Reinhold Zwerger and Klaus Schöpfleuthner, Wohlmutstrasse 8, A 1020 Wien, Austria. It is often on sale for about $8 in Uranópoli, but if you want to make sure of snagging a copy write to the publishers in advance at the above address. The entire peninsula is covered, and while it is not perfect, the cartographers cannot be blamed for such inaccuracies as the new road between Morfonú Bay and Meyístis Lávras.

Another very useful aid is the sketch map prepared by Theodhoros Tsiropoulos of Thessaloníki (☎ (031) 430 196). This small A4 sheet has no contour lines, but shows the complete surviving trail network on the Mountain, as signposted with red placards bearing white Byzantine lettering between 1980 and 1989 by Tsiropoulos and others. There are a few minor errors, especially on the coast between Arsanás Zográfu and Dhokhiaríu monastery, but in general this is an extremely reliable itinerary-planning device. If you are unable to contact Mr Tsiropoulos at the number provided, you might try SEO-Thessaloníki at (031) 224 710.

Korfes has regazetted Mt Áthos in issues 97 and 98, but despite improvements on the previous effort the map is a poor substitute, as would be the YIS 1:50,000 *Áthos* and *Kariaí* sheets on which it's based. Coverage on the *Korfes* map only extends as far as Dhokhiaríu on the south-western coast and Stavronikíta on the north-eastern shore – this plus the Tsiropoulos map together would still not do as well as the Austrian sheet.

Because of the availability of two decent maps and the existence of the red signposts, the trail descriptions in the stages below will not be on a rock-by-rock basis, but will concentrate on point-to-point walking times, so that you don't end up being locked out of a monastery by arriving too late.

Stage 1: Esfigménu to Pandokrátoros via Vatopedhíu

(5½ hours)
After obtaining your dhiamonitírion at Arsanás Hilandharíu, stay on the boat until the next stop, the monastery of Esfigménu. This, built directly at sea level, is reportedly one of the strictest houses on the Mountain, and a banner recently hung out the window of an upper floor, reading 'Orthodoxy or Death' (in Greek) would seem to bear this out – and does not encourage a casual visit. Do disembark, though, for the three-hour path south-east to Vatopedhíu. Much of the way this does not follow the shore, but keeps 500 to 700 metres inland, climbing to a low saddle before dropping down to the edge of Vatopedhíu's vast bay.

Vatopedhíu compares with Meyístis Lávras (see Stage 2) in wealth and importance, and exceeds it in size; the cobbled, slanting courtyard with its free-standing belfry seems more like a central European town plaza, surrounded by stairways and cells for more than 300.

The *katholikón* (main church), one of the oldest on Áthos, is noteworthy for two mosaics of the Annunciation and the Deisis (Christ, the Virgin and John the Baptist shown together) flanking the door of the inner narthex (porch). The refectory is engaging, with well-lit 18th-century frescoes.

Forty monks live here, mostly young and

two-thirds Cypriot but also nine Australians and, at last look, some French novices. Also present are whole families of cats, in brazen violation of the ávaton but a fairly common monastic foible. This is a popular monastery to visit, but the old-fashioned arhondaríki is also quite large, so space should not be a problem if you wish to stay.

Continuing to Pandokrátoros, you'll initially walk an hour up a dusty track, passing two signed turn-offs to the hermitage of Kolítsu; the short-cut path shown on the Austrian map is marked at its start but quite badly overgrown.

In either case, at the top of the grade, beyond the second Kolítsu turn-off, follow the marker towards Pandokrátoros, pointing down an abandoned driveway. Within 15 minutes this has dwindled to a path again by a dry fountain; an hour from the track you have your first glimpse of Pandokrátoros and Stavronikíta. The descent is steady, often sharp, but the occasionally cobbled trail is good under foot despite obstructing bushes. It's a total of 2½ hours walking to the door of Pandokrátoros.

The setting is superb, on a hill overlooking the arsanás, which is more a fishing harbour;

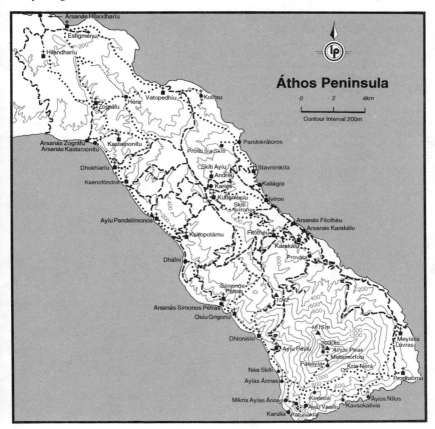

the courtyard with its eight ornamental orange trees suggests Andalucía. Most of the 35 monks are welcoming, with a bit of that air of the old gentlemen's club which the new wave of novices so disparages. Unless the community succumbs soon to pressure from its peers, this will be your only chance to stay at a large idiorrhythmatic institution. A lay worker cooks for pilgrims, the guest wing overlooks the sea, and there is even a cold shower. In a valley overhead poke the spires of the enormous Profíti Ilía skíti, built during the 19th-century Russian expansion drive and today home to just nine monks.

Stage 2: Pandokrátoros to Meyístis Lávras via Stavronikíta & Ivíron

(1¾ hours plus boat)

Head south over the creek bridge, passing the arsanás, to find the marked start of the coastal path to Stavronikíta. It's 50 minutes' walk door-to-door – fairly easy going with some ups and downs. Stavronikíta is one of the more interesting monasteries architecturally, with some of the best views of Áthos peak by virtue of its position. Essentially a fortified tower surrounded by neat, aqueduct-fed kitchen gardens, it was recently renovated rather starkly. The katholikón occupies most of the gloomy courtyard, and the refectory, normally opposite, had to be positioned upstairs in a sparse stone-and-wood room enlivened only by 16th-century fresco fragments of the Last Supper and the death of Saint Nicholas, the monastery's patron. It has always been one of the poorest houses, and is currently home to 15 monks (including several Australians), but they're hard pressed to handle the relatively large number of visitors and it no longer rates as one of the more outgoing foundations. The guest quarters, despite another wondrous shower, are cramped, fill quickly and for the most part face inland.

From Stavronikíta it's again just under an hour to Ivíron, by trail as far as the tower of Kaliágra (officially the arsanás of Kutlusmusíu monastery) and on a mixture of path and beach track thereafter. Despite the name – 'of the Iberians' (Caucasian Georgians) – the last

Georgian died in the 1950s, and today it is home to 35 Greek monks, many of whom moved over from Stavronikíta. If you meet him, Father Sinesios is particularly welcoming.

The monastery's pride is the miraculous ikon of the Portaítissa ('She Who Guards the Gate'), housed in a special chapel to the left of the entrance. Great disasters will visit Áthos if She ever leaves the Mountain, it is said. The katholikón is among the largest on Áthos, with an 11th-century mosaic floor and more recent, undistinguished frescoes. More impressive are the assorted decorative items such as the Persian-influenced gold crown of the chandelier, two Hellenistic columns with ram's-head capitals from a Poseidon temple which once stood here, and a silver-leaf lemon tree crafted in Russia.

A signposted trail leads up within one hour 20 minutes to the monastery of Kutlumusíu, at the edge of Kariés, much the most pleasant way of walking there if you need to. From there an onward, marked path takes you via the skíti of Ivíron within 2¼ hours to the monastery of Filothéu, and from there a track then a trail to Karakálu in 40 minutes more, but I'd advise against this route for several reasons: the path system between Karakálu and Meyístis Lávras has been completely destroyed in recent years, neither Filothéu or Karakálu are of surpassing architectural or artistic interest, and both houses forbid non-Orthodox attendance at liturgy and trápeza. If you do go, you'll find relatively comfortable guest quarters and good food at Filothéu; Karakálu was swept by fire in 1988, a fairly common occurrence on Áthos, and has a very limited capacity to host guests until repairs are completed, with preference given to Orthodox pilgrims.

To finish the basic stage, take instead the midday boat from Ivíron to Meyístis Lávras – do not in any circumstances attempt to walk the distance on the road. Rides are not forthcoming and it will take you nearly seven hours!

Meyístis Lávras is the oldest and first in rank of the ruling monasteries, and physically the largest structure on Áthos. No less than 15 chapels sprout in its enormous court-yard, and (uniquely) it has never been ravaged by fire – though there are a substantial number of additions from late Ottoman times, including the rambling guest wing. The treasury and library are accordingly rich, though the non-Orthodox traveller is unlikely to get a look. As is usual in such cases, several monks of the 25 here have complementary keys which must be turned in unison to enter.

What you will certainly see over a meal are the superior frescoes in the trapezaría, painted by Theophanes the Cretan in 1535. Alongside the apse the Saints march into Paradise, having undergone grisly martyr-doms, while a Tree of Jesse (the genealogy of Jesus) grows in the southern transept. Athanasios the founder lies dying opposite, and the Apocalypse breaks out to the left of the main entry.

In the western apse the Last Supper is being eaten, an understandably popular theme in Greek Orthodox refectories.

Just outside the door stands a huge fount, largest on the Mountain, with pagan columns supporting the canopy. The katholikón – admission only for services – contains more excellent frescoes by Theophanes.

Stage 3: Meyístis Lávras to Ayías Ánnas via Katunákia or Kavsokalívia
(5½-6½ hours)
This stage encompasses some of the most beautiful and wild country on Áthos, hopefully never to be desecrated by a road. Not surprisingly it was a favourite home of the earliest Athonite anchorites, and there are still a number of hermitages and idi-orrythmatic skítes clustered near the sea.

Heading south from Meyístis Lávras (at 200 metres), take the direct, right-hand, upper trail signposted for Ayías Annas; the lower option to the nominally Romanian skíti of Prodhrómu, a cenobitic dependency of Meyístis Lávras, quickly becomes a dreary track of over an hour's duration. The high trail leads, within the same period of time, with a final sharp right turn over a small pass, to a cross and a wooden bench at 500

metres for enjoying the views over the sea. From here you can, if you wish, bear left and down to visit Prodhrómu at the expense of an extra half hour. But the old Romanian monks whom I met in 1981, conversing with the outside world in rough French, seem all to have disappeared, and there seems every reason to press on with what will be a very demanding day.

Almost immediately past the cross there's a fork down to the hermitage of Áyios Nílos and the skíti of Kavsokalívia; this is a beautiful route, but involves an 800-metre altitude change (300 down, 500 up) to rejoin the main trail later, and will consume an extra hour compared to the usual path.

This continues, shunning another left fork five minutes later, for 20 minutes to an unreliable tap wired to an oak tree. An hour past the cross, twist through a densely forested ravine and reach another signed turning to Kavsokalívia. Within another quarter of an hour, or 2¼ hours from Meyístis Lávras, the permanent Kría Nerá stream spills over the trail in deep shade, making a fine lunch stop.

Coming onto the three-hour mark of the day, you'll pass two more turn-offs down to Kavsokalívia, and shortly after a pair to the colony of Kerasiá, an oasis in a valley between two rocky spurs. A four-way junction at about 760 metres, the high point on the traverse, is reached 3½ hours from your start. Right (north) and up is the path leading to Áthos peak; ideally you would stay at Kerasiá the night before an ascent, but there are no formal facilities for guests there. Straight ahead leads to Ayías Ánnas, but since you will very likely be coming up this at dawn of the next day, take instead the left-hand (south-westerly) option for an extremely 'scenic route' via Katunákia with little extra effort (since the altitude change is identical), and only an additional hour of walking.

Ignore an almost immediate, unmarked level option to Ayíu Vasilíu and keep to the marked path right which drops within a hour to about 325 metres elevation as it crosses the ravine cutting through the cottages of Katunákia hermitage. The large building above and to the right is the Dhanieléon, a small academy devoted to the perfection of sacred chanting. Cottages fleck the rocks and terrraces, with a chapel here and there; the tenants are elusive, and you'll need more than the extra hiking hour to await their return or find an occupied hut.

There is another collection of even more severe hermitages down the cliff to your left, known as Karúlia ('Pulleys') after the preferred method of hoisting supplies from passing boats before any of the precipitous access trails were opened. Here live dwindling numbers of the most isolated hermits on the mountain, dividing their lives between prayer, meditation, and the crafting of devotional articles. The last of the French-speaking Russians who arrived after the 1917 revolution, the famous Father Nikon, died a few years back (in rather murky circumstances, according to Maximos's book) and was arguably on the path to sainthood; others may be simply half mad from a surfeit of hardship and solitude.

Bearing right around the bend brings you level, within 20 minutes, with the skíti of Mikrís Ayías Ánnas, where newish 'villas' would not disgrace a Greek holiday island. The monks here must be relatively comfortable with their solar water heaters and electric power. Like all the cottage-dwellers hereabouts, they spend much of their time producing articles such as ikons, wood carvings, incense and jewellery for sale in the curio shops at Kariés, Meyístis Lávras and secular Greece. If you are not Orthodox you will generally not be expected to show interest in buying them, but patronage is gladly accepted.

Beyond this haven the path climbs briefly to a pass giving onto one of the most stunning perspectives on Áthos: much of the south-western coast of the peninsula, doubtless glimmering in the afternoon sun, with the buildings of Ayías Ánnas tumbling down its ravine just like in the old woodcuts, Néa Skíti down by the sea, and the monasteries of Dhionisíu and Osíu Grigoríu visible upcoast. After no more than two hours from the four-way junction you should be at the gate of the kiriakón, having just filled water bottles from the cascade below.

Ayías Ánnas, like the entire south-western tip of Áthos, enjoys a balmy climate capable of coaxing lemons to ripeness; for this reason it has been a favourite site of idiorrhythmatic and anchoritic settlement, and a preferred target of Greek pilgrims who often fill the place. There is a guest wing at Ayías Ánnas, but the food may leave something to be desired; still, it is the closest likely bed to the peak if you don't have a sleeping bag with you.

Sidetrip: Up Áthos Peak

(8 hours return)

You can arrange to leave a full pack at Ayías Ánnas while you tackle the summit in the morning. The dhíkeos has an exaggerated fear of the mountain, and if you tell him of your plans he may insist that you take a companion. As long as the weather is holding, though, the ascent of Point 2030 is no more daunting than that of any other major Aegean hill such as Fengári (Samothráki) or Kérkis (Sámos).

From the kiriakón, it's one hour 15 minutes up with a daypack to the four-way crossroads. Bearing north here towards the peak you'll pass a concrete trough which was a healthy spring a decade ago but is now dried up and filled with rubbish, whatever its appearance on maps. Another one hour 45 minutes will see you along a marked trail through oak and fir to the treeline, and the chapel-shelter of Panayía on a grassy saddle at just over 1500 metres. There's a well inside, some wooden pallets for spreading sleeping bags, and a fireplace. If you overnight here, you'd have the opportunity of being on the summit for sunrise.

Carrying on to the peak, zig-zag up to the ridge visible on the north, where a few stubborn firs cling to life up to the 1900-metre contour. You've just over an hour up to the prominent hogback, followed by a sharp left into a defile flanked by boulders. You'll glimpse the iron cross atop the chapel of Metamórfosi (Transfiguration) just ahead, where there's a visitors' book to sign and another cistern, with tastier water than at Panayía. On clear days (rare in summer) you should be able to see from Mt Ólimbos on the west to Ánatolia on the east; more often, though, you'll see nothing more than the peninsula at your feet – and the reason why you've been hiking the perimeter and the south of Áthos: roads everywhere, and the great scar from a 1989 fire.

Coming down, it's 50 minutes to Panayía and nearly one hour 45 minutes back down to the junction. Returning to Ayías Ánnas, a brief level stretch precedes a sharp descent, an hour in all, luckily in partial shade even in the afternoon. Don't dawdle at Ayías Ánnas (300 metres) after retrieving your pack, since you'll certainly want to reach a monastery by evening and must allow for the possibility of your first choice being full.

Stage 4: Ayías Ánnas to Dhionisíu
(2 hours)

It's barely half an hour to the turn-off for Néa Skíti (Theotóku), with a spring just before. Within another 30 minutes you emerge at the intersection with the track heading 10 minutes up to Ayíu Pávlu monastery, impressively visible above the shrubbery for some moments before. The view, with a northern spur of Áthos peak plunging down, hasn't changed much since Edward Lear painted it in the 1850s, except for the jagged scar of the modern road heading in. About 35 monks, mostly from the island of Kefalloniá, live here today, in this most castle-like of the Athonite houses, squeezed into the head of a valley out of reach of pirates.

Daylight permitting, you may wish to proceed to Dhionisíu. The track leads down to the pebbly bay, where it ends near a spot secluded enough for a swim – if armadas of disgusting white jellyfish aren't already there. The onward route seems to be bottled up by an impassable cliff, but waymarks point you inland towards the phone lines and over the problematic spur. An hour's total trek separates Ayíu Pávlu from Dhionisíu.

This recently renovated house, perched defensively on a coastal cliff, has overcome a former reputation for grimness and is one of the better monasteries to stay at, and an interesting one in the bargain. The food is usually good – the arkhondáris seems to know that many pilgrims come here directly from the peak, hungry – and so is the monastery's very own Monoksilítiko wine, produced at a remote kellí.

Dhometios and Chrisostomos, two of among 40 monks, tend to greet pilgrims, showing them to the neat and airy arhondaríki which compares well with often claustrophobic facilities elsewhere. Unusually they may also offer, unbidden, a tour of Dhionisíu's points of interest. The buildings themselves, largely spared from fire, dated mostly from the 16th century before the remodelling regrettably stripped the half-timbering from the exterior. The monastery is electrified cleanly by a water turbine installed up the canyon behind.

The library, curated by a Cypriot monk, boasts illuminated Gospels on silk-blended paper, a wooded carved miniature of the Passion week, and ivory crucifixes. You've little chance, though, of seeing the great treasure, the three-metre-long chrysobull (imperial charter) of the Trapezuntine emperor Alexios III Comnene.

It is also difficult to see, even when guided, the 16th-century frescoes by the Cretan artist Tzortzis in the dim katholikón (as ever the monastery perimeter blocks out sunlight), but not so the brilliant contemporary ones by Theophanes on the inside and outside of the refectory. The interior features the Entry of the Saints into Paradise and the mystical Ladder to Heaven; the exterior wall is ablaze with a version of the Apocalypse, complete with something akin to a nuclear mushroom cloud.

Stage 5: Dhionisíu to Dháfni via Osíu Grigoríu & Símonos Pétras
(2¾ hours and boat)

The path from Dhionisíu to Osíu Grigoríu is rougher than the preceding coastal stretches, and would be out of the question after a day spent going up and down the peak.

Curl down anticlockwise around the base

of Dhionisíu, cross the scrappy beach, and make the stiff climb to a point about 225 metres up, some 40 minutes out. Then plunge down on a kalderími surface before climbing again to another saddle of the same height 15 minutes later – you can see Símonos Pétras far ahead.

Now you drop into a major ravine, roller-coaster a bit more on the way out of it, and finally, one hour 20 minutes beyond Dhionisíu, find yourself at the door of Osíu Grigoríu, the only monastery to be built virtually at sea level. In the wake of a devastating 18th-century fire there are few buildings or treasures of note – except perhaps the quirky palm tree in the courtyard – and Osíu Grigoríu was always hierarchically unimportant. But it has long been one of the friendliest, most gracious monasteries and an excellent place to gain a better understanding of Orthodoxy. In the comfortable guest study you can read a small collection of English material on monasticism while gazing out at the northern Aegean just beyond.

Take the onward path to Arsanás Símonos Pétras (45 minutes), entering the edge of the fire-damage zone dating from 1989 – not an appealing prospect for further walking. From the arsanás it's nearly 40 minutes up to Símonos Pétras (Simópetra), sprouting from a pinnacle like a Tibetan lamasery. The name, meaning 'Rock of Simon', stems from the foundation legend that the hermit Simon was moved to build a monastery by a mysterious light hovering over the sheer pinnacle here.

The most externally spectacular of the monasteries on this coast, Símonos Pétras is visible (as you'll probably have noticed already) from as far away as 10 km. Its original walls were destroyed in a devastating 1891 fire, but the plaster-and-cement replacement still manages to attract numerous admirers. The creaky wooden balconies which girdle the top four floors of the 10-storey structure are not for the acrophobic – directly underneath yawns a 250-metre slanting drop to the sea.

Along with Filothéu, Símonos Pétras is one of the most vigorous communites on Áthos, with more than 50 monks from nearly a dozen countries in residence. Unlike Filothéu, you are allowed, even encouraged, to attend the liturgy, and the chanting here is particularly fine. Unfortunately, because of its reputation, Símonos Pétras is frequently crowded with foreigners and might best be admired from a distance in high season.

Quality walking stops here for the time being – there are no surviving onward trails to Dháfni, and you're advised to cover that distance on the morning boat. For a suitable fee, the skipper can often be persuaded to take groups a bit further, to the monastery of Ayíu Pandelímonos, before returning to meet the main ferry from Uranópoli and take passengers back to Ayías Annas. This is a wise investment, since the coastal trail from Dháfni to Ayíu Pandelímonos is not the greatest.

Dháfni itself consists of a post office for mailing your postcards, some rather tacky souvenir shops, and a customs station – the baggage of all departing passengers is inspected, to impede the traffic in smuggled treasures. Beware of the secular police in their distinctive eagle-brooch caps, always ready to pounce on real or imagined breaches of the rules by pilgrims. There's also one taverna where you can get a beer and a bowl of soup, but there are no grocery shops for topping up your stock of trail food.

Stage 6: Ayíu Pandelímonos to Zográfu via Ksenofóndos, Dhokhiaríu & Kastamonítu

(4½ hours)

It might be worth your while taking the regular noon ferry beyond Ayíu Pandelímonos to either Ksenofóndos or Dhokhiaríu to save some time if you intend to spend the night inland at either Kastamonítu or Zográfu – since while the coastal hiking here is mostly on trails, the scenery doesn't compare to that of south-west Áthos, and you could save your stamina for the more beautiful paths slipping over the Áthos crest to the inland monasteries.

For completeness's sake, the stage

description will start at Ayíu Pandelímonos, also known simply as the Rusikó (Russian) after the origins of most of its 38 monks. This ethnic predominance is strongly reflected in the onion-shaped domes and the different style of the frescoes. Most of the buildings were erected virtually overnight in the latter half of the 19th century, as the leading edge of Czarist Russia's campaign for preeminence on the Mountain, and have a utilitarian, barracks-like quality that was not improved when the outer dormitories were gutted by fire in 1968. The sole outstanding features are the corrosion-green roofs and the enormous bell (second largest in the world) over the refectory, which often provokes speculation as to how they got it up there. If you're an architecture buff, Rusikó can probably be skipped without regret; aficionados of Belle Epoque kitsch will be delighted, however, with the mass-printed liturgical calendars, gaudy reliquaries of assorted saints' bones, and a cornucopia of gold (or perhaps just gilded) fixtures in the top-storey chapel.

The small population fairly rattles around the echoing halls, though the collapse of the Soviet system means Ayíu Pandelímonos can look forward to a material and spiritual renaissance. Already large groups of Russian pilgrims nearly fill the place in the weeks following the 27 July (9 August to the outside world) festival of the patron saint. If you are permitted to attend liturgy, do so for the sake of the Slavonic chanting, though you can anticipate that the residents, already rather indifferent to those who are not Slavic Orthodox, will be paying progressively more attention to their newly free-to-travel flock.

The trail between Rusikó and Ksenofóndos takes an hour, with some thornbush in the middle and moments of tractor-track at the start and end. It's not so roller-coasterish as the section between Dhionisíu and Grigoríu, but you do climb to nearly 100 metres at points. Ksenofóndos's busy sawmill lends it a vaguely industrial atmosphere, accentuated by ongoing extensive reconstruction. The enormous, sloping, oddly shaped court, expanded upward

during the 1800s, is unique in possessing two kathólika.

The smaller, older one – with exterior frescoes of the 16th-century 'Cretan' School – was outgrown and replaced during the 1830s by the huge upper one, where two fine mosaic icons can be worshipped once restoration has been completed. The guest accommodation occupies a modern wing overlooking the sea at the extreme southern end of the perimeter.

A half-hour walk, begun by going up anticlockwise around Ksenofóndos' outer walls, leads to Dhokhiaríu, invitingly picturesque when glimpsed from sea but not conspicuously welcoming and in the throes of remodelling. The repairs haven't yet included the primitive but clean guest quarters, which see few foreigners. An exceptionally tall, large katholikón nearly fills the court, though its Cretan School frescoes, possibly by Tzortzis, were clumsily done over in 1855. Much better are those from the late 17th century in the long, narrow refectory, with its windows to the sea making it one of the nicest on Áthos. Even Orthodox pilgrims have trouble gaining permission to worship the miraculous ikon of the Virgin housed in a chapel between the church and trapezaría, near the fine pebble-mosaic floor of the outer narthex.

The direct trail to Kastamonítu (Konstamonítu) monastery shown on the Tsiropoulos map has been reclaimed by the forest. To get there you must first follow the pine-fringed shore for 45 minutes (half on bulldozed beach pebbles, half on a trail) to its arsanás, then climb 10 minutes on a dirt track through a hillside olive grove, with a final 35 minutes, nearly doubling back on your initial course, on cobbles to the monastery at 250 metres elevation.

The most noteworthy feature of Kastamonítu is its enchanted, rural setting at the top of a wooded valley; the place itself seems as poor and bare as you'd expect from the lowest-ranking monastery, with more grass growing up through the cracks in the courtyard pavement than is usual at the more energetic houses. Orthodox and heterodox are segregated here, and few foreigners stop, preferring to continue to Zográfu.

The path to Zográfu there leads north-west over the forest hills within 90 minutes to this most inland of the 20 monasteries, which has been exclusively Bulgarian-staffed since 1845. Though the vast rows of abandoned cells far outnumber the few remaining monks, Zográfu can, like Rusikó, anticipate something of a revival with the end of communism in Bulgaria – provided that the Greek civil authorities assent to this. If you're curious as to the feel of a Slavic foundation, this is a good choice for a night's pause, well poised also for the final walking stage.

Stage 7: Zográfu to Hilandharíu or Esfigménu

(3 hours)

West of Zográfu is a multiple path junction around the ravine bridge. The eastern (left) bank route leading up the main canyon brings you within three hours and a maximum elevation of 250 metres to Esfigménu, easily in time for the afternoon boat to Ierissós (weather permitting).

The path on the far bank of the bridge heads steadily north-west up a side gully before levelling off at a plateau and dropping to Hilandharíu after 2½ hours. This irregularly shaped monastery was generously funded by the 13th-century Serbian kings and has since then remained a Serbian foundation (and lately a focus of Serbian nationalism). The frescoes of the katholikón, originally dating from the 14th century, were for once skilfully retouched in 1801; as you'd expect for a life raft of medieval Serbian culture, the library and treasury are well endowed.

Allow 45 minutes to reach the arsanás along the connecting track, though you will possibly be able to arrange a ride there in a service vehicle.

If for some reason you wish to return to Vatopedhíu, a trail leads directly from Zográfu, via the 350-metre-high crossroads called Héra, to that monastery within two hours. In all cases you will need to leave Zográfu early enough, possibly missing the first meal of the day, to be sure of meeting the afternoon boat to Ierissós.

Samothráki

This island belongs to no archipelago, and since it has always been linked administratively and communications-wise with the mainland opposite, I've included it as part of Thráki.

Samothráki, or the 'Samos of Thrace', was a place of pilgrimage for thousands of years, when suplicants were initiated into a mystery religion at the Sanctuary of the Great Gods, tucked into a small valley in the north-eastern quarter of the island. These Great Gods or *Kabiri* were originally pre-Olympian, local Thracian deities, later identified by the Samian colonists as the Dioskuroi; similarly, an Anatolian mother-goddess also revered here was syncretised with Demeter. As in the case of the rites of Eleusis, little is known about the ceremonies here, except that unusually they were open to all, including women and slaves, and that – in a foretaste of Christianity – confession, absolution and baptism were administered, along with a smattering of ethical precepts.

Samothráki has more recently earned a reputation among European nature lovers by virtue of its striking natural beauty. Few other Greek islands are as dramatic seen from the sea; the enormous mass of Mt Fengári (Sáos) looms over your approaching ferry like some higher celestial ship. The northern face of Samothráki resembles the mainland across the water: a relatively broad coastal plain, furrowed by streams and burgeoning with planes and beeches, preceding the sudden eruption of Fengári. The southern flanks of Fengári drop off equally steeply, sometimes sheerly, from Lákkoma to the Kípos cape, but heavily cultivated flatlands occupy the entire south-western tip of the island. As with most large islands in the Aegean, the southern shore is warmer and drier, with primarily evergreen vegetation in uninhabited regions.

The premier hike on Samothráki is the ascent of 1611-metre Fengári, highest point of the Aegean islands (excluding Crete). Thérma (Lutrá), with its shady groves and hot springs, is the most popular starting point, though accommodation is limited and uniformly full in July and August – you might end up at the camping ground on the shore nearby. Attractive (if windy) Hóra is preferable to the ugly, functional port of Kamariótissa as a base, being close to the south-coast stroll described and also acting as a less used jump-off point for the peak.

Season

Recommendation as for Áthos.

Maps

YIS 1:50,000 *Nísos Samothráki** or British WWII 1:50,000 map *Samothráki*.

Access

There's a ferry to Sámothraki from Alexandhrúpoli at least daily in summer, usually after 1 pm, and another two or three times weekly from Kaválla. During the off season these frequencies drop to thrice and once weekly respectively.

Upon disembarking you should check the current bus schedule, posted in the little waterfront park. Historically there have been almost hourly departures to Thérma; up to five well-spaced services to Hóra, except for Sunday when there are just three; and two or three daily buses to Lákkoma and Profítis Ilías, the last at 2 pm.

Trek 1: Ascent of Fengári

(5½-6 hours)

This is most quickly and safely done from Thérma. From the bus turnaround area, proceed up the muddy street going parallel to the stream; this soon narrows to a donkey track. Do not pass a large concrete water tank, but instead turn left just before – the path up the mountain starts behind a huge, open-boled plane tree close to the overflow outlet of the tank.

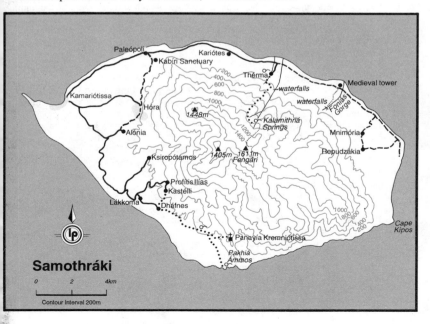

Samothráki

0   2   4km

Contour Interval 200m

Toil uphill through a big fern brake until you find an old, roofless stone chapel – the very clear trail continues just to its left. For the next hour the route charts an obvious course through arbutus and heather; about 30 minutes along you can see and hear giant waterfalls in a canyon to your left. The arbutus-heather environment suddenly becomes a beech community on a ridge devoid of underbrush; it's important during this second hour to keep an eye peeled for cairns, since the path is no longer hemmed in by shrubbery and is none too easy to pick out in the forest gloom.

After about a two-hour march, the trail veers off this ridge and crosses a gully just a few paces east of the spot where the Kalamithriá spring gurgles over the path. From the bed of this ravine you've a 20-minute climb to a meadow on a knoll just at the treeline. Cairns, and with a stretched imagination a trail, continue a little further up the peak, but for the most part it's an hour-plus cross-country scramble through bracken and boulders up the ridge hovering just ahead of you to the south-west. Once on the crest you should see two trig points to your left. The nearer, 1600-metre column was erected in 1942 by the Bulgarian occupation force; however the true (1611-metre) peak is indicated by the Greek survey marker a little beyond.

Fengári ('Moon') lives up to its name – great crags and boulder slides break up the barren landscape in all directions. To the west, Mt Áthos and the top of Thássos island ride above the ocean's heat haze, with the mainland peaks of Pangéo (left) and Falakró (right) flanking Thássos to either side. To the north, the Rodhópi range huddles beyond Komotiní, and in exceptional conditions Ulu Dağ above Bursa in Turkey is visible to the east. If Poseidon did in fact watch the progress of the Trojan War from this peak, as the legend states, he couldn't have picked a better vantage point.

It's well over three hours up the mountain, slightly less coming down; allow at least 5½ hours in motion. There is also a fairly well frequented route up from Hóra, initially on a path and then cross-country after the first spring, but you must have a detailed map for route-finding.

Fengári's volcanic heart pumps out a steady supply of free, just-right hot water in the rickety old public bathhouse, behind the fancy new spa in Thérma. If the enclosed pool is too hot (about 42°C) or occupied, there's a cooler (37°C) open-air tub about 50 metres beyond, and a soak in either makes a perfect reward for the completion of the trek.

Trek 2: Waterfalls Above Foniás
(1½ hours return)

If it's high summer perhaps you'd rather have a cold bath. Walk down from Thérma to the coast road, turn right and continue 4.3 km (about one hour unless you hitch) to the vicinity of the medieval tower of Foniás. There's a bridge on the road, just before the tower, over the Foniás stream flowing down from the falls.

Find a red 'B' (perhaps a German waymark, for *baden*) and a green paint splodge, which together mark the beginning of the route up to the cascades. Sporadic red dots guide you along the essentially pathless left (west) bank of the stream for the entire 40-minute walk; if you lose the way, don't panic: you can't miss the cascades as long as you stay by the water.

At the end of the marked route, 12-metre falls plunge into a large, deep swimming hole that seems more like an abandoned quarry than a natural basin. The water is absolutely frigid – come at midday if you intend to get in. Further progress up this valley is complicated by towering rock walls on three sides.

Trek 3: Southern Shore –
Lákkoma/Profítis Ilías to Pakhiá Ámmos
(2 hours)

You may need to have spent the previous night in either Hóra or Kamariótissa to make the bus connections necessary to reach the trailhead. Take an early departure from Kamariótissa to either Lákkoma or Profítis Ilías. If you alight from the bus at Lákkoma it's a pretty straightforward affair to walk

Top: Skíathos: Rooflines of Evangelistrías monastery (MD)
Bottom: Náxos: Áyii Apóstoli with piggy-back chapel, Tragéa (MD)

Top: Folégandhros: July barley reaping at Áno Meriá (MD)
Bottom: Folégandhros: Barley-toting donkey, Áno Meriá (MD)

east along the dirt track to Dháfnes hamlet and then continue to Pakhiá Ámmos as described here. There's no harm, though, in staying on until the end of the bus line at Profítis Ilías; the hike is not any longer from there, and the scenery satisfying.

This higher village, alive with the sound of running fountains, also has two psistariés (but unfortunately no accommodation as yet), and is one of the best places on the island to watch the sunset.

From Profítis Ilías (about 300 metres), follow the asphalt road to its end in Kastélli hamlet, five minutes below. From the uppermost three houses, a good mule trail at '10 o'clock' winds its way down the ridge towards the Lákkoma-Dháfnes-Pakhiá Ámmos track. Your path links up with the latter just east of Dháfnes after about 20 minutes. Much of this road barely deserves the label, being just passable to motor trikes – it's more of a glorified donkey track through peaceful countryside smothered in olives.

About 45 minutes beyond the Kastélli trailhead a spring feeds a trough just left of the track; 20 minutes later is an important fork. The left option leads up within half an hour to Panayía Kremniótissa chapel, perched atop one of a group of pinnacles. Outriders of Fengári stand guard behind and to the north-west, and there are sweeping prospects over the entire southern coast. In clear weather you can glimpse the Turkish island of Imvros a bit to the south-east. The chapel itself is of no great antiquity or architectural interest, and there's no water nearby.

The right-hand fork leads, also within 30 minutes, to the bay of Pakhiá Ámmos ('Broad Sand'), Samothráki's best beach. Olives yield to a landscape of stunted oaks, wild apples and aloe, and the last dependable water on the trail, a tiny creek, lies about 10 minutes past the junction.

The strand itself extends for nearly a km, closed off at either end by two gaunt headlands and lapped by crystal water. It gets busy in summer, when boat excursions call from Kamariótissa (a possible means back) and a certain number of tents sprout. Some visitors never find the tiny, freshwater spring in a cleft in the rocks at the beach's extreme eastern end. Here water trickles into two potholes just a few inches above sea level!

Thessalía, Magnisía & Évvia

Mt Ólimbos, often considered a part of Makedhonía, actually straddles the border with Thessalía and has been included in this chapter. The geologic record shows that it, like neighbouring peaks to the south, is a result of a single surge of mountain-building activity that took place some 70 to 80 million years ago.

Much later, the prehistoric inland sea that inundated the plain of Thessalía finally succeeded in boring an exit to the Aegean, thus creating the celebrated vale of Témbi and further separating Kíssavos and Pílion from their massive sibling to the north-east.

Further south, the Pagasitic flatlands at the base of Mt Pílion were home to the earliest humans to settle in what is now Greece. Looking at the rich agricultural breadbasket west of the arc of mountains, it's easy to see what induced these Neolithic pioneers to grow roots here, but it's equally obvious that there is little to detain the trekker or day hiker.

Your attention is best directed back to the slopes of Pílion and Kíssavos, still as thickly covered with trees as they were in the days when the centaurs were said to dwell there. These horse-men were probably a mythologisation of an aboriginal tribe that retreated to the hills after the Dorians invaded in the 12th and 11th centuries BC, and were reputed by the latter to be proficient in all sorts of doctoring and sorcery, including the ability to change shape. Hikers caught in the elemental force of a storm on a forested slope of these areas will find it easy to believe that every rustling branch hides a lurking character out of a Rousseau painting.

Pílion falls within the ancient territory and modern boundary of Magnisía province, which also includes the Sporádhes islands, geologically and climatically a continuation of Pílion. Unhappily, they are not as rewarding for walking as you might hope: too many bulldozer tracks and (on Skíros) out-of-bounds military areas.

Separated from the mainland at one point by a mere 30-metre channel, Évvia is officially the second-largest Greek island after Crete. However, you'd be hard pressed to put a finger on any definite island character, and the place seems, even more than the Sporádhes, an extension of the mainland opposite. The main advantages of peak-climbing on Évvia are the almost instant access from Athens and adaptability to tight schedules.

Ólimbos

The legendary abode of the ancient Greek gods is today still outstanding among the Greek mountains in every category you might consider. Ólimbos (Olympus) attracts the most Greek and foreign visitors annually, and in the quantity, colour and variety of wildflowers in a country which overall is distinguished with respect to alpine flora. Its marked trail system is on a par with that in the north Píndhos, and two important staffed alpine shelters are found here. The range constitutes the core of one of the first national parks to be established in Greece and – more ominously – is the number-one killer of mountaineers who fail to respect the peak's idiosyncracies.

Ólimbos is actually a fairly complex massif, arranged in a horseshoe around the wild Mavrólongos (Enipévs) gorge and culminating in 2917-metre Mítikas ('The Beak'), second-highest peak in the Balkans between Austria and Turkey. (Top honour, by a mere eight metres, goes to Musala in Bulgaria.) The watershed traces the border between Thessalian Lárissa province and Makedhonian Piéria province, and makes a strong impression on visitors due to its abrupt rise from a narrow coastal strip.

Mt Ólimbos is something of a morphological oddity: the ruggedly beautiful limestone pinnacles, walls and saddles above the treeline belong to the same geotectonic belt as Gamíla in the Píndhos, and have nothing to do with the schist that forms the rest of Thessalía and Magnisía. This is because the mountain was once far higher, its top consisting of the surrounding schist beds folded and uplifted. As they wore away over the ages, the limestone underneath, joined deep in the earth's crust with the Píndhos, was exposed. This tectonic 'window' is unique on mainland Greece.

Its closeness to the Thermaïkós gulf means that Ólimbos acts as a trap for moist air; local weather is therefore fickle even by Greek alpine standards, and can change with a rapidity more typical of tropical volcanos. Mists which boil up to the crests from the deep canyons to the east and west are a particular hazard. All this dampness fosters a dense blanket of mixed forest on the lower slopes, mostly beech, black pine and Balkan pine; above the 1900-metre contour few deciduous species can survive. The best meadows for wildflowers lie between 1700 and 2200 metres, with the treeline for the last Balkan pines at about 2300 metres.

Some recent and possible future developments have major implications for the enjoyment of trekking on one of Greece's premier mountains. In 1984-85 the European overland trailblazers reopened a forgotten path through the Mavrólongos ravine as part of the E4 trail, thus allowing walkers to enjoy that superb canyon and also relieving them of the obligation to either pay for transport into the park or tramp many km of dreary road to get there.

But if a proposed development is sanctioned, it will destroy Ólimbos as we know it. Already unnecessary roads have been bulldozed up to the southern and western edges of the alpine horseshoe, and ski resort promoters continually pressure the authorities for permission to construct massive facilities on the east-facing slopes (there is already a small ski lift, used to train the army alpine squad, at Vrisopúles). Not content with just ski pylons and bulldozed runs, the promoters envisage a touristic téléférique up

the Mavrólongos ravine to the peaks, fake ancient temples to gawk at when you get there, and a 'model' city on the north-eastern slopes of the mountain, incorporating convention and shopping centres, hotels, casinos – in short, a high-altitude Disneyland.

The Greek chapter of Mountain Wilderness is devoting most of its resources to fighting these pernicious proposals; if you would like to help after appreciating Ólimbos as it is, send donations to Mountain Wilderness, PO Box 30736, 100 33 Athens, Greece.

HUT-HOPPING AROUND MAVRÓLONGOS

Good campsites and permanent springs are rare owing to the steepness and porosity of the rock strata, and in any case camping is technically illegal within the park boundary, which includes most of the upper reaches of Mavrólongos. The handful of refuges scattered around the summit zone, staffed and sponsored by a number of organisations, partly fill the need for protected overnight camps. You will, however, need to bring extra supplies to free yourself from complete dependency on the huts.

Rating & Duration

Hiking on Ólimbos is moderately strenuous but should not be too demanding for anyone in good physical condition. With few exceptions trails climb sharply, though surfaces are generally fair to good.

Some recommended itineraries include:

Day 1: Gortsiá to SEO refuge;
Day 2: climb summit and descend to Spílios Agapitós refuge;
Day 3: hike out to Litókhoro via the Mavrólongos gorge

Day 1: as above
Day 2: day hikes to summit and Spílios Agapitós, returning to the SEO refuge;
Day 3: SEO refuge to Livadháki refuge via Kalóyeros;
Day 4: Livadháki to Litókhoro via Gólna and the lower Mavrólongos Gorge

Day 1: Litókhoro to Ayíu Dhionisíu, and,after, either of the abovementioned itineraries.

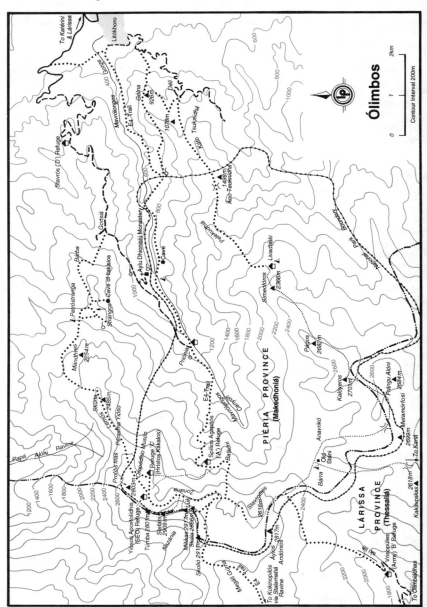

Season

The two most important alpine refuge schedules are given in the main body of the text and should be borne in mind along with the following factors. The annual Olympic wildflower explosion commences in mid-May, but many of the higher altitude routes do not come out from under snowpack until late June; before that you'll want an ice axe, crampons and gaiters for territory above 2200 metres.

Weather is only relatively stable on Ólimbos in any case, with summer days often marred by rain or clouds. Veteran climbers declare late September and early October the best months, as with many other maritime mountains, and I'd have to agree – of my three visits (in May, July, September) the autumn trip was the clearest. Be patient in any season – storms gather and disperse fairly rapidly.

Supplies

You will find an adequate range of supplies in Litókhoro's shops, but don't go overboard unless you're planning to camp at Ayíu Dhionisíu or Livadháki. You are not allowed to use the stoves in the two staffed refuges, as the staff expect you to give them some additional business.

Maps

You should preferably get the giant folding map entitled *Olympus*, published by *Korfes*/EOS Akharnés with Roman lettering, or make do with the original *Korfes* 45-46 magazine sheets. The older products are actually a bit easier to read but are not as accurate as the later single sheet.

Both items are available either from the *Korfes* offices in Akharnés, or more conveniently from the youth hostel in Litókhoro, which also carries the very optional maps from *Korfes* 47-48 covering rarely visited sides of the mountain. The single foldout sheet is about double the price of the four old centrefolds put together, but has useful trilingual text on the verso.

Access

Litókhoro, a rather nondescript army town at the mouth of the Mavrólongos gorge, is the base for most trips up the mountain. It's linked by rail with Athens, Vólos and Thessaloníki several times a day, but the railway station is nine km out of town. There's a fairly regular bus connection up to Litókhoro, courtesy of the direct bus service from Kateríni and Thessaloníki, but you may want to use a taxi to save time. The most convenient train departures from Athens are at 10 am, 2.40 pm and midnight (no sleepers on this last one, though); from Vólos at 6 am and noon; and from Thessaloníki at 7.10, 8.20, 9.35 and 11.30 am.

Near Litókhoro's upper platía are the information booths of the EOS and SEO, each plumping (and making reservations) for their respective shelters on the mountain; they are also a possible source of maps.

The staff at both offices take long afternoon naps, but don't panic if you miss their opening hours – this book contains everything you need to get up and down the mountain safely. As for reservations, the municipal tourist office, which has a much shorter siesta, may be able to provide this service for you. The Spílios Agápitos refuge has its own phone anyway (see Stage 2B).

If you've arrived too late in the day to start up the hill, you'll need to stay in Litókhoro. There's the often oversubscribed youth hostel (☎ (0352) 81 311) at the top end of town, and a few relatively inexpensive hotels such as the Park (☎ (0352) 81 252), Afrodhiti (☎ (0352) 81 415) and Markesia (☎ (0352) 81 831). Groceries can be bought along Ikosiogdhóïs Oktovríu, the lane winding up south-west from the upper square, and good meals are available at To Pazari on the same street – Litókhoro's other restaurants range from the bad to the worse.

In terms of beginning a hike, the youth hostel is in effect one trailhead – the characteristic black-on-yellow E4 diamonds begin within sight of it, and almost everyone will pass this way going in at least one direction, if not both.

If you have a vehicle or the funds to hire

one, a road snakes nearly 18 km into the heart of the mountain. (Hitching is also a possibility.) Three km along there's a recently erected national park control booth; your nationality will be recorded and you'll be handed a small flyer schematically detailing the park rules and some of the more popular hikes. Expect an admission fee to be charged here in the very near future. The asphalt ends at the Km 6 mark; at Km 10 you pass the 40-bunk Stavrós ('D') refuge (☎ (0352) 81 687), of possible interest if you want a bed fairly close to the Gortsiá (Dhiakládhosi) trailhead, which is at Km 14; the Priónia taverna and roadhead are at Km 17.7; and the 1700-metre-long driveway heading down to the ruined monastery of Ayíu Dhionisíu takes off in between, slightly closer to Gortsiá than to Priónia.

Stage 1: Litókhoro to Priónia or Gortsiá via the Mavrólongos Gorge
(4½ hours)
Starting from the youth hostel (about 300 metres), just follow the E4 waymarks along the driveway toward the conspicuous mouth of the river gorge ahead, passing the cemetery and the Mili restaurant after 15 minutes. The well-engineered and marked trail from here on is a delight, soaring and dipping alongside (and occasionally across) the lively river, with occasional ladder-assisted scambles providing some commando-type training. However, you will see people of all ages and abilities, admittedly often with just daypacks, moving up and down this route.

Depending on your pace and load it's from 2¾ to three hours up to the cave of Ayíu Dhionísiu, out of which pours delicious water. Within 20 minutes you'll reach the final river crossing at about 800 metres, a popular area to pitch tents without harrassment, and signs direct you either upstream to Priónia (another hour) or a few moments uphill to Ayíu Dhionisíu monastery (850 metres) – or what's left of it.

This used to be a wonderful spot to stay, but is now well worth avoiding on summer weekends especially, when every car-tripper in the Balkans seems to show up here. Its ruinous state is due to the Nazis having blown it up during April 1943 in reprisal for the monks sheltering resistance fighters; a long-standing sign relating these events was recently removed, perhaps in the interests of good relations within the EC. The monks were all relocated to a replacement monastery near Litókhoro, leaving just one monk-caretaker, none too good-tempered, to control the appalling vandalism that is still perpetrated on the premises – the cots and blankets in the cells I slept in on my first visit have long since been stolen or burnt in the fireplaces. You'll probably only want to stop to collect water.

Priónia itself can offer a log-cabin taverna, a huge parking area beloved of trekking-tour buses and private cars, but no place to stay.

To reach Gortsiá from the cave, simply head up the vehicle driveway serving the monastery (no short cuts possible) and turn right when you reach the main dirt road. It takes about 45 minutes in all to reach Gortsiá (1050 metres), passing en route one more generous spring, your last chance to fill up for quite some time. A relatively recent but already faded placard gives a schematic rundown of the trail ahead, which begins as a driveway up to a small parking area.

Stage 2A: Gortsiá to Yiósos Apostolídhis (SEO) Refuge & Summit Zone
(5½-7 hours)
This is by far the more beautiful approach to the summit zone, much preferable to Stage 2B, though judging from the emptiness of the path most people are put off by the long trek up to the SEO shelter. Many people also get lost right at the outset. The trick is to take the narrow trail heading up and left from the car park, not the overly inviting forest track going down and right nor the path going up behind you to the right. There is supposed to be a marker-sign at the base of the correct path, but it is often helpfully uprooted and tossed aside.

Bárba meadow (1450 metres), an hour along, has fine wildflowers in May. Keeping well to the right of the ridgetop, and taking all left forks when presented with the choice, you'll reach, after 45 more minutes, a knoll with a bench at about 1625 metres and the first good views down into the Mavrólongos.

Two hours along there's a messy junction with a new water tank and a placard. The side trail left leads within 10 minutes to a rock overhang which was walled in as a rustic studio by the eccentric painter Vassilis Ithakisios in the 1920s. The right-hand option is a new trail heading directly to Petróstrunga, while 10 minutes straight up the ridge stands another battery of signs at the site known as Strángos at about 1700 metres. One of these points left to a tank-type spring hidden in a cliff face about 10 minutes slightly below; this is the only permanent water en route.

Continuing on the main trail, you'll arrive at Petróstrunga at just over 1900 metres, some 2½ hours above the road; there's a summer colony of shepherds here, since you're now well out of the national park area. You could camp here and enjoy more flowers, provided the dogs let you. Just beyond, at a signposted right fork, the proper trail veers briefly north, allowing a glimpse of the Petróstrunga crag (the name means 'Rock Corral') before curling back west-south-west around Mándhres knoll.

Leave the forest 4¼ hours out, angling south-west up to a metal sign at the base of Skúrta hill (2425 metres; the legend '2485' refers to the trig point). This you pass a few minutes later, to be treated – weather permitting – to your first complete views of the high peaks.

Next the trail negotiates, with little altitude change, the length of the Lemós ('Neck') which, as the name suggests, is a long narrow ridge joining Skúrta with the Pérasma Yiósu, a small couloir named in honour of a late president of SEO. The Mavrólongos canyon yawns on your left, while a more gentle grade tilts down the opposite side into the Papá Alóni ravine. The route wiggles through Yiósu and puts you out onto the Oropédhio Musón ('Plateau of the Muses', about 2600 metres) 5¼ hours from the roadhead.

On your left you'll see the first of a series of marker poles, presumably for nordic skiers. At the only possible junction the left fork heads for Refuge 'C' (or Hrístos Kákalos, in honour of the local guide who was the first Greek to climb the mountain), visible on the ridge ahead and generally locked. The right turning brings you to the SEO refuge within 25 minutes, for an elapsed walking time from Gortsiá of just over 5½ hours. With rests and lunch, you should allow seven hours.

This shelter, named for Yiosos Apostolidhis, enjoys unrivalled views of Stefáni Peak, nicknamed the 'Throne of Zeus', from its 2740-metre perch. It is open from July to mid-September, though owing to staffing problems this cannot be entirely relied on and you should phone SEO Thessaloníki (☎ (031) 224 719) or (0352) 81 773 in Litókhoro) for this year's schedule. SEO members used to take turns as wardens here, but in 1991 a forest service employee and his family were here on a one-year contract. Beds and meals cost about $6 and $9 respectively, but owing to its altitude the SEO inn is not nearly as crowded as Refuge 'A' and usually has a space among its 80 bunks when the lower shelter is full. Thanks also to the height, bad weather (particularly whiteouts) can last for some days up here and you're smart to bring more money than you think you'll need to pay for your upkeep if trapped here. The outer door of the refuge is locked at 10 pm, so allow enough time to get up here from Gortsiá if you've made an afternoon start.

In the same vein, it's worth knowing that the glassed-in front porch is supposed to be kept unlocked all year round as a potentially life-saving measure. 'Green' electrical power is supplied by wind and solar generators. You're advised not to drink the washroom sink water, which is laced with mud and minerals; in snow-free times you can tap a pair of cisterns down in the gulch at the base of Stefáni. (The nearer one, paradoxically, supplies Refuge 'C').

Stage 2B: Priónia to Spílios Agapitós ('A'} Refuge & Summit Zone

(3 hours)

This doesn't quite qualify as a full stage – the energetic could complete Stage 1 and 2B together in a single walking day.

The Priónia trailhead (about 1100 metres) is the start of the very popular ascent, along the continuation of the E4, to the equally crowded, staffed shelter above. A waterfall just past the parking area is the sole water source for the three-hour climb, so top bottles up. The forest on the way up is pleasant, if a bit gloomy; frequented as it is, this is not yet true wilderness.

Refuge 'A', 2100 metres up at the site Balkóni, is open continuously from 15 May to 31 October, and it's a good idea to reserve one of the 80 bunks by phone (☎ (0352) 81 800) especially in July and August when the shelter is apt to be full every night. Beds and food cost the same as at the SEO refuge ($6 and $9 respectively).

The warden of many years standing is Kostas Zolotas, who can be contacted in Litókhoro (☎ (0352) 81 329) when he's not on the mountain. Mr Zolotas speaks Greek, German and English but may take some warming up to – stay on his good side by letting him know immediately if you intend to overnight here, and by not breaking any of the rather numerous rules. Lights-out happens soon after the outer door is locked at 10 pm; Zolotas will make sure you get an early start attempting the peak by gleefully switching on those same dorm lights at the crack of dawn.

Sidetrips: The Summit Zone

Using either of the two refuges as a base, you can cover virtually all of the following terrain in a day, equipped with a light pack and given stable weather.

Ascent of Mítikas via Skála Above Spílios Agapitós the E4 continues, passing two important junctions, to the base of Skála peak. The turn-off for the Zonária trail (see following description) to Oropédhio Musón

is marked by a sign on a tall iron pole 45 to 60 minutes above the refuge, depending on snowpack, at about 2600 metres. About 15 minutes further the second split is also marked by a pole, just visible from the first. The E4 proceeds straight here (see Other Descent Routes off Ólimbos); you bear right, following the red arrows and dots on the rock pointing you towards Mítikas.

One hour above the junction the trail reaches Skála peak (2866 metres) and deteriorates to a series of dots, dashes and arrows directing you through the scree and the crags. On your left there's a 500-metre drop into the chasm of Kazánia ('Cauldrons'), so it's not an exercise for those afraid of heights, but there is little actual danger in dry conditions since you've a bit of ridge protecting you. The drop on the right is drastic but not sheer. During snowmelt the way is slippery and dangerous, and an ice axe and maybe a length of rope wouldn't go amiss.

The final 20 minutes of the nearly three-hour course from the hut are the worst, as you drop slightly from Skála, traverse a neck, squeeze around a nasty spot and then scramble the final distance to Point 2917, a small 'table top' with a metal Greek flag and a climber's register. Before the midday cloud boils up you should have a 200-km view in every direction. It is possible that nobody had enjoyed this panorama prior to the first recorded Swiss-Greek ascent in 1913, though the sporting sultan Mehmet IV made an unsuccessful attempt on the peak in 1669.

Rather than retrace your steps, it is possible to return to a point on the trail described in the next section by stepping out north of the summit in an apparent suicide leap, but in fact ending up safely at the top of the Lúki couloir. The main danger is not to you but to climbers ascending this gallery exposed to rockfalls (and snow avalanches in spring); a pained expression crosses Zolotas's face at Refuge 'A' if you mention ambitions to use this route (understandable, since if you know it he is the one who has to summon the army helicopters and notify the next of kin). You will save an hour or so by this 45-minute descent to the Zonária trail, but check on conditions first, and allow for Mr Zolotas' pessimism.

Spílios Agapitós to Oropédhio Musón via Zonária At the first iron-poled junction above Spílios Agapitós refuge noted previously, turn right onto the good trail heading north which is, however, only open after snowmelt. Zonária means 'stripes' and soon enough you're among alternating bands of rock and earth. Just over 35 minutes along you'll see the well-marked base of the Lúki couloir, heading up to Mítikas – look for the word 'MITIKAS' and orange arrows on the rocks just after a sign announcing that the SEO shelter is 20 minutes distant. The climb up takes just under an hour, threading through the goblin needles that are a big attraction of this area, but again this is where people tend to die on Ólimbos – at an average rate of one a year over the past decade.

Shortly beyond you reach the high point on the trail, at about 2750 metres, where there's another marked turn-off to climb 2909-metre Stefáni – the name's written in Greek characters on the rocks, followed by red dots. This ascent takes the same time as Lúki, but is even steeper and definitely not for the timid – at the very top the required maneouvres will have the inexperienced whimpering.

In the last moments of the hour-long traverse to the SEO hut, the main trail snakes along the base of magnificent fan-shaped Stefáni, in which is embedded a six-name memorial plaque to climbers who died here in a single accident. Just before the shelter, you'll see the grave of Yiosos Apostolidhis, killed here as well in 1964 and a further reminder of the mountain's lethal power.

Spílios Agapitós to Oropédhio Musón via Direct Route Two red arrows adorn the main trail towards Skála and Zonária about 200 metres above Refuge 'A'. One, accompanied by a cryptic '9', points left; the other, also marked '9', points right, and you follow it. A faint and narrow (but not impossibly so) path winds up, steeply at times, to the Oropédhion Musón within one hour 45

minutes. If you have a full pack, don't take this route – use the Zonária trail; and going up is easier than coming down.

The way first crosses the highest forested slopes, then a scree-littered gully (snow-blocked in spring) and next climbs steeply up, along the base of Zonária, to a pass. Finally it threads across the plateau to the two shelters, 10 minutes apart and mutually visible. For the SEO hut, follow the red numbers up to '72', and continue from there by line of sight.

Those numerals on the rocks, which guide you the entire way, are supposed to be the serial order of curves in a proper, graded trail. However, funding is not forthcoming to improve what is currently little better than a surveyed goat path, so for the foreseeable future this shortcut will remain just an interesting option for starting a loop through Zonária.

Stage 3: Summit Zone to Livadháki via Kalóyeros Peak

(5½–6½ hours)
This stage begins at the junction of the E4 and the Zonária trail (see the previous description of Sidetrips: The Summit Zone); if you're coming south from the SEO refuge, it's less than an hour to this point, since you're losing altitude. The itinerary takes you through some of the least frequented parts of Ólimbos; while initially a bit dull, it later on compares scenically to the trail between Gortsiá and the SEO hut – plus you'll very likely have the countryside all to yourself. The only drawback is the necessity of hauling two to three litres of water with you.

Face west, along the axis of the E4, and bear left onto a minor path going south, away from both the E4 and the summit route beginning to scale the ridge of Skála. This leads after 20 minutes to a grassy area (2650 metres) at the foot of 2815-metre Áyios Andónios, topped by a ruined meteorological station. Turning around to look north one last time, you'll see 2911-metre Skolió on the left, a popular viewpoint for Mítikas's west face, and Skála with its ant-trains of climbers in front of you.

Now traverse, without significant elevation change, the base of Áyios Andónios, passing the two knolls of Stavroitiés flanking the head of the Mavrólongos canyon, to a saddle overlooking the Bárra (Piyés) grazing land. This will take another 25 minutes, moving cross-country; the 'O2' route shown on the recommended map is not only traced too high, but does not exist yet except as a gleam in EOS's eye.

From the saddle you've an hour down to an apparently abandoned stáni with two stone corrals and a trap-door cistern (unreliable) at about 2325 metres. You could camp here in an emergency. Go up the grassy slope to the east, then drop down into the cramped limestone dell of Anavrikó, with ruined walls and corrals. Head upstream along the watercourse draining off the base of Metamórfosi; the EOS map tracing is correct for once, though it's still a cross-country route, not a trail, that sees you up at a 2560-metre saddle on the shoulder of Metamórfosi, 50 minutes past Bárra. A cluster of ruined bivvy rings tells you you're at the right spot.

Now turn sharp left (east-north-east) and begin to trace the watershed. Pass Frángu Alóni well to its north, skimming along the abyss to the left in the space of a level 10 minutes. Drop slightly before climbing the back side of Kalóyeros, adhering vaguely to the 2650-metre contour. The first peak, with a metal swivel-flag on top, is 2701-metre Kalóyeros itself, reached an hour past Metamórfosi. Just below is the dilapidated, twisted national park boundary fence, which has failed miserably in its office of keeping poachers out and chamois in.

Stay high; don't veer down and right with the remains of the fence. Págos, with a standard concrete trig point, is the next surveyed peak (2682 metres), 15 minutes past Kalóyeros, and 45 minutes further you'll pass Point 2366 of Simeofóros. Now bear east, until catching sight of the little hut at Livadháki (2140 metres); you've a final, steep half-hour descent for a total elapsed time from the E4 junction of 5½ hours.

The tiny Livadháki shelter is sound, if bare, and can hold four people at a pinch. At least the fireplace draws well, and knowing trekkers there will always be a supply of burnable trash to get logs going. The biggest problem is the giant but empty cistern here, which apparently has a leak; there's usually some water in the take-out basin in the nettles by the door, but it's suspect at the best of times, fit for washing and boiling only. In compensation the area above the shelter is a botanist's paradise, and with clear weather you've an unconventional sunset view of the high peaks.

Stage 4: Livadháki to Mavrólongos via Gólna

(4¾ hours)

Don't be misled by the direct trail to Priónia shown on EOS maps – it no longer exists. The following is the quickest, safest and most scenic way of returning towards Litókhoro.

The trail down begins at the north-north-east corner of Livadháki meadow; after a couple of minutes take the downward right-hand option at a Y-fork (left is the abandoned, impassable path to Priónia). Cairns guide you down the 40-minute descent to a bare saddle at about 1800 metres, where you bear right (east) off it. This is Pelekudhiá ridge, as a sign on a tree at about 1750 metres announces.

Past the sign the path improves and the sporadic cairns of higher up disappear, but the way becomes blocked by weeds as you pass through a patch of burnt forest, a sad detraction from the route's appeal. Wild strawberries in July are a consolation. You've another 50 minutes from Pelekudhiá to another saddle and an erosion zone at the base of the 1498-metre crag of Áno Tsuknídha, plus 20 minutes more to the national park boundary fence at the end of the ridge.

Cross the broad saddle between Áno and Káto Tsuknídha before grunting down a sharp drop on eroded switchbacks to a gully at the base of Point 1078. Some 3¼ hours out of Livadháki you'll arrive at the exposed, grassy ridge of Déli (850 metres), where the path drops right (south) a quarter of an hour more to the seven-km access road from Litókhoro. Don't bother with that, however, as you can continue with quality hiking.

Just at the kink in the trail approaching Déli, where it plunges down and right to the road, take the faint left-hand trail doubling back north-west into the ravine. Over the next half an hour you'll bottom out in the shady canyon, then climb up an often double or triple trail to the bare ridge of Gólna. A cairn marks Point 926, and a faded metal EOS sign identifies the place.

A well-worn trail, apparently coming up from near Litókhoro, initially climbs slightly and then falls off the north flank of the ridge into Mavrólongos. As you round a particular bend, you start to drop in earnest; there is an incredible view straight up the canyon, with Ayíu Dhionisíu monastery dead ahead and bits of the E4 already visible snaking among crags below.

Some 45 minutes beyond Déli, bear down and right at a fork into a disgraceful mess left by woodcutters virtually at the boundary of the national park. You appear to be lost, but persist, following red survey numbers on rock as the path snakes down. An hour and a quarter out of Déli you'll reach a small brook, the first reliable water since the refuges. Immediately after – back up and do it again if you don't see it – the faint trail plunges steeply right, spilling you out onto the E4 within five minutes. You're at about 700 metres here, some two hours above Litókhoro and 90 minutes below the ruined monastery. The total hiking time from Livadháki to this point will be over 4½ hours.

Other Descent Routes off Ólimbos Except for some patches of forest around Kariá and Stalamatiá, the Thessalía side of the range is pretty bleak compared to the eastern routes. There are a few other possibilities for leaving the mountain in this direction, none of them used much by summer trekkers and all of them fraught with logistical or aesthetic problems. They're summarised here for completeness's sake.

The E4 continues west from the busy junction at the base of Skála, around Skolió on its gentle southern flank, before descending south-west through Megáli and Mikrí Gúrna to a stáni at about 2150 metres, reached after two hours. There is a concrete cistern here but the water is no better than at Livadháki. This route continues, bearing west-north-west now, through the Stalamatiá ravine before ending, 4½ to five hours out, at the large village of Kokinopilós. There are restaurants and accommodation here, but it would be a bit of a bother getting out – buses to Elassóna or Kateríni pass regularly only along the main road, four km downhill.

You can head south from Bárra along the proposed O2 route to the 2500-metre pass between Metamórfosi and Kakávrakas peaks, from where you can descend to the village of Kariá at 900 metres within four hours. Unfortunately a dirt road has recently been pushed all the way up to the pass, thus negating any appeal of this traverse. Kariá itself is pleasant enough, with a single ksenónas, but you'd have quite a time getting out the 25 km of half-paved road to the main Elassóna-Kateríni highway, since there's no bus. The road in the other direction is even worse, with little traffic, so rides east to the coast cannot be expected.

By turning the flank of Áyios Andónios to the south-west rather than dropping into Bárra, you'll come to a path leading down to the ski lift, army installation and refuge at Vrisopúles (1800 metres) within two hours.

However, from here you can look forward to 20 km of dirt track to the village of Olimbiádhas, where asphalt and bus services begin. This route is used principally uphill in winter by downhill and nordic skiers who wish to come to grips quickly with the slopes of Áyios Andónios.

Kíssavos

Kíssavos (Óssa) has always done badly in comparison with its five-star neighbour Ólimbos, starting in mythological days when the Titans reputedly used the peak as a doormat and front step on their way to the latter mountain to do unsuccessful battle with the Olympian gods.

The denigration continued in medieval Greek folk literature, in which a personified Ólimbos disparagingly refers to Kíssavos as Turkopatiméni ('Turk-trampled') in contrast to itself, teeming with bandits and guerrillas.

Today's hikers are likely to whiz past Kíssavos through the vale of Témbi, on their way to the greater attractions of Ólimbos, or if they do stop and climb the 1978-metre peak, it's only to get an unusual look at the higher summits to the north. While this is certainly a good reason to make the ascent, it's not the only one – if EOS Lárissa cleans up and remarks certain trails, you will be able to make an interesting, complete traverse of the mountain, either to the beach resort of Stómio or the high village of Anatolí.

Rating & Duration

The simple ascent of the peak is an easy exercise, though forays into the dense low-altitude forests to the east and south are another story.

Because Spiliá's facilities are so minimal, it's wise to get there on the morning bus, planning an overnight at the Kánalos refuge, or in the long days of summer leaving Spiliá early enough in the afternoon to reach Kánalos by dark.

Season

Don't underestimate Kíssavos because of its modest altitude – snow lingers late, and three to four metres of winter pack is the norm. The peak is almost as prone to mist as Ólimbos, and below-freezing temperatures are recorded frequently from November to May. There is a very prominent memorial below the alpine refuge to two local youths who froze to death in the snow here in 1983, and another accident was narrowly avoided in 1984.

Supplies

Get your supplies in Lárissa.

Maps

Use *Korfes* 37, unhappily out of print; or the 1:100,000 sketch map, showing most forest roads and (theoretical) trails, published by EOS Lárissa and available either at their Lárissa branch (☎ (041) 220 097, Vasilísis Sofías 6, or at the Kánalos refuge. Failing either of these, try the YIS 1:50,000 sheet *Rapsáni & Karítsa*, and possibly *Platíkambos* and *Ayiá* as well.

Access

From Lárissa, the capital of Thessalía, there are two buses daily to Spiliá (early morning and mid-afternoon), two to Anatolí, and three, oddly spaced, to Stómio.

SPILIÁ TO POINT 1978 VIA KÁNALOS, RETURN

Spiliá (780 metres) is a tiny village at the headwaters of the Sikuríu stream. There is a handful of grill places, but the only conventional accommodation is booked continually by staff of the OTE tower up on the mountain.

Leave Spiliá on the road heading northeast, and after 15 minutes you'll see a sign reading 'Poría óres 2½...EOS Lárissa' pointing right towards the shelter. Red arrows and a trail begin climbing through sturdy oaks; turn right at the top of the first rise, marked by a crumbled ikónisma. Bear right a second time upon reaching the first meadow; you must look carefully to spot a small arrow nailed halfway up a tree on the upper margin of the pasture.

The path becomes distinct once again as it ascends through more oaks to a chapel and a hairpin left turn about half an hour above Spiliá. Some 45 minutes out of the village, the route emerges from the oak groves and begins switchbacking up a bare hogback on a progressively better-defined trail. The Ólimbos foothills and various valleys running parallel to Témbi appear to the north-west; the cone of Kíssavos itself, with the very summit still hidden, looms just to the south-east.

Approximately two hours from Spiliá you'll cross the forest road serving the

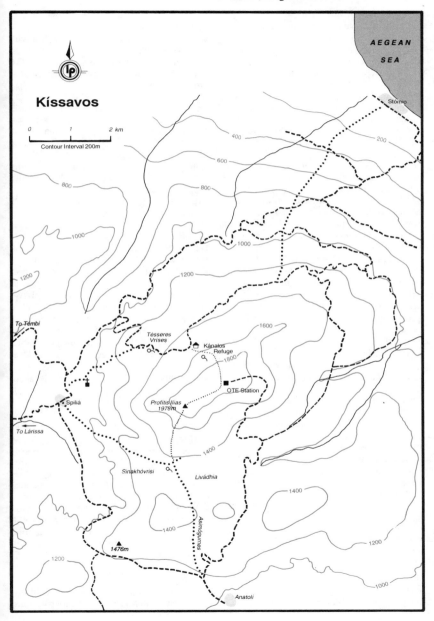

refuge; follow red blazes along a rock shelf on the other side. Soon you recross the road, and the path, now rather haphazard, goes directly up a moderately pitched, almost treeless hillside. Within another 30 minutes is the drippy spring of Tésseres Vríses ('Four Springs' – no sign of the other three), the only water before the refuge. It takes nearly three hours with a full pack to reach Kánalos refuge (☎ (0495) 51 485) at 1600 metres, not the 2½ hours suggested by the EOS sign near Spiliá.

The 35-bed shelter itself is an appealing, rambling structure, well-appointed inside with a fire going on chilly spring or autumn days. It is usually in use on weekends, though you should phone ahead to confirm this. If nobody's here you could easily camp on the surrounding pasture, which is dampened by a handful of reliable springs.

To reach the summit, follow the rather optimistic, too-short ski towrope, and then power poles, for 30 minutes up to the OTE relay station on the brow of the ridge above the refuge. From there head right and proceed west-south-west another 30 minutes up the ridge on a path well grooved into the soft turf.

Profítis Ilías, as the 1978-metre peak is known, has a free-standing belfry and an odd, burrow-like chapel in addition to the usual trig point. To the north the serrated crest of Ólimbos rears up in miniature; downstream from the Témbi gorge the channels of the Piniós river delta meander, and to the north-east the triple prong of the Halkidhikí peninsula is just discernible. Closer in, the wave patterns of the aquamarine northern Aegean lapping apparently at your feet make it look as if you could dive in, and the dense beech forests to the east and south seem a continuation of the surf line. (A radius of about two km from the summit is a bare circle, once dense with fir trees but logged off years ago.) Finally, the northern flank of Pílio rides above the hazy hills to the south-east.

Return the same way to Spiliá or choose one of the options mentioned next in Other Routes; this will depend on whether or not the paths are transitable.

OTHER ROUTES

The following traverses or approaches will only be feasible if the EOS has acted on its intentions to rehabilitate disappearing trails – check in Lárissa or the refuge before attempting them.

To Anatolí From the summit of Profítis Ilías, descend south to the 1200-metre meadows around Sinakhóvrisi, where you may see a disused trail coming up from Spiliá. Next climb slightly over the wooded Asimógurnes spur (about 1400 metres) before dropping down to Anatolí at 920 metres. All this will take the better part of four hours, and you can expect to dodge a fair bit of recently opened forest road.

To Stómio The path down to Stómio from the refuge still exists in stretches, but at last look was mostly overgrown by one of the densest forests in Greece, with many red waymarks lost or damaged. Assuming that it has been reconditioned, you have a good five hours, again cutting perpendicular to half a dozen logging tracks, until arriving in Stómio. The enormous beach and estuary teeming with birdlife make this a desirable destination, so don't expect to have the place to yourself in midsummer. Apart from July and August, however, when Stómio is taken over by Serbians, there are plenty of dhomátia and places to eat.

Pílion Peninsula

The great crab claw of land extending southeast of Vólos towards the Sporádhes islands, the Pílion peninsula, is one of the most popular destinations on the Greek mainland. Blessed with fine scenery, good beaches and interesting villages, and poised almost exactly halfway between Athens and Thessaloníki, it could hardly be otherwise.

More than anywhere else in Aegean Greece, the climates and habitats of the two sides of the Pílion crest are markedly different. The north-eastern slope bears the brunt of the severe, damp winter weather, with heavy snowfall down to elevations of a few hundred metres. The climate has encouraged dense beech and chestnut forests and extensive apple, pear and walnut orchards. On the southern and western sides of the watershed, however, much milder conditions encourage a quasi-Mediterranean biome of olives, oak and other plants adapted to drought and warmth. The separation is not hard and fast, though – microclimates create pockets of scrub and thick stands of deciduous trees at unpredictable places on the 'wrong' side.

The villages here seem like a version of Zagória transplanted to a more jungly environment, and the analogy holds; as in Ípiros this was a semi-autonomous district during the Ottoman era, with very similar architecture – including sumptuous mansions – and cultural trappings. Here too a few of the settlements are protected 'museum pieces', though the greater economic activity has ensured that all too many of them are thoroughly defaced with ugly new construction.

There should be infinite opportunities for trekking on Pílion, given the lie of the land and the arrangement of the villages, but unfortunately there are not. Tourism – most obvious at the half a dozen beach resorts on either coast and at the high-altitude ski resort – and agricultural activity have guaranteed that there's little area unscathed by bulldozer tracks. Virtually every apple tree has a driveway to it, and the neglected paths that aren't destroyed outright soon vanish under the riotous vegetation. Much of the 1600-metre-plus crest itself is an off-limits military area. I have not been to the southern third of the peninsula, but in three visits to the north and centre the following admittedly very satisfying one-day hikes are all I have been able to discover.

DAY TREKS FROM TSANGARÁDHA

Tsangarádha, divided like several of the larger Pílion villages into widely scattered parishes, makes the best base for a modest bit of walking. There are various places to stay (expensive, and no single occupancy) and to eat. From some of the ridges over which the districts are draped you can see Skiáthos and Skópelos islands to the south.

If you let on that you're interested in walking, locals tend to automatically point you towards the spectacular kalderími down to Damúkhari bay, which begins in the parish of Ayía Paraskeví. Less known but equally rewarding is the much longer path linking Ksoríkhti, the next village south of Tsangarádha, and Miliés (Miléës, Mileái), an important community on the western slopes. Before the Metaxas dictatorship built the road around the hill via Lambinú and Kalamáki in 1938, this was the principal link between the narrow-gauge railway ending at Miliés and the Tsangarádha area.

Incidentally, all of these trails are waymarked with three serial dots in red paint, courtesy of a German hiking tour leader. If you happen to find these elsewhere on Pílion, you're probably on to something interesting.

Rating & Duration, Season, Supplies
These are all moderate, half-day or less outings. It is best done in spring or early autumn.

Map
YIS 1:50,000 *Zagorá*.

Access
There are just two buses a day along the Vólos-Miliés-Tsangarádha route, in the morning and early afternoon; you're relying on the latter service to return to Tsangarádha after hiking over the ridge.

Trek 1: Tsangarádha to Damúkhari & Beyond
(3 hours)
The path to Damúkhari (and a bit further) begins in the Ayía Paraskeví district of Tsangarádha, just below the post office at about 500 metres elevation. You'll see an international 'no entry' sign at the top of the kalderími, a sign advertising the hotel Villa ton Rodhon, and another blue rusty one reading 'Pros Ayían Kiriakín/Damúkharin'.

In the first 15 or 20 minutes there are four

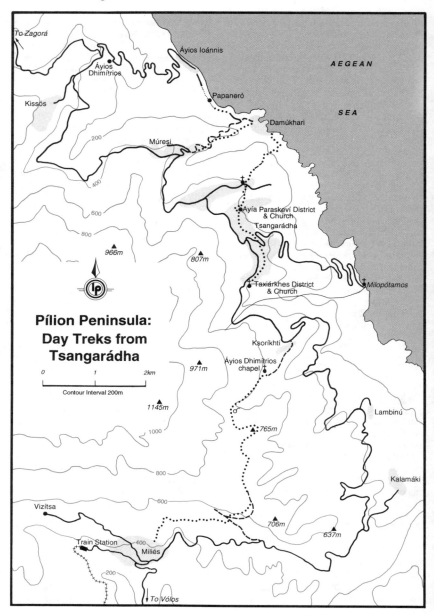

To Zagorá

Áyios Ioánnis

Áyios Dhimítrios

AEGEAN

Papaneró

Kissós

SEA

Damúkhari

Múresi

200

400

600

800

966m

807m

Ayía Paraskeví District & Church

Tsangarádha

Milopótamos

Taxiárkhes District & Church

Pílion Peninsula: Day Treks from Tsangarádha

Ksoríkhti

Áyios Dhimítrios chapel

971m

0   1   2km

Contour Interval 200m

1145m

765m

Lambinú

1000

800

Kalamáki

600

Vizítsa

706m

637m

Train Station

400

Miliés

200

To Vólos

road crossings; the only ambiguity is at the third one, where you head down towards the belfry of the church that is probably Ayía Kiriakí. At the final one, cross the asphalt to a small sign reading 'Pros Aktí Damúkhari'.

About half an hour along you'll reach a concrete drive; follow this until it ends, then bear slightly left onto the resumption of the kalderími, away from the dirt track going right. Soon you have a marvellous view of the coast north to the popular resort of Áyios Ioánnis and beyond as the route zig-zags skilfully down through the maquis. It's just under an hour's walking downhill to the southerly swimmers' cove of Damúkhari, essentially the mouth of the deep gorge separating Tsangarádha from the village of Múresi.

There is a single taverna here, and you may continue north to the small-craft anchorage cove of Damúkhari, where there's another place to eat and stay. Thereafter, the marked path collides with the car park of the new road down from Múresi, next to a church. Turn left and walk up this about 300 metres to a cluster of plane trees, then bear right onto a dirt track which after 200 metres becomes a path down and right to the long beach of Papaneró, the southern annex of Áyios Ioánnis but considerably quieter. There are tavernas here too; you're just 20 minutes beyond Damúkhari. The return trip to Tsangarádha takes about 90 minutes, over an hour of this on the steep kalderími.

Trek 2: Múresi to Damúkhari
(1½ hours return)

This partly cobbled, waymarked path between the western edge of Múresi and Damúkhari takes 40 minutes going downhill. Since the road – or rather, roads – down were built it's a bit sliced up and can't compare scenically with the Tsanagarádha route, but if you've been for a bite to eat at Múresi's tavernas, the best in the area, it may come in handy.

The path starts at a scooped-out portion in the asphalt on the low side of the main road down to the sea. At the next encounter with the road, near some new villas, go right for about 15 metres, then down on the path's continuation. Go straight across the next time you hit the road. At an apparent fork, bear left – the cobbles are partly visible. You'll be spilled again onto a narrow dirt track, but just take a sharp right down onto the resumed kalderími after a couple of minutes. Next you'll tangle with a bulldozed area; the trail reappears about three minutes later, down and to the right.

There's no more trouble of this sort for the balance of the time down to the car park and church at the main road's end. If you're reversing the directions given, look for the phone lines leading up the slope, and a lone ramshackle house on the hillside above a baby olive plantation – this flanks the trail.

Trek 3: Tsangarádha to Miliés via Ksoríkhti
(4 hours)

A short link trail joins the Tsangarádha-Damúkhari kalderími with the platía of Ayía

Pílion Peninsula: Descending *kalderími* from Tsangarádha to Damúkhari (near the top)

Paraskeví, should you need to use it. Once at the square with its famous 18-metre-diameter plane tree, follow the distinctive triple-dot waymark out of the rear corner – there's also a 'XORIHTI' legend. Bear left and down at a small church in the trees, and cross an asphalt drive about 15 minutes along, continuing straight. At the next ambiguous point, a four-way junction, bear down and left again. The path now approaches Taxiárkhes district, passing numerous substantial, well-tended houses. You'll reach the platía of Taxiárkhes some 40 minutes along.

Here there's another fine parish church, a fountain, and some kafenía and snack bars. You'll have to turn up right onto the highway and walk for half an hour to Ksoríkhti, over the Milopótamos ravine, with no possible short cuts.

Once there, get up to Ksoríkhti's platía and adopt the ridge track heading south-west and marked by a sign reading 'Pros Áyio Dhimítrio'. This track ends 20 minutes later upon arriving at the ksoklísi and splits into three among some orchards. You want the newish, ugly left-most one, below all the young tree plantations, since it rapidly becomes the old trail with sporadic triple marks to lead you on.

A ravine will have opened up to the left; edge high along its north bank, progressing through the scrub typical of the south and west Pílion. About 50 minutes out of Ksoríkhti, this growth gives way suddenly to a damp, beech-shaded gully, past the apparent end of a black irrigation hose which you've been following. Cross the watercourse and head up left; just on the far bank, below the kalderími, drips a weak spring.

You reach the highest elevation en route, about 750 metres, still under the beeches about 70 minutes out of Ksoríkhti. The path's course has curled from south-west to southerly. Shady vegetation persists as you bend south-west again, emerging 90 minutes along into low scrub again, with your first view of the Pagasitic gulf ahead.

Twenty minutes further on, the trail, now dirt, becomes a track, but three minutes later

the path resumes on your right and continues through a chestnut grove. Soon, however, you're forced to rejoin the track, descending to a three-way junction some two hours out. Take the left-most option, and walk about 250 metres down to a clump of plane trees in a scraped-out, disorientating area.

Bear onto the right-most track here; you should immediately pass a concrete water pillbox (potable) on the right, and then on the left a large, deep irrigation tank (bath time?). The track has narrowed to a lane, then a path, and cobbles and waymarks reappear.

Now you've a beautiful, final half-hour descent through forest to a concrete driveway just above Miliés village. Turn left onto this, for the 10-minute downhill course, using short cuts through the village to the main road. The total walking time from Ksoríkhti will be 2¾ hours, plus the 70 minutes from Tsangarádha; you'll need to have had an early start to make the afternoon bus back, which passes through between 1.45 and 2 pm. Next to the bus stop is a wonderful bakery dishing out all kinds of local pies, cakes and turnovers, as well as cool drinks. It's famous, with a drive-in trade from all over the region; a better post-hike lunch is difficult to imagine.

If you show up with a full pack and want to stay in Miliés, there is a limited amount of accommodation up by the main platía, and (more costly) down by the old railway station which is soon to be reactivated. The village is interesting enough, but most outsiders stay and eat in the showcase of the region, Vizítsa, three km to the west.

OTHER TREKS ON THE PÍLION PENINSULA
Makrinítsa to Surviás Monastery, return
(7½ hours return)

Makrinítsa, the most heavily visited of the Pílion communities, was founded in 1204 by refugees from the Latin sacking of Constantinople, and is still graced by six architecturally notable churches plus several dozen mansions in assorted states of repair. There are also a couple of tavernas, two small shops (though you'll do better in

Vólos) and a handful of inns. Some of these are housed in restored traditional houses, and all tend to be expensive for what they are, with singles nonexistent. (You'll find this true almost everywhere in Pílion.)

The featured hike from Makrinítsa heads north, angling towards the summit ridge but eventually crossing the deep gorge of Leskaní to arrive at a half-ruined, almost forgotten monastery. This is remote, wild country, with only a tiny hamlet and an occasional shepherd to relieve the loneliness.

Map YIS 1:50,000 *Vólos*. No map is provided in this book.

Access Nine buses make the 50-minute trip every day up the steep 17-km road from Vólos.

Route Directions Makrinítsa is built on a slope, so its altitude ranges from 500 to 700 metres. Leave the village from its upper quarter, on the road passing the convent of Áyios Yerásimos; this road snakes up the ridge dividing the well-watered canyon in which much of Makrinítsa nestles from the bare gully to the west.

The village slips out of sight behind you near a spindly blue ikónisma, where the road changes to the other side of the ridge and begins to bear north as the dry ravine to your left (west) comes up to meet you. A small vineyard with a low fence just left of the track marks the easiest spot to adopt the foot trail, which actually begins near the ikónisma; it's heavily used and you may notice it long before the fence.

Cross the head of the canyon with its handful of plane trees and begin climbing the hillside opposite to complete the first half an hour of walking. Fifteen minutes past the streambed you'll top a ridge near an iron cross embedded in a cairn. Approximately one hour above Makrinítsa you should see a corral to the left and a stock-watering pond in a meadow straight ahead.

Here the trail becomes vague; veer left, passing between the corral and the pond, and find an initially faint continuation which

marches more and more definitely over the low ridge beyond. Aim for the bare spot on the ridge. Soon there's a descent to a rough but double-treaded track which must carry tough trucks at some point in the year; this takes you to a giant concrete-trough spring about 30 minutes past the corral. From the spring continue along the track as it bears further left (north-west) and becomes narrower and stonier over the subsequent 15 minutes up to a T-junction with a much larger jeep track.

The far side presents a myriad of possible continuations; the correct choice is a narrow, slightly uphill donkey track just left of straight on. Within a few moments you should, peering carefully, be able to spy the monastery roof peeking out from the woods on the opposite side of the Kaliakúdha canyon. From this first glimpse of your destination, the rocky path descends in a leisurely fashion through juniper and holly oak, heading west towards the large hilltop meadow of Lútsa with its 689-metre trig point. You arrive here some two hours out of Makrinítsa; beyond the peak the routes continues down the grassy slope past a dry well.

Now the path steepens and becomes a kalderími about halfway down to Leskaní hamlet, which has been visible since just before Lútsa. The juniper-scrub oak vegetation begins to yield to a lush mix of oak and beech. Close to three hours along you cross the ravine at 450 metres via a fine stone bridge, whose three arches can only be seen by clambering down into the riverbed. Leskaní is just 10 minutes further; 'downtown' consists of a spring dated 1888 and shaded by the usual plane tree, a single cottage and the nearby chapel of the Panayía. The village was once occupied all year round, but since the civil war the population has fled, or was forcibly removed, to the lowlands.

From the chapel proceed right and slightly uphill; the path becomes constricted again in the streambed between two more farmhouses. The final climb up to Surviás takes 45 minutes, bringing the total elapsed hiking time from Makrinítsa to just under four hours. The path is fairly distinct for the first 35 to 40 minutes to a large spring flanked by three poplars, where you bear left through trackless walnut groves to reach the monastery (700 metres).

Surviás Monastery Your first thought on arrival might be to ask yourself why you've bothered coming here: the monastery's crumbled perimeter walls and ruined cells promise nothing of interest within, and the dry fountain behind the katholikón reinforces the air of desolation. Once inside the church, with a moment or two for eyes to adjust to the dim light, opinions improve. Every sq cm of the interior is covered with vivid 16th-century frescoes which, with their warmth and humaneness, are a relief from the usually austere Byzantine imagery. But only fragments of what was an intricate altar screen remain, and many ikons were stolen during the 1950s. Bring a powerful torch to illuminate the walls, though there are often some candles about; if you open some of the windows to admit daylight, close them completely when you've finished to prevent further deteriorartion of the frescoes.

There is an interesting, if macabre, legend associated with the destruction of the monks' quarters which, while taking place during WW II, was for once not the fault of occupying armies. At some point during the winter of 1943-44, a shepherd passed the night in a vacant cell. He lit a fire and left the next day without dousing it properly. An ember found its way in to the straw one floor below, igniting it and thus devastating both wings of cells. A year to the day afterward, a hungry wolf appeared out of the snow to prey on the shepherd's flocks which were grazing at Sésklo, near Vólos. The guilty shepherd went out to confront it, whereupon the wolf ate him. The story is considered by its tellers a striking example of divine justice, administered only after a year's grace in which the herdsman failed to offer restitution to the church.

You can stay overnight (no fires please) in one of two 2nd-floor cells that have been restored – if they haven't had locks installed,

or if modern shepherds from Purí, one of the most north-eastern villages of Pílion, haven't occupied them. They tend to appear in autumn to graze their flocks here and raid the nut trees.

It used to be possible to hike on trails to Purí itself, four hours distant, or within 3½ hours to the still-active monastery of Flamúri, but the landscape has been so thoroughly chewed up by forestry tracks that it's hardly worth the bother. Flamúri is more easily reached by a shorter path from the village of Véneto (see the next hike in this section).

Retracing your steps to Makrinítsa may take as little as 3½ hours now that you know the way.

Véneto to Purí via Limniónas

(7-10 hours)
This trek, in the very far north-east of Pílion, would seem to be one of the best coastal walks in mainland Greece. The shore is unspoiled, with no anchorages for large boats, and said to be teeming with wildlife, including seals, wild boars and (in spring) spectacular butterflies.

I have not done this walk. The account I read made it sound good enough to try out.

Maps YIS 1:50,000 *Ayiá* and *Panayía Ayiás*.

Access Bus connection, if any, will be from Vólos. There is definitely a service as far as Kanália, less than halfway, with the option of a taxi from there on.

Route Directions First it's worth mentioning that a well-defined path connects the tiny village of Véneto with the historic monastery of Flamúri (90 minutes), contemporary of Surviás and open to men only – you could probably stay the night if you asked nicely.

The main itinerary follows an up-and-down trail going south parallel to the wild and majestic shoreline here, beginning at 250 metres elevation and attaining as much as 400 metres while occasionally dipping to almost sea level. The surface is often cobbled but the way is frequently blocked by thick, sometimes thorny scrub.

Some 3½ walking hours along you'll reach the hidden pebble cove of Limniónas, one of the most unspoiled in the Pílion owing to the lack of road access. Have a swim but remember that you're only halfway done. From here the path climbs steadily to meet a forest road coming north from Purí; there's the first potable water of the route near the junction, but the trail here is also almost impassable by virtue of the vegetation. However, it's wise to persevere with the path, since it shortcuts most of the 19 km of track to the village, crossing at one point a fine old stone bridge over a dry ravine.

The total walking time is seven hours, but you should allow nearly 10 hours for swimming and fighting through the bushes – best done in late spring when the days are long and the butterflies are out in force. Púri (400 metres) is a friendly enough village but has no tourist facilities. For those you'll have to press on four km to Zagorá, or 12 km more to the agreeable beach resort of Horeftó. Take a taxi from Zagorá to Horeftó, or hope to coincide with one of three daily buses – the trail short cut is badly mangled and not worth bothering with.

Skiáthos

That the smallest and most commercialised of the Sporádhes should have arguably the best hiking may come as a surprise, but good, shaded trail surfaces, a variety of scenery, and unique perspectives on Pílion and neighbouring islands make a convincing case. The massive influx of tourists may have had the lucky side effect of preserving certain footpaths across the island, since solo foreigners and organised walking tours seeking to escape the beach crowds seem all too happy to use them.

The two easy routes detailed both end at the *kástro* (fortified old town) at the extreme northern tip of Skiáthos, joined to the body of the island by steps replacing a long-vanished drawbridge. This village was abandoned in 1825 after the islanders presumably decided that the new Greek state could and would protect them from piracy at the new town site. The place last entered history in 1941, when it was a popular hideout for Allied stragglers, mostly New Zealanders and Australians, waiting to be smuggled out of occupied Greece by boat to Turkey.

Season
In the Greek tourism league tables, Skiáthos is well up in the top 10 regarding crowds and cost. Don't show up in midsummer. The weather will be pretty muggy then anyhow.

Map
YIS 1:50,000 *Skiáthos*.

Access
Depending on the season, one to four daily standard ferries link Skiáthos with Vólos and Skópelos island, with one connection as well to Alónisos island and the mainland port of Áyios Konstantínos. Once (spring/autumn) or twice (summer) a week there is a very useful direct ferry link with Thessaloníki, Skíros, Tínos, Páros, Thíra and Iráklio (Crete).

According to demand, hydrofoils ply from Vólos, Áyios Konstantínos, Kími (Évvia) and Thessaloníki to all of the Spóradhes, but these are more than twice as expensive as the already high prices on the standard steamer lines.

If you're in a hurry and can afford it, you can fly from Athens – the flight frequency varies from three weekly in winter to five daily in the peak season.

Trek 1: Hóra to Kástro via Áyios Apóstolos
(2½ hours)
Walk north from the dock of Skiáthos harbour on the asphalt road towards the airport. Some 15 minutes out of town, the road bears sharply right, and you should veer left onto a dirt track prominently marked by red dots on a tree, a 'W' (perhaps for German

weg) and, most obviously, a multicoloured sign reading 'Panayía Evangelístria'.

Climb along this jeep track for another quarter of an hour until a wooden cross and a white and green ikónisma mark the actual start of the trail (the track going straight goes to Evangelistrías monastery – see the next hike description). Turn left onto the footpath and proceed an occasionally steep 15 minutes more on a well-worn surface to another white and green ikónisma marking a confusing intersection. Here red dots and a

sign seem to suggest you take a left fork, but the right turning actually works better.

About an hour from town you'll reach the fountain of Áyios Dhimítrios, identified with a plaque. Within another 10 minutes you'll meet a new logging road; turn right (north) and walk a few paces to the point where the trail resumes on the far side. Soon cobbling appears and the route enters shade; some 20 minutes above the road, ignore an uncobbled fork on the right and pass an unreliable cistern recessed into the hillside on the left

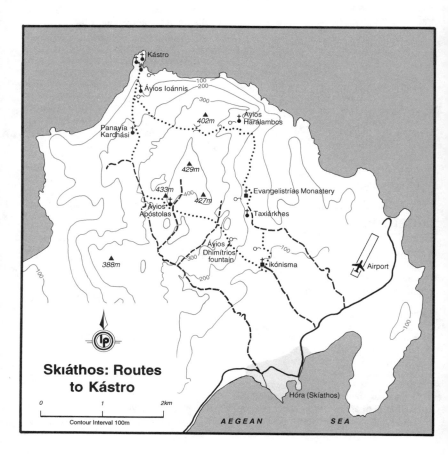

Skiáthos: Routes to Kástro

0   1   2km

Contour Interval 100m

of the path. Just 90 minutes from Hóra, the kalderími is briefly disrupted by another bulldozer track in the vicinity of a red and white ikónisma. Cross the road-disrupted saddle, aiming for the ochre ksoklísi of Áyios Apóstolos, set at the 433-metre summit of the island just north of the path's continuation.

In the next 15 minutes the cobbles resume and dip down to meet another dirt road on its way to the north coast. Turn right and walk a few paces to yet another ikónisma on the right verge, painted with the word 'KASTRO' and a red arrow pointing to the onward path. Within 15 minutes of leaving the road on this path, keep going straight towards the chapel of Panayía Kardhási. Here the belfry has the form of a ship's mast with a crow's nest, and glass fishing floats whimsically stud the roof line. Within another 15 minutes you'll reach the well-maintained grounds of Áyios Ioánnis monastery, complete with surging fountains, flower beds and picnic tables. Another 10 minutes, or 2½ hours from the harbour, brings you to the entrance of Kástro.

The town itself is a heap of vine-shrouded ruined foundations; only the gate (permanently ajar) and three churches remain intact. The most interesting of these, Hristú, contains some fine frescoes and a massive carved témblon (altar screen) . Observe the little sign near the entrance that reads 'Klíste pórta yiatí béynun pondíkia' ('Close the door, because the mice get in').

Behind the church, a couple of picnic tables and water piped down from Áyios Ioánnis make a good place for a lunch stop. The higher points of the ruins offer superb views east to Glóssa village on Skópelos, west to Pílion, and back over the island; the open sea stretches without interruption to Halkidhikí. A fine beach in the lee of the Kástro cape, to the east, is only crowded with excursion-boat passengers until mid-afternoon; a stream with drinkable water empties onto the shore here for the benefit of campers, and there is also one (expensive) snack bar.

Trek 2: Hóra to Kástro via Evangelistrías Monastery & Áyios Harálambos

(2½ hours)

The route directions for this trek are identical to the previous route up to the first green and white ikónisma. From there go straight instead of left. After a few minutes take a right turn off the jeep track, onto a prominent path which passes a spring and shortly collides with the concrete road heading towards Evangelistrías.

Turn left and continue on the road past the tiny monastery of Taxiárkhes, which is just before a rise with a flagpole, a threshing cirque and the end of the road. From some chapels near the flagpole a path leads the last few moments down to the gate of Evangelistrías, one hour's hiking from the harbour.

The monastery, the only one on the island still inhabited, commands the head of a peaceful valley plunging to the just-visible sea. Most of the structure dates from 1806, but the beautiful katholikón with its intriguing roof lines and carved témblon is probably two centuries older. Evangelistrías is a good example of the historically close association of Orthodoxy and Greek nationalism, for it is claimed that here, in 1807, the Greek flag in its present form was first raised, and saluted, by assembled future heroes of the war of independence.

To continue to Kástro, duck out the back gate of the monastery and clamber down some steps to a shaded fountain and picnic area; from here a clear trail proceeds up the opposite side of the stream valley. The locked monastery of Áyios Harálambos, half an hour beyond Evangelistrías, was where the Skiathote novelist Alexandhros Moraitis, a contemporary of his more famous fellow islander Papadiamantis, retired to in 1929.

From a junction five minutes before Áyios Harálambos, a marked trail continues up to the saddle between Points 402 and 429, before dropping down the other side to a point between Panayía Kardhási and Áyios Ioánnis within 45 minutes.

You can of course combine the two routes to make a very pleasant loop hike. Do the

Evangelistrías leg in the morning, to be sure of seeing that monastery, since the remaining monks shut it for a long nap at noon.

Dhírfis

The imposing summit of Évvia, perfectly pyramidal when seen from the south-west, dominates the middle of Dhírfis and, along with its offshoot Ksirovúni, offers a day or two of surprisingly challenging climbing. Between the the northern Aegean and the crest joining the two peaks lies some of the most rugged and deserted terrain on Évvia – a potential target for those with the right map and kit.

Rating & Duration
The basic route is a moderately difficult full-day hike. Allow another day for attempts on Ksirovúni.

Season, Supplies
It is too hot to trek here in midsummer, but at other times it is fine. A clear day in winter would be good if you were equipped with snow gear. Get supplies in Athens or Stení.

Map
YIS 1:50,000 *Stení Dhírfios*. No map is provided in this book.

Access
There are 17 mini-trains daily from Athens to Halkídha, the industrial Évvian capital at the narrow straits; from there, five buses daily ply to Stení, the village at the foot of the mountains.

Stení is a shady, attractive community built on the southern slope of a deep, well-watered hollow at about 400 metres. Several grills cater to carnivores, but groceries are spotty (pick them up in Athens or Halkídha) and the hotels are a bit on the expensive side, with no singles available.

SUMMIT ASCENT
(7 hours return)
There's a placard in Stení, erected by the Halkídha chapter of EOS, which helps visualise the route, but it's schematic and rather faded.

From the Stení bus stop, walk up the ascending asphalt road, passing the last psistariá on the right and a spring and chapel on the left. Just beyond a soccer pitch the foot trail starts in the streambed to the right of an abandoned hotel. Initially on the true left bank, it changes to the right side after a few moments, where a thick forest of chestnut and fir begins almost immediately.

About half an hour above the trailhead, cross a jeep road; the path resumes directly across the track, but from here on it might be littered with fallen branches and boulders. The trail also becomes wide and rather erratic, with many oxbows, short cuts and splits, but always adheres to the spine of the ascending ridge. The cone of Dhírfis is a constant landmark on your left.

Cross the road once again; the path becomes much neater until, 90 minutes above Stení, you reach the saddle between Dhírfis and Ksirovúni. Here you'll find a snack bar-café and the perpendicular intersection of a large dirt road – from Stení to Strópones and Metókhi north-east of the ridge – and the smaller track running almost parallel to the crest. The base of Ksirovúni, lower but much more rugged than Dhírfis, is an hour's walk south-east from here; there is supposed to be a marked climbing route to the summit, but I have not done it.

A rusty sign points north-west towards the EOS shelter. After half an hour you come to the powerful trough spring of Lirí, and then to the refuge at 1150 metres a little beyond. It may be open on weekends (☎ (0228) 51 285 for further information). From the hut a red-blazed mule track continues for 25 minutes to the base of Dhírfis itself, passing some roofless stone shelters. At the foot of the peak, a bit to the left, is another trough spring; on the right a path snakes down a valley towards the tiny, isolated hamlet of Ayía Iríni.

From the second spring it's a 75-minute climb, following red dots along the southeast spine, to the 1743-metre trig point and a rough-hewn cross. The peak gives an impression of greater elevation owing to a low (about 1200-metre) treeline and comprehensive panoramas of central Évvia, Skíros and the Aegean. The final ascent is fairly demanding, with a sharp 400-metre elevation gain; coming down takes about as long, since the 'trail' surface is miserable scree most of the way.

You can vary the return to Stení, making a loop trip of sorts. Retrace your steps to the EOS lodge, cross the little ski run just beyond it, and begin following red waymarks, first on rocks and next on trees. These bracket the initially healthy trail that descends through the firs. After 15 minutes you'll cross a forest road (not the one from Stení to Metókhi) for the first time; after another 15 minutes, the path meets it again and expires. From here on efforts to find patches of trail between the road's curves are not very productive, and you've a dusty 1½ hours more to the outskirts of the village. Try hitching the frequent traffic, and don't consider this route for the ascent.

Kikládhes (Cyclades) Islands

The 20-plus islands of the Kikládhes (Cyclades) floating south-east of the Attic Peninsula conjure stereotypic travel-poster visions in the heads of potential visitors; for many people, this *is* Greece. Gleaming whitewashed villages sprawl like beached starfish on rocky spurs, or mimic snowbanks in the folds of a hill. Groves of windmills once harnessed the prevailing north-west wind to grind late-summer grain, though today they mostly stand ruined or converted to dwellings. The celebrated cubist architecture hereabouts is not unique – try telling that to an Andalusian or a Yemenite – but much of it has passed beyond into the realm of folk sculpture.

In antiquity the archipelago was far more wooded and populated, but by medieval times the ravages of shipbuilders, livestock, earthquakes, massacres and piracy had combined to send most of the islands into decline. Every so often one of them, by virtue of strategic location, a fine port or a commodity suddenly in demand, would enjoy a brief renaissance before subsiding again into obscurity like an exhausted supernova.

As modern Greece expanded northward, annexing more arable land, the Kikládhes ceased to play much of a role in the national economy and again served, as they had under the classical Greeks, Romans and Byzantines, mainly as places of exile for political troublemakers. Because of this neglect and a relatively brief period of Ottoman rule, these islands became havens of traditional Greek customs, bloodlines and dialect.

A recent invasion of nude bathers, villas, discos and boutiques has certainly made inroads on this culture, but not as much or in as many places as you would think. Take the case of the chain of tiny islets behind Náxos, only recently given mains electricity and still for all intents and purposes stuck 20 years back, versus busy, growing Náxos itself with its new airport and estate agents for villa sales.

The people themselves are much of the attraction of travelling and walking here. Physically, they are as a rule small-boned, dark, energetic and (truth to tell) more than a little inbred. The *evzónes* (parliamentary guard), requiring strapping lads two metres high, doesn't recruit much locally. Allowing for pockets of dourness here and there, they are both open-hearted and dignified, especially if you happen to be crossing their grain fields, vineyards or hamlets on foot.

Sérifos

The third in the western Kikládhes (after Kéa and Kíthnos), Sérifos is one of the less visited in the entire group and has always lain outside the mainstream of history. Just why is mysterious, because Sérifos is blessed with one of the highest water tables in the archipelago, and many sheltered anchorages. Iron and copper were mined here until cheaper African deposits dealt the industry its deathblow.

Serifos's stony and rugged profile – perhaps a result of Perseus's legendary return here with the Gorgon's petrifying head – seems off-putting when seen from an approaching ferry, but it hides an interior where numerous streams bubble through oases of calamuses, willows, figs, olives poplars and the occasional palm tree on their way to various sandy coves. The north and centre of the island are a walker's joy, with clear, used trails, plenty of drinking water and well-spaced villages.

ISLAND CIRCUIT FROM HÓRA
This six-hour, mostly road-free itinerary loops through the most attractive settlements and terrain on Sérifos; every bend in the trail allows another look over a fertile valley, hamlet or patch of ocean washing the indented perimeter of the island.

Rating & Duration

This easy to moderate outing can be done in one long day. Splitting it in two is complicated by the total absence of conventional lodging en route and the fact that camping at Sikamiá Bay is illegal.

Map

YIS 1:50,000 *Nísos Sérifos*.

Access

Almost daily ferries from Pireás link Sérifos with Kíthnos, Sérifos and Mílos, with two or three services weekly to/from Kímolos, Folégandhros, Síkinos, Íos and Thíra. One service weekly to Síros, and to Crete and certain of the Dodecanese.

Route Directions

Most visitors stay in Livádhi, the harbour settlement, so first you'll need to get yourself to Hóra, the striking village that pours like milk over the rocky hogback overhead. There are hourly buses up the hill, but the way is simple, appealing and brief enough (45 minutes) to walk; near the power plant, leave the asphalt road in favour of the old

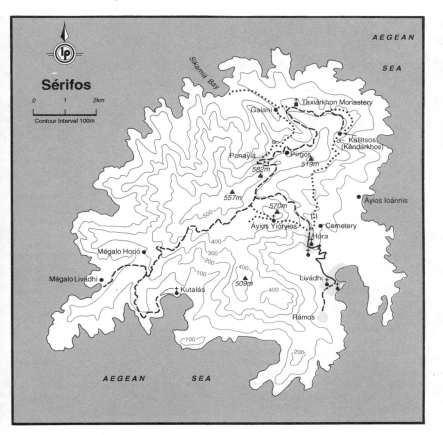

stair-path zig-zagging up through Káto and Áno Hóra.

Leave Hóra from the café near the bus stop. Descend north on a stair-street, following a 'Kéndarkhos' sign, then head north out of town on the paved track to the graveyard. Ten minutes along, veer left off the concrete onto a dirt mule track; two red dots flank the 'exit'. After another 10 minutes you'll cross an old bridge; just upstream is an elaborate, recessed cistern-fed trough where you can fill water containers.

Beyond the bridge, the path climbs out of this first stream valley and passes a fork right; follow the red dots straight ahead. To your right, notice a small modern bridge over a second creek; you can detour below this bridge to visit the giant rock pools that are the year-round homes of terrapins and thousands of the frogs for which Sérifos is famous.

Soon you should reach a lone farmhouse and an adjacent chapel before bottoming out in yet a third creek drainage. Go parallel to the stream briefly, then cross it some 45 minutes out of Hóra on a comparatively recent bridge. After a short claustrophobic stretch between rock walls you climb slightly, passing a well partly hidden by reeds.

Approximately an hour out of Hóra you'll attain a ridge from which the beach hamlet of Áyios Ioánnis is just visible to the right; in front of you spreads yet another rivulet gully. Keeping all greenery below and to your right, bear left and up towards two white buildings above the vegetation. After a messy interval the trail curves above this pair and soon becomes a proper kalderími. As you reach the high point on the leg to Kállitsos, you're treated to comprehensive views over the entire south-eastern quarter of Sérifos.

From this crest the cobbled way descends towards Kállitsos (Kéndarkhos), poised attractively above an oasis where wild plums ripen in July. Just over 90 minutes of walking separates the platía in Áno Hóra from the one in Kállitsos, where there's a shady bench, a fountain and a taverna.

Once away from this spot, it's another 20 minutes to a level zone of terraces and vineyards beyond the last house of the village. As you cross a jeep track bearing off the main road into Kállitsos, a prominent ksoklísi and Kíthnos island appear simultaneously. Cross the driveway leading down to this chapel (nothing remarkable), maintaining a course towards the hamlet visible on the next ridge. Avoid the Kállitsos-bound road above on the left – it's easy to continue on the path threading its way through a grove of oaks growing just over two hours out of Hóra. To your right a pair of dovecotes, clusters of calamus and vegetable patches indicate where water surfaces.

Half an hour past the oaks, the trail is ground under the dhimósio for the moment. A few faint traces cross a new stream canyon in the direction of the hamlet, but it's simplest to take the road for the remaining 15 minutes to the monastery of Taxiárkhon, the most important on the island. The katholikón inside the fortifications dates from at least the 15th century and is decorated with partly damaged frescoes depicting in exquisite detail the tortures of the damned in Hell. Entry is via a Lilliputian door at the top of a few stone steps, but there is lately just a single monk in residence, often away on ecclesiastical business. If you have your heart set on gaining admission, it's wisest to contact a travel agency in Livádhi beforehand to make arrangements.

From the fortress-cloister proceed 10 minutes more along the road until reaching a concrete path on the right, which you should follow down within another 10 minutes to the village of Galaní. This appealing place overlooks the sandy but exposed bay of Sikamiá to the west, accessible by a side path. A combination store/taverna at Galaní provides simple fare, but there is only one bus service daily.

Instead of returning to the road, leave Galaní on the pedestrian street which quickly becomes a trail heading east-south-east and up a well-watered valley. Shun the tempting path crossing the ravine in the direction of a red-roofed chapel. Twenty minutes beyond

Galaní you'll cross the creek on a small dam; a two-metre-deep pool just downstream is large enough to soak two friends on a hot afternoon.

From a pair of sheds on the opposite bank, the trail – with intermittent cobbling – climbs briskly, switchbacking past a chapel and a palm tree. At a prominent hilltop junction 20 minutes above the stream, take a fork going slightly right – not the one that goes left and up towards the road and Pírgos hamlet. Within a few moments you should arrive at a large, concrete-improved spring at the head of a second valley draining down to Sikamiá.

An hour above Galaní you'll come out on a ridge in the vicinity of the cemetery for Panayiá, the village visible a few hundred metres to the left. Once across the graveyard's access drive, the trail meanders through fields of acanthus before stopping in front of the village school.

Panayiá boats a handful of kafenía and the 10th-century church of the Virgin from which the settlement takes its name; however, all the frescoes inside have vanished and only several recycled Roman columns supporting the dunce-cap cupola remain.

To continue, find a prominent kalderími at the top of the village, near the town-limits sign. The first 15 minutes are in decent repair, with good views back over both Galaní and Panayiá, but by the time you pass a small chapel and intersect the road back to Hóra the path is in bad shape. It does in fact persist below and to the left of the road as you head south-west, but is so rubble-strewn and buried that it's safest to stick with the road. At the junction almost in the geographical centre of the island, take the fork signposted towards Mégalo Livádhi and Kutalás.

Ten minutes past this, or 40 minutes from Panayiá, you'll come to a plateau distinguished only by a few low, white buildings and an undependable cistern. Turn left into this unpromising landscape and pass the last farm, then locate a white cubic structure ahead in a nest of rocks. A fairly distinct trail heads toward it; this is the other, most obvious side of Sérifos,

lunar and mountainous. Your path merges with another coming up from Kutalás, just before your arrival at the square, belfryless ksoklísi of Áyios Yióryios, guarding a narrow, windy pass an hour from Panayiá. Slip through for an unconventional look at Hóra just below, then enjoy the last 20 minutes of the loop on a fine kalderími descending to the highest windmill of Hóra.

Sífnos

The next island south of Sérifos is about the same size but very different in character – paradoxically better-tended despite less ground water, its villages merging into one another on a fertile central plateau. Large vegetation is principally a vast amount of olive trees – of the Kikládhes, only Náxos has more. In ancient times Sífnos was famous for its gold and silver mines, but these have long since been exhausted, and today the island is celebrated for its ceramic workers and popular architecture. 'Celebrated' is an understatement in July and August, when Sífnos is absolutely overrun with trendy Athenians with and without holiday homes here, and discerning French and Italians.

Season
Spring and autumn are best seasons to walk in, not only to avoid the summer crowds but because there is no shade, and potable water is oddly spaced.

Maps
Best is the 1:40,000 topo map prepared by John-Birkett Smith and available on the island for about $1.50; it's quite accurate except that the position of the new road towards Vathí is badly traced. Otherwise, use YIS 1:50,000 *Nísos Sífnos*.

Access
The island has the same ferry service as Sérifos, plus in summer a small-boat link with Páros, usually cancelled in rough

weather and dwindling to two or three times weekly in spring or autumn. Once a week in season there is a useful connection with Crete and certain of the Dhodhekánisos islands.

ISLAND TRAVERSES FROM KATAVATÍ

These traverses through the heart of the island connect outstanding typical churches and monasteries, while passing through rugged scenery. Vathí, a relatively remote settlement on the shores of a funnel-shaped bay, is an ideal goal for lunch or even an overnight stop. It is possible to loop back to Katavatí by a lower, shorter route, but this once-magnificent kalderími has been largely destroyed by an ugly new road which once completed threatens to turn Vathí into a resort like any other.

Rating & Duration

The basic traverse, including a detour to Profítis Ilías, is an easy to moderate 4½-hour outing. The more strenuous route via Ayía Marína and Áyios Nikólaos requires 2¾ hours; add an extra half-hour for the sidetrip to Áyios Andhréas. Many walkers choose to return to the north of the island with the rather expensive kaïki – last departure from Vathí at about 5pm – which brings you back to Kamáres, the main harbour.

Katavatí to Vathí via Profítis Ilías

This is the classic transect of the uninhabited portion of Sífnos, and the only route to survive completely unaffected by road-building.

Katavatí is the southern extension of Apollonía, the central inhabited district served by frequent buses from Kamáres port. Walk though this 'suburb' on its central stair-street, past the Hotel Galini, to a well-signed junction: 'Mávro Horió (in Greek) and 'Vathy' (in English) are painted on a wall, plus there's a free-standing metal sign reading 'Profítis Ilías' in Greek.

Additionally, a scheme is given for waymarks: cross-in-a-square-grid, or blue paint splodges. Turn right here and curl around some fields, heading away from the

just-visible disused monastery of Firáyia (Piyés). The fieldstoned path roller-coasters along a canyon and within 20 minutes reaches a cement causeway over a dry gulley on the right.

Here is the well-signed turn-off for the monastery atop Profítis Ilías. It's 45 minutes, without any ambiguity, along zig-zags up through gorse, juniper and terebinth to the mountain-top – a sharp climb, but not horrific. On the summit (variously listed as 695 or 681 metres), you've the expected views, and in calm weather at least the unlocked grounds of the fortified, partly unwhite-washed monastery are well worth the trip. Inside there's reliable tap water, and an imposing, vaulted refectory of early medieval date, most active at festival time (18-19 July). The katholikón or main church has a naive 18th-century altar screen, with a dome upheld on four ancient columns.

Ascending, you are fairly sheltered by the bulk of the mountain even on windy days until reaching the peak. Women should beware of a well-known local muleteer and lecher, who inveigles you up on his beasts for a photo opportunity in return for copping a feel (to men he merely delivers a lecture on the transience of sexual powers). Descent back to the causeway takes 35 minutes; it is not possible to cut cross-country down to any other point on the main trail.

The waymarked onward route to Vathí and Mávro Horió proceeds straight at the causeway and soon crosses to the north-west bank of the ravine; bear right at a fork, ignoring cairns. Curling up the valley, 15 minutes past the causeway you'll pass below the beautiful country chapel of Taxiárkhis, surrounded by the crumbled remains of a monastery; there are 18th-century frescoes needing maintenance inside.

Twenty minutes above Taxiárkhis, the path rises to a saddle and almost immediately forks; bear left with red and blue arrows. The desired route continues west, 45 minutes past the turn-off for Profítis Ilías, towards the ancient tower-base of Órnos, just to the right of the trail. You *don't* want to take a second left, despite its waymarking and initially

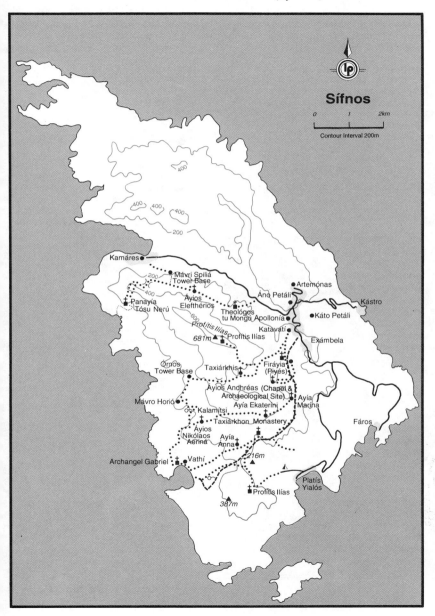

Sífnos

0   1   2km

Contour Interval 200m

Kamáres

Mávri Spiliá
Tower Base

 Áyios
Elefthérios

Theológos
tu Mongú

Panayía
Tósu Nerú

Profítis Ilías
681m

Ornos
Tower Base

Mávro Horió

Kalamítsi

Taxiárkhis

Áyios Andhréas (Chapel &
Archaeological Site)

Ayía Ekaterini

Taxiárkhon Monastery

Áyios
Nikólaos
Aerina

Ayía
Anna

Archangel Gabriel   Vathí

216m

387m

Profítis Ilías

 Artemónas

Áno Petáli

Apollonia

Katavatí

Firáyia
(Piyés)

Ayía
Marína

Kástro

Káto Petáli

Exámbela

Fáros

Platís
Yialós

Profítis Ilías

easier surface – this option climbs unnecessarily, and misses the important (and unique) water source further along. Just after passing the sunken, four-metre stump of the Hellenistic watchtower, do bear left.

In the next half hour the trail descends past a flat-roofed, belfryless chapel on your right to Mávro Horió, all of two cottage, an alóni and some ancient wall remnants on a bluff, one hour 15 minutes past the ravine bed. You may have to vault some thorn barriers on your way down; don't despair, this is the right way. The onward path to Vathí does not actually enter Mávro Horió, but curves left and down some 50 metres before to angle across the Kalamítsi creek valley.

In the next quarter of an hour the trail loses

Kiklládhes: Taxiárkhis Chapel, Sífnos

more altitude, crosses a tiny bridge in the drainage bottom and the passes the only spring since Katavatí as you begin to climb out of Kalamítsi.

During the next half hour the trail rollercoasters up and down, passing a giant rock outcrop 500 metres to its left – avoid a dead-end trail heading down to the base of the pinnacle. Instead veer around it in a clockwise fashion, as blue waymarks of the 'main' trail descended from high above reappear. As you attain a ridge and round a bend, walls enclose the trail; after a few moments descending between them, you'll have your first look at the bay of Vathí – and the ugly new road in on the far shore. The final descent takes place through the houses (and litter piles) at the far north-west corner of the bay.

Not counting the 1½-hour detour to Profítis Ilías, you'll need just over three walking hours to reach the shore at Vathí. Here the miniscule monastery of the Archangel Gabriel guards the tiny fishing harbour from its own jetty, with a welcome water tap just the other side of the monastery's arcade. Several tavernas operate in season, arguably the best restaurants on an island which in general no longer lives up to its former reputation for good cooking. There are also numbers of inexpensive dhomátia, though sometimes not enough to go around for the Germans who favour the place – if these dhomátia are full camping is tolerated. The main attraction, though, is the long beach and the idyllic sense of isolation about to be shattered by the road, set for completion in 1993.

Katavatí to Vathí via Áyios Nikólas Aeriná

This marked route involves a high-level crossing of montane Sífnos, and provides another, slightly quicker way to reach Vathí.

At the marked junction in Katavatí, go straight instead of left; the pedestrian street becomes a trail which is cut by the road a few minutes later, next to the disused monastery of Firáyia (Piyés). Just 10 metres up the road, the trail erupts on the left, but some 15

Top Left: Tínos: Approaching Ksinára on the old trail (MD)
Top Right: Tínos: Exóburgo peak and Trípotamos (MD)
Boitom Left: Amorgós: Looking south-west past Hozoviotíssas monastery (MD)
Bottom Right: Amorgós: Cobbled trail up to Tholária from Egiáli (MD)

Top: Sífnos: Monastery atop Profítis Ilías peak (MD)
Bottom: Náxos: Komiakí as seen on descending trail from Stavrós (MD)

minutes out of Katavatí you are forced back up onto the road again. A few paces south is a saddle, from which the conspicuous 15-minute side-trail takes off up to Áyios Andhréas.

This handsome ksoklísi dominates the east of the island from amid the hilltop ruins of an extensive Bronze Age town, the whole surrounded by a double wall. The side trail up from the road is obvious, and in clear weather you can make out the islands of (going clockwise) Síros, Páros, Andíparos, Íos, Síkinos and Folégandhros, plus all the main villages of Sífnos.

Return to the road and continue a few minutes more to the chapel of Ayía Marína, immediately to the right of the roadcut, next to which a red-dot-waymarked uphill trail resumes. Bear right at the next fork, to curl west around and under Áyios Andhréas with its tuft of trees, shunning the new road. Frequent red dots and dashes keep you on course.

Climb through junipers until, an hour out of Katavatí, you emerge onto a high plateau with the chapel of Ayía Ekateríni on your left (south) beyond some stone fencing. After going through a gate, the path becomes a corniche route high above the beach of Platís Yialós, the ugly new road, and Taxiárkhon monastery. After another gate, you climb some more (keep right when given the choice) to a knoll and saddle 80 minutes along, offering your first glimpse of Vathí.

From here, the path finally begins descending, curling across the head of a ravine beneath two cottages, the only whitewashed buildings around 1½ hours into the walk. Some 15 minutes more of progress through low scrub and past stone pens drops you suddenly atop the chapel-monastery of Áyios Nikólaos Aeriná ('Saint Nicholas of the Winds' – most days you'll see how it got this name).

The red waymarks end here, and indeed you seem to have made distressingly little progress down towards Vathí. But beyond the little monastery an unmarked but obvious path drops briskly to the blue-dotted path not used in Katavatí to Vathí via Profítis Ilías, at a point above Kalamítsi spring and the isolated outcrop. Directions to Vathí are the same as in the previous account from here on.

Optional Return to Katavatí

The new road to Vathí has also destroyed roughly half of one of the finest kalderímia in Greece, though enough remains of it to make for a relatively pleasant return to Katavatí should you not take the boat back to Kamáres.

Begin at house No 50 on the Vathí waterfront, to the left (with your back to the sea) of Manolis Taverna/Rooms. Some 200 metres up this dry wash, a green rock-painted 'To Apollonia' message directs you right onto a marvellous stair-path. The first landmark, 25 minutes along, is a pair of whitewashed cottages and a threshing cirque atop a knoll; more follow, plus the chapel-monastery of Ayía Ánna atop a saddle, 35 minutes out. Here's a rain cistern with a sikláki (can-on-a-string) for fetching the water. Ten minutes later you must descend to the new road; five minutes north on this are some currently dry fountain-niches below the rural monastery of Taxiákhon, but between the extensive ongoing renovations and the ugly new roadcut, the magic of the place has fled.

Beyond Taxiárkhon no more usable trail has survived the bulldozers, except for one loop down past another spring, until a bit beyond the turnoff for Áyios Andhréas.

Just past the saddle you can bear down and right onto the cairned, surviving 15-minute stretch of the old path, which reaches Firáyia monastery and continues into Katavatí, for a total two-hour time course – just over half of it on a dusty road, which the wonderful surviving patches of trail only make you regret the more.

OTHER HIKES ON SÍFNOS
Vathí to Platís Yialós

Many people wish to link these two beach resorts, and certainly in pre-bulldozer days this was a popular trip. But now the following hints are included mainly as an anti-recommendation for the walk.

The path used to start in the sandy wash with a brightly painted well at the far end of the main Vathí beach. However, when complete the new road will have chewed up most of the trail; even if the first 20 minutes of path has survived, you will then be forced up onto the road as far as the saddle between the two bays. Here you can theoretically bear right (south) onto a private driveway to pick up the surviving remnant of high trail which, flanked by cairns, descends parallel to and above a deep ravine towards the highest buildings of Platís Yialós and its uninspiring campsite. But the route, via the chapel of Profítis Ilías, is hard to follow – more so if darkness is approaching – and from the campsite you must walk another 15 minutes on dirt road out to the asphalt and bus stop, for a total of one hour 45 minutes, well over half of that spent road-tramping. It's really best only as an emergency bail; going in the opposite direction, what's left of the path would be difficult if not impossible to find.

Apollonía to Panayía Tósu Nerú

This transect shows Sífnos at its wildest, rockiest and also most forested! Still, it's not an itinerary for extremely windy or hot days. You needn't retrace your steps, but can descend on another trail to Kamáres.

Leave Apollonía on the Kamáres-bound road; just past the first bridge, take the cement driveway south, and bear right into the cluster of houses to reach the start of the actual trail. You'll reach the beautiful rural monastery of Theológos tu Mongú 25 minutes along; bear left at the fork just beyond for the proper path towards Áyios Elefthérios and an adjacent radar reflector, visible up ahead.

You've one hour 15 minutes to Áyios Elefthérios, another, smaller isolated monastery with a rain cistern and bucket – fill up, this is the last water. The path continues past the reflector, and just over half an hour later you get your first glimpse of Kamáres, and pass some old mining works below to the right.

Once over a very windy pass, you drop into thick juniper forest. After a corniche stretch with little elevation change, there's a sharp, zig-zag drop in airless conditions to your goal, the rural monastery of Panayía Tósu Nerú – there's no water to be had other than the usual cistern contents. It is, however, possible to continue to the cove below for a swim. The total time course from Apollonía is three hours.

To vary the return, some 10 minutes beyond the saddle, angle down cross-country through scrub to the base of the ruined Mávri Spiliá tower, and then look left to find the top of a very ancient trail down to Kamáres.

This was once a superbly engineered kalderími, and faint red-dot waymarks indicate that, until recent years, it was used for climbing uphill. It has, however, been badly affected by landslides in places today and demands good footwear and concentration. Forty-five minutes below the tower ruins, you end up at a round water tank above the highest hotels of the expanding resort.

Folégandhros

Seen from an approaching boat, Folégandhros exhibits a forbidding aspect of sheer cliffs, unrivalled elsewhere in the Kikládhes except at Amorgós and Thíra. Some visitors never venture further than Karavostási harbour, intimidated both by the palisades and the thorny wilderness glimpsed beyond the port.

But only the eastern half of the island is semi-arid, and a marvellous *hóra* (main village) perches out of sight at the brink of the northern palisades. Áno Meriá, Folégandhros's other settlement, extends for some distance along an English-style high street which is merely an old cart track intermittently paved, not an eyesore roadcut like so many of the new roads on other elongated islands.

The northern portion of Folégandhros, beyond the tapering that almost pinches it in two like a dividing amoeba, is especially beautiful, with striking chapels, terraces and alónia, and there are adequate wells and springs for thirsty walkers. The best trails have been selected from many, including those leading to a string of beaches at convenient distances from Áno Meriá or Hóra.

Folégandhros was inhabited in ancient days, but mostly by political exiles; more recent Greek regimes have used it similarly. In the Middle Ages it was depopulated three times by corsairs; the current islanders are descendants of Creto-Venetian refugees who came in the 1600s, which accounts for numerous Italianate surnames (Dhanásis, Gerárdhis, Lizárdhos, etc) and a heavy Cretan accent.

Numerous curious legends surround the island, worth summarising before moving on to the hike descriptions. A valuable silver ikon of the Virgin was among the booty plundered at each sacking and massacre, but three times it came floating back across the waves to Folégandhros. Once it was accompanied by a Christian prisoner, who had been manacled in a boat with the fleeing pirates. A great wave capsized the vessel; the captive alone was saved by clinging to the ikon, which washed ashore at the base of the cliff on which now stands the gigantic church of the Assumption.

Hrisospiliá, the Golden Cave, is also below the church and takes its name from another incident during the cycle of depredations. The outgunned islanders had descended from the fortified heart of the hóra to this cave via a secret staircase, taking with them a large fortune in gold jewellery. (The stairs have long since vanished and the grotto is accessible now only by sea.) The enemy found the hideout, plugged the entrance with brushwood, and set it ablaze. When the last wave of immigrants came to resettle the island, they found among the ashes the gold of their luckless predecessors.

Season
Folégandhros gets busy in midsummer, with a fairly young international crowd. Hiking, though, is not out of the question with

cooling winds and the barley harvest to lend some relief and interest.

Maps
YIS 1:50,000 *Folégandros* and *Síkinos* – annoying for such a small place, 12 km long and four broad at the most. This book's offering should be adequate for direction finding.

Access
Folégandhros is connected to Pireás, Kíthnos, Sérifos, Sífnos, Mílos, Kímolos, Síkinos, Íos and Thíra by three to five weekly ferries, and with Síros, Páros and Náxos somewhat less often. There is also a once-or twice-weekly link with Crete and some Dhodhekánisos islands.

DAY TREKS FROM HÓRA OR ÁNO MERIÁ
All of the following are designed to be completed in well under a day, with time left for a swim and returning to base. Several daily minibuses plying between Hóra and Áno Meriá get you off to a good start for more remote walks – the official bus stops are often the trailheads themselves. Áno Meriá even has a few small stores and a tiny taverna if you forget to buy victuals in Hóra.

Trek 1: Hóra to Lustriá Bay
(2 hours)
This walk cuts through the heart of the dry eastern half of Folégandhros, with good swimming at the end.

Beginning in Hóra, find the crossroads just below a sign announcing Fani-Vevis's rooms to rent. Turn left onto the concrete road leading down to Karavostási, and after 100 metres bear right onto a wide, walled-in donkey track. Twenty minutes out of town, an enclosed almond grove, the only greenery in a desert of thorns and herbs, grows to the right; a bit beyond and left, a stérna supplies water appetising only to animals.

Some 20 minutes past the almonds you'll attain a slight rise from where Síkinos island is visible to the left and the hamlet of Petúsi shows dead ahead; off the path to the right

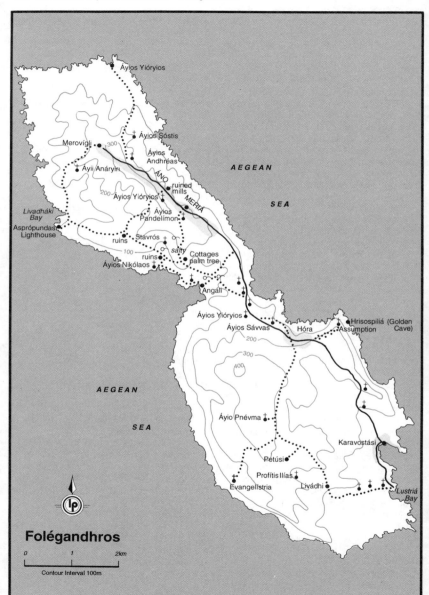

Folégandhros

0   1   2km

Contour Interval 100m

huddles the ksoklísi of Áyio Pnévma. Shortly after, ignore a right fork to the isolated chapel of Evangelístria near some olive trees, the first of many on the relatively fertile plateau here which supports the hamlet.

Soon, just under an hour out of Hóra, a right fork near some more stunted olives leads the last few paces to Petúsi, a summer colony of about 10 people who produce barley, grapes, olives and dairy products. If you're lucky you may get to taste *surotó*, a soft, sweet sheep cheese; *ksinógalos*, a curdled milk product like sour yogurt; and *ksinótiro*, the same substance made into a hard cheese.

Retrace your steps to the junction and continue down to the south, passing below and left of Profítis Ilías chapel on its height some 15 minutes from Petúsi. Ninety minutes from Hóra you'll approach the outskirts of Livádhi, slightly bigger than Petúsi. Lustriá Bay appears in the distance, so it's impossible to get lost from here on.

Below Livádhi the trail widens to a driveway, passing a couple of wells and a trio of ksoklísia on the left. Lustriá's sand is coarse and pebble-studded, but after two hours of walking nobody seems to care, least of all the dozens of 'free' campers from the tamarisk or those from the official campsite nearby. Karavostási, with tavernas and a bus service back to Hóra, is 20 minutes north via the wide coastal track.

Trek 2: Hóra to Angáli & Áyios Nikólaos
(1-1½ hours)
Angáli is justifiably the most popular beach on the island: sheltered, scenic and sandy.

From Hóra walk half an hour along the road to Áno Meriá, then turn left at the blue sign just before two small ksoklísia; the dozen houses of Angáli soon appear at the sandy mouth of the canyon opening below you. You've 20 minutes down to a stream, fed by three sluggish springs, and a left turn onto another path running parallel to the creek bed. From this muddy junction walk 15 minutes seaward (south-west) to Angáli, a pleasant place with a few tavernas, places

to stay and a crop of tents. A faint trail hugs the shore closely for the final 20 minutes west to Áyios Nikólaos, a waterless but protected beach where clothing is optional.

On your way back from either beach you can continue up the stream valley past the springs and onto a kalderími, which emerges onto the Hóra to Áno Meriá track a km or so north of the two small landmark chapels noted. You may also find the pair of paths which exit the west side of Hóra and pass below and north of the concrete road to Áno Meriá. These shortcuts wind through terraces of wind-sculpted olive trees and come out between the two chapels of Áyios Sávvas and Áyios Yióryios, thus halving the amount of road-walking necessary.

Trek 3: Áno Meriá to Áyios Nikólaos
(¾ hour)
Turn down and south from the Áno Meriá 'high street' at the Elpis store, passing the venerable church of Áyios Pandelímon with its brown and blue doorway. A 20-minute descent on a clear kalderími brings you to a turnout with a spring, just above Stavrós ksoklísi.

From the fountain, climb slightly and veer east as the path swoops tantalisingly past Áyios Nikólaos and then appears to forsake it entirely. But half an hour from the store, take a right turn just before a pair of small cottages guarded by a single palm tree. Within 10 more minutes you come to an abandoned hilltop hamlet, from where it's a brief scramble down to Áyios Nikólaos beach.

Continuing on the main trail past the palm tree huts takes you within 20 minutes to the trio of springs above Angáli.

Trek 4: Áyios Andhréas to Áyios Yióryios Bay
(1 hour)
Take a bus to Áyios Andhréas church at the northern end of Áno Meriá, alighting at the labelled *stégastro* (bus-stop shelter). From the kiosk a distinct path descends northwards, keeping the hilltop ksoklísi of Áyios Sóstis to its right, in one uncomplicated hour

to the bay and chapel of Áyios Yióryios. The beach is quite big, but it's only usable on the rare occasions when a north-west wind is not blowing.

Trek 5: Merovígli to Áyios Nikólaos
(2¼ hours)

The next bus stop beyond Áyios Andhréas, Merovígli, is also the end of the line. From here continue straight along the gravelled track, forking left after five minutes. (Keeping straight leads past assorted ksoklísia to small holdings on the extreme northern tip of the island.) This left-hand path curls down and past the church of Áyii Anáryiri on its knoll, after which the going gets much rougher. The Asprópundas lighthouse is a good navigation aid for Livadháki Bay, a partly sheltered cove (no fresh water) some 45 minutes below the Merovígli stop.

Locate an inconspicuous series of rock stairs on the southern flank of Livadháki cove, which lead within 15 minutes to the grounds of the lighthouse. There the onward trail is difficult to find; start at the power and phone poles, then veer gradually away to the right, following the general bearing of a prominent stone wall. As the path becomes more obvious, Hóra pops into sight to the south-east.

About half an hour above the lighthouse, take a right turn upon meeting some olive trees and two abandoned cottages. (Proceeding straight through this intersection leads, after half an hour, to a group of ruined windmills on the Áno Meriá high street, very close to the church of Áyios Yióryios – not the one near Hóra – and a taverna.) Drop 20 minutes from the pair of derelict cottages to a brackish pool just below Stavrós chapel, and then climb five minutes to the two abandoned cottages and palm tree described in the route from Áyios Pandelímon. From there you can turn down to the beaches or maintain your course towards the springs above Angáli.

Barley in the Kikládhes
The cultivation of barley is possibly the single largest remaining commercial tie between these islands and the rest of Greece. The grain, harvested in July, is sent to the mainland to be brewed into beer; the rest of the plant is kept as animal feed.

Heavy machinery is useless on the rugged terrain of hillside terraces, so reaping is done by hand, as is winnowing. Two or three-mule teams do the threshing in the alónia, which are usually located at the outskirts of villages but may occasionally be found by isolated fields. It is common to meet donkey or mule caravans on their way home completely hidden by bundled sheaves, like a portion of Birnam Wood on the move against Macbeth. Seen silhouetted against the horizon at dusk, such a procession of bristly cubes on four legs is a startling sight.

It takes two Folegandhriots such as Dhimitris Karistinaios and his cousin Nikitas Marinakis about five days to gather barley from a seven-strémma (1¾-acre) field. In the midsummer heat a sensible working day is 8 am to noon, and then from 4 pm until sunset. Their field, like many others, is rented from absentee landlords in Athens – ex-islanders who have gone on to more profitable occupations.

Tínos

One of the windiest and bleakest members of the larger Kikládhes, Tínos is also one of the more beautiful by virtue of its fine domestic architecture and decorative arts, and its hidden, well-watered valleys. There are claimed to be over 60 villages large and small, inhabited in varying proportions by the island's nearly equal Catholic and Orthodox population, whose sectarian competition in past centuries is supposedly responsible for the numerous extraordinarily tall belfries. Of all places in Greece, the Venetians ruled here the longest and the Ottomans the briefest, Tínos changing hands only in 1714. The Venetians naturally encouraged the Catholic contingent during their long tenure and introduced the practice of pigeon breeding, of which the hundreds of fanciful *peristereónes* (dovecote towers) are witness.

Half Catholic or not, Tínos is also one of the principal focuses of Orthodox pilgrimage in Greece, by virtue of the huge shrine which dominates the harbour town. The atmosphere of holiness generated, and the relative lack of sheltered beaches, has until recently kept a leash on some of the wilder aspects of island tourism, and the local artisans' tradition has attracted instead Greek, German, Swiss and French artists.

Many of the most interesting villages are grouped around the 500-metre-plus fortified crag of Exóburgo, never taken by enemy fire but surrendered cravenly by the last Venetian commander. The best hiking on Tínos is to be had within sight of it, threading through the villages at its base as well as up to the top.

LOOP AROUND EXÓBURGO
(7 hours)
This itinerary, starting and ending in the harbour hóra, visits most of the important villages in the south-central island, cutting perpendicular to the road system on a variety of trail surfaces except for a few unavoidable periods. Almost every settlement has something different of interest, and frequently somewhere to eat, so there's no need – at least in the tourist season – to lug large amounts of picnic supplies with you. Make it something of a gastronomical tour: Tínos wine is good and the local sausages and dairy products are excellent.

Rating & Duration
This is a moderate outing, mostly because of some long climbs and drops but also the six to seven hours needed.

Season
Because of the constant breeze it never gets extremely hot on Tínos, and it can be bitterly cold in spring or autumn. Avoid the two main pilgrimage dates of 25 March and 15 August, and summer weekends, and you should always find accommodation.

Maps
YIS 1:50,000 *Tínos*.

Access
Tínos is one of the better-connected isles in the Aegean by virtue of having both religious and secular tourism. There are connections at least daily to the mainland ports of Pireás and Rafína, and to Ándhros, Síros, Míkonos; two to four weekly (depending on the season) to Páros, Náxos, Amorgós and Íos; one or two a week to Skiáthos, Thessaloníki, and Iráklio; one to three weekly to Ikaría and Sámos; and one or two weekly to Astipálea, Kálimnos, Kós, Nísiros, Tílos and Ródhos in the Dhodhekánisos.

In addition to these main-line services, there are expensive hydrofoils linking Tínos daily in the tourist season with Síros, Páros, Náxos, Amorgós and the islets between the latter two.

Route Directions
In Hóra, begin at the Taverna Fanaria on the seafront north of the centre. Head up the lane going inland – you should see a sign identifiying the street as 'Ayíu Nikólau' within 200 metres; at a square with a capped fountain, the name changes to Ayías Varváras. Passing behind and left of the vast pilgrimage basilica of Evangelístria, the way becomes a broad kalderími which climbs within 45 minutes over the hills to a chapel decorated with a relief of the Virgin and Child, one of the many examples of the marble carver's art which abounds on Tínos.

Just beyond is a permanent stream crossed by a fine arched bridge; you can detour over it through the trees and up the hill 15 more minutes to visit Ktikádhos, one of the prettiest villages on the island, with an excellent taverna.

Back at the main trail, continue up to the the island's main lengthwise road, passing under a bridge made especially for it; bear up towards the ridge with windmills here. An hour or so along the principal route out of Hóra you'll see the enormous convent of Kekhrovuníu on its namesake mountain off to the right, and the rooftops of Ksínara ahead to the north. Fork right just past the windmills, and enter Ksínara, seat of the Roman Catholic bishopric, one hour 15 minutes along. Many of the wholly or partly Catholic communities are either well-sheltered from the wind or have ample flat land and water, or both, a legacy of the Venetians' favouritism, and Ksinára is no exception.

Once in the village, fork left at the small platía by the church (right leads to a strong fountain and the direct ascent of Exóburgo or Ksobúrgo), curling around the south-east flank of the pinnacle. Preferably, begin descending north; when you hit the road, bear right. You'll reach Lutrá, with its Ursuline convent and carpet-weaving school, half an hour beyond Ksinára.

There's an unavoidable patch of road-walking here; when the asphalt forks, go right up to Skaládhos, away from Krókos. Just past the taverna – a lunch possibility – head perpendicularly up and right on a stair-street to the top of the village and the road again.

After 10 to 15 minutes' southerly progress on this road, bear east onto a red-blazed trail going down into some oleanders. After following the drainage here it shakes free and makes directly for Vólakas (Vólax), named for the weird boulder field behind it, arriving on the outskirts half an hour beyond Skaládhos (2¾ hours into the day).

Vólakas is a small Catholic community famous for its basket weavers, who unfortunately are a dying breed; of the dozen active in 1981, only six remain. When the workshops are not open, you can buy a basket from a combination bar/sales boutique run

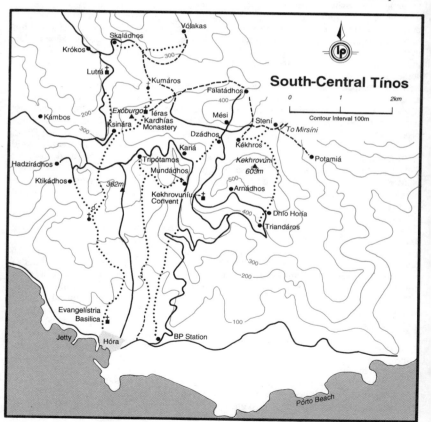

by a German-Greek couple. Considering the quality, they are not overpriced – one of mine has given more than a decade's faithful service.

Retrace your steps to the trailhead, which is just at the edge of Kumáros. Carry on straight through the village arcades (one kafenío here) as the lane becomes a stair-trail climbing the north-eastern slopes of Exóburgo, past fields being planted with potatoes in early spring. Twenty minutes above Kumáros, you'll reach the Catholic monastery of Iéras Kardhiás ('Sacred Heart'), where a right turn leads up the steep, 20-minute stair-path to Exóburgo summit.

The views are even better than you'd expect from the top of an island, arguably the most comprehensive in the Kikládhes, though gale-force winds may prevent your ascent. Examining the crumbled but sheer perimeter walls, you'll understand why nobody ever took all of Tínos by force even when the lowlands were overrun; this hill was the capital, and last refuge of the population, throughout the Venetian centuries, and was only permanently abandoned in the mid-1800s.

From the base of the mountain, a narrow dirt track leads 20 minutes east-north-east to the large village of Falatádhos, where you face a choice in the matter of how to finish the day.

You might head 15 minutes south along the road to the adjacent hamlets of Mési and Dzádhos; at the latter's church begins a fine 20-minute trail which descends the wooded valley between Kariá and Mundádhos, just five minutes south from where the path debouches. Another excellent trail links Mundádhos with Tripótamos, one of the handsomest villages on the island, bought up and refurbished by outsiders in the space of 10 years. After touring the lanes there you can take an onward path which descends the ridge straight south, just below the new 'express' road into the interior, within an hour.

Alternatively, go straight on the road beyond Mundádhos for half an hour, bearing right at the big road junction, then a quick

left onto the kalderími descending in half an hour to the BP petrol station at the edge of Hóra.

The best return to Hóra from Falatádhos, however, involves crossing the cultivated valley on farm lanes to Kékhros, the village seen to your right as you look south (the left-hand village is Stení). Leave Kékhros on Odhós Ayíon Anaryíron, which quickly becomes a south-east-bound kalderími skirting 603-metre Kekhrovúni. Five minutes along, bear right at a Y-fork where the feeder trail comes up from Stení. Next make a right at a T-intersection, then another immediate right bearing. About 25 minutes out of Kékhros you'll draw level with the oasis village of Potamía away to the left down in its valley, and Míkonos island appears on the horizon. Ten minutes later a minor trail crosses yours at right angles; go right for about 10 metres, then left again, levelling out at a 500-metre-high saddle with some ruined mills.

From there the descent to Dhío Horiá, reached 45 minutes beyond Kékhros, is unambiguous. In this village there's a kafenío on the enormous square with a view of the sea; the marble-sheathed cave fountains with their elaborate shrines attest to the artistry and piety of the islanders.

When you meet the road, bear right and look below for the path continuing 10 minutes to Triandáros, where there's a good taverna – though scarcely any village life, since the place has been almost completely bought up by foreigners intent on holiday homes.

To close the final gap back to Hóra, you can either road-walk west two km to the junction one km or so south of Mundádhos and follow the kalderími to the harbour described previously, or take your chances with paths and tracks leading south down the valley below to Pórto beach and a late afternoon swim – or rather a sunset swim, for you will have been hiking for nearly seven hours, not counting stops.

Náxos

The largest of the Kikládhes, Náxos has always been the cultural and commercial centre of the archipelago, and is rapidly developing into a (if not the) touristic one. It is that rare thing in the islands, a combination of indelible character and historical interest, and every sybaritic comfort or facility that you can imagine.

Rich archaeological finds at Neolithic (3000-2000 BC) and Geometric (850-700 BC) sites demonstrate very early human occupation of Náxos. Perhaps the first travellers to call in were Theseus and Ariadne, escaping from the labyrinth of Crete; Theseus abandoned his rescuer here, whereupon the god Dionysos is supposed to have replaced him in her affections. Náxos was important in Byzantine times, as evidenced by numerous small but exquisite churches, many with frescoes, found in a profusion unequalled on other medium-sized islands.

After the Kikládhes fell to the Venetians in the wake of the Fourth Crusade, the successive Sanudo and Crespi dynasties chose the island as the seat of their insular duchies; accordingly there are also some very fine monuments dating from those years, including not only the upper fortified kástro of the busy harbour hóra, but also a generous sprinkling of fortress-towers in remote places.

Theseus and Ariadne were not the last Cretans to happen by, since like several other of the Kikládhes, large number of refugees from the fall of Crete settled here some centuries ago.

The marble of Náxos is coarser than that found on nearby Páros or Tínos, but since ancient times has been highly prized for sculpture – for example the *kouroi* (singular *kouros*; idealised figures of youths aspiring to be gods) found at two sites. Emery was also until recently quarried for export to Germany, and with its fertile interior Náxos is probably the only island of the group that could be entirely self-sufficient without tourism.

Not that it shows any signs of abandoning this new source of wealth: vacation facilities expand exponentially each year, and Hóra is losing its former atmosphere of a farmers' market town at a similar rate. Naxos' fate has been sealed by the recent opening of an airport – though the runway can't accommodate big jets, and built as it is on a former salt marsh will probably spend much of the time flooded or buckled.

Walking across the island is often the best, and sometimes the only, way to reach the more remote places. As so often in Greece, a forbidding rocky perimeter and hedonistic beaches conceal surprisingly untouched monuments or lush garden spots. Some trails have been waymarked, though these and others are apt to be clogged with thornbush since the construction of parallel roads. The main flow of traffic across Náxos moves east between Hóra and Filóti, and then with a sharp bend north to Apíranthos and Apóllonas. If you know what you're doing, it's possible to hike between these points while only rarely touching down on asphalt, and that is the gist of the two routes outlined below. If you plan to spend a long time on the island, Christian Ucke's locally available, English-translated guide *Walking on Naxos* (C & M Hofbauer, Munich) is a worthwhile investment, though some of the itineraries are only 30 or 40 minutes long – and at DM26.80 or over 3500dr, it is an investment.

Season

Naxos' interior is big enough to shelter you from the meltémi wind in summer, which makes for sweaty hiking and the risk of a chill once you emerge onto exposed ridges. As in most parts of Aegean Greece, visit in spring or autumn if you can.

Maps

YIS 1:50,000 *Filótion* and *Náxos* – for the north and centre only.

Access

Next to Páros, Náxos has some of the best ferry connections in the central Aegean.

There is a steamer service at least daily to and from Páros, Íos, Thíra, Síros and the mainland ports of Rafína and Pireás, several weekly to Amorgós, Ikaría, Sámos, Síkinos, Folégandhros and Crete, and even one to many of the Dhodhekánisos.

In addition, there are hydrofoils and a daily kaïki service running between Míkonos and Amorgós, with a dozen stops in between including Náxos. The newly opened airport is so far served by just two very daily flights from Athens.

HALKÍ TO APÓLLONAS VIA THE CENTRAL RIDGE

This trek from the fertile Tragéa valley in the middle of the island to a quiet resort near the northern tip can be split into four self-contained sections, with road access and possibilities of overnight accommodation between each.

Rating & Duration

A tough walker could conceivably accomplish the total of 25-plus km in one day, but would leave themselves little leeway against nightfall, and the unexpected sights and encounters that are the staples of island life inland.

Access

During summer, buses leave Hóra six times daily for Halkí; the 9.30 and 11 am, 1 and 3 pm go all the way to Apóllonas via Stavrós and Komiakí, allowing you to tailor your route if you don't wish to spend a night out in the villages.

Between early October and early May the winter timetable is in effect, with the consequent deletion of the 3 pm service to Apóllonas and the corresponding 5.30 pm return trip. In any case, it is wise to check first at the KTEL office at the base of the ferry jetty.

Stage 1: Halkí to Stavrós

(2¾ hours)

From the road junction next to the high school, follow the main Filóti road for 100 metres before turning left onto a track opposite a

bakery. This takes you past a modern olive-oil press to Kalóxilos (300 metres), with its blue-domed church, within 10 minutes. Follow the main street north, keeping right at the next fork and leaving the village centre along a high-walled alley, passing the chapel of Áyii Apóstoli and Ayia Ekateríni, and the cemetery immediately after on the right.

At the last houses, don't take the concrete road left, but continue straight on the track, soon a path across a small stream with oleanders. The path zig-zags left and then right to break the slope ahead, before attacking it perpendicularly.

You may need to hurdle some spiky branch or metal mesh barriers against livestock to stay on the sporadic kalderími up to a gentle ridge.

Looking back, the fine view over the Tragean olive groves, church domes, and Venetian towers peeking out here and there is ample reward for the first half an hour of effort. The route now levels out and veers right, but you take the second left turn, following red dots, onto a shady trail with little altitude change. After 20 more minutes between tended fields, Moní village (440 metres) appears on the slope opposite. Now the path drops steeply, merges with a trail coming in from the left, crosses a small stone bridge and does the final climb to the village, bringing your walking total from Halkí to one hour.

There is a hotel in Moní (☎ (0285) 31 902, Katerina Kondopidhou) with 12 beds, should you wish to break up the hike – though you've only come 40 minutes so far. Leaving Moní, follow the asphalt road for several hundred metres to a ridge and junction north of the village, where you turn left towards Kinídharos. After about a km, drop to a bridge, with a possible short cut of one curve. Just after the bridge, bear right onto a mesh of bulldozer tracks and aim north-east over a swampy plateau for a few hundred metres. If you stray too far left you will slip onto the path which drops towards the Artemídhos valley; it is best, if in doubt, to keep right, as the large hill to the east will put you back on target.

You should intersect a broad but shrub-riddled kalderími within 20 minutes of the asphalt road; the cobbles head purposefully east-north-east between the large hill above and a smaller outrider on the west, climbing steadily to straddle a ridge after half an hour. Finally it curves left to deposit you on the side road to Keramotí 30 minutes later still, 2½ hours from Halkí and some minutes below Stavrós Pass and its chapel up on the main trans-island road. Ask nicely and you can probably arrange a bed or two in Keramotí (500 metres), a tiny village at the head of the Artemídhos valley.

Stage 2: Stavrós Pass to Komiakí
(2¼ hours)

At the chapel, pause to enjoy the view over both Náxian coasts, with Amorgós island thrown in on a clear day. From Stavrós Pass, follow the asphalt road north-east (towards Kóronos village) for 50 metres before forking left onto a wide, scree-covered live-stock track. Diverging slowly but steadily from the main road, this takes you past a sheep pen and veers left beneath power poles and wires to the base of conical Mt Kóronos, at 997 metres the second-highest point on Náxos (by a mere two metres). Here you can

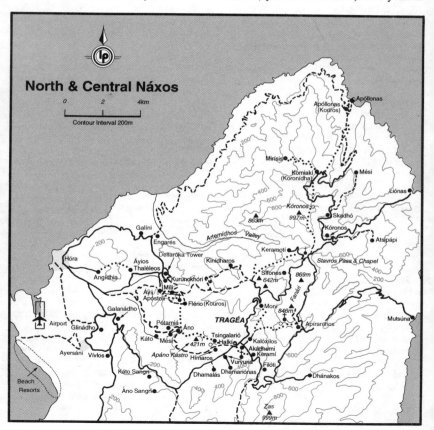

North & Central Náxos

0   2   4km

Contour Interval 200m

either adopt the more direct onward path left or circle more gently around on the right-hand track.

Within 10 minutes you'll draw even with a marble quarry. Keeping left of this, but right of a dry-stone wall, pick your way along a tracery of paths heading north-west, passing a square-walled sheep pen and a curious boulder garden. From here you should see the patchwork of white and grey roofs in Kóronos and Skadhó below, the principal emery-miners' villages.

Now the path is clearer (and flatter), reaching a few minutes later a col with a hut built in the lee of a boulder 45 minutes out of Stavrós Pass. This is the best departure point for a hike up to the summit. The view from up top encompasses layer upon layer of jagged hills to the south, as well as the coast-to-coast breadth of Náxos. If you're lucky, you may be treated to a display of whirling and diving by the local population of goose vultures.

Returning to the hut, the level path continues, now heading almost due north, to emerge on a saddle north-east of the peak in 15 minutes, or about one hour 15 minutes out of Stavrós Pass including the summit-climb. The next stretch is rather overgrown, and can be avoided by following the ridge on the right towards its gentle summit, and then cutting down to the left where the going seems more uncluttered. You should aim for a threshing cirque (alóni) above a series of terraces in varying hues of green and yellow.

The direct path, for those with tough skin or trousers, curves left through a sandy depression; where the thornbush hinders further progress, about 10 minutes from the saddle, cut down to the dry streambed on your right. Hop down this for another 10 minutes (there are a couple of small drops) to the edge of the highest terrace, between the alóni and a small tree. Follow the rim right for a minute, jump down to the next level, and find a spring just below, which gushes out (except in autumn) from between two boulders under a tree. You should be about 1½ hours beyond Stavrós Pass.

Here a goat trail leads left, starting along the terrace and later twisting down in a northerly direction, to bring you onto the asphalt road at a bend within 20 minutes. A third of the way down you'll pass a pair of derelict houses with a bed frame propped between as a sort of gate. If you hurdle or open this, turning right and following the edge of a vegetable patch for a few moments, you come to a beautiful spring and stone basin. From the ruined cottages you can also plunge cross-country over the terraces, veering right, to a shady creek; the road is a few minutes' rock-hopping downstream.

The path continues below the bend, 250 metres left (west) of the stream canyons after an international 'curve' sign. After fighting your way through thick broom and weaving down the right-hand side of a walled, sloping field finally becoming a vineyard, you level out at a leftward curve at the base of a wall enclosing the vines. Within 15 minutes, drop sharply to another stream and climb up the far bank, before resuming level progress. Shun a left fork and descend slightly to yet another gully within five minutes, crossing this to climb the final few paces onto the road.

Komiakí (Koronídha) lies just a few minutes downhill; take the concrete access drive left and either follow it five minutes up to a weaving workshop (accommodation can be arranged here), or branch right at the first bend and follow this alley for 10 minutes to the centre of the village – either way, count on about 2¼ hours' hiking from Stavrós.

Its flat-roofed white houses arranged in tiers and festooned with vines, Komiakí (600 metres) is one of the most attractive of the Naxian hill-villages, reputedly also the original home of *kítron*, the island's citron liqueur. If you stay the night, a very worthwhile detour before finishing the main route is to take the amazing kalderími down to the hamlet of Mirísis. Head north out of Komiakí on the path to the ridge, where you'll see the cobbles coiling down to that tiny garden spot, a summer-only annexe of the high village. Unfortunately its Shangri-la quality has been compromised somewhat by the recent introduction of a road, and you will have to climb back up to resume the main itinerary – a difference in height of over 200 metres.

Stage 3: Komiakí to Apóllonas
(2 hours)

Leave the village on the main road, passing the modern church and graveyard – which, incidentally, has a fine Byzantine chapel hiding behind. Just after the first hairpin, a red sign indicates where you should leave the road.

Initially, the path bumbles vaguely along a terrace but, after a right curve, clears up and takes you north-north-east down a spur well above the road. The kalderími is still largely intact, but the view east towards the road is rather depressing in the wake of a recent fire in the walnut orchards. After 45 minutes you'll pass a smelly sheep corral; 15 minutes later, on a shoulder just above the road, take the steeper left-hand option to the concrete road bridge.

As well-concealed red waymarks indicate, you must turn right onto the road at the bridge to stay on the path; at the first bend, 50 metres along, the path dips down to the left again. Descend between bramble bushes to the unpotable stream, cross it and veer right. A pile of sand from a half-built house may still be obstructing the way 15 minutes below the bridge, but it is dodgeable.

Just under half an hour from the bridge you'll emerge for good on the road, now dirt-surfaced, about two km before Apóllonas.

Instead of road-walking the entire remaining distance, turn left at the fork halfway along to visit the famous kouros of Apóllonas. After 500 metres, there is a sign pointing up and left to where the colossal 10½ metre statue lies, abandoned some time around 600 BC owing to a flaw in the marble. From the sign, either of two paths cuts down directly to the seaside village, for two hours of total walking from Komiakí. Perhaps because of its exposed location, Apóllonas has never really taken off as a beach resort, so except in the very high season you should find a bed here. The last bus back to Hóra is at 5.30 pm.

APÍRANTHOS TO THE MÉLANES VALLEY

For a representative sampling of Náxos's interior, this transect across some of its most monument-studded territory is hard to beat. Despite the modest amount of actual walking, there are so many potential distractions along the way that you may have trouble completing the tour in one day!

Rating & Duration

This is basically a moderate hike involving less than five hours of walking, but by the time you've done some sightseeing and had lunch you should count on nearly eight hours. Except at Halkí, very early in the itinerary, there is no possibility of a place to stay the night, so you'll need to complete the route in one day. You should also allow for a possible extra obligatory walk from Áyii Apóstoli to the main road.

Access

The 9.30 am bus to Apíranthos gets you off to too late a start to catch the 3.40 pm bus back from Áyii Apóstoli (Mélanes), the hike's end, unless you hurry; a taxi from the latter to Hóra costs about US$8.

Stage 1: Apíranthos to Halkí
(2 hours)

Before starting the walk, take some time out to explore Apíranthos, the most Cretan-like of the Náxian interior villages – as you'd expect where the population is almost totally of refugee descent. Seen from the approaching bus, the place seems a study in greys and browns, but once inside, the low, narrow alleys prove to be paved in a lighter marble, and the house walls whitewashed as in any other island village.

The initially broad, walled-in path west starts from just north of an abandoned windmill next to the highest cistern and church in Apíranthos (600 metres); after 200 metres take a hairpin left onto a stair-path marked with some red dots and an arrow. (The 'main' path apparently continues north towards Stavrós Pass.) At the outset, a newly-built cistern forces a slight detour. For the first 20 minutes up to the saddle on the southern flank of Mt Fanári, you have great views over to Dhonúsa, Amorgós and Mt Zas. Once on top you can add perspectives on Moní, Kinídharos, and the entire west and centre of Náxos. It is possible to detour 15 minutes to the chapel perched atop 820-metre Fanári summit; this is in fact where the red waymarks go.

The cobbles and revetment of your trail fade away as you descend west; 10 minutes below the saddle and to the right there's a reliable spring, but don't expect to continue down the faint trail below it. Despite appearances this never gets to Moní or the Tragéa, but shortly becomes hopelessly entangled in fences and gorse. Instead angle left across the top of the ridge until reaching the head of another well-engineered switchbacking kalderími – you should be able to see it from the spring.

You've 45 minutes' descent down this to a fenced-in terrace next to a shallow ravine. Descend between rock walls and past olean-ders to a big T-junction, and bear left and down. Approaching the hour mark downhill, the surface deteriorates to that of the streambed. Once past two gates the way levels out, and at a concrete tank an actual walled-in trail resumes on the left, going south-south-west. Going right, incidentally, leads to Moní. Now you're at the edge of the Tragéa, a vast, olive-swathed bowl in the heart of Náxos. The trail forges ahead pur-posefully: sometimes cobbled, sometimes not, but always sunk two or three metres below the level of the surrounding orchards.

Ten minutes along the resumption of the proper trail, you collide with a newish track system; after 10 minutes more, bear left upon reaching a big T-intersection of paths on a bedrock surface. Bear left for almost immediate entry into Kalóxilos, a pretty community just off the Halkí to Moní road. Your path becomes the main longitudinal pedestrian street of the village, and then a concrete driveway, hitting the Halkí to Filóti asphalt road after another 20 minutes, or nearly two hours into the day.

Here you can cross the road directly to pick up the walkway through the village of Akádhemi, but instead you might turn left at the bakery junction. Walk 400 metres up to the narrow drive opposite the church of Taxiárhes at the edge of Keramí hamlet, and folow it down to the 11th or 12th-century church of Áyii Apóstoli. This is always locked, like most of the historical country churches on Náxos, but the exterior profile is the thing: a peculiar piggy-back chapel above the narthex, where the nobles who funded the shrine could worship in private.

Continue on the lane below the front door for 450 metres, then turn right up a narrower one leading to the centre of Halkí, famous for its Grazia tower of the Venetian era and the Byzantine church of Panayía Protothrónis with its recently cleaned 11th and 12th-century frescoes.

They're adjacent, and often open until noon – a good reason perhaps to skip the detour via Akádhemi and come straight here from Kalóxilos. In any case you should plan on lunch in the pleasant square, since you'll have been walking for over two hours now and will find nothing more substantial for the rest of the day.

Stage 2: Halkí to the Mélanes Valley
(2½-3½ hours)
Proceed west on the cement driveway leading towards the twin hamlets of Tsingalarió (Áyios Ioánnis) and Hímaros. After a couple of hundred metres the con-crete ends; beyond, just past a bridge, bear right onto a wide trail leading up to Tsingalarió within 15 minutes. On the way up you'll certainly pause to gape at the central Tragéa, with all its tower-tops and church-domes, and the spectacle of Filóti sprawled on the hillside opposite.

Fill up at the trough-spring where the kalderími collides with a concrete drive; clear the village on this drive as it eventually becomes a rocky trail again, heading up through a bare landscape. Ahead looms Apáno Kástro, whose crumbling Venetian fortifications were built in the 13th century on the foundations of a Byzantine castle. It's another quarter of an hour, with sporadic red waymarks, past the ksoklísi under the fort to a pass. An often ample cobbled trail erupts next to a second, ancient chapel west of and below Apáno Kástro, descending gradually through more moonscape within 25 minutes to the edge of Áno Potamiá village.

Cross the road here and descend to a small platía at a T-intersection where there's a keyless tap, in front of an evening-only kafenío. Bear right towards a large church at the top of this valley, one of the many oases tucked into the island's interior but invisible from the sea. You'll see more red and blue waymarks; the legend 'KOUROS 2ND' in blue Roman letters is everywhere. At the big church with a plaza and all-day cafe across from it, the path continues to its right, and blue metal signs announce 'Kouros' at every possible ambiguity. From Áno Potamiá, it's 45 hiking minutes over this low, pleasingly vegetated ridge to another concrete drive in the Mélanes valley. Turn right here and follow more signs a few moments to the kouros at Flério.

This kouros is considerably smaller, newer (by an estimated 50 years) and more finished than the Apóllonas one, though it too had to be left in eternal slumber – whether the broken leg was the reason, or a later accident, is unclear. It was discovered during 1943 inside a walled orchard, and the family concerned still supervises visits. At the adjacent cafe, there are drinks, snacks and perhaps fruit of the season on offer, and one of the sons may offer to guide you up the rubbly slope behind it to see another similarly abandoned effigy.

From the cement-paved Flério-bound drive, you have a choice of onward routes. The start of both options, despite a helpful red dot, is badly mangled by a new bulldozer track; head levelly north on a narrow surviving path, just below the road, to a white chapel.

To relocate the direct path to Áyii Apóstoli (shown on many maps and bus schedules as Mélanes, in confusion with the valley), go down from the chapel and then left along the edge of someone's kitchen garden. Next slip through a gap in the stone

fence and proceed just 30 metres across a waste ground of rocks and thorn to pick up a narrow trail towards Áyii Apóstoli. This in turn quickly joins the main kalderími whose start had been so badly muddled up on the road. You've no more than half an hour from the chapel to the village by this direct route, with fine views across the lush valley to Míli. Red dots guide you more or less through Áyii Apóstoli; the critical juncture is a hard left uphill towards two of the grills.

For the indirect way, don't drop towards the market gardens from the white chapel, but stay level to clear attractive Míli on a cemented walkway; just past the last structure, as Korúnokhóri with its imposing Dellaróka tower comes into view, the way becomes a stair-path plunging left into the ravine bottom, then labouring up to Áyii Apóstoli. This roundabout option is a bit longer, some 45 minutes from the Flério-bound road.

In Áyii Apóstoli there are dhomátia and several grills, like O Dekes – which is open all day and has a phone to summon a taxi. Unless you got an early start and walked briskly, you will have missed the single afternoon (3.40 pm) bus out; a taxi should cost about $9 back to the harbour. The minimum elapsed time from Halkí, not counting the kouros visit, will be 2½ hours.

From either Áyii Apóstoli or Kurunokhóri, worth visiting for the sake of its mini-castle, you've a 45-minute road-walk, with no possibility of a path, to Áyios Thaléleos, and nearly as much again down to the main road, where you'll be able to flag a bus until 6.40 pm.

Alternatively a trail leads from Áyios Thaléleos over the saddle in the hill above to Angídhia in as much time again, debouching very close to a lively taverna. On a long summer day the crawl over the hill with the sunset before you, and the prospect of a meal (and taxi ride down the final three km to Hóra) immediately afterwards might be a fitting finish to the hike, but in all honesty most quality hiking ends at Áyii Apóstoli.

Amorgós

The easternmost of the Kikládhes is shaped like a 33-km-long man with hands clasped in front of him. His spine, the south-eastern flank, is a row of imposing mountains dropping sharply to the sea in a severe cliffscape. Most water flows north-west towards numerous secluded bays, some with miniscule beaches; villages and cultivated terraces surround the various springs, while the high ridges are exceptionally windswept and arid. But Amorgós is more than a larger mirror-image version of Folégandhros, which it does resemble in some respects. There are substantial ancient sites near present-day Arkesíni, Katápola and Egiáli. More recent monuments, above all the well-preserved hóra and one of Greece's most unusual monasteries, are no less compelling.

Because of its topography and (until recently) lack of roads, Amorgós is in effect two islands, with the north-eastern and south-western ends having quite different characters. Nearly all ferries call at each of the two harbours, Katápola and Egiáli, and are still much the fastest way of moving from one part of the island to another. The recently built lengthwise road, despite rumours of imminent paving, is atrocious, subject to washouts and cutting mostly perpendicularly to the extensive path system; thus these are still used regularly by both locals and visitors, and remain in excellent condition.

For many years the only visitors were compulsory ones; ancient and modern regimes alike exiled political dissidents to Amorgós. One of the more prominent recent transportees was George Mylonas, briefly Minister of Culture in 1989, who was confined here by the 1967-74 junta. He managed to elude his guards during one of his daily swims and was spirited off the island in a speedboat piloted by his son-in-law, an adventure retold in the unfortunately out-of-print *Escape from Amorgós*. It would have made as good a movie as Luc Besson's *The Big Blue*, which was partly filmed here and

put the island on the map touristically. The original German and British pioneer foreigners have been joined by flocks of French and Italians who come to pay their respects to the film location.

With this belated discovery Amorgós is slowly being transformed. Even so short a time ago as the colonels' regime, exile here must have been uncomfortable, because as late as the early 1980s tourist facilities were quite primitive, and the island could be cut off for a week at a time by a combination of minimal ferry scheduling and bad weather. All that is history: food and beds are as good (and often as expensive) as elsewhere, and you can come or go at will almost daily in summer. Development-wise, the place is perhaps at an ideal early-adulthood juncture – things can only go downhill from here, with a large polluting yacht marina proposed for Egiáli Bay.

Fortunately, it seems that the road builders have done their damage, so the hikes are described with some confidence. They are popular with foreigners, many of whom come specifically to walk on the island, so you'll usually have company. In general, routes in the south-west are short (under half a day) and easy; north-east of a line between Katápola and Hóra, outings are more advanced.

Season

The best time to visit is the usual late spring/early autumn recommendation for Aegean Greece, with the stress on 'late' – if Force 7 gusts blow you into a thornbush in March or April, you'll spend the rest of the day plucking the spines out with tweezers.

Supplies

Amorgós's grocery stores have resisted the pressure of change and are still as funky – and haphazardly stocked – as you'd expect for an isolated island. Luckily, tavernas and snack bars are more elaborate and well placed for on-trail refreshment, and I have highlighted them.

Maps

Dr Georg Perreiter has prepared a very accurate topographic map in two versions; prefer the large photocopied 1:50,000 sheet, which has useful notes, to the smaller 1:75,000 colour product. Both are on sale in Katápola and Egiáli for a nominal price. The YIS 1:50,000 quads *Amorgós* and *Aiyiáli* are really only for purists.

Access

There is a daily connection in the tourist season with Náxos, the minor islets in the straits between, Páros, and Míkonos via a small but reliable kaïki which calls mostly at the south-western port of Katápola. Larger ferries link Amorgós with Dhonúsa (one of the islets), Páros, Tínos, Míkonos, and Síros three or four times weekly in season, and with Íos, Thíra, Astipálea and Kálimnos (a well-connected Dhodhekánisos) one or two days a week.

Most of these main-line ferries call at the north-eastern harbour of Egiáli as well. There are also fast and expensive hydrofoils from Katápola only back to Pireás and Rafína on the mainland, via a variable sequence of intermediate island stops.

SOUTH-WEST AMORGÓS

The following itineraries assume you will use Katápola or Hóra as your base; Katápola is slightly more practical, Hóra more full of character (and nearer better beaches). Amorgiots have a reputation for being reserved, though certainly not hostile – this is more obvious at this end of the island. The French and Italians concentrate here, closer to the wreck of the *Olympia* at the western tip which was featured in the movie.

Trek 1: Katápola to Arkesíni

(3¼ hours)
This route offers sweeping views of Amorgós's windward coast and the inland sierra. From Vrútsi you can detour to Kastrí, a wedding-cake-shaped rock banded with medieval walls and the remains of classical Arkesíni.

The trail ends within sight of the Hellenistic tower-fort at modern Ayía Triádha, and with a reasonably early start you can catch the daily afternoon bus back to base.

The route begins on a stairway behind the highest blue-domed church at the top of Katápola. A steady 25-minute climb, the last

Kikládhes: Hellenistic Stockade at Ayía Triádha, Amorgós

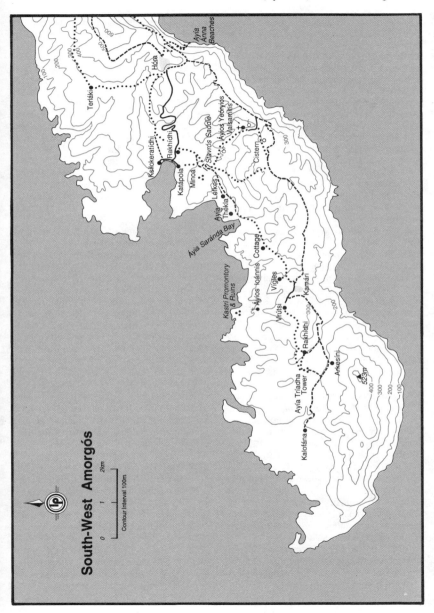

South-West Amorgós

0   1   2km

Contour Interval 100m

15 to 20 minutes on an ugly new road, brings you to the saddle known as Stavrós, not to be confused with several others on Amorgós. Little remains of ancient Minoa to the right of the track other than some polygonal wall four or five courses high, the foundations of an Apollo temple, a crumbled Roman-era structure, and piles of unsorted pottery shards, most recently excavated in 1981 and 1986. Only the site, visible from both Hóra and ancient Arkesíni, is memorable.

Some 100 metres further, bear right on the track towards the 10 houses and church of Léfkes hamlet, 10 minutes beyond; the old trail exists for a while just below the new road. Once over two bridges you come to a large oasis; a spring below and right of the progressively narrowing track is dry by summer, though not the more reliable trough spring to the left. The track, not so unpleasant since Stavrós, ends at Ayía Thékla hamlet, half an hour past Minoá.

Here, the old trail resumes with a right fork down towards the bay and dirty beach of Áyia Saránda. After crossing the streambed feeding both, tackle 30 minutes of uphill switchbacks, topping out at another crest with a lone stone cottage. From here you can tick off, going anticlockwise, most of the minor islets between Amorgós and Náxos; the Kástri promontory studded with its ruins; the conspicuous modern church of Áyios Ioánnis on its own hill; the hamlet of Vígles, a handful of houses on still another knoll; and a portion of Kamári village.

Just under half an hour of hiking – down, up and then level – separates you from Vígles, with Kamári appearing a few minutes later. The path, already a wider lane again, intersects the main island trunk road just over two hours into the day, next to a lumpy, belfryless, triple church. On your left stands a taverna, a lunch possibility; a right turn onto the concrete sideroad leads within 10 minutes to Vrútsi village.

Vrútsi is the point of departure for the overgrown, mostly cross-country detour to the ruins at Kastrí, via Áyios Ioánnis – allow an extra hour. Continuing on the main itinerary, pass two kafenía on the left and adopt a kalderími at the village outskirts, some 20 minutes from the taverna up on the main road.

This dips to a well and then winds towards the hamlet of Rakhídhi (Rakhúla); if you look carefully west, you may already glimpse the ancient tower of Ayía Triádha on its hillock. If you want to go directly there, the path actually forks before Rakhídhi, with the right-hand option the short cut. Otherwise you wind through the village – either way it's about 40 minutes past Vrútsi.

This most important pre-Christian monument on Amorgós dates from about 200 BC, and its outer masonry and lone doorway are still in good condition. However, the interior has collapsed and the construction of a maze of pig pens has been permitted around it – wall-climbing attempts may be rebuffed by indignant grunts and squeals.

A dirt drive leads the final distance, for three-plus hours of hiking, to modern Arkesíni village, confusingly remote from its classical predecessor and not much to write home about. There is a single 'rooms' and evening-only taverna, but most importantly the afternoon bus back towards Hóra and Katápola. It is supposed to head back from Kalofána, the nearby terminus village, at 4 pm, but on my last visit it came back at 3.40 – don't dawdle, it's a long and dusty trudge back on the road if you miss it.

Incidentally the villages at this end of the island are often known collectively as Káto Meriá, a term which may appear on bus schedules or windshield destination displays.

Link Trail: Hóra to Katápola After spending the balance of the afternoon around Hóra or at the beaches below – an excellent plan – you may need to get back to Katápola. There is a frequent shuttle bus in season, but it's more fun (and nearly as quick) to walk along the short-cutting path, at least downhill. From the base of the village on the northwest, locate the sign for the heliport; just beyond, an obvious trail goes down into the canyon. Bear left almost immediately (veering right goes to Terláki and Ríkhti, a useful alternative start of the Hóra to Egiáli route). The first 45 minutes of descent are very pleasant, passing a spring, a well and a cistern, with views over the ravine. But you're brought jarringly down to earth by the Katápola rubbish dump and the final 20 minutes of dirt driveway down to Ksilokeratídhi district.

Trek 2: Áyios Yióryios Valsamítis Loop
(3 hours)

This hike is about the same duration as the one to Ayía Triádha, but frees you from reliance on public transport – and makes an equally pleasant morning out of Katápola.

Directions are the same up to Stavrós saddle, but this time you bear uphill and left past a French-renovated cottage, then left again up a narrow trail away from a new track, then take another left at a final path junction – all within the space of 200 metres from the saddle. Some 20 minutes above Stavrós, you'll pass a church and orchard on your left and arrive at a spring and oasis in a kink of the walled path – a fine rest spot.

Beyond a ridge-top farm the way curls south, ending up just over an hour out of Katápola at the recently restored convent of Áyios Yióryios Valsamítis. The water from its famous oracle spring has been piped mostly out of sight, but the terrace or gardens make a good picnic spot. The church itself probably dates originally from Byzantine times, since a plaque over the door states it was repaired in the late 17th century.

Beyond this peaceful spot the concrete access drive passes just under a visible section of the partly cobbled old trans-island trail, all that remains since the bulldozing of the Hóra to Arkesíni road. Scramble up towards the power lines, and adopt the trail going south-west. Ninety minutes out of Katápola there's a potable cistern by the trail, near two abandoned chapels, and 15 minutes later you'll hit the road again at a concrete culvert.

Within five minutes, the power lines jog left at a bare spot. This is your prompt to bear right, through a gap in a stone fence onto the start of the return trail. There's a lonely farm on the valley floor some two hours into the day; once over a pass behind it you have a magnificent prospect over the northern coast. It's another half an hour down to the renovated cottage at Stavrós Pass. Incidentally, from one of the new bulldozer curves below Minoá, a fairly obvious path winds down to and across the fields to the Rakhídhi district of Katápola, for a total of three hours hiking.

NORTH-EAST AMORGÓS

North of the Hóra to Katápola road the trails are in better condition and more spectacular, the villages are more substantial and (though such things are rather subjective) the islanders are more extroverted. Egiáli tourism is more low key than in the south-west, with a mostly German and English-speaking crowd.

Trek 1: Hóra to Egiáli via Hozoviotíssas Monastery
(4¼ hours)

The premier Amorgiot hike is the half-day trek from Hóra to Egiáli, a fairly representative traverse of Amorgós with often bleak but always striking scenery. There's a net altitude drop of over 300 metres to Egiáli, but it's not a straightforward one, with lots of up and down. You'll need a litre or two of water per person, since the wells en route are not reliable.

Access

You may find yourself doing this route with a full pack, like it or not, given the spotty transport between the Hóra and Egiáli. The latter is so pleasant that it's hard to imagine not wanting to stay at least one night.

If you're determined to do it as a day hike only, boat and van logistics are complicated and require double-checking. Some mornings the kaïki or a hydrofoil leaves Katápola for Egiáli very early, allowing you to walk with the sun at your back (though initially uphill). Some days there is a main-line ferry back from Egiáli to Katápola in the evening. If you do this walk in reverse, you might be able to use a private shuttle van which plies

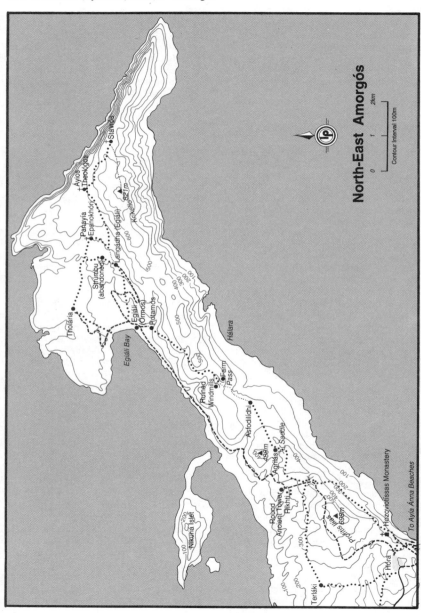

North-East Amorgós

0   1   2km

Contour Interval 100m

Stavrós
Ayios
Theológos
Panayía
Epanokhóri
Kíkellos
321m
Langádha (Egiáli)
Strúmbu
(abandoned)
Tholária
Egiáli
Órmos
Potamós
Egiáli Bay
Hálara
Farm
Pass
Ruined
Windmills
Asfodílidhi
Saddle
458m
Ayía
Ághia
Robad
Ancient Tower
Ríkhti
Profítis Ilías
698m
Nikuría Islet
100
200
Tertáki
Hóra
Hozoviotíssas Monastery
To Ayía Ánna Beaches

late in the afternoon from Katápola to Egiáli; this belongs to the single luxury hotel in Egiáli, with preference given to guests arriving on the afternoon ferry at Katápola. Still, it might be worth trying to reserve a seat by phoning (☎ (0285) 73 244) in Egiáli or by going to the signed storefront there. It is very unreliable, though, and things will only improve when the road is finally paved and a KTEL bus service introduced.

Route Directions To get under way, leave Hóra past the secondary school and the tiny terrace park where a solitary bench overlooks the sea – there will be a sign pointing towards the monastery. The obvious kalderími snakes down towards the modern road serving both Hozoviotíssas and the beach at Ayía Ánna; just 10 minutes downhill, an inconspicuous right-hand path takes you nearly all the way to the beach within 40 minutes – nearly as fast as the bus going downhill.

The main route continues left to the road, which you leave at the bus shelter and obvious track leading to the resumption of the cobbled way up to the monastery of Hozoviotíssas, reached just over half an hour out of Hóra. This freakish, wedge-shaped building abuts a reddish cliff 320 metres above the sea, and is considerably larger inside than it looks, with more than enough room for the handful of monks remaining. The present foundation dates from Byzantine Emperor Alexis Comnene's patronage between 1080 and 1088, but tradition asserts that there was some sort of religious community here from the early 9th century. Monks fleeing the iconoclast controversy brought a beloved ikon of the Virgin here from either a town or another cloister named Hozova somewhere in the Middle East – thus the name.

Visiting hours are 8 am to 2 pm and 5 to 7 pm in summer, with slight variations off-season; leg and arm coverings are available at the door if you forget modest dress. A long entrance stairway, tunnelled through solid rock, leads up to a reception room, and then to the rooftop church and balcony from

where you can sometimes see Astipálea island, 45 km to the south-east.

To carry on towards Egiáli, go through the wooden gate and pass the toilets teetering on the brink to the right. The trail, occasionally faint, labours for 75 minutes through a featureless thornbush desert until attaining a saddle with a well; just below passes the modern road. Don't go down to this, but veer up right towards a stone corral and two giant stone pillars; multiple goat traces soon consolidate into a single path.

Within 15 minutes you round a bend, with a glimpse allowed of the ancient round tower below at the hamlet of Ríkhti. You will also notice the debouchement of the prominent trail coming from Terláki hamlet and Hóra,

Kikládhes: Outside Hozoviotíssas Monastery, Amorgós

and indeed if you've already seen the monastery on a short excursion you might prefer this more scenic valley route up to here. The islanders say that this was in fact the main high road in years past, and they only used the path via Hozoviotíssas when north winds made the Terláki alternative impassable.

However you reach this point, continue towards the abandoned hamlet of Agrílas, with the bleak islet of Nikuriá, almost touching Amorgós, always before you; it was used as a leper colony until this century. Agrilás and its warren of fences, two hours along, occupies a saddle – highest point along the way – between Hill 488 with its trig point and some knobby outcrops. The path here threads between the dry-stone walls, then descends the other side of the pass rather faintly, with some cairns and red waymarks (facing you coming from Hóra) to guide you.

Reach the church at the western edge of Asfodilídhi (Asfodhilítis) 2½ hours into the day; unlike Agrilás, Asfodilídhi is partly inhabited in summer. The trail widens and gets revetment at a potable well, before bearing up and left on a mixed slag and cobble surface to the second-highest pass (about 350 metres, 2¾ hours out) of the route. It's distinguished by power lines, a single farm and two decapitated windmills; a conspicuous side turning leads down toward the hidden beach of Hálara.

(Some walkers, ascending from Egiáli, get lost here – *don't* stray off towards the northerly mill and an abandoned hamlet, but follow the power lines south-west.)

Curl around the head of a ravine and climb slightly, just over three hours out, to a chapel with end-on views of Nikuriá. From now on it's all downhill on a good kalderími to the edge of Potamós, the village just above Egiáli. Curve below the giant church here for the last bit of road to Egiáli, where you arrive after 4¼ hours of trekking. Except in August there should be no problem about accommodation; even if you're not staying the night, it would be a shame not to enjoy the beaches here before returning to the other end of the island.

Trek 2: North-Eastern Village Loop & Áyios Theológos

(2½-4¼ hours)

Dirt roads and frequent seasonal shuttle buses serve the two villages above Egiáli Bay, but most of the old paths still exist and make for modest half-day outings. Confusingly, Egiáli, the harbour settlement, is officially called Órmos, while Langádha, the southerly inland village, is formally Egiáli. (Everyone agrees that the northerly one is Tholária.) East of Langádha a clear but rugged trail leads to a fascinating early church and, eventually, to the summit of the island.

Begin on Órmos's main beach; at the northern end, hop up between stone walls and, upon reaching the new road, turn left and then immediately right past a chapel onto the path's continuation. It's just under an hour to Tholária's church, on the far side of which is a handsome café-snack bar, one of three in town and more like a mainland mountain magazí with its wood flooring. The name Tholária ('Vaults') refers presumably to the numerous Roman-era tombs which are the chief traces of the ancient town on a nearby hill; you'll need local assistance to find most of them.

The onward trail to Langádha exits the lower corner of the village, a small blue and white sign in Greek lettering pointing the way. Five minutes out of town, bear left at a fork to avoid unnecessary altitude loss; the path curls around the valley, seemingly in the wrong direction, but then swings south on a level course.

Half an hour out of Tholária there's a conspicuous junction. Straight ahead goes directly to Langádha, via the abandoned hamlet of Strúmbu (Strímbo). Take the left fork instead for 15 minutes to the commandingly sited church of Panayía Epanokhóri and its giant festival grounds, which come alive on 15 August. Continuing on past the church you'll intersect the broad kalderími between Áyios Theológos and Langádha; turn down and right. It's just an hour total from Tholária to the latter.

If you have had an early enough start, take

the time to bear left up towards the saddle and, after 50 occasionally cairned minutes, to the unusual church of Áyios Theológos. The lower walls consist of 5th-century masonry; there are fresco fragments in the apse, and the fascinating ground plan features two attic-like chapels elevated above the level of the nave. From here the trail continues up and around the flank of the mountain on a corniche route to the ksoklísi of Stavrós Pass and then cross-country west to the 821-metre trig point of Kríkello.

However, most people will leave that for another day, descending to Langádha in not much less time than it took to come up: there are two very sharp grades above the turn-off to Panayía Epanokhóri, and the kalderími is not a true one but mostly hacked out of rough rock. Allow one hour 40 minutes for the detour just to Áyios Theológos.

Langádha has a good lunch spot, a Greek-German-run affair at the lower end of the village. Leaving from the very bottom end of town, take the left fork at the cistern well (right goes down to the agricultural plain, and fizzles out). It's 35 minutes down to Órmos, the last five minutes an obligatory road tramp, for a total on the basic loop of just over 2½ hours.

Crete (Kríti)

The southernmost island of Europe suffers even more than the rest of Greece from a popular misconception that it is merely the seat of distantly past and vanished glories, in this case those of the Minoans. This view ignores a quirky Graeco-Venetian culture that flourished in three post-Byzantine centuries, followed by a bizarre, brutal Ottoman interlude of almost equal duration. Semi-autonomous status in 1898 was a prelude to union with the mainland 15 years later.

It's equally little known that Crete (Kríti) possesses some of the most striking wilderness in Greece, with rough-and-ready mountaineers, never completely subdued by occupying powers, to go with them. As you proceed west along the length of the island, past the isolated peaks of Dhíkti and Psilorítis to the imposing range of the Lefká Óri, both terrain and inhabitants assume legendary, larger-than-life proportions. A Cretan patriarch all got up in *tsalvária* (baggy pants), high boots, vest, leather apron and *saríki* (headband) invites you onto his porch for a *tsikudhiá* (terebinth spirits), and soon it's clear that, for him anyway, the heroic age is not over. Memories of the resistance against the German occupation during WW II are still fresh, and an enormous oral tradition keeps alive memories of Crete's (largely unsuccessful) struggle for independence against invaders from Byzantine to modern times.

Other Greeks regard the Kritikí (Cretans) with a mixture of amusement, fear and respect, stereotyping the island as the first and last bastion of freedom, and an arena for outrageous behaviour which has long since disappeared elsewhere in the nation. The locals in turn look down on the mainlanders, never missing an opportunity to remind visitors that Crete – *O Megalónisos* or 'The Great Island' in their parlance – is arguably the only portion of Greece that could go it alone. As recently as 1987, an armoured transport and a tank were discovered hidden in the hills after being stolen from an armoury on the island – whether as a prank or part of a serious plot by secessionists was unclear.

Even foreigners may form the opinion that the Kritikí embody all the Greek virtues and vices, but at triple strength. Nothing is done at half-measure: blood feuds, marriage by abduction, drunken three-day festivals, banditry, suicidal resistance against hopeless odds, and self-denying generosity were until quite recently staples of life – and have not yet disappeared entirely. Tune into Iráklio or Haniá radio stations and you can listen to the sheep-rustling report along with the evening news: '...stolen yesterday from the herdsman Tito Manusakis, at the location Dhafnólakkos, three rams, six three-year old ewes and four spring lambs, by an unknown person or persons...'

All this and too many late-night reruns of *Zorba* have contributed to the image of the islanders as super-Greeks, a reputation that they seem perfectly happy to bask in. Stripped of the hype, however, the Cretan character can best be summarised in one untranslatable word – *levendiá* – implying physical grace, musicality, eloquent wit, high spirits in the face of adversity, and self-sufficient pride. It's a quality prized in men and women alike.

Annoy a Cretan and you'll certainly catch the rough side of their tongue – in every sense, as the local accent and vocabulary are eccentric and the sorrow of beginners. In trying to understand the occasional overweening stance, it's as well to remember the words of the Sicilian Don Fabrizio in *The Leopard*, which apply equally here: 'They have come to teach us good manners! But they won't succeed, because we are gods.'

Maps

For a general journey-planning map, try the 1:200,000 Nelles Verlag or Geobuch publication, usually not available on Crete. This even occasionally shows trails correctly, though the scale is too small for navigating by landforms.

Access

All sea lanes, it seems, and quite a few air corridors, lead to Crete. There are boats in the tourist season every week to Italy, the former Yugoslavia, Turkey, Cyprus, Israel and Egypt; the last three destinations remain served through most of the winter as well. The assortment of international air charters from northern Europe – no scheduled flights directly to the island as yet – is too legion to list here.

Iráklio gets a daily direct overnight boat from Pireás, plus five to six weekly services in season from the most popular of the Kikládhes (Páros, Náxos, Íos and Thíra). Less often – perhaps twice weekly – there are links with Ródhos and Kárpathos in the Dhodhekánisos, as well as Míkonos, Tínos, Skíros, Skiáthos and Thessaloníki. Daily hydrofoils from many of the Kikládhes supplement the steamer schedules.

Réthimno's boat connections are restricted to the recently inaugurated four-times-weekly ferry from Pireás and an occasional hydrofoil from the Kikládhes. But the town makes a wonderful introduction to the island.

Haniá has a nightly service from Pireás, but no longer any links with Thessaloníki. If you're planning to visit Crete in tandem with the Pelopónnisos, it's well worth knowing about the little-publicised subsidised line (ágoni grammí) between certain tiny Arkadhian ports, Monemvassía, Yíthio, Kíthira island and Kastélli (west of Haniá); for years it has chugged through the Peloponnesian stops on Monday and Thursday afternoon and night, to arrive at Kastélli the next morning.

Iráklio gets at least four plane flights daily throughout the year from Athens, as well as one or two weekly from Thessaloníki and two or three from Ródhos, depending on the season. In summer, there are also three weekly air links with Thíra. Haniá is also well served from Athens, with three daily flights throughout the year; there is also one flight weekly from Thessaloníki.

I have not listed specific connections for the eastern towns of Sitía and Áyios Nikólaos since they are very remote from the trekking routes, but they too have extensive ferry links with the Kikládhes and the Dhodhekánisos, in addition to Sitía's plane flights from Kárpathos and Athens.

Psilorítis (Ídhi)

At 2456 metres, Psilorítis is Crete's highest summit by a scant three metres. Scenically it can't compare to the convoluted runner-up Lefká Óri to the west, and many hikers dutifully climb it just because it's there. The small sierra's chief claim to fame is the presence of two caves in its flanks. One, the Spíleon Kamáron on the southern slope, is of great archaeological significance; the Idhéon Ándron, at the edge of the Nídha plateau on the northern side, is similarly important and is also claimed (in rivalry with another cavern on Mt Dhíkti) to be the mythological birth chamber of Zeus.

CRETE'S HIGHEST POINT

The final ascent of the peak itself typically begins from the Nídha plateau, after a low-altitude approach from the southern side of the range. This in some ways is more interesting, but it is threatened as ever by recent road construction.

Rating & Duration

This is a moderately strenuous trek, with the effort apportioned over at least two days: the first day to get up to a campsite within striking distance of the peak, the second day involved in the round-trip climb from base camp, and possibly even a third day to get all the way down again.

Season

Spring (April) snowpack lends some interest to the alpine climb but will also slow you down – and hide the waymarks.

Supplies

Try to get your supplies in the provincial capital of Iráklio; stores in Kamáres and Vorízia are fairly basic.

Maps

Harms sheet No 3, *Iraklion*; otherwise use the British 1:50,000 wartime map *Crete Sheet 18 Timbákion* and *YIS 1:50,000 Timbákion** and *Anóyia**.

Access

Two daily buses ply from Iráklio to the villages of Kamáres and Vorízia on the southern side of the Psilorítis massif. If you are coming from the south, there is also at least one daily bus up from Míres on the Messarian plain.

Both Kamáres and Vorízia (three km east) are somewhat nondescript villages at about 660 metres elevation, with a hotel, a couple of seasonal tavernas and a store apiece. If you show up on the afternoon bus and wish to begin hiking immediately, the storekeepers will be happy to point you to the start of the paths; most villagers have caught on to the fact that foreigners come here principally to climb to the peak or the caves.

Stage 1: Kamáres/Vorízia to the Nídha Plateau

(4½ hours)

The path actually begins most distinctly in Vorízia; on my visit I tracked diagonally, cross-country, up from Kamáres until intersecting it. In either case the first hour involves a cruel climb over a juniper-tufted ridge, with views east over the villages of Záros and Nívritos. As the grade slackens, the hills of Alikadhám and Hafossokefála should be in front of you to the right. After another half an hour you'll arrive at a high tree-studded plateau with two stone corrals.

The now-faint path plunges into the welcome shade of a kermes oak grove as it parallels the ridgeline dividing the heads of two valleys to either side. Míra spring bubbles out about halfway up the escarpment looming behind the oak forest; look for a small trough, and the inevitable discarded rusty cans, just off the main trail about 2½ hours along.

Once past the spring (which is below the trail, in case you find the water but briefly lose the way), climb stiffly up a small, shallow gully next to a hogback; 20 minutes further along some red dots appear and help pull you over the difficult terrain. The rocky but waymarked path negotiates the pass separating the Psilorítis massif from its neighbour to the east, and then some 3¼ hours in the day arrives at the stáni of Kutsunára.

You can't miss the sturdy *kúmos* here, a type of stone roundhouse particular to alpine Crete whose design has roots in Neolithic times. Ten minutes beyond the kúmos (sometimes also called a *mítato*) many rivulets and a large trough spring gush forth from the depths of the mountain. It's a magic, favoured spot, with amazing perspectives over the foothills and Messará plain to the south; if you've had a late start out of Vorízia you could do far worse than camp here.

Four walking hours above your start, the high point (about 1500 metres) on the route to Nídha is marked by another kúmos; next you drop through limestone badlands towards an ugly new military road which has obliterated everything, including waymarks, in its wake. Hopefully the bulldozers will pass considerably below the trail description thus far but this cannot be depended on. Half an hour of walking separates you from the current trail's end and the margins of the Nídha plateau.

Nídha (a corruption of *stin Ídha*) is an oval, turfy basin about three km by two at an average altitude of 1360 metres. As you approach, three buildings come into sight: Análipsi chapel on the upper left and the EOS shelter and its gushing spring at the nearby site of Prínos, both just above the road; and a forlorn-looking taverna-inn ('Taverne Idain Andron...There is some beds') just below the track. It appears that this is no longer a going concern and that you'll have to camp on the thick green turf of the plateau, awaking to the nightingale-like singing of the *arfíkhtalo*, a bird indigenous to Nídha. The only possible sustenance other than what you brought along comes from the stáni consisting of a stone corral and a kúmos very close to the abandoned tourist facilities. The friendly shepherds may offer you some sheep's milk (an excellent breakfast) in exchange for helping them pen their sheep for milking – and possibly also a ride north off the mountain if you climb the peak as an out-and-back excursion.

Stage 2: Nídha Plateau to Tímios Stavrós

(7 hours return)

The classic route up to the Tímios Stavrós chapel on Psilorítis' summit begins at the EOS hut. Red dots lead you past Análipsi, its festival grounds, and the tombs of heroes of the 1866 and 1941-44 insurrections, to the side drive leading up to the Idhéon Ándron (closed indefinitely for ongoing archaeological excavation). The actual footpath begins at the second bend in the drive and mounts

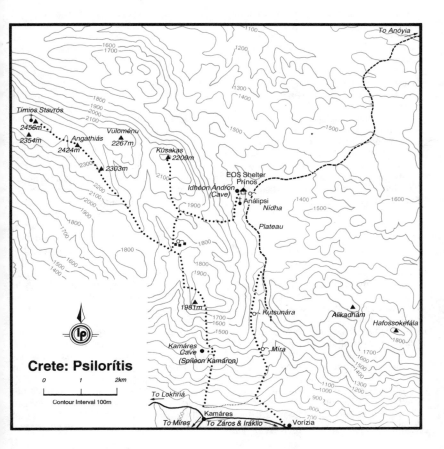

Crete: Psilorítis

0   1   2km

Contour Interval 100m

gradually up a ridge, going south-south-west.

After half an hour you'll reach a ravine, where you turn west so that your back's to Nídha and begin gaining height more sharply along a rocky path on the southern bank. You'll arrive at an exposed rise with a stone hut about one hour 45 minutes along. Don't follow the most prominent path here, which only goes to the secondary summit of Kúsakas, but follow the ridge downhill and south instead, as unproductive as this seems.

Within 10 minutes you'll arrive at a depression (about 1800 metres) where several trails meet, with more stone huts and another spring. Turn right (north-west) and adopt the obvious uphill trail, which will take you all the way to the 2456-metre peak in just under two hours. Because of the mountain's whaleback shape, however, it's only in the last few minutes that the peak becomes visible, as the slopes steepen on either side of you.

The chapel on top is a double-domed dry-stone affair with a small belfry. A cistern nearby under piled rocks is usually potable, with a handy can for fetching the water, but it's best not to count on this. Nor can you rely on the panorama, which is often ruined by heat haze or storm clouds. You should, in fact, be equipped and ready to seek shelter at any of the stone structures along the way, since Psilorítis's weather can turn nasty at short notice.

A round trip from Nídha shouldn't take more than seven hours; however, if you've taken a full pack as far as the spring and huts at the 1800-metre depression, halfway along, a more attractive option might be to adopt the southerly trail here which eventually ends up in Kamáres after five hours. Midway through this you pass the side trail to the huge Kamáres cave – Spíleon Kamáron – (c 1400 metres), in which a large trove of painted Minoan urns were discovered. From here down to Kamáres the way is marked and fairly heavily trodden, since the cave by itself is a fairly popular destination from Kamáres village. If the new road between Nídha and Vorízia has in fact obliterated the

lower trail described, you may well want to take the cave route both ways.

Lefká Óri & the Sfakiá Coast

Draw a line from Súyia to Frangokástello on Crete's south-western coast, and you have the diameter of Sfakiá, a roughly semicircular district in Haniá province that constitutes one of the most rugged, inaccessible and fascinating areas of the island. The Lefká Óri ('White Mountains') form the heart of it, rearing up from sea level to over 2400 metres elevation less than 10 km inland. These karstic peaks take their name from their dazzling appearance, which lends a cruel illusion of snow cover even in summer, when nothing could be further from the truth – this is essentially high-altitude desert, with not a drop of water or a blade of grass to be found in most spots.

On their northern flanks the Lefká Óri rise, marginally more gently, from the fertile, well-watered coastal plain beyond Sfakiá. On the south, however, as the mountains plunge precipitously to the shore, they are riven by more than a dozen deep, dramatic gorges – that of Samariá is the most celebrated and hiked through. Where water, herds of goats or a past vocation at smuggling and livestock-rustling permitted, tiny villages still barely hold on, lately given a new lease on life by tourism. Until recently no roads penetrated this district, and many of these settlements are still linked by good trails used more now by foreigners than locals.

French and German-speaking visitors predominate, and apparently the French trekking company Terre l'Aventure pioneered many of the high-altitude routes as far as outsiders are concerned.

If you'd like a guide for a traverse not described here, it might be a good idea to contact EOS Hani (☎ (0821) 24 647), at Dzanakáki 90. This branch is supposed to be open nightly from 8.30 to 11 pm; see if Sifis Pendhrakis (that's a man) or Tatiana (a woman) are in town – they once worked at the Astráka shelter in Ípiros, know the Lefká Óri well, and can speak enough English to work with foreigners.

Warning

You'll generally have some company even on the lonlier traverses, and in October 1992 EOS Haniá members spent some time waymarking the more popular routes. This is the most deadly wilderness area in Greece, with fatalities recorded nearly every year – admittedly as much because of greater numbers compared to Ólimbos as owing to intrinsic danger. Always carry far more water than you think you'll need, and do not leave the marked trails or cross-country routes detailed below without a large-scale map and a local guide – and I don't mean any of the foreign trek leaders, who often get their groups into the worst trouble.

If you think I'm being alarmist, you'll see what I mean once you get up in the high country. The hut warden at Kalérgi and the national park authorities at Samariá regularly summon rescue helicopters, and are tired of doing so – sometimes they find the lost individual half dead, other times they're too late, and occasionally not even the numerous vultures find the body. Even experienced mountaineers from Haniá are reduced to tears of frustration, wandering in karst mazes where identical, uncountable pinnacles and needles can only be distinguished by subtle colour differences. Goats, who normally fear people, may approach you hoping for a drink of water. It's that sort of country.

Rating & Duration

Treks hereabouts all earn a moderate to difficult rating, depending on the season and your pack weight. This applies equally to the mass-tourist Samariá gorge traverse, attempted by far too many out-of-condition, bus-borne tour customers. Routes combining mountains and gorge will certainly exceed 30 km, possibly 40 km, with potential altitude changes of over 4800 metres.

Because of the circular nature of the trail system described, you could conceivably spend a week here, never walking any sector twice. Most people will choose between the gorge route and the Lefká Óri traverse, finishing with some coastal trekking, which can be comfortably done in three or four days respectively.

Season

Along with some of the smaller Dhodhekánisos islands, this is one of the most torrid parts of Greece in midsummer, which here can be considered to be from mid-June to the first week of September. If you are thinking of hiking here at that time – in a word, don't. All of the safety problems described above are aggravated by the real danger of heatstroke at sea level and the potential drying-up of the few water sources on the peaks. Spring snowbanks, as long as they're not so thick as to hide the high trails, might save your life if you need to melt snow for drinking.

Easter on Crete usually features ideal trekking weather, though the sea is generally too cold for swimming. September has the best coastal swimming, but of course the summer drought higher up persists. The famous gorge itself is closed owing to flood danger from November to late April. In September/October it is plagued by dangerous falls of boulders set rolling by the Cretan ibex descending the crags in search of water and greenery.

Supplies

The most satisfying shopping trip is at the covered central market in Haniá, where there's a wealth of dried, cured and fresh goodies packaged in a trekker-friendly manner. A corkscrew-like walking stick made of extremely sturdy abelitsia wood (*Zelkova abelicea*, a dwarf relative of the elm, which grows in the Lefká Óri) might be a wise investment; these are getting rare as the little trees are being afflicted by the local version of Dutch elm disease. You can also efficiently stock up in Réthimno if you're coming from that direction.

Maps

British 1:50,000 wartime maps *Crete, Sheet 5, Voukoliés Lákkoi*; *Crete, Sheet 6, Soúdha Vámos* (only for the high traverse); *Crete, Sheet 15, Khóra Sfakíon* (for both high traverse and the coast); and *Crete, Teménia, Sheet 14* (for the gorge of Samariá and the Gíngilos-Kustoyérako link trail); or YIS 1:50,000 *Vatólakkos**and *Vrísai**. Finally available is Harms sheet No 1, *Hania*.

Access

From Haniá there are four buses daily from May to October at 6.15, 7.30 and 8.30 am, and at 4.30 pm, to Ksilóskala at the top of the Samariá gorge, also the trailhead for the Kalérgi refuge and the Gíngilos-Kustoyérako route. The bus goes back immediately on arrival, which is 90 minutes later. If you opt for one of the early departures, bus-station staff assume that you're day-tripping down the gorge and will automatically attempt to sell you an extra ticket from Hóra Sfakíon to Haniá – if you don't want this, say so. If you're attempting the Gíngilos day hike or the full Lefká Óri traverse, the 8.30 am and 4.30 pm departures respectively are fine – in spring you'll reach the refuge just at twilight.

Coming from Réthimno, the first buses of the day (at 6.15 and 7 am) to Haniá either continue themselves to Ksilóskala or make a direct connection in Haniá. The initial 5 am Kastélli to Haniá bus behaves in the same fashion.

If you'd rather forgo the high-altitude walks and stick to the coast, your starting point will be either Hóra Sfakíon or Anópoli. The former has three daily services from Haniá, at 8.30 and 11 am, plus 2 pm, with a prompt turnaround two hours later. There is also one daily service in the high season, at around 10 am, from the popular beach resorts of Plakiás and Frangokástello to the east.

Approaching Hóra Sfakíon or Anópoli from Réthimno, you'll have to change buses at Vríses, halfway to Haniá; allow an hour to get there. Anópoli, 12 twisty km above Hóra Sfakíon, has one daily service from Haniá at 1 pm, passing through Hóra at 4 pm.

The footsore can catch a lift along some or all of the Sfakiá coast by the small passenger ferries which link Hóra, Lutró and Ayía Rúmelli (at the bottom of the Samariá gorge) up to five times daily from mid-

June to September; perhaps two or three a day during May and October; and according to a skeletal schedule tfor the rest of the year for the benefit of the locals. The exact date when extra departures kick in varies from year to year, depending on the tourist load; check at the Haniá port police or tourist information office.

HIGH-LEVEL TRAVERSE & COASTAL TREKS

Despite the Lefká Óri's grim reputation, the rewards are in proportion to the dangers. The mineral colours and landforms are striking, and up top you really do lord it over the western end of Crete, from the Aegean to the Libyan seas. No desert mirage ever looked better than the little port of Lutró after a north-to-south traverse of the summit area. And there's a big difference between a beach that can only be walked to and one targeted by excursion boats and roads.

Stage 1: Ksilóskala to Pákhnes via Katsivélli

(7¾ hours)
This stage was waymarked in red paint during September 1992.

From Ksilóskala (1200 metres), set off on the signposted trail up to Kalérgi refuge which begins climbing north-north-east from the wood-fenced area at the top of the gorge of Samariá. After about half an hour the trail ends at a bend in the recent dirt road coming up from the nearly circular plain of Omalós, which has been in sight for much of the way. Turn right and follow this jeep track uphill to a summit, where there's a kúmos and a memorial plaque to a shepherd executed here by German occupation forces during WW II.

Bear right here again for the last few minutes of the one hour 20 minutes up to the Kalérgi refuge at 1680 metres. This is open from May to October inclusive, and managed by Austrian Josef Schwemmberger in cooperation with EOS Haniá. Accommodation consists of six quads (US$9 per person) and an eight-bunk dorm (US$6 apiece) with sheets and other bedding

Top: Sfakiá Coast, Crete: Áyios Pávlos Chapel, between Ayía Rúmelli and Lutró (MD)
Left: Lefká Óri, Crete: The Sidherespórtes of the gorge of Samariá (MD)
Right: Sfakiá Coast, Crete: Trekking from the Sellúdha to Áyios Ioánnis (MD)

Sími: Bay & chapel-monastery of Áyios Vasílios (MD)

included in the fee. Half-board is available, and the hut, possibly the most comfortable staffed shelter in Greece, also has heating, a water tank on a trailer outside for tapping when no-one's home, a CB radio for summoning help in emergencies, and a phone (☎ (0821) 54 560). It is strongly suggested that you phone to reserve bunks in the high season. Josef, who speaks English and some French as well as German, has it rigged to ring either up on the mountain or down on his boat in Haniá harbour if he's there. Josef or his Greek assistant will provide any extra information you need on the area and also a photocopy of the German wartime map, inferior to the British product but sufficient to get you to Anópoli safely as long as you stay on the designated route; unhappily their copy does not adequately show the trail below Amutséra – trust the directions in this book.

After enjoying the morning views across to Gíngilos peak and down into the gorge, proceed east along the track 50 minutes to the outcrop-studded saddle of Poriá (1500 metres), with a bracken meadow and a shepherds' colony successively to the north.

The recently extended track bends northeast now and begins to climb slightly; you leave it about one hour 15 minutes along, ascending a ravine flanked by red numbers '25' and '26' painted on the rock at about 1600 metres. There's no trail, but the grade is tolerable.

Some 2½ hours into the day you'll emerge on the saddle just south-west of 2030-metre Mávri summit, to be treated to an awesome look down into the far corner of the Samariá gorge system. Pick up a faint but cairned trail going east-north-east towards Melidaú, the double-humped peak on the east, with distinctive folded bands of rock on its steep southern face. Within 10 minutes you'll come out on the prominent, windswept 2000-metre saddle between Mávri and Melidaú. In addition to the new red paint splodges, older yellow dots and arrows begin to appear, indicating the onward route; there are fine views from here over Haniá town and the north-eastern corner of the national park of Samariá.

A bit over three hours along you'll attain a small plateau just short of Melidaú's 2133-metre trig point. The path is now faint, but yellow and sometimes red paint splodges, courtesy of the Kalérgi refuge staff, guide you along the southern flank of the peak and then off the mountain towards limestone dells ahead. You'll notice a single pasture down and right at the edge of an abyss. By 3¾ hours you should be at the head of this chasm, where you bear south-east into a level dirt-patch 'bowling alley' at about 2000 metres. Soon a trail of sorts resumes, descending to Plakosélli pasture (1800 metres) 4¼ hours along. Here there's a large (three-metre-wide) open well whose water is a bit murky and is best purified or treated.

Now waymarks take you south-south-east down a shallow gully to the next pasture and cistern at Pirrú, 4½ hours into the day. However, unlike at Plakosélli, the water level here is far below the surrounding ground; if the shepherds are not on hand to fetch it for you with their buckets, you'll have to devise something with your kit.

Continue south from Pirrú, following blazes slightly up and left away from the apparent 'main' trail which leads down to another well and pastoral colony at Potamús. This is at the head of the Eliyía gorge draining past Áyios Ioánnis village, but again don't attempt passage without the best map available and a local escort. Instead, round the hillside with little altitude change until swerving sharply east and beginning to climb away from Potamús. A well-designed and sometimes revetted trail appears, snaking through a maze of limestone dells and potholes, and waymarks accordingly diminish. The higher summits of Lefká Óri, most noticeably conical 2224-metre Modháki, glow in what is now certainly late afternoon light.

Nearly 6½ hours along, arrive at the stáni of Katsivélli (1970 metres), where there's a proper spring and three kúmi roundhouses whose Anópoli tenants are armed to the teeth against rustlers. Fill up with as much water as you can carry here, since sources from now until close to Anópoli are unreliable.

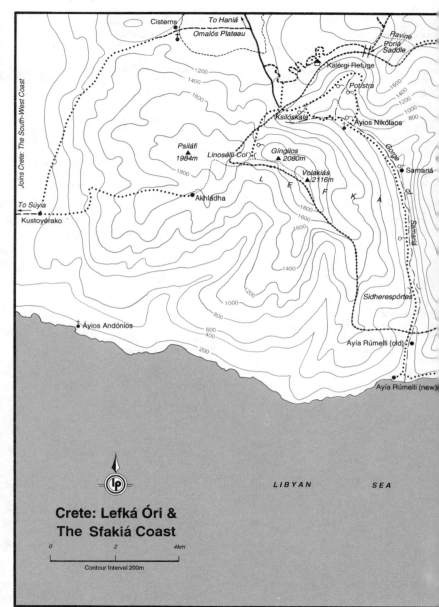

Cisterns

To Haniá

Omalós Plateau

Ravine
Poriá
Saddle

Kalérgi Refuge

1200

1400

1600

Potístra

Ksilóskala

1600
1400
1200
1000
800

Áyios Nikólaos

Psiláfi
1984m

Linosélli Col

Gíngilos
2080m

Volakiás
2116m

L E F K Á

Gorge

Samariá

Joins Crete: The South-West Coast

1800

To Súyia

Kustoyérako

Akhládha

1800

1600
1600

Samariá
of

1400

Sidherespórtes

1200

Áyios Andónios

1000

800
600
400

200

Ayía Rúmeli (old)

Ayía Rúmeli (new)

LIBYAN   SEA

**Crete: Lefká Óri &
The Sfakiá Coast**

0   2   4km

Contour Interval 200m

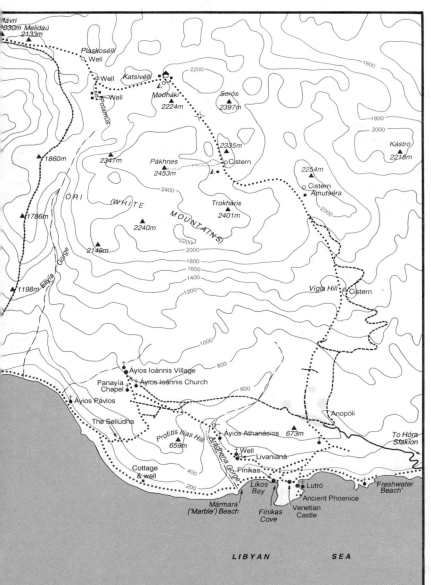

Mávri
2030m Melidaú
2133m

Pláskosélli
Well

Well   Katsivélli

Well   Modháki
2224m

Sorós
2397m

Kástro
2218m

2335m

1860m   2347m   Pákhnes
2453m   Cistern

2254m

Cistern
Amutséra

2400

ÓRI   (WHITE)   Trokháris
2401m

1786m   MOUNTAINS

2000

2240m

2149m

1198m   Elivía Gorge

Vígla Hill   Cistern

1000

800

Áyios Ioánnis Village

Panayía   Áyios Ioánnis Church
Chapel

Áyios Pávlos

Anopóli

The Sellúdha

To Hóra
Sfakíon

Profítis Ilías Hill   Áyios Athanásios   673m
659m

Well

Livanianá

Cottage   Fínikas
& well

Líkos
Bay   Lutró

Freshwater
Beach

Mármara   Ancient Phoenice
('Marble') Beach   Fínikas   Venetian
Cove   Castle

LIBYAN   SEA

A large (100-bunk) but presently unstaffed refuge, built by EOS Haniá in 1992, stands in a gully to the west; you'll have passed it on your way in. East of the shepherds' colony you may notice waymarking for a new trail in from Askífu, a village on the Haniá-Hóra Sfakíon road.

Now you've a 20-minute climb to a saddle at about 2100 metres, offering a good look at the main summits to the south-west. The route then threads along a ridge between deep depressions in the surrounding moonscape to the next saddle, in front of you to the right at about 2200 metres, just under an hour out of Katsivélli.

After another 20 minutes you'll reach a third saddle at about the same height, at the foot of which is an open cottage suitable for three persons, several bivvy barriers, and a concrete cistern. This is the base of Pákhnes, and your home for the night, since you'll have been walking for more than 7½ hours. You may have to fish for the water with a roped container and secure your food against mice, which amazingly survive in this desolate landscape.

Sidetrip: Ascent of Pákhnes

A climb of the peak is best done as a wake-up exercise before moving on to the next stage. It is a fairly straightforward ascent, with sporadic cairns and scooped-out climbers' traces. First skirt a group of dells west of the hut, then crawl up along the northern flank of an initial cairned false summit, aiming for a saddle west of this. Next you claw your way up scree piles to another false peak, but the worst is over – from there it's just an easy walk along the ridge to the very ordinary true summit, 50 minutes above your base camp. There's a visitors book in a plastic box to sign, just at the base of the 2453-metre marker. The panorama is not as good as you'd hope, owing to a confining ring of other peaks; make for the next flat-topped cairn to the west for better views towards Samariá. The return to the hut takes nearly as long owing to the terrain and surface underfoot.

Stage 2: Pákhnes to Lutró via Anópoli
(6¼ hours)

The clearly defined trail south of Pákhnes twists through some of the harshest, most lunar terrain yet – the limestone is anything but white here, including a rather grisly black variety, and there are a couple of sinkholes by the trail down which it would be easy enough to disappear in poor visibility. After one hour 15 minutes of this you'll arrive at Amutséra (1800 metres), where there's a two-person shelter and a cistern provided with a bucket. Unfortunately, the cistern seems to have a cracked bottom, as the water was almost gone in June following a wet winter.

Within 10 minutes of leaving Amutséra you'll collide with the ugly new road; just a few moments along this, about 20 minutes worth of old trail survives to considerably short cut the road to its west, to just above the 1600-metre level. Walk a few minutes more on the joint road-trail, and then bear right into the head of a shallow ravine; there are occasional cairns and waymarks.

The path, unmolested from here on, plunges purposefully south along the canyon bed, between rows of horizontal cypresses; scrub oaks and maples pop up below 1600 metres. At the base of Vígla hill, 2½ hours below Pákhnes base camp, a very handsome old vaulted cistern at about 1350 metres is reliable, but again you'll have to go fishing for a drink.

Beyond this point, well-engineered and buttressed switchbacks tackle a very abrupt drop; at about 1200 metres pines appear, and at just under 1100 metres a gap in the trees some three hours below Pákhnes allows your first look at Anópoli on its wide *kámbos* (agricultural plain).

You'll reach the mouth of this ravine, with a kink in the new road passing by and an ikónisma and a kúmos adjacent, nearly four hours along, at about 750 metres. The path continues downhill and a few moments later crosses another road perpendicularly for a more gentle descent through pines. Finally, the trail system runs out at a curve in the track; go straight, then around a concrete barn with a well to its right. Cover the last few minutes of the 4½ hours from the foot of Pákhnes to the upper, kafenío-bus stop plaza of Anópoli (600 metres). Have a drink here, but unless you want to stay the night – a possibility – leave enough time for the final descent to Lutró.

At the main, lower, platía with its monument to Dhaskaloyannis (an unsuccessful 18th-century rebel against Ottoman rule), the town hall and the handful of places to eat and stay, find 'LOUTRO NO CAR' scrawled on a wall across from a small shady cafe. Virtually all lanes and paths, as well as the indicated vehicle track, dwindle and converge on a footpath among the southernmost houses of Anópoli, with a splendid view over the fertile basin and the flanks of Lefká Óri to the north.

The landmark to aim for, reached some 20 minutes from 'downtown', is the chapel perched on a bluff. Fifteen minutes past the crest separating the high upland from the sea, take the right fork; there's little possibility of confusion from here on, since your goal lies before you (albeit in toy-like dimensions) and the steep palisade is as bare and grim as can be imagined. Forty minutes further down the limestone slope, the direct trail to Fínikas forks right (west); pass it. Stray vegetation begins appearing and soon you meet the Hóra Sfakíon-to-Lutró trail between a white ikónisma and the ruined easternmost house of Lutró. A few paces more into the hamlet itself brings the elapsed time from Anópoli to one hour 40 minutes, for a walking total on the day (not counting the Pákhnes climb) of well over six hours.

Lutró has been 'discovered' in recent years and is no longer quite the cold-saltwater-only rustic resort it once was. All creature comforts are on offer, at a price – but after two days of roughing it you'll gladly treat yourself at one of the new generation of pensions that's mushroomed here. It's still accessible only by boat or on foot, and the locals, plus the somewhat escapist clientele, seem happy to keep it that way. Stroll past the half a dozen tavernas of an evening, and you'll soon meet everybody – an intimacy

abetted by the somewhat claustrophobic scenery. For breakfast try *kalitsúnia*, the delicious local cheese-and-herb turnovers. The rocky beach is nothing to get excited about, but kayaks and snorkelling gear are rented for forays to better coves nearby. Alternatively, walk.

Sidetrips: Day Hikes around Lutró
Lutró to Hóra Sfakíon This route, which begins at the ikónisma and abandoned house noted in Stage 2 previously, is heavily travelled and hemmed in between the sea and vertical rock faces most of the way, so this trail description is not meticulous. Instead, it's a freak of nature about halfway to Hóra that merits attention.

The famous 'Freshwater Beach' lies about an hour east of Lutró, just past a white chapel on a promontory. Fresh water percolates down from the cliffs above into several potholes in this 700-metre arc of pebbles. A semipermanent colony of nudist campers here does a good job of keeping the beach and sea clean, and asks you not to lather up in the drinking 'wells'. The only other facilities are a tiny taverna at the western end of the beach, and occasional excursion boats from Lutró and Hóra. There used to be caves for sheltering out of the sun, but two collapsed in 1992, killing two bathers in the process.

The trail east to Hóra was badly damaged by storms in 1991 at a point 15 minutes above the beach, and may very well be impassable to those with a full pack (you'd probably prefer the ferry to Hóra anyway, with 18 kilos on your back). Beyond the landslide zone, good cobbling resumes until you intersect the Hóra-to-Anópoli asphalt road as it first swerves inland. Walking 40 minutes down the road brings you to Hóra, some 2¼ hours out of Lutró. Should you be reversing these directions, you can easily recognise the trailhead by the dirt turning area where cars are always parked; Freshwater Beach is visible to the west.

Loop via Livanianá & the Lower Arádhena Gorge In Lutró, begin behind the

main church and the waterfront kiosk – don't take the trail south around the cape, which merely ends among sparse ruins, possibly those of ancient Phoenice. Zig-zag up 10 minutes to the ruined Venetian castle and a vaulted cistern, which you pass about 100 metres to its north. After shunning the waymarked turn-off right to Anópoli, dip briefly towards the cove of Fínikas with its two dhomátia establishments. Climbing once more, cut across a section of ugly new road, following blue paint splodges that draw you across terraces to the crest of a bluff with some pens, which divides Fínikas from the remoter bay of Líkos.

The trail splits again here; bear right, go through a gate and cross a portion of ugly new road twice, always ascending towards LivaniMná, visible among its olive trees. A good kalderími takes over now, bringing you to the usually reliable well at the edge of the village, just under an hour out of Lutró. You'll see another section of road high above you to the right which may eventually reach the hamlet and disrupt the trail debouchement, but for now the project seems stalled and in any case will not save Livanianá from dereliction. The very hospitable population has fallen to 35, and there's no mains electricity or kafenío.

Head up now to the church at the top of the village and an adjacent cistern at about 250 metres elevation. Go straight through a gap in some fencing, then bear right and slightly down with a blue arrow; don't go hard right and up along the ridge, as this only leads to Anópoli or the head of the new road. Note the position of the small ksoklísi of Áyios Athanásios on a 350-metre-high knoll to the north; you'll need to head there by line of sight over abandoned olive terraces, since the trail fizzles to nothing over the next 20 minutes.

Once there, head north-west from the front door, over thornbush terraces studded with wild pear trees. A single path on this bearing snakes down to the bed of the Arádhena gorge, which you reach 40 minutes out of Livanianá. Just before the bottom, a grotto on the right contains a mossy drip-spring

filling a trough; take advantage, as this is the most water you'll see all day.

Ignore for now the marked continuation on the far bank of the gorge, but turn left instead, following cairns downstream. The Arádhena gorge is a very respectable second to the more famous canyon of Samariá, and its traverse is an increasingly popular outing from Lutró. The upper reaches, between the bridge by Arádhena village and where the trail has just entered, is Tarzan stuff, with a lot of rope ladders and iron spikes, some recently storm-damaged. The 45 minutes below the trail to the sea is much easier, but there are still some long drops and scrambles. Follow the cairns, even when this seems illogical – there's always a good reason why. About halfway down there's another, much weaker spring, if you neglected to fill up before.

The small pebbly cove where you exit the oleander-choked gorge is called Mármara, or 'Marble Beach'. Though much smaller and less popular than Freshwater, it too has an afternoon boat back to Lutró. If you miss it, it's a simple and fairly pleasant matter to walk back to Lutró in 50 minutes. First there's about 20 minutes on a ledge just above the water, until dipping to sea level just before the first taverna of reefy Líkos Bay; the onward path has been enterprisingly waymarked in blue through the terraces of two of the businesses here. Once beyond these the path climbs up to the fenced crest, to rejoin your outbound trail.

Stage 3A: Lutró to Ayía Rúmelli via the Coast
(4½ hours)
This is a heavily used path, accordingly well waymarked in red and yellow blazes. However, much of the scenery is dull, and there's little shade and no water along the way. With a light pack you may well want to consider Stage 3B instead.

Simply reverse the directions given at the end of Stage 2 to get from Lutró to Mármara; once there continue up the western flank of the bay for a half-hour slog over to a hillock, where you'll have your last look at Fínikas and its castle. After another 45 minutes you pass a lonely cottage by a stock trough and unreliable well, and within as much time again, having entered the first fringes of pine forest, you reach an important junction: straight for Ayía Rúmelli, hairpin right up to Áyios Ioánnis (see Stage 3B).

Fifteen minutes of gradual descent brings you to the beach at Áyios Pávlos, a 13th or 14th-century chapel (with damaged frescoes) marooned on a pebbly ledge with sand dunes all around. On this spot the apostle Paul is said to have made the first of his several landfalls on Crete, baptising converts at a spring here. 'Spring?' you may laugh, as you fling your heat-maddened self into the water to find it surprisingly chilly, even in summer. The reason is a phenomenon identical to that at Freshwater Beach. Dig down about 30 cm in the sand here, and the hole will fill with more or less drinkable water – the only evidence of the fountain which ran out in the open until a hundred years ago. Boat captains used to heave to offshore here and lower buckets to collect the cold, sweet water gushing from the shallow ocean floor.

It's just over another hour, for a total of 4½ hours, from here to Ayía Rúmelli. Though the path surface varies from sand to pebbles to packed dirt, it's difficult to get lost, what with power poles to mark the way.

Reverse Itinerary If for some reason you're reversing this stage of the trek, you need to look for a small, way-marked gap in the eastern bank of the alluvial debris where the Samariá gorge meets the sea. The only other possible moments of confusion are just above Áyios Pávlos – where you may have to fetch about for the resumption of the trail in the pines – and of course the all-important fork a few moments later (go right to stick with the coast).

Stage 3B: Lutró to Ayía Rúmelli via Áyios Ioánnis

(5¾ hours)

Despite some fierce altitude changes, you may well prefer this to Stage 3A. You don't miss out on Áyios Pávlos beach, much more of the way is in shade, and Áyios Ioánnis is well placed for a lunch stop. Waymarking on this route is technicolour – red, blue, even yellow.

Follow the directions from Lutró, through Livianá, up to the trail-crossing of the Arádhena gorge. This time, do head up the other bank; faint old red dots and cairns guide you up 25 minutes of tight, initially overgrown switchbacks. Don't go up the right-hand ravine when the gully splits. The grade lessens and the still-faint trail straightens out, skirting a livestock pen straddling the head of the gulch here. Ninety minutes out of Livianá, or 50 minutes above the gorge bed, cross a larger trail coming in on the left from Profítis Ilías hill. A few minutes later you'll see scattered bits of fencing and more pens; intersect a new secondary track from Arádhena village and walk under the power lines going directly to Ayía Rúmelli.

Turn left onto the narrow track, then keep straight, for once ignoring red arrows pointing left again to who-knows-where. Five minutes later, an old trail veers off to the right through pine woods. Adopt it, and 25 minutes later you'll be at the outskirts of Áyios Ioánnis (800 metres), some two hours above Livianá.

In the last few moments you'll arrive at a T-junction with another, bigger path. Down and left leads to Ayía Rúmelli; however, turn right to go up to the village entrance, with a gate across the ugly new access road from Anópoli, a well and the 'Kafe Taverna'.

The village's story is a sad and revealing one, which you may learn anyway if you have lunch here. As late as the early 1980s, Áyios Ioánnis had a population of about 100 and enough children to support a primary school. But it had no electricity or a road, and a chronic water shortage. Disgusted at the government's neglect, the inhabitants drifted away until today there are barely 20 permanent inhabitants, and the school has become the taverna. The bulldozers and power lines came too late (in 1987-88), as the villagers may bitterly tell you. And the water has not yet arrived, if it ever will. Under the circumstances the destruction of the beautiful cobbled trail from Anópoli via Arádhena was fairly pointless; Arádhena itself had pretty much emptied out after 1948, when an interclan feud over some sheep caused the deaths of a dozen men in a single day.

To resume progress towards Ayía Rúmeli, descend the stony path between the double-nave church of Áyios Ioánnis and the smaller white one of Panayía, but keep right, following yellow waymarks and avoiding the narrower trail on the left along which you arrived. In the next few moments you'll pass a corral on your right, and cross a track leading to a well on your left. Some 15 minutes beyond the village, approach a second pen, but rather than pass it, turn right across a small dry wash. The faint trail rapidly becomes an obvious right-of-way as you climb out of the gully and head for the brink of the 600-metre-high coastal cliffs.

From the edge Ayía Rúmelli is just visible to the west, as part of a sweeping vista over 20 km of shoreline. An extremely rocky but nonetheless magnificent kalderími, called the Sellúdha, zig-zags an hour down to the coast, merging as it levels out with the seaside trail from Lutró described in Stage 3A. (However, much of it is currently badly obstructed by fallen trees and boulders dislodges by the freak snows of 1991-92, and needs cleaning to be comfortably passable). From here on the route directions are identical.

Total hiking time from Lutró via this inland itinerary is about 5¾ hours, or only 75 minutes more than the coast route – assuming no getting lost. People hike *up* the Sellúdha fairly frequently, but that's best done with a very early start out of Ayía Rúmelli. A very keen day hiker could turn left at the base of the Sellúdha and return to Lútro in about 2½ hours, or seven hours in total.

ASCENT OF THE SAMARIÁ GORGE

The passage of the majestic gorge of Samariá is certainly the single most popular walking tour on the whole island, and possibly in all of Greece. Inevitably, the reality suffers in comparison to the tour-company hyperbole,

and the sheer numbers of people parading up and down have largely compromised any feel of wilderness, but no trek through the Lefká Óri would be complete without the traverse.

At over 16 km in length, the gorge (as you'll be told endlessly when here) is the longest in Europe. It opens out abruptly just beyond the Omalós highland, the upper reaches nestled between Gíngilos peak and the Kalérgi spur, and then curls from an east-south-east orientation to an almost due south one as it undergoes most of the elevation drop involved. A bit closer to the top than midway is the empty hamlet of Samariá, inhabited until 1962 almost exclusively by members of the Viglis clan. Many of them were notorious sheep rustlers, and all of them were involved in an ongoing feud with the village of Lákki, below the Omalós. So when the authorities created the national park in 1962 to protect the local natural resources, they dealt with several other problems simultaneously by evacuating the village.

Incidentally, the name 'Samariá' has nothing to do with either the Biblical kingdom or the Virgin Mary, but is a contraction of Osia Maria ('Mary the Beatified'). This minor Egyptian saint is one of the most curious in the Orthodox iconographic cycle. A much-desired Alexandrine courtesan, Osia Maria repented of her ways and retired to the desert for 40 years. She was found on the point of death by Zozimas, abbot of a nearby monastery, and is traditionally shown in frescoes as a withered, simian figure being spoon-fed by him like an infant.

Contrary to almost unanimous belief, an uphill trek as described here is not that difficult an exercise; the only severe altitude change occurs in the highest five km, in generally cool alpine conditions. It's certainly not in the same league as the tortuous 800-metre ascent from sea level to Áyios Ioánnis via the Sellúdha, over scarcely three horizontal km.

There is also the added advantage of enjoying the gorge in relative solitude, since you only meet the oncoming hordes briefly, part way through, rather than having to pass and be passed repeatedly as will happen if you start lemming-like with almost everyone else from Ksilóskala.

Also, morning at the bottom and late afternoon at the top are quite pleasant, requiring a minimum of clothing changes, while dawn starts at the head of the gorge are close to freezing and afternoon arrivals at the sea are only made bearable by the thought of a swim.

Furthermore, you can leave your own or hired transport at Ksilóskala, and finish a loop comprising the four stages described.

Rules & Regulations The gorge is open from 1 May to 31 October, with variations in the exact dates according to local conditions. At the discretion of the wardens, you may be allowed through before or after these dates if it's been determined that there is no danger of flash-flooding. The restrictions were instituted after several hikers drowned in head-high waters at the narrowest points in the gorge. The park area is open from 6 am to 3.30 pm for full traverses, with entry allowed only to the first two km at either end between 3.30 pm and sunset.

At both the upper and lower boundaries of the park, next to the path, large placard-maps summarise the botanical biomes of the reserve and pinpoint water, shelter or firefighting locations along the trail. Another sign lists prohibitions against flower gathering, littering, hunting or otherwise molesting animals, fires or smoking, radios, leaving the main trail, bathing in the streams, and camping.

At each entry to the canyon there's also a staffed 'traffic control' post where, in exchange for an admission fee (currently US$5), you're issued a dated ticket which you must surrender at the opposite end. If you lose this you might have to pay the entry charges again, and if you present a day-old ticket it will be assumed that you've camped illegally in the park.

Stage 1: Ayía Rúmelli to Ksilóskala
(6 hours)

Ayía Rúmelli, at least the new settlement on the shore near the mouth of the gorge, is a relentlessly functional place strictly dedicated to processing the waves of tourists descending the gorge (and the trickle venturing up). The hotels and eateries here are uniformly overpriced – a good 33% more than at Lutró – owing to a combination of a captive audience and the cost of transporting supplies. The only real asset, aside from the obvious kiosk selling boat tickets out, is the huge pebble-and-sand beach here.

Campers will want to pitch tents either behind that beach, where some of the tavernas may let you use their showers if you eat there, or in the favoured areas east of the village around the gorge mouth, where those tank-trap-like things are part of a solar power generation plant.

Leaving new Ayía Rúmelli, the trail keeps to the left (west) bank of the gorge which narrows drastically about 500 metres inland from the last walls of the old village, almost completely abandoned since the end of WW II and the beginning of mass tourism. Near the edge of this ghost town is the lower national checkpoint.

Much of the way through the gorge is studded with km signposts, but while the entire hike is actually over 16 km, only the distance contained within the park boundaries – some 13 or 14 km – is actually marked. So for example Samariá hamlet, at '6' ascending or '7' descending, is really between nine and 10 km from the sea. This somewhat cruel deception (especially coming downhill expecting a swim at Km '0') can cause no end of bafflement or argument unless recognised. In the following route notes the signed distances are given, with the true distance in parentheses.

Shortly after Km 3 (6), the gorge narrows to a mere two metres at the famed Sidherespórtes ('Iron Gates'), where rock walls tower nearly 300 metres overhead. In spring you don't hike this portion of the route so much as wade it; there may be up to a dozen water crossings on either side of the narrows.

Once through this bottleneck, the path, often little more than a slight disturbance in various rock piles, climbs gradually to some pine and cedar groves before passing a point, eight to nine km along, where the river gushes forth from subterranean channels in the canyon bed. If this fails to appear, there are springs and rest stations at Kefalovrísi (eight true km inland) and Neró tis Pérdhikas (nine km).

The empty hamlet of Samariá, with its 14th-century church to the Egyptian saint, fountains, warden's post and picnic tables, lies on the eastern bank of the gorge, accessible by a foot bridge between the Km 6 and 7 markers. There is also supposed to be a physician on duty here but the warden who used to run mule-train rescue patrols has retired, and supporting paramedic staff are currently inadequate for the frequent incidents in the gorge.

Beyond this point the grade stiffens en route to the chapel and spring of Áyios Nikólaos, roughly 10 (13½) km beyond Ayía Rúmelli. This ksoklísi is surrounded by some of the tallest and oldest cypresses on Crete, possibly descendants of an original grove here sacred to Britomartis, a Cretan version of Artemis. The little church is almost certainly built on the foundations of a pagan temple. Nearby, the main Samarian stream has resurfaced, at least until July, and early in the year you may find yourself, as at Sidherespórtes, repeatedly donning and shedding your boots for crossings (there's no rule against foot baths, luckily).

From the last river fording at Km 11 (14), the trail switchbacks very steeply, gaining nearly half of the 1200-metre elevation change entailed from the ocean up to Ksilóskala at the head of the gorge. Except for one fountain at Km 12 (15), there is no more reliable water along the way. Most walkers reach Ksilóskala, Km 14 (17), about six hours after leaving Ayía Rúmelli. If you don't take the evening bus down to Haniá, you can stay either at the Kalérgi alpine refuge (☎ (0821) 54 560; phone ahead from Ayía Rúmelli if the weak circuits permit it), or at several hotels and dhomátia in Omalós hamlet, five km to the north. Despite what you might read elsewhere, there is no longer any accommodation in the conspicuous

tourist lodge above the bus turnaround area – the last beds were removed and the place was converted to a luxury bar-restaurant in 1991.

Reverse Itinerary Going down the gorge, it's 2½ hours along the main trail from Ksilóskala to Samariá hamlet, and from there another two hours down to Ayía Rúmelli. If you do not intend to stay the night there or walk out to the east, be quick about nabbing a boat ticket, as these sometimes sell out.

Thirty minutes below Ksilóskala, you might want to consider taking the alternative trail passing through Potístra, if only to lose some of the habitual crowds near the top. To do so legally you need to contact the Dhasarhío (Forest Directorate) in Haniá (☎ (0821) 22 287) and have a good reason handy (a university degree in biological sciences might do). Permission is currently rarely granted, owing to the danger from boulder-slides and stray bullets from the poachers who frequent this area. The actual path, clear but much narrower than the canyon-floor route, crawls high up the flanks of Melidaú peak before looping down to rejoin the main trail within sight of Áyios Nikólaos. The Potístra detour is not as shaded as the usual way, but ample compensation is offered by the views to the peaks west and the sense of solitude almost completely lacking on the conventional descent.

There are two springs along the way, which is (at most) half an hour longer than the main path to Áyios Nikólaos.

Stage 2: Ksilóskala to Kustoyérako via Gíngilos
(8 hours)

Seen from Ksilóskala, Gíngilos peak to the south seems off limits to all but technical climbers, who do in fact delight in the face that's visible. But the relatively gentle saddle west of it is a very popular hikers' target, and many people make the climb up as a day hike while based at the Kalérgi refuge.

It is well worth allowing extra time for it, since the 2080-metre peak, while nowhere near the highest point in the Lefká Óri, has far better views than the Pákhnes area. And although you are in often within the boundaries of the national park, there is no admission fee and none of the regimentation attendant on the gorge traverse. I even met a German gentleman coming up with a hang glider on his pack, intending to fly off Gíngilos (a novel way of avoiding park fees if there ever was one). With a full pack, experienced trekkers also have the option of continuing more conventionally to Kustoyérako from the strategic col, along a little-used trail.

The signposted path begins just behind the bar-restaurant west of the roadhead at Ksilóskala. You climb intially sharply, with the national park boundary fence to your left, before slipping through a gap in the fence some 35 minutes along. Now there's a level stretch, followed by a slight descent to a natural rock tunnel (1550 metres) exactly an hour out. There are no waymarks but the trail is impossible to miss. Ten minutes later, pass a large rock overhang cave, and then in as much time again you'll reach the only reliable water en route, a spring at about 1550 metres feeding four consecutive troughs.

Now the path acquires some waymarks and cairns as it switchbacks up a scree-laden slope to the col of Linosélli (1775 metres).

Sidetrips: Volakiás & Gíngilos Peaks

Although the good trail ends at Linosélli col, the onward way to the top of Gíngilos is signalled by sensible painted arrows in the rocks to the east. It takes 50 minutes (2½ hours in total) to reach a false summit, where there is a cairn; the going is OK except at the very start, where there are two deep, vertical cave mouths which you don't want to be above, as it's slippery. Near the end a path of sorts even resumes.

The true top of Gíngilos lies an additional 25 minutes east-north-east from the false summit; this final stretch has few cairns, and the rock is fairly rotten underfoot.

In any event the views from either point are virtually identical and spectacular. Going anticlockwise you'll see a patch of Haniá to the north; Theodhóru islet; the peninsulas of

Rodhópu and Gramvúsa, with the bay of Kastélli in between; the peninsula at Paleohóra; the islet of Gávdhos; adjacent Volakiás peak to the south-east; and to the east, the entire Lefká Óri summit zone east of the gorge, probably shining pinkish-orange rather than white in the afternoon light.

A detour to 2116-metre Volakiás from Gíngilos's false top will consume an additional 90 minutes. It's all cross-country scrambling down to the broad saddle separating the two peaks, then across it, and finally up again. Around here you're more likely to see the *kri-kri* or rare Cretan ibex, logo of the national park, or some of the vultures and lammergeiers who nest in the sheer palisades above the gorge.

The return to Linosélli saddle takes just 35 minutes, and from there back to Ksilóskala it's another two hours. On the way down you'll probably be in more of a mood to notice the twisted cypresses and small-leafed Cretan maple along the trail. Once out of park territory, you might (in June or July) want to gather some *malotíra*, the sweet-scented Cretan sage with fuzzy grey leaves that is the finest of the Greek 'mountain teas'.

Beyond Linosélli paths are neglected and relatively untrodden since the war, making the trek to the village of Kustoyérako from here a quite advanced trekking exercise. If you feel you're up for it, face south-west from the col; the faint path does not drop into the obvious gorge, but stays high on your right to reach the pair of huts and a cistern at Akhládha after two hours. Past here the trail improves for the final four hours, much of it through pine forest, to Kustoyérako, which is 8½ km up a side track from the main road into Súyia.

Alternative Approach The easier route to Kustoyérako, and the one favoured by French trekking groups, takes off from the west edge of the Omalós plateau. Follow the dirt road which snakes off between a chapel and some cement cisterns; soon this becomes a good path, with some cobbled surface, tending first west and then south. From the cisterns to Kustoyérako it's 4½ hours of downhill walking, with one spring en route.

However you arrive, Kustoyérako is a much-rebuilt village with a taverna, a frescoed Byzantine church and a distinguished record of resistance to almost every foreign occupier of the island. You'll probably get permission to camp by or in the school if you're unable to arrange a lift the same evening along the final 13 km to the fleshpots at Súyia.

The South-West Coast

Except for the two port resorts of Súyia and Paleokhóra, the Cretan coast between Ayía Rúmelli and Elafonísi is every bit as thinly settled and attractive as the Sfakiá shore, though once beyond Súyia you no longer have the Lefká Óri as a dramatic backdrop.

The section between Ayía Rúmelli and Súyia constitutes the 'missing link' in the coastal trail system; there is a two-hour path east of Súyia as far as the chapel of Áyios Andónios, but nothing substantial beyond. The intervening countryside is steep and rugged, with the same warnings – and record of tourist fatalities – applying here as for the Lefká Óri. Engage a local guide from Ayía Rúmelli or Súyia if you're bold enough to attempt the traverse.

SÚYIA TO ELAFONÍSI

The coast between the small resort of Súyia and the beach islet of Elafonísi, while less dramatic than that fronting the Lefká Óri, is well strewn with beaches small and large which are one of the main attractions of walking here. Paths, like those further east, are fairly well marked; also, if boat services between Syia and Paleokhóra are not running, this is a fairly common way of getting between the two.

Rating & Duration

This two-stage coastal walk is considerably

easier than those in the Sfakiá area, and by exploiting the pertinent boat services can also be done as day hikes.

Season

People regularly accomplish these routes in high summer, since the brevity of the stages makes it possible to finish them before noon with a dawn start.

Supplies

Súyia has a small store or two, and you've lots of choice of supplies in Paleokhóra.

Maps

Use the British 1:50,000 wartime maps *Crete, Sheet 14, Teménia* (for most of the way from Súyia to Paleokhóra) and *Crete, Sheet 13, Palaiokhóra* (for the conclusion, and the section beyond to Elafonísi); YIS 1:50,000 *Vatólakkos* *and *Palaiokhóra*. Harms sheet No 1, *Hania*, is now available.

Access

Unless you've trekked from Ksilóskala to nearby Kustoyérako, you've the following choices for reaching Súyia. There's just one daily kaïki from Ayía Rúmelli to Súyia and Paleokhóra, leaving at about 4 pm and reaching Paleokhóra about two hours later, having stopped at Súyia halfway. It goes back the same way the next morning between 8 and 8.30 am. This service runs on a reliably daily basis only from June to September, with perhaps three services a week in May and October, and nothing at all in winter.

Súyia also has two daily buses from Haniá, at 8.30 am and 1.30 pm, and Paleokhóra has at least five between 8 am and 5.30 pm. Reverse frequencies are the same, except that the first buses tend to leave the resorts at dawn.

Stage 1: Súyia to Paleokhóra via Ancient Lissós

(4¾ hours)

Súyia is a growing resort which before WW II was merely the harbour annex of Kustoyérako. Architecturally it is not fabulous, consisting of a collection of concrete tourist facilities and a modern olive press (follow your nose). Next to this stands a church built clumsily on the foundations of an earlier 6th-century one, whose Byzantine mosaic floor has been lately recognised as a treasure and been mostly removed for 'repairs'. The beach, including a nudist cove at the eastern end, is the main attraction, with lots of people always camped behind it – including, illegally, among the scanty ruins of ancient Súyia. Prices are a bit lower than at Lutró, reflecting the clientele.

To begin, head down to the ferry/fishing harbour, where an unsigned path heads up the ravine behind the dock. There are green and red waymarks, plus cairns, but most of the way through the mini-gorge choked with oleanders, pines and carob trees is clear. Some 20 minutes along, overhanging walls seem more appropriate to the American South-West or the US outback; a few minutes later there's a definite veering up towards the true right (south) bank of the ravine, marked by a small pine tree growing directly out of a boulder. You climb quickly to a sparsely wooded plateau at about 150 metres elevation, allowing views of the ground covered so far and the western flanks of the Lefká Óri.

A few minutes of level progress beyond this overlook, the bluff drops sharply into the valley containing ancient Lissós. From the edge you can spy two ksoklísia, a small pebbly bay, and the gaping tombs of a plundered Roman necropolis on the opposite slope of the vale; Hellenistic Lissós is not immediately obvious. The onward route, however, is – look for a distinct notch in the hillside to the west, just right of the necropolis; the trail threads up this.

For now the path zig-zags about 20 minutes down the bluff face, past a cave mouth and through some olives, until bottoming out at the valley floor. Turn right off the main trail to find an old 'Lissos' sign and the fenced-in highlight of the archaeological zone, one hour 15 minutes along. If the grounds are locked you'll have to first visit the guard's hut 100 metres ahead for the keys.

This *asklipion* or therapeutic temple of Lissós was only discovered in 1957. The healing spring used to issue from among maidenhair fern and mint just below the massive walls of the 3rd-century BC sanctuary, but has lately been capped and diverted down to a huge tank near the warden's cottage. Inside are extensive, handsome floor mosaics from the 1st century AD, and the outer walls are rasped with numerous Greek inscriptions. Nearby, but hard to find, are traces of the baths used by the sick, a priest's residence and pilgrims' quarters.

Proceed next to the concrete water pool, following the hose pipe just off the yellow and red-blazed trail, to fill bottles for the dry spell ahead. Just above the warden's cottage stands the usually open chapel of Áyios Kiriákos, dating to the 13th or 14th century. Among numerous faded frescoes, only those

Crete: Roman-era mosaic floor in the Asklipion Sanctuary at ancient Lissós, west of Súyia

of 'Áyios Yióryios and the Dragon' and 'The Presentation' are recognisable. Downstream from the pool many tiny paths wander through vegetable patches and the Roman graves on their way to the beach. A few minutes before the cove is a Byzantine chapel of the Panayía, incorporating ancient columns, pediments and plaques to form a gingerbread exterior. The central curative shrine must have supported a sizeable town, perhaps as late as the pirate raids of the 9th century, since ancient foundations poke up through the weeds everywhere between the sea and the fenced temple.

Above the warden's cottage, where you can often get a soft drink, the red and yellow blazes, plus the occasional green one, take you over a series of tree-studded terraces. If you're floundering, the best orientation point is a stone-threshing cirque which you must pass to its right. From there on the trail is unmistakeable as it curls around north and up through the gap in the bluff ahead, which becomes a fair-sized gully close up.

After climbing through prickly shrubbery with the aid of the waymarks, you'll top out on an exposed plateau some 20 minutes out

of Lissós valley. On the hillside to the north you'll notice a track up to a cistern and catchment basin. Proceed straight west until arriving at a perpendicular junction with another track 45 minutes out of Lissós, at about 250 metres elevation. Follow cairns across the track; once on the other side your path briefly becomes a double-rutted track also, but as soon as the sea and coast ahead reappear (2¼ hours along) it reverts to a path again. Within five minutes you can look straight into the sea below to the left, and ahead to a cove which makes an excellent lunch stop. Now the trail drops steeply before levelling out just before that cove glimpsed from above, reached 2¾ hours into the day. There are actually two little bays here, separated by rock formations.

Continuing west, the path roller-coasters, always near the sea, wading through arbutus and thornbushes; there are one or two minor scrambles through steep little gullies. Just under 3½ hours into the day you'll cross a broad, sandy naturist beach with swimming so good that you won't care about being all salty from here on.

From the far end of this beach, head a

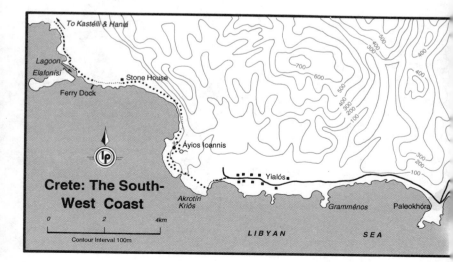

couple of hundred metres up the gully responsible for all the nice sand; you cannot follow the shoreline the whole way to Paleokhóra, so you must find the continuation of the path on the far bank of the riverbed – it's well cairned. The trail climbs up onto a headland, the base of which is lapped by the sea and therefore impassable, before dropping within 15 minutes to the end of a long pebble beach. Cars appear, and after 10 more minutes so does the end of the drive-able track. You've no choice but to adopt for this the final 45 minutes into the centre of Paleokhóra, for a total of 4¾ hours from Súyia; beyond the town's official campsite the track becomes a proper asphalt road.

Paleokhóra has everything you could possibly want in a resort, and then some – except perhaps rooms in August. It had a reputation as a hippie haven in the 1970s, when penniless youths picked fruit and tomatoes, living on as little as possible all winter, but now the place is, if not entirely up-market, solidly package and family-orientated. Back in the old days it was probably easier to see that this is in fact the capital of the county (*eparkhía*) of Sélino, and indeed its former name is

Kastél Selínu. The castle in question, built by the Venetians in 1279, is crumbling away on the headland beyond the spit on which the town is built.

Reverse Itinerary Reversing the itinerary, especially as a day hike with Paleokhóra as a base, has the advantage that you can easily find a taxi to take you at least to the end of the asphalt and save almost an hour of road-tramping. However, you'll have the sun in your face much of the way, and must pay constant attention to the time in order to catch the afternoon boat back from Súyia. Perhaps a better strategy would be to take the morning boat to Súyia, and arrange to have a sympathetic taxi driver meet you at road's end at a prearranged time.

Stage 2: Paleokhóra to Elafonísi
(2½ hours)
Elafonísi, one of Crete's most unusual beaches, is generally approached by excursion boat from Paleokhóra or bus from Haniá. However, it's a very fine walk there except perhaps for the last few confusing moments, and a one-way boat ride back is

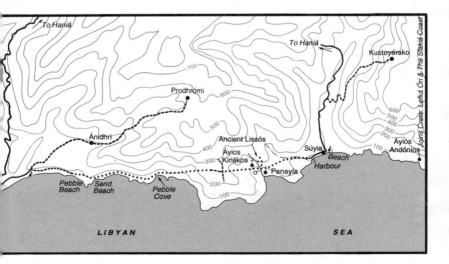

easily arranged – or, for those with a full pack, an onward bus north.

The hike starts not in Paleokhóra itself but eight km west in the district of Yialós; persuade your taxi driver (there's no bus) to drop you near the last villa on the shore here. Set out on the dirt track leading below this onto a pebble cove; at the far end of this you'll see red dots and an arrow on the rocks marking the start of the actual path.

Fifteen minutes along you'll top the rear of the cape Akrotíri Kriós, with the sea and the faint outline of Elafonísi visible beyond. Red waymarks are positively dense as you descend to a cove studded with boulders, skim the shore and then climb north-west to a corniche section about 40 minutes out of Yialós. From this point all of Elafonísi is seen, including its famous lagoon.

Round the bend here to see the ksoklísi of Áyios Ioánnis in front of you. The trail as waymarked appears to go needlessly above it, but you're being taken to a weak spring, the only water en route, tucked in a clump of oleanders. The unremarkable church a few minutes below is effectively the one-hour mark out of Yialós.

The path beyond Áyios Ioánnis is steep, slippery, and only has cairns, with no more coloured waymarks. Half an hour further, you reach the edge of a sand and rock bay, with a dune slope behind. Once over a rock pile at the beach's far end, the path reappears more distinctly, leading to an orange-toned stone house on a hill after another 30 minutes. Bear left and down here for the final 30 minutes to Elafonísi, passing just above where the excursion boats from Paleokhóra dock. Don't go too far inland from the orange house, or you'll be stopped by a new fence that's fairly difficult to scale – keep well left (south) of the few holiday villas that have gone up so far. The walking total is about 2½ hours.

Elafonísi is tethered to the mainland by a shallow sandbar, across which you wade in thigh-high water to get to the prime sunbathing spots on the islet. It is always popular, but there's generally enough space to flop out next to your choice of the warm, protected lagoon water or the more boisterous open sea. Despite the number of visitors there's just one real place to stay – camping is the norm – and just two trailer cantinas offering the most basic of snacks. Double check with the captains as to the time of the last boat back to Paleokhóra, anywhere from 3.30 to 5 pm depending on the season. The bus towards Kastélli and Haniá leaves at about 4 pm.

It would be difficult, though certainly not impossible, to find the way in reverse, but you'd have to go late in the afternoon to avoid the heat, and risk being caught by darkness if you got lost – not to mention the extra trudge from Yialós into Paleokhóra, since very probably no taxi would be available.

Dhodhekánisos (Dodecanese) Islands

The remotest of the Greek archipelagos from the mainland was only incorporated into modern Greece in 1948, after 500 years of occupation by the Latin Knights of St John, the Ottomans, the Italians, the Germans and the British. While not so fertile as the Ionian or north-east Aegean islands, the Dhodhekánisos have suffered this fate mostly as a result of lying squarely astride the fast lane of history. Any imperial power with designs on the eastern Mediterranean was obligated to subdue or at least control the Dhodhekánisos. Through it all, the islanders have maintained their Greek cultural identity, reacting especially strenuously to the repressive Italian sanctions against the Greek language and Orthodox church during the period 1919-43. On the plus side the Italians were the only occupiers ever to do anything on behalf of the islands, undertaking massive archaeological excavations and restorations, plus more mundane public works, to make them the showcase of Mussolini's 'Aegean Island Empire'.

Geographically, members of the Dhodhekánisos display a marked schizophrenia. Dry limestone outcrops such as Kálimnos, Sími, Kássos, Hálki and Kastellórizo alternate with the sprawling sandy giants of Ródhos, Kos and Léros. Nísiros and (to some extent) Tílos are volcanic, while Astipálea and Pátmos at the fringes of the group resemble more the Kikládhes. The rugged and occasionally forested contours of the limestone isles are actually the last stretch of the great subduction-generated arc connecting Crete with Anatolia.

Like so many other parts of Greece, the Dhodhekánisos ceased to have much economic importance after the collapse of the Ottoman Empire and the establishment of frontiers in the east Aegean. During Turkish times, the wealthier islands were heavily garrisoned and exploited, while the more austere islets were left to the industrious devices of the natives. Most of these made their living in some way from the sea, usually shuttling goods to or from Anatolia, with the Sultan's involvement being confined to the yearly collection of a *maktú* or tribute in money or kind, in exchange for wide-ranging privileges. With the coming of the Italian fascists and – truth be told – the centralised Greek administration, the minor Dhodhekánisos lost their autonomy and usually their economic reason for existence. Massive emigration to the USA and Australia ensued, with the peace of the grave settling on the abandoned villages. Very often these small, underdeveloped islets offer excellent hiking.

This island group, especially the ones covered here, is renowned for its balmy weather and long tourist season. You could attempt virtually any of the hikes here all year round, given stable conditions. February and March are apt to be the worst months, but even then there are many exceptional days.

Ródhos

The largest of the Dhodhekánisos is a thumping disappointment for walkers. Hummocky but not rugged enough to protect itself from the bulldozers, Ródhos (Rhodes) is crisscrossed by jeep tracks that go nearly everywhere. Arsonists have recently been very hard on the forests here, and the general mass-tourism ethic certainly does not help preserve the countryside.

Access (Ródhos)

Given its role as a medium-sized provincial capital as well as a five-star tourist centre, Ródhos is simple to get to by boat or plane. International ferries call from Cyprus and Israel every four or five days in season, every

10 days or so out; there are also anywhere from two to seven weekly short-hop boats from Marmaris in Turkey throughout the year. Domestic connections are too many to list exhaustively, but if you wait long enough – a matter of a few days in season – something will take you to Ródhos; the only island groups where this isn't true are the Sporádhes and the Ionians. The most convenient and important services from a hiker's standpoint are the twice-weekly (one direct, one with a layover in Kálimnos) links to/from Sámos; the daily service, either excursion or line ferry, to/from Sími; four or five weekly links with Tílos and Nísiros; three to five weekly trips to/from Crete; and most of the Kikládhes except the very far north-western members at least once a week.

Like to Crete, there are not yet any direct scheduled flights from northern Europe to Ródhos, only charters (lots of them) – but this will change as the European air industry is deregulated after 1993. Internal flights from Athens arrive four or five times daily in summer, nearly as often in winter. There are additional summer connections with Thíra, Iráklio, Páros, Míkonos, Kárpathos, Kássos, Kastellórizo, Kos and Thessaloníki two or three times weekly in season, with only the first four Kikládhes services disappearing in winter.

HILL-WALKING ON RÓDHOS

Despite heavy tourism, there are two notable hill walks. These lead to the island's two highest summits, which are well worth doing even if you've primarily come to Ródhos, like most people, to enjoy the medieval city, the superb beaches, and the scattered ancient ruins and Byzantine frescoes.

Rating & Duration

Both of the hikes described are easy to moderate, involving well less than a full day's effort.

Supplies

Get your supplies in Ródhos town before setting out – hard as it is to believe when you're in the tourist bustle of the north, the trailhead villages are small and relatively primitive.

Access

Public bus service is not one of Ródhos's long suits, at least for the remote south-west where both hikes are located. Áyios Isídhoros has no bus links and Siána and Monólithos have just one weekday service in the early afternoon, too late to start walking. Only on Sunday is the pattern reversed, with a morning departure from Ródhos and an afternoon return.

I strongly recommend staying the night in Áyios Isídhoros or Monólithos – a beautiful corner of the island with lots to see and acceptable food and lodging. Your other alternatives include getting a taxi from the nearest village served by buses – in all cases Kalavárdha, nearly 40 km away – or arriving on hired transport. A rented buggy is preferable, even though you don't make full use of it on walking days, since by the time you pay for the round-trip taxi fare you may as well have hired a car.

Trek 1: Ascent of Mt Atáviros

(5 hours return)
At 1215 metres, Atáviros is the highest point on Ródhos. The climb up is not the most exciting, but the trail from Áyios Isídhoros is clear and mostly gradual, leaving you free to enjoy the fantastic views. On top is an archaeological site, the foundations of a classical temple dedicated to Zeus.

Maps Italian 1:25,000 occupation maps *Monte Attairo* and *Alaerma*; YIS 1:50,000 sheet *Émbonas*.

Route Directions The path starts at the north-eastern edge of Áyios Isídhoros (350 metres), heading directly away from the town-limits sign and running parallel to the wall of an olive grove. Do not go up and left. Within two minutes, you should reach a livestock barrier and a red waymark or two; five minutes along, you're down in the bed of a ravine. Cross it and adopt a trail on the far bank after a few minutes more.

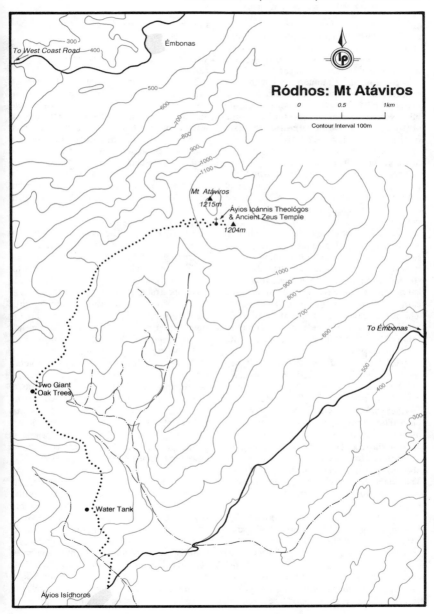

Now you begin snaking steadily up on a north-westerly bearing, attaining the ridge above and ignoring a left fork. Just over half an hour along, draw even with a concrete livestock cistern which you can tap. Above this you pass three stunted trees with your first view of the summit, 50 minutes out. The path now curls around to a northerly bearing just over an hour along, levelling out on a 900-metre-plus saddle dividing a giant ravine system – not the one you came up – on the east from the Ródhos coast and views to Hálki and islets to the west.

There is little net altitude change up to the one hour 20 minute mark, where two giant oaks flanking the path offer the only shade en route. Once past these the path begins to bend around progressively more north-east, skirting a precipice from where, one hour 50 minutes along, you glimpse the rooftops of Émbonas village. The trail tracing on the Italian occupation map, accurate thus far, stops just before this, but the actual path keeps going, zig-zagging with occasional cairns and waymarks up to the Zeus Temple. This is just to one side of Point 1204; the true summit is a few minutes of cross-country scrambling to the north-west, tufted with some metal poles and modern ruins.

What remains of the temple is aligned west-to-east, like all good pagan shrines; nearby is a tiny chapel to Áyios Ioánnis Theológos (Saint John the Theologian or the Divine), which is what the locals call the place. Here is one of the more obvious examples in Greece of the saint of the Apocalypse appropriating Zeus's former place of worship; the transition was made easy by the shared eagle symbolism, and the Theologian's churches always preside over awesome scenery at the edge or the top of the visible world.

The return trip to Áyios Isídhoros takes just under two hours, at a fairly brisk pace – five hours for the entire journey is a reasonable estimate, allowing for rests and pottering about the ruins. Incidentally some people climb the peak from Émbonas, but there's no path, the grade averages 45% (and sometimes exceeds that) and there seems no reason to recommend such a strategy, especially downhill.

Trek 2: Mt Akramítis Traverse
(2-2½ hours)

Although considerably lower (825 metres) than Atáviros, Akramátis, the second peak of the island, is far more interesting botanically and topographically. The attraction here is not the summit, but two bowl-like meadows hidden by the summit ridge, the healthy forest below, and the front-seat views of the sea as you descend.

Maps Italian 1:25,000 occupation map *Monòlito*; YIS 1:50,000 *Émbonas* and *Khálki*.

Route Directions The way up starts by the Siána cemetery (450 metres), about 700 metres west-south-west of the village on the asphalt road to Monólithos. There is space to park a car or a scooter by the boundary wall. Take the track beginning opposite on the high side of the road; a few metres up this stands a roofless structure, next to which a trail, well marked by red blazes and cairns, heads north up the hill through cypress, pine and other typical Aegean shrubbery.

Less than half an hour along, the vegetation (and the trail) thins out upon reaching a cleared, gentler slope. Bear left (west) now, following sporadic waymarks which stay in the higher trees up to a group of ruined stone huts at about 600 metres elevation. Keep these below you and head up towards a phone pole on the hillside above – a re-emerged path leads to it.

A few moments later, the way forks: right to a fire lookout tower and the peak, left up through a ridge. To traverse the south-western ridge, keep a good 300 metres left (south) of the lookout – get too close to it, and you'll find an unmanageable drop coming off the ridge higher up. Angle west-south-west without a clear path towards a second ledge, prompted by a blue blaze; then red ones (and a path of sorts) resume again, leading you through a thick pine grove.

Suddenly, just over an hour above the

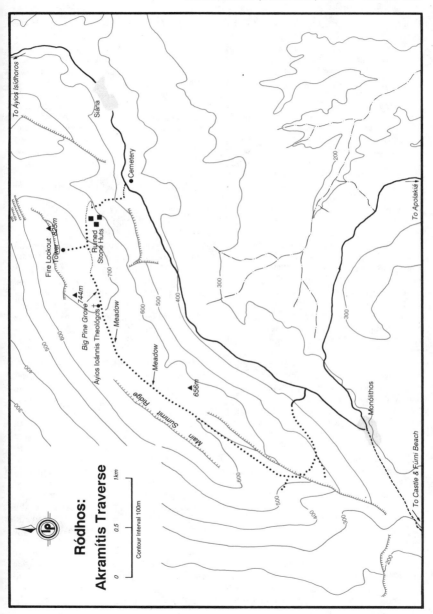

**Ródhos:
Akramítis Traverse**

Contour Interval 100m

0   0.5   1km

To Áyios Isídhoros

Siána

Cemetery

Fire Lookout
Tower 825m

Ruined
Stone Huts

Big Pine Grove
Áyios Ioánnis Theológos
744m

700

Meadow

600

500

400

300

Meadow

656m

Main Summit Ridge

500

600

500

400

300

200

300

300

200

To Apolakiá

Monólithos

To Castle & Fúrni Beach

cemetery, you virtually stumble on the unwhitewashed chapel of Áyios Ioánnis Theológos (700 metres), alone in a giant courtyard containing a cistern with potable water. With the main Akramátis crest running just behind, it's an impressive, wild spot.

From here, follow the waymarks, still on a west-south-west course, to a third ledge, and worm down the far side of this on a faint path through sage plants. You'll land in a long, grassy meadow that needs about 10 minutes to cross – it's best in spring when the turf is fresh and the wildflowers on display. There are no more blazes for now but there is telltale flattening of the grass where people and livestock have been by.

After a very brief scrub-covered incline you'll end up on another smaller meadow, 600 metres above sea level and 20 minutes past Áyios Ioánnis Theológos, with some stone ruins at the upper end. Climb slightly out of the pasture to the clear resumption of the trail through pine and cypress forest. The path soon widens considerably and acquires a masoned edge as it stays level or even climbs slightly until, 40 minutes beyond Áyios Ioánnis Theológos, you emerge onto a 180° view of Apolakiá Bay – and the start of the sharp drop off the secondary crest behind which you've been sheltered.

Fifteen minutes downhill, ignore a fork on the right with a blue arrow – the side trail ends at a viewpoint. You'll finish on the asphalt road (360 metres) just over an hour below the chapel, proceeding against the blue arrows for the last 10 minutes. Turn right and stroll a few moments downhill to Monólithos; if you've left a vehicle back at the cemetery, it's a 25-minute trudge to get there, for a 2½ hour loop.

Sími

Closer to Anatolia than Ródhos, and possessing a jagged outline correctly implying rocky terrain, Sími might not initially impress a map browser as a good venue for day hikes. But along with Ródhos and the summit of Kos, it is the only member of the archipelago to have retained a substantial portion of its original forests, and (despite a number of new roads) an excellent trail network remains.

Visits begin auspiciously at the port of Yialós, whose imposing mansions and waterfront attest to the wealth of the 19th-century sponge-fishing fleets and merchant marine. But 10 years of war between 1913 and 1923, the invention of synthetic sponges, nearby Kálimnos's increasing domination of the sponge trade, and German-perpetrated destruction in 1944 together spelt disaster for the island, so it's a sad and faded tableau of past glories that meets the eye.

Sími is slowly being restored architecturally, but by wealthy foreigners and Athenians, not the locals who prefer to build anew if they can flout the preservation order in effect. Yialós blends without demarcation into Horió, which covers the high ridge and hidden valley to the south, and the two communities are known collectively as Sími. The only other significant habitations are at the nearby bays of Pédhi and Embório.

ACROSS THE ISLAND

Venture beyond Sími and you find a striking, largely unspoiled and deeply indented isle with numerous protected bays. Sandy stretches are few but swimming off the pebble shores is excellent on calm days. In the south and west particularly, extensive stands of juniper, cypress and pine enliven bare rocks. You're unlikely to meet anyone away from the town, and the silence is broken only by the occasional bleat of a goat or the hum of bees in the herb bushes.

Sími rivals Pátmos and certain of the Kikládhes in the sheer number – close to 200 – of ksoklísia and small monasteries scattered uniformly over the landscape. The island is as poor in natural ground water as it is rich in shrines, but almost all of the latter have rain cisterns, so if someone hasn't made off with the necessary siklákli (can on a string), you need never go thirsty.

Season

Between June and September Sími is possibly the hottest of all Greek islands. The local taxi-boats to the remoter beaches do a brisk trade then.

Supplies

The small bazaar in Yialós is adequate for supplies.

Maps

Use the Italian 1:25,000 occupation map *Isola di Simi*, or YIS 1:50,000 *Nísos Sími**. The 1:33,000 tourist map produced by Ioannis Koza and sold on the island is good enough to get by on, in conjunction with this book's offering.

Access

Twice weekly that workhorse of the minor Dhodhekánisos, the *Kálimnos*, calls in each direction on its run between Ródhos and Kálimnos, offering direct links with Kos, Nísiros and Tílos as well; once a week in high season a larger ferry sails between here, Crete and a changing selection from among the Kikládhes.

There are also daily tourist excursion boats (expensive) and hydrofoils (worse) from Ródhos in the morning. You are under some pressure to buy a return ticket, whether it's desired or not, and you won't be told about the *epivatikó* (local passenger) departures. Three days a week, usually dovetailing well with the bigger ferries, either the *Simi I* or its sister ship the *Simi II* leaves Ródhos for Sími at about 2 pm, returning the next morning at dawn. This is the 'shopper's special' for the benefit of the islanders, and not surprisingly costs about half as much as the tourist sailings.

Trek 1: Yialós To Áyios Emilianós

(6 hours return)

This delightful walk heads west-south-west past Sími's oldest and second largest monastery, continues through fine woods and ends at one of the most peculiar spots on the island.

Rating & Duration This is a moderate transect of the island, with almost half of the route shaded by trees; allow six hours for the round trip, plus stops.

Route Directions Leave the waterside platía by the highest, most inland lane, then bear up and left behind the Hotel Haris. Follow the main stair-street as it zig-zags up and out of town; incorrect turnings finish in dead ends. When confirming directions simply ask for 'Mikhaíl', the informal abbreviation for your first probable destination, the monastery of Taxiárkhis Mikhaíl Rukuniótis.

You'll go through a livestock gate by a ruined lone house 15 minutes along; avoid, five minutes later, a tempting straight continuation to the conspicuous chapel of Áyios Fanúrios – go left round the hairpin instead to stay with the revetted principal trail. After 10 more minutes, having passed through a small grove of valonea oaks, you attain the first ridge en route; here there's a junction of two jeep tracks (not on the tourist map), a clump of young eucalyptus trees and a pair of footpaths.

The more direct trail resumes on the opposite side of the jeep track; this narrow, uncobbled but well-worn path descends, skirting the very edge of an army truck depot, on its way to the small convent of Áyii Anáryiri, one hour out of Yialós.

In the courtyard grow two enormous, ancient pomegranate trees, and the katholikón has fresco fragments from the 18th century.

You might prefer to detour via the monastery of Mikhaíl, plainly visible from the ridge, by taking the kalderími which continues briefly to the right before being swallowed by the descending dirt drive. A giant, umbrella-shaped cypress shades the gate of the monastery, also about an hour out of the harbour. If you're lucky, the elderly caretaker couple who live there will be home, and will admit you to the highly unusual katholikón. It is a double sanctuary, with a relatively recent church stacked directly atop a much older, sunken one, which figured in the dream sequences of

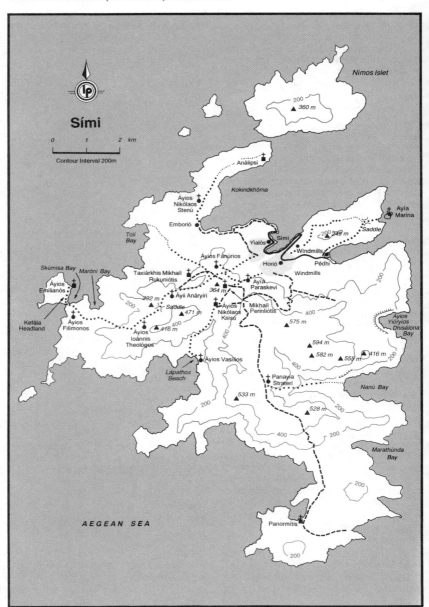

Sími

0   1   2   km

Contour Interval 200m

Nímos Islet

▲ 360 m

Análipsi

Kokindkhóma

Áyios Nikólaos Stenú

Emborió

Toli Bay

Áyios Fánúrios

Yialós   Sími

Horió

Windmills

Pédhi

Windmills

▲ 249 m   *Saddle*

Áyia Marína

Skúmisa Bay   *Maróni Bay*

Áyios Emilianós

Taxiárkhis Mikhaíl Rukuniótis

Áyii Anáryiri

▲ 292 m   *Saddle*

Áyia Paraskeví

Mikhaíl Perinliótis

Kefála Headland

Áyios Filímonos

▲ 471 m

Áyios Nikólaos Ksisú

▲ 418 m

Áyios Ioánnis Theológos

▲ 575 m

Áyios Yióryios Dhisálona Bay

▲ 594 m

▲ 582 m   ▲ 555 m   ▲ 416 m

Áyios Vasílios

Lápathos Beach

Panayía Straterí

Nanú Bay

▲ 533 m

▲ 528 m

Marathúnda Bay

AEGEAN SEA

Panormítis

Eugenia Fakinou's novel *Astradeni* (Kedros, Athens, 1991). Almost certainly it was a pagan temple, but has today been abandoned to damaging mildew; the upper shrine has a fine carved témblon and lurid 18th-century frescoes which, if not great art, are engaging. Their subject matter resembles those of Ródhos's Byzantine-era country chapels: Old Testament stories to the left, the Acts of Christ on the right, and a rare depiction of the Holy Trinity rather than the Pantocrator (Christ in Glory) up in the dome. The patron saint's festival takes place on 8 November.

The jeep track serving Mikhaíl Rukuniótis continues to just before Áyii Anáryiri; once there, hunt around on the left (south, high) side of the compound for the onward trail – red dots, at first faint and then clearer, help you. Continue straight now, aiming for a low saddle, marked by a neat clump of juniper, in the hills ahead. At this next and final high point of the walk stands a complex of half-ruined stone huts and pastures. Keep all of these well to your right and angle 40° left onto a clear trail skirting the base of an increasingly well-forested hillside.

As you descend along this, fine views west open up on a clear day: Turkish Datça on its peninsula to the north-west, and Tílos and Nísiros ahead on the horizon. Half an hour beyond Áyii Anáryiri, you'll arrive at the small monastery of Áyios Ioánnis Theológos; the water tap here is unreliable, but from the terrace you can see the monasteries of Áyios Filímonos and Áyios Emilianós and the bays of Maróni and Skúmisa below.

Shortly after Theológos the path forks; bear right for half an hour of steady descent through vegetation, past Maróni, before the trail frays into aimless goat traces. Proceed by line of sight and the occasional cairn to Áyios Filímonos, usually locked but said to contain faded frescoes; the well with a bucket to the left of the main gate should be accessible. To the right of this gate a cemented path leads down to Skúmisa bay and a small dock – good swimming off it if there's no wind or sea urchins. Faint goat tracks exist for the final 300-metre push to

Emilianós, 20 minutes beyond Filímonos, or just under three hours from Yialós in total.

Áyios Emilianós sits on an islet linked by a long, wave-lashed causeway to the headland of Kefála. The monastery is not architecturally or historically exceptional, merely remarkable for its setting. William Travis, in his most recommendable book *Bus Stop Symi* (Rapp & Whiting, London, 1970), recounts a summer spent here, and I will not plagiarise his excellent work other than to say that the grave of a young girl killed nearby in uncertain circumstances during the last war, which used to stand next to the gate, has vanished since the 1960s. You could overnight here, though only the 'kitchen' (first door on the right inside, with a *stérna*, fireplace and sleeping platform) is permanently open. You can swim from the lee side of the islet, but beware of sea urchins.

On your way back you might consider swimming at Maróni, though quite a lot of tar and garbage can wash up here. More importantly, there are two wells with buckets behind a modern cottage, which is generally occupied in summer.

Uphill from Áyios Emilianós to the ridge above Theológos takes just under an hour, now that you know the way, and from there to Áyii Anáryiri requires another 25 minutes. You might wish to vary the final leg home as follows: at the eucalyptus ridge, veer right onto a level path instead of descending directly to Yialós via the kalderími, and reverse the initial moments of the Horió to Áyios Vasílios route described in the next hike, when this link trail meets up 10 minutes later. This return via Horió is about 30 minutes longer, but allows terrific late-afternoon perspectives on the harbour and the Bozburun area in Turkey. Fifteen minutes before the edge of Horió, the chapel of Ayía Paraskeví has a much-needed cistern and bucket.

Trek 2: Sími to Áyios Vasílios
(3½ hours return)
This fairly demanding hike leads to one of the best Simiot beaches, accessible only on

foot, as well as yet another improbably situated chapel-monastery.

Rating & Duration Though only a half-day of walking is involved, the grade is often steep and the surface uneven near the end.

Route Directions Ascend from the platía of Yialós to Horió via the stairway known as Kataráktis, after an adjacent drainage system. Find the uppermost right-hand (westerly) street in Horió, distinguished by three grouped belfries on the hillside south of the castle. Follow this lane out of Horió; very soon after leaving the last house behind, ignore a left fork. Do take a left fork about 200 metres after passing the ksoklísi of Ayía Paraskeví with its giant oak tree, some 20 minutes past the base of the Kataráktis stairs. (The right-hand path is the alternative return for the Áyios Emilianós hike.) About half an hour along, the path intersects a modern dirt road; just the other side are the sprawling (but locked) grounds of the Mikhaíl Perinliótis monastery.

Take the new bulldozer track just to the left of Perinliótis' perimeter walls, marked by a red and white sign in Greek and English pointing towards Áyios Vasílios. After barrelling straight ahead through the relatively green plateau of Ksisós towards a prominent notch in the landscape, the track ends about 50 minutes out of Horió at the door of Áyios Nikólaos Ksisú monastery, where there's a cistern and an outsized pine tree.

A trail begins behind a red-fenced pen left of the track's end and drops between drystone walls to a lone gate; blazes and cairns begin to appear profusely. The gap in the landscape resolves into a canyon yawning below the last oak trees of Ksisós – and will probably keep the bulldozers away from Áyios Vasílios forever. The path improves, passing a small white cottage and a barbwire-topped goat pen. You now zig-zag over to the right of the rapidly plunging ravine as the trail parallels the gully for some 20 minutes before the sea appears.

Your route crosses another wash one hour 20 minutes from town, is briefly shaded by junipers, and then levels out on a plateau dense with thyme and oregano. Here, keep well right of a stone corral and locate cairns leading down towards the Aegean. Nearly 45 minutes from Áyios Nikólaos Ksisú, the path appears to halt at a natural rock balcony from where you first glimpse Áyios Vasílios, 20 metres downhill; a few paces from here an improvised stairway drops down to the tiny monastery, depositing you at the door one hour 35 minutes from Yialós.

The chapel boasts unexpected frescoes and one of those pebble-mosaic floors that grace many churches and mansions in the south-eastern Dhodhekánisos; a water cistern, cooking area and a sleeping platform can be found in the building to one side. If the blinding light or heat is not too debilitating, you can laze on the terrace between the two buildings and gaze at the cobalt-blue bay 50 metres below. For most, it is irresistible; turn right at the top of the access stairway – there's a painted legend 'SEA' with an arrow above – and carefully pick your way down a stable rock pile to Lápathos, a clean sand-and-pebble beach. Wooded slopes plummet down on all sides to shelter the bay and any visitors from the wind; at times other than summer you'll probably have the place to yourself.

Retracing your steps, it's just over an hour from the beach to the road; just over 1½ hours to the edge of Horió; and another 10 minutes to the bottom of Kataráktis, or the same one hour 45 minute time as outbound – which makes sense for a walk from sea level to sea level.

Trek 3: Sími to Ayía Marína

(1-1¼ hours)

Once again a small church crowns an islet, but this time there's no causeway – you must swim out to it. Unfortunately the bucket for the cistern was missing on my last visit, and there's no water along the way, so come prepared. The walking route itself is not particularly remarkable, nor is it long.

Climb up to Horió via the other monumental stairway known as the Kalí Stráta and find the row of windmills on the ridge to the north-east. The trail begins to the left of the highest group of six, though there are nearly a dozen in all, some restored. Once through a livestock gate of cyclone fencing, the path, faint though traceable, hugs the left flank of the hillside and is sporadically marked by the letters 'BK' and cairns.

One hour along you'll reach a large, fenced-off meadow at the base of a large hill; the path ends here. Skirt the enclosed pasture, keeping it on your left, and climb the saddle to the right of the rocky knob looming beyond the flat area. Ayía Marína islet and its baby monastery are plainly visible from the saddle, which has some rudimentary terraces and grazing areas on top. A followable trail does resume through the exact middle of the valley dropping sharply down to the shore opposite Ayía Marína. Despite an absence of fresh water it's a favoured spot, with fine swimming in the shallow, sandy-bottomed cove.

Many people arrive here from Pédhi, following a decent trail waymarked with green and blue paint splodges. This starts from the last house on the left as you face the bay at Pédhi, and is a little shorter than the route described above – about an hour. You might construct a loop hike by coming or going on this trail.

OTHER TREKS ON SÍMI
Análipsi Monastery
From the bay of Emborió, a trail leads north a bit beyond the monastery of Áyios Nikólaos Stenú and stops well before the Italian map tracing, which shows it going as far as Kokindkhóma. The idea on everyone's minds is to get to the exquisitely set sea-level monastery of Análipsi, but you'll soon learn why most people come by boat – the terrain is very rough beyond Kokindkhóma, and I had to turn back. If you succeed, it's probably a 4½-hour round trip from Yialós.

Nanú Bay
Another popular mini-walk is the hour-plus descent to the good beach at Nanú bay; the trail takes off from the chapel of Panayía Stareri, about halfway along the jeep road from Yialós to the southern monastery of Panormítis. Probably the best strategy here would be to hire a moped for riding up to the ksoklísi, though that would rule out hitching a ride back to town on one of the excursion boats which serve Nanú.

Tolí Bay
From the access track down to Mikhaíl Rukuniótis, a trail takes off going north-west, through rolling farming country, to the very swimmable bay of Tolí. Your goal is in sight much of the way so it's difficult to get badly lost. Allow four to 4½ hours for the round trip from town.

Tílos

Just 400 people live permanently on Tílos, perhaps the least visited of the 12 main Dhodhekánisos islands. The inhabitants are swamped by tourists (mostly German and Greek) for perhaps six weeks in midsummer, leaving the place as an escape artist's dream for the rest of the year.

It is not an island that reveals its assets on a flying visit, as day trippers from Kos and Sími discover to their loss. After a few days of low-key walking and lazing on the beach (one often a necessary prelude to the other), you may have discovered several of the seven small castles of the Knights of Saint John which drape themselves on various summits, or gained entry to some of the camouflaged medieval chapels, some with frescoes or pebble mosaics, clinging to hillsides. Though nearly barren on the heights, Tílos – unlike Sími – has quite a bit of water, mostly pumped up from the agricultural plain behind Eristós. There are oak and terebinth trees near the cultivated areas, plus pumice beds and red lava sand beaches, courtesy of the volcano on nearby Nísiros.

AROUND LIVÁDHIA
Most of the walking is near the eastern town and harbour of Livádhia, which is slightly more geared up to handle visitors than

Eristós beach or Megálo Horió, the western village. There is a rather advanced trek from the monastery of Ayíu Pandelímonos around the south-western tip of the island to Eristós, but I was unable to do this and have been told that the trail is in shaky condition much of the way. Most people will content themselves with short strolls around Livádhia – one soon loses the inclination to do much else on relaxed Tílos.

Maps

Italian 1:25,000 occupation map *Isola di Piscopi* (Episcopi was a medieval name for Tílos); YIS 1:50,000 *Nísos Tílos**.

Access

Tílos has much the same service as Sími, except links with the Kikládhes are more reliable, and that there are no daily excursion or shoppers' boats from Ródhos.

Instead an excursion kaïki based in Kos calls occasionally, and additionally there is one weekly ferry to/from Ródhos, Nísiros, Kos, Míkonos, Tínos, Ándhros and Rafína.

Eastern Loop

(4-6 hours)

Although this strange, circular trail doesn't seem to go anywhere in particular, you get a good sense of inland Tílos – and there are possible detours to a spring, another ghost hamlet, a handful of beaches and a castle.

Rating & Duration The basic circuit is an easy-to-moderate walk on a mostly clear trail, not exceeding half a day; allow considerable extra time for sidetrips.

Route Directions Starting from the eastern end of the pebble beach of Livádhia, head initially south-east then north-east on the obvious path, past the little fishing port at Áyios Stéfanos, to the hilltop chapel of Áyio Ioánnis. You'll reach this 35 minutes out, and after another 15 minutes southwards you'll come to a Y-junction.

You should make time to detour left on the broader path, which ends after half an hour at the abandoned pastoral hamlet of Ierá.

Along the way a faint trail goes down towards the sea, ending above the spring of Tu Dhespóti Toh Neró, which many people never find despite the telltale line of water-loving vegetation in the descending ravine. The trick is to follow the shore south-east from the tiny islet until you stumble on the spring, barely 10 metres in from the sea. Beyond, in the crook of land formed by the Kútsuva headland and the body of the island, a small beach nestles, usable on calm days.

To continue with the main circuit, return to the Y-junction and take the other fork, prompted by a cairn and a blaze. This narrower turning climbs 10 minutes up to a walled orchard, and then to a fenced-off well under a boulder overhang to the left of the path; you could get at the water if you were really determined. From here you've another quarter hour up to a ruined house up on a saddle, among various minor 300 to 400-metre-high hills. Here there's a good view south to the sea, and west towards a re-appeared kalderími which will carry you the rest of the way. Painted red dashes and arrows are thick in the vicinity of the saddle, so you can't get lost.

Within 10 more minutes you emerge at the true pass between Áyios Nikólaos and Mastíkha peaks, from where you can look south-east to Áyios Séryios beach (difficult to reach) and, more compellingly, north-west over the entire bay and plain of Livádhia. At your feet are the grounds of the Panayía Polítissa monastery, where celebrations are held on 23 August.

After 25 more minutes, first travelling level and then sharply descending on the wide path, you arrive at the best possible detour to Áyios Séryios. Erosion scars in a red-dirt bank mark the start south from a bend in the main route, but it's no picnic – you very quickly must veer away from the head of a nasty ravine, and then drop across a hillside for nearly an hour. The trail tracing on the otherwise reliable Italian map is a bit optimistic here.

Back on the main track, another 15 minutes along from the trail to Áyios Séryios beach, the more heavily used side trail for

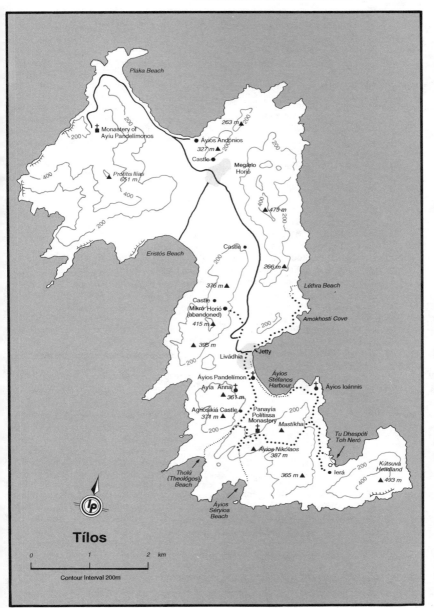

Plaka Beach

Monastery of
Ayiu Pandelímonos

200

200

Profítis Ilías
651 m

400

400

263 m ▲

Áyios Andónios
327 m ▲
Castle ●

Megálo
Horió

400 200

▲ 475 m

200

Eristós Beach

Castle ●

200

266 m ▲

376 m ▲

Léthra Beach

200

Castle ●
Mikró Horió ●
(abandoned)

Amokhósti Cove

415 m ▲

200

▲ 395 m

200

Livádhia

✝ Jetty

Áyios Pandelímon ●
Ayía Anna ✝
▲ 361 m

Áyios
Stéfanos
Harbour

Áyios Ioánnis ●

Agnosikiá Castle ●
371 m ▲

Panayía
Politissa
Monastery

200

Mastíkha
▲

Tu Dhespóti
Toh Neró

Kútsuva
Headland

▲ Áyios Nikólaos
387 m

▲ 493 m

365 m ▲

200

400

Ierá ○

Tholú
(Theológos)
Beach

Áyios
Séryios
Beach

Tílos

0   1   2 km

Contour Interval 200m

Tholú (a corruption of Theológos) beach appears on the left. This ends after 10 minutes at a ledge, allowing a glimpse of your destination below at the mouth of a deep valley. Cairns guide you the final 30 minutes down to the sand, with the route drifting slightly west across a tributary ravine in the final minutes. The *thólos* or domed vault of the name stands to the eastern side of the beach – whether a church, tomb or mine works is uncertain. Nudists love the place, but in spring there's still quite a lot of debris washed up from winter storms here.

Returning to the main trail takes just 30 minutes, owing to better uphill footing; just past the reunion is your opportunity, on the left, to scale the Agriosikiá castle from behind. (Approaching from Livádhia, it's a rockclimber's exercise.) A final half hour separates you from the cemetery of Livádhia, where the path becomes a motor-trike track. While you're here, hunt out the nearby church of Áyios Pandelímon, with the Byzantine mosaic floor of its predecessor exposed for viewing – a few animal figures are discernible.

The route as described, with the detour to Tholú, requires four hours; allow well over an hour for each additional side trip to Ierá, Áyios Séryios or the castle.

From Livádhia

Léthra Beach From Livádhia, hop up to the houses just above the ferry jetty, and find the obvious broad trail heading out towards the mouth of the bay some metres above the water. It does not show up on the Italian map because, amazingly, it was opened as late as the 1950s. There is no possibility of confusion on the 70-minute course to Léthra bay, with some 600 metres of pebbles and red sand; people camp here and disport themselves in the nude despite a lack of fresh water. About 15 minutes before the bay you can scramble down on goat traces to the hidden sandy cove of Amokhostí. Almost every visitor to the island, including small children, seems to make this walk at some point.

Mikró Horió An interesting short hike from Livádhia is up to the ghost village of Mikró Horió. Follow the cemented road towards Megálo Horió and Eristós, bearing right under power poles onto the old path when the road swings left. It's 30 minutes up to the saddle from where you have your first view of the ruins; cross the road for the remaining 15 minutes of trail hiking. The place was abandoned in favour of Livádhia during the 1950s because the inhabitants had to go too far for water; just the church, with a castle overhead, is intact, but opens only on the 15 August festival. Don't bother following red dots north towards Megálo Horió – there's no longer any trail worth mentioning since the road was improved.

Ayía Ánna Just a km inland, due south from 'downtown' Livádhia, the ksoklísi of Ayía Ánna is said to be the oldest on the island and has excellent Byzantine frescoes inside, as well as a pebble-mosaic floor. It's even closer than Mikró Horió, but to ensure entry ask around first in Livádhia for the key.

Nísiros

The nearly round island of Nísiros isn't merely volcanic – it *is* a volcano which last erupted in the 19th century. There is no drinkable ground water – everyone has cisterns – but oak, almond, olives and a few grapevines flourish in the fast-draining pumice soil. The climate is mild enough to rain-farm in the winter, which is just as well since most people can't afford to import water from Ródhos during the hot months.

Most of the population has left for Astoria (New York), and those who do remain make a fair living from quarrying pumice and gypsum – the islet of Yialí, between Nísiros and Kos, is a solid lump of minerals. Substantial tourism has only recently begun, and probably won't expand much – the island hasn't enough good beaches to satisfy the mass trade, and most visitors are day trippers from Kos who are whisked up in tour coaches to see the volcanic crater. Don't imitate them: Nísiros is well worth a few days' stay, with friendly inhabitants and a few good walks from Mandhráki, the main port and capital, up to the villages of Emborió and Nikiá, via the volcano.

Nisirians have a reputation for being fun-loving and a trifle unambitious. There are numbers of jolly fisherfolk here with red carnations behind their ears who wink at you, whether you're a man or a woman. The only thing that gets them worked up is the prospect of geothermal power, which they are almost uniformly against. The very bad behaviour on the part of the DEI (Greek public power corporation) on volcanic Mílos island is a warning of what could happen here, as far at the islanders are concerned, and they have so far succeeded in obstructing further exploitation of the crater's steam fields.

The DEI, for its part, is raring to go, hoping to expand from the one successful bore to date up to five, and sell the excess of the two megawatts of power generated to Kos, Kálimnos and Léros by undersea cable. As bait, they dangle the prospect of surplus electricity to run the island's desalination plant, which stands idle for lack of sufficient electricity to run it. The islanders retort that they will realise no benefit from the project, and on the contrary will see their agricultural and tourist livelihood ruined by the visual and atmospheric pollution.

It must be said that the DEI is off to a bad start, having messily abandoned an unsuccessful well and, in 1991, bulldozed a totally unnecessary road around the south-western flank of Nísiros. Worst, from the hiker's standpoint, was the simultaneous destruction of the 600-year old kalderími from Mandhráki to Nikiá, which was one of the finest in Greece, thus precisely halving the amount of walking on Nísiros. It took just one month to destroy a millennial work, and those responsible should be ashamed of themselves. Still, the trails that remain should keep you busy for a day or two.

Season

No freshwater sources, little shade, Dhodhekanisian climate – in other words, wonderful early spring or late autumn walking. A little rain makes Nísiros even greener than it normally is, and the February almond-blossom display is one of the most stunning in Greece.

Maps

Italian 1:25,000 occupation map *Isola di Nisiro*; YIS 1:50,000 *Nísos Nísiros**.

Access

Nísiros Nísiros has the same twice-weekly connections on the Kálimnos-Ródhos route as Tílos and Sími, as well as two boats a week, like Tílos, to selected Kikládhes islands and either Rafína or Pireás. Depending on the season, there are three to seven daily boats from Kardhámena on Kos opposite, with sometimes an additional unpublicised afternoon departure; more expensive, and strictly tourist, are the excursion kaïkia from Kos town.

Trailheads Nísiros bus services are a bit haphazard. In theory there are departures from Mandhráki to Nikiá at about 10 am and 1.30 pm, the latter being your way down when it turns around. In practice, however, one of the two vehicles is always broken down, with unannounced cancellations the result, or has been commandeered for a special tour and won't stop for you. In that case Stage 3B through Emborió will necessarily interest you.

ACROSS THE ISLAND

This itinerary cuts through some of the most impressive scenery on the island, allowing you (with an early start) to beat the mid-morning tour groups up to the volcano and to enjoy the destination village of Nikiá before catching the afternoon bus back if desired.

Rating & Duration

Despite a modest three-hour time for the basic outing, this is a moderately strenuous walk owing to the loose pumice surface and the occasional sharp grade.

Stage 1: Mandhráki to Evangelístria
(1 hour)

Leave Mandhráki via the stair-streets leading up from the inland platía, near Zervo's pastry shop and the public library. Once you're clear of the houses, bear onto the concrete drive that snakes uphill, passing a giant municipal cistern system on your left. Soon the pavement splits; in the angle of the fork a red-and blue-dotted path begins between dry-stone walls. This old donkey trail collides repeatedly with the road, which soon becomes dirt; bear left at the first road crossing, and keep your eyes peeled for the waymarks at each subsequent crossing. Finally, 40 minutes above town, you've no choice but to follow the bulldozed track for 15 minutes more to Evangelístria (250 metres). A giant pepper tree ringed by a concrete apron provides a good rest spot; inside the recently renovated monastery grounds there's a well with a bucket.

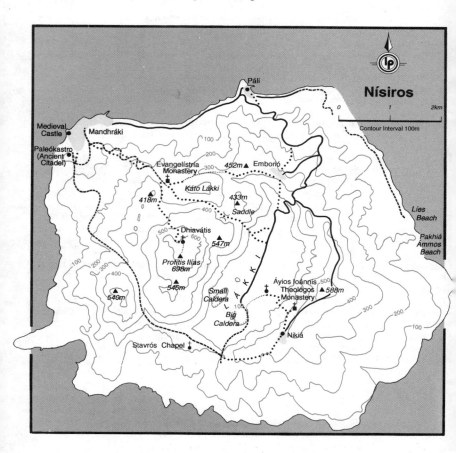

Nísiros

Top: Sími: Áyios Emilianós bay and headland, seen from the trail at Theológos (MD)
Left: Sími: Yialós, seen from Ayía Paraskeví with the islet of Nímos beyond (MD)
Right: Nísiros: The distinctive round upper platía of Nikiá (MD)

Top: North-west Sámos: Crossing Mikró Seïtáni cove (MD)
Left: North-west Sámos: Ayía Triádha hill seen from Paleó (Áno) Karlóvassi (MD)
Right: West Sámos: Kímisis Theotóku Convent under snow, Mt Kerkis (MD)

Sidetrip: Profítis Ilías Summit

(2½ hours return)

This is a magnificent sidetrip for a clear, calm day. Backtrack about 150 metres from the pepper tree and find a path bearing south and uphill. 'Pros Dhiavátis' ('To Dhiavatis', the monastery just below the summit) is very faintly splashed in white paint on a rock at the trailhead. Avoid the new bulldozer track down to the left; 15 minutes up the correct trail you'll pass a cistern and a small hut. Fork left immediately after, following a faint white arrow.

From this junction it's a one-hour climb along an occasionally messy but always traceable path to the farm-like monastery of Dhiavátis, tucked in a hollow just north of the peak. The trail ends here; scramble another 15 minutes by line of sight to the chapel atop 698-metre Profítis Ilías, roof of the island. Going clockwise from due south, you should see the islet of Sírna (southwest), Astipálea (west), Kos (the entire northern horizon), Kálimnos and Psérimos (partial views, behind Kos), the Reşadiye Peninsula in Turkey (north-east), Sími (east) plus Tílos and sometimes Ródhos (southeast).

There is no easy or safe direct way down to the volcano floor from this mountain – retrace your steps to Evangelístria and proceed to Stage 2.

Stage 2: Evangelístria Monastery to the Volcano

(1¼ hours)

Find, on the eastern edge of the pepper-tree circle, the start of the onward footpath. There are red and blue waymarks, and at one point the legend 'Volcano' in English. You almost instantly dip into, cross and climb out of the volcanic gully known as Káto Lákki. As you inch up the far side you can turn around to see Yialó islet, the Kríkello headland on Kos, and part of Kálimnos.

Soon the path levels out and slips through a pass in a volcanic moonscape about 35 minutes past Evangelístria and 1½ hours from Mandhráki. If you're alert you'll spot a stray steam vent on the high side of the trail.

The descent from the saddle is marred somewhat by a slippery haphazard trail, but waymarks deposit you on the asphalt road leading to the crater, near a stone house and a well, one hour 50 minutes out of Mandhráki. Turn right and walk 20 minutes through progressively thinning vegetation until you reach the moonscape. The entire volcanic valley, known locally as Lákki, is actually the magma chamber floor of a much larger volcano that collapsed in 1522.

Today, two small caldera slump still deeper below the level of the four-sq-km plateau. The primary, round, easterly crater is obvious and noisy: hissing fumaroles are encrusted with sulphur crystals, scalding water sometimes trickles to the surface, and everywhere there's the porridge-like sound of mud boiling a few inches below your shoes. Hidden at the western edge of the pumice desert lies the secondary crater, a bit quieter but more visually dramatic and too deep to get into. A drink stand between the two operates when tours are about, and marks the start of the 10-minute path up to the higher caldera.

Stage 3A: Volcano to Nikiá

(¾ hour)

From the drink stall, walk to the northeastern corner of the volcanic zone, some 400 metres north of the main caldera. The trail heads initially straight back and then zig-zags upslope from the vicinity of a small chapel and an abandoned geothermal wellhead, the metal litter of which so angers the islanders. The start is inconspicuous, but look for red paint-splodges. About 20 minutes up the path is a water tank, often cruelly empty; 40 minutes from the floor of Lákki you have the option of forking left to visit the attractive monastery of Áyios Ioánnis Theológos, 300 metres away. As usual for the shrines of the evangelist of Revelations, this contemplates the abyss, and hosts a lively festival on the night of 25 September.

Resuming your course, it's just a few minutes more, for a total of about 45 minutes from the drink stand, to the bus turnaround point of Nikiá. Hikers wishing to reverse the above instructions will see small bilingual signs below the bus stop pointing towards 'Áyios Ioánnis/St John' and 'Iféstio/Volcano'.

Nikiá, the highest of Nísiros's four villages, has incomparable views of both the sea and the crater, and is well-preserved, particularly the uniquely round upper platía, which comes alive for the 21 November festival. It would be a shame to arrive without time to explore Nikiá before the downhill bus leaves; you can even get a simple lunch at the kafenío roughly halfway between the upper platía and the bus turnaround area. Unlike Emborió, this village is still a going concern, and even house-owners in the diaspora are reluctant to sell out.

Stage 3B: Volcano to Emborió & Beyond

(¾–2 hours)

If you miss the bus down, you might want to know about some or all of this stage.

Upon meeting the asphalt road hiking into Lákki from Evangelístria, turn left instead of right; within a few minutes you'll reach the start of the mule path up to Emborió village, just visible on the cliff overhead. It's a stiff,

25-minute climb along this kalderími to this largely desolate, ruined village; all but about 10 people have moved to Páli or Mandhráki, and the abandoned houses are slowly being bought up and renovated by outsiders. A single kafenío serves cold drinks and little else.

To continue down to Páli, where there is food, lodging and up to six daily buses back to Mandhráki, find the kalderími which drops from the centre of the village (in a northerly direction). After a few moments it hits the road, which you're obliged to follow for about 40 minutes before the old trail cuts in on the right again and takes you down for the final 10 minutes to the water.

Purists might like to use the abandoned, overgrown trail leading directly from Emborió to Evangelístria. Climb to the top of Emborió and fork left before reaching the cemetery. The first 20 minutes are ordinary enough, but once around the mountain west of the village the trail fizzles out and you'll spend the next 25 minutes shuffling along the northern edge of Káto Lákki. What's left of the trail, whose former course is shown correctly on the Italian map, meets the more prominent path you probably took to Lákki about 50 metres short of the pepper tree.

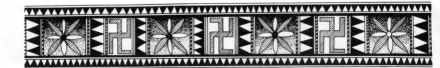

North-East Aegean Islands

The islands of the north-eastern Aegean are not quite a real archipelago, having little in common other than a similar date of union with Greece in late 1912 and a sense of being chunks of mainland adrift in the sea. Geologically this is literally true in the case of Sámos, Híos and Lésvos, all three islands having been at one time joined to Anatolia. It's a fact duly referred to by modern Turkey in its ongoing propaganda battle with Greece concerning continental shelves and territorial waters in the eastern Aegean.

Military tensions here are the most perceptible in the country outside of Thráki. Be alert to the international 'no photography' signs and be prepared to have tracks and trails not described here end up at army watchtowers or bunkers.

For their part the Greeks point to the enduring Hellenic presence on the Anatolian mainland opposite, which only ended in 1923. The three islands noted have always served as stepping stones in the transmission of Greek culture and merchandise, whether headed east or west, and the most tangible modern evidence of this is the mirror-imaging of architectural styles on the islands and their former counterparts across the water. The rickety wood-and-plaster townhouses of Sámos can also be seen in Kuşadası; the bazaar in Híos looks very much like the one in İzmir; and the warm-toned volcanic-stone houses of Lésvos are reflected at Turkish Ayvalık and Behramkale. After the 1923 peace treaty with Turkey, these islands received large numbers of Anatolian Greek refugees, thus adding to their Oriental flavour.

As in the Dhodhekánisos, the establishment of frontiers in the straits here after 1923 was an economic disaster for the islands concerned; however, the main towns were simply too big and important to completely go to seed, as often happened further south. Today they are still all medium-sized provincial capitals, spoilt in varying degrees by concrete eyesores and home to the scattered faculties of the University of the Aegean – a bureaucratic compromise that must be a logistical headache. While not exactly industrial, neither are they the marshmallow-cute towns of a Kikládhes promotional poster, and probably more than one traveller has been intimidated into staying on the ferry rather than disembarking. In all cases you should quell first impressions and enjoy the harbours for what they are – busy commercial centres – before pressing on into the often startlingly empty interiors.

It must be stressed that all of these islands are big, and public transport is poor compared to the more heavily visited Kikládhes or Crete. You'll want to establish yourself in one resort and explore its environs, and the hike descriptions for each island are tailored around a particular home base.

Sámos

One of the greenest islands in the Aegean, Sámos is also definitely the closest to Turkey – just over a nautical mile from the south-western coast to the mainland. Physically it is an enchanted isle, with high mountains, dense forests, a rainbow spectrum of wild-flowers, carefully terraced vineyards, lonely stretches of coast, and an aquamarine sea. Pythagoras was only the first of numerous mystics to be drawn to it.

Because of its fertility and position, Sámos has nearly always been important – and coveted. The ancient capital of Polycrates at present-day Pithagório was one of the great cities of Ionia, and in Byzantine times the island was wealthy enough to constitute its own *theme* (administrative division) within that empire.

Yet there is little evidence of this past greatness today, and not just because ancient and Byzantine ruins are thin on the ground.

Sámos was completely depopulated by Turkish pirates in the late 15th century, and remained empty for more than 100 years, enough time for complete discontinuity with its past. Even the fabled Sámian wine of Byronic fame is a product of recent French 'missionary' effort; nobody knows what the ancient stuff was like. When an Ottoman admiral received permission to resettle it, he did so with Greek Orthodox refugees gathered from every corner of the empire, with few questions asked by either party. So the island has been saddled with a permanent identity crisis and lack of distinctive cultural traits.

The new Samians acquitted themselves well in the war of independence, but rather than being united with Greece they were granted a unique semi-autonomous status for nearly a century, a period known as the Iyimonía, when the island was ruled by an appointed Christian prince and enjoyed a mild renaissance. An especially harsh WW II experience and mass emigration again sent the island into decline – and set the stage for the advent of mass tourism.

This began slowly at the end of the 1970s, gathering speed by the middle of the next decade until things, quite frankly, began to get out of hand. Sámos has now overdrawn its water supply, and the few remaining permanent streams are drying up. Arsonists have set to work, burning the best forest off the eastern third of the island; because of dense undergrowth and a lack of firebreaks, even the smallest blaze can be devastating. And the effect of the sudden influx of wealthy foreigners on the unsophisticated, unprepared local villagers has been equally catastrophic; about the politest thing one can say is that there are nice people everywhere in Greece, and there are just proportionately fewer of them on Sámos. There has simply not been the time to adjust gracefully, as in the broadly similar cases of Tenerife and Madeira.

Part of the social problem is the island's awkward size and demographics: too large to be intimate, too small to be cosmopolitan. It's the most countrified of the north-east

Aegean islands, and something of a two-headed monster with the rival towns of Karlóvassi and Vathí at opposite ends, each with about 25% of the Sámian population of 25,000.

Despite this grim capsule summary, the island is still very much worth a walking visit. Friends tell me that Sámos was a labyrinth of trails until the 1970s, when it must have been a trekker's paradise, because the number of surviving paths is still impressive. The most rewarding areas for hikes are the north-centre and western end of the island, on the shadier side of the central ridge which catches all moist air shuttling in either direction. Something in the landscape appeals to Germans, Dutch and Scandinavians, who flock here by the jet-full; the package season lasts from late April to late October, at other times the place is extremely quiet.

Season

Sámos has a relatively warm, damp climate that can be quite trying unless you're prepared for it. Areas facing south and east are drier and hotter in the summer, while the shaggier north gets the lion's share of cooling afternoon breezes, tempering the jungly humidity a bit. It's unwise to schedule midsummer hikes, especially in the shadeless north-east; May and September/October are usually delightful, whether along the north-west coast or up in the two mountain ranges. Being relatively far south, winter hikes at lower altitudes are more than feasible, but you'll find all tourist services outside Vathí and Karlóvassi completely shut down, and the buses offer a skeleton service at best.

Access (Sámos)

Ferry connections with Sámos are good, owing more to the island's central location in the eastern Aegean than recent touristic development. The two main harbours on Sámos are Karlóvassi in the north-west and Vathí in the north-east; nearly all ferries stop at both. Depending on the time of year, there are three to six weekly sailings from Ikaría and Pireás; something between two and five

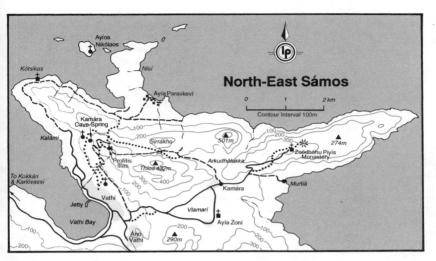

North-East Sámos

of these also call at a selection among Páros, Náxos, Síros, Tínos, Míkonos, and Fúrni.

Fúrni also sends its own kaïki to Karlóvassi twice a week, and similarly often through most of the year a small boat, the *Hioni* or its sister ship *Kapetan Stamatis,* calls from Híos, looping once weekly through Fúrni and Ikaría as well. The *Nisos Kalimnos* appears with similar frequency, linking Sámos – Pithagório harbour in this case – with most of the Dhodhekánisos, large and small.

In addition there's a once-weekly subsidised ferry (ágoni grammí) sailing in each direction between either Kaválla or Thessaloníki, stopping at all the bigger north-east Aegean islands and Dhodhekánisos on the way.

Domestic flights are currently restricted to three daily connections with Athens only. International charter arrivals fit the nationalities and time periods cited above; there are as yet no scheduled services from northern Europe.

NORTH-EAST LOOP

(3-5 hours)

This circuit out of Vathí and around grey,

bald Mt Thíos is the ideal winter or early spring hike, when clouds can still obscure the remoter corners of Sámos. The views across the indented coast here to Turkey are unrivalled; a big minus is the necessity of a certain amount of road-walking.

Rating & Duration

This is an easy hike of three to five hours, depending on whether you make either of the optional detours.

Maps

Use the British 1:50,000 wartime map *Sámos East*; YIS 1:50,000 *Sámos**. The latest edition of the Vasilis Valis 1: 75,000 tourist map, while devoid of contour lines, does feature a number of suggested hikes, including this one, traced crudely on insets.

Route Directions

From the Vathí waterfront, head inland past Olympic Airways and the post office to the junction known as Plátanos named after the big plane tree in the middle of the road. There's a supermarket on the right, and the Kotopula taverna on the left; a sign on the tree points left to 'Vlamarí, 4' – follow it.

About 100 metres further, where the asphalt winds up and left, go straight back and level on a concrete surface to the start of the old kalderími up to Vlamarí.

There's one point, a few minutes along, where you hit the road again, but simply veer right to the resumption of the kalderími to one side of a pension. It's a total of 20 minutes up to a pass flanked by a small monastery and a taverna; here the cobbles end and you must follow the road slightly down onto the vast, sparsely populated Vlamarí upland, devoted to grapes and other crops.

Upon reaching the fork in the road, bear left, and within 15 more minutes you'll be at the large hamlet of Kamára, all of 15 houses and two tavernas. The latter are too early on in the walk to be very compelling, but if you do the detour suggested later they'll come in handy afterwards.

Continue through Kamára on the asphalt until, five minutes beyond the edge of the village, there's a junction. On the right is a hilltop army installation, straight down leads to the fishing anchorage of Murtiá, and the asphalt curls left, slightly uphill. Follow it for perhaps 150 metres until you see a well-designed path taking off right over a wooden bridge with railings. This is the start of the old way to Zoödhóhu Piyís monastery, the most spectacularly set on the island.

About 20 minutes along, the kalderími makes a hairpin back left to meet the road again; the straight-ahead path was abandoned in the 1970s when the road was opened. Turn right on the road and, after perhaps three minutes, notice the resumption of a stair-trail worming up in a ravine. A couple of moments up is a cistern with some places to sit – a good rest stop. Soon the kalderími grade slackens, and you can see the monastery ahead to the north-east.

You arrive at the gate some 45 minutes above Kamára. Founded in the late 18th century, Zoödhóhu Piyís is not of any particular historical or artistic interest, but it still functions with two or three monks in residence, and is for all intents and purposes the parish church of Kamára, well attended on Sundays and festivals. Behind and above,

still further north-east, is a broad mesa with a large ikónisma and terrific views of the straits between here and Turkish Kusadasi. It is inadvisable to proceed further, as this is a military area.

Retrace your steps to Kamára, a 40-minute exercise; before reaching either of the two tavernas, bear right (north) onto a drive leading up to the highest visible houses and a giant plane tree. Pass this, continuing on the dirt track going north by the very last houses of the hamlet. In a few moments a large, hidden valley, the Arkudhólakka, opens out at your feet, and the motor-trike track veers around left. There are some tempting-looking trails up on the left, but they go nowhere any longer; stay on the track until, about 20 minutes out of Kamára, more productive paths with a few waymarks angle up and left on the hillside towards a prominent pass overhead. If you miss the paths and follow the track too long, you'll end up in a low gully near some goat pens and a concrete cistern – back up.

The saddle (250 metres) is reached half an hour beyond Kamára; turn around to see Turkey and the Zoödhóhu Piyís headland beyond Arkudhólakka. Point 432 of Thíos is immediately south, and the lower hump of Sirrákho flanks the pass on the north. The recently extended road cuts the path just east of the saddle; merely cross it to resume course on the other side, guided by cairns and 1992-repainted waymarks.

Descend west-north-west now, aiming for a nearly level clearing flanked by some pine trees offering welcome shade, reached within 15 minutes. There are some vague moments in the path, but heed the occasional red paint splodges and the way clears up over the next quarter of an hour to a lone ruined farm presiding over some terraces. Now you can look north over some of the most jagged coast on Sámos, with the nearly deserted southern shore of Turkey's Çesme peninsula beyond. The chapel of Profítis Ilías will be seen just a bit overhead.

Unlikely as it looks, the ruined house and terraces mark two major junctions. If you go out the property's boundary fence on the west, following waymarks, you'll have the choice of bearing uphill (south-west) towards the chapel (320 metres), reached within 20 minutes, with a slight detour off the 'main' path in the last few moments. It used to be that you could continue along that path all the way back to Vathí as an alternative to what's described below, but the new road in the vicinity has considerably diminished its appeal and made finding the way difficult even on this short scramble (use the newly painted waymarks, but reverse their sense).

It's best, then, after admiring the view from Profítis Ilías, to descend to the derelict cottage and terraces again and continue slightly downhill, west-north-west, towards a shallow gully studded with a pair of cypresses. Despite some cairns the way is ambiguous here; the trick is to avoid the tempting valley bottom, staying a bit high on the left until the trail clearly kicks in again at the base of the hill, alongside a stone wall.

If you were instead to angle north through the low scrub and out of the gully to the very low crest ahead, you'd eventually collide with the waymarked, narrow path down to Ayía Paraskeví, the inhabited cove to the right of the indented Nisí peninsula. Before the coast road around via Kalámi and Kótsikas was built, this was the only overland way into Ayía Paraskeví.

Assuming you've left that for another day, proceed along the resumed main trail as it slips through a defile, emerging onto a panorama over Vathí bay. Vegetation, including some huge oaks, suddenly becomes lusher, and 20 minutes beyond the terraces and ruin you'll see why: the cave-fountain of Kamára (no relation to the hamlet), on the left of the trail and brimming over with water in a normally wet winter or spring. Below the often soggy trail, accessible via some steps, is the chapel of Zoödhóhos Piyí ('Life-giving Spring'), a tribute to the cave.

From here the trail south towards Vathí is obvious, with no complications except for a brief spell through what looks like an abandoned army obstacle training course. Some 20 minutes beyond Kamára is a side trail on

the left marked with a blue chapel symbol that is the start of the most frequented, 35-minute hike up to Profítis Ilías.

Despite the new, ugly road cut, most of the path is still negotiable. Some 10 minutes up it, you hit the road at a curve – the debouchement is flanked by cairns, as is the trail resumption 200 metres uphill. When this happens again 15 minutes later, walk up the road 150 metres, past the first cairn to another atop the slippery road embankment – that is the true path continuation. You hit the road again in a few moments, but this time access to the resumption right is on a firmer set of steps hacked out of the schist; you won't see the road again until up top, when it passes just east of the little chapel.

The main descending path, now a kalderími, curls down past a chapel on a terrace to a T-junction within five minutes; bear right here, away from the first block of flats at the edge of town, and emerge instead at the top of Ikosiosdhóïs Oktovríu St, which you then follow steeply down to near the ferry dock.

The basic loop from Plátanos junction to this point takes about three hours; add 90 minutes for a side-trip to Zoödhóhou Piyís monastery, and another half hour for the scramble up to Profítis Ilías from the old farm.

NORTH-CENTRAL VILLAGES

This is the classic Sámian walk, waymarked for more than a decade, the first walk that most people attempt, and now even on the list of package day tours. Unfortunately, one leg of the trail has recently been destroyed by road-building above it, and the track met below Manolátes is due to be extended towards Vurliótes, so it's uncertain whether you'll be able to complete the entire itinerary in the future. There are, however, numerous bail-outs and alternative sectors, so you will probably still be able to piece together something satisfactory.

Rating & Duration

This is a moderate hike of less than five hours, but most people make an easy day of it with frequent stops for food and drink in the villages along the way.

Maps

Use the British 1:50,000 wartime maps *Sámos East* and *Sámos West*; YIS 1:50,000 *Sámos** & *Néon Karlovásion**. The Vasilis Valis tourist map, cited before, has a schematicised route.

Access

If you're not already staying in Kokkári, get one of the earlier departures of the nine daily

bus services from Vathí. This frequency applies only from early June to mid-September; in spring and autumn there may only be five or six departures, with one less in the morning.

Stage 1A: Kokkári to Vurliótes

(1½ hours)

Begin at the very south-western edge of Kokkári resort, where the new bypass road meets the town service road by the Milos Beach Hotel. From the 'Stop' sign by the

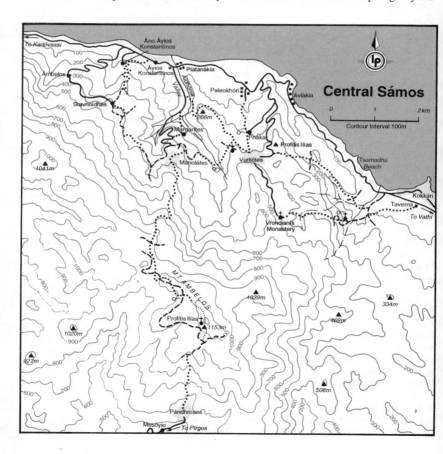

Central Sámos

0   1   2 km

Contour Interval 100m

hotel, head up (south) along the initially asphalted street, which becomes dirt after a few moments. Some 300 metres along, near a water tap, bear right at a Y-junction; this slips over a slight rise, from where you see a lush valley with greenhouses. Descend, keeping left of all cultivation, as the track narrows and becomes a trail passing under the arch of an abandoned aqueduct, with an ikónisma wedged in the buttress. Waymarks are useful here; cross the stream soon met at the best ford, and head up west to the power pole on the hillside ahead, where the old trail becomes much more distinct. All of this shouldn't take more than 15 minutes.

A couple of minutes later, a recent jeep track scissors across the trail, which continues, cairned and well-grooved into the terrain, just the other side. As the path climbs gradually on the north-eastern flank of the forested canyon here, there are no other potential sources of confusion until, about 40 minutes out of Kokkári, another new track slices over the path; again, simply head straight across onto the resumption.

Now the route dips slightly on its way to a rocky ravine and the base of the final kalderími approach to Vurliótes. This is the steepest portion of this stage, but still manageable; the main complaint people seem to have, hiking up in the morning, is their inability to get a decent photo aiming east over Kokkári. The trail debouches inconspicuously on the low side of a service drive leading within 100 metres to the concrete apron on the paved road up to Vurliótes, one hour 15 minutes along; a half-unbolted sign here points down the way you've come, indicating the path to Kokkári.

Another quarter of an hour along the access road takes you to the photogenic platía of Vurliótes, where a number of small tavernas cater to walkers. Snack Bar Kiki is the most consistent, offering *revithó-keftedhes* (chickpea croquettes) and their own expensive but good *moskháto* dessert wine, which can be made more versatile by dilution with soda water. Owing to good land and abundant water, Vurliótes is the most thriving of the north-central hill villages,

though the population is still down to 500 from its heyday of about 1200.

Stage 1B: Paleokhóri to Vurliótes
(50 minutes)

This alternative approach to Vurliótes is also useful descending, particularly if you're staying at Platanákia and can't be bothered with getting a bus to or from Kokkári.

Coming from Vathí, ask the bus driver to set you down near the side road up to Vurliótes; the main coastal highway is too narrow to stop at the actual trailhead, about 700 metres further, where a cluster of houses to the south flank an initially concrete drive signposted 'Paleokhóri'. Wind up past the houses to the chapel of Profítis Ilías; just past this a chain stretched across the track is your cue to veer left onto a narrow trail which quickly becomes a kalderími.

Half an hour above the main road you reach the small hamlet of Pnáka, with a triple-spouted fountain and a summer-only taverna. From here you've another 20 minutes up to Vurliótes, where successive left and right turns will lead you up to the platía.

Stage 2A: Vurliótes to Kokkári via Vrondianís Monastery
(1½ hours)

This is a popular way back to Kokkári, especially if you've come over Ámbelos from Pándhrosos (see Ascents of Mt Ámbelos) or are reversing the northern village loop.

From the eastern edge of Vurliótes, walk for half an hour on the track to the monastery of Vrondianís (Vrónda, Vrondú; no possibility of trail short-cutting). This is the oldest on the island, dating from the 16th-century resettlement, but sadly the army is using it as a barracks and have made some horrific architectural adulterations. The local festival, on or about 8 September (the Birth of the Virgin), is one of Sámos's liveliest, taking place both here and at Vurliótes.

The curious epithet Vrondianís ('Our Lady the Thunderer') comes from a local weather superstition: the islanders claim that there will always be a severe, unseasonable storm in the week preceding or following 8 September, and this is almost always true.

To head downhill, find a large, flat expanse like a soccer pitch some 150 metres below and north-east of the monastery building. Here a hand-drawn blue-on-white sign says 'Monopáti Kokkári' in Greek. Some 10 minutes along you'll descend through the ruined cottages of an abandoned hamlet into a stream valley, crossing the water (if any) a few moments later.

Once on the other side the trail becomes a dramatic corniche route, level or even slightly uphill, high up on the right bank of the stream valley which has become a plunging gorge. You'll see nearly bare cliffs on the far side, and a frontal view of Kokkári and (weather permitting) Kuşadası as you approach the half-hour mark out of Vrondianí. Some 45 minutes along, cut across the curves of a dirt track ending near some scattered farmhouses; the trail continues below them – be alert for the red waymarks. Next you'll have to curl down through some terraces, cross a track again, and then plunge down steeply on an over-grown section of path to a spring shaded by giant plane trees. Immediately below is a white ksoklísi, one hour along.

Below the chapel the trail is temporarily swallowed by the track, which you adopt going seaward for 10 minutes to a four-way junction. Barrel straight on, using more path for a 10-minute section to a final track inter-section. Bear right a few paces to the trail's resumption in some olive terraces. From here it's 20 minutes more, for a 1½-hour walk from out of Vrondianís monastery, along a somewhat overgrown trail tunnelling through dense vegetation. The stage ends literally on top of the Hriso Varelli taverna, where you can recover from those last few moments of bush-whacking.

Stage 2B: Vurliótes to Manolátes
(1¼ hours)

The onward path to Manolátes village starts at the western edge of Vurliótes, by the cemetery (about 300 metres elevation). A few moments down the slope here it's vital to take the left-hand, red-dotted option at a Y-fork, not the blue-blazed trail on the right. There's another less obvious junction about 10 minutes beyond the cemetery in more open scrub – it's easy to go straight onto the route for Stage 2C without meaning to, so be sure to hairpin back and left here. (Both options are waymarked.) Some 15 minutes out of Vurliótes you'll arrive at a ksoklísi guarding a pass and an ugly new dirt road at about 280 metres, with a nose-to-nose view of Manolátes across a big valley – which you'll have to cross.

From the chapel the path drops down within 15 more minutes to a permanent stream (150 metres) which runs beneath tall trees and creepers in all but the driest years. Most walkers insist on resting at this beauti-ful spot for a few minutes; the water is drinkable. When you're ready to move on don't cross the creek directly, but proceed about 50 metres upstream then west and uphill; numerous red waymarks on rocks and stumps point the way. The climb ahead is softened by the dense shade of the copses arching over the trail at times, centuries of donkeys and rain having excavated it well below the surrounding ground level.

The path winds up past an isolated cottage on a rise above the vegetation tunnels, just before the first market gardens of Manolátes. Then, 45 minutes out of Vurliótes, it slams into the end of an ugly modern service track pushed this far in 1987, and slated to be extended to Vurliótes, hopefully above the streambed crossing, at some time in the future.

You're forced to take this; almost immediately make a left turn. This curls up onto a higher contour and reaches another junction within 10 minutes, by a newly ren-ovated cottage. Turn sharply left and uphill, prompted by a faded red dot left over from the time this was a trail, and watch very carefully for the resumption of the path between dry-stone walls on the right within 200 metres. This leads without further prob-lems to a concrete lane on the north-eastern edge of Manolátes within 10 minutes, or one hour 10 minutes out of Vurliótes. If you haven't already done so, turn around and gaze at the vine terraces below, like the background landscape in a Renaissance painting.

It's another few minutes to the centre of the village, where you've a choice of two or three snack bar-cafés. The most popular, by virtue of its location on the fountain platía, is Yioryidhes, though Tria Alfa lower down is slightly better. In September they both serve stuffed squash flowers, a wonderful delicacy. Manolátes once had 450 people but now can only muster 150, with just three children in the primary school. However, the population seems to have stabilised as a few young adults, fed up with town, move back to ancestral homes.

Stage 2C: Vurliótes to Platanákia
(¾ hour)
This is a useful alternative route for getting quickly to and from Platanákia, the eastern 'suburb' of Áyios Konstantínos.

Follow the directions for Stage 2B until, about 10 minutes beyond the cemetery, you go straight, rather than left towards the chapel. The waymarks take you along the seaward side of a low ridge thick with small oaks, arbutus and carob; some 10 minutes later, ignore a tempting right fork and curl left and down away from a rural cottage. You'll descend past another, and then level out at the edge of a well-tended olive grove. Beyond this the path drops steeply on its way to a grassy meadow and the same stream as encountered in Stage 2B, only much lower down. Cross it on half-submerged rocks and find yourself, a bit over half an hour from the junction, on the road from Manolátes to Platanákia, just 700 metres inland from the latter. The debouchement is marked with a red dot for the benefit of those wishing to head uphill; this takes no more than 40 minutes to the junction.

Stage 3A: Manolátes to Áno Áyios Konstantínos via Stavrinídhes
(1¼ hours)
From the fountain platía, descend a few paces and then bear left (west) onto a down-

hill jeep track which is initially concreted. It's easy to miss; you want to go down by the yellow building housing the rural clinic (agrotikó iatrío). About five minutes later the track swings left; there's a hand-lettered sign formerly pointing to the start of the old trail to Stavrinídhes uprooted and propped up against the embankment. Opposite are crude barriers across the old trailhead, with more hand-lettering warning you not to enter.

Not content with the existing forest track winding into the mountains, those folks who love to squander EC grant money or community funds have opened a rough track, currently impassable to vehicles, between Manolátes and Stavrinídhes. Some 600 metres of the wonderful old trail lies permanently buried under the rubble and boulders displaced by blasting and bulldozing higher up. You have no choice but to continue along the older track, forking right after a few moments onto the new one. After passing two stone huts, this ends 20 minutes out of Manolátes, for the moment some distance short of the leg coming to meet it from Stavrinídhes.

Cairns guide you over the mess at the end of the bulldozed zone to a steep, impromptu trail hacked out through some scrub; this quickly deposits you onto a proper path feeding you onto what is left of the old main trail, down and to the right. This dips into a second canyon about half an hour out of Manolátes. Shortly after, you've no choice but to adopt the Stavrinídhes-originating branch of the dirt road just overhead, which brings you to a saddle within 10 more minutes.

Go neither left on the new track nor straight on an older one towards an isolated bluff, but hunt out the resumption of a trail on the western side of the older dirt road. This drops into a final wet canyon, with a spring at the bottom, and then up the slope through the fringes of Stavrinídhes, about an hour from Manolátes.

Stavrinídhes (275 metres) is a sleepy place, the least imposing of the three villages on this itinerary, with little in the way of food or drink – though there are a couple of rooms to rent. It has recently acquired some notoriety, in a country where the Orthodox church is all but a state religion, as a haven for Jehovah's Witnesses. To finish the trek, clear the village and bear down and right onto the lane passing the cemetery.

Beyond this point over-eager earth movers have been at it again, and you're obliged to track-walk about 10 minutes past the graveyard. If you look carefully you can still see broken-up sections of the old kalderími to either side. When the jeep road hairpins sharply inland you'll see a red dot and the reemergence of the trail to seaward. From here it's 25 minutes on the weedy but still enjoyable path down to the highest houses of Áno Áyios Konstantínos. Turn right when you reach the T-junction, and stroll a few minutes to the fountain and the (usually locked) medieval chapel just below.

Leaving the village along the side drive towards the coast road, watch for the kalderími taking off at right angles, bound for the centre of lower Áyios Konstantínos; this will save a few minutes of road-walking. The last bus towards Kokkári and Vathí passes by at about 6.45 pm in summer, or 4.45 pm in spring and autumn.

Stage 3B: Manolátes to Platanákia via the Aïdhónia Valley

Although not as satisfying as a conclusion down to Áno Áyios Konstantínos, this stage is well suited to those who can't stand track walking, or are running late.

Leave Manolátes on the main paved access road, going north; after a couple of curves, some 500 metres out of town, take the stair-path that appears on the right of the pavement. Within five minutes you'll hit a dirt track; turn right onto this, but very shortly take the path's resumption left, between walls, down to a visible chapel; don't curl around on the track to a farmhouse.

Once below the chapel there are no further complications, though within a few minutes you might wish to detour down and right to the well-concealed, abandoned hamlet of Margarítes. All that remains intact are a frescoed church (usually locked) and a spring. The main trail eventually emerges between two cottages on the Platanákia-Manolátes concrete road some 20 minutes below the latter. It's about as much time again down to the coast road and the Platanákia bus stop through the densely wooded valley of Aïdhónia.

ASCENTS OF MT ÁMBELOS (KARVÚNIS)

The second-highest summit of Sámos is not a very striking peak, but the climb up from either of two trailhead villages is beautiful, passing through venerable forests of long-needled Calabrian pine which so far have escaped the firebugs. You can reverse one of the two approaches – preferably the Manolátes route – to make a point-to-point traverse rather than an out-and-back.

Rating & Duration

This is a moderate climb, whether done as a traverse or round trip, involving four to 4½ hours of hiking.

Maps

Use the British 1:50,000 wartime map *Sámos East*; YIS 1:50,000 sheet *Sámos**. The Vasilis Valis map route goes a different way.

Ascent 1: Approach from Manolátes
(4½ hours return)

This is easily appended to the northern villages trek, especially since the latter will be rather brief without the Manolátes-Stavrinídhes leg. It is also the more commonly done climb, since public transport connections to nearby Platanákia are so good.

Start from the fountain, dated 1876, in the platía (350 metres) opposite the Yioryidhes snack bar; climb past it, bearing left, until you see many red arrows pointing up Odhós Dhexamenís (Reservoir St). Follow this lane to the edge of the village, where more red dots and arrows point to a right fork leading past the tank in question and up onto a distinct trail.

The path is well grooved into the land-scape for the first half an hour up to a ridge with the last, well-tended grapevines of the village. Beyond here the trail fades a bit as it winds through dense, occasionally obstructive vegetation, but there is usually a timely waymark, scrap of rubbish or worn spot to guide you. About an hour along, cross the end of a bulldozer track at a high, abandoned vineyard; the way is particularly ambiguous above here across some grassy turf, but within 15 minutes of westerly then south-ward progress you end up next to a rocky outcrop, a false 900-metre summit of Ámbelos.

Descend slightly from this for 10 minutes to a forest road which you go directly across, heading up the steep bank opposite. Within another 15 minutes through an impressive forest of Calabrian pine, a relatively uncommon tree for Aegean Greece, you'll approach the road again. Some 70 metres before meeting it, follow red dots curling left (south-east) through the trees, parallel to a small ridge. You see road again briefly, but do not use it, as it curves away from the faint trail when you emerge from behind the low ridge. You'll reach the island's watershed at just under 1000 metres elevation, one hour 45 minutes above Manolátes, where the trail ends for now at the forest road that runs parallel to it.

After glimpsing the ocean south of Sámos, turn left; some red dots on the opposite side of the track beckon, but much of the onward path has been destroyed. Still, purists can trace many portions of the old route to either side of the little-used track, especially about 15 more minutes along, just before a rocky hogback plummets to meet the road as it curls up and right. Some 100 metres before this, a stretch of old trail drops briefly right to a gulch and then climbs slightly to a little rock-lined pool about 30 metres below the level of the road. This slow spring also lies just below a gentler ridge on the high side of the forest road, flecked with red waymarks, allowing the easiest access to the summit.

Once across the road, trail traces of sorts continue through the last trees but mostly

just follow the blazes until they stop in the middle of a rock-ladder; by now the final distance to the true peak is fairly obvious, moving cross-country on the open ridge just above the treetops. You go clockwise along the watershed, avoiding the big 'bowl' to the south; red waymarks resume. Twenty-five minutes above the spring, or a brisk 2½ hours from Manolátes, should see you at the 1153-metre peak of Profítis Ilías with its squat chapel. There are also two peculiar structures nearby, military relay antennae installed by NATO in 1977 with the aid of helicopters.

The view is the best on Sámos – take out a compass to identify the following high-lights on a clear spring or fall day: Kuşadası, 60°; Vathí, due east; Samsun Dağ in Turkey, the ancient Mt Mikale, 120°; Agathónisi, 150°; Lipsí and Léros, due south; Arkí and Pátmos, 200°; Fúrni and Thímena, 240°; Ikaría, 260°; and Mt Kérkis (Kerketévs), the island's loftiest peak, due west.

Returning to Manolátes by the same route requires just over two hours – not as quick as you'd think, as the downhill grade is sharp and hard on the knees.

Ascent 2: Approach from Pándhrosos
(2½ hours return)

This is a much shorter climb – 80 minutes in total – since the trailhead is both higher and closer to the peak. However, public transport in is poor: on weekdays only there is a 7.45 am bus from Vathí to Pírgos, the large village six km below Pándhrosos, from where you'll have to get a taxi to the trailhead. There's also a 2 pm departure, but this gets you to Pándhrosos too late to complete a traverse by dark except perhaps a week either side of the summer solstice. It makes little sense to come down this way, unless you can afford a long taxi ride or a hired vehicle left parked here.

Once in Pándhrosos (Áno Arvanítes, 640 metres), find the highest of three platías, which has the main church in the far corner. Don't cross the square, however, but turn onto a waymarked cobbled street going up and left; this soon curls around to head north

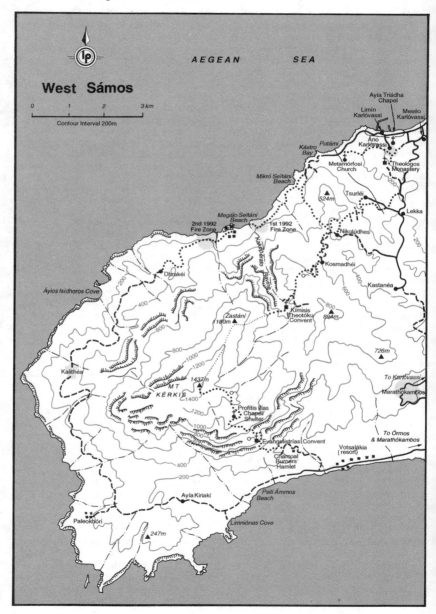

AEGEAN   SEA

West Sámos

0   1   2   3 km

Contour Interval 200m

Ayía Triádha Chapel
Limín Karlóvassi
Meséo Karlóvassi
Áno Karlóvassi
Kástro Bay
Potámi
Metamórfosi Church
Theológos Monastery
Mikró Seitáni Beach
524m
Tsurléi
Lekka
Megálo Seitáni Beach
2nd 1992 Fire Zone
1st 1992 Fire Zone
Nikolúdhes
Kakó Peráto
Dhrakéi
Kosmadhéi
Kastanéa
Áyios Isidhoros Cove
200
400
600
800
Zastáni 180m
Kimísis Theotóku Convent
894m
726m
Kalithéa
600
1000
1200
MT KÉRKIS
1437m
1400
To Karlóvassi
Marathókambos
1200
Profítis Ilías Chapel/Shelter
1000
800
Evangelistrías Convent
Votsalákia (resort)
To Órmos & Marathókambos
Charcoal Burners' Hamlet
400
200
Ayía Kiriakí
Psilí Ámmos Beach
Paleokhóri
247m
Limniónas Cove

and out of the village, through fields. Just over 10 minutes along, bear left with some waymarks, away from what seems to be the main path; five minutes later, take another left up and over a tiny aqueduct.

From here on the path is simple to follow, though badly overgrown once you're above the last tilled plots of land. But 35 minutes along you'll hit a new jeep road; cross the curve here and continue to the next and final tangling with it five minutes later. Turn right and follow it through the Calabrian pines up to the one-hour mark, where a yellow sign reading 'Pros Prof. Ilía/Karvúnis' in Greek indicates a left at a fork. There's a brief trail shortcut early along this, but most of the final quarter of an hour of the one hour 20 minutes up to the summit is cross-country over bare, stony hillside – leave the track when you think best.

To set off correctly from the chapel towards Manolátes, the proper compass bearing is 330-340°. There are a few waymarks on the initially open ridge here, but they're more orientated for people ascending from Manolátes.

Should you have a compelling reason to return to Pándhrosos, the descent on the same route takes just over an hour.

ASCENTS OF MT KÉRKIS (KERKETÉVS)

The second-highest point in the Aegean after Samothráki's Mt Fengári is an impressive mountain, a partly volcanic extrusion in what is otherwise mostly schist. The peak, riddled with shrines and caves, has always attracted legends as well as streamers of cloud; local fisherfolk claim, for instance, that an aurora seen around the summit in certain weathers is the spirit of Pythagoras.

You can make a short, sharp climb from the beach resort of Votsalákia in the south-west of the island, or opt for the longer, gradual approach via a string of villages between Karlóvassi and the peak. There is also a useful link trail between this latter route and the north-west coast.

As with Ámbelos, it is possible to reverse one of the routes given (preferably the one

from Votsalákia) to fashion a traverse, but in that case you're probably better off doing it as a two-day trek with a camp near a spring below the summit.

There is also said to be a route up from Kalithéa village, though I have not done it; the local shepherds are familiar with it.

Rating & Duration

This is the most difficult walk on Sámos, whether done as an out-and-back or a traverse; allow seven to eight hours of walking time.

Season

This hike should only be attempted in stable conditions between May and October. The peak gets a fair bit of snow in winter, which will obscure the route, but more dangerously can wave a big streamer of cloud and mist at any time – the cause of the worst aviation disaster in Greek history.

Maps

Use the British 1:50,000 wartime map *Sámos West*; YIS 1:50,000 *Néon Karlo-vásion**. The Vasilis Valis map's schematic route is roughly correct.

Access

If you are not already staying in Votsalákia, take any of the two to four daily buses there from Karlóvassi – exact timings vary with the season, though it is obviously best to aim for the earliest one. You may have to pay for a taxi back to Karlóvassi in the afternoon, as the last bus back historically goes between 3 and 4 pm.

Trek 1: Votsalákia to Kérkis via Evangelistrías Convent

(7 hours return)

Head west out the developed portion of Votsalákia until reaching a dirt track going inland, just past a small bridge; there should be some red dots and a sign in Greek reading 'Evangelistrías'. Five minutes along, turn left at a T-junction by a house and continue north-west towards the toes of the mountain. Upon reaching a charcoal burners' hamlet 20 minutes along, turn left again, cued by a red dot on a rock, and a couple of minutes later repeat the manoeuvre, following a hand-lettered sign. You must stay on this track through olive groves until, 40 minutes above the coast road, you'll see a dot and a cairn above and right, marking the start of the old trail up to the convent.

You're not entirely clear of the dirt road yet, as it chews up the path at two more curves; look for a red arrow on an olive tree on one occasion. Phone wires leading up to the monastery are the most reliable waymarks. Just over an hour under way you'll reach a natural ledge with fine views west over the Fúrni archipelago and the bay of Limniónas.

From here the often cobbled trail zig-zags purposefully north until arriving, 1½ hours along, at the convent of Evangelistrías, set in a pine grove at 675 metres elevation. Collect plenty of water at the spring here, as sources higher up are not entirely reliable. The four elderly nuns here welcome climbers with a

Sámos: Charcoal-burners mound at foot of Mt Kérkis (below Evangelistrías Convent)

shot of ouzo and will express voluble concern for your safety if they feel that either your kit or the weather are not what they should be. The katholikón is of no great artistic or historic interest – the superb balcony setting's the thing. Proper dress is required to visit the interior; both sexes will have to change out of the shorts they're likely to be wearing.

Continue behind the buildings, leaving the grounds through a gate at their north-eastern corner for the path's continuation through the tall trees. Almost immediately the trail angles up and left, marked by a series of blue paint splodges and crosses, very helpful since the way is often faintly visible.

Some two hours along you go through a gate marking the upper boundary of the monastery holdings, just below the treeline at about 900 metres. Curl across a small ravine and then north up a spur through a mix of rocks and grass to a small plateau at 2¼ hours, from where you'll first see the actual double-humped peak to the north-west.

Now the way veers slightly north-east to arrive at the chapel of Profítis Ilías (1150 metres) 2¾ hours along. Here there's an extra room with a fireplace that makes a suitable emergency shelter. Beyond this point bear north-west again to a saddle laced with a few trails, where you could camp if necessary. The most prominent of these paths, initially red-dotted, leads north with little altitude change to another double-humped ridge at the top of the valley to the left. From here on all the way to the summit you'll find lemon-scented mint that makes excellent tea, and (in late spring) tiny pink and red ranunculus.

Three hours out, to the right of the route, is a little spring that runs well into summer after a normally wet winter. Just beyond the spring you'll attain the saddle, behind which another deep valley leads down to the convent of Kímisis Theotóku (see Trek 2: Karlóvassi to Kérkis). Turn left to pass a damaged blue metal ikónisma atop a rise at 1225 metres, 10 minutes above the spring. Facing west now, skirt the second knoll and adopt one of the many faint traces curling south-west around a hill temporarily obscuring the summit. These eventually consolidate into a single, main path which ends up on a final east-west saddle at the base of the peak. Worm your way up more traces and livestock gouges to the 1437-metre summit at 3¾ hours.

This is indeed the true summit, though the northerly of the two bumps seems higher when you're actually up there. The view is apt to be a bit disappointing, since so much of the island lies to the east, blocking views in that direction, and convoluted Kérkis itself limits perspectives closer up. Below the secondary summit, on 3 August 1989, an Olympic Aviation STOL plane flying in from Thessaloníki crashed in a thick mist with the loss of all 34 aboard – a blot on the safety record of Olympic Airways and its subsidiary, and a tragedy still remembered on the island. Most of the wreckage was cleaned up, but you will still notice some pieces.

The way down to Votsalákia takes 3¼ hours, with the particularly steep grade between Profítis Ilías and Evangelistrías slowing you down considerably. If you have daylight and stamina to spare, treat yourself with a swim at either Psilí Ámmos or Votsalákia beaches – a good enough reason for spending a night or two here rather than rushing for the afternoon bus out, or splurging for a taxi.

Trek 2: Karlóvassi to Kérkis via Kímisis Theotóku

(6 hours one way)

Karlóvassi is a scattered, not particularly distinguished town divided into four districts: Néo, Meséo, Áno or Paleó, and Limín. This trek – as well as the north-western coast route in the next section – actually starts in Áno, the most attractive and well-sited of the neighbourhoods.

If you begin from Néo, cross to Meséo by the steeply pitched bridge over the riverbed, adapted today to carry cars but dating from the 19th century. Just less than 10 minutes along, turn left onto a narrower lane flanked by a palm tree. This street leads pleasantly

through Meséo Karlóvassi; a few minutes later, having passed the signed side road up to Lékka and Kosmadhéi, take a left onto a concrete driveway heading in the general direction of the hilltop chapel of Ayía Triádha, as soon as the asphalt starts tending towards the coast.

This lane soon becomes a dirt track suitable only for motor trikes and mules, flanked by an orange dot or two. Within 10 minutes more, follow a white arrow and orange dot left onto an uphill kalderími; upon arriving in Áno Karlóvassi, bear left and continue along the narrow street threading lengthwise through the village to the car-park platía with the Mikro Parisi snack bar-café (sporadically open).

Head up the concrete steps to one side of the Mikro Parisi, turning left at the top of the stairway onto a concrete lane – there are some red blazes. Then take the old cobbled trail on the right, signposted 'Ioánnis Theológos', avoiding the tempting left-hand option curling around the other side of the stream valley.

Within 10 minutes you should hit the driveway coming down to end at the monastery of Theológos, just to your right; bear left onto this sporadically paved track to emerge on the main asphalt road up to Lékka in yet another 10 minutes, or roughly half an hour above the base of Ayía Triádha hill.

Turn right onto the asphalt, but about 200 metres further heed waymarks indicating a path resuming between two functional concrete and composition-block structures. More dots guide you on the initially level and then slightly downhill course through olive terraces, making successive left and right forks. You must cross a new jeep track about four minutes before coming out on the narrow Lékka to Tsurléi road, nearly 40 minutes along.

Turn right at the road, passing Lékka's garbage dump, and then bear left after a minute at a Y-fork which descends into a small valley within five minutes. The track reaches a second, year-round stream a few moments later, just after a small ksoklísi on the left. Here bear right off a curve, prompted by a red dot, across the creek and up onto a trail through forest; bear left with waymarks at the first fork, and again, around the one-hour mark of march, at a T-junction. (The right-hand option here descends to the rather gloomy, half-abandoned hamlet of Tsurléi.)

Now climb more steeply south, parallel to the aqueduct bringing water to Tsurléi; within five minutes you intersect a new road – cross straight over it. You're moving south-west along the northern flank of a densely wooded canyon leading up to Nikolúdhes village; some pointy hills protrude above the pines on the far bank, and there are a few pleasant cobbles underfoot.

Some 20 minutes above the aqueduct fork, you reach another critical junction: straight leads directly to Nikolúdhes village (no facilities) within 10 minutes, but it's more appropriate, if you're aiming for the peak, to swing up and right, following waymarks, on a more scenic path.

Within 10 minutes you leave the trees for now in favour of an open ridge, and after five minutes more – just under two hours from the base of Ayía Triádha hill – you emerge on a hairpin curve in the dirt road between Nikolúdhes and Kosmadhéi.

Just before this you'll have noticed a side trail coming up from below – this is the link trail down to the north-western coast itinerary. Turn right at the curve, and you'll notice another ending of this same trail system a few minutes along.

From the curve up to Kosmadhéi village it's about 35 minutes, using the old path as a short cut most of the way. The first trail section occurs at a red dot right off a left curve in the road, just after a lone shed.

Upon meeting the road again, watch for a very obvious stretch of trail heading straight west off of a hairpin twist; you emerge onto the road again near a couple of structures and the start of a track dropping down almost to Megálo Seïtáni (see The North-West Coast).

The path resumes immediately to the left of these barns, a bit overgrown but quite efficient on its way further up, being cut by the road only once more.

At 620 metres elevation, Kosmadhéi is by a whisker the second-highest village on the island – not a very prepossessing place architecturally, but there is a kafenío and the setting is magnificent. In late 1991 a freak storm deposited two metres of snow here, killing off the valuable budding wood of many olives below, so the community may face some hard times ahead.

Exit Kosmadhéi along the trail beside the tall stone water cistern on the hill overhead. Next the route dips a bit to cross the head of the valley beyond, then curls west to pass a spring near the base of a shallow gully. Assisted by red dots, worm up this to a saddle at about 660 metres with some goat pens to the right and a newly constructed chapel on the left, 35 to 40 minutes out of Kosmadhéi.

You must now descend into the vast, recessed valley which eventually meets the sea as the awesome gorge of Kakopérato at Megálo Seïtáni – however, you don't lose much altitude, and the trail, waymarked by blue crosses, remains delightful. Just over an hour out of the village, or nearly 3¼ hours from Meséo Karlóvassi, you'll meet a jeep track and stream; turn right for the final 10 minutes down to the two-nun convent of Kímisis Theotóku (also known as Panayía Kakopérato, to the Virgin of Bad Passage, named after the impassable gorge below it) more like a farm-plus-a-church in its wooded hollow at 550 metres.

There is a spring here, better for drinking from than the seasonal stream, and this is the best campsite if you're doing an overnight traverse of the Kérkis range.

The distinctive pyramidal peak towering above here is only the secondary summit of Kérkis, Zastáni (about 1180 metres). The true summit is still over 2½ hours distant, reached most easily via Zastáni. Once past the convent, a trail of sorts initially veers towards the head of the Kakopérato ravine before climbing up onto a neck of land parting this gorge from the southerly one coming down from the saddle with its blue ikónisma mentioned in Trek 1. The path soon disappears as you proceed cross-country, up onto two successive 'ledges' in the terrain ahead. Avoiding sheer aretes on the right, you reach Zastáni 1½ hours above Theotóku, climbing onto its back rather than the summit mass. Once there, simply turn southwards and ridge-walk another hour to the true summit of Kérkis.

THE NORTH-WEST COAST

This spectacularly scenic corner of Sámos has the least packaged and touristed feel, and is a favourite with independent, active travellers. West of Karlóvassi a mixture of pine, arbutus, olive and juniper completely blankets a landscape dominated by imposing spurs plunging down to the sea on the right or merging into the folds of Mt Kérkis inland. Mostly shaded paths roller-coaster gently up and down, right and left, narrowing to dirt furrows in olive groves and expanding to kalderímia or stairs of polished rock on the saddles.

These trails offer arguably the finest coastal walk in Greece, though doubtless partisans of western Crete will dissent loudly – two medium-sized fires in July 1992 diminished its appeal somewhat. The indisputably best beach on the island lies roughly midway, a perfect rest and recreation stop. In keeping with the natural splendour here, this beach supposedly forms the heart of a monk-seal refuge, so it's unlikely that a road will ever ruin it.

The only problem with this trek is logistical – you may have to choose between reversing the instructions as given in order to accomplish the walk as a day hike, or planning on a possible overnight at the endpoint.

Rating & Duration

This is a moderate trek of nearly four hours duration, perhaps best done in September or early October when you can really enjoy a swim at the Seïtáni beaches.

Maps

Use the British 1:50,000 wartime map *Sámos West*; YIS 1:50,000 *Néon Karlovásion**. The Vasilis Valis map diagram is correct.

Access

Reaching Karlóvassi presents no problems; the sticky wicket is getting into or out of Dhrakéi and Kalithéa, the two villages at the end of the hike as I've described it. For years now, the May-to-September bus schedule has featured just four services a week, two each on Monday and Friday between Karlóvassi and Dhrakéi via Kalithéa: 4.45 am and 12.30 or 1 pm outbound, 6.15 am and 2.30 or 2.45 pm back from the end of the line.

During the school year there may be extra services, but this cannot be relied on, and indeed one recent autumn schedule showed the morning departure eliminated. You are wise to check current bus-station placards and plan accordingly. From late May to late June, the longer days of the year, it is quite easy to arrive in Dhrakéi with the midday bus and finish a reverse itinerary well before dark.

During days and seasons when there is no bus, a taxi from Kalithéa does a 'shopper's special' run every morning to Karlóvassi for a reasonable fee per person. However, this is often prebooked and so cannot be entirely depended upon.

Stage 1: Áno Karlóvassi to Potámi Beach

(1 hour)

The directions up to the Mikro Parisi café in Áno Karlóvassi are the same as given previously in Ascents of Mt Kérkis. This time, however, instead of going south up the concrete stairs, take a lane going west under an archway formed by the upper storey of a house. Grope to the chapel with a terrace at the western edge of the village, on the next-to-highest lane; beside it an obvious kalderími appears. There are red waymarks here and there, and all the villagers know where you're going – just ask '*Áyios Andónios?*' if in doubt.

Within 10 minutes the cobbles mount to a saddle and the ikónisma of Áyios Andónios, before starting the fairly steep descent towards Potámi. Just a couple moments further, a side trail leads briefly down to a monastery on a terrace shaded by a giant tree;

it's a fine spot, and in wet years a spring drips in an adjacent cave.

Past this, the main trail surface is often slippery with pine needles, as gaps in the trees permit glimpses of Potámi bay and the Taco Bell-style spire of the hideous modern chapel of Áyios Nikólaos. About half an hour from Áno Karlóvassi the trail dumps you on a track; turn right, and after a couple of moments drop left onto the resumption of the trail as the dirt road drifts off to the right. Some 45 minutes along you'll come out on the asphalt coast road from Limín Karlóvassi, a bit south of the Iliovasilema taverna (recommended for lunch or supper).

Purists can go right, past the Iliovasilema, and down a short path onto Potámi beach, which takes about 15 minutes to cross. Others will prefer to follow the asphalt south for just a few paces – the reason being a signposted side-track up to the 11th-century Byzantine church of Metamórfosi ('Transfiguration'). No frescoes remain, but architecturally this narrow, tall shrine is the most interesting on the island.

Beyond it a waymarked path continues 20 minutes up the shady canyon of the same stream which you'd cross higher up on the hike to Nikolúdhes, until reaching an impassable cul de sac. The only way onward is by swimming into the chilly, often deep water – preferably at high noon. After about 100 metres through a maidenhair-flecked rock gallery, you reach a chamber in the strata filled by a short waterfall. To get further upstream you'll need trainers or rock-climbing shoes, and some rope.

Stage 2: Potámi Beach to Megálo Seïtáni
(1½ hours)

Having returned to the main beachfront road, it takes about 10 minutes to reach the pavement's end. Walk up the continuing dirt track, forking right a few minutes along just before a summer cottage. Do not bear right some 10 minutes past Potámi onto the wide obvious trail down to Kástro bay, but wait until, a few minutes later, there's a second turn-off flanked by cairns and waymarks.

There are usually knots of parked cars and bikes nearby and a light traffic with other walkers coming out of the bushes.

Once on the trail, most people need about 25 minutes to reach the cove of Mikró Seïtáni, passing an isolated farm and coiling briefly through a ravine running down to Kástro bay. Mikró Seïtáni itself is 150 metres of sand and gravel flanked by sculpted rock formations offering valuable shade. Being so close to the roadhead it is very popular in season.

On the south-western rock wall here, head up the partially reinforced steps (the bottom one is storm-damaged) leading to a rocky point, where you can first see the broad crescent of Megálo Seïtáni ahead. The steps then veer inland to become a dirt path through still-tended olives. It's 30 to 40 minutes to the big beach, ignoring – just before the final descent to the sand – a signed path above and left which eventually becomes the jeep track up to Kosmadhéi. The last 15 minutes passes through the area damaged by fire in 1992; you should expect some trail damage from winter landslides in future years.

You trade cobbles for sand at the mouth of the severe gorge coming down from Kímisis Theotóku convent about one hour 20 minutes past Potámi. There's no fresh water, no shade and no dress code at this purported wildlife refuge – all factors which have so far kept away developers, road builders, campers and litter. The pristine sea, though apparently no longer home to seals, is warm quite early in the year – enjoy.

Stage 3: Megálo Seïtáni to Dhrakéi
(1½ hours)

It takes about 10 minutes to cross the 700-metre-long beach to a group of seven or eight illegal summer bungalows. The onward trail is initially faint and poorly marked; you must take first the left then the right of two forks as you meander up a gentle slope planted with olive trees. Within a few minutes you should see some caves on the left of the trail as you negotiate a ravine.

The path, often an impressive corniche

route, is unambiguous from here to the high point of this stage, just over an hour beyond Megálo Seïtáni. You've come up, first through coastal scrub and then through pines, to a weathered-limestone saddle with the crags of Kérkis hovering overhead. There was a bad fire here in 1992, though not as devastating as that east of Megálo Seïtáni. Ikaría and (on a clear day) Turkey can be seen out to sea.

Now you drop slightly towards a valley, with an ikónisma (which you'll eventually pass) visible on the far bank. Cross the dry streambed on the valley floor, bearing right not left. You'll by now have noticed two green 'Karlóvassi' signs pointing against you and a few red waymarks and cairns. When you meet another path on the far side of the ravine, bear right.

Very suddenly, just less than 1½ hours from Megálo Seïtáni, you're in Dhrakéi (280 metres), a surprisingly large village for such an out-of-the-way place. But there is only a kafenío – for food you'll have to road-walk six km to Kalithéa, where in addition to a simple grill there's a somewhat expensive four-bed inn which may be rented by the schoolteacher during the academic year. If you don't overnight in the area you'll have to retrace your steps to Karlóvassi – a quite tiring seven to eight-hour walking day.

Link Trail: Kérkis to North-West Coast
This is useful to know about, whether coming off Kérkis craving a swim or varying Stage 1 with a climb first towards Nikolúdhes instead of over to Potámi.

Instead of bearing right onto the main trail to the Seïtáni beaches, follow the dirt road up from Potámi to its end, some 10 minutes later. Here a trail begins, going straight and level before veering sharply up and left from some terraces. It climbs without ambiguity on a variety of surfaces for an hour up to the ridge just beside the Nikolúdhes to Kosmadhéi road, though at the very top the path frays into two separate debouchements. Coming down it takes 50 minutes; you can barrel straight through the terraces to a per-pendicular intersection with the main trail to Mikró Seïtáni.

Híos

Until recently one of the least touristed large Aegean islands, Híos still retains a strong local flavour, the result of reclusive but prosperous inhabitants and a tumultuous history. The Genoese controlled the island for a critical two centuries between the Byzantine and Ottoman periods, leaving behind some of Greece's most distinctive villages, reminiscent of Italy or Yemen, scattered in the south and the centre.

Hiots traditionally have either owned, or worked on, ships, and distinguished themselves as canny traders. Many of them are quite wealthy, though because there's less ostentation than usual in Greece, the islanders have a reputation for being tight-fisted. Aristotle Onassis, though born in Anatolia, was brought up in Híos, and his saga set the tone for a dozen similar moguls from Híos and the satellite island of Inússes. Life here has a distinctly US-East-Coast flavour as well as a maritime one, since many islanders have spent as much time in New York as in staffing freighter radio-rooms, and English is widely spoken.

The island itself is predominantly a huge chunk of limestone, with evidence of past volcanic activity at Mávra Vólia beach on the very south tip. More of the best beaches line the central-west coast, but are difficult to get at without your own transport. The name 'Híos' is related to hióni, the Greek word for snow, and indeed on a full-moon night you can drive across the bare limestone heights without headlamps, so great is the reflectivity of the rock.

Unfortunately, the landscape is a good deal more naked than it ought to be: a devastating series of fires in the 1980s wiped out most of Híos' extensive pine forests, particularly in the middle of the island. The only decent hiking territory left is in the far north, depopulated by the Ottoman massacres of

1822 and mass emigration. Best bases for a walking holiday are either Mármaro (Káto Kardhámila) or Langádha.

Season

Híos has a dry, healthy climate as touted in the tourist literature – what they don't tell you about are the fairly severe winds which buffet the north of the island and make winter or early spring walking up there unpleasant. Summers are hot, but not unpleasantly so, ripening the mandarins for which the island is famous.

Access

Four to nine early-evening ferries weekly sail from Pireás to Híos town, with two additional, later services from Rafína. Other possible mainland points of embarkation are Kaválla (once or twice weekly), Thessaloníki (once or twice weekly) and Vólos (once weekly in season only).

Inter-island connections have improved lately but are still not terrific. You can go to and from Lésvos at least daily in season; Límnos four times a week; and Sámos, Ikaría, Pátmos, Léros, Kálimnos, Kos and Ródhos once a week on a big ferry most of the year. Additionally the *Hioni* or its sisterships the *Kapetan Stamatis* and *Psara* sail fairly reliably twice a week year-round to and from Sámos, with one weekly foray as far as Fúrni islet and Ikaría. At unpredictable intervals in summer there is a link with Tínos, mostly for the benefit of religious pilgrims.

Internal air links are restricted to two or three daily flights from Athens. International air charter arrivals are minimal and cannot be predicted accurately from year to year.

ASCENT OF MT PILINÉO

Pilinéo is the highest mountain on Híos, and impressive enough seen from the north. The classic trailhead is the village of Amádhes, set at the mouth of a valley running down from the high crest, and there is a decent path part of the way up. The early-morning bus ride out here actually turns out for the best, since there are few trees along the way, and

during mid-summer you'll appreciate making the initial climb in whatever shade is offered by a ridge east of the route.

Rating & Duration

This is a moderately strenuous trek of about five hours total.

Maps

Use the British 1:50,000 wartime map *Volissós (Khíos Sheet 1);* or YIS 1:50,000 *Volissós* & Khíos – Vrondádhos**

Access

Take the 5.30 am bus from Híos town (which passes Mármaro about an hour later) to Amádhes, two villages before the end of the line at Kambiá. The bus back in the afternoon leaves Kambiá at about 3.20 pm, passing through Amádhes 10 minutes later.

Route Directions

Once in Amádhes (375 metres), take a concrete lane climbing above the main road, near the bus stop, to a cluster of houses on the hillside. Turn left (south) through a narrow gap between the buildings, to find the start of the obvious trail, below and to the right of a cement water tank. Within 10 minutes you go past some cypress trees, and soon, to the right of the path, you'll begin to see the smashed, asbestos-lined pipes of an abandoned aqueduct down to Amádhes.

This trail ends after just over an hour at the ksoklísi of Áyios Yióryios (720 metres), by some trees. There's a spring behind the chapel, actually the source of the aqueduct, the water being easier to get at in a sort of 'tomb'-bunker than from the more obvious standpipe-with-hatch-cover.

From Áyios Yióryios, turn south-west into the valley leading up to the summit ridge, following livestock traces or walking in the ravine bed in lieu of a proper trail; it's hard to get lost from here on, since the summit with its blue chapel is visible most of the way.

Climb steeply onto an east-to-west spur, flanked by limestone crags, heading towards an obvious col in the crest ahead of you – a very rough path begins just below it, bearing north-north-west towards the small, corrugated-iron chapel of Profítis Ilías on the summit. The villagers claim that this route was once passable to the mules used to haul up the building materials for the church. You'll arrive at the trig point some two hours 45 minutes out of Amádhes; the view includes the island of Psará to the west-north-west as well as the entire north of Híos.

It's wisest to retrace your steps to Amádhes for the afternoon bus out. Some tour groups scramble down to (or up from) Spartúnda, the village south-west of the peak, but there's a fair bit of bulldozer-track walking involved and no public transport out – more trouble than it's worth.

WALKS OUT OF PITIÚS

Pitiús is an interesting village with a single fortified tower, guarding the pass in the back road between Mármaro and the south-west of the island. The main problem with starting walks here is that there's no public tranport in or out.

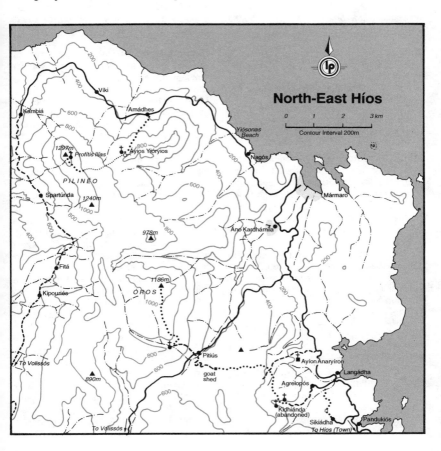

Ascent of Mt Óros
(4½ hours)

At 1186 metres, Óros is the second highest point on Híos, though the British wartime map incorrectly gives the elevation as 1125 metres. Up top there's what appears to be a derelict radio transmitter, with its mast visible from Kardhámila and the main road between there and Langádha.

Rating & Duration This is an easy-to-moderate walk of half a day.

Maps Use the British 1:50,000 wartime map *Volissós (Khíos Sheet 1);* or YIS 1:50,000 *Khíos – Vrondádhos*.*

Access If you're staying in Áno Kardhámila or Langádha, your best bet is to take a taxi up to Pitiús. From Híos town, take the earliest of the several daily bus services to Áno Kardhámila and either alight at Langádha to look for a taxi, or get down at the side turning to Pitiús and resign yourself to the prospect of road-walking uphill for seven km.

Route Directions From the platía of Pitiús (450 metres), walk north-west to the war memorial, and then adopt a track continuing in the same direction, climbing slightly to a white ksoklísi on the hillside beyond. Just before the chapel, a path veers off to he right and zig-zags north-east up onto a rocky hogback. From this ridge the summit mast is visible. Make your way over boulders and loose stones, following the route of the old power poles. There's no shade en route, apart from a large tree about half-way to the summit.

The peak itself is a bit disappointing because of all the crumbled buildings; if you need shade you're forced to rely on their ruined walls. But the views are magnificent, especially east to Turkey. Virtually at your feet you can see a deep gorge slashing through the terrain between Pitiús and Áno Kardhámila, but those who have attempted it report that it is fairly rough, with some dangerous scrambling in places.

Descend to Pitiús by the same route; the round-trip will take about four hours 30 minutes. Given the village's isolation, you may as well continue with the next hike to get back to a main road.

Pitiús to Langádha or Sikiádha
(3-4 hours)

The upland scenery south-east of Pitiús is just as bare as that in the opposite direction; the village really is an oasis, like so many in the mountainous heart of the island. Nonetheless this is a very enjoyable, mostly downhill walk, worth doing for its own sake; both Langádha and Sikiádha have some good evening tavernas in which to refresh yourself at hike's end.

Rating & Duration This is an easy walk of three to four hours, depending on whether you stop in Langádha or Sikiádha.

Maps Use the British 1:25,000 wartime map *Volissós (Khíos Sheet 1)*, plus *Khíos (Khíos Sheet 2);* or YIS 1:50,000 *Khíos – Vrondádhos*.*

Route Directions From the Pitiús plaza, take a narrow street south-east for about 50 metres; once past a public phone in a crude lean-to, turn right immediately. Continue past a church to a concrete road leading south-west out of the village; this becomes a dirt track after crossing a bridge to the left. After climbing in zigzags, the track turns east across a stony plateau, ending at a masonry building which serves as a goat barn.

A path continues east, making for a gap in the hills; it's fairly easy to follow, but keep left when in doubt. Some 35 minutes beyond the goat-barn, the trail reaches a rocky height with a circular bivvy shelter. From here you'll have your first view down to Langádha and the numerous bays around it. You can also make a short detour north across the limestone boulders to a trig point.

From the bivvy circle, descend east along the path towards a handful of trees and some corrals. Just before the trees you'll cross a recently bulldozed dirt road coming up from the vicinity of Ayíon Anaryíron monastery.

Continue due east from the corrals over more uneven ground. The trail veers right, goes through a dry-stone wall and then drops down through a gap in the landscape to the south.

Soon you reach some cultivated patches and the abandoned village of Kidhiánda. Just beyond you'll see two white churches; your trail, sporadically walled in, curls around to the left-hand (eastern) church, from where an intermittently paved jeep track drops still further to the hamlet of Agrelopós.

Across the gorge below, high overhead, lies the village of Sikiádha. To get there, start down the cement road towards Langádha, and as it bears sharp left just past the ravine bridge, adopt the mule track bearing up and right (south) behind a path.

This path, often indistinct, climbs steeply up the slope, keeping a walled enclosure to its right. About 25 minutes up from the bridge, a newer, wider track is reached; follow this right and uphill towards an older communications tower and a newer mast. Just before reaching these, turn left across rough ground for about five minutes, and then pick up another mule track. This threads between dry-stone walls past a farm to arrive at the edge of Sikiádha about an hour above the ravine bridge.

In summer, the last bus from Sikiádha or Langádha towards Híos passes at about 4 pm; towards Mármaro, about an hour later.

Lésvos

Lésvos is the third largest Greek island after Kríti and Évvia, though owing to the closeness of Turkey, the often distant sea, and the extensive areas devoted to stock-raising and grain-growing, there's even more of a mainland feel than is usual for the north-east Aegean. Some visitors consider the landscape, clothed at its best in thick, unburned pines and supposedly five million olive trees, drab and repellent – ditto the busy harbour capital. Others find both the volcanic terrain and local architecture, a mix of Genoese castles and Turkish-influenced plaster or stone mansions, rich and satisfying. This matter of taste, the relatively short summer season, and sparse ferry connections have until now kept Lésvos as a connoisseur's island: more visited than Híos, but far less so than Sámos.

As on Híos, the locals until recently didn't actively court tourism, preferring to either emigrate (mostly to Australia or the USA) or subsist on their olives, fish, animal husbandry and ouzo. The last, arguably the best in the country, is responsible both for the highest local rate of alcoholism in Greece and musical, tables-and-dancing-in-the-streets summer village festivals which can last for days. The numbers of tourists who do appear haven't succeeded in cramping the islanders' dignified, old-fashioned style, and tend to concentrate in just three widely separated resorts: Eressós, Plomári, and Mólivos.

Of the three, Mólivos is the most developed and is closest to what quality hiking there is on Lésvos. At 968 metres in elevation, nearby Mt Lepétimnos is the island's highest point by a single metre, partly covered in a mix of scrub, stubby oaks, poplars and (on the wetter north slope) a few deciduous trees. A dozen or so villages ring the peak, and make logical trailheads – though as always new roads have been pushed between them in recent years, destroying several paths.

Those that remain are used by well-advertised local donkey-and-horseback tour operators, taking advantage of the island's plentiful supply of livestock. If you choose to patronise them, you'll probably find yourself covering some of the routes below, in about the same time, but more restfully.

Season

The climate on Lésvos is relatively gentle considering its northerly location. Although you're out of the citrus zone, except for some hardy lemons, the island claims to have even more sunny days per year than Ródhos. Wind is not as much of a problem as elsewhere, given the shelter of nearby Anatolia.

Winters in the hills are very cold, though, despite the sun, and tourist facilities almost non-existent from late October to mid-April. The long, lingering springs are perhaps the best time, when Lepétimnos is at its greenest.

Access

Connections are pretty much identical with those for Híos, except that there is no direct, small-boat link with Sámos or Fúrni, only the once-weekly service from Ródhos and intervening islands.

Domestic flights include two or three daily from Athens and four to six weekly, depending on season, from Thessaloníki and Límnos. There are also a certain number of charters from northern Europe – more from Germany and Scandanavia, much less from England and France – though not yet any scheduled flights.

AROUND LEPÉTIMNOS

While it is not possible to circle the mountain entirely on trails, the described stages can be combined for a traverse of whatever length you desire. There are enough permanent springs to make this a comfortable autumn hike, and the views over the Lesvian coast, the hill villages and across to Turkey are superb. Unfortunately, a very useful link trail between Petrí and Stípsi was recently destroyed by bulldozing, forcing you to choose between trailheads.

Rating & Duration

These are all easy to moderate stages, entailing, however, a total of over seven hiking hours.

Maps

Use the British 1:50,000 wartimes maps *Ay. Paraskeví (Lésvos Sheet 4)* and *Míthimna (Lésvos Sheet 2);* or YIS 1:50,000 *Míthimna* & Ayía Paraskeví**.

Access

I've assumed that you're based in either Mólivos (Míthimna) or Pétra, the two main resorts in the north of the island. There are five well-spaced buses per workday from Mitilíni, the port/capital, dwindling to three or four on weekends. You can take the reverse schedules part-way back to the actual trail-head villages of Petrí or Stípsi, but in both cases you'll have to walk or take a taxi for a final four km along the respective side turnings from the main road.

Stage 1A: Stípsi to Vafiós
(2¾ hours)

Stípsi is a surprisingly large village at about 400 metres tucked in the south-west folds of the Lepétimnos massif, with a view south-east to the Kalloní gulf, rather than the much closer bay of Pétra to the west.

Leave Stípsi on the wide track going up from east to west, behind the village (north side); soon this acquires a northerly course as it slips through a pass at about 500 metres. About 20 minutes out of town, past a trough-spring, take the prominent path taking off on your right, having ignored a left-hand option at the same time. You cross one switchback in the dirt road and then you'll see no more of it.

Half an hour along this trail, some cobble surface appears near a spring staked by poplars. The kalderími zig-zags for about 20 minutes more, down through bracken and oak, to a clump of plane trees in a streambed. A bit less than 10 minutes later, having passed through a gate and some nettle patches, you reach the junction with the trail coming over from Petrí (see Stage 1B), at a point overlooking a ruined mill, an aqueduct and some odd buttressings on the canyon wall below.

The cobbles continue downhill a few moments to the bed of this bigger ravine (c 200 metres), where a pool containing turtles, frogs (and sometimes hikers) persists until late in the summer. This place is called Pigádhos or Platáni locally, but is shown on maps as Akhiliopigádha or Khiliopigádha.

Heading north-west up the far bank for five minutes, you'll come to a PVC-pipe aqueduct; don't turn right or left here, but go straight across it. The path improves in the next 10 to 15 minutes to a ruined farm, with a spring feeding an open irrigation tank

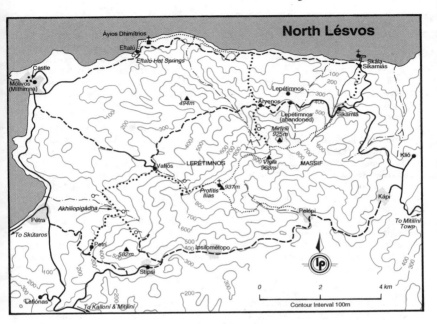

North Lésvos

among some poplars to the left of the trail (another possible bath on a hot day).

Ten minutes beyond this, ignore a hairpin right turn, but 25 minutes along, having scaled a barrier of branches, you *must* bear right onto an apparently 'minor' trail; from the junction it's just half an hour to Vafiós. The first 10 minutes are very weedily overgrown, but once atop a saddle you'll see the rooftops of Vafiós ahead. Pass two successive gates, and then bear hard right onto the clear, east-north-east continuation of the trail.

Vafiós is a friendly village with a good taverna on the outskirts and a pair of simpler, more traditional kafenía in the centre. You can either return to Mólivos on the partly paved road west (few trail short cuts) or preferably continue with Stage 2.

Stage 1B: Petrí to Vafiós
(1¾ hours)
For a slightly easier start, you can begin the traverse in Petrí (200 metres) – a small hamlet with about 40 residents) overlooking the sea. There is a small snack bar-café in the centre. The trail to Akhiliopigádha begins at the north edge of the village and is waymarked with red dots for most of the 40 minutes down to the ravine. The initial moments are flat and obvious before the descent to the junction mentioned in Stage 1A, after which the route is the same. This alternative stage takes just under two hours, as opposed to two hours 40 minutes for Stage 1A, and is suggested if you're going to attempt finishing at Sikamiá instead of Eftalú (see Stage 3).

Stage 2: Vafiós to Profítis Ilías of Lepétimnos
(1½ hours one way)
Leave Vafiós (300 metres) along a stony path taking off from an aqueduct outfall in the obvious ravine behind; don't return all the way to the bridge carrying the trail in

from Stípsi and Petrí. Climb east, more or less parallel to the aqueduct, up through the streambed alive with poplars, planes and (in springtime) water-trickles. Ignore a fork left; after about 25 minutes you pass through a gate and find yourself suddenly amid parched scrub. Within another 10 minutes, you'll reach a weak spring in a plane-shaded hollow; this is the last reliable water for some time.

Turn right here, up a fainter path going parallel to this side ravine on its south-west flank. Soon there's an ambiguous spot at a false ridge with a rock hut and outcrops; the proper trail continues north-east, following the canyon up to its head. The path crosses the upper reaches of the watercourse; once having reached the spur on the opposite bank, detour up and right, cross-country, towards the chapel and secondary summit of Profítis Ilías (937 metres) for a good look around. You'll need a hour to get here from the weak fountain in the hollow.

You can retrace your steps to Vafiós, or complete a traverse by descending east-south-east along the ravine leading to Pelópi (Yeliá), the ancestral village of 1988 US presidential candidate Mike Dukakis, but you will probably prefer to continue along the mountain.

Stage 3: Profítis Ilías of Lepétimnos to the North Coast

(3-4 hours)

Walk one hour, with no trail, north-east along the open ridge from Profítis Ilías to Vígla, the 968-metre summit of Lepétimnos. In the canyon enclosed by Vígla and 925-metre Mirivíli (from which the local novelist Stratis Stamatopoulos Myrivilis took his pen-name), a trail of north-north-east bearing can be seen just below thick bracken. You'll need to get over onto the north flank of Mirivíli to see both ferns and trail-top. The path quickly acquires bits of masoned border on its clear, hour-long course down to Áryenos village. Halfway along is a trough spring, the first water since the canyon above Vafiós.

Áryenos (450 metres) is a passably attrac-

tive village on a knoll overlooking both the mountain and the sea, in particular Skála Sikamiás to the north east. One of the kafenía can provide simple *mezédhes* (in season only) before the final leg down to the shore.

The onward path starts below the village, below a sharp bend in the main road (currently dirt but eventually to be paved), marked by several street-lamps and two park-benches. Fetch around in the mess of bulldozer scars here below the curve until finding the current trailhead. Cobbled in places, the trail zig-zags pleasantly north-north-west and down for just under an hour to the sea; there is some scree but the way, through low oaks and olive plantations, is simple to follow, with just a left bearing about 45 minutes along to maintain downhill progress.

Once on the coast, where a new, rough, direct track has been bulldozed between Skála Sikamiás and Mólivos, turn left; you can actually avoid the dirt road and stay on the pebble shore, except when crossing the first headland, for the 45 minutes to the decent beach and shuttered monastery at Áyios Dhimítrios. Five minutes beyond squats the dome of the somewhat neglected thermal baths at Eftalú (with a small admission fee in summer), a fitting end to the trek. However the shallow pool inside is *extremely* hot and best appreciated either on a cool day or coming straight from the sea here. Civilisation in the form of Mólivos is still more than an hour's tedious road-walk away.

Upper Sikamiá (Sikaminiá, 360 metres) village, Myrivilis' birthplace, is the most attractive of the Lepétimnos settlements, and might be another possible endpoint to a traverse. However, from Vígla, you need to go east-north-east without a trail to the head of the tree-cloaked canyon descending to Sikamiá, with a rather dubious path down from there – a leg of at least 90 minutes.

Your reward would be two very characterful *mezé-kafenía* on the village square, and a delightful 40-minute kalderími down to Skála Sikamiás, Lésvos' self-styled 'Ye Olde Fishing Village'. The fish *is* good, however, and fairly reasonable; guarding the picturesque anchorage is the rock-perched chapel of Panayía Gorgóna, which figured so prominently in Myrivilis' novel of that name.

The main problem with finishing your trek here is getting back to Mólivos or Pétra; the late-morning bus (summer only) goes south-east back to Mitilíni town, not west. You have to taxi or hitch the 16 km of road back to the northern resorts, or walk 10 km more directly along the coast.

Glossary

ádhia paramonís – residence permit
ágoni grammí – unprofitable shipping line
agoréo – collective taxi
agrofílakas – guard
agrotikó iatrío – clinic
alóni – threshing cirque
amaxostihiés piótital – intercity express train
arsanás – seaside chapel fortress
asklipion – therapeutic temple

bakáliko – grocery store

dhasikó – forest
dhexamení – capped water tank
dhimósio – inter-village track
dhomátia – rooms
dhrómos – road, way (general)

eklisía – church
enikiazónteydhomátia – rented rooms
epivatikó – local passenger
estiatória – 'restaurant'

féribot – ferry

gámma – 3rd class of boat
galaktozaharoplastío – milk bar

hóra – main village; also Hóra

ikónisma – shrine

kámbos – agricultural plain
kástro – fortified old town
kafenío/kafenía – drinks café/s
kaïki – type of boat
kalderími – old cobbled trail
karélli – suspended river crossing
katástima – store, eg **katástima athlitikó** · sports store
katafíyia – alpine shelters or refuges
katholikón – main church
kinótiko grafio – community records office
kolimvitírio – natural swimming hole
kouros – sculpted figure of youth; pl. kouroi

ksenón(as) – inn, eg **ksenón meótitos** – youth hostel
ksoklísi – rural church
KTEL – bus company
kúmos – stone round-house
kutrúmbulo – cairns
kyllos – cavity or sinkhole

limeharhío – port authority
livádhia – meadow

magazí – combined store/café/taverna
mándhra – synonymous with *stáni*
mandróskila – watchdogs
megalón dhiadhromón – long-distance trail
meltémi – warm wind
mília – nautical miles
mítato – synonymous with *kúmos*
Monastíri – the Monastery of...
monopátia – trails

néfos – chronic Athenian smog

oropédhio – alpine basin or flats
oséh – OSE (Organismós Sidherodhrómon Elládhos – state rail organisation)
otostop – hitching
ouzádhika – eating place
ouzerí – eating place

pandopolíon – grocery store
paneyíria – festivals
pansions – type of accommodation
peratária – equivalent to a karélli
períptero/a – kiosk
peristereónes – dovecote towers
pírgos – accommodation
platiá – town square
Profítis – the Prophet...
psistariés – grills

sírma – wire
siklákli – can on a string for fetching water from a well
sinikíes – settlements

350

skála – stairway or engineered path
skíti – smaller dependency of Áthonite
   monastery
stáni/stánes – shepherd's hut/s
stégastro – bus-stop shelter
sténoma – narrowing of a gorge
ston odhondotó – rack-and-pinion railway

takhidhromía – post offices
tavérnes – restaurants/grills
taverna – inns

témblon – altar screen
tréna – train
tréno-ksenodhohío – sleeper-only train
trívio – rock-crushing mill
tsaï vunú – mountain tea

vapória – type of boat

yeniká nosokomia – public hospital
yípedho – soccer pitch
yimnásio – secondary school

Index

Lonely Planet guides to Europe

Eastern Europe on a shoestring
This guide has opened up a whole new world for travellers – Albania, Bulgaria, Czechoslovakia, eastern Germany, Hungary, Poland, Romania and Yugoslavia.
'...a thorough, well-researched book. Only a fool would go East without it.' – *Great Expeditions*

Mediterranean Europe on a shoestring
Details on hundreds of galleries, museums and architectural masterpieces and information on outdoor activities including hiking, sailing and skiing. Information on travelling in Albania, Andorra, Cyprus, France, Greece, Italy, Malta, Morocco, Portugal, Spain, Tunisia, Turkey and former republics of Yugoslavia.

Scandinavian & Baltic Europe on a shoestring
A comprehensive guide to travelling in this region including details on galleries, festivals and museums, as well as outdoor activities, national parks and wildlife. Countries featured are Denmark, Estonia, the Faroe Islands, Finland, Iceland, Latvia, Lithuania, Norway and Sweden.

Western Europe on a shoestring
This long-awaited guide covers all of Western Europe's well-loved sights and provides routes for cycling and driving tours, plus details on hiking, climbing and skiing. All the travel facts on Andorra, Austria, Belgium, Britain, France, Germany, Ireland, Italy, Liechtenstein, Luxembourg, Netherlands, Portugal, Spain and Switzerland.

Finland – travel survival kit
Finland is an intriguing blend of Swedish and Russian influences. With its medieval stone castles, picturesque wooden houses, vast forest and lake district, and interesting wildlife, it is a wonderland to delight any traveller.

Iceland, Greenland & the Faroe Islands – travel survival kit
Iceland, Greenland & the Faroe Islands contain some of the most beautiful wilderness areas in the world. This practical guidebook will help travellers discover the dramatic beauty of this region, no matter what their budget.

Poland – travel survival kit
Poland's 1000-year history survives in magnificent cities such as Krakow and Gdansk; and its tranquil lakes and rugged mountains are hardly known to travellers. This reliable guide will help you make the most of this safe and friendly country.

USSR – travel survival kit
Invaluable advice on getting around and beating red tape for individual and group travellers alike. This comprehensive guide includes an unsanitised historical background and complete information on art and culture. Over 130 reliable maps, and all place names are given in Cyrillic script. (includes the independent states)

Trekking in Spain

Aimed at both overnight trekkers and day hikers, this guidebook includes useful maps and full details on hikes in some of Spain's most beautiful wilderness areas.

Trekking in Turkey

Few people are aware that Turkey boasts mountains with walks to rival those found in Nepal. This book gives details on treks that are destined to become as popular as those further east.

Also available:
Eastern Europe phrasebook

Discover the most enjoyable way to get around and make friends in Bulgarian, Czech, Hungarian, Polish, Romanian and Slovak.

Mediterranean Europe phrasebook

Ask for directions to the galleries and museums in Albanian, Greek, Italian, Macedonian, Maltese, Serbian & Croatian and Slovene.

Scandinavian Europe phrasebook

Find your way around the ski trails and enjoy the local festivals in Danish, Finnish, Icelandic, Norwegian and Swedish.

Western Europe phrasebook

Show your appreciation for the great masters in Basque, Catalan, Dutch, French, German, Irish, Portuguese and Spanish (Castilian).

Moroccan Arabic phrasebook

Essential words and phrases for everything from finding a hotel room in Casablanca to asking for a meal of *tajine* in Marrakesh. Includes Arabic script and pronunciation guide.

Turkish phrasebook

Practical words and phrases that will help you to communicate effectively with local people in almost every situation. Includes pronunciation guide.

Russian phrasebook

This indispensable phrasebook will help you get information, read signs and menus, and make friends along the way. Includes phonetic transcriptions and Cyrillic script.

Lonely Planet Guidebooks

Lonely Planet guidebooks cover every accessible part of Asia as well as Australia, the Pacific, South America, Africa, the Middle East, Europe and parts of North America. There are five series: *travel survival kits*, covering a country for a range of budgets; *shoestring guides* with compact information for low-budget travel in a major region; *walking guides*; *city guides* and *phrasebooks*.

Australia & the Pacific

Australia
Bushwalking in Australia
Islands of Australia's Great Barrier Reef
Fiji
Melbourne city guide
Micronesia
New Caledonia
New Zealand
Tramping in New Zealand
Papua New Guinea
Papua New Guinea phrasebook
Rarotonga & the Cook Islands
Samoa
Solomon Islands
Sydney city guide
Tahiti & French Polynesia
Tonga
Vanuatu

South-East Asia

Bali & Lombok
Bangkok city guide
Myanmar (Burma)
Burmese phrasebook
Cambodia
Indonesia
Indonesia phrasebook
Malaysia, Singapore & Brunei
Philippines
Pilipino phrasebook
Singapore city guide
South-East Asia on a shoestring
Thailand
Thai phrasebook
Vietnam, Laos & Cambodia
Vietnamese phrasebook

North-East Asia

China
Mandarin Chinese phrasebook
Hong Kong, Macau & Canton
Japan
Japanese phrasebook
Korea
Korean phrasebook
North-East Asia on a shoestring
Taiwan
Tibet
Tibet phrasebook
Tokyo city guide

West Asia

Trekking in Turkey
Turkey
Turkish phrasebook
West Asia on a shoestring

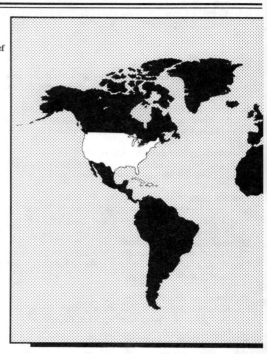

Middle East

Arab Gulf States
Egypt & the Sudan
Egyptian Arabic phrasebook
Iran
Israel
Jordan & Syria
Yemen

Indian Ocean

Madagascar & Comoros
Maldives & Islands of the East Indian Ocean
Mauritius, Réunion & Seychelles

Mail Order

Lonely Planet guidebooks are distributed worldwide. They are also available by mail order from Lonely Planet, so if you have difficulty finding a title please write to us. US and Canadian residents should write to Embarcadero West, 155 Filbert St, Suite 251, Oakland CA 94607, USA ; European residents should write to Devonshire House, 12 Barley Mow Passage, Chiswick, London W4 4PH; and residents of other countries to PO Box 617, Hawthorn, Victoria 3122, Australia.

The Lonely Planet Story

Lonely Planet published its first book in 1973 in response to the numerous 'How did you do it?' questions Maureen and Tony Wheeler were asked after driving, bussing, hitching, sailing and railing their way from England to Australia.

Written at a kitchen table and hand collated, trimmed and stapled, *Across Asia on the Cheap* became an instant local bestseller, inspiring thoughts of another book.

Eighteen months in South-East Asia resulted in their second guide, *South-East Asia on a shoestring*, which they put together in a backstreet Chinese hotel in Singapore in 1975. The 'yellow bible' as it quickly became known to backpackers around the world, soon became *the* guide to the region. It has sold well over half a million copies and is now in its 7th edition, still retaining its familiar yellow cover.

Today there are over 100 Lonely Planet titles – books that have that same adventurous approach to travel as those early guides; books that 'assume you know how to get your luggage off the carousel' as one reviewer put it.

Although Lonely Planet initially specialised in guides to Asia, they now cover most regions of the world, including the Pacific, South America, Africa, the Middle East and Europe. The list of *walking guides* and *phrasebooks* (for 'unusual' languages such as Quechua, Swahili, Nepalese and Egyptian Arabic) is also growing rapidly.

The emphasis continues to be on travel for independent travellers. Tony and Maureen still travel for several months of each year and play an active part in the writing, updating and quality control of Lonely Planet's guides.

They have been joined by over 50 authors, 48 staff – mainly editors, cartographers, & designers – at our office in Melbourne, Australia and another 10 at our US office in Oakland, California. In 1991 Lonely Planet opened a London office to handle sales for Britain, Europe and Africa. Travellers themselves also make a valuable contribution to the guides through the feedback we receive in thousands of letters each year.

The people at Lonely Planet strongly believe that travellers can make a positive contribution to the countries they visit, both through their appreciation of the countries' culture, wildlife and natural features, and through the money they spend. In addition, the company makes a direct contribution to the countries and regions it covers. Since 1986 a percentage of the income from each book has been donated to ventures such as famine relief in Africa; aid projects in India; agricultural projects in Central America; Greenpeace's efforts to halt French nuclear testing in the Pacific and Amnesty International. In 1991 $68,000 was donated to these causes.

Lonely Planet's basic travel philosophy is summed up in Tony Wheeler's comment, 'Don't worry about whether your trip will work out. Just go!'